standard catalog of®

3rd Edition

CADILLAC

1903-2005

John Gunnell

©2005 KP Books
Published by

An imprint of F+W Publications, Inc.

700 East State Street • Iola, WI 54990-0001
715-445-2214 • 888-457-2873

Our toll-free number to place an order or obtain
a free catalog is (800) 258-0929.

Library of Congress Catalog Number: 2004114244

ISBN: 0-87349-289-7

Designed by Brian Brogaard
Edited by Tom Collins

Printed in the United States of America

Acknowledgments

The heritage of the Standard Catalog® series of books continues with this 3rd edition of the Standard Catalog of Cadillac: 1903-2005.

The original concept has been carried on with a format that assists the hobbyist, historian, collector and professional dealer in finding helpful information.

Chester L. Krause, founder of the former Krause Publications, created the concept of the Standard Catalog series and David V. Brownell did preliminary work on the project while serving as editor of Old Cars Weekly during the 1970s. John A. Gunnell assumed the project in 1978.

This latest edition was made possible thanks to the efforts of many people. The team of Jamie Griffin and Brian Brogaard updated the traditional Standard Catalog series design.

Credit for many of the images in this book goes to the members of the Cadillac-La Salle Club, Inc. who showed overwhelming generosity in sharing color slides, color prints and digital images of their cars. Their carefully preserved cars are on display throughout the book. Many of the images they contributed were not able to be used because of space limitations.

Others who contributed to this work were Angelo Van Bogart, author of Cadillac: 100 Years of Innovation and associate editor of Old Cars Weekly who reviewed many of the pages and contributed commentary and photos. The work of Mary Sider, Ken Buttolph, Ron Kowalke, Jim Lenzke and B. Mitchell Carlson on earlier editions cannot be overlooked.

Professional photographers Tom Glatch, Bob Harrington and Tom Jevcak as well as literature collector Phil Hall and automotive hobbyists David Lyon and Elton McFall contributed many images to the book.

In addition, several images and sources used in the book are part of the Old Cars Weekly Archives including magazine advertisements, historic General Motors press releases and images, and the collection of Henry Austin Clark, Jr.

The *Standard Catalog of Cadillac: 1903-2005* is intended to help the reader appreciate the car that has become "The Standard of the World."

Contents

Acknowledgments
3

Introduction
6

SECTION ONE
Cadillac

SECTION TWO

Price Guide

Introduction

Henry Martyn Leland learned precision machining with Samuel Colt in Connecticut and with Brown and Sharpe, makers of tools and machinery in Rhode Island. Leland may have been remembered for developing a hair clipper that made a barber's work easier for years to come.

In 1890, Leland took his family and talents to Detroit, Michigan, and aligned himself with wealthy lumberman Robert C. Faulconer and tool designer Charles H. Norton. Eventually, their company became Leland & Faulconer Engineering Company, precision gear makers and engine makers.

Leland was contracted to produce an engine by Olds Motor Works for its curved dash Oldsmobile. The Leland engine was rejected by Oldsmobile in 1901 but a year later, it helped Leland convince two financial backers of Henry Ford's original automotive company, William Murphy and Lemuel W. Bowen, to remain in the automotive business.

The Cadillac Automobile Company was born, named after Le Sieur de Cadillac, Antoine de la Mothe, the adopted name and title of the French explorer born Antoine Laumet who founded Detroit.

The first Cadillac was completed on October 17, 1902 and was displayed at the New York Automobile Show in January 1903. Orders for 2,286 cars were taken at the show and Cadillac was on its way.

Over the course of its long history, Cadillac has been a leader. The concept of interchangeable parts was introduced to the automotive industry by Cadillac in 1908, winning the prestigious Dewar Trophy in the process. It was the basis for the phrase "Standard of the World."

In 1912, Cadillac became "The Car That Has No Crank" with the introduction of the Delco self-starter and electric lights developed by Charles F. Ketterling. A Cadillac hallmark, the V-8 engine, was introduced in 1914, inspired by the DeDion V-8 of 1910.

Detachable cylinder heads arrived on Cadillacs in 1918 and an inherently-balanced crankshaft in the V-63 of 1924. Four-wheel brakes also were introduced with that Cadillac.

Above: **The 1903 Cadillac (left) and 1906 Cadillac (right) are rare treasures.**

Jack Tallman

In 1928, Harley J. Earl designed the Series 341 Cadillacs. The following year, synchromesh transmission and safety glass appeared in Cadillacs. The famous V-16 and V-12 engines appeared during 1930.

The decade of the 1930s brought such achievements as Ride Control in 1932, no-draft ventilation in 1933, independent front suspension in 1934 and the Fisher all-steel turret top in 1935. A steering-column-mounted gearshift lever arrived in 1938.

Cadillacs followed Packard's lead in 1940 with air conditioning as well as no-shift Hydra-Matic Drive that had debuted previously in the Oldsmobile line.

After producing tanks in World War II, Cadillac continued a trendsetting pace in engineering in the post-war era. In 1949, a compact, sturdy, overhead valve V-8 became the new Cadillac power source.

In the 1950s, Cadillac innovations included the Florentine Curve roof, bumper tip dual exhausts, purposeful-looking "egg crate" grilles and the simulated air vent rear fenderline treatment.

Cadillac marked its 50th season as an automaker in 1952 and the 40th consecutive years of V-8 engine availability in 1954. The Eldorado Brougham was an automotive landmark in 1957 with its advanced airplane fuselage styling, its price above $13,000, plus a few features never before seen on any car.

Like the 1958 Edsel, the 1959 Cadillac has come to represent a cultural symbol of its day. In 1964, Cadillac introduced Comfort-Control heating and air-conditioning which became a new industry standard.

From the beginning, Cadillac had been nearly synonymous with luxury. People spoke of countless products as "The Cadillac" of their category.

Cars like the front-wheel-drive luxury Eldorado of 1967 and the Allante of 1987 continued Cadillac's record of automotive innovation. By 1990, Cadillac also enhanced its images as a safety-conscious company. Improvements were made in roof crush performance, side rail reinforcement in the engine compartment and a reinforced front floor pan, among other improvements.

Anti-lock brakes became standard equipment on 1991 Cadillacs. In 1993, the 90th Anniversary of Cadillac was marked with the introduction of the pioneering Northstar engine.

Perfectionist Henry Leland originated the quality reputation of Cadillac. Others, like the Fisher brothers of body-making fame and designer Harley Earl contributed to the car's refined and striking good looks. Many have contributed to Cadillac technology and innovation.

Throughout the 20th century and now in the 21st century, the slogan long associated with the car still is true as Cadillac remains the "Standard of the World."

By 1927, Cadillac was known for large, reliable cars like the Series 314 sedan.

A 1903 Cadillac leads this modern edition of the London to Brighton race.

Cadillac

1903-2005

SECTION ONE

The Car That Became "Standard of Excellence!"

It might have been called many things but when a new car was created from a reorganized auto company in Detroit in 1902, the name it was given was *"Cadillac."* Henry Leland, the elderly Civil War veteran whose efforts helped reorganize the previous car company, offered the namesake of the explorer who founded Detroit, Michigan.

Ironically, Cadillac used a borrowed name. Antoine Laumet, born near Castelsarrasin, France, followed the custom of young military officers of his time and dropped his given surname in favor of the more appealing and dashing title *"de la Mothe, Sieur de Cadillac."* While the adopted name brought a hint of nobility, no title was conferred on Laumet.

Soldier Laument, forever known as Cadillac, also became an explorer. And in 1701, on behalf of the French government of Canada, founded *"Ville d'Etroits,"* the "village by the straights," referring to the river straights between Lakes St. Clair and Erie.

Perfectionist Leland was proud to produce a car with such high quality expectations that it became known as the "Standard of the World." He'd christened his prized vehicle after a rogue explorer who sought a better life. It's ironic that the car named in his honor often has set another standard. It's been the status symbol of the nouveau riche and those seeking upward mobility, a measuring stick of achievement.

1903

OVERVIEW

The earliest Cadillacs were the automotive world's first rebels. They climbed the steps to government buildings, they tempted competitors in contests of speed and stamina and they dared the early automobile establishment to match their innovation. Though the first cars are often called Model As, Cadillac did not use the "A" designation in 1903. However, later Cadillac publications combined references to 1903 "Cadillac" and "1904 Model A" and used "Model A" in reference to all single-cylinder cars with two front springs and angle steel frame.

I.D. DATA

Serial numbers were not used. Engine numbers were stamped two places on crankcase: 1. Top, right edge of cylinder flange, near water outlet. 2. Right, front face, just below top cover. (Blank spaces on patent plate are for additional patent dates, not engine number.) Engine No.: 1- 2500 (Includes three prototypes built in 1902.)

MODEL A—ONE-CYLINDER

The chassis of the first Cadillac incorporated an angle steel frame. Two half-elliptic springs were used front and rear.

Above: **1903 Cadillac, Model A, rear entrance tonneau touring**
David Lyon

Up front was a straight, tubular axle. Right-hand steering with a steering wheel (not a tiller) was featured. The driving controls were to the right. Adjustable rack-and-pinion steering gear was used. The single-tube tires were mounted on wood wheels. Power came from a Leland & Faulconer "Little Hercules" horizontal, single-cylinder engine mounted to the left-hand side, under the front seat. It was water cooled using impeller-pump circulation through a front-mounted and sloping fin-tube radiator. The detachable, special-alloy cast-iron cylinder had a copper water jacket. Also detachable was the combustion/valve chamber. The vertical valves were arranged in line and perpendicular to the cylinder bore. Exiting at the bottom was and exhaust system operated by a rocker-and-push-rod arrangement via a cam on a gear-driven, half-speed shaft in the crankcase. The inlet at the top was operated by a rocker activated by a sliding cam driven by an eccentric on the half-speed shaft. The fulcrum for the sliding cam was adjustable by movement of a lever on the steering column, giving variable lift to the inlet valve and, thus, throttle adjustment for the engine. A gravity-feed system delivered fuel, from a tank under the driver's seat, to an updraft mixer that automatically supplied the amount of fuel demanded by the inlet valve opening. Internal lubrication was splash-type from a single-pipe, gravity feed oiler. External points, including the mains, were lubricated

by grease and oil cups. Cranking could be accomplished from the right or left side of the vehicle, through jackshaft and chain, to the crankshaft. The driveline included a two-speed planetary transmission. Low speed was on the left foot pedal, high and reverse were on the controller lever at the right. A single chain ran to the spur-gear differential. A foot-pedal-operated mechanical braking system operated on the inboard ends of the rear half axles. The engine could be used for additional braking by easing the controller lever into reverse. The Cadillac featured a two-passenger runabout body that could be converted into four-passenger car by bolting on a rear-entrance tonneau. A sloping, curved dashboard was in front of the driver. The car's body could be lifted from the chassis without disconnecting any wiring, plumbing or controls. Alanson P. Brush, of Leland & Faulconer, held patents on the copper water jacket, variable-lift-inlet valve system, fuel mixer, planetary transmission and adjustable rack-and-pinion steering. By 1906, the impact of the Brush patents would start a drastic change in Cadillac design.

Model Number	Body Type & Seating	Factory Price	Shipping Weight	Production Total
A	Runabout-2P	750	1,370	Note 1
A	Tonneau-4P	850	1,450	Note 1

Note 1: Cadillac model year total was 2,497.

ENGINE

Horizontal, with cylinder to rear. One cylinder. Cast iron cylinder, with copper water jacket. Bore and stroke: 5 x 5 inches. Displacement: 98.2 cid brake horsepower: "Higher than advertised or calculated horsepower" Advertised horsepower: 6-1/2. Main bearings: Two. Valve lifters: Mechanical. Carburetion: Updraft mixer, manufactured by Cadillac.

CHASSIS

Wheelbase: 72 inches. Overall length: 9 feet 3 inches. Height: 5 feet. Front/Rear Tread: 54-1/2 inches. Tires: 28 x 3 single tube.

TECHNICAL

Planetary transmission. Speeds: 2F/1R. (3:1 low, reverse direct high). Controls: low—foot pedal. Reverse, high—lever to right. Low, reverse—bands. High—disc clutch. Chain drive. Spur gear differential. Overall ratio: 3.1:1 to 5:1. Mechanical brakes on two wheels—contracting on inboard drums. Wood wheels—12 spoke (14 spoke on prototype). Wheels: 22 inches.

DRIVE TRAIN OPTIONS

Different combinations of 9- or 10-tooth driving sprocket with 31-, 34-, 38-, 41-, or 45-tooth driven sprocket gave 10 possible ratios from 3.1:1 to 5:1. Lower ratios for runabout to be run on smooth, level roads to higher ratios for loaded delivery to be run on rough, hilly roads. Instructions for changing sprockets were furnished to owners, but the change involved disassembly of the transmission and rear axle, definitely not a "quick-change" set-up.

OPTIONS

Tonneau ($100). Leather top with side curtains and storm apron ($50). Rubber top with side curtains and storm apron ($300). Lights.

HISTORICAL

The first Cadillac was advertised in November 1902, but was not at auto shows until January 1903. Innovations included the use of interchangeable parts. Calendar-year sales and production was 2,497 cars (all models). The president of Cadillac was C. A. Black. Although period photos exist of stripped single-cylinder Cadillacs in speed contests, the as-delivered cars were only fast enough to travel at reasonable speeds on the roads of the time. However, the cars soon gained a reputation for reliability, ease and economy of maintenance and remarkable pulling and climbing capability. Publicity shots show Cadillacs pulling heavily loaded wagons up slopes and climbing the steps of public buildings. The first Cadillac exported to England was entered by its promoter, F. S. Bennett, in the July 1903 Sunrising Hill Climb—"The worst hill in England." The entry finished seventh in a field of 17, being the only one-cylinder in a field otherwise made up of two- and four-cylinder cars with up to four times the displacement of the Cadillac. The same car was entered in the September 1903 1,000-Mile Reliability Trial in England. It finished fourth in its price class on total points, but first in its price class on reliability scoring.

1903 Cadillac, Model A, rear entrance tonneau touring with top

1904

OVERVIEW

The 1904 Model A was a continuation of the 1903 Cadillac. The new Model B Cadillac was the same as the Model A, except for a few details.

I.D. DATA

Serial numbers were not used for the Model A or B. Engine numbers were stamped two places on the crankcase: 1. Top, right edge of cylinder flange, near water outlet. 2. Right, front face, just below top cover. (Blank spaces on patent plate are for additional patent dates, not engine number.) Model A engine Nos.: 3500—4018 with B. 8200—8350 with CEF (1905). 13501—13706 with CEF (1905-special). Model B engine Nos.: 2500—3500. 3500—4018 with A. 4200—5000 with EF.

MODEL A —ONE-CYLINDER

In 1904, Cadillac added a delivery body, This model came with a detachable top. The horsepower rating was upped to 8-1/4 hp. Clincher tires were now standard equipment. A 60-inch tread was an available option. A pressure-fed multiple oiler was introduced.

Above: **1904 Cadillac, Model B, runabout with tonneau**

Tom Jevcak

MODEL B —ONE-CYLINDER

The Model B chassis had a pressed steel frame and axles. A girder-style front axle was employed and it was not made available with the wider tread). A single transverse half-elliptic front spring was used. Cranking was done counterclockwise and at the left side only. Compression relief was provided for cranking. A safety device that prevented the crank from being inserted when the spark-control lever was in its advanced position was another new feature. The Model B's horsepower rating was also 8-1/4 hp and the increase reflected confidence, rather than any engine design changes. The Model B body was an inverted box and the sloping, curved dash design was replaced. A vertical radiator was mounted below the frame. A joint in the body, at the dash, allows the body to be slid off with no lifting. A surrey body style with a side entrance detachable tonneau was added. The top on the delivery model was no longer detachable. The weight of all body styles was reduced by as much as 70 pounds. Prices increased by $50.

Model A

Model Number	Body Type & Seating	Factory Price	Shipping Weight	Production Total
A	Runabout-2P	750	1,370	—
A	Tonneau-4P	850	1,450	—
A	Deluxe-2P	850	1,525	—

Model B

Model Number	Body Type & Seating	Factory Price	Shipping Weight	Production Total
B	Runabout-2P	800	1,300	—
B	Touring-4P	900	1,420	—
B	Surrey-4P	900	1,400	—
B	Deluxe-2P	900	1,525	—

ENGINE

Horizontal, with cylinder to rear. One. Cast iron cylinder, with copper water jacket. Bore and stroke : 5 x 5 inches. Displacement: 98.2 cid Brake horsepower: "Higher than advertised or calculated horsepower" Advertised horsepower: 8-1/4. Main bearings: Two. Valve lifters: Mechanical. Carburetion: Updraft mixer, manufactured by Cadillac.

CHASSIS

MODEL A

[Except Delivery] Wheelbase: 72 inches. Overall length: 9 feet, 3 inches. Height: 5 feet. Front/Rear Tread: 54-1/2 inches (60 optional). Tires: 28 x 3 Clincher. [Delivery] Wheelbase: 72 inches. Overall length: 9 feet, 3 inches. Height: 7 feet, 1-inch. Front/Rear Tread: 54-1/2 inches. Tires: 28 x 3 Clincher.

MODEL B

[Except Delivery] Wheelbase: 76 inches. Overall length: 9 feet, 4 inches. Height: 5 feet. Front/Rear Tread: 54-1/2 inches. Tires: 30 x 3 Clincher. [Delivery] Wheelbase: 76 inches. Overall length: 9 feet, 4 inches. Height: approximately 7 feet. Front/Rear Tread: 54-1/2 inches. Tires: 30 x 3-1/2 Clincher.

TECHNICAL

MODEL A

Planetary transmission. Speeds: 2F/1R (3:1 low, reverse direct high). Low-foot pedal, reverse, high—lever to right. Low, reverse bands, High disc clutch. Chain drive. Spur gear differential. Overall ratio: 3.1:1 to 5:1. Mechanical brakes on two wheels—contracting on inboard drums. Wood wheels—12 spoke (14 spoke on prototype).

MODEL B

Planetary transmission. Speeds: 2F/1R (3:1 low, reverse direct high). Low-foot pedal, reverse, high—lever to right. Low, reverse bands, High disc clutch. Chain drive. Spur gear differential. Overall ratio: 3.1:1 to 5:1. Mechanical brakes on two wheels—contracting on inboard drums. Wood wheels—12 spoke (14 spoke on prototype).

DRIVE TRAIN OPTIONS

Different combinations of 9 or 10 tooth driving sprocket with 31, 34, 38, 41, or 45 tooth driven sprocket gave ten possible ratios from 3.1:1 to 5:1. Lower ratios for runabout to be run on smooth, level roads to higher ratios for loaded Delivery to be run on rough, hilly roads. Instructions for changing sprockets were furnished to owners, but the change involved disassembly of the transmission and rear axle, definitely not a "quick-change" set-up.

OPTIONS

MODEL A

Tonneau ($100). Leather top with side curtains and storm apron ($50). Rubber top with side curtains and storm apron ($300). Lights.

MODEL B

Bulb horn. Lights. Leather top with sides and storm apron ($50). Rubber top with sides and storm apron ($30). Deck to replace tonneau on touring or surrey ($10).

HISTORICAL

The Cadillac Model A was introduced 1903. The Model B was introduced January 1904. Calendar-year sales and production for both models combined was 2,319. The president of Cadillac was C. A. Black. The Cadillac factory burned down in the spring of 1904, reducing production to almost nothing for 45 days. Deposits on 1,500 orders were returned. Cadillac's volume of sales still exceeded those of any other make in the country. When the street was muddy, cars with a rear-entrance tonneau were backed in perpendicular to the sidewalk so passengers didn't have to walk in the mud. The side-entrance surrey ended this inconvenience.

1904 Cadillac, Model B, rear entrance touring

1905

OVERVIEW

The 1905 Model B was a continuation of the 1903 Model B Cadillac was the same as the Model A, except for a few details. Cadillac's new Model C was a midyear offering and featured a reduced price. The Cadillac Model D was a five-passenger touring car with side-entrance tonneau doors. The new Cadillac Model E was the same as a 1904 Cadillac, except that it had a more conventional-looking "hood" with sharp corners and side louvers. The Model F had the same chassis as the Model E, but it rode on a two-inch longer wheelbase.

I.D. DATA

Serial numbers were not used on any of these models. Engine numbers were stamped two places on crankcase. 1. Top, right edge of cylinder flange, near water outlet. 2. Right, front face, just below top cover. (Blank spaces on patent plate are for additional patent dates, not engine number.) Model B engine Nos.: 4200-5000 with EF (1904). Model C engine Nos.: 6600-8200 with EF, 8200-8350 with AEF, 13501-13706 with AEF-special. Model D engine numbers were stamped on top of crankcase—in front of and to the left of number one (front) cylinder. Starting: 10001. Ending: 10156. Model E engine Nos.: 4200-5000 with EF (1904), 50006600 with F, 6600-8200 with CF, 8200-8350 with ACF, 13501- 13706 with ACF-special. Model F engine Nos.: 4200-5000 with BE (1904).

Above: **1905 Cadillac, Model E, "Doctor's Delight" runabout with top**

5000-6600 with E, 6600-8200 with CE, 8200-8350 with ACE, 13501-13706 with ACE special, 13728-14200.

MODEL B—ONE-CYLINDER

The Cadillac Model B was unchanged from 1904. Its horsepower was now rated at 9. The type of optional wide-tread front end available on Model Bs in 1904 was no longer offered. A tubular axle with a 61-inch tread could now be ordered to replace the pressed steel axle with the standard tread.

MODEL C—ONE-CYLINDER

The new Model C was a Model B with a Model F hood and radiator. Cadillac called the Model C "an accommodation to customers who want a detachable tonneau." The Model F was non-detachable. This was probably a car designed to liquidate remaining Model B chassis.

MODEL D—FOUR-CYLINDER

The Model D's body was made of wood, but an aluminum skin was available at extra cost. It had runningboards, an aluminum dash, a lubricator and a running fuel tank with gravity feed to the mixer. The storage fuel tank was located at the rear of the chassis. Fuel transfer to the running tank was generated by exhaust pressure. The Model D chassis emphasized strength and durability. It used a pressed-steel frame. There were two half-elliptic springs up front and a platform spring at the rear. Right-hand steering was fitted, with the controls to the right. The brake lever operated the service brakes on the rear drums, while a foot

pedal operated the emergency brake on the drive shaft. Application of either brake system disengaged the flywheel clutch through an interlock. The engine and transmission were mounted in a tubular subframe. A double-syphon muffling system was employed. The driveline incorporated a three-speed planetary transmission (3:1, 2:1, direct) operated by a progressive shift with all speeds on single lever. There was a twin-disc clutch in the flywheel, a disc clutch and three bands on the transmission and an emergency brake drum behind the transmission. Shaft drive, with two U-joints, connected to the bevel gear. The live rear axle had a spur gear differential. The four-cylinder vertical in-line L-head engine cranked counter-clockwise. It had individual cylinders with copper water jackets and detachable heads. A two-piece crankcase was employed and the lower section carried the main bearings and a patented sloping-trough splash-lube system that ensured lubrication to each cylinder, even when the car was climbing up a grade. A horizontal commutator shaft projected forward, into a cavity in the radiator. The commutator could be serviced from the front of vehicle. With the number one cylinder over the front axle and a stretched out accessory section on the front of the engine, the radiator extended forward of the front tires. The hood took up one-quarter of the length of the car. The engine throttle control was a complicated variation of the one-cylinder throttling arrangement. The L-head valves were operated by in-line pushrods and by roller tappets riding on extra-wide cams on a spring-loaded, sliding camshaft. The exhaust cams were of constant cross section, but the inlet cams were cone shaped to effect a varying lift and timing as the camshaft moved along its axis. Axial motion of the camshaft against its return spring was controlled by a hydraulic piston that received pressure from an engine-driven pump. The throttle control on the steering column operated a bypass valve in the hydraulic loop. The position of this valve regulated the percentage of system pressure acting on the camshaft piston and therefore controlled the nominal axial position of the camshaft. Governor action was automatic, due to interaction between engine-driven pump speed, hydraulic pressure and cam position. Raising the speed too high increased pressure and drove the cam back to a lower-speed position. As on the one-cylinder engine, the inlet valve opening automatically determined the amount of fuel supplied by a mixer. The fuel mixer was identical to the one-cylinder car's mixer, except for the addition of an auxiliary air intake valve. In addition to patents pertaining to one-cylinder cars, Alanson Brush also held patents on the splash lubrication system and the muffler system used on the Model D Cadillac. Although not patented, counterclockwise cranking was also a Brush "trademark" that he later used on the first Oakland.

MODEL E—ONE-CYLINDER

The Model E had a radiator that raised up to fit shape of the hood. A detachable tonneau was not available. The front axle was now of tubular design and was arched, with a truss. A rocker shaft between the front axle and spring was introduced at mid-year. The Model E had a balanced linkage on its transmission bands. The Models E, F, K, M, S, T were not six distinct models. The E, K and S designations covered runabouts while Models F, M, T encompassed all other body styles.

MODEL F—ONE-CYLINDER

The Model F was the first Cadillac one-cylinder touring car with a non-detachable tonneau and two side doors for tonneau entrance. A delivery body was available.

Model B

Model Number	Body Type & Seating	Factory Price	Shipping Weight	Production Total
B	Surrey-4P	900	1,450	—

Model C

Model Number	Body Type & Seating	Factory Price	Shipping Weight	Production Total
C	Runabout-2P	750	1,330	—
C	Touring-4P	850	1,450	—

Model D

Model Number	Body Type & Seating	Factory Price	Shipping Weight	Production Total
D	2D Touring-5P	2,800	2,600	156

Model E

Model Number	Body Type & Seating	Factory Price	Shipping Weight	Production Total
E	Runabout-2P	750	1,100	—

Model F

Model Number	Body Type & Seating	Factory Price	Shipping Weight	Production Total
F	2D Touring-4P	950	1,350	—
F	Deluxe-2P	950	1,400	—

ENGINE

MODELS B, C, E, F

Horizontal, with cylinder to rear. One cylinder. Cast iron cylinder, with copper water jacket. Bore and stroke: 5 x 5 inches. Displacement: 98.2 cid Brake horsepower: "Higher than advertised or calculated horsepower" Advertised horsepower 9. Main bearings: Two. Valve lifters: mechanical. Carburetion: Updraft mixer, manufactured by Cadillac.

MODEL D

Vertical, in-line, L-head. Four cylinder. Cast iron cylinders, cast singly, copper water jacket. Bore and stroke: 4-3/8 x 5 inches. Displacement: 300.7 cid Advertised horsepower: 30. Main bearings: Five. Valve lifters: Mechanical, roller tappets, variable lift inlet. Carburetion: Cadillac updraft mixer with auxiliary air valve.

CHASSIS

MODEL B

Wheelbase: 76 inches. Overall length: 9 feet, 4 inches. Height: 5 feet. Front/Rear Tread: 56-1/2 (61 inches optional). Tires: 30 x 3 Clincher.

MODEL C

Wheelbase: 76 inches. Overall length. 9 feet, 4 inches. Height: 5 feet. Front/Rear Tread: 56-1/2 inches Tires: 30 x 3 Clincher.

MODEL E

Wheelbase: 74 inches. Overall length: 9 feet. Height: 4 feet, 8 inches. Front/Rear Tread: 56-1/2 (61 inches optional) Tires: 28 x 3 Clincher.

MODEL F TOURING

Wheelbase: 76 inches. Overall length: 9 feet, 4 inches. Height: 5 feet., 4 inches. Front/Rear Tread: 56-1/2 (61 inches optional) Tires: 30 x 3-1/2 Clincher.

MODEL F DELIVERY

Wheelbase: 76 inches. Overall length: 9 feet, 4 inches. Height: approximately 7 feet. Front/Rear Tread: 56-1 /2 inches. Tires: 30 x 3-1/2 Clincher.

MODEL D TOURING

Wheelbase: 100 inches. Overall length: approximately 12 feet, 10 inches. Height: approximately 5 feet, 9 inches. Front/Rear Tread: 56-1/2 inches. Tires: 34 x 4-1/2 Dunlops.

TECHNICAL

MODELS B, C

Planetary transmission. Speeds: 2F/1R (3:1 low, reverse—direct high). Controls: low foot pedal, reverse, high lever to right low, reverse bands, high—disc clutch. Chain drive. Spur gear differential. Overall ratio: 3.1:1 to 5:1. Mechanical brakes on two wheels contracting on inboard drums. Wood wheels 12 spoke. Wheels: 24 inches.

MODEL D

Planetary transmission. Speeds: 3F/1R. Right-hand drive, controls to right. Clutch: twin disc in flywheel, disc and three bands on transmission. Shaft drive. Live axle, bevel drive, spur gear differential. Mechanical brakes on two wheels—service-lever-rear drums—emergency-pedal- drive shaft. Wood artillery wheels, 12 spoke. Wheels: 25 inches.

MODEL E

Planetary transmission. Speeds: 2F/1R (3:1 low, reverse direct high). Controls: low—foot pedal, reverse, high—lever to right. Low, reverse—bands. High disc clutch. Chain drive. Spur gear differential. Overall ratio: 3.1:1 to 5:1. Mechanical brakes on two wheels—contracting on inboard drums. Wood wheels — 12 spoke. Wheels: 22 inches.

MODEL F

Planetary transmission. Speeds: 2F/1R, (3:1 low, reverse—direct high). Controls: low—foot pedal, reverse, high—lever to right. Low, reverse bands, High—disc clutch. Chain drive. Spur gear differential. Overall ratio 3.1:1 to 5:1. Mechanical brakes on two wheels contracting on inboard drums. Wood wheels—12 spoke (14 spoke on prototype). Wheels: 23 inches.

DRIVE TRAIN OPTIONS

Different combinations of 9 or 10 tooth driving sprocket with 31, 34, 38, 41, or 45 tooth driven sprocket gave ten possible ratios from 3.1:1 to 5:1. Lower ratios for runabout to be run on smooth, level roads to higher ratios for loaded delivery to be run on rough, hilly roads. Instructions for changing sprockets were furnished to owners, but the change involved disassembly of the transmission and rear axle, definitely not a "quick-change" set-up.

OPTIONS

MODEL B

Bulb horn. Lights. Rear deck to replace tonneau ($10).

MODELS C, F

Bulb horn. Lights.

MODEL E

Bulb horn. Lights. Leather top with sides and storm apron ($50). Rubber top with sides and storm apron ($30).

HISTORICAL

Calendar-year sales and production of all models was 4,029. The Model D, introduced in January 1905, featured several innovations including a three-speed planetary transmission, a governed throttle and the first variable-lift inlet valve gear on a multi-cylinder engine. Calendar-year sales and production of this model was 156 units. The president of Cadillac was C.A. Black. After designing the one-cylinder and Model D Cadillacs, Alanson Brush left Leland & Faulconer and Cadillac and extracted lump-sum and royalty payments for use of his patents. This action triggered a plan to purge Brush's influence from the design of Cadillac products. Cadillac Automobile Co. and Leland & Faulconer merged in October 1905 to form Cadillac Motor Car Co. Henry Leland became general manager of the new company. Maximum production capability was one car every 10 minutes of each 10-hour working day. The new Model F was introduced in January 1905. Its new front-end styling was recognized as a desirable improvement. Cadillac updated its Model B with the Model F hood and radiator to create the Model C. In addition, the owners of A and B Models had the new nose grafted to their cars. There was even an aftermarket supplier of kits to update the styling,

1906

OVERVIEW

The one-cylinder Cadillac retained a 76-inch wheelbase. The Leland-built engine produced more than the rated 10 hp. Prices began at $750 for the Model K two-passenger runabout. The 1906 Models can be identified by their long muffler and the severe cant at the front of the front fenders.

I.D. DATA

Models K, M serial numbers on plate on rear of body (with engine number). Engine numbers were stamped two places on crankcase: 1. Top, right edge of cylinder flange, near water outlet. 2. Top surface of left, front mounting leg. Also on plate on rear of body with serial number. Blank spaces on patent plate are for additional patent dates, not engine or serial number. Engine Nos.: 8350-10000 with M, 20001-21850 with M, 21851-22150 with M (1906-1907). Model L serial numbers on plate on rear of body or on dash (with engine number). Engine numbers were stamped on top surface of crankcase—in front of and to the left of number one (front) cylinder. Model H serial numbers on plate on rear of body or on dash (with engine number). Engine numbers were stamped on top surface

Above: **1906 Cadillac, Model M, light touring**

Long Island Auto Museum

of crankcase—in front of and to the left of number one (front) cylinder. Engine Nos.: 10201-10709 (1906-1908).

MODEL K — ONE-CYLINDER

The 1906 Model K had the chassis as 1905. The spark control was now on the steering column and the oiler had mechanical feed from a cam on the hub of the flywheel. Straight-side Dunlop tires were now standard equipment. The bodies were restyled. All one-cylinder passenger car bodies were now of Victoria style. The dashboard was now made of pressed steel and hood corners were rounded. This hood-and-dash treatment was used through 1908. Tops were not shown in sales catalogs, but undoubtedly were available. Cadillac was setting up its own top department and would be offering Cadillac-made tops by1907.

MODEL M — ONE-CYLINDER

The Model M was the same as the 1906 Model K, except for body styles and a two-inch longer wheelbase.

MODEL L — FOUR-CYLINDER

The Model L was based on the 1905 Model D. This series offered Cadillac's first enclosed limousine body and was the first Cadillac to use rear-facing auxiliary seats in the touring car's tonneau. This gave the Model L a

seven-passenger seating capacity. The engine's bore was increased from 4-3/8 inches to 5 inches. The fuel mixer was replaced by a throttled, float-feed, jet-type carburetor. The hydraulic governor was replaced by a centrifugal ring-type governor linked to the "butterfly" type throttle valve in the carburetor. The variable-lift inlet-valve feature was dropped. A new vertical (instead of horizontal) commutator shaft was featured. This change in the type of commutator drive allowed for a shorter hood. The dash was now made of pressed steel. The wheelbase was lengthened to 110 inches. The service and emergency brakes both acted on the rear drums.

MODEL H — FOUR-CYLINDER

The Model H was the same as the Model L, except no limousine was offered and the touring car was a five-passenger model. A runabout and the first production Cadillac coupe were also included. Early ads, advance catalogs and the *1906 ALAM Handbook* listed the wheelbase of the Model H as 100 inches, rather than the actual 102 inches.

Model K

Model Number	Body Type & Seating	Factory Price	Shipping Weight	Production Total
K	Victoria Runabout-2P	750	1,100	—

Model M

Model Number	Body Type & Seating	Factory Price	Shipping Weight	Production Total
M	2D Victoria Touring-4P	950	—	—
M	Delivery-2P	950	—	—

Model L

Model Number	Body Type & Seating	Factory Price	Shipping Weight	Production Total
L	2D Touring-5/7P	3,750	2,850	—
L	2D Limousine-7P	5,000	3,600	—

Model H

Model Number	Body Type & Seating	Factory Price	Shipping Weight	Production Total
H	2D Touring-5P	2,500	2,400	—
H	Runabout-2P	2,400	—	—
H	2D Coupe-2P	3,000	2,500	—

ENGINE

MODELS K, M

Horizontal, with cylinder to rear. One. Cast iron cylinder. With copper water jacket. Bore and stroke: 5 x 5 inches. Displacement: 98.2 cid Brake horsepower: "Higher than advertised or calculated horsepower" Advertised horsepower: 10. Main bearings: Two. Valve lifters: Mechanical. Carburetion: Updraft mixer, manufactured by Cadillac.

MODEL L

Vertical, in-line, L-head. Four. Individual cast iron cylinder, copper water jacket. Bore and stroke: 5 x 5 inches. Displacement: 392.7 cid Advertised horsepower: 40. Five main bearings. Valve lifters: mechanical. Carburetion: throttled, float feed, jet type made by Cadillac.

MODEL H

Vertical, in-line, L-head. Four. Individual cast iron cylinder, copper water jacket. Bore and stroke: 4-3/8 x 5 inches. Displacement: 300.7 cid. Advertised horsepower: 30. Main bearings: Five. Valve lifters: Mechanical. Carburetion: throttled, float feed, jet type made by Cadillac.

CHASSIS

MODEL H

Wheelbase: 102 inches. Tires 32 x 4.

MODEL K

Wheelbase: 74 inches. Overall length: 9 feet, 2 inches. Height: 4 feet, 6 inches. Front/Rear Tread: 56 inches (61 optional). Tires: 28 x 3.

MODEL M TOURING

Wheelbase: 76 inches. Overall length: 9 feet, 7 inches. Height: 5 feet, 6 inches. Front/Rear Tread: 56 inches (61 optional). Tires: 30 x 3-1/2.

MODEL M DELIVERY

Wheelbase: 76 inches. Front/Rear Tread: 56 inches. Tires: 30 x 3-1/2.

MODEL L TOURING

Wheelbase: 110 inches. Overall length: approximately 13 feet, 3 inches. Height: approximately 6 feet, 3 inches. Front/Rear Tread: 56-1/2 inches. Tires: 36 x 4 front, 36 x 4-1/2 rear.

MODEL L LIMOUSINE

Wheelbase: 110 inches. Overall length: approximately 13 feet, 6 inches. Height: approximately 7 feet, 5 inches.

1906 Cadillac, Model K, light runabout with buggy top

Front/Rear Tread: 56-1/2 inches. Tires: 36 x 4 front, 36 x 5 rear. [Model H] Wheelbase: 102 inches. Front/Rear Tread: 56-1/2 inches. Tires: 32 x 4.

TECHNICAL

MODEL K

Planetary transmission. Speeds: 2F/1R (3:1 low, reverse—direct high). Controls: low—foot pedal, reverse, high —lever to right. Low, reverse—bands, High—disc clutch. Chain drive. Spur gear differential. Overall ratio: 3.1:1 to 5:1. Mechanical brakes on two wheels—contracting on inboard drums. Wood wheels 12 spoke. Wheel size: 22 inches.

MODEL M

Planetary transmission. Speeds: 2F/1R (3:1 low, reverse—direct high). Controls: low—foot pedal, reverse, high —lever to right. Low, reverse — bands, High—disc clutch. Chain drive. Spur gear differential. Overall ratio: 3.1:1 to 5:1. Mechanical brakes on two wheels—contracting on inboard drums. Wood wheels 12 spoke. Wheel size: 23 inches. Drivetrain Options: Different combinations of 9 or 10 tooth driving sprocket with 31, 34, 38, 41, or 45 tooth driven sprocket gave 10 possible ratios from 3.1:1 to 5:1. Lower ratios for runabout to be run on smooth, level roads to higher ratios for loaded delivery to be run on rough, hilly roads. Instructions for changing sprockets were furnished to owners, but the change involved disassembly of the transmission and rear axle, definitely not a "quick-change" set-up.

MODEL L

Planetary transmission. Speeds: 3F/1R. Right-hand drive, controls to right. Clutch: Twin disc in flywheel, disc and three bands on transmission. Shaft drive. Live axle, bevel drive, bevel differential. Mechanical brakes on two wheels—service and emergency on rear drums. Wood artillery wheels, 12 spoke. Wheels: 28 front, touring rear 27, limousine rear 26 inches.

MODELS L, H

Planetary transmission. Speeds: 3F/1R. Right- hand drive, controls to right. Clutch: Twin disc in flywheel, disc and three bands on transmission. Shaft drive. Live axle, bevel drive, bevel differential. Mechanical brakes on two wheels—service and emergency on rear drums. Wood artillery wheels, 12 spoke. Wheels : 24 inches.

OPTIONS

MODEL K

Bulb horn. Lights. Rubber top with sides and storm apron ($30). Leather top with sides and storm apron ($50).

1906 Cadillac, Model M, light touring with surrey top

Long Island Auto Museum

MODEL M
Bulb horn. Lights. Cape cart top for Touring ($75).

MODEL L
Bulb horn. Lights. Touring top ($150).

MODEL H
Bulb horn. Lights. Touring top ($125). Runabout top ($50).

HISTORICAL

The Model K and Model M were introduced in January 1906. Calendar-year sales and production was 3,650 for both models combined. The Model L was introduced in January 1906. Calendar year-sales and production are unknown, but probably very limited. The president of Cadillac was C. A. Black. Wm. K. Vanderbilt, Jr. owned a Model L Cadillac, but high-profile customers were rare. Cadillac needed high production to make the concept of interchangeable parts pay off. The Model H was introduced in January 1906. Sales and production was 509 units (1906-1908). Cadillac began to purge Alanson Brush design features from its cars this year so the fuel mixer and variable-inlet valve openings were no longer used on four-cylinder Cadillacs. The real start of the purge was the design of the Model G for 1907.

1906 Cadillac, Model K, light runabout

Mr. and Mrs. David Gish

1906 Cadillac, Model M, "tulip-bodied" light touring with top

Jack Tallman

1906 Cadillac, Model M, light touring car

Henry Austin Clarke Jr. Collection

1906 Cadillac, Model K, light runabout

Mr. and Mrs. David Gish

1907

OVERVIEW

This year Cadillac came out with its new Model G four. It represented a "Thoroughly high-grade, medium-powered and medium-sized automobile at a price somewhat lower than the large touring cars." The use of shaft drive eliminated the complicated chain-and-sprocket system used up to this time. Other 1907 Cadillacs were carryover models with minor refinements.

I.D. DATA

Model G and Model H serial numbers on plate on rear of body or on dash (with engine number). Engine numbers were stamped on top surface of crankcase—in front of and to the left of number one (front) cylinder. Model G engine Nos.: 30003-30425 (1907), 30426-30500 (1907-1908). Model H engine Nos.: 10201-10709 (1906-1908). Model K and Model M serial numbers on plate on rear of body (with engine number). Engine numbers were stamped two places on crankcase. 1. Top, right edge of cylinder flange, near water outlet. 2. Top surface of left, front mounting leg. Also on plate on rear of body with serial number. (Blank spaces on patent plate are for additional patent dates, not engine or serial number.) Engine No. 2185122150 with

Above: **1907 Cadillac, Model K, light runabout**
David Lyon

Model M (1906-1907), 22151-24075 with Model M, 24075-24350 with Models M, S and T.

MODEL G—FOUR-CYLINDER

Although the Model L Cadillac limousine had a planetary transmission and 5 x 5-inches bore and stroke, like the single-cylinder Cadillac runabout, the two models were entirely opposite in concept. The single-cylinder car was a horseless carriage for the masses, while the Model L was a Nabob's throne-on-wheels. Whether due to the Alanson Brush patent squabble, acute marketing perception or both, Cadillac came up with a four-cylinder design that met the expectations of customers who wanted just a bit more than the best one-cylinder car could offer. The new Model G was an inexpensive, easily-maintained, long-lasting, precision-built car—a "single-cylinder Cadillac with four cylinders." Bodies available on the Model G chassis included a two-door five-passenger touring car and a three-passenger (single rumble seat) runabout. Both models carried a wooden dash. Cadillac-built tops were available at extra cost.

MODEL H—FOUR-CYLINDER

The 1907 Model H was the same as the 1906 Model H, except that the body lines of the touring car were simplified and a five-passenger limousine was offered.

MODEL K—ONE-CYLINDER

The 1907 Model K had a much shorter muffler with an outlet at the front rather than the side. The oiler system was changed from cam drive to pulley-and-belt drive. An engine/transmission drip pan was added. Runabout bodies remained the same as in 1906, but the front fenders were changed. The "nose" of the fender was now flattened and an inside skirt was added, but early-1907 catalogs still showed the canted fenders. For the first time, only a factory-installed Victoria top was offered, as well as a buggy top. The prices on all 1907 Cadillacs varied somewhat from one catalog or ad to another, possibly due to a severe economic crisis in 1907. The most-quoted (highest) prices are used in this book.

MODEL M — ONE-CYLINDER

The Model M chassis was the same as that of the Model K, except for two-inch longer wheelbase. Additional body styles were offered. A folding tonneau was new. The tonneau folded up to look like a runabout (this body was not available on the shorter Model K chassis). The Model M lineup offered the first production-type one-cylinder Cadillac coupe.

Model G

Model Number	Body Type & Seating	Factory Price	Shipping Weight	Production Total
G	2D Touring-5P	2,000	—	—
G	Runabout-2P	2,000	—	—
G	Runabout-3P	2,000	—	—

Model H

Model Number	Body Type & Seating	Factory Price	Shipping Weight	Production Total
H	2D Touring-5P	2,500	—	—
H	2D Limousine-6P	3,600	—	—
H	Runabout-2P	2,400	—	—
H	2D Coupe-2P	3,000	—	—

Model K

Model Number	Body Type & Seating	Factory Price	Shipping Weight	Production Total
K	Victoria Runabout-2P	800	1,100	—
K	Victoria top	925	—	—

Model M

Model Number	Body Type & Seating	Factory Price	Shipping Weight	Production Total
M	2D Straight line Touring-4P	950	1,350	—
M	2D Victoria Touring-4P	950	—	—
M	Folding Tonneau-4P	1,000	—	—
M	2D Coupe-2P	1,350	—	—
M	Deluxe-2P	950	—	—

ENGINE

MODEL G

Vertical, in-line, L-head. Four. Individual cast-iron cylinder, copper water jacket. Bore and stroke: 4 x 4-1/2 inches. Displacement: 226.2 cid. Advertised horsepower: 20. Main bearings: five. Valve lifters: mechanical. Carburetion: throttled, float feed, jet type made by Cadillac. The Model G engine had the cylinders cast singly. It also featured, copper water jackets, a detachable combustion valve chamber, main bearings that were replaceable without removing the crankshaft, interchangeable inlet and exhaust valves operated by pushrods and a roller cam follower on a single gear-driven camshaft, a belt driven fan, a water pump, an oiler, a splash lubrication system, a three-point engine-suspension system, a float-feed carburetor controlled by foot throttle or automatic ring-type governor and clockwise cranking.

MODEL H

Vertical, in-line, L-head. Four. Individual cast iron cylinder, copper water jacket. Bore and stroke: 4-3/8 x 5 inches. Displacement: 300.7 cid. Advertised horsepower: 30. Main bearings: five. Valve lifters: mechanical. Carburetion: throttled, float feed, jet type made by Cadillac.

MODEL K

Horizontal, with cylinder to rear. One cylinder. Cast iron cylinder, with copper water jacket. Bore and stroke: 5 x 5 inches. Displacement: 98.2 cid Brake horsepower: "Higher than advertised or calculated horsepower" Advertised horsepower: 10. Main bearings: two. Valve lifters: mechanical. Carburetion: updraft mixer, manufactured by Cadillac.

MODEL M

Horizontal, with cylinder to rear. One cylinder. Cast iron cylinder, with copper water jacket. Bore and stroke: 5 x 5 inches. Displacement: 98.2 cid Brake horsepower: "Higher than advertised or calculated horsepower" Advertised horsepower: 10. Main bearings: two. Valve lifters: mechanical. Carburetion: updraft mixer, manufactured by Cadillac.

CHASSIS

MODEL G

Pressed steel frame, two half-elliptic front, two full-elliptic rear springs, foot brake internal, hand brake external on rear drums, worm and sector steering mechanism. Wheelbase: 100 inches. Front/Rear Tread: 56 inches. Tires: 32 x 3- 1/2.

MODEL H

Wheelbase: 102 inches. Front/Rear Tread: 56-1/2 inches. Tires: 32 x 4.

MODEL K

Wheelbase: 74 inches. Overall length: 9 feet, 2 inches. Height: 5 feet, 6 inches. Front/Rear Tread: 56 inches (61 optional). Tires: 30 x 3.

MODEL M TOURING

Wheelbase: 76 inches. Overall length: 9 feet, 7 inches. Height: 5 feet, 2 inches. Front/Rear Tread: 56 inches (61 optional). Tires: 30 x 3-1/2.

MODEL M (EXCEPT TOURING)

Wheelbase: 76 inches. Front/Rear Tread: 56 inches (61 optional). Tires: 30 x 3-1/2.

TECHNICAL

MODEL G

Leather-faced cone clutch, selective sliding gear transmission, independently attached to frame, single universal in drive shaft to bevel driveline rear axle with spur gear differential. Speeds: 3F/1R. Right-hand drive, controls to right. Leather-faced cone clutch. Shaft drive. Live axle. Mechanical brakes on two wheels—service and emergency on rear drums. Wood artillery wheels, 10 spoke front, 12 spoke rear. Wheels: 25 inches.

MODEL H

Planetary transmission. Speeds 3F/1R. Right-hand drive, controls to right. Twin disc in flywheel. Disc and three bands on transmission. Shaft drive. Live axle, bevel drive, bevel differential. Mechanical brakes on two wheels—service and emergency on rear drums. Wood artillery wheels, 12 spoke. Wheels: 24 inches.

MODEL K

Planetary transmission. Speeds: 2F/1R (3:1 low, reverse direct high). Low—foot pedal, reverse, high—lever to right. Low, reverse bands, high—disc clutch. Chain drive. Spur gear differential. Overall ratio: 3.1:1 to 5:1. Mechanical brakes on two wheels—contracting on inboard drums. Wood wheels—12 spoke. Wheel size: 24 inches.

MODEL M

Planetary transmission. Speeds: 2F/1R (3:1 low, reverse direct high). Low—foot pedal, reverse, high—lever to right. Low, reverse bands, high—disc clutch. Chain drive. Spur gear differential. Overall ratio: 3.1:1 to 5:1. Mechanical brakes on two wheels—contracting on inboard drums. Wood wheels—12 spoke. Wheel size: 23 inches.

DRIVE TRAIN OPTIONS

MODEL K

Different combinations of 9 or 10 tooth driving sprocket with 31, 34, 38, 41, or 45 tooth driven sprocket gave 10 possible ratios from 3.1:1 to 5:1. Lower ratios for runabout to be run on smooth, level roads to higher ratios for loaded delivery to be run on rough, hilly roads. Instructions for changing sprockets were furnished to owners, but the change involved disassembly of the transmission and rear axle, definitely not a "quick-change" set-up.

MODEL M

Different combinations of 9 or 10 tooth driving sprocket with 31, 34, 38, 41, or 45 tooth driven sprocket gave 10 possible ratios from 3.1:1 to 5:1. Lower ratios for runabout to be run on smooth, level roads to higher ratios for loaded delivery to be run on rough, hilly roads. Instructions for changing sprockets were furnished to owners, but the change involved disassembly of the transmission and rear axle, definitely not a "quick-change" set-up.

OPTIONS

MODEL G

Bulb horn. Lights. Cape cart top for touring ($120). Note: Tops now being manufactured by Cadillac.

MODEL H

Bulb horn. Lights. Touring top ($150).

MODEL K

Bulb horn. Lights. Rubber top with side curtains and storm apron ($40). Leather top with side curtains and storm apron ($70).

MODEL M

Bulb horn. Lights. Rubber cloth cape cart top for touring ($100).

HISTORICAL

The Model G was introduced in January 1907. Calendar-year sales and production was 1,030 cars in the 1907 and 1908 period. The president of Cadillac was C. A. Black. The Model G was the first Cadillac that did not reflect the design influence of Alanson Brush in a major way. The Model H was introduced in 1906. Calendar-year sales and production was 509 cars from 1906 to 1908. The Model K and Model M were introduced in 1906. Calendar-year sales and production was 2,350 combined with production of the M, K, S and T models. In February and March 1908, three late-1907 Model K Cadillacs successfully completed the Royal Automobile Club's Standardization Test. As a result of these test results, the Cadillac Automobile Company was awarded the Dewar Trophy for 1908. The actual award date was February 1909. The Dewar Trophy was an annual award for the most important advancement of the year in the automobile industry.

1907 Cadillac, Model H, limousine

1908

OVERVIEW

Only 2,377 automobiles left the Cadillac factory in 1908. The Model G was carried over. This car represented a compromise design, but it formed a solid basis for the 1909 to 1914 Model Thirty. The 1908 Model H was introduced in June 1907. The Model H was the last of the four-cylinder Cadillacs with a planetary transmission and counter-clockwise cranking. The 1908 Model M was a continuation of the car introduced in 1906. The Model S and Model T were introduced in November 1907. Cadillac employees were kept busy converting the plant to build an all-new Model Thirty. It was introduced in August 1908.

I.D. DATA

Model G & H serial numbers on plate on rear of body or on dash (with engine Nos.). Engine numbers were stamped on top surface of crankcase—in front of and to the left of number one (front) cylinder. Model G engine Nos.: 30426-30500 (1907-1908), 30501-31032 (1908). Model H engine Nos: 10201-10709 (1906-1908). Model M, S, & T serial numbers on plate on rear of body with engine number. Engine numbers were stamped two places on crankcase: 1. Top, right edge of cylinder flange, near

Above: **1908 Cadillac, Model S, runabout with "dickey" seat**

water outlet. 2. Top surface of left, front mounting leg. Also on plate on rear of body (with serial number). (Blank spaces on patent plate are for additional patent dates, not engine or serial number.) Model M engine Nos.: 24075-24350 with K, S, T (1907). Model S engine Nos.: 24075-24350 with K, M, T (1907), 24351-25832 with T. Model T engine Nos.: 24075-24350 with K, M, S (1907), 24351-25832 with S.

MODEL G—FOUR-CYLINDER

The latest Model G Cadillac was the same as the 1907 version, but a limousine was added to the line. In addition, one-or two-passenger rumbleseats were available and both were of a different design than the single rumble seat of 1907. There were no changes in the Model G engine for 1908, but the advertised horsepower rating was increased. This was due to the newly instituted ALAM horsepower formula, which gave the Model G a horsepower rating of 25.6. Cadillac had always been conservative with its horsepower ratings. The ALAM rating was also conservative and gave the same rating to every engine with the same bore and number of cylinders. There was no allowance for design, accuracy or precision of manufacture, superior practice in fits and tolerances, etc. Cadillac, although having had a voice in establishing the ALAM formula, soon took exception to being rated the same as

the least sophisticated manufacturer. Although engines were tested for actual developed horsepower, it was to be many years before horsepower curves were publicized.

MODEL H—FOUR-CYLINDER

The Model H was also the same as in 1907, except that the coupe body was dropped from the line and the touring car body was now similar to that used on the Model G chassis. It had a continuous molding across center of doors. An engine-speed governor and interlock between brakes and clutch were no longer supplied. The tire size increased to 34 x 4.

MODEL M—ONE-CYLINDER

For 1908, the Model M Cadillac was offered only with the delivery type body. It was the same as the 1907 delivery, except that the price now included two oil side lamps, an oil tail lamp and a bulb horn. Headlights were not standard equipment until 1910.

MODEL S—ONE-CYLINDER

The Cadillac Model S chassis was the same as 1907, except the wheelbase used with all body styles was increased and full runningboards replaced step plates. Single and double rumbleseat options were offered. Straight line or Victoria styles were available on runabouts. If rumble seat passengers were to be carried regularly, it was recommended that 30 x 3-1/2 tires be used.

MODEL T—ONE-CYLINDER

The Cadillac Model T used the same chassis as the Model S, but the Model T coupe did not have runningboards. Other bodies were same as used with the 1907 Model M, except that the folding tonneau body was dropped. A Victoria style top now available for to cover the Victoria Touring model's rear tonneau.

1908 Cadillac, Model T, "straight-line" touring with surrey top

Model G

Model Number	Body Type & Seating	Factory Price	Shipping Weight	Production Total
G	2D Touring-5P	2,000	—	—
G	2D Limousine-5P	3,000	—	—
G	Runabout-3P	2,000	—	—
G	Runabout-4P	2,025	—	—

Model H

Model Number	Body Type & Seating	Factory Price	Shipping Weight	Production Total
H	2D Touring-5P	2,500	—	—
H	2D Limousine-6P	3,600	—	—
H	Runabout-2P	2,400	—	—

Model M

Model Number	Body Type & Seating	Factory Price	Shipping Weight	Production Total
M	Delivery-2P	950	—	—

Model S

Model Number	Body Type & Seating	Factory Price	Shipping Weight	Production Total
S	Straight Line Runabout-2P	850	—	—
S	Victoria Runabout-2P	850	—	—
S	Victoria Runabout with single rumble	875	—	—
S	Straight Line Runabout with double rumble	885	—	—

Model T

Model Number	Body Type & Seating	Factory Price	Shipping Weight	Production Total
T	2D Straight Line Touring-4P	1,000	—	—
T	2D Victoria Touring-4P	1,000	—	—
T	2D Coupe-2P	1,350	—	—

ENGINE

MODEL G

Vertical, in-line, L-head. Four. Individual cast-iron cylinder, copper water jacket. Bore and stroke: 4 x 4-1/2 inches. Displacement: 226.2 cid. Advertised horsepower: 25. Main bearings: five. Valve lifters: mechanical. Carburetion: throttled, float feed, jet type made by Cadillac. The Model G engine had the cylinders cast singly. It also featured, copper water jackets, a detachable combustion valve chamber, main bearings that were replaceable without removing the crankshaft, interchangeable inlet and exhaust valves operated by pushrods and a roller cam follower on a single gear-driven camshaft, a belt driven fan, a water pump, an oiler, a splash lubrication system, a three-point engine-suspension system, a float-feed carburetor controlled by foot throttle or automatic ring-type governor and clockwise cranking.

MODEL H

Vertical, in-line, L-head. Four. Individual cast iron cylinder, copper water jacket. Bore and stroke: 4-3/8 x 5 inches. Displacement: 300.7 cid. Advertised horsepower: 30. Main bearings: five. Valve lifters: mechanical. Carburetion: throttled, float feed, jet type made by Cadillac.

MODEL M

Horizontal, with cylinder to rear. One cylinder. Cast iron cylinder, with copper water jacket. Bore and stroke: 5 x 5 inches. Displacement: 98.2 cid Brake horsepower: "Higher than advertised or calculated horsepower" Advertised horsepower: 10. Main bearings: two. Valve lifters:

mechanical. Carburetion: updraft mixer, manufactured by Cadillac.

MODEL S

Horizontal, with cylinder to rear. One cylinder. Cast iron cylinder, with copper water jacket. Bore and stroke: 5 x 5 inches. Displacement: 98.2 cid Brake horsepower: "Higher than advertised or calculated horsepower" Advertised horsepower: 10. Main bearings: two. Valve lifters: mechanical. Carburetion: updraft mixer, manufactured by Cadillac.

MODEL T

Horizontal, with cylinder to rear. One cylinder. Cast iron cylinder, with copper water jacket. Bore and stroke: 5 x 5 inches. Displacement: 98.2 cid Brake horsepower: "Higher than advertised or calculated horsepower" Advertised horsepower: 10. Main bearings: two. Valve lifters: mechanical. Carburetion: updraft mixer, manufactured by Cadillac.

CHASSIS

MODEL G

Pressed steel frame, two half-elliptic front, two full-elliptic rear springs, foot brake internal, hand brake external on rear drums, worm and sector steering mechanism. Wheelbase: 100 inches. Front/Rear Tread: 56 inches. Tires (Except Limousine): 32 x 3-1/2. Tires (Limousine): 34 x 4.

MODEL H

Wheelbase: 102 inches. Front/Rear Tread: 56-1/2 inches. Tires: 34 x 4.

MODEL K

Wheelbase: 74 inches. Overall length: 9 feet, 2 inches. Height: 5 feet, 6 inches. Front/Rear Tread: 56 inches (61 optional). Tires: 30 x 3.

MODEL M

Wheelbase: 76 inches. Front/Rear Tread: 56 inches (61 optional). Tires: 30 x 3-1/2.

MODEL S

Wheelbase: 82 inches. Overall length: 10 feet, 1 inch. Height: 5 feet, 4 inches. Front/Rear Tread: 56 inches (61 optional). Tires: 30 x 3.

MODEL T

Wheelbase: 82 inches. Overall length: 10 feet, 2 inches. Height: 5 feet, 4 inches. Front/Rear Tread: 56 inches (61 optional). Tires: 30 x 3-1/2.

TECHNICAL

MODEL G

Selective sliding gear transmission. Speeds: 3F/1R. Right-hand drive, controls to right. Leather-faced cone clutch.

Shaft drive. Live axle, bevel drive, spur gear differential. Mechanical brakes on two wheels—service and emergency on rear drums. Wood artillery wheels, 10 spoke front, 12 spoke rear. Wheels: Touring and Roadster 25 inches, Limousine 26 inches.

MODEL H

Planetary transmission. Speeds: 3F/1R. Right-hand drive, controls to right. Twin disc in flywheel, disc and three bands on transmission. Shaft drive. Live axle, bevel drive, bevel differential. Mechanical brakes on two wheels—service and emergency on rear drums. Wood artillery wheels, 12 spoke. Wheels: 26 inches.

MODEL M

Planetary transmission. Speeds: 2F/1R (3:1 low, reverse—direct high). Low—foot pedal, reverse, high—lever to right. Low, reverse—bands, high—disc clutch. Chain drive. Spur gear differential. Overall ratio: 3.1:1 to 5:1 (see drive train options). Mechanical brakes on two wheels—contracting on inboard drums. Wood wheels—12 spoke. Wheel size: 23 inches.

MODEL S

Planetary transmission. Speeds: 2F/1R (3:1 low, reverse—direct high). Low—foot pedal, reverse, high—lever to right. Low, reverse—bands, high—disc clutch. Chain drive. Spur gear differential. Overall ratio: 3.1:1 to 5:1 (see drive train options). Mechanical brakes on two wheels—contracting on inboard drums. Wood wheels—12 spoke. Wheel size: 23 inches.

MODEL T

Planetary transmission. Speeds: 2F/1R (3:1 low, reverse—direct high). Low—foot pedal, reverse, high—lever to right. Low, reverse—bands, high—disc clutch. Chain drive. Spur gear differential. Overall ratio: 3.1:1 to 5:1 (see drive train options). Mechanical brakes on two wheels—contracting on inboard drums. Wood wheels—12 spoke. Wheel size: 24 inches.

DRIVE TRAIN OPTIONS

MODEL M

Different combinations of 9 or 10 tooth driving sprocket with 31, 34, 38, 41, or 45 tooth driven sprocket gave ten possible ratios from 3.1:1 to 5:1. Lower ratios for runabout to be run on smooth, level roads to higher ratios for loaded delivery to be run on rough, hilly roads. Instructions for changing sprockets were furnished by owners, but the change involved disassembly of the transmission and rear axle, definitely not a "quick- change" set-up.

MODEL S

Different combinations of 9 or 10 tooth driving sprocket with 31, 34, 38, 41, or 45 tooth driven sprocket gave ten

possible ratios from 3.1:1 to 5:1. Lower ratios for runabout to be run on smooth, level roads to higher ratios for loaded delivery to be run on rough, hilly roads. Instructions for changing sprockets were furnished by owners, but the change involved disassembly of the transmission and rear axle, definitely not a "quick-change" set-up.

MODEL T

Different combinations of 9 or 10 tooth driving sprocket with 31, 34, 38, 41, or 45 tooth driven sprocket gave ten possible ratios from 3.1:1 to 5:1. Lower ratios for runabout to be run on smooth, level roads to higher ratios for loaded delivery to be run on rough, hilly roads. Instructions for changing sprockets were furnished by owners, but the change involved disassembly of the transmission and rear axle, definitely not a "quick-change" set-up.

OPTIONS

MODEL G

Headlights. Rubber, leather and mohair tops in three-bow, cape cart and victoria styles ($90 to 200).

MODEL H

Headlights. Lined cape cart top for touring ($150).

MODEL M

Headlights.

MODEL S

Headlights. 30 x 3- 1/2 tires on runabouts with rumble ($50). Rubber top with side curtains and storm apron (60). Leather top with side curtains and storm apron ($80).

Victoria style top, factory installed only ($175). Storm front with windows to replace storm apron ($15).

MODEL T

Headlights. Cape cart top ($115). Victoria style top, factory installed only ($175).

HISTORICAL

The president of Cadillac was C.A. Black. The concept of precision manufacturing of interchangeable parts was a new one for the automobile industry in 1908. Cadillac's adoption of the concept won the company the Dewar Trophy—the first ever for an American car—in 1908 and was the basis for the sales slogan "Standard of the World," which Cadillac adopted a few years later. Had Alanson Partridge Brush's design concepts been perpetuated at Cadillac, the nameplate may well have failed to survive. By 1908, the only remaining Brush features were the copper water jacket and the splash lube system and both of these were used by Cadillac through 1914. The new four-cylinder cars, with their bulky and complicated planetary transmission, were a giant leap from the single-cylinder models, which had become passé. The fours were aimed at the luxury market. Several hundred of the approximately 16,000 single-cylinder Cadillacs produced through 1907 still exist and are in the hands of collectors all over the world. A prominent Australian collector visiting the Antique Automobile Club of America's National Fall Meet in Hershey, Pennsylvania, remarked, "Anyone wanting to restore, drive and enjoy a one-cylinder car best find a Cadillac." To this we say, "No argument, mate!"

1908 Cadillac, Model G, limousine

1909

OVERVIEW

The new Model Thirty was the only Cadillac offered in 1909. It was a moderately-priced car, based on the Model G. The Thirty came as a sporty Roadster, a four-passenger Demi-tonneau (similar to a convertible) and a five-passenger Touring car. All three models carried the same price.

I.D. DATA

Serial numbers on plate on rear of body or on dash (with engine number). Engine numbers were stamped on top surface of crankcase—in front of and to the left of number one (front) cylinder. Starting: 32002. Ending: 37904.

MODEL THIRTY—FOUR-CYLINDER

The market for the one-cylinder cars that Cadillac built its reputation on was vanishing. After an inauspicious entry into the luxury-car field, the company settled down with a design that originated as the 1906 to 1908 Model G. By moving totally to in-house production and focusing on just a single line of cars, Cadillac could offer a high-quality car at a moderate price ($600 less than the price of the Model G). The "Thirty" differed from the Model G in that

---

Above: **1909 Cadillac, Thirty, touring**

no closed bodies were offered. A detachable tonneau was made available again. The Roadster and Demi-Tonneau had a steel cowl and steel doors. The Model G's flaring and twisted front fenders were replaced by flat fenders with fillers between the fenders and frame. Full running boards and running board dust shields were used on all bodies. There were no louvers in the hood. The bodies were painted by Cadillac. The gear-type drive for the water pump and oiler used on the Model G was changed from external-belt drive to internal gears. The gear-driven accessory shaft allowed for an optional magneto. A speed governor was no longer used.

Model Number	Body Type & Seating	Factory Price	Shipping Weight	Production Total
30	2D Touring-5P	1,400	—	—
30	2D Demi-Tonneau-4P	1,400	—	—
30	Roadster-3P	1,400	—	—

ENGINE

Vertical, in-line, L-head. Four-cylinder. Individual cast iron cylinders. Copper water jacket. Bore and stroke: 4 x 4-1/2 inches. Displacement: 226.2 cid Brake horsepower: 30. ALAM horsepower: 25.6. Main bearings: five. Valve lifters: mechanical-pushrod-roller cam followers. Carburetion: float feed, made by Cadillac.

CHASSIS

Wheelbase: 106 inches. Front/Rear Tread: 56 inches (61 inches optional). Tires: 32 x 3-1/2. Chassis: 3/4 platform rear spring system. Single dropped frame. Wheelbase lengthened to 106 inches. In midyear, brake drum diameter was increased to 12 inches.

TECHNICAL

Selective, sliding gear transmission. Transmission refined and mounted at three points to frame cross members rather than at four points to frame side rails. Universal joint housed in ball joint at rear of transmission. Speeds: 3F/1R. Right-hand drive, controls to right. Leather-faced cone clutch. Shaft drive. Plain live rear axle, bevel drive, bevel gear differential. Rear axle with bevel-gear differential made by American Ball Bearing. Overall ratio: Touring car and Demi-tonneau 3.5:1, Roadster 3:1. Mechanical brakes on two wheels. Foot-operated service brake, contracting type. Lever-operated emergency brake, lever-operated. 10- and 12-spoke wood artillery wheels with quick-detachable rims. Wheel rim size: 25 inches. Optional final drive ratios: 3:1, 3.5:1, 4:1.

OPTIONS

Seat covers ($45-75). "Rubber," mohair, or leather tops ($55-$125). Bosch, Dow, Eisemann, or Splitdorf magnetos ($100-$126). Rushmore style B headlights with Rushmore No. 1 generator ($46.50). Rushmore style B headlights with with Prest-O-Lite style B tank ($59.50). Metzger windshield ($50). Gabriel horns, styles 1, 2, 3, 4 ($15-35). Stewart & Clark speedometer ($15-40).

HISTORICAL

Introduced in December 1908. Calendar-year sales and production: 5,903. The president and general manager of Cadillac was Henry Leland. On July 29, 1909, Cadillac Motor Car Co. became a wholly-owned subsidiary of General Motors Co. and Henry Leland became president and general manager of Cadillac Motor Car Co.

1910

OVERVIEW

Refinements to the 1910 Cadillac included a new ignition system designed by Charles F. Kettering's Dayton Engineering Laboratories, which later became the Delco Division of General Motors. Open-car prices were increased a stiff $200. Close-bodied models arrived after April 1910. A limousine came first and a coupe was added in later sales catalogs. The closed bodies were built by Fisher Body Company, which also became part of General Motors. The Demi-Tonneau's body was made of wood and it had a large detachable rear passenger compartment. When it was removed, the car became a two-passenger runabout. All of the doors were made of steel.

I.D. DATA

Serial numbers on plate on rear of body or on dash (with engine number). Engine numbers were stamped on top surface of crankcase —in front of and to the left of number one (front) cylinder. Starting: 40001. Ending: 48008.

MODEL THIRTY — FOUR-CYLINDER

The wheelbase of the Model 30 grew. The new limousine had an even longer whellbase. Engine displacement also grew, thanks to an increase in bore size. The new dual-

ignition setup included a Delco four-coil electrical system and a low-tension magneto. A midyear change added a centrifugal water pump. Acetylene headlights and a gas generator were supplied with all Cadillacs. A taillight, gas side lights, a horn, a tool kit, a tire pump, a tire repair kit and a tire holder were also standard equipment. At midyear, the rear axle was changed to a Timken semi-floating type.

Model Number	Body Type & Seating	Factory Price	Shipping Weight	Production Total
30	2D Touring-5P	1,600	—	—
30	2D Demi-Tonneau-4P	1,600	—	—
30	Roadster-2P	1,600	—	—
30	Roadster-3P	1,600	—	—
30	2D Limousine-7P	3,000	—	—
30	2D Coupe-3P	2,200	—	—

ENGINE

Vertical, in-line, L-head. Four. Individual cast iron cylinder, copper water jacket. Bore and stroke: 4-1/4 x 4-1/2 inches. Displacement: 255.4 cid Brake horsepower: 33. ALAM horsepower: 28.9. Main bearings: five. Valve lifters: mechanical-pushrod-roller cam followers. Carburetion: float feed—made by Cadillac.

CHASSIS

[All except limousine] Wheelbase: 110 inches. Front/Rear Tread: 56 inches (61 optional). Tires: 34 x 4. [Limousine] Wheelbase: 120 inches. Tires: 34 x 4-1/2.

Above: **1910 Cadillac, Thirty, touring**

TECHNICAL

Selective, sliding gear transmission. Transmission refined and mounted at three points to frame cross members rather than at four points to frame side rails. Universal joint housed in ball joint at rear of transmission. Speeds: 3F/1R. Right-hand drive, controls to right. Leather-faced cone clutch. Shaft drive. Plain live rear axle, bevel drive, bevel gear differential. Rear axle with bevel-gear differential made by American Ball Bearing or Timken semi-floating rear axle. Overall ratio: (except Limousine) 3.5:1, (Limousine) 4:1. Mechanical brakes on two wheels. Foot-operated service brake, contracting type. Lever-operated emergency brake, lever-operated. 10- and 12-spoke wood artillery wheels with quick-detachable rims. Wheel rim size: (except Limousine) 26 inches, (Limousine) 25 inches. Optional final drive ratios: 3:1, 4:1.

OPTIONS

Seat covers ($40-60). "Rubber" or mohair tops ($55-95). Prest-O-Lite style B tank ($25). Windshield ($30). Jones speedometer No. 29, 33, 34 ($25-35). Foot rail ($3.50).

HISTORICAL

Introduced November 1909. Innovations included a new Delco ignition system. Model-year sales were 8,008. Henry Leland was President and general manager of Cadillac. In the early days of automobiling in America, open cars and poor travel conditions precluded winter motoring. Manufacturers displayed samples at the winter auto shows and took orders for spring and summer delivery. Cadillac's model year coincided with the calendar year and the year's production was presold. In 1910, Cadillac got more heavily into closed cars and had a solid reputation for quality and value. With a ready demand for their full factory capacity, they introduced the 1911 models in late summer of 1910 and had delivered a significant percentage of the 1911 model production by the start of the calendar year. Cadillac was now producing below demand and customers were willing to accept delivery at any time or wait as long as necessary for delivery.

The 1911 Cadillac Thirty was considered a wonderful car in this 1910 ad.

In addition to model selection, Cadillac promoted electric starting in 1913 ads.

1911

OVERVIEW

The model lineup included the "Gentleman's Roadster," the quickly-convertible (into a runabout) four-passenger Demi-tonneau, the five-passenger Touring, the Limousine and the inside-drive coupe. This was the first year that a front door ("fore door") was incorporated in open Cadillac bodies. The front door was found only on the left-hand side of the fore-door Touring and fore-door Torpedo Roadster.

I.D. DATA

Serial numbers on plate on dash (with engine number) Engine numbers were stamped on top surface of crankcase — in front of and to the left of number one (front) cylinder. Starting: 50000. Ending: 60018.

MODEL THIRTY — FOUR-CYLINDER

The 1911 Touring body and the Coupe body was interchangeable with a Demi-tonneau body to permit year-round motoring. Other changes included a longer wheelbase lengthened, larger-diameter brake drums and a double-dropped frame. A new full-floating Timken axle was used. The Thirty also featured a torsion arm and two universal joints in its drive shaft. Acetylene headlights, a

Above: **1911 Cadillac, Thirty, touring**

David Lyon

gas generator, a taillight, gas side lights, a horn, a tool kit, tire-repair equipment and a tire holder were standard.

Model Number	Body Type & Seating	Factory Price	Shipping Weight	Production Total
30	2D Touring-5P	1,700	—	—
30	2D Demi-Tonneau-4P	1,700	—	—
30	3D Fore-door Touring-5P	1,800	—	—
30	3D Torpedo-4P	1,850	—	—
30	Roadster-2P	1,700	—	—
30	Roadster-3P	1,700	—	—
30	2D Limousine-7P	3,000	—	—
30	2D Coupe-3P	2,250	—	—

ENGINE

Vertical, in-line, L-head. Four. Individual cast iron cylinder, copper water jacket. Bore and stroke: 4-1/2 x 4-1/2 inches. Displacement: 286.3. cubic inches. ALAM horsepower: 32.4. Main bearings: five. Valve lifters: mechanical-pushrod-roller cam followers. Carburetion: float feed: Schebler Model L. Bosch high-tension magneto and Delco single-coil system used for dual ignition.

CHASSIS

Wheelbase: 116 inches. Front/Rear Tread: 56 inches (61 inches optional). Tires: [Except Limousine] 34 x 4, [Limousine] 36 x 4-1/2.

TECHNICAL

Selective, sliding gear transmission. Speeds: 3F/1R. Right-hand drive, controls to right. Leather-faced cone

clutch. Shaft drive. Full-floating rear axle, bevel drive, bevel gear differential. Overall ratio: 3.43:1 (Roadster 3.05:1, Limousine 3.66:1). Mechanical brakes on two wheels. Foot-operated service brake, contracting type. Lever-operated emergency brake, lever-operated. 10- and 12-spoke wood artillery wheels with quick-detachable rims. Wheel rim size: (except Limousine) 26 inches, (Limousine) 27 inches. Optional final drive ratios: 3.43:1, 3.66:1.

OPTIONS

Seat covers ($40-60). Mohair tops ($65-90). Prest-O-Lite style B tank ($25). Windshield ($40). Jones electric horn, with storage battery ($40).

HISTORICAL

Introduced August 1910. Model year sales were 10,019. Model year production was 10,019. The president and general manager of Cadillac was Henry Leland.

1911 Cadillac, Thirty, touring

1911 Cadillac, Thirty, touring

1911 Cadillac, Thirty, touring

1911 Cadillac, Thirty, touring

1912

OVERVIEW

The 1912 Cadillac Model Thirty was the same as the 1911 model, except that the basic price increased to $1,800. A number of significant changes were made to update body styling. A new carburetor and a Delco 6-/24-volt starting-lighting-ignition system were supplied.

I.D. DATA

If serial numbers were used they were on the plate on dash (with engine number). Engine numbers were stamped on top surface of crankcase—in front of and to the left of number one (front) cylinder. Starting: 61001. Ending: 75000.

MODEL THIRTY — FOUR-CYLINDER

The Model Thirty Demi-tonneau and four-door Touring were replaced by a single Phaeton. The 1912 Coupe accommodated an extra passenger on a folding seat. At this time, Cadillac offered the only fully-enclosed, standard, four-cylinder limousine. The bodies on open cars were made of steel. The closed cars had aluminum bodies. A full set of doors was used on all body styles. Cadillac reverted to a louvered hood. Runningboard dust shields covered the frame and runningboard brackets. Exterior trim was nickel plated. The electric side lights had external wiring. All controls were inside the car, except for the brake lever on open-bodied models.

Model Number	Body Type & Seating	Factory Price	Shipping Weight	Production Total
30	4D Touring-5P	1,800	—	—
30	4D Phaeton-4P	1,800	—	—
30	4D Torpedo-4P	1,900	—	—
30	2D Roadster-2P	1,800	—	—
30	4D Limousine-7P	3,250	—	—
30	2D Coupe-4P	2,250	—	—

ENGINE

Vertical, in-line, L-head. Four. Individual cast iron cylinder, copper water jacket. Bore and stroke: 4-1/2 x 4-1/2 inches. Displacement: 286.3 cid Brake horsepower: 40 plus. ALAM horsepower: 32.4. Main bearings: five. Valve lifters: mechanical pushrod-roller cam followers. Carburetion: float feed, made by Cadillac to C.F. Johnson patents.

CHASSIS

Wheelbase: 116 inches. Front/Rear Tread: 56 inches (61 optional). Tires: 36 x 4.

Above: **1912 Cadillac, Four, phaeton**

Jack Tallman

TECHNICAL

Selective, sliding gear transmission. Speeds: 3F/1R. Right-hand drive, controls to right. Leather-faced cone clutch. Shaft drive. Full-floating rear axle, bevel drive, bevel gear differential. Overall ratio: 3.92:1 (phaeton and torpedo 3.66:1, roadster 3.43:1). New brakes with larger 17-inch drums were fitted. Mechanical brakes on two wheels. Foot-operated service brake, contracting type. Lever-operated emergency brake, lever-operated. 10- and 12-spoke wood artillery wheels with quick-detachable rims. Wheels: 28 inches. Optional final drive ratios: 3.05:1, 3.43:1, 3.66:1.

OPTIONS

Front bumper ($18). Clock ($15). Seat covers ($32-50). Mohair tops ($60-90). Windshields ($35-40). Trunk rack ($10). Kamlee No. 1000 trunk ($30). Demountable rims ($25). Electric horn ($25). Power tire pump ($35). Handy lamp ($2).

HISTORICAL

Introduced September 1911. Innovations for 1912 included an electric starting-ignition-lighting system. Model year sales and production were 13,995. The president and general manager of Cadillac was Henry Leland.

1912 Cadillac, Four, phaeton

1912 Cadillac, Four, phaeton

1912 Cadillac, Four, phaeton

1913

OVERVIEW

Cadillac production and sales reached new heights in 1913. Cadillac also won its second Dewar Trophy for its new Delco electric self-starter. No other manufacturer ever won the coveted Dewar Trophy twice. The 1913 models included some significant mechanical updates. All controls were inside the cars. Cowls were seen on all bodies, except the Coupe. New front fenders had a reverse-curve design. Overall, Cadillac bodies had a smoother, more integrated appearance.

I.D. DATA

If serial numbers were used, they could be found on plate on the dash (with engine number). Engine numbers were stamped on top surface of crankcase—in front of and to the left of number one (front) cylinder. Starting: 75001. Ending: 90018.

MODEL THIRTY—FOUR-CYLINDER

Standard equipment for the 1913 Model Thirty included a top and a windshield. The sidelight wiring was concealed. Cadillacs used a longer wheelbase. The engine had major bottom-end changes including a longer stroke. There were

---

Above: **1913 Cadillac, Four, "Princely coupe"**

Jack Tallman

now main bearings in the upper half of the crankcase and the lower half became the oil pan. A chain-driven camshaft and accessory shaft were used. The engine mounting points were moved to the top of the crankcase and the engine was suspended from arched cross members. The valve stems were enclosed. The electrical starting-and-generating system was simplified. It was now a six-volt-only system and had a more compact design. A ring governor was used again, but for spark control rather than speed control. An engine-driven tire pump was optional.

Model Number	Body Type & Seating	Factory Price	Shipping Weight	Production Total
30	4D Touring-5P	1,975	—	—
30	4D Torpedo-4P	1,975	—	—
30	4D Touring-6P	2,075	—	—
30	4D Phaeton-4P	1,975	—	—
30	2D Roadster-2P	1,975	—	—
30	4D Limousine-7P	3,250	—	—
30	2D Coupe-4P	2,500	—	—

ENGINE

Vertical, in-line, L-head. Four. Individual cast iron cylinder, copper water jacket. Bore and stroke: 4-1/2 x 5-3/4 inches. Displacement: 365.8 cid Brake horsepower: 40-50. ALAM horsepower: 32.4. Main bearings: five. Valve lifters: mechanical-pushrod-roller cam followers.

Carburetion: float feed, made by Cadillac to C.F. Johnson patents.

CHASSIS

Wheelbase: 120 inches. Front/Rear Tread: 56 inches (61 inches optional). Tires: 36 x 4-1/2.

TECHNICAL

Selective, sliding gear transmission. Speeds: 3F/1R. Right-hand drive, controls to right. Leather-faced cone clutch. Shaft drive. Full-floating rear axle, bevel drive, bevel gear differential. Overall ratio: 3.43:1 (roadster 3.05:1, limousine 3.66:1). Mechanical brakes on two wheels. Foot-operated service brake, contracting type. Lever-operated emergency brake, lever-operated. 10- and 12-spoke wood artillery wheels with quick-detachable rims. Wheels: 27 inches. Optional final drive ratios: 3.43:1, 3.66:1, 3.92:1.

OPTIONS

Front bumper ($15). Clock ($35). Seat covers ($32.50-65). Runningboard trunk ($33). Tire trunk ($16.50). Electric horn ($25). Power tire pump ($25). Handy lamp (2). Weed chains ($8).

HISTORICAL

Introduced August 1912. Model-year sales and production were 15,018. The president and general manager of Cadillac was Henry Leland. The famous Cadillac slogan "Standard of the World" was first used by the company in the fall of 1912, when it appeared in ads for the 1913 models.

1913 Cadillac, Four, "Princely coupe"

1913 Cadillac, Four, "Princely coupe"

1913 Cadillac, Thirty, touring

1913 Cadillac, Fisher-bodied coupe

1914

OVERVIEW

After six years the highly-successful four-cylinder Model Thirty was getting old fashioned. Cadillac updated it a bit by converting to left-hand drive. The gasoline tank was now rear mounted. The 1914 Cadillac offered a comprehensive seven-model line up.

I.D. DATA

There were no serial numbers for the 1914 Cadillac. Engine numbers were stamped on top surface of crankcase — in front of and to the left of number one (front) cylinder. Engine Nos.: 91005-99999, A-1 A-5008.

1914 CADILLAC — FOUR-CYLINDER

The Thirty was the same as in 1913 except Torpedo bodies were no longer available. The Coupe got a new Landaulet treatment. A five-passenger "inside drive limousine" (actually a center-door sedan) was a new style. A new hinged steering wheel and hinged driver's seat cushion facilitated entrance and exit for front seat passengers at right side of car. With smaller side lamps, Cadillac bodies now had the appearance of enclosing the occupants and all

Above: **1914 Cadillac, Thirty, touring**

Vintage Automobiles of Northfield, MA

the machinery. The speedometer drive was now located in the left-hand steering knuckle. The rear axle was changed to a two-speed Timken type. Cadillacs carried a second ignition system for auxiliary use only and had only one distributor and one set of spark plugs. A hand pump on the dash pressurized the new rear-mounted fuel tank for starting and a camshaft-driven pump was used for fuel delivery while the car was running. A power tire pump was standard equipment.

Model Number	Body Type & Seating	Factory Price	Shipping Weight	Production Total
30	4D Touring-7P	2,075	—	—
30	4D Touring-5P	1,975	—	—
30	4D Phaeton-4P	1,975	—	—
30	2D Roadster-2P	1,975	—	—
30	2D Landaulet Coupe-3P	2,500	—	—
30	4D Standard Limousine-7P	3,250	—	—
30	2D Inside Drive Limousine-5P	2,800	—	—

ENGINE

Vertical, in-line, L-head. Four. Individual cast iron cylinder, copper water jacket. Bore and stroke: 4-1/2 x 5-3/4 inches. Displacement: 365.8 cid Brake horsepower: 40-50. N.A.C.C. horsepower: 32.4. Main bearings: five. Valve lifters: mechanical-pushrod-roller cam followers. Carburetion: float feed, made by Cadillac to C.F. Johnson patents.

CHASSIS

Wheelbase: 120 inches. Front/Rear Tread: 56 inches (61 optional). Tires: 36 x 4-1/2. Special chassis. Wheelbase: 134 inches.

TECHNICAL

Selective, sliding gear transmission. Speeds: 3F/1R. Right-hand drive, controls to right. Leather-faced cone clutch. Shaft drive. Full-floating two-speed rear axle. Bevel drive. Bevel-gear differential. Overall ratio: 3.67:1 and 2.5:1. Mechanical brakes on two wheels. Foot-operated service brake, contracting type. Lever-operated emergency brake, lever-operated. 10- and 12-spoke wood artillery wheels with demountable rims. Wheels: 27 inches. Optional final drive dual ratio: 4.07:1 and 2.5:1.

OPTIONS

Seat covers ($32.50-65). Handy lamp ($2).

HISTORICAL

Introduced July 1913. Innovations included the production-type two-speed rear axle. Model year sales and production was 14,003. The president and general manager of Cadillac was Henry Leland. The 1914 Model Thirty was the last four-cylinder Cadillac for 67 years and marked the final use, by Cadillac, of Alanson P. Brush's design features. A 1914 Cadillac Touring car (engine number 92,524) was awarded the 1913 Dewar Trophy for electrical-system and two-speed-axle performance during a 1,000-mile test conducted in September and October 1913.

Mr. and Mrs. David Gish

1914 Cadillac, Thirty, five-passenger touring

1915

OVERVIEW

Cadillac's new-for-1915 Type 51 model was had a V-8 engine and marked a significant advance in American automobile history. Cadillac's reputation for engineering leadership was further enhanced. Though certainly not the first engine of its type, the Type 51 power plant was the first V-8 used in a mass-produced, series-production automobile. Also in 1915, the embryonic General Motors Corporation paid its first dividends to investors.

I.D. DATA

Serial numbers were not used. Engine numbers stamped on the crankcase just back of the right hand bank of cylinders and on a plate on the dash. Starting: A-6000. Ending: A-19001.

TYPE 51 — V-8

The coachwork used on the Type 51 chassis was similar to 1914 bodies, but some differences were also apparent. The sidelights were smaller, the hood top panels blended more smoothly into the hood side panels and the shape of doors was changed. A three-piece "Rain Vision" windshield was used on closed cars. The roof line of closed cars

Above: **1915 Cadillac, Type 51, touring**

David Lyon

was raised at the front. A Cadillac "one-man" top with inside operating curtains that opened with the doors was standard equipment. The top fastened to the windshield, eliminating the need for straps. The four-passenger Phaeton was replaced by a two-door Salon (sedan) with a passageway between the individual front seats. The right front seat revolved. The "Inside Drive Limousine" of 1914 was now designated a "five-passenger Sedan." A Berline – or enclosed-drive Limousine–was added. The designation "Imperial" used in conjunction with any body style denoted a regular sedan with a glass partition added between the front and rear compartments.

Type 51

Model Number	Body Type & Seating	Factory Price	Shipping Weight	Production Total
NA	4D Touring-7P	1,975	—	—
NA	4D Touring-5P	1,975	—	—
NA	2D Salon-5P	1,975	—	—
NA	2D Roadster-2/4P	1,975	—	—
602	2D Landaulet Coupe-3P	2,500	—	—
601	2D Sedan-5P	2,800	—	—
583	4D Limousine-7P	3,450	—	—
NA	4D Berline Limousine-7P	3,600	—	—
715	4D Imperial Sedan-5P	—	—	—

ENGINE

Ninety degree L-head. Heads not detachable. Cast iron blocks of four on aluminum crankcase. Bore and stroke: 3-1/8 x 5-1/8. Displacement: 314 cid. Compression ratio:

4.25:1. Brake hp: 70 at 2400 rpm. Taxable hp: 31.25. Torque or Compression Pressure: 180 at 1800-2200 rpm. Main bearings: three. Rockers with roller cam follower. Crankcase capacity: 1.5 gal. Cooling system capacity. 5.25 gal. Carburetor: float feed, auxiliary air control; manufactured by Cadillac under C.F. Johnson patents. Water jackets and combustion chambers integral. Water circulation and temperature control is by an impeller-type pump with thermostat for each block of cylinders. Three 1-7/8 inch diameter bearings on crankshaft with four throws all in one plane. Fork and blade connecting rods. Rod bearings available standard, 5 under and .020 under. Three rings, solid wall pistons and cylinder blocks available standard, first and second oversize. Single camshaft with eight cams. Camshaft and generator shaft driven by silent chain. Motor/generator/distributor at rear, two-cylinder power tire pump at front, inside engine vee. Updraft carburetor, water- heated intake manifold and log-type exhaust manifolds located inside vee. Dual exhaust system with no balance pipe. Valves 1-9/16 inches diameter, 5/16 lift. Exhaust valves flat, intake valves tulip shaped. Valves actuated by adjustable tappets that are activated by rocker arms with roller riding on cams. Firing order is: 1L-2R-3L-1R-4L-3R-2L-4R, where R(right) and L(left) are as viewed from the rear and each bank is numbered one through four from the front. Valve chamber caps are stamped H, L, or LL for high or low compression ratios. Engine has three-point suspension. Ball and socket at front and solid at rear, forming an additional frame cross member. Before Engine No. A-7710, oil relief valve is cast integral with starter gear housing. Starting with Engine No. A-7710, oil relief valve is a separate unit mounted on angular face of crankcase. The lubrication system is recirculating, pressure fed from a gear-type oil pump. The pump draws oil from the crankcase and forces it through a header pipe running inside the crankcase. Leads run from this pipe to the main bearings and thence through drilled holes in the crankshaft to the connecting rod bearings. Pistons, cylinders, etc., are lubricated by oil thrown from the lower ends of the connecting rods. Oil from the rear end of the header pipe runs to the pressure relief valve. Overflow from this valve is gravity fed to the camshaft and chains, then drains back to the crankcase.

CHASSIS

[Standard Type 51] Wheelbase: 122 inches. Front/Rear Tread: 56 inches (61 inches optional). Tires: 36 x 4-1/2. Wood wheels with 10 spokes in front, 12 spokes in rear. Speedometer drive changed to right steering spindle. Rear springs three-quarter platform, front springs half-elliptic, six inches longer than in 1914. Ladder-type frame changed to six-inch deep "H" frame with three cross members.

[Special Type 51 Chassis Without Body] Wheelbase: 145 inches. Chassis: First left-drive Cadillac (right-drive available as an option).

TECHNICAL

Selective sliding gear transmission. Aluminum case in unit with engine. Speeds: 3F/1R. Left drive, center control (right-hand drive optional). Multiple disc, dry plate, 15 discs, 7-3/4 inches diameter. Alternate discs (plates) faced with wire mesh asbestos. Tubular drive shaft with two universal joints. Torque arm. Spiral bevel drive in full floating rear axle. Overall ratio: 4.44:1. Mechanical brakes on two wheels, one external, one internal. Wood artillery wheels, demountable rims (wire wheels optional). Wheels: 27 inches. Optional drive ratio: 3.94:1, 5.07:1.

OPTIONS

Seat covers ($35-65). Handy lamp ($2).

HISTORICAL

Introduced in September 1914. Innovations included the first high production V-8 engine. Model-year sales and production was 13,002. Henry Leland was the president and general manager of Cadillac.

1915 Cadillac, Type 51, coupe

1916

OVERVIEW

The 1915 Cadillac V-8 was a spectacular success and the 1916 model had a new Type 53 designation. Minor styling and engineering improvements were made to the hood and cowl. Performance of the V-8 increased by 10 percent, thanks mostly to an enlarged intake manifold and carburetor modifications.

I.D. DATA

Serial numbers were not used. Engine numbers were stamped on the crankcase just back of the right-hand bank of cylinders and on a plate on the dash. Starting: A-20000. Ending: A-38003.

TYPE 53—V-8

The bodies used on Type 53 Cadillacs were similar to Type 51 bodies, except that the hood line was raised so that the transition in the cowl is less abrupt. The roof line of closed bodies was raised again at the front, so that the entire roof line became one gentle curve. The door shape was also changed. The five-passenger Touring was dropped, the Salon now had four doors and a new Victoria body

Above: **1916 Cadillac, Type 53, seven passenger touring**

Dr. Thomas Dawson

replaced Landaulet Coupe. A four-passenger coupe, built by Cadillac, was added at midyear. A five-to seven-passenger Brougham replaced the two-door sedan. This car had two "emergency" seats in the rear passenger compartment, compared to a true seven-passenger car with folding auxiliary seats. The emergency seats were rear-facing, upholstered shelves that were hinged to fold down from the back of the front seat. A Touring body on a special 132-inch chassis was also offered. Police patrol, ambulance and hearse bodies were also constructed on a special 145- inch-wheelbase chassis.

Type 53

Model Number	Body Type & Seating	Factory Price	Shipping Weight	Production Total
NA	4D Touring-7P	2,080	—	—
NA	4D Salon-5P	2,080	—	—
NA	2D Roadster-2/4P	2,080	—	—
1517	2D Victoria-3P	2,400	—	—
NA	2D Coupe-4P	2,800	—	—
1518	4D Brougham-5/7P	2,950	—	—
1744	4D Limousine-7P	3,450	—	—
1519	4D Berline-7P	3,600	—	—
NA	4D 132-inch Touring	—	—	—
NA	Ambulance	3,455	—	—
NA	Police Patrol	2,955	—	—
NA	Hearse	3,880	—	—

ENGINE

L-head. Heads not detachable. Cast iron blocks of four on aluminum crankcase. Bore and stroke: 3-1/8 x 5-1/8.

Displacement: 314 cid. Compression ratio: 4.25:1. Brake hp: 77 at 2600 rpm. Taxable hp: 31.25. Torque or Compression Pressure: 180 at 1800-2200 rpm. Main bearings: three. Rockers with roller cam follower. Crankcase capacity: 1.5 gal. Cooling system capacity. 5.25 gal. Carburetor: float feed, auxiliary air control; manufactured by Cadillac under C.F. Johnson patents. The distributor was moved from the rear to the front of the engine. The fan blades were curved. The exhaust manifolds redesigned with curved connector pipes feeding into collector.

CHASSIS

[Type 53] Wheelbase: 122 inches. Front/Rear Tread: 56 inches. (61 opt). Tires: 36 x 4-1/2. [Special Chassis] Wheelbase: 145 inches., 132 inches.

TECHNICAL

Selective sliding gear transmission. Case in unit with engine. 3F/1R. Left drive, center control (right-hand drive optional). Multiple disc, dry plate clutch, 15 discs. Shaft drive. Spiral bevel, full-floating rear axle. Overall ratio: 4.44:1. Mechanical brakes on two wheels, one external, one internal. Wood artillery wheels, demountable rims (Rudge-Whitworth wire wheels optional). Wheels: 27 inches. Optional drive ratio: 3.94:1, 5.07:1. The power tire pump moved from engine to transmission.

OPTIONS

Seat covers ($35-65).

HISTORICAL

The 1916 models were introduced in July 1915. Model year sales and production were 18,004. The president and general manager of Cadillac was Henry Leland. In May 1916, Erwin G. "Cannonball" Baker and Wm. F. Sturm drove a V-8 Cadillac roadster from Los Angeles to New York City in seven days, 11 hours, 52 minutes. They bettered their previous time, driven in another make of car, by three days, 19 hours, 23 minutes.

1916 Cadillac, Type 53, seven passenger touring

Dr. Thomas Dawson

1917

OVERVIEW

In 1917, the United States entered World war I and the Lelands left Cadillac. V-8s continued with the Type 55, which featured several new body styles and upgraded styling and technology. The range included 15 models including hearses and patrol wagons. The standard wheelbase grew by three inches.

I.D. DATA

Serial numbers were not used. Engine numbers were stamped on the crankcase just back of the right hand bank of cylinders and on a plate on the dash. Engine No.: 55-A-1 through 55-A-1000, 55-B-1 through 55-B-1000, etc., through 55-S-2.

TYPE 55—V-8

Appearance changes included new black enameled headlights and a one-inch wide molding around the upper edge of all open bodies. New crown fenders appeared. The elimination moldings on hood panels and around the doors gave a smoother appearance overall. The phaeton and roadster had a six-degree slope to their windshield.

Above: **1917 Cadillac, Type 55, touring**

The Salon was replaced by a Phaeton with a front bench seat. A new Club Roadster was added. A new Convertible Touring (sort of a "four-door hardtop") was manufactured by Cadillac and had a vee windshield. A Coupe with a cast-aluminum body was also manufactured by Cadillac. The Victoria model became a five-window car with a fixed top and removable roof pillars. The Berline became the Imperial (undoubtedly due to nasty connotation of "Berlin" at the time). A Landaulet body style was also added. One listing of closed body styles by Fisher mentioned a "Touring Couplet," but gave no description of this car. The headlight rims, previously plain, were now embellished with the stylized outline of a shield and crown emblem.

Type 55

Model Number	Body Type & Seating	Factory Price	Shipping Weight	Production Total
NA	4D Touring-7P	2,240	—	—
NA	4D Phaeton-4P	2,240	—	—
NA	2D Roadster-2/4P	2,240	—	—
NA	2D Club Roadster-4P	2,240	—	—
NA	2D Convertible Victoria-4P	2,710	—	—
NA	2D Coupe-4P	2,960	—	—
NA	4D Convertible Touring-7P	2,835	—	—
2460	4D Brougham-5/7P	3,110	—	—
2450	4D Limousine-7P	3,760	—	—
2440	4D Imperial-7P	3,910	—	—
2620	4D Landaulet-7P	3,910	—	—
2470	Touring Couplet	—	—	—
NA	Ambulance	3,760	—	—
NA	Police Patrol	3,160	—	—
NA	Hearse	4,040	—	—

ENGINE

Ninety degree V-8. L-head. Heads not detachable. Cast iron blocks of four on aluminum crankcase. Bore and stroke: 3-1/8 x 5-1/8 inches. Displacement: 314.5 cid S.A.E./N.A.C.C. horsepower: 31.25. Main bearings: three. Valve lifters: rockers with roller cam follower acting on mechanical lifters. Carburetion: float feed, auxiliary air control, manufactured by Cadillac under C.F. Johnson patents. Lighter pistons of "belted" design with large oil return holes in the piston walls were used starting in 1917. The exhaust manifolds had shorter connector pipes. Split, tapered collars were used to retain the valve-spring "feet."

CHASSIS

[Type 55] Wheelbase: 125 inches. Front/Rear Tread: 56 inches. Tires: 36 x 4-1/2. [Type 55 limousine, landaulet, imperial] Wheelbase: 132 inches. Front/Rear Tread: 56 inches. Tires: 37 x 5. [Special Chassis] Wheelbase: 145 inches. Frame depth was increased to eight inches and two tubular cross members were added. An optional wider tread was no longer available.

TECHNICAL

Selective sliding gear transmission. Case in unit with engine. Speeds: 3F/1R. Left drive, center control (right-hand drive optional). Multiple disc, dry plate clutch, 17 discs. Shaft drive. Spiral bevel, full-floating rear axle. Overall ratio: 4.44:1. Mechanical. brakes on two wheels, one external, one internal. Wood artillery wheels, demountable rims (Rudge-Whitworth or Houk wire wheels were optional). Wheels: 27 inches. Optional drive ratio: 3.94:1, 5.07:1. The number of clutch plates was increased to 17.

HISTORICAL

The 1917 Cadillacs were introduced in August 1916. Model year sales and production was 18,002. General Motors Corp. was incorporated October 13, 1916, in Delaware. General Motors Co. was taken over by General Motors Corp. August 1, 1917. General Motors Corp. then became the "operating" company and Cadillac Motor Car Co. became a Division of General Motors. Henry Leland left Cadillac in June 1917 and Richard H. Collins became the division's president and general manager.

1917 Cadillac, Type 55, limousine for Gen. John "Black Jack" Pershing

1918

OVERVIEW

Cadillac built more than 20,000 cars in its old factory during 1918. Plans for a new plant were in the works. The year's Type 57 had few changes. A higher radiator and a higher longer hood were seen and all models sported a new cowl. There were 17 models on two wheelbases.

I.D. DATA

Serial numbers were not used. Engine numbers were stamped on the crankcase just back of the right-hand bank of cylinders and on a plate on the dash. Also stamped on the fan shaft housing. Engine Nos.: 57A-1 through 57-Z- 1000 with 1919.

TYPE 57—V-8

The Type 57 was similar to the Type 55 except that the top line of the hood and cowl was now a continuous straight line to the windshield on most body styles. The headlight reflectors could be tilted by a mechanical linkage running to a lever on the steering post. The nine hood louvers were tilted at six degrees. Windshields on all open cars tilted six degrees. The Club Roadster, the Coupe, the Convertible

Above: **1918 Cadillac, Type 57, Victoria opera coupe**

Touring and the Touring Couplet were dropped from the line. A Town Limousine and a Town Landaulet were added. The main compartment of these two bodies was approximately four inches narrower than that of the standard Limousine. A Suburban sedan was added at midyear.

Type 57

Model Number	Body Type & Seating	Factory Price	Shipping Weight	Production Total
NA	4D Touring-7P	2,590	4,035	—
NA	4D Phaeton-4P	2,590	3,925	—
NA	2D Roadster-2/4P	2,590	3,865	—
2750	2D Convertible Victoria-4P	3,075	3,970	—
2730	4D Brougham-5/7P	3,535	4,290	—
NA	4D Brougham-7P	4,145	—	—
2740	4D Limousine-7P	4,085	4,425	—
2820	Limousine	—	—	—
2680	4D Town Limousine-6P	4,100	4,295	—
3110	U.S. Govt. Limousine	—	—	—
2760	4D Imperial-7P	4,285	—	—
2770	4D Landaulet-7P	4,235	4,510	—
2840	4D Town Landau-6P	4,250	4,350	—
2910	4D Suburban-7P	4,090	4,350	—
NA	Police Patrol	3,850	—	—
NA	Ambulance	4,350	—	—
NA	Hearse	4,685	—	—

ENGINE

Ninety degree V-8. L-head. Heads detachable. Cast iron blocks of four on aluminum crankcase. Bore and stroke: 3-1/8 x 5-1/8 inches. Displacement: 314.5 cid S.A.E./ N.A.C.C. horsepower: 31.25. Main bearings: three.

Valve lifters: rockers with roller cam follower acting on mechanical lifters. Carburetion: float feed, auxiliary air control manufactured by Cadillac under C.F. Johnson patents. The "belted" pistons used previously were replaced by ultra lightweight pistons.

CHASSIS

[Type 57] Wheelbase: 125 inches. Front/Rear Tread: 56 inches. Tires: 35 x 5. [Type 57 Roadster] Wheelbase: 125 inches. Front/Rear Tread: 56 inches. Tires: 34 x 4-1/2. [Type 57 Lmousine, Imperial, Landaulet, Town Limousine, Town Landaulet] Wheelbase: 132 inches. Front/Rear Tread: 56 inches. Tires: 35 x 5. [Special Chassis] Wheelbase: 145 inches.

OPTIONS

Selective sliding gear transmission. Case in unit with engine. The transmission was redesigned and was not interchangeable with the transmission used in Types 51, 53 and 55. Speeds: 3F/1R. Left drive, center control (right-hand drive optional}. Multiple disc, dry plate clutch, 17 discs. Shaft drive. Spiral bevel, full-floating rear axle. Overall ratio: 4.44:1. Mechanical brakes on two wheels, one external, one internal. Wood artillery wheels, demountable rims (R-W wire wheels optional). Wheels: 25 inches. Optional drive ratio: 3.94:1, 5.07:1.

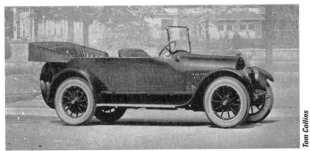

1918 Cadillac, Type 57, touring

HISTORICAL

The 1918 Cadillacs were introduced in August 1917. Model year sales were 45,146 cars for 1918-1919 combined. Model year production was the same. The president and general manager of Cadillac was Richard H. Collins.

1918 Cadillac, Type 57, touring

1919

OVERVIEW

Cadillac reverted to peacetime production in 1919. The Type-57 models saw few changes. The 1919 offerings 1919 included 10 standard body syles on two wheelbases. Smaller models rode a 125-inch wheelbase chassis and the larger cars were on a 132-inch wheelbase chassis. In addition, some purpose built models like the police patrol wagon were available on special order.

I.D. DATA

Serial numbers were not used. Engine numbers were stamped on the crankcase just back of the right-hand bank of cylinders and on a plate on the dash. Also stamped on the fan shaft housing. Engine Nos.: 57-A-1 through 57-Z- 1000 with 1918 and 57-AA-1 through 57-TT-146.

TYPE 57 — V-8

Very few changes were made to 1919 models. The hood had 25 vertical louvers. The phaeton was1-1/2 inches lower. The Victoria was no longer "convertible" and had an aluminum (rather than leather) roof and rear quarter. The Brougham was replaced by a Sedan with a full-width front seat and no emergency seats. The Town Limousine

Above: **1919 Cadillac, Type 57, touring**

David Lyon

was renamed the Town Brougham. The Landaulet, Town Landaulet and Hearse were dropped. As Fisher Body Company made minor changes in details on the Victoria, Suburban and Sedan, the bodies were identified as 57-A and 57-B. This was a body designation only, not a Type designation. There was no Type 57-B Cadillac. The 57-B bodies had a square effect at the body, door and window corners and the lower edge of the windshields. It followed the curve of the cowl.

Type 57

Model Number	Body Type & Seating	Factory Price	Shipping Weight	Production Total
NA	4D Touring-7P	3,220	4,035	—
NA	4D Phaeton-4P	3,220	3,925	—
NA	2D Roadster-2/4P	3,220	3,865	—
3040	2D Victoria-4P	3,990	3,970	—
3050	4D Sedan-5P	4,215	—	—
3260	Imperial Sedan	—	—	—
3210	4D Limousine-7P	4,520	4,425	—
NA	4D Imperial-7P	4,620	—	—
NA	4D Town Brougham-6P	4,520	4,295	—
2830	Limousine-8P	—	—	—
3140	4D Suburban-7P	4,465	4,350	—
3140-PI200	Imperial Suburban	—	—	—
NA	Police Patrol	4,050	—	—
NA	Ambulance	4,550	—	—

ENGINE

L-head. Heads detachable. Cast iron blocks of four on aluminum crankcase. Bore and stroke: 3-1/8 x 5-1/8. Displacement: 314 cid. Compression ratio: 4.25:1.

Brake hp: 77 at 2600 rpm. Taxable hp: 31.25. Torque or Compression Pressure: 180 at 1800-2200 rpm. Main bearings: three. Rockers with roller cam follower. Crankcase capacity: 1.5 gal. Cooling system capacity. 5.25 gal. Carburetor: float feed, auxiliary air control; manufactured by Cadillac under C.F. Johnson patents.

CHASSIS

[Type 57] Wheelbase: 125 inches. Front/Rear Tread: 56 inches. Tires: 35 x 5. [Type 57 roadster] Wheelbase: 125 inches. Front/Rear Tread: 56 inches. Tires: 34 x 4-1/2. [Type 57 Limousine Suburban] Wheelbase: 132 inches. Front/Rear Tread: 56 inches. Tires: 35 x 5. [Special Chassis] Wheelbase: 145 inches.

TECHNICAL

Selective sliding gear transmission. Case in unit with engine. Speeds: 3F/1R. Left-hand drive, center control (right-hand drive optional). Multiple disc, dry plate clutch, 17 discs. Shaft drive. Spiral bevel, full-floating rear axle. Overall ratio: 4.44:1. Mechanical brakes on two wheels, one external, one internal. Wood artillery wheels, demountable rims (Rudge-Whitworth wire wheels optional). Wheels: 25 inches. Optional drive ratio: 3.94:1, 5.07:1.

OPTIONS

Front bumper ($12.50). Rear bumper ($12.50). Cigar lighter ($5). Seat covers ($13.50-125). Spotlight ($7.50). Set of five Rudge-Whitworth wire wheels ($150). Tire chains ($9). Rear view mirror ($3.75).

HISTORICAL

The 1919 Type 57 was a continuation of 1918 Type 57. Model year sales and production for 1918-1919 combined were 45,146 cars. Cadillac built over 20,000 of its 1919 models alone. The president and general manager of Cadillac was Richard H. Collins.

1920-1921

OVERVIEW

The dawn of the Roaring Twenties changed Cadillac's big V-8-powered Touring cars very little. However, many new body styles joined the company's list of models. Due to a postwar business slump and corporate upheavals within General Motors, the 1920 series cars were carried over into 1921 without major revisions. Some Fisher Body Company references identify three different "designs" of cars in these years and designate the first, second and third designs as 59-A, 59-B and 59-C, respectively. These designs differ only in detail and did not have significant styling changes. The -A, -B, -C suffixes refer only to bodies, not type, so there was no Type 59-A, Type 59-B, or Type 59-C Cadillac. A two-passenger Coupe appeared only in early Type 59 catalogs and, if produced at all, was dropped by April 1920. On April 1, 1920, Cadillac advanced all of its list prices by $200 and the two-passenger Coupe was no longer listed. On May 1, 1920, the price of the Town Brougham increased to $5,690. This body style was not shown in 1921 catalogs, but was revived later.

I.D. DATA

Serial numbers were not used. Engine numbers were stamped on the crankcase just back of the right-hand bank of cylinders and on a plate on the dash. Engine Nos.: 59-A-1 through 59-Z-1000 and 59-AA-1 through 59-BB-12. Job (Body) number is stamped on right front door sill.

TYPE 59 — V-8

The smaller sidelights were used and they were mounted closer to the windshield. A shield-shaped pattern on the headlight doors was changed to a narrow bead with curved sides. It had a detachable emblem at the top. Headlights and sidelights were optionally available in full nickel. A new Touring car was on the 132-inch wheelbase. The front wheels changed from a 10-spoke design to a 12-spoke design. The frame was stiffened by lengthening its deep section. The radiator water condenser was moved to the outside of the frame. An extra-length chassis was no longer available. The speedometer drive mechanism was moved from the front axle to the transmission.

Above: **1920 Cadillac, Type 59, town car**

TYPE 59

Model Number	Body Type & Seating	Factory Price	Shipping Weight	Production Total
—	4D Touring-7P	3,740	—	—
—	4D Phaeton-4P	3,590	—	—
—	2D Roadster-2/4P	3,590	—	—
4000	2D Victoria-4P	4,340	—	—
—	2D Coupe-2P	4,290	—	—
4010	4D Sedan-5P	4,750	—	—
4020	4D Suburban-7P	4,990	—	—
4030	4D Limousine-7P	5,090	—	—

Model Number	Body Type & Seating	Factory Price	Shipping Weight	Production Total
4050	4D Imperial Limousine-7P	5,190	—	—
4040	4D Town Brougham-7P	5,090	—	—

2nd Design

Model Number	Body Type & Seating	Factory Price	Shipping Weight	Production Total
—	4D Touring-7P	3,940	—	—
—	4D Phaeton-4P	3,790	—	—
—	2D Roadster-2/4P	3,790	—	—
4130	2D Victoria-4P	4,540	—	—
—	2D Coupe-2P	—	—	—
4140	4D Sedan-5P	4,950	—	—
4120	4D Suburban-7P	5,190	—	—
4150	4D Limousine-7P	5,290	—	—
4170	4D, Imperial Limousine-7P	5,390	—	—
4160	4D Town Brougham-7P	5,290	—	—

3rd Design

Model Number	Body Type & Seating	Factory Price	Shipping Weight	Production Total
—	4D Touring-7P	3,940	—	—
—	4D Phaeton-4P	3,790	—	—
—	2D Roadster-2/4P	3,790	—	—
4290	2D Victoria-4P	4,540	—	—
—	2D Coupe-2P	—	—	—
4270	4D Sedan-5P	4,950	—	—
4300	4D Suburban-7P	5,190	—	—
4360	4D Limousine-7P	5,290	—	—
4350	4D Imperial Limousine-7P	5,390	—	—
—	4D Town Brougham-7P	5,690	—	—

ENGINE

L-head. Cast iron blocks of four on aluminum crankcase. Bore and stroke: 3-1/8 x 5-1/8. Displacement: 314 cid. Horsepower: 79 at 2700 rpm. Taxable hp: 31.25. Main bearings: three. Rockers with roller cam follower. Cooling system capacity. 6 gal. Carburetor: float feed, auxiliary air control; manufactured by Cadillac under C.F. Johnson patents.

CHASSIS

Type 59 phaeton, roadster, victoria, coupe, sedan] Wheelbase: 125 inches. Front/Rear Tread: 56 inches. Tires: 34 x 4-1/2. [Others] Wheelbase: 132 inches. Front/Rear Tread: 56 inches. Tires: 35 x 5.

TECHNICAL

Selective sliding gear transmission. Case in unit with engine. Speeds: 3F/1R. Left drive, center control (right-hand drive optional). Multiple disc, dry plate clutch. Shaft drive. Spiral bevel, full-floating rear axle. Overall ratio: 4.44:1, 5.07:1. Mechanical brakes on two wheels, one external, one internal. Wood artillery wheels, demountable rims, 12 spoke. Wheels: 25 inches. Optional drive ratio: 3.94:1.

OPTIONS

All nickel headlights, sidelamps and hubcaps. Rudge-Whitworth wire wheels.

HISTORICAL

The Type 59 Cadillac was introduced in January 1920. Model-year sales and production was 24,878 cars. In 1920, the president and general manager of Cadillac was Richard H. Collins. H.H. Rice became president as of May 1921. The general state of the postwar economy, shortages of materials, railway strikes and the completion and occupation of a new factory resulted in a production slump at Cadillac during the 1920-1921 period. This was not due to lack of interest in the product itself. The World War I-era Type 57 had always been a sell out, so Cadillac entered the 1920s with long waiting lists of eager customers. It was simply hard for the company to build enough cars to meet demand. Due to reconstruction pressures in the nation and in the company—Cadillac continued building the new Type 59 for two years without significant styling or mechanical changes. 1920 was an eventful year for General Motors and for Cadillac. Colorful William C. Durant lost control of GM for the second and last time. The flamboyant and ambitious entrepreneur had again overextended himself in his enthusiasm to expend the corporation. He was finally ousted by a concerned board of directors. This meant that a major reorganization was needed. Pierre S. Dupoint was named president and Alfred P. Sloan instituted a new management structure that eventually made GM the largest and most successful company in the world. Also in this period, Charles F. Kettering (inventor of the self-starter) organized the GM Research Corporation.

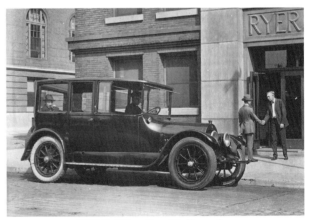

1921 Cadillac, Type 59, limousine

1922-1923

OVERVIEW

The new Type 61 Cadillac could most easily be identified by the taller hood louvers used on all models. The top of each ventilating louver was almost even with the apex of the front fender openings. Some body styles featured distinctive-looking sill plates that are characteristic of these models. Some other new details are described below. The 1922 series was carried over into 1923.

I.D. DATA

Serial numbers were not used. Engine numbers were stamped on the crankcase just back of the right-hand bank of cylinders and on a plate on the dash. Engine Nos: 61-A-1 through 61-Z-18006.

TYPE 61—V-8

The Type 61 had higher radiator and the "shoulders" of the hood were raised. The hood was made of aluminum. Despite having the same ground clearance as earlier models, the new Cadillacs had a lower center of gravity. Exterior door handles were provided on all doors, except the front doors of the Limousine. Closed cars had a soft-type roof construction. A fixed, leather-covered visor was also supplied on closed cars. Also seen on most Cadillacs

was a trunk rack and vertical rub strips on the rear of the body to protect the finish when luggage was carried. The five-passenger Sedan and Phaeton had and runningboard kick plates. The headlights were mounted on a single post

1922 Cadillac, Type 59, limousine

Albert Ketchum

Above: **1922 Cadillac, Type 61, five-passenger touring**

David McWalter

rather than forked one. The shield-shaped bead on the headlight doors had straight, rather than curved, sides. Optional equipment included nickel-plated lights and a nickel-plated radiator shell offered. The horn was moved to a new spot under the hood. New walnut steering wheel, without a hinge jutted out from a new instrument panel. A windshield cleaner and rearview mirror were now standard equipment. Two body styles, the two-passenger Coupe and the Town Brougham, were revived and a new five-passenger Coupe was added to the line along with a Landau Sedan for 1923. The 1923 Victoria had a roomier interior and doors that were hinged at the front.

TYPE 61

Model Number	Body Type & Seating	Factory Price	Shipping Weight	Production Total
	4D Touring-7P	3,940	4,025	—
	4D Phaeton-4P	3,790	3,955	—
	2D Roadster-2/4P	3,790	3,920	—
4420	2D Victoria-4P	4,540	4,115	—
4470	2D Coupe-2P	4,540	3,980	—
4440	2D Coupe-5P	4,690	4,130	—
4430	4D Sedan-5P	4,950	4,220	—
4400	4D Suburban-7P	5,190	4,420	—
4450	4D Limousine-7P	5,290	4,400	—
4460	4D Imperial Limousine-7P	5,390	4,450	—
4480	4D Town Brougham-7P	—	—	—
5160	4D Landau Sedan-5P	—	—	—

2nd Design

Model Number	Body Type & Seating	Factory Price	Shipping Weight	Production Total
	4D Touring-7P	3,150	4,025	—
	4D Phaeton-4P	3,150	3,955	—
	2D Roadster-2/4P	3,100	3,920	—
4430	2D Victoria-4P	3,875	4,115	—
5080	2D Coupe-2P	3,875	3,980	—
5050	2D Coupe-5P	3,925	4,130	—
5040	4D Sedan-5P	4,100	4,220	—
4410	4D Suburban-7P	4,250	4,420	—
5060	4D Limousine-7P	4,550	4,400	—
5070	4D Imperial Limousine-7P	4,600	4,450	—
	4D Town Brougham-7P	—	—	—
	4D Landau Sedan-5P	—	—	—

3rd Design

Model Number	Body Type & Seating	Factory Price	Shipping Weight	Production Total
	4D Touring-7P	2,885	4,025	—
	4D Phaeton-4P	2,885	3,955	—
	2D Roadster-2/4P	2,885	3,920	—
5090	2D Victoria-4P	3,675	4,115	—
	2D Coupe-2P	—	3,980	—
	2D Coupe-5P	3,750	4,130	—
	4D Sedan-5P	3,950	4,220	—
5030	4D Suburban-7P	3,990	4,420	—
	4D Limousine-7P	4,300	4,400	—
	4D Imperial Limousine-7P	4,400	4,450	—
	4D Town Brougham-7P	—	—	—
	4D Landau Sedan-5P	3,950	—	—

NOTE: Introductory prices were much the same as for the Type 59. In January 1922 there was a drastic price reduction. This was followed by a smaller reduction in December 1922. These were the first price reductions for Cadillac and followed an industry trend. Increased production schedules, higher efficiency in the new manufacturing facilities and economic pressures combined to make the reductions possible as well as necessary.

ENGINE

L-head. Cast iron blocks of four on aluminum crankcase. Bore and stroke: 3-1/8 x 5-1/8. Displacement: 314 cid. Brake hp: 79 at 2760 rpm. Taxable hp: 31.25. Compression Pressure: 180 lbs.-ft. at 2,000 rpm. Main bearings: three.

1922 Cadillac, Type 61, coupe

Walter Miller

Rockers with roller cam follower. Torque compression 180 lbs.-ft. at 2,000 rpm. Crankcase capacity: 6 qt. Cooling system capacity. 6 gal. Carburetor: float feed, auxiliary air control; manufactured by Cadillac under C.F. Johnson patents. Engine changes first seen in 1922 included a new carburetor with two-inch (5.08 cms) intake, a thermostatic fuel-mixture-control system (manual choke still used during cold starting), easily-accessible water drain valves that could be opened with a screwdriver, a camshaft drilled to provide internal oil passage and a two-pole generator in place of the previous four-pole ytpe.

[1923]

L-head. Cast iron blocks of four on aluminum crankcase. Bore and stroke: 3-1/8 x 5-1/8. Displacement: 314 cid. Brake hp: 79 at 2760 rpm. Taxable hp: 31.25. Compression Pressure: 180 lbs.-ft. at 2,000 rpm. Main bearings: three. Valve lifters: Rockers with roller cam follower. Crankcase capacity: 7 qt. Cooling system capacity. 6 gal. Carburetor: float feed, auxiliary air control; manufactured by Cadillac under C.F. Johnson patents.

CHASSIS

[Type 61] Wheelbase: 132 inches. Front/Rear Tread: 56 inches. Tires: 33 x 5. Chassis: Smaller wheels, giving lower

1923 Cadillac, Type 61 seven-passenger Suburban

Frank Williams

center of gravity. All bodies on 132 inches. wheelbase. Self-lubricating bushings at many points in brake and clutch linkage. New piston-type grease cups at other lube points.

TECHNICAL

Selective sliding gear transmission. Case in unit with engine. Speeds: 3F/1R. Left drive, center control (right-hand drive optional). Multiple disc, dry plate clutch. Shaft drive. Spiral bevel, full-floating rear axle. Overall ratio: 4.50:1, 4.91:1. Mechanical brakes on two wheels, one external, one internal. Wood artillery wheels, demountable rims, 12 spoke. Wheels: 23 inches. Optional drive ratio: 4.15:1. Driveline: Rear axle housing redesigned to maintain road clearance with smaller wheels. Final drive ratios now 4.50:1, 4.91:1 and 4.15:1 (special). Transmission lock provided.

OPTIONS

All nickel headlights, sidelamps, hubcaps and radiator shell. Rudge-Whitworth wire wheels.

HISTORICAL

Introduced September 1921. Model-year sales and production for 1922-1923 was 41,001. The president and general manager of Cadillac was Herbert H. Rice. During this period Cadillac invested $2,000,000 in plant improvements to combat its production problems.

Albert Ketchum

1922 Cadillac, Type 61, seven-passenger touring

1924

OVERVIEW

The 1924 Cadillac had a wider radiator, new drum-shaped headlights and a distinctive radiator shell design with angular lines at the upper corners. Duco nitrocellulose lacquer, manufactured by duPont de Nemours Company, greatly speeded up the paint-drying process and produced a much better finish on car bodies. This paint was first developed for General Motor's Oakland division and was soon adopted by other divisions like Cadillac. It reduced the time it took for auto paint to dry properly from weeks to hours. Finished cars no longer had to be stored at the factory, waiting for the paint to dry. This freed up already-existing factory space for additional car production.

I.D. DATA

There were no serial numbers used on the Cadillac V-63. Engine numbers were stamped on the crankcase just back of the right-hand bank of cylinders and on a plate on the dash. Starting: 63-A-1. Ending: 63-H-1550.

TYPE V-63–V-8

The 1924 Cadillac Type V-63 was similar to the 1923 Type 61, with a few exceptions. The hood was longer and the radiator sat one inch higher. The roof and rear quarter

Above: **1924 Cadillac, Series V-63, seven-passenger touring**

Tom Jevcak

lines of closed cars were softened. Liberal use was made of non-functional landau bars. The new headlights were bowl shaped, instead of bell shaped. The closed cars had a lower seating position and more interior room. Ventilator doors were set flush in the cowl. The windshield posts were 1-1/2 inches narrower. Full-width, curved division windows were used in some models. An automatic, vacuum-operated windshield cleaner was standard equipment. The two-passenger coupe now had a blind-rear-quarter roof treatment. A five-passenger sedan with an Imperial-type division window was offered. A new seven-passenger sedan was introduced at midyear. The Touring car featured dull finish black leather seat trim with an extra-heavy pebble grain texture. The Phaeton and the Roadster had bright-finish black leather with a long-grain texture. The Touring and phaeton had a fully-lined top while the roadster had a Sport Top. A plate glass backlight was incorporated into all tops. Open cars came with side curtains and the large, transparent areas in the curtains were fitted with double flaps on the lower edge which were tagged to facilitate easy attachment. The upper panels on all curtains could be opened to make hand signals and for ventilation. The side curtains came in a special container bag that had inserts to protect the "lights" or window sections. Closed cars featured selected mohair velvet or cloth fabrics over cushion springs of Cadillac design. The cars also had a waterproof toolbox with a long-grain textured covering

and a lock mounted in the right-hand dust shield. The upper and lower windshield sections were adjustable. Closed cars also had a sun-and-rain visor covered with a leather-grain fabric. Closed cars (except the Coupe) came equipped with dome lights and all models had a dash-mounted 8-day clock. A second such clock was fitted in the rear passenger compartment of the open Limousine, the Brougham de Ville, the Imperial Suburban and the Imperial Sedan. Instrumentation included a speedometer (which was visible from the rear compartment) a combination ammeter, air and oil pressure gauge, an electric motor horn, a foot rail (except Coupe and Roadster) , a robe rail, license tag holders, a rear view mirror, an automatic windshield cleaner, an electric cigar lighter (except open Limousine and Town Brougham), a portable underhood inspection light on a 14-ft. reel and a tire holder (with lock) for two spare tires.

TYPE V-63

Model Number	Body Type & Seating	Factory Price	Price Weight	Factory Total
NA	4D Touring-7P	3,085	4,280	—
NA	4D Phaeton-4P	3,085	4,200	—
NA	2D Roadster-2/4P	3,085	4,190	—
5490	2D Victoria-4P	3,275	4,380	—
5380	2D Coupe-2P	3,875	4,270	—
5280	2D Coupe-5P	3,950	4,370	—
5270	4D Sedan-5P	4,150	4,480	—
5290	4D Landau Sedan-5P	4,150	4,480	—
5460	4D Imperial Sedan-5P	4,400	4,600	—
5260	4D Suburban-7P	4,250	4,560	—
5310	4D Imperial Suburban-7P	4,500	4,640	—
5470	4D Sedan-7P	3,585	4,610	—
5300	4D Limousine-7P	4,600	4640	—
5370	4D Town Brougham-7P	4,600	4,530	—

ENGINE

L-head. Heads detachable. Cast iron blocks of four on aluminum crankcase. Bore and stroke: 3-1/8 x 5-1/8. Displacement: 314 cid. Compression ratio: 4.25:1. Brake hp: 80 at 3000 rpm. Taxable hp: 31.25. Main bearings: three. Rockers with roller cam follower. Crankcase capacity: 7 qt. Cooling system capacity: 6 gal. Carburetor: float feed, auxiliary air control; manufactured by Cadillac under C.F. Johnson patents. Two-plane crankshaft 90-degree counter-balanced.

NOTE: Starting in 1924 the Cadillac 90-degree V-8 used a "compensated" crankshaft. The crank throws were 90 degrees apart and the crankshaft was fitted with compensating weights. It was claimed that the new crankshaft "rotates with unprecedented smoothness." The use of a fully-counterweighted two-plane crankshaft meant that all primary and secondary forces were balanced and engine smoothness was improved. The spark plug firing order was changed to: 1L-4R-4L-2L-3R-3L-2R-1R. Flywheel weight was reduced as a result of the increased flywheel effect of compensators and the larger (2-3/8—inch-diameter) crankshaft. There were 16 cams on the new camshaft. The rocker arms and plate were redesigned. Chain adjustment was no longer needed as a result of the 1/4-inch wider chains and greater smoothness of the engine.

CHASSIS

[V-63] Wheelbase: 132 inches. Front/Rear Tread: 56 inches. Tires: 33 x 5. [Special Chassis] Wheelbase: 145 inches. Front/Rear Tread: 56 inches. Tires: 33 x 5. Chassis: Front wheel brakes added. Service brake pedal acts on rear external and front internal bands. Emergency brake lever acts on rear internal bands. Front axle/steering knuckle design changed to reversed Elliott type. New tie rod with adjustable ball and socket ends moved from front to rear of axle. Two cross members added to frame. 145 inches. wheelbase special chassis once more made available.

TECHNICAL

Selective sliding gear transmission. Case in unit with engine. Speeds: 3F/1R. Left drive, center control (right-hand drive. optional). Multiple disc, dry plate clutch. Shaft drive. Spiral bevel, full-floating rear axle. Overall ratio: 4.50:1, 4.91:1. Mechanical brakes on four wheels. Wood artillery wheels, demountable rims, 12 spoke. Wheels: 23 inches. Optional drive ratio 4.15:1. Driveline: No significant changes.

OPTIONS

All nickel headlights, radiator shell and hubcaps. Wire wheels. Disc wheels. Five balloon tires on disc wheels ($140). Six balloon tires on disc wheels, plus double carrier for spares ($215). Five balloon tires on wire wheels ($225). Six balloon tires on wire wheels, plus double carrier for spares ($315).

HISTORICAL

The 1924 Cadillac was introduced September 1923. Innovations included a compensated, inherently-balanced, two-plane crankshaft and four-wheel brakes. Model-year sales and production were 35,500 for 1924-1925 combined . The president and general manager of Cadillac was Herbert H. Rice.

1924 Cadillac, Series V-63, seven-passenger touring

1924 Cadillac, Series V-63, touring

David Lyon

1925

OVERVIEW

Additional nickel-plated trim and softer curves in the upper radiator corners were 1925 Cadillac characteristics. A new raised, upswept molding carried the Cadillac crest. Other new features included vertical radiator shell shutters, crowned elliptical and tool boxes mounted at the front of the running boards.

I.D. DATA

Serial numbers were not used. Engine numbers were stamped on the crankcase just back of the right-hand bank of cylinders and on a plate on the dash. Starting: 63-H-1551. Ending: 63-M-2572.

TYPE V-63 — V-8

The year 1925 brought a continuation of the 1924 line with a new "Custom" line added. The Custom line was introduced in October 1924. Five "custom" bodies were shown in the sales catalog, but a total of eight were built according to actual job numbers. With these cars, the customer could choose from 24 color harmonies and 10 upholstery patterns. The introduction of Duco finish started a color explosion. A new nickel-plated radiator shell and nickel-plated headlights became standard. A

"scrolled" radiator shell, first used only on Custom line models, was soon adapted to the Standard line. Custom line cars were distinguished by their sloping windshield and double belt molding. A two-door, five-passenger coach was added to the Standard line. Blue, Waverley Gray and Arizona Gray Duco finish was available for cars in the Standard line. Custom models were available any color upon 60 days notice, although six standard colors were also offered. A number of Cadillacs with custom bodies by various coachbuilders were exhibited at auto shows and built to customer order.

1925 Cadillac, Series V-63, Custom coupe

Above: **1925 Cadillac, Series V-63, Custom Victoria**

David Lyon

TYPE V-63

Model Number	Body Type & Seating	Factory Price	Shipping Weight	Production Total
1149	4D Touring-7P	3,185	—	—
1150	4D Phaeton-4P	3,185	—	—
1151	2D Roadster-2/4P	3,185	—	—
5690	2D Victoria-4P	3,485	—	—
6150	4D Sedan-5P	3,835	—	—
5700	4D Landau Sedan-5P	3,835	—	—
5680	4D Sedan-7P	3,885	—	—
6030	4D Imperial Sedan-7P	4,010	—	—
6010	2D Coach-5P	3,185	—	—

"Custom" Body Styles

Model Number	Body Type & Seating	Factory Price	Shipping Weight	Production Total
5750	4D Sedan-5P	4,550	—	—
5720	4D Suburban-7P	4,650	—	—
NA	4D Imperial Sedan-5P	—	—	—
5760	4D Limousine-7P	—	—	—
5730	4D Imperial Suburban-7P	4,950	—	—
5770	4D Town Brougham-7P	—	—	—
5740	2D Coupe-5P	4,350	—	—
5710	2D Coupe-2P	3,975	—	—

ENGINE

L-head. Heads detachable. Cast iron blocks of four on aluminum crankcase. Bore and stroke: 3-1/8 x 5-1/8. Displacement: 314 cid. Compression ratio: 4.25:1. Brake hp: 80 at 3000 rpm. Taxable hp: 31.25. Main bearings: three. Rockers with roller cam follower. Crankcase capacity: 7 qt. Cooling system capacity. 6 gal. Carburetor: float feed, auxiliary air control; manufactured by Cadillac under C.F. Johnson patents. Two-plane crankshaft 90-degree counter-balanced.

Note: Crankcase ventilation system to eliminate dilution and condensation used on the last 2,000 units of the Cadillac V-63 models built in late 1925 and continued on the 1926 and later Model 314 "New Ninety Degree Cadillac"

CHASSIS

[All standard body styles and custom two-passenger coupe] Wheelbase: 132 inches. Front/Rear Tread: 56 inches. Tires: 33 x 5. Special chassis. Wheelbase: 145 inches.

Front/Rear Tread: 56 inches. Tires: 33 x 5. [All custom body styles except two-passenger coupe] Wheelbase: 138 inches. Front/Rear Tread: 56 inches. Tires: 33 x 5.

TECHNICAL

Selective sliding gear transmission. Case in unit with engine. Speeds: 3F/1R. Left drive, center control (right-hand drive optional). Multiple disc, dry plate clutch. Shaft drive. Spiral bevel, full-floating rear axle. Overall ratio: 4.50:1, 4.91:1. Mechanical brakes on four wheels. Wood artillery wheels, demountable rims, 12 spoke. Wheels: 23 inches. Tires: 33 x 6.75 low-pressure type. Optional drive ratio: 4.15:1, 5.55:1.

OPTIONS

Black radiator shell. Wire wheels. Disc wheels. Five balloon tires on disc wheels ($140). Six balloon tires on disc wheels, plus double carrier for spares ($215). Five balloon tires on wire wheels ($225). Six balloon tires on wire wheels, plus double carrier for spares ($315).

HISTORICAL

The 1925 Cadillac V-63 was a continuation of the 1924 series with the all-new Custom line added in October 1924. Model year sales and production was 35,500 for 1924-1925 combined. The president and general manager of Cadillac in early 1925 was Herbert H. Rice. Lawrence P. Fisher of Fisher Body Company took over as head of Cadillac in April 1925. A Cadillac factory-building program was almost completed with a $2 million additional investment for seven new foundries on a seven-acre site. In September the Fleetwood Body Corporation was purchased by General Motors. Six Duco color schemes were standard, but any color scheme was available with 60 days notice.

1926

OVERVIEW

In July 1925, the Cadillac 314–promoted as "The New Ninety-degree Cadillac"—replaced the V63. The new model was characterized by its more rounded nickel—plated radiator shell. The 314 represented a transition from the famed engineering of Henry Leland to the styling-dominated tenure of Earnest Seaholm and Harley Earle. According to one 1926 product catalog, all bodies were Fisher-built, but later in the year, custom Fleetwood bodies became available on individual order. Cadillac's V-8 was the third engine-design variation since the 1914-15 V-8. It had the same bore and stroke, crankshaft and architecture as the previous Cadillac V-8s. A new single-pump cooling system incorporated thermostatically-controlled radiator shutters. A new Delco 2-unit electrical system featured a vertical starter motor and separate generator. Longitudinal, semi-elliptic rear springs brought Cadillacs closer to the ground. With more power and less weight, the 1926 Cadillac had snappier road performance. Other Cadillac features included "Silico-chrome" valves, a 4-pole generator that was belt-driven from the camshaft, an Exide 130-amp-hour six-volt battery, tilt-beam headlights, a clutch with two fewer (15) carbon steel plates, 6.75 x

33 balloon tires and a choice of three gear ratios: 4.91:1, 4.5:1 and 4.15:1. Open cars were transferred to the long-wheelbase Custom line and the two-passenger Custom coupe was transferred to Standard line. A rear quarter window was added. The Coach became the Brougham. The Landau Sedan, Limousine and Town Brougham were dropped. Cadillac's semi-commercial chassis now had a 150-inch wheelbase. Cadillac offered funeral coaches and a Superior-bodied ambulance, plus an armored car.

I.D. DATA

Serial numbers were not used. Engine numbers were stamped on crankcase immediately above the base of the oil filler spout and on plate on dash. Engine numbers for Series 314 cars consist of six digits, starting with the figure 1. Unit numbers for Series 314 cars consist of the figure 1, followed by a dash, followed by one to five digits. Starting: (1926) 114250. Ending: (1926) 142020. Up to the Series 314, Cadillac had used the engine number as the key identifying number for the vehicle and all changes made during a model production run were recorded by engine number. Parts orders listing the part and the engine number ensured receipt of the correct version of the part, including correct paint color, if applicable. Starting with the Series 314, a "unit and car number" scheme was put into effect. Each car was assigned an engine number, which was stamped on the engine and on a plate on the firewall

---

Above: **1926 Cadillac, Series 314, five-passenger sedan**
Dr. Thomas Dawson

just before the car was shipped. This engine number, as before, was the identifying number of the vehicle—to be used for registration, etc. However, changes were recorded, for the most part, by unit number, vehicle was the number stamped on each main assembly of the vehicle as that assembly was completed. Engine number and engine unit number bore no relation to each other. A change made at engine unit number 138009 might or might not have been included on the car carrying engine number 138009.

NOTE: Various Cadillac manuals and parts books detail the various changes by unit number or, in rare cases, by engine/car number, but no cross reference exists. If the factory kept any cross reference of unit numbers against engine/car numbers, they did not pass it along with the car. Dealers were urged to make a unit number record for each of their customer's cars, so as to be able to service and supply parts for the car according to the exact requirements of the particular configuration of that vehicle. The various numbers are located as follows: [Chassis/Frame Unit Number] On the upper surface of the left-hand side bar, opposite the steering gear; [Body Unit Number and Job/Style Number] On right front sill or on metal plate on the front face of the dash; [Steering Gear Unit Number] On housing, near lubrication fitting; [Transmission Unit Number] On top of flange holding brake and clutch pedal bracket; [Clutch Unit Number] On front and rear retaining plates; [Front Axle Unit Number] On upper surface of axle I-beam; [Rear Axle Unit Number] On rear surface of the housing, just to right of cover plate; [Carburetor Unit Number] On left-hand rear face of flange by which carburetor is attached to intake header; [Generator Unit Number] On side of generator and [Starter Unit Number] On side of starter.

SERIES 314 STANDARD — V-8

Both Standard and Custom models had a higher, narrower radiator with the new thermostatically controlled shutters in place of the old valve-type shutters. The hood and cowl panels were longthened and long, sweeping front fenders carried the battery and tool boxes. A one-piece windshield was used on all cars. The windshield used on open cars swung from a pivot at its top. A vertical "Vision & Ventilating" or (V.V.) windshield was used on closed cars. Fourteen louvers decorated the rear section of the hood sides. The new nickel-plated radiator shell had the Cadillac emblem set on a shield-shaped background. All front doors were now hinged at the windshield post. No sidelights were used. The new drum-type headlights (9-inch diameter on Standard models) contained parking light bulb and double filament bulbs that provided a "tilting beam." At the rear, the taillight was mounted on the left fender, instead of on the tire carrier. A motor-driven horn was attached to the left-hand headlight bracket, instead of intake manifold. In the spring of 1926, effective at Chassis Unit Number 1-25000, the battery and the tool boxes were moved from the front fenders to a location behind the runningboard dust shields. All 1926 Cadillac had a 65-point lubrication system. Even the 1926 Standard line was said to embody "Cadillac's highest ideals of travel comfort and of beauty. The standard models had flatter, vertical windshield and nickel-plated door handles. Standard models included the two-passenger Coupe, the 5-passenger Sedan, the 7-passenger Sedan, the 4-passenger Victoria and the 5-passenger Brougham. Standard equipment included patent-construction armrests, inner doors garnished with walnut window moldings, sturdy doors with outside door handles and double safety catches, combined interior door and pull handles and an instrument board with walnut inset panels. Closed cars were upholstered in selected Mohair-velvet or cloth fabrics. They had cushions and back springs of special design encased in fabric. Standard jobs had cotton bats in plain pleats. The rigid metal running boards had ribbed-rubber matting and a white metal binding with a black facing. Other regular features included a large cowl ventilator, a horn button in center of the steering wheel, a universal key starting switch, a tire carrier, a gearshift lever, door locks, a combined cigar lighter and inspection lamp on a 12-ft. cord, an 8-day dashboard clock, a foot rail in all models except coupes, a power air-compressor for tires, a robe rail, license tag holders, a rearview mirror, an automatic windshield cleaner, a tire carrier with approved lock and a vanity case. The Brougham and the five-passenger sedan had a trunk rack.

SERIES 314 CUSTOM — V-8

Later in the year, custom Fleetwood bodies became available on individual order. Custom line Cadillacs were built mainly on the 138-inch wheelbase and most models could be immediately identified by their sloping, single-panel, swing-out windshield. The Touring Roadster and Phaeton had special slanting windshields. A one-piece windshield with vent wings was seen on open cars. Other custom characteristics included 10-inch drum headlights, a special flush roof bead molding (or rain gutter), a Motometer on top of the radiator grille, outside door handles with hard rubber finish, a double-bar front bumper with twin bumperettes, a rear bumper, an automatic dome light, panel lights and molded-rubber running board mats. Rich, inlaid, hardwood panels decorated the interior door panels. Also inside were an electric gasoline gauge, detachable vanity and smoker cases, a solid-hinged robe rail with end handles, silk cord assist handles, cable-type window lifters and seats with special, fabric-encased springs. The Phaeton and the five-passenger Sedan came standard with a trunk rack. The Cadillac's 33 x 6.75 tires could be mounted on wood-spoke, steel-disc or wire-spoke

John Koll

1926 Cadillac, Series 314, custom touring

wheels. Custom line body types included a five-passenger Sedan, a five-passenger Coupe, a two-passenger Roadster with three-bow top (on the smaller wheelbase), a four-passenger Phaeton with a four-bow top, a seven-passenger Suburban, a seven-passenger Imperial Suburban and the seven-passenger Touring with five-bow top. On the latter model the top was covered in heavy black leather-like fabric and a full headlining was provided, along with side curtains that opened with the doors. Seven Duco color treatments were standard.

SERIES 314—Standard body styles

Model Number	Body Type & Seating	Factory Price	Shipping Weight	Production Total
6400	2D Brougham-5P	2,995	4075	—
6430	2D Coupe-2P	3,045	4040	—
6490	2D Victoria-4P	3,095	4115	—
6420	4D Sedan-5P	3,195	4,155	—
6410	4D Sedan-7P	3,295	4,240	—
6440	4D Imperial-7P	3,435	4,360	—

"Custom" body styles (August 1925)

Model Number	Body Type & Seating	Factory Price	Shipping Weight	Production Total
1154	4D Touring-7P	3,250	4,300	—
1155	4D Phaeton-4P	3,250	3,960	—
1156	2D Roadster-2/4P	3,250	3,920	—
6460	2D Coupe-5P	4,000	4,190	—
6470	4D Sedan-5P	4,150	4,190	—
6450	4D Suburban-7P	4,285	4,250	—
6480	4D Imperial Suburban-7P	4,485	4,355	—

"Custom" closed body styles (January 1926) replacing closed bodies of August 1925 (sloping windshield)

Model Number	Body Type & Seating	Factory Price	Shipping Weight	Production Total
6680	2D Coupe-5P	4,000	4,465	—
6690	4D Sedan-5P	4,150	4,465	—
6670	4D Suburban-7P	4,285	4,580	—
6700	4D Imperial Suburban-7P	4,485	4,615	—

Midyear additions to "Custom"

Model Number	Body Type & Seating	Factory Price	Shipping Weight	Production Total
6680-L	2D Cabriolet Coupe-5P	—	—	—
6690-L	4D Cabriolet Sedan-5P	—	—	—
6670-L	4D Cabriolet Suburban-7P	—	—	—
6700-L	4D Imperial Cabriolet Suburban-7P	—	—	—

Semi-commercial line

Model Number	Body Type & Seating	Factory Price	Shipping Weight	Production Total
NA	5D Custom Limousine Funeral Coach	—	—	—
NA	5D Imperial Limousine Ambulance	—	—	—
NA	5D Imperial Limousine Funeral Coach	—	—	—
NA	3D Armored Car	—	6500	—

ENGINE

L-head. Cast iron blocks of four on aluminum crankcase. Bore and stroke: 3-1/8 x 5-1/8. Displacement: 314.4 cid. Compression ratio: 5.0:1. Brake hp: 87 ay 3000 rpm. Taxable hp: 31.25. Main bearings: three. Rockers with roller cam follower. Crankcase capacity: 8 qt. Cooling system capacity. 5.5 gal. Carburetor: float feed, auxiliary air control; manufactured by Cadillac under C.F. Johnson patents.

Note: A crankcase ventilation system to eliminate dilution and condensation continued on the 1926 and later Cadillacs using this engine family. Oil filter added. Oil level indicator on right side of crankcase instead of inside "vee." Oil filler cap screw type instead of hinged. Camshaft bearing fed full oil pressure, not overflow from regulator. Rocker arms eliminated. Valves and tappets placed at angle to the cylinder bores to line up with cams. One water pump at left. Detachable elbow on cylinder heads. Oil pump at right front corner of crankcase, in place of second water pump. Oil and water pumps driven directly from cross shaft. Starter and generator separate units for first time on Cadillac. Starter vertical at top of flywheel housing, driving through teeth on rear face of flywheel. Generator in front, in vee. Generator/fan driven by belt, eliminating one chain. Tension on single chain maintained by idler sprocket. Front cover of engine made of steel instead of aluminum. Intake manifold now a separate piece.

CHASSIS

[All Standard cars plus Custom roadster] Wheelbase: 132 inches. Front/Rear Tread: 56 inches. Tires: 33 x 6.75 low pressure. [All Custom cars except roadster] Wheelbase: 138 inches. Front/Rear Tread: 56 inches. Tires: 33 x 6.75 low pressure. [Semi-commercial] Wheelbase: 150 inches. Front/Rear Tread: 56 inches. Tires: 33 x 6.75 low pressure. Semi-elliptic rear springs with ball-and-socket shackles were used. The spring seats no longer oscillated on the rear axle housing. Custom models had metal spring covers. The torque arm was relocated from the right-hand side to the left-hand side and was now connected to the frame through a fabric hanger. Watson stabilator shock absorbers were now used. In the spring, at steering gear unit number 1-23500 the steering mechanism was changed from worm-and-sector type to split-nut design.

TECHNICAL

Selective sliding gear transmission. Case in unit with engine. Speeds: 3F/1R. Left drive, center control (right-hand drive optional). Multiple disc clutch. Shaft drive. Spiral bevel, full-floating rear axle. Overall ratio: 4.91:1, 4.5:1, 4.15:1. Mechanical brakes on four wheels. Wood artillery wheels, split rim, 12 spoke (wire and disc optional). Wheels: 21 inches. Optional drive ratio: 5.33:1 (Standard on armored car). Driveline: Axle shafts have 14 drive teeth instead of 6 lugs. Fuel capacity: 16.67 imperial gallons (75.7 liters). The Cadillac radiator was now of cellular design and an additional radiator-to-cowl brace was required. The balloon tires were mounted on split rims with no side rings. New brake drums were bell-shaped to give clearance for balloon tires.

OPTIONS

Front bumper for Standard cars ($24). Rear bumper for Standard cars ($24). Heater ($32). Spring covers for Standard cars ($20). 33 x 5 tires on wooden wheels (NC). Tonneau windshields ($90-120). Trunks ($56-72.50).

Note: Cadillac still took the stand that its cars were complete and ready for entirely acceptable service as built.

However, accessories were recognized and dealers were encouraged to handle this business. Accessory catalogs were published by factory branches and the factory put out bulletins to dealers. It would be a few more years

before the factory put out an accessory catalog directly to the public.

HISTORICAL

The 1926 Cadillacs were introduced in August 1925. New features included a crankcase-ventilation system. Calendar-year sales was 27,771. Calendar-year production was 27,771. Model-year sales and production for 1925-1926 (actually August 1925 through September 1927) was 50,619. The president and general manager of Cadillac was Lawrence P. Fisher. The 200,000th Cadillac built was sold in January 1926 to Glenn H. Curtiss, a famous inventor and manufacturer of airplanes and hydroplanes. A new Cadillac administration building, started in 1919, was completed in 1926. Cadillac claimerd that, "Public preference for the Cadillac is pronounced only because public confidence in Cadillac mechanism, coachwork, and policies has never been betrayed." Cadillac chief engineer Ernest Seaholm was largely responsible for the new 314's design. He worked with assistant chief engineer C.W. Strickland in designing the car. Engineer Frank Johnson handled transmission design, H.H. Gilbert was the research engineer, G.E. Parker was the designer and W.N. Davis was body engineer.

Dr. Thomas Dawson

1926 Cadillac, Series 314, five-passenger sedan

1927

Overview

The 314-A Series cars were introduced in July 1926 and produced through the following August. There was a new radiator and fender design with inside compartments for the battery and tools (which were no longer carried in boxes on the fenders). Fifty body styles were offered and 11 were updated or all-new models. There were 18 Fisher bodies of which five were new styles. Eleven other bodies were new or modified. Brunn, Fleetwood and Willoughby offered custom bodies for the Custom Series chassis. A new 150-inch wheelbase was used for professional cars, such as the hearses and ambulances built by Meteor Body Works of Piqua, Ohio. Most standard body types matched those of 1926.

I.D. DATA

Serial numbers were not used on the 1927 Cadillac. Engine numbers stamped on crankcase immediately above the base of the oil filler spout and on plate on dash. Starting: 142021. Ending: 150619.

SERIES 314A STANDARD – V-8

For 1927 the battery box and tool-box were removed from running boards and were instead carried in compartments built into the body sills. The new radiator shell had sharp corners between the top and front surfaces and a round, colored Cadillac emblem on a black background. Roadsters and phaetons have forward-folding windshields. The hood had 14 louvers again. Large drum headlights were now fitted to models, instead of to just the Custom Series models. Cadillac's new walnut instrument board had handsome silver inlays. Five new "Cabriolets" were actually closed cars with leather-covered rear roof quarters. Cadillacs also featured a new push-pull type ignition switch, a new steering-wheel-mounted light switch, windshields on roadsters and phaetons, an adjustable roadster seat, nickel side lamps and a new Delco ignition system. A Sport Coupe and Sport Sedan were added to Standard line. A new 138-inch wheelbase was used on the Standard seven-passenger sedan and a new Standard Victoria could be converted into a five-passenger car by removal of the parcel compartment. The vibrator-type horn had a "bent" trumpet section. Front and rear bumpers, a motometer and fender wells were standard on the Sport Coupe, Sport Sedan and Sport Phaeton.

Above: **1927 Cadillac, Series 314, sedan**

David Lyon

SERIES 314A CUSTOM – V-8

A new Convertible Coupe and a Dual-Cowl Sport Phaeton were added to the Custom line, which was available with bodies by Fleetwood, Brunn, Willoughby and other body builders. The new 138-inch wheelbase was used for Imperial Sedans. The monogram panel on Touring and Phaetons models extended to the cowl. The vertical moldings in front of the rear doors were moved to the back of the doors. "Custom" cars (and Standard sport models) had a nickel cowl band and nickel-plated sidelights. The headlight bodies on Custom models were nickel plated. Front and rear bumpers and a motometer were standard on Custom line models.

SERIES 314A—Standard Body Styles

Model Number	Body Type & Seating	Factory Price	Shipping Weight	Production Total
6970	2D Brougham-5P	2,995	4,170	—
6980	2D Coupe-2P	3,100	4,105	—
7000	2D Sport Coupe-2P	3,500	4,460	—
7030	2D Victoria-5P	3,95	4,90	—
6990	4D Sedan-5P	3,250	4,270	—
7040	4D Sport Sedan-5P	3,650	4,590	—
7050	4D Sedan-7P	3,400	4,370	—
7010	4D Imperial-7P	3,535	4,480	—

Factory "Custom" Body Styles

Model Number	Body Type & Seating	Factory Price	Shipping Weight	Production Total
7020	2D Convertible Coupe-2/4P	3,450	4,300	—
6680	2D Coupe-5P	3,855	4,465	—
6690	4D Sedan-5P	3,995	4,465	—
6670	4D Suburban-7P	4,125	4,580	—
6700	4D Imperial-7P	4,350	4,615	—
6680-L	2D Cabriolet Coupe-5P	3,955	—	—
6690-L	4D Cabriolet Sedan-5P	4,095	—	—
6670-L	4D Cabriolet Suburban-7P	4,225	—	—
6700-L	4D Cabriolet Imperial-7P	4,450	—	—
1165	2D Roadster-2/4P	3,350	4,220	—
1164	4D Phaeton-4P	3,450	4,275	—
1164-B	4D Dual-Cowl Phaeton-4P	3,975	4,465	—
1163	4D Touring-4P	3,450	4,285	—

Fleetwood Custom Body Styles

Model Number	Body Type & Seating	Factory Price	Shipping Weight	Production Total
2891	Limousine Brougham	5,525	—	—
2925	Town Cabriolet (seats forward)-7P	5,750	—	—
3200	Town Cabriolet (opera seats)-7P	5,500	—	—
3202	Coupe with rumble-2P	4,775	—	—
3260	Imperial-5P	4,975	—	—
3260-5	Sedan-5P	4,875	—	—
3261	Imperial Cabriolet-5	5,125	—	—
3261-5	Sedan Cabriolet-5P	4,975	—	—
3275	Imperial-7P	5,150	—	—
3275-5	Sedan-7P	4,975	—	—
3276	Imperial Cabriolet-7P	5,375	—	—
3291	Limousine Brougham	5,525	—	—
3078	Cabriolet-7P	—	—	—
3012	Transformable Cabriolet-7P	—	—	—
2950	Convertible Cabriolet-7P	—	—	—

Note: A Fleetwood convertible coupe, 2935, also was available.

Brumm and Willoughby Custom—Brumm Body Styles

Model Number	Body Type & Seating	Factory Price	Shipping Weight	Production Total
1810	Collapsible Cabriolet-4P	—	—	—
1836	Sedan-4P	—	—	—
1915	Sedan Landau-6P	—	—	—
NA	Town Cabriolet	4,800	—	—

Willoughby Body Styles

Model Number	Body Type & Seating	Factory Price	Shipping Weight	Production Total
NA	Town Cabriolet	4800	—	—

Semi-commercial line: Continuation of 1926.

ENGINE

L-head. Cast iron blocks of four on aluminum crankcase. Bore and stroke: 3-1/8 x 5-1/8. Displacement: 314 cid. Compression ratio: 4.25:1. Brake hp: 87 ay 3000 rpm. Taxable hp: 31.25. Main bearings: three. Rockers with roller cam follower. Crankcase capacity: 8 qt. Cooling system capacity: 4.5 gal. Carburetor: float feed, auxiliary air control; manufactured by Cadillac under C.F. Johnson patents. Early in 1927, at Engine Unit Number 1-41001 (Chassis Unit Number 1-40994), practically everything on the outside of the engine, except the carburetor, was relocated. The overall appearance, except for the location of the starter, now resembled that of the soon-to-be-introduced 303-cid LaSalle engine. The generator and water pump were moved to the lower right front corner of

This Cadillac ad from 1927 appealed to affluent customers.

the engine and were driven by a common chain. The fan was once more on a separate bracket and still belt driven. The distributor went from the rear to the front of the engine and onto a common shaft with the oil pump, now inside the engine. The fuel-pressure pump was now at the rear of the engine, driven by a connecting rod. The starter was moved forward. It was now driven through gear teeth cut on the front face of the flywheel.

CHASSIS

[All Standard cars except seven-passenger sedan and Imperial. Custom roadster and convertible coupe] Wheelbase: 132 inches. Front/Rear Tread: 56 inches. Tires: 33 x 6.75 low pressure. [Semi-commercial models] Wheelbase: 150 inches. Front/Rear Tread: 56 inches. Tires: 33 x 6.75 low pressure. [All Custom Series except Roadster and Convertible Coupe. Standard seven-passenger sedan and Imperial.] Wheelbase: 138 inches. Front/Rear Tread: 56 inches. Tires: 33 x 6.75 low pressure.

TECHNICAL

A vision of elegance was apparent in this 1927 Cadillac ad.

Selective sliding gear transmission, case in unit with engine. Speeds: 3F/1R. Left-hand drive, center control (right-hand drive optional). Multiple dry-disc clutch. Shaft drive. Spiral bevel, full-floating rear axle. Overall ratio: 4.91:1. Mechanical brakes on four wheels. Wood artillery wheels, split rim, 12 spoke. (See Note). Wheels: 21 inches. Disc wheels were standard on the Standard sport coupe and sedan. Wire wheels were standard on the Custom sport phaeton. At Steering Gear Unit Number 1-44906, steering gear was changed back to worm and sector type.

OPTIONS

Front bumper for Standard cars ($25). Rear bumper for Standard cars ($25). Tire cover(s) ($6.25-17.50). Black radiator shell (NC). Heater ($40). Trunk rack ($50). Trunks ($55-91). Armrest on Standard line ($25). Motometer on Standard line ($10). Cowl lamps on Standard line ($75). Nickel headlights on Standard line ($10). 33 x 5 high pressure tires (NC). Disc wheels set of five (NC). Disc wheels set of six with dual carrier ($25). Wire wheels set of five ($140). Wire wheels set of six, with dual carrier ($175). Six wire wheels, fender wells ($350). Six disc wheels, fender wells ($240). Six wood wheels, fender wells ($200).

HISTORICAL

Calendar year sales were 8,599. Calendar year production was 8,599. A total of 50,619 Cadillacs were built and sold in the model year running August 1925 through September 1927. The president and general manager of Cadillac was Lawrence P. Fisher. "Fifty body styles and types —Five hundred color and upholstery combinations" was Cadillac's catch phrase for its new program to individualize the motor car. Change was constant and everything was tried. Pilot models were sold but not cataloged. The catalog was only a starting point—the customer could pick almost any combination of bits and pieces and have a unique motor car without the expense of a full custom. The authenticity of surviving cars may be in question because of the multitude of possible variations. In the final analysis, if it has a vertical starter motor, it's most likely a 314. Many Cadillac dealers staged a "Silver Anniversary Salon" in October 1926 to officially launch the 1927 models. One Chicago dealer exhibited 30 models in huge tent, transformed into a garden, where full orchestra entertained nightly. The show drew 2000 visitors a day. The La Salle debuted as a companion car to the Cadillac. Also, 1927 was the first year that specific Fleetwood body styles with the familiar four-digit Job Numbers were listed for Cadillac. All Fleetwood closed sedans had rear-hinged front doors. Town cars had flat windshields and leather cabriolet roofs.

1928

OVERVIEW

With a new 341-cid V-8, the 1928 Cadillacs used a matching Series 341 designation. Thanks to a new 140-inch wheelbase for passenger cars, all Cadillacs looked longer and more streamlined. The longer wheelbase, combined with a rear axle mounted below the springs in "underslung" fashion, allowed for long, low-slung body lines. A deeper and narrower cellular-type radiator was mounted lower in the frame. The hood had multiple narrow louvers that stopped short of the radiator shell. At the rear a ribbed fuel tank cover emphasized the streamlining. Cone-shaped headlights were used. Fisher-bodied models, formerly divided into Standard and Custom lines, were now all in one series and 26 basic body styles were offered. The Victoria was dropped. The two-door Brougham was replaced by the four-door Town sedan. Funeral coaches, ambulances used a new 152-inch wheelbase and Superior bodies. By 1928, General Motors owned Fisher Body Co. and Fleetwood Body Co. They had become GM Divisions in June 1926 with Fleetwood becoming a division of Fisher. Practically all of Fleetwood's output was now on the Cadillac or LaSalle chassis and most Cadillac bodies, whether catalog designs or full customs, were built by Fleetwood.

Above: **1928 Cadillac, Series 341, Fisher Custom town sedan**

I.D. DATA

There were no serial numbers used. Engine numbers were stamped on plate on front of dash and on crankcase just below the water inlet on the right side. Starting: 300001. Ending: 320001.

SERIES 341-A—FISHER—V-8

The top of the hood and radiator shell on the 1928 Cadillac were flattened and 30 narrow louvers were set toward the rear of the hood side panels. Dual ventilator doors were used in the top of the cowl on open cars and in the sides of the cowl on closed cars. Massive 12-inch bullet-type headlights were mounted on a crossbar between the fenders. A monogram rod was attached between the headlights and nickeled wire-conduit stanchions were placed between the headlights and the frame. Windsplits on the lights were also featured on the panels and moldings of the hood and cowl. An extra wide single-belt molding blended into the cowl and hood, as well as closed-car body pillars. Matching sidelights were mounted on the cowl. Dual ball-shaped taillights were mounted on the rear fenders. The monogram panel on four-door open bodies ran back to the rear doors only. At the 24th NY Automobile Salon that opened on December 2, 1927, Fisher exhibited only three "custom" bodies on the Cadillac chassis, but at least 15 were available. Standard

1928 Cadillac, Series 341, Fisher Custom sport phaeton

equipment for 1928 Cadillacs included a compensated 90-degree V-8 engine, a new-design clutch, a 21-gallon gas tank, a vibrator horn, tilt-beam headlights, dual side lights, dual rear lights (right-hand stop light and left-hand taillight), automatic step lights in the dust shield, 16-inch brakes, a 19-inch diameter rubber-composition steering wheel, and instrument board (with windshield-wiper control, carburetor heat control, spark control, oil-pressure gauge, carburetor enriching device, instrument light switch, speedometer, ammeter, electric fuel gauge, 8-day clock, ignition lock, engine temperature indicator and combined inspection light and cigar lighter, one-piece, full-crown fenders, a 4.75:1 final drive ratio, 32 x 6.75-inch balloon cord tires and artillery-type hickory wheels with steel felloes.

SERIES 341-A—FLEETWOOD CUSTOM —V-8

Fleetwood bodies featured a molding sweeping down and forward on the sides of the cowl, except on the transformables, which had a bold molding sweeping up

1928 Cadillac, Series 341, Fisher Custom sport phaeton

the cowl, which coachbuilders called a "coupe pillar." It swept forward across the top of the hood. Other body details included 3-1/2 inch wider rear compartment (rear tread had been increased by two inches), adjustable front seats on all but Imperials and bumpers as standard equipment on all cars. There were a dozen basic Fleetwood bodies, some of which were made available as later V-16 styles with "55S" model designations. By using several variations and combinations of treatment above the belt line on a few basic body shells, Fleetwood was able to satisfy most customer's special desires and still offer short delivery (three to seven weeks). For the few who wanted something truly unique, Fleetwood produced full customs to order for those willing to wait four months to take delivery. Cadillac advertisements showcased over 50 Fleetwood bodies. Fleetwood designs exhibited at 1928 auto salons included an art deco Town Car with numerous rich appointments, an All-Weather Division Window Phaeton, a five-passenger Sedan with small rear quarter windows, a Metal Back Town Brougham with rear quarter windows, a five-passenger Club Cabriolet, a seven-passenger Town Car and a seven-passenger limousine.

SERIES 341-A—INDIVIDUAL CUSTOM —V-8

A small number of body designs for the Cadillac chassis were exhibited at 1928 auto salons by "outside" custom body builder. These included a three-position Town Car by Hibbard & Darrin that converted into a Landualet or a Touring Car and a Hibbard & Darrin Convertible Sedan. Kellner and Million-Guiet offered Town Car proposals that may or may not have been produced.

Fisher—140 in. wheelbase:

Model Number	Body Type & Seating	Factory Price	Shipping Weight	Production Total
1173	2D Roadster-2/4P	3,350	4,590	—
1171	4D Touring-7P	3,450	4,630	—
1172	4D Phaeton-4P	3,450	4,640	—
1172-B	4D Sport Phaeton-4P	3,950	5,145	—
7920	2D Coupe-2/4P	3,295	4,820	—
7980	2D Convertible Coupe-2/4P	3,495	4,665	—
7970	2D Coupe-5P	3,495	4,760	—
7950	4D Sedan-5P	3,595	4,880	—
7960	4D Town Sedan-5P	3,395	4,875	—
7960-L	4D Town Sedan-5P	3,395	4,875	—
7930	4D Sedan-7P	3,695	4,965	—
7990	4D Imperial Sedan-5P	3,745	4,925	—
7990-L	4D Imperial Cabriolet-5P	3,745	4,925	—
7940	4D Imperial Sedan-7P	3,895	5,025	—
7940-L	4D Imperial Cabriolet-7P	3,895	5,025	—

Semi Commercial—152-in. wheelbase:

Model Number	Body Type & Seating	Factory Price	Shipping Weight	Production Total
NA	Limousine Funeral Coach	—	—	—
NA	Limousine Ambulance	—	—	—
Fleetwood — 140-in. wheelbase				
8020	4D Sedan-5P	4,095	5,120	—
8020-L	4D Sedan (leather back)-5P	—	—	—
8030	4D Imperial Sedan-5/7P	4,245	5,085	—
8030-L	4D Imperial Sedan (leather back)-5/7P	—	—	—
8025	4D Sedan Cabriolet-5P	4,095	5,120	—
8035	4D Imperial Sedan Cabriolet-5/7P	4,245	5,085	—
8045	4D Sedan Cabriolet-5P	4,095	5,120	—
8045-C	4D Collapsible Landau-5P	4,795	—	—
8055	4D Imperial Sedan Cabriolet-5/7P	4,245	5,085	—
8055-C	4D Collapsible Landau-5/7P	4,945	—	—
8000	4D Sedan-7P	4,195	5,040	—
8000-L	4D Sedan (leather back)-7P	—	—	—
8010	4D Imperial-7P	4,445	5,180	—
8010-L	4D Imperial (leather back)-7P	—	—	—
8005	4D Sedan Cabriolet-7P	4,195	5,040	—
8015	4D Imperial Cabriolet-7P	4,445	5,180	—
3525	4D Transformable Town Cabriolet-7P	5,500	5,180	—
3525-C	4D Touring Town Cabriolet, Collapsible rear quarter-7P	6,200	—	—
3512	4D Transformable Town Cabriolet-5/7P	5,000	5,180	—
3512-C	4D Transformable Town Cabriolet, Collapsible rear qrtr.	5,700	—	—
3520	4D Transformable Town Cabriolet-7P	5,500	5,180	—
3520-C	4D Transformable Town Cabriolet, Collapsible rear qrtr.-7P	6,200	—	—
3591	4D Transformable Limousine Brougham-7P	5,500	5,180	—
3591-C	4D Transformable Limousine Brougham, Collapsible rear qrtr.	—	—	—
3550	Full Collapsible Cabriolet (on order)	—	—	—
3550	Fully Collapsible, Transformable Cabriolet	—	—	—

Note: The following body styles are listed as Fleetwood 341, 341-A, 341-B, but are unconfirmed. All are on 140-inch. wheelbase except as noted. Included must be full customs and one-off variations of catalog customs.

1928/1929 Cadillac Series 341-A, 341-B

Model Number	Body Type & Seating	Factory Price	Shipping Weight	Production Total
3015	Limousine-7P (138-inch wheelbase)	—	—	—
3097	Limousine-5P	—	—	—
3133	All Weather Touring-5P	—	—	—
3135	Special Town Cabriolet	—	—	—
3144	Sedan-4P (132-inch wheelbase)	—	—	—
3174	Sport Cabriolet-5P	—	—	—
3185	Sedan-7P	—	—	—
3199	Coupe-2P	—	—	—
3208	Imperial Cabriolet-5P (152-inch wheelbase)	—	—	—
3238	Club Cabriolet-5P	—	—	—
3274	Sport Cabriolet Sedan-5P	—	—	—
3300	Convertible Cabriolet-7P	—	—	—
3360	Sedan-5P	—	—	—
3360-5	Imperial-5P	—	—	—
3361	Sedan-5P	—	—	—
3361-5	Imperial-5P	—	—	—
3375	Sedan-7P	—	—	—
3375-5	Imperial-7P	—	—	—
3376	Sedan-7P	—	—	—
3412	Town Car-7P (152-inch wheelbase)	—	—	—
3435	Town Car-7P (152-inch wheelbase)	—	—	—
3475	Limousine-7P	—	—	—
3512-P	Town Car-5P	—	—	—
3512-C-P	Town Car-5P	—	—	—
3515	Limousine-7P	—	—	—
3520-P	Town Car-5P	—	—	—
3520-C-P	Town Car-7P	—	—	—

1928/1929 Cadillac Series 341-A, 341-B

Model Number	Body Type & Seating	Factory Price	Shipping Weight	Production Total
3525-P	Town Car-7P	—	—	—
3525-C-P	Town Car-7P	—	—	—
3591-P	Town Car-7P	—	—	—
3591-C-P	Town Car-7P	—	—	—
3885	Convertible Sedan	—	—	—
3891	Imperial Sedan-7P	—	—	—

ENGINE

L-head. Cast iron block on copper/aluminum crankcase. Bore and stroke: 3-5/16 x 4-15/16. Displacement: 341 cid. Compression ratio: 4.8:1. Brake hp: 90 at 3000 rpm. Taxable hp: 35.1. Torque: 208 lb.-ft. Compression 90-92 psi at 1,000 rpm. Main bearings: three. Valve lifters: Mechanical with rollers riding on cams. Crankcase capacity: 8 qt. Cooling system capacity. 6 gal. Carburetor: manufactured by Cadillac under C.F. Johnson patents.

L-head. High compression cylinder head. Cast iron block on copper/aluminum crankcase. Bore and stroke: 3-5/16 x 4-15/16. Displacement: 341 cid. Compression ratio: 5.3:1. Brake hp: 90 at 3000 rpm. Taxable hp: 35.1. Torque: 208 lb.-ft. Compression pressure: 105-107 psi at 1,000 rpm. Main bearings: three. Valve lifters: Mechanical with rollers riding on cams. Crankcase capacity: 8 qt. Cooling system capacity. 6 gal. Carburetor: manufactured by Cadillac under C.F. Johnson patents.

Note: Cadillac expert Jim Schild says the 1928 service manual shows the low compression V-8 as a special order engine with the high compression (5.3:1) engine standard. "They are essentially the same engine except for the heads," he writes.

CHASSIS

Wheelbase: 140 inches. Overall length: 213-1/4 inches. Front/Rear Tread: 56/58 inches. Tires: 32 x 6.75 (7-20). [Series 341-A Commercial Chassis] Wheelbase: 152 inches. Front/Rear Tread: 56/58 inches. Tires: 32 x 6.75 (7-20).

TECHNICAL

Selective transmission. Speeds: 3F/1R. Left-hand drive, center control (right-hand drive optional). Twin disc clutch. Shaft drive (torque tube). Full-floating rear axle. Spiral bevel drive. Overall ratio: 4.75:1 standard, 4.39:1, 5.08:1 optional. Mechanical brakes on four wheels.-inch rear drums. 16-inch front drums (17-inch front midyear). Artillery wheels (wire and disc optional). Wheels: 20 inches. Rear springs underslung. Fuel tank filler neck extended outside frame side rail. Hydraulic shock absorbers.

OPTIONS

Folding trunk rack ($25). Step plate ($3.25 ea.). Tire mirrors ($30). Wind wings ($15-30). Trunks ($65- 100). Herald ornament ($12). Seat covers ($5.25). Spotlight ($35). Tire covers ($10). Tonneau windshield ($120). Natural wood wheels ($10 extra). Five disc wheels ($20). Six disc wheels, fender wells, two spares ($175). Five wire wheels ($95). Six wire wheels, fender wells, two spares ($250). Fender wells for wood wheels, two spares ($140).

HISTORICAL

The 1928 Cadillacs were introduced in September 1927. Model-year sales and production was 20,001 cars. The president and general manager of Cadillac was Lawrence P. Fisher. The new engine marked the first change for the Cadillac V-8 since the Type 51. The transition that had started with the final version of the Series 314 engine was now complete. The 341-cid Cadillac engine and the 303-cid LaSalle engine were practically identical in configuration. The 341-cid V-8 had offset blocks, side-by-side connecting rods, a single exhaust system, a horizontal starter along the right side of the transmission, the oil filter mounted on engine and an oil-level indicator behind the right-hand block. With this new engine manifold vacuum, plus a vacuum pump, operated the fuel-feed system and windshield wipers. Aside from differences due to displacement and power, the only noticeable difference between the Cadillac and LaSalle engines was the enameled heat deflector over the Cadillac carburetor.

David Underwood

1928 Cadillac, Series 341, Fisher Custom sport phaeton

1929

OVERVIEW

The 1929 Cadillac had a large number of important improvements, although its outer appearance was changed very little. The parking lights were moved to the front fenders. Security-Plate safety glass was now used in all windows and windshields. All brightwork was chrome plated. Electric windshield wipers were adopted. The chassis featured new Duplex-mechanical brakes with internal shoes at all four corners of the car. A "Silent Synchromesh" transmission was introduced. The connecting rods were drilled to give pressure lubrication to the small ends. Metric spark plugs were used in Cadillac engines beginning at mid-model year.

I.D. DATA

The serial number was stamped on plate on front of dash and on crankcase just below the water inlet on the right side. The motor number was the same as the serial number. Starting: 320101. Ending: 499999.

SERIES 341-B—FISHER—V-8

Other new 1929 Cadillac features included adjustable front seats (except in Imperial models), ball-and-socket

Above: **1929 Cadillac, Series 341-B, dual cowl phaeton**
David Lyon

type rear spring shackles and double-barrel shock absorbers. There were 11 model included in the Fisher Body offerings. These were considered the "standard" bodies for the 140-inch wheelbase Cadillac chassis.

SERIES 341-B — FLEETWOOD CUSTOM — V-8

In addition to the 11 standard Fisher body styles, the Series 341-B Cadillac was available with an equal number of special Fleetwood bodies. These premium bodies were called the "Fleetwood Custom" line, although some were produced in quantity. Fleetwood models continued to show the sweep panel across cowl and hood on most body styles, now including all sedans. The Transformable Town Cabriolets and All-Weather Pheaton now had rear-hinged front doors. In 1929, Fleetwood introduced a new body style that it called the All-Weather Phaeton. Slightly modified versions of each body were sometimes produced to customer orders, resulting in a lengthy list of 33 Fleetwood models.

SERIES 341-B — INDIVIDUAL CUSTOM — V-8

Outside body builders onstructed a Fully-Convertible Cabriolet, an Open-Front Town Car and a Landau Limousine. A long-wheelbase Pullman Cabriolet was done by German body builder Papler.

341-B Fisher Bodies—140-in. wheelbase

Model Number	Body Type & Seating	Factory Price	Shipping Weight	Production Total
1182	4D Touring-7P	3,450	4,774	—
1183	4D Phaeton-7P	3,450	4,635	—
1183-8	4D Sport Phaeton-4P	3,950	5,110	—
1184	2D Roadster-2/4P	3,350	4,678	—
8620	4D Sedan-7P	3,795	5,145	—
8630	4D Imperial Sedan-7P	3,995	—	—
8640	4D Sedan-5P	3,695	5,027	—
8650	4D Imperial Sedan-5P	—	—	—
8660	4D Town Sedan-5P	3,495	5,028	—
8670	2D Coupe-5P	3,595	4,887	—
8680	2D Convertible Coupe-2/4P	3,595	4,796	—
8690	2D Coupe-2/4P	3,295	4,909	—

Semi-Commercial—152- in.wheelbase

Model Number	Body Type & Seating	Factory Price	Shipping Weight	Production Total
NA	Limousine Funeral Coach	—	—	—
NA	Limousine Ambulance	—	—	—

Fleetwood Custom Bodies— 140-in. wheelbase

Model Number	Body Type & Seating	Factory Price	Shipping Weight	Production Total
3830	4D Imperial-5P	4,345	5,130	—
3830-S	4D Sedan-5P	4,195	5,120	—
3830-C	4D Collapsible Imperial-5P	5,045	—	—
3830-SC	4D Collapsible Sedan-5P	4,895	—	—
3830-L	4D Imperial (leather back)-5P	4,450	—	—
3830-SL	4D Sedan (leather back)-5P	4,295	—	—
3861	4D Imperial Town(club) Sedan-5P	—	—	—
3861-S	4D Club Cabriolet-5P	4,395	5,120	—
3861-C	4D Collapsible Imperial Club. Cabriolet-5P	—	—	—
3861-SC	4D Collapsible Club Cabriolet-5P	5,095	—	—
3855	4D Imperial Cabriolet-5P	4,345	5,130	—
3855-S	4D Sedan Cabriolet-5P	4,195	5,120	—
3855-C	4D Collapsible Imperial Cabriolet-5P	5,045	—	—
3855-SC	4D Collapsible Sedan Cabriolet-5P	4,895	—	—
3875	4D Imperial-7P	4,545	5,210	—
3875-S	4D Sedan-7P	4,295	5,200	—
3875-C	4D Collapsible Imperial-7P	5,245	—	—
3875-L	4D Imperial (leather back)-7P	4,645	—	—
3875-SL	4D Sedan (leather back)-7P	4,395	—	—
3875-SC	4D Collapsible Sedan-7P	4,995	—	—
3875-X	4D Imperial (full leather quarter)-7P	4,795	—	—
3875-SX	4D Sedan (full leather quarter)-7P	4,545	—	—
3180	All-Weather Phaeton-5P	5,750	5,130	—
3880	4D Imperial All-Weather Phaeton-5P	5,995	5,140	—
3512	4D Transformable Town Cabriolet-5/7P	5,250	5,180	—
3512-C	4D Collapsible Touring Town Cabriolet-5/7P	5,950	5,180	—
3520	4D Transformable Town Cabriolet-7P	5,500	5,180	—
3520-C	4D Town Cabriolet-7P, Collapsible rear qrtr.	6,200	5,180	—
3525	4D Transformable Town Cabriolet-7P	5,500	5,180	—
3525-C	4D Town Cabriolet-7P, Collapsible rear qrtr.	5,500	5,180	—
3591	4D Touring LimousineBrougham-7P	5,500	5,180	—
3591-C	4D Town Brhm.-7P, Collapsible rear qrtr.	6,200	5,180	—
3550	4D Collapsible, Transformable Cabriolet-7P	6,700	—	—

ENGINE

L-head. Cast iron block on copper/aluminum crankcase. Bore and stroke: 3-5/16 x 4-15/16. Displacement: 341 cid. Compression ratio: 4.8:1. Brake hp: 90 at 3000 rpm. Taxable hp: 35.1. Compression 90-92 psi at 1,000 rpm. Main bearings: three. Valve lifters: Mechanical with rollers riding on cams. Crankcase capacity: 8 qt. Cooling system capacity. 6 gal. Carburetor: manufactured by Cadillac under C.F. Johnson patents. L-head. Cast iron block on copper/aluminum crankcase. Bore and stroke: 3-5/16 x 4-15/16. Displacement: 341 cid. Compression ratio: 5.3:1. Brake hp: 90 at 3000 rpm. Taxable hp: 35.1. Compression pressure 105-107 psi at 1,000 rpm. Main bearings: three. Valve lifters: Mechanical with rollers riding on cams. Crankcase capacity: 8 qt. Cooling system capacity. 6 gal. Carburetor: manufactured by Cadillac under C.F. Johnson patents.

CHASSIS

[Series 341-B] Wheelbase: 140 inches. Overall length: 213-1/4 inches. Front/Rear Tread: 56/58 inches. Tires: 7-20 (32 x 6.75). [Series 341-B Commercial Chassis] Wheelbase: 152 inches. Front/RearTread: 56/58 inches. Tires: 7-20 (32 x 6.75).

TECHNICAL

Selective synchromesh transmission. 3F/1R. Left drive, center control (right-hand drive optional). Twin disc clutch. Shaft drive (torque tube). Full-floating rear axle, spiral bevel drive. Overall ratio: 5.08:1 standard, 4.75:1, 4.39:1 optional Duplex-mechanical brakes on four

Henry Austin Clark Jr. Collection

1929 Cadillac, Series 341-B, Fleetwood town car

1929 Cadillac, Series 341-B, five-passenger coupe

wheels. All shoes inside drums. 16-1/2-inch. drums. Wood artillery wheels (wire and disc optional). Wheels: 20 inches.

OPTIONS

Folding trunk rack ($25). Step plate ($3.25 ea.). Tire mirrors ($30). Wind wings ($15-30). Heater ($32). Trunks ($65-100). Herald ornament ($12). Seat covers. ($25.25). Spotlight ($35). Tire covers ($10). Tonneau windshield ($120). Natural wood wheels ($10 extra). Five disc wheels ($20). Six disc wheels, fender wells, two spares ($175). Five wire wheels ($95). Six wire wheels, fender wells, two spares ($250). Fender wells for wood wheels, two spares ($140).

HISTORICAL

The 1929 Cadillacs were introduced in August 1928. Model-year sales and production was 18,103 cars. The president and general manager of Cadillac was Lawrence P. Fisher. In December 1929, Fisher sent Cadillac dealers a letter announcing the V-16 series for 1930. The first showing of the V-16 took place on January 4, 1930, at the Grand Central Palace in New York City.

1929 Cadillac, Series 341-B, roadster

1929 Cadillac, Series 341-B, seven-passenger sedan

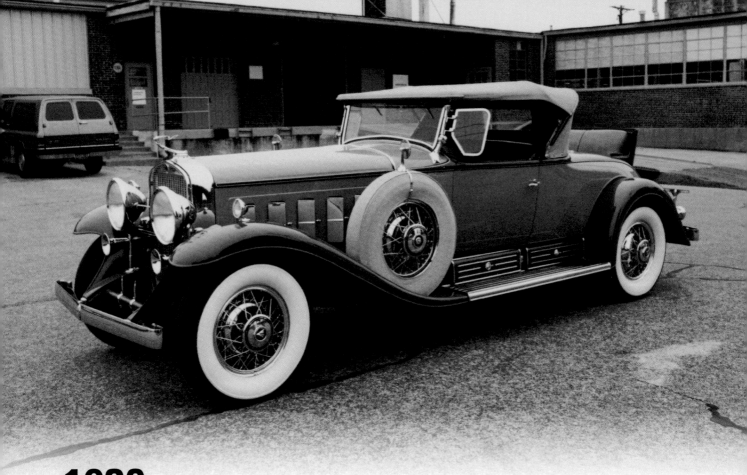

1930

OVERVIEW

America was sliding into an economic disaster called the Great Depression when the 1930 Cadillacs arrived in September 1929. The Cadillac V-8 was enlarged to 353 cubic inches, which created a new Series 353 line. It included just seven models with Fisher coachwork. These cars were now promoted as Fisher Custom line models. A Fleetwood Special Custom line was also available with the same V-8 and the same 140-inch wheelbase chassis. There were also 11 basic Fleetwood bodies, but numerous modified versions of those bodies were also cataloged. In December, Cadillac management announced that a new line powered by a 452-cubic-inch V-16 was being readied for the New York Automobile Salon in January 1929. A five-passenger Imperial Landau Sedan was the only car actually exhibited at that venue. The V-16 utilized a 148-inch wheelbase. Before long, an array of 54 semi-custom body styles by Fleetwood was available. Series 452 prices started at a little over $5,000 and ran as much as $10,000. That compared to $435 for a 1930 Model A Ford roadster.

Above: **1930 Cadillac, Series 452, Fleetwood "Fleetdown" V-16 roadster**

I.D. DATA

[V-8 Series 353] There were no serial numbers on the 1930 Cadillac Series 353. Engine numbers were stamped on crankcase just below the water inlet on the right-hand side. Starting: 500001. Ending: 511005.

[V-16 Series: 452A] Serial numbers were not used on the 452A series. Engine numbers were stamped on crankcase right-hand side, on the generator drive chain housing. Starting: 700001. Ending: 700288 (approximate).

SERIES 353—FISHER CUSTOM—V-8

The 1930 Series 353 Cadillac V-8 was an extension of the Series 341-B, with some notable changes. The louvers in the sides of the hood now extended well to the front of the car. A wider radiator and larger headlights were used. The headlights had a 12-inch-diameter lens and measured 13 inches overall. The windshield now sloped a few degrees and a short, cadet-type sun visor was used on closed cars. A new valance across the rear of the car covered the fuel tank and frame and joined the rear fenders. Inside, a new recessed instrument board was seen and Cadillacs had four-inch wider rear seat cushions. All but a few bodies were prewired for the installation of a radio and a radio antenna was built into the top. Ball-and-socket rear spring shackles were no longer used. The front tread

increased from 56 inches to 59 inches and the rear tread increased from 58 inches to 59-1/2 inches. The use of a third rear shoe for emergency brake was dropped. A lever now operated the rear service brakes. The tailpipe had a fan-shaped end. Demountable wood wheels were offered as an extra-cost option. A steering modulator was seen on the front end of the left spring. All cars had a 3/4-floating rear axle. The V-8 had a 1/16-inch bore increase. A new reduction-type starter was used. The cooling fan was now lubricated by engine-oil return pressure. The spark plugs were covered and a new distributor had wires running out of the rear into a single conduit. The Fisher (now Fisher Custom) line was reduced to seven bodies, including a Convertible Coupe.

SERIES 353 — FLEETWOOD SPECIAL CUSTOM — V-8

Models in the Fleetwood Special Custom were crafted from 14 basic semi-custom bodies. Cadillac offered many variations of each style and cataloged 37 different ones. Fleetwood models continued to show the sweep panel across the cowl and hood. Open-bodied Fleetwood models had attractive louvers in the sides of the cowl that matched the hood louvers.

1930 Cadillac, Series 353, five-passenger sedan

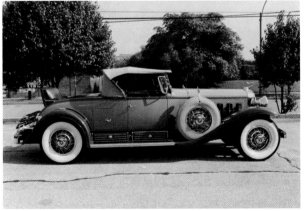

1930 Cadillac, Series 452, Fleetwood "Fleetdown" V-16 roadster

Series 353 - V-8 - Fisher

Model Number	Body Type & Seating	Factory Price	Shipping Weight	Production Total
30152	4D Town Sedan-5P	3,495	5,040	—
30158	2D Coupe-2/4P	3,295	4,955	—
30159	4D Sedan-5P	3,695	5,070	—
30162	4D Sedan-7P	3,795	5,170	—
30163	4D Imperial-7P	3,995	5,210	—
30168	2D Convertible Coupe-2/4P	3,595	4,860	—
30172	2D Coupe-5P	3,595	4,945	—

Fleetwood built-to-order

Model Number	Body Type & Seating	Factory Price	Shipping Weight	Production Total
4150	4D Full Collapsible Transformable	—	—	—
4157	4D Tour.-7P	—	—	—
4160	4D Sport Phaeton-5P	—	—	—
4160-A	4D Sport Phaeton-5P	—	—	—
4160-B	4D Sport Phaeton-5P	—	—	—
4161	4D Sedan or Imperial Sport Cabriolet-5P	—	—	—
4164	4D Transformable Brougham-5P	—	—	—
4164-B	4D Transformable Brougham with cane work-5P	—	—	—
4176	2D Convertible Coupe-2P	—	—	—
4185	2D All Weather Coupe-4P	—	—	—
3350	Transformable All Weather Phaeton (152-inch wheelbase)-7P	—	—	—
3950	Town Car with Full Collapsible Top-7P	—	—	—
3902	2D Roadster-2/4P	3,450	4,625	—
3930	4D Imperial-5P	4,395	5,220	—
3930-5	4D Sedan-5P	4,195	5,150	—
3930-C	4D Collapsible Imperial-5P	5,195	—	—
3930-SC	4D Collapsible Sedan-5P	4,995	—	—
3955	4D Imperial Cabriolet-5P	4,445	5,240	—
3955-5	4D Sedan Cabriolet-5P	4,245	5,200	—
3955-C	4D Collapsible Imperial Cabriolet-5P	5,195	—	—
3955-SC	4D Collapsible Sedan Cabriolet-5P	4,995	—	—
3975	4D Imperial-7P	4,595	5,320	—
3975-5	4D Sedan-7P	4,295	5,280	—
3975-C	4D Collapsible Imperial-7P	5,395	—	—
3975-SC	4D Collapsible Sedan-7P	5,095	—	—
3975-P	4D Imperial (plain hood)-7P	4,845	—	—
3981	4D Sedanette Cabriolet-5P	4,500	5,070	—
3982	4D Sedanette-5P	4,595	5,070	—
3980	4D All Weather Phaeton-5P	4,700	4,990	—
3912	4D Transformable Town Cabriolet-5/7P	4,995	5,230	—
3912-C	4D Collapsible Transformable Town Cabriolet-5/7P	5,745	—	—
3920	4D Town Cabriolet (quarter window)-7P	5,145	5,150	—
3920-C	4D Collapsible Town Cabriolet (quarter window)-7P	5,945	—	—
3925	4D Transformable Town Cabriolet (no quarter window)-7P	5,145	5,150	—
3925-C	4D Collapsible Touring Town Cabriolet (no quarter window)-7P	5,895	—	—
3991	4D Transformable Limousine Brougham-7P	5,145	5,320	—
3991-C	4D Collapsible Touring Limousine Brougham-7P	5945	—	—

SERIES 452A — FLEETWOOD - V-16

Body details introduced on the 1930 V-16 included single-bar bumpers, dual horns, a concave monogram bar, a radiator screen, 13-inch Guide "Tilt-Ray" headlights, dual rear lights matching the headlights, triple moldings on the dust shield panels of straight-sill styles, five doors in the hood, a single matching door in the side of the cowl and none, one or two rectangular vent doors in the

top of the cowl. Most bodies with recessed hood/cowl had one triangular door in the top of the cowl. Although full-custom bodies were built by Fleetwood, Murphy, Waterhouse, Saoutchik, Vanden Plas, Pinin Farina and others, most were "catalog customs" built by Fleetwood. A few cars had Fisher bodies. Only about one-fifth were open or convertible models, two-thirds were five- or seven-passenger Sedans or Imperial Sedans and the rest were Coupes or Town Cars. More than 50 body styles were offered, but the list consisted of only a few basic body shells with several variations each. For instance, buyers could chose from metal or leather quarters with or without rear quarter windows, from fixed or collapsible (landau) quarters with or without an Imperial-type division window, from straight sills or coach sills and from plain or recessed hood and cowl styles and so on. With a few exceptions, the "41" styles had a plain hood and straight sills, the "42" styles had a plain hood and coach sills and the "43" styles had a recessed hood and cowl and straight sills. Windshield treatments varied from vertical vee to 22 degree sloping, as follows: 1) a vertical vee swing-out type windshield was used on styles 4130 and 4155 (this is known as the "Pennsylvania" windshield, based on the fact that Fleetwood Body Company was located there); 2) a 7-degree flat swing-out windshield was used on styles 4212, 4220, 4225, 4264 and 4291; 3) a 7-degree vee-type swing-out windshield was used on styles 4312, 4320, 4325, 4335, 4376, 4380 and 4391; 4) a 7-degree flat crank-up Vision & Ventilating windshield was used on styles 4330, 4355, 4361, 4375 and 4381; 5) a 16-degree flat swing-out, folding windshield was used on style 4302; 6) an 18-degree flat crank-up Vision & Ventilating "Madame X" windshield was used on styles 4130, 4155, 4161, 4175, 4276 and 4476; 7) a 21-degree flat swing-out windshield was used on style 4235 and 8) a 22-degree flat, divided windshield was used on style 4260. The sobriquet "Madame X" is not prominent, if used at all, in Cadillac promotional literature. Perhaps the only place Cadillac printed it is in body style listings found in various parts lists as early as March 1930. The term is associated with the cars having job/style numbers 4130, 4155, 4161, 4175, in plain, -S, -C or -SC variations. In later parts lists, job number 4476 is listed as having a "Madame X" windshield. "Madame X" has a Hollywood flavor, but is no more inappropriate than other Fleetwood Body Company style designations such as "Fleetbourne" and "Fleetdown." The term must have arisen from a distinctive styling feature common to the four basic body styles. Further, the term more likely came from Detroit than from the Pennsylvania Dutch country where Fleetwood was located. The most distinctive styling feature of the "41" series bodies, which were built in Detroit, Michigan, was the 18-degree flat, crank-up Vision & Ventilating windshield. It is unlikely that the Pennsylvania versions,

with their vertical-vee swing-out windshields were thought of as "Madame X" bodies. Job/style number 4276, being style 4476 with coach sills, also has a "Madame X" windshield. Chrome-plated window reveals were used on "41" bodies, but were not unique to those styles. Although early body specs listed chrome-plated reveals, revised body specs from July 1930 specified painted window reveals on "41" bodies. Painted window reveals on "Madame X" bodies are probably as rare as the "standard" rear-mounted spare tire. In simplest terms, 1930 Fleetwood four-door bodies with the 18-degree windshield, mounted on the Cadillac V-16 chassis, were "Madame X" styles and two coupe body styles also used the "Madame X" windshield. The V-16 frame was similar to that used under the Series 353 V-8 models, except for a five-point engine mount on the V-16. The brake system had a vacuum-assist function controlled by manifold vacuum, not a vacuum pump. The big V-16s used 16-1/2-inch diameter brake drums. Specially-balanced whitewall tires were used. The driveline featured a rear engine support at the tail of the transmission. Heavier clutch linings were used at first, but chassis unit 7-2991 and later cars produced used the same thinner clutch lining as V-8 models. Rear axle shafts were of the same design used on Series 353 V-8s, but were made of special steel. A 3.47:1 optional final drive ratio was dropped in mid-model year. The appearance of the V-16 was a beautiful example of outstanding industrial design and much attention was paid to its eye appeal. It looked neat with its polished aluminium parts, bright enamel finish and shielded wires. Covers were used on the engine and dashboard to hide the plumbing and controls. Twin ignition coils were mounted in recesses in the radiator top tank. The spark plug wires came out the rear of the double-decker distributor cap and disappeared under the cover inside the vee. The narrow (45 degree) vee allowed for outboard mounting of manifolds and dual carburetors. Intake pipes from higher in the engine compartment were added at engine number 702502 to eliminate the problem of road splash entering the carburetors. Fuel feed was by dual vacuum tanks operated by vacuum pump. Engineer Owen Milton Nacker designed the all-new engine with a three-inch bore and four-inch stroke. It was basically two straight eights sharing a common crankshaft. Each bank of cylinders had its own fuel-distribution system and exhaust system. The overhead-valve engine featured hydraulic valve silencers. It was capable of propelling these very heavy cars at speeds ranging from 80-100 mph. The only faster American car was a "Doosey." By May 1930, the chrome-plated vacuum tanks were superseded by painted units. The dual exhaust system ended in fan-shaped tailpipe tips. To silence the overhead valve system, hydraulically-rotated eccentric bushings were used in the rocker arms. The early use of a different head thickness for various compression ratios was replaced by the use of

1930 Cadillac, Series 452, Fleetwood "Fleetdown" V-16 roadster

Dick Blazich

a single head with gaskets of different thicknesses. Right and left heads and blocks were interchangeable. One row of head studs went through the block to the crankcase, the second row seated in the block. Engine lubrication was full pressure from an oil pump mounted on the rear main bearing cap. At engine unit number 7-1038, the oil level indicator was moved from the rear of right-hand cylinder block to the left side of the crankcase. The belt-driven fan was mounted on ball bearings and lubricated by grease fitting, not engine oil pressure. Crankshaft thrust was taken by the center main bearing. A harmonic balancer was mounted on front end of crankshaft. A single chain to drive camshaft and generator was provided with an automatic adjuster incorporated in an idler acting on the outside of the chain. A thermostat was used to close the crankcase ventilation intake at higher engine temperatures. The double-outlet water pump on the right side of the engine was driven by an extension shaft from the rear of the generator. A cooling system condenser tank was used once again. The engine and transmission assembly was mounted at the four corners of the engine, with a dual mount at the rear of the transmission. The front mounts were supported by diagonal members in the frame.

Series 452A - V-16-Fleetwood

Model Number	Body Type & Seating	Factory Price	Shipping Weight	Production Total
4108-C	4D Imperial Landau Cabriolet-5/7P	—	—	—
4130	4D Imperial-5/7P	7,300	5,920	—
4130-5	4D Sedan-5P	6,950	5,850	—
4155	4D Imperial Cabriolet-5/7P	7,350	5,940	—
4155-C	4D Imperial Landau Cabriolet-5/7P	—	—	—
4155-5	4D Sedan Cabriolet-5P	7,125	5,900	—
4155-SC	4D Landau Sedan Cabriolet-5P	—	—	—
4161	4D Imperial Club. Sedan-5P	—	—	—
4161-C	4D Imperial Landau Club. Sedan-5P	—	—	—
4161-5	4D Club. Sedan-5P	6,950	5,740	—
4175	4D Imperial-7P	7,525	6,020	—
4175-C	4D Imperial Landau-7P	—	—	—
4175-5	4D Sedan-7P	7,225	5,980	—
4200	4D Sedan Cabriolet-7P	—	—	—

Model Number	Body Type & Seating	Factory Price	Shipping Weight	Production Total
4206	2D Coupe-2/4P	—	—	—
4207	2D Coupe-2/4P	—	—	—
4208	4D Imperial Cabriolet-5/7P	—	—	—
4212	4D Transformable Town Cabriolet-5/7P	8,750	5,915	—
4212-C	4D Collapsible Transformable Town Cabriolet-5/7P	—	—	—
4220	4D Transformable Town Cabriolet-7P	8,750	5,850	—
4220-B	4D Transformable Town Cabriolet-7P	—	—	—
4225	4D Transformable Town Cabriolet-7P	8,750	5,850	—
4225-C	4D Collapsible Transformable TownCabriolet-7P	—	—	—
4235	2D Convertible Coupe-2/4P	6,900	5,670	—
4243	4D Phaeton	—	—	—
4244	4D Phaeton	—	—	—
4246	4D Phaeton	—	—	—
4257-A	4D Touring-7P	—	—	—
4257-H	4D Touring-5P	—	—	—
4260	4D Sport Phaeton-5P	6,500	—	—
4260-A	4D Sport Phaeton-5P	—	—	—
4260-B	4D Sport Phaeton-5P	—	—	—
4262	4D Imperial Cabriolet-7P	—	—	—
4264	4D Town Brougham-5/7P	9,200	5,765	—
4264-B	4D Town Brougham-5/7P	9,700	5,675	—
4275	4D Imperial Sedan-7P	—	—	—
4275-C	4D Imperial Landau Sedan-7P	—	—	—
4276	2D Coupe-2/4P	6,850	5,765	—
4280	4D All Weather Phaeton-4P	7,350	5675	—
4285	4D All Weather SportCabriolet-5P	—	—	—
4291	4D Transformable Limousine Brougham-7P	8,750	6,020	—
4302	2D Roadster-2/4P	5,350	5,325	—
4312	4D Transformable Town Cabriolet-5/7P	7,000	5,930	—
4312-C	4D Collapsible Transformable Town Cabriolet-5/7P	—	—	—
4320	4D Transformable Town Cabriolet-7P	7150	5850	—
4320-C	4D Collapsible Transformable Town Cabriolet-7P	—	—	—
4325	4D Transformable Town Cabriolet-7P	7,150	5,850	—
4325-C	4D Collapsible Transformable Town Cabriolet-7P	—	—	—
4330	4D Imperial-5/7P	6,300	5,920	—
4330-5	4D Sedan-5P	5,950	5,850	—
4335	2D Convertible Coupe-2/4P	5,900	5,655	—
4355	4D Imperial Cabriolet-5/7P	6,350	5,940	—
4355-C	4D Collapsible Imperial Cabriolet-5/7P	—	—	—
355-5	4D Sedan Cabriolet-5P	6,125	5,885	—
4361	4D Imperial Club Sedan-5P	—	—	—
4361-5	4D Club Sedan-5P	5,950	5,740	—
4375	4D Imperial-7P	6,525	6,020	—
4375-C	4D Collapsible Imperial-7P	—	—	—
4375-5	4D Sedan-7P	6,225	5,980	—
4376	2D Coupe-2/4P	5,800	5,750	—
4380	4D All Weather Phaeton-5P	6,650	5,690	—
4381	2D Coupe-5P	5,950	—	—
4391	4D Transformable Limousine Brougham-7P	7,150	6,020	—
4391-C	4D Collapsible Transformable Limousine Brougham-7P	—	—	—
4412	4D Transformable Town Cabriolet-5/7P	—	—	—
4476	2D Coupe-2/4P	5,800	5,765	—
3289-A	4D Transformable Town Cabriolet-7P	—	—	—
3981	4D Sedan Cabriolet-5P	—	—	—
3991	4D Transformable Limousine Brougham-7P	—	—	—
2950-X	4D Sedan-7P	—	—	—
2901-LX	4D Sedan-7P	—	—	—
2951-LX	4D Sedan-7P	—	—	—
30-X	4D Sedan-7P	—	—	—
LX-2905	4D Town Sedan-5P	—	—	—
LX-2913	2D Coupe-5P	—	—	—

30-152	4D Town Sedan, Fisher-5P	—	—	—
30-158	2D Coupe, Fisher-2/4P	—	—	—
30-159	4D Sedan, Fisher-5P	—	—	—
30-168	2D Convertible Coupe, Fisher-2/4P	—	—	—
30-172	2D Coupe, Fisher-5P	—	—	—

(*) A few 1930-1931 Cadillac V-16s had Fisher bodies.Most had "custom" coachwork selected from the Fleetwood catalog. Some catalog bodies may have been built only one year or not at all. Full-custom bodies were built by Fleetwood, Murphy, Waterhouse, Saoutchik, Vanden Plas, Pinin Farina and other custom coach builders.

ENGINE

BASE V-8

L-head. Cast-iron block on silicon/aluminum crankcase. Bore and stroke: 3-3/8 x 4-15/16. Displacement: 353 cid. Compression ratio: 5.15:1. Brake hp: 96+ at 3000 rpm. Taxable hp: 36.45. Main bearings: three. Valve lifters: Mechanical with rollers riding on cams. Crankcase capacity: 8 qt. Cooling system capacity: 6 gal. Carburetor: manufactured by Cadillac under C.F. Johnson patents.

OPTIONAL V-8

L-head. Cast-iron block on silicon/aluminum crankcase. Bore and stroke: 3-3/8 x 4-15/16. Displacement: 353 cid. Compression ratio: 5.03:1. Brake hp: 96+ at 3000 rpm. Taxable hp: 36.45. Main bearings: three. Valve lifters: Mechanical with rollers riding on cams. Crankcase capacity: 8 qt. Cooling system capacity: 6 gal. Carburetor: manufactured by Cadillac under C.F. Johnson patents.

V-16

45 degree, overhead valve V-16. Cast nickel-iron blocks on silicon/aluminum crankcase. Bore and stroke: 3 x 4 inches. Displacement: 452 cid C.R.: 5.35:1 early standard, 5.11:1 standard, 4.98:1 optional Brake horsepower: 175-185 @ 3400 rpm. SAE/Taxable horsepower: 57.5. Main bearings: five. Valve lifters: pushrod/rocker arm with hydraulic rotary eccentric silencer in rocker arm. Carburetion: float feed, auxiliary air control, manufactured by Cadillac under C.F. Johnson patents.

CHASSIS

[V-8 Series 353] Wheelbase: 140 inches. Length: approximately 210-5/8 inches. Front/Rear Tread: 59/59-1/2 inches. Tires: 7-19. [Commercial Chassis] Wheelbase: 152 inches.

[V-16 Series: 452A] Wheelbase: 148 inches. Overall length: approximately 222-1/2 inches. Front/Rear Tread: 59/59-1/2 inches. Tires: 7-19 early, 7.50-19 mid-model.

TECHNICAL

[V-8 Series 353] Selective, synchromesh transmission. Speeds: 3F/1R. Left drive, center controls (right-hand drive optional). Twin disc clutch. Shaft drive (torque tube). 3/4 floating rear axle spiral bevel gears. Overall ratio: 5.08:1 standard, 4.39:1, 4.75:1 optional (4.75:1 made standard in midyear). Safety-mechanical brakes on four wheels. (16-1/2-inch. drums). Wood artillery wheels (disc, wire, wood demountable optional). Wheels: 19 inches.

[V-16 Series: 452A] Selective, synchromesh transmission. Speeds: 3F/1R. Left drive, center control, (right-hand drive optional). Twin disc clutch. Shaft drive, (torque tube). 3/4 floating rear axle, spiral bevel drive. Overall ratio: 4.39:1 standard, (3.47:1), 4.07:1, 4.75:1 optional vacuum assisted mechanical brakes on four wheels. Wood artillery wheels (wire, disc, demountable wood optional). Wheels: 19 inches.

OPTIONS

[V-8 Series 353] Tire cover(s) ($6.50-30). Wind Wings ($25- 55). Tonneau Shield ($185). Radio ($175). Heater ($42.50). Radiator ornament ($25). Trunks ($80-115). Seat covers ($26.75-230.25). Spotlight/driving lights ($15.50-80). Tire mirrors ($32/pair). Five wire wheels ($70). Six wire wheels with fender wells, trunk rack ($210). Five demountable wood wheels ($50). Six demountable wood wheels with fender wells, trunk rack ($190). Five disc wheels ($50). Six disc wheels with fender wells, trunk rack ($190).

[V-16 Series: 452A] Mirrors ($10-32). Sidemount cover(s) ($5-40). Tonneau windshield ($185). Wind wings ($47.50). Radio ($200). Heater ($41-55). Heron or Goddess ornament ($20). Auxiliary lights ($37.50-75). Seat covers ($26.75-73.50). Trunks ($100-119). Five wire wheels ($70). Six wire wheels, fender wells, trunk rack ($210). Five demountable wood wheels ($50). Six demountable wood wheels, fender wells, trunk, rack ($190). Five disc wheels ($50). Six disc wheels, fender wells, trunk rack ($190). Fenders other than black ($100).

HISTORICAL

The president and general manager of Cadillac was Lawrence P. Fisher. The 1930 Cadillac V-8 line was introduced in September 1929. Most bodies pre-wired for radio, with aerial built into the top, and radios were available. Model-year sales came to 13,892 cars of which

1930 Cadillac, Series 452-B, Fleetwood V-16 roadster

11,005 were V-8 models and 2,887 were 1930 V-16s. The V-16 line was introduced January 4, 1930 at the New York Auto Show. About 20,000 people viewed the new Cadillac "Supercar" at the show, held at the Astor Hotel. Two V-16s were displayed. The first was a version of the Madam X Landaulet, a Harley Earl design of 1929. The V-16 version had a longer hood with louver doors, but was otherwise a direct take off built at Fleetwood Metal Body Company's old plant in Fleetwood, Pennsylvania. It was designated the Job No. 4108C3 Fleetwood Imperial-Landaulet. All enclosed V-16s with four doors then became known as Madame X cars, whether they had the "Pennsylvania" type windhield (a vertical "V" type) or the "Detroit" style flat windshield with an 18-degree slope. Although a token number (approximately one percent) of the V-16 chassis were sold to domestic and foreign coachbuilders, all body styles advertised by Cadillac were "Catalog Customs" by Fleetwood. The customer was able to order limited variations in the "Catalog Customs," or a full-custom creation. It is remarkable that Fleetwood was able to turn out 400 to 500 bodies per month at a time when activities at the Pennsylvania shop were being phased out and "production" at a new location in Detroit was being set up. Fleetwood closed down its East Coast operation in the spring of 1930. Subsequent Madame X models were built in the Chevrolet Annex, behind the General Motors Building in Detroit. They were painted in the Research Building located across the street. Through the fall of 1930, Cadillac dealers were required to furnish the factory with weekly and monthly owner reaction and service reports on each V-16 car delivered. Outside body builders continued to offer a number of individual custom designs for the Cadillac V-8 chassis. European body builder Van den Plas constructed a Fully-Convertible Cabriolet, an Open-Front Town Car and a Landau Limousine. A long-wheelbase Pullman Cabriolet was done by German body builder Papler.

1930 Cadillac, Series 452, Fleetwood V-16 Imperial landau sedan

1931

OVERVIEW

Model-year 1931 represented the apex of Cadillac's model–line expansion with the addition of a new V-12 series to fill the gap between the V-8 and the V-16. The company spanned the entire luxury-car niche with Fisher and Fleetwood bodies, 134-, 140- and 143-inch wheelbases and three different types of V-block engines. This was the beginning of a trend that eventually led to Cadillac's total domination of the fine car field in terms of unit sales. All of Cadillac's four passenger car lines were extensively restyled for 1932. The V-8-powered Series 355A models arrived in September 1930 and offered 12 models. The new Series 370A Cadillac V-12 entered production in October with the same 12 Fisher bodied models, plus 10 semi-custom Fleetwood-bodied models. The V-16 was a continuation of the fabulous 452A Series introduced in 1930.

I.D. DATA

[V-8 Series 355A] Serial numbers were not used. Engine numbers were stamped on crankcase just below the water inlet on the right hand side. Starting: 800001. Ending: 810717.

Above: **1931 Cadillac, Series 370-A, Fleetwood V-12 phaeton**

[V-12 Series 370A] Serial numbers were not used on the 1931 Cadillac Series 370-A. Engine numbers were stamped on the right- hand side of the crankcase, on generator drive chain housing. Starting 1000001. Ending 1005733.

[V-16 Series 452A] Serial numbers were not used on the 452A series. Engine numbers were stamped on crankcase right- hand side, on the generator drive chain housing. Starting: 702888. Ending: 703251 (approximate).

SERIES 355A—FISHER—V-8

The Series 355A Cadillac V-8s of 1931 were similar to the Series 353 models of 1930 except for a number of changes. They had new bodies that were longer and lower. A longer hood featured five hood ports or "doors." Matching doors were located in the sides of the cowl. A modified coach-type door sill was used. It had no storage compartments in the splash pan. The battery and tool compartments were now under the front seat. Metal floor boards were another advance. The new oval instrument panel had the same grouping of gauges as before. The front end resembled that of the 1930 V-16 with a radiator screen, a single-bar bumper and dual horns. The diameter of the headlights was reduced one inch. Cadillac's new V-8 frame featured divergent side rails. The rear springs

were mounted directly under the frame rails with metal covers on the springs. The radiator was mounted lower in the frame. The cooling system had a new condenser tank. Engine displacement was the same as that of last year's 353 V-8 series, so the Model code no longer matched the actual displacement. The V-8 now used a 4-point engine suspension, similar to that introduced on the V-16. An intake muffler was added. The distributor was 1-1/2 inches higher than on the 353 and the fan was positioned lower to match up properly with the lower radiator.

1931 Cadillac, Series 452, Fleetwood V-16 roadster

SERIES 355A—FLEETWOOD SEMI CUSTOM—V-8

Beyond its standard range of semi-custom bodies for the Cadillac V-12 and V-16 chassis, the new Fleetwood factory in Detroit, Michigan, built seven limited-production semi-custom bodies for the 1931 Series 355A V-8 chassis.

Series 355A – V-8 - Fisher

Model Number	Body Type & Seating	Factory Price	Shipping Weight	Production Total
31252	4D Town Sedan-5P	2,845	4,675	—
31258	2D Coupe-2/4P	2,695	4,480	—
31259	4D Sedan-5P	2,795	4,660	—
31262	4D Sedan-7P	2,945	4,760	—
31263	4D Imperial Sedan-7P	3,095	4,835	—
31272	2D Coupe-5P	2,795	4,500	—

Series 355A – V-8 - Fleetwood

Model Number	Body Type & Seating	Factory Price	Shipping Weight	Production Total
4502	2D Roadster-2/4P	2,845	4,450	—
4503	4D Sedan-7P	—	—	—
4535	2D Convertible Coupe-2/4P	2,945	4,450	—
4550	4D Transformable Town Cabriolet-7P	—	—	—
4557	4D Touring-7P	3,195	—	—
4560	4D Phaeton-4/5P	2,945	4,395	—
4580	4D All Weather Phaeton-5P	3,795	4,685	—

SERIES 370A—FISHER—V—12

The newly-introduced Cadillac V-12 resembled the V-16 with its radiator screen, five ventilating ports on each side of the hood and ventilating doors on each side of the cowl. But there were differences beyond the figure "12" mounted on the headlight tie bar. To begin with, the hood was four inches shorter than that used on the V-16, but five inches longer than the V-8 style hood. The headlights were one inch smaller in diameter than the V-16 type. There were dual horns, but they were slightly smaller than those used on the V-16 models. The modified "coach" style body sills

had a single molding on the splash shield. The battery was mounted in right front fender. The dual taillights were ball-shaped like the V-8-style lights. The frame has divergent side rails like those on the Series 355A V-8. The rear springs were mounted under the frame rails. The V-8 and V-12 shared the same front tread width. The V-12's brakes were vacuum-assisted with vacuum drawn from the left manifold only. Fifteen-inch brake drums were used. In addition to 140- and 143-inch-wheelbase passenger car chassis, a 152-inch wheelbase chassis was offered for semi-commercial use. The V-12 engine had dual-intake silencers that were slightly smaller than the single-intake type used on V-8s. They were positioned at the rear, where the V-16 had its vacuum tank mounted. The carburetors were similar to the V-16 type, but were reversed so that air inlet was at the rear. The single vacuum tank was mounted at the center of the dash, where the V-16's oil filter was. An oil filter was mounted on the left side of the crankcase. The 12-cylinder engine's bore was 1/8 inch larger than that of the V-16 engine. The rear center (No. 3) main bearing took the thrust. The V-12 exhaust manifolds had two sections, rather than the V-16's three. Also, the spark plug wires came out the top of the distributor cap, rather than the rear. Fisher-bodied V-12s were made in 12 styles, but were not common. Even the Fisher bodies had Fleetwood interiors. The V-12's instrument panel was similar to the V-8's.

1931 Cadillac, Series 370, Fleetwood V-12 sedan

SERIES 370A—FLEETWOOD—V—12

Ten bodies were cataloged by Fleetwood for the Cadillac V-12 chassis, but several variations brought the total model count up to 14 according to a 1934 *NADA Official Used Car Guide.*

Series 370A – V-12-Fisher 140-inch wheelbase

Model Number	Body Type & Seating	Factory Price	Shipping Weight	Production Total
31158	2D Coupe 2/4P	3,795	5,135	—
31172	2D Coupe-5P	3,895	5,155	—
31159	4D Sedan-5P	3,895	5,315	—
31152	4D Town Sedan-5P	3,945	5,330	—

	Transformable Town Cabriolet-5P	--	5,655	--

Fisher 143-inch wheelbase

Model Number	Body Type & Seating	Factory Price	Shipping Weight	Production Total
--	Touring-7P	4,295	5,005	--
31162	4D Sedan-7P	4,195	5,445	--
31163	4D Imperial Sedan-7P	4,45	5,520	--

Fleetwood 140-inch wheelbase

Model Number	Body Type & Seating	Factory Price	Shipping Weight	Production Total
4702	2D Roadster2/4P	3,945	5,010	--
4735	2D Convertible Coupe-2/4P	4,045	5,105	--
4760	4D Phaeton-5P	4,045	5,050	--
4780	4D All-Weather Phaeton-5P	4,895	5,340	--
4830-S	Sedan-5P	4,995	5,350	31
4830	Imperial Sedan-5P	5,200	5,420	14
4855-S	Sedan Cabriolet-5P	5,095	5,400	41
4855	Imperial Cabriolet-5P	5,300	5,440	18
4875-S	Sedan-7P	5,075	5,480	28
4875	Imperial Sedan-7P	5,275	5,520	39
4812	Opera Seat Town Cabriolet	5,700	5,430	12
4820	Quarter Window Town Cabriolet	5,850	5,350	8
4825	Formal Quarter Town Cabriolet	5,850	5,350	12
4891	Transformable Brougham Limousine-5P	5,850	5,520	14

SERIES 452A — FLEETWOOD (*) - V-16

The 1931 Cadillac V-6 was a continuation of the 1930 Series 452A car line. The characteristics of these cars were the same for both years. Engine numbers and other sources indicate that just 363 of these cars were built in 1931. Despite the Depression, the Fleetwood Plant in Detroit continued to turn out a wide range of semi-custom body styles for the V-16 chassis. Due to the low production numbers, it is likely that actual production of some of the body styles available in the Fleetwood catalog was not carried out this year. The 1931 V-16 Fleetwood bodies continued the same designs used in 1930 with many body styles continuing to use sweep panels and seven-degree slanted V-shaped windshields.

Series 452A - V-16 – Fleetwood

Model Number	Body Type & Seating	Factory Price	Shipping Weight	Production Total
4108-C	4D Imperial Landau Cabriolet-5/7P	—	—	—
4130	4D Imperial-5/7P	7,300	5,920	—
4130-5	4D Sedan-5P	6,950	5,850	—
4155	4D Imperial Cabriolet-5/7P	7,350	5,940	—
4155-C	4D Imperial Landau Cabriolet-5/7P	—	—	—
4155-5	4D Sedan Cabriolet-5P	7,125	5,900	—
4155-SC	4D Landau Sedan Cabriolet-5P	—	—	—
4161	4D Imperial Club. Sedan-5P	—	—	—
4161-C	4D Imperial Landau Club. Sedan-5P	—	—	—
4161-5	4D Club. Sedan-5P	6,950	5,740	—
4175	4D Imperial-7P	7,525	6,020	—
4175-C	4D Imperial Landau-7P	—	—	—
4175-5	4D Sedan-7P	7,225	5,980	—
4200	4D Sedan Cabriolet-7P	—	—	—
4206	2D Coupe-2/4P	—	—	—
4207	2D Coupe-2/4P	—	—	—
4208	4D Imperial Cabriolet-5/7P	—	—	—
4212	4D Transformable Town Cabriolet-5/7P	8,750	5,915	—
4212-C	4D Collapsible Transformable Town Cabriolet-5/7P	—	—	—

Model Number	Body Type & Seating	Factory Price	Shipping Weight	Production Total
4220	4D Transformable Town Cabriolet-7P	8,750	5,850	—
4220-B	4D Transformable Town Cabriolet-7P	—	—	—
4225	4D Transformable Town Cabriolet-7P	8,750	5,850	—
4225-C	4D Collapsible Transformable TownCabriolet-7P	—	—	—
4235	2D Convertible Coupe-2/4P	6,900	5,670	—
4243	4D Phaeton	—	—	—
4244	4D Phaeton	—	—	—
4246	4D Phaeton	—	—	—
4257-A	4D Touring-7P	—	—	—
4257-H	4D Touring-5P	—	—	—
4260	4D Sport Phaeton-5P	6,500	—	—
4260-A	4D Sport Phaeton-5P	—	—	—
4260-B	4D Sport Phaeton-5P	—	—	—
4262	4D Imperial Cabriolet-7P	—	—	—
4264	4D Town Brougham-5/7P	9,200	5,765	—
4264-B	4D Town Brougham-5/7P	9,700	5,675	—
4275	4D Imperial Sedan-7P	—	—	—
4275-C	4D Imperial Landau Sedan-7P	—	—	—
4276	2D Coupe-2/4P	6,850	5,765	—
4280	4D All Weather Phaeton-4P	7,350	5,675	—
4285	4D All Weather SportCabriolet-5P	—	—	—
4291	4D Transformable Limousine Brougham-7P	8,750	6,020	—
4302	2D Roadster-2/4P	5,350	5,325	—
4312	4D Transformable Town Cabriolet-5/7P	7,000	5,930	—
4312-C	4D Collapsible Transformable Town Cabriolet-5/7P	—	—	—
4320	4D Transformable Town Cabriolet-7P	7,150	5,850	—
4320-C	4D Collapsible Transformable Town Cabriolet-7P	—	—	—
4325	4D Transformable Town Cabriolet-7P	7,150	5,850	—
4325-C	4D Collapsible Transformable Town Cabriolet-7P	—	—	—
4330	4D Imperial-5/7P	6,300	5,920	—
4330-5	4D Sedan-5P	5,950	5,850	—
4335	2D Convertible Coupe-2/4P	5,900	5,655	—
4355	4D Imperial Cabriolet-5/7P	6,350	5,940	—
4355-C	4D Collapsible Imperial Cabriolet-5/7P	—	—	—
355-5	4D Sedan Cabriolet-5P	6,125	5,885	—
4361	4D Imperial Club Sedan-5P	—	—	—
4361-5	4D Club Sedan-5P	5,950	5,740	—
4375	4D Imperial-7P	6,525	6,020	—
4375-C	4D Collapsible Imperial-7P	—	—	—
4375-5	4D Sedan-7P	6,225	5,980	—
4376	2D Coupe-2/4P	5,800	5,750	—
4380	4D All Weather Phaeton-5P	6,650	5,690	—
4381	2D Coupe-5P	5,950	—	—
4391	4D Transformable Limousine Brougham-7P	7,150	6,020	—
4391-C	4D Collapsible Transformable Limousine Brougham-7P	—	—	—
4412	4D Transformable Town Cabriolet-5/7P	—	—	—
4476	2D Coupe-2/4P	5,800	5,765	—
3289-A	4D Transformable Town Cabriolet-7P	—	—	—
3981	4D Sedan Cabriolet-5P	—	—	—
3991	4D Transformable Limousine Brougham-7P	—	—	—
2950-X	4D Sedan-7P	—	—	—
2901-LX	4D Sedan-7P	—	—	—
2951-LX	4D Sedan-7P	—	—	—
30-X	4D Sedan-7P	—	—	—
LX-2905	4D Town Sedan-5P	—	—	—
LX-2913	2D Coupe-5P	—	—	—
30-152	4D Town Sedan, Fisher-5P	—	—	—
30-158	2D Coupe, Fisher-2/4P	—	—	—
30-159	4D Sedan, Fisher-5P	—	—	—
30-168	2D Convertible Coupe, Fisher-2/4P	—	—	—
30-172	2D Coupe, Fisher-5P	—	—	—

ENGINE

V-8s:

L-head. Cast-iron block on aluminum crankcase. Bore and stroke: 3-3/8 x 4-15/16. Displacement: 353 cid. Compression ratio: 5.26:1. Brake hp: 95+ at 3000 rpm. Taxable hp: 36.45. Compression pressure: 104 at 1000 rpm. Main bearings: three. Valve lifters: Mechanical. Crankcase capacity: 8 qt. Cooling system capacity: 6 gal. Carburetor: Cadillac/Johnson with intake silencer.

L-head. Cast-iron block on aluminum crankcase. Bore and stroke: 3-3/8 x 4-15/16. Displacement: 353 cid. Compression ratio: 5.35:1. Brake hp: 95+ at 3000 rpm. Taxable hp: 36.45. Compression pressure: 104 at 1000 rpm. Main bearings: three. Valve lifters: Mechanical. Crankcase capacity: 8 qt. Cooling system capacity: 6 gal. Carburetor: Cadillac/Johnson with intake silencer.

V-12

45 degree overhead valve V-12. Cast-iron on aluminum crankcase. Bore and stroke: 3-1/8 x 4 inches. Displacement: 368 cid C.R.: (5.38:1) 5.20:1 standard, 5.03:1 optional.

Brake horsepower: 135 @ 3400 R.P.M. SAE/taxable horsepower: 46.9. Main bearings: Four. Valve lifters: Mechanical, with hydraulic silencer on rocker bushing. Carburetion: dual Cadillac/Johnson, with intake silencer.

V-16

45 degree, overhead valve V-16. Cast nickel-iron blocks on silicon/aluminum crankcase. Bore and stroke: 3 x 4 inches. Displacement: 452 cid C.R.: 5.35:1 early standard, 5.11:1 standard, 4.98:1 optional. Brake horsepower: 175-185 @ 3400 rpm. SAE/Taxable horsepower: 57.5. Main bearings: five. Valve lifters: pushrod/rocker arm with hydraulic rotary eccentric silencer in rocker arm. Carburetion: float feed, auxiliary air control, manufactured by Cadillac under C.F. Johnson patents.

CHASSIS

[V-8 Series 355A] Wheelbase: 134 inches. Overall length: approximately 203 inches. Height: 72-1/2 inches. Front/Rear Tread: 57-1/4/59-1/2 inches. Tires: 6.50 x 19. (7 x 18 on optional wheels). [V-8 Series 355A Commercial Chassis.] Wheelbase: 152 inches.

[V-12 Series 370A] Wheelbase: 140 inches. except seven-passenger sedan and Imperial 143 inches. Overall length: 210-220 inches. Height: 72-1/2 in Front/Rear Tread: 57-

1931 Cadillac, Series 370, Fleetwood V-12 convertible coupe

1/4/59-1/2 inches. (see note). Tires: 7:00 x 19 whitewall. (7.50 x 18 on optional wheels). [Series 370-A Commercial chassis] Wheelbase: 152 inches. Note: 60-1/2 inches. rear tread on Town Sedan beginning with chassis unit number 10-2720.

[V-16 Series: 452A] Wheelbase: 148 inches. Overall length: approximately 222- 1/2 inches. Front/Rear Tread: 59/59-1/2 inches. Tires: 7-19 early, 7.50-19 mid-model year and later.

TECHNICAL

[V-8 Series 355A] Selective, synchromesh transmission. Speeds: 3F/1R. Left-hand drive, center controls, right-hand drive optional. Twin disc clutch. Shaft drive, (torque tube). 3/4 floating rear axle, spiral bevel drive. Overall ratio: 4.75:1 standard, 4.07:1, 4.54:1 optional. Mechanical brakes on four wheels. Wood artillery wheels standard (wire, disc, demountable wood optional). Wheels: 19 inches standard, 18 inches with optional wheels.

[V-12 Series 370A] Selective, synchromesh transmission. Speeds: 3F/1R. Left-hand drive, center control, right-hand drive optional. Twin disc clutch. Shaft drive (torque tube). 3/4 floating rear axle, spiral bevel drive. Overall ratio: 4.54:1 standard, 4.07:1, 4.91:1 optional. Mechanical brakes on four wheels, with vacuum assister. 15-inch drums. Wood artillery wheels standard (wire, disc, demountable wood optional). Wheels 19 inches standard (18 inches with optional wheels).

[V-16 Series: 452A] Selective, synchromesh transmission. Speeds: 3F/1R. Left drive, center control, (right-hand drive optional). Twin disc clutch. Shaft drive, (torque tube). 3/4 floating rear axle, spiral bevel drive. Overall ratio: 4.39:1 standard, (3.47:1), 4.07:1, 4.75:1 optional. Vacuum assisted mechanical brakes on four wheels. Wood artillery wheels (wire, disc, demountable wood optional). Wheels: 19 inches.

OPTIONS

[V-8 Series 355A] Trunks ($100-119). Tonneau windshield ($185). Wind wings ($25-47.50). Tire cover(s) ($5-40). Mirrors ($10-32/pair). Radio (price on application). Heater ($41-55). Auxiliary lights ($37.50-75). Seat covers ($26.75-73.50). Heron or Goddess mascot ($20). Five wire wheels ($70). Six wire wheels with fender wells, trunk rack ($240). Five demountable wood wheels ($50). Six demountable wood wheels with wells and rack ($230). Four natural wood wheels ($10).

[V-12 Series 370A] Trunks ($100-119). Tonneau windshield ($185). Wind wings ($24-47.50). Tire cover(s) ($5-40). Mirrors ($10-32/pair). Radio (price on application). Heater ($41-55). Auxiliary lights ($37.50-75). Seat covers ($26.75-73.50). Heron or Goddess mascot ($20). Five wire wheels ($70). Six wire wheels with fender wells, trunk rack ($240). Five demountable wood wheels ($50). Six demountable wood wheels with wells and rack ($230). Four natural wood wheels ($10).

[V-16 Series: 452A] Mirrors ($10-32). Sidemount cover(s) ($40). Tonneau windshield ($185). Wind wings ($47.50). Radio ($200). Heater ($41-55). Heron or Goddess ornament ($20). Auxiliary lights ($37.50-75). Seat covers ($26.75-73.50). Trunks ($100-119). Five wire wheels ($70). Six wire wheels, fender wells, trunk rack ($210). Five demountable wood wheels ($50). Six demountable wood wheels, fender wells, trunk, rack ($190). Five disc wheels ($50). Six disc wheels, fender wells, trunk rack ($190). Fenders other than black ($100).

HISTORICAL

The president and general manager of Cadillac was Lawrence P. Fisher. The Series 355A Cadillac V-8 was introduced in August 1930. Model year sales and production were 10,717 cars. The Series 370A V-12 was introduced in October 1930. One V-12 Roadster was used as a pace car at the Indianaplis 500-Mile Race. Model year sales and production of V-12s came to 5,733. Approximately 363 Cadillac V-16s were made this year. Full-custom bodies by outside body builders were a rarity on the V-8 chassis. In his book *80 Years of Cadillac-LaSalle* (Crestline), Walter P. McCall pictures a handsome Victoria Cabriolet with coachwork by the French body builder Saoutchik, based on a V-16 chassis. More individual custom bodies were turned out for the V-12 and V-16 chassis.

1931 Cadillac, Series 370, Fleetwood V-8 phaeton

1932

OVERVIEW

Handsome bodies, an automatic vacuum-operated clutch with freewheeling, a Silent Synchromesh transmission and a carefully-worked-out shock-absorber-control system operated by the driver were the outstanding features of all three chassis in the 1932 Cadillac line. Details that improved the Cadillac's handsome lines included a radiator shell that flared at the top, a sloping windshield, more flaring fenders and curved running boards with heavy beads. All models had twin taillights and twin backing lights. A new type of four-beam headlight was used. Promoted as "Super-Safe Lighting," this advance featured three-filament bulbs and four control positions for degree and angle of illumination. Cadillacs also introduced a new type of door bolt that snapped softly into place. Two adjustable sun visors were provided and the doors could now be locked from the inside. All three Cadillac series were introduced in January 1932, along with the new LaSalle. The Series 355B V-8, the Series 370B V-12, the Series 452B Cadillac V-16 and the LaSalle all had slightly smaller dimensions and a stronger family resemblance. They were very handsome cars.

Above: **1932 Cadillac, Series 355-B, V-8 seven-passenger Imperial sedan**

I.D. DATA

[V-8 SERIES 355B] There were no serial numbers used for the Series 355B Cadillac. Engine numbers were stamped on crankcase near the water inlet on the right-hand side. Starting: 1200001. Ending: 1202700.

[V-12 SERIES 370B] Serial numbers were not used. Engine numbers were stamped on the right-hand side of the crankcase on the generator drive chain housing. Starting: 1300001. Ending: 1301740.

[V-16 Series 452B] Serial numbers were not used. Engine numbers were stamped on the right-hand side of the crankcase on the generator drive chain housing. Starting: 1400001. Ending: 1400300.

SERIES 355B — FISHER — V-8

Like other Cadillac products, the V-8 had a longer and lower body and an entirely restyled front assembly. The roof line was lowered one to three inches. A longer hood featured six vents. The new front-end styling included a flat grille built into the radiator shell, streamlined bullet-shaped headlights, similar side lights and no fender tie-bar or monogram bar. The trumpets of the dual horns projected through headlight stanchions. The new headlight lenses were 9-1/2 inches in diameter. The taillights matched the

headlights. The front license plate was mounted on the bumper. The runningboards curved to match the sweep of the front fenders and blended into the rear fenders. The tail of the rear fenders was blended into the fuel tank valance. The trunk on the Town Coupe, Town Sedan and five-passenger Convertible Coupe was integral with the body. Driving vision was increased by 30 percent as a result of eliminating the outside visor and using a new windshield and new corner posts with a 12-degree slope. There was a large ventilator in the top of the cowl, but none in the sides of the cowl. All separate body moldings were eliminated. A three-spoke steering wheel afforded an easy view of the instrument cluster in front of the driver. The right side of the instrument board had a "locker." The Cadillac frames were redesigned, using more box-type construction and no front or rear tubular cross members. Cast molybdenum brake drums were introduced and the "Cardan" shaft used previously was replaced by cable control for the front brakes. A new "Full Range Ride Control" system permitted driver adjustment of the shock absorber valves. V-threaded spring shackle pins were adopted to control side play. Wire wheels became standard, with optional full chrome covers available to simulate disc wheels. Also available were optional demountable wood wheels that fit the same hubs as the wire wheels. A "Triple-Silent Synchro-Mesh" transmission used constant-mesh helical gears with a ground-and-lapped tooth profile for all forward gears. The rear axle was redesigned to be lighter and stronger, through use of improved heat treatments. Final drive ratios were changed, but the use of smaller tires gave the same net effect. A "Controlled Free Wheeling" feature was operated by vacuum assist on the clutch, which was controlled by a foot button. Depressing the button released the clutch, while releasing the button or depressing the accelerator re-engaged the clutch. The 1932 V-8 provided a 21 percent increase in power, mostly due to a new manifold design, plus carburetor revisions. The intake manifold was redesigned to give an equal-length path to each cylinder. The location of the inlet and exhaust valves was interchangeable on the middle cylinders of each block. The inlet valves sat side by side at the center, so that one leg of the inlet manifold could service both middle cylinders. The exhaust manifold was on top of the intake manifold and a single exhaust pipe ran to the rear. An air filter was added to the intake muffler. The tailpipe had an external tuning chamber. A mechanical fuel pump replaced the use of vacuum-tank-type fuel feed. There was a separate vacuum pump for the windshield wipers. A new Cuno self-cleaning oil filter was mounted along the left side of the crankcase. On the V-8s, this was cleaned by manually turning the handle on top of the unit. The storage battery and air-cooled generator were both of greater capacity. Cadillac eliminated the used of manual advance on the distributor. A six-point engine suspension

1932 Cadillac, Series 355-B, V-8 convertible coupe

system (with mounts on all four corners of the engine, plus a dual mount at the rear of the transmission) was employed. The cooling fan was now mounted closer to the radiator. The close-fitting fan shroud was adjustable and moved up or down on the radiator as the fan assembly was moved for adjustment of the fan belt tension. The Cadillac radiator featured full-bonded-fin construction. The use of thermostat-controlled shutters was retained. For 1932, there were 13 basic Fisher bodies. They included open models such as the Roadster, Convertible Coupe and four different versions of the Phaeton. The styling of the 1932 Fleetwood bodies was less distinctive and was very similar to the Fisher body styles. All listed Fleetwood bodies were closed styles for 1932. Most body designs were shared across the engine-chassis lines.

SERIES 355B— FLEETWOOD — V-8
Seven Fleetwood semi-custom bodies were cataloged for 1932, but variations in some of the basic bodies raised the model count to nine as shown in the tables below.

Series 355B-Fisher 134-inch wheelbase

Model Number	Body Type & Seating	Price Weight	Factory Total	Production Total
32-8-155	2D Roadster-2/4P	2,895	4,635	—
32-8-178	2D Coupe-2/4P	2,795	4,705	—
32-8-168	2D Convertible Coupe-2/4P	2,945	4,675	—
32-8-159	4D Standard Sedan-5P	2,895	4,885	—

Fisher 140-inch wheelbase

Model Number	Body Type & Seating	Price Weight	Factory Total	Production Total
32-8-256	4D Standard Phaeton-5P	2,995	4,700	—
32-8-280	4D Special Phaeton-5P	3,095	4,750	—
32-8-273	4D All-Weather Phaeton-5P	3,495	5,070	—
32-8-279	4D Sport Phaeton-5P	3,245	4,800	—
32-8-272	2D Coupe-5P	2,995	4,715	—
32-8-259	4D Special Sedan-5P	3,045	4,965	—
32-8-252	4D Town Sedan-5P	3,095	4,980	—
32-8-262	4D Sedan-7P	3,145	5,10	—
32-8-263	4D Imperial Sedan-7P	3,295	5,150	—

Fleetwood 140-inch wheelbase

Model Number	Body Type & Seating	Price Weight	Factory Total	Production Total
4930-5	4D Sedan-5P	3,395	4,965	—
4975-5	4D Sedan-7P	3,545	5,110	—
4975	4D Limousine-7P	3,745	5,150	—
4981	2D Town Coupe-5P	3,395	4,915	—

4912	4D Town Cabriolet-5/7P	4,095	4,990	—
4991	4D Limousine Brougham-7P	4,245	5,100	—
4925	4D Town Cabriolet-7P	4,245	5,100	—
4975-H4	4D Limousine-7P	—	—	—
4985	2D Convertible Coupe-5P	—	—	—

SERIES 370B—FISHER—V-12

The overall styling and appearance of the Cadillac V-12 was identical to that of the V-8 model, except for the emblems designating the engine type. The 1932 V-12 had a stiffer frame than the 1931 model. It had nine-inch side rails. Mechanical features were also shared with V-8s, except for minor differences dictated by the V-12's increased power and weight. For example, it used different standard and optional gear ratios. The V-12's dual exhaust system had tuning chambers in the mufflers, rather than attached to tailpipes. Dual ignition coils were mounted on the top radiator tank. The engine was basically the same one used in the 370A, but the fuel-feed system was changed from vacuum tank to mechanical fuel pump. The V-12 also had a new Cuno disc-type self-cleaning oil filter mounted at the right-hand side of the clutch housing. On the V-12 (and V-16) version, it was connected to the starter pedal linkage. Whenever the starter pedal was depressed, the discs rotated and cleaned the filter. New dual Detroit Lubricator carburetors were used, marking the first time in 20 years that a Cadillac/Johnson carburetor was not used. There were 13 Fisher bodies cataloged for the V-12 chassis.

SERIES 370B— FLEETWOOD — V-12

A total of 22 Fleetwood semi-custom bodies were cataloged for the 1932 Cadillac V-12 chassis. Like the V-8 designs, the 1932 V-12 Fleetwood bodies were mostly closed styles and were very similar to the Fisher bodies. The V-12 Convertible Coupe and Town Cabriolet bodies essentially were modified closed-body designs.

Series 370B-Fisher 134-inch wheelbase

Model Number	Body Type & Seating	Factory Price	Shipping Weight	Production Total
32-12-155	2D Roadster-2/4P	3,595	4,870	—
32-12-178	2D Coupe-2/4P	3,495	4,085	—
32-12-168	2D Convertible Coupe-2/4P	3,645	5,060	—
32-12-159	4D Standard Sedan-5P	3,595	5,175	—

Fisher 140-inch wheelbase

Model Number	Body Type & Seating	Factory Price	Shipping Weight	Production Total
32-12-236	4D Standard Phaeton-5P	3,695	5,240	—
32-12-280	4D Special Phaeton-5P	3,795	5,290	—
32-12-273	4D All-Weather Phaeton-5P	4,195	5,385	—
32-12-279	4D Sport Phaeton-5P	3,945	5,340	—
32-12-272	2D Coupe-5P	3,695	5,220	—
32-12-259	4D Special Sedan-5P	3,745	5,345	—
32-12-252	4D Town Sedan-5P	3,795	5,370	—
32-12-262	4D Sedan-7P	3,845	5,460	—
32-12-263	4D Imperial Sedan-7P	3,995	5,500	—

Fleetwood 140-inch wheelbase

Model Number	Body Type & Seating	Factory Price	Shipping Weight	Production Total
5030-S	4D Sedan-5P	4,095	5,345	—
5075-S	4D Sedan-7P	4,245	5,460	—
5075	4D Limousine-7P	4,445	5,500	—
5081	2D Town Coupe-5P	4,095	5,225	—

5012	4D Town Cabriolet-5/7P	4,795	5,380	—
5091	4D Limousine Brougham-7P	4,945	5,580	—
5025	4D Town Cabriolet-7P	4,945	5,580	—

Fleetwood 140-inch wheelbase Special

Model Number	Body Type & Seating	Factory Price	Shipping Weight	Production Total
5029	Imperial-5P	—	—	—
5030	4D Imperial Sedan-5P	—	—	—
5030-FL	4D Imperial Cabriolet-5P	—	—	—
5030-SFL	4D Sedan Cabriolet-5P	—	—	—
5031	Imperial Sedan-5P	—	—	—
5031-5	Sedan-5P	—	—	—
5055	Imperial Sedan-5P	—	—	—
5055-C	Collapsible Imperial Sedan-5P	—	—	—
5056	Imperial Cabriolet-5P	—	—	—
5057	Touring-7P	4,895	5,295	—
5065	Imperial Sedan-7P	—	—	—
5075-FL	4D Limousine Cabriolet-7P	—	—	—
5075-H4	Imperial Sedan-7P	—	—	—
5082	Sedan-5P	—	—	—
5085	2D Convertible Coupe-5P	4,995	5,200	—

SERIES 452B—FISHER—V-16

For the first time in 1932, a series of Fisher bodies were available on the Cadillac V-16 chassis. Some of these were extremely rare automobiles. Styling and appearance features were generally the same as those of the V-8 and V-12 models, except for emblems and longer hood with seven ports. With the longer wheelbase and more power and weight, some mechanical details were beefed up from V-8 and V-12 specifications. The V-16 had deeper 10-inch frame rails, heavier axles, 18-inch wheel rims, an 11-inch clutch, 16-inch brake drums, different final gear ratios, a bigger battery and a higher-output generator. The engine remained basically the same as in 1930-1931. As on the V-12, new Detroit Lubricator carburetors and a Cuno disc-type self-cleaning oil filter were used. Fuel feed was by mechanical pump. Intake silencers with a filter took the place of the vacuum tanks on the dashboard. In a departure from the smooth, uncluttered look of the earlier V-16, the spark plug wires sprouted from the top of the distributor cap. This was a more efficient and dependable design, but did not look as neat.

SERIES 452B — FLEETWOOD — V-16

Seven Fleetwood bodies were offered on a V-16 chassis with a 149-inch wheelbase. Twenty Fleetwood Specials were available on the same wheelbase. Rare was a 165-inch wheelbase Fleetwood Imperial Sedan. A few Fleetwood body styles had an 18-degree windshield, instead of the typical 12 degree windshield. Some body styles achieved the ultimate proportions—radiator over

1932 Cadillac, Series 355-B, coupe

front axle, windshield midway between the axles and all seating between the axles. Some V-16 Fleetwood bodies were shared designs and were less distinctive than earlier models. The five styles with 18-degree windshields were still considered Madame X models. There were no 1932 Fleetwood roadsters or phaetons.

Series 352B-Fisher 143-inch wheelbase

Model Number	Body Type & Seating	Factory Price	Shipping	Production Total
32-16-155	2D Roadster-2/4P	4,595	5,065	—
32-16-178	2D Coupe-2/4P	4,495	5,530	—
32-16-168	2D Convertible Coupe-2/4P	4,645	5,505	—
32-16-159	4D Standard Sedan-5P	4,595	5,625	—

Fisher 149-inch wheelbase

Model Number	Body Type & Seating	Factory Price	Shipping	Production Total
32-16-256	4D Standard Phaeton-5P	4,695	5,400	—
32-16-280	4D Special Phaeton-5P	4,795	5,450	—
32-16-273	4D All-Weather Phaeton-5P	5,195	5,525	—
32-16-279	4D Sport Phaeton-5P	4,945	5,500	—
32-16-252	4D Town Sedan-5P	—	—	—
32-16-259	4D Special Sedan-5P	—	—	—
32-16-262	4D Sedan-7P	—	—	—
32-16-263	4D Imperial Sedan-7P	—	—	—
32-16-272	2D Coupe-5P	—	—	—

Fleetwood 149-inch wheelbase

Model Number	Body Type & Seating	Factory Price	Shipping	Production Total
5130-S	4D Sedan-5P	5,095	5,735	—
5175-S	4D Sedan-7P	5,245	5,865	—
5175	4D Limousine-7P	5,445	5,905	—
5181	2D Town Coupe-5P	5,095	5,605	—
5112	4D Town Cabriolet-5/7P	5,795	5,775	—
5191	4D Limousine Brougham-7P	5,945	5,935	—
5125	4D Town Cabriolet-7P	5,945	5,935	—

Fleetwood 149-inch wheelbase Special

Model Number	Body Type & Seating	Factory Price	Shipping	Production Total
5112-C	4D Collapsible Town Cabriolet-5/7P	—	—	—
5120	4D Transformable Town Cabriolet-7P	—	—	—
5125	4D Transformable Town Cabriolet-7P	—	—	—
5125-C	4D Collapsible Touring Town Cabriolet-7P	—	—	—
5125-Q	4D Transformable Cabriolet-7P	—	—	—
5129	4D Imperial-5P	—	—	—
5130-FL	4D Imperial Cabriolet-5P	—	—	—
5130-SFL	4D Sedan Cabriolet-5P	—	—	—
5131	4D Imperial Sedan-5P	—	—	—
5131-S	4D Sedan-5P	—	—	—
5140-B	Special Sedan-5P	—	—	—

1932 Cadillac, Series 355-B, roadster

Model Number	Body Type & Seating	Factory Price	Shipping	Production Total
5155	4D Imperial Sedan-5P	—	—	—
5155-C	4D Collapsible Imperial Sedan-5P	—	—	—
5156-C	4D Collapsible Imperial-5P	—	—	—
5164	4D Transformable Town Brougham-7P	—	—	—
5165	4D Imperial Limousine-7P	—	—	—
5175-C	4D Collapsible Limousine-7P	—	—	—
5175-FL	4D Limousine Cabriolet-7P	—	—	—
5175-H4	4D Imperial Sedan-7P	—	—	—
5185	2D Convertible Coupe-5P	—	—	—

Fleetwood 165-inch wheelbase Special

Model Number	Body Type & Seating	Factory Price	Shipping	Production Total
5177	4D Imperial-8P	—	—	—

ENGINE

1932 BASE V-8

L-head. Cast-iron block on aluminum crankcase. Bore and stroke: 3-3/8 x 4-15/16. Displacement: 353 cid. Compression ratio: 5.38:1. Brake hp: 115 at 3000 rpm. Taxable hp: 38.1. Compression pressure: 112 at 1000 rpm. Main bearings: three. Valve lifters: Mechanical. Crankcase capacity: 8 qt. Cooling system capacity: 6.5 gal. Carburetor: Cadillac/Johnson.

OPTIONAL "HIGH-COMPRESSION" V-8

L-head. Cast-iron block on aluminum crankcase. Bore and stroke: 3-3/8 x 4-15/16. Displacement: 353 cid. Compression ratio: 5.70:1. Brake hp: 115+ at 3000 rpm. Taxable hp: 38.1. Compression pressure: 112 at 1000 rpm. Main bearings: three. Valve lifters: Mechanical. Crankcase capacity: 8 qt. Cooling system capacity: 6.5 gal. Carburetor: Cadillac/Johnson.

OPTIONAL "LOW-COMPRESSION" V-8

L-head. Cast-iron block on aluminum crankcase. Bore and stroke: 3-3/8 x 4-15/16. Displacement: 353 cid. Compression ratio: 5.20:1. Brake hp: 115 at 3000 rpm. Taxable hp: 38.1. Compression pressure: 112 at 1000 rpm. Main bearings: three. Valve lifters: Mechanical. Crankcase capacity: 8 qt. Cooling system capacity 6.5 gal. Carburetor: Cadillac/Johnson.

V-12

45 degree overhead valve V-12. Cast-iron on aluminum crankcase. Bore and stroke: 3-1/8 x 4 inches. Displacement: 368 cid C.R.: 5.30:1 standard, 5.08:1, 4.90:1 optional Brake horsepower: 135 @ 3400 R.P.M. SAE/Taxable horsepower: 46.9. Main bearings: four. Valve lifters: mechanical with hydraulic silencer on rocker bushing. Carburetion: Detroit Lubricator Type L-13, R-13/Model 51.

V-16

45 degree overhead valve. Sixteen cylinders. Cast-iron on aluminum crankcase. Bore and stroke: 3 x 4 inches. Displacement: 452 cid C.R.: 5.36:1 standard, 5-00:1,

4.90:1 optional Brake horsepower: 165 @ 3400 R.P.M. Taxable horsepower: 57.5. Main bearings: five. Valve lifters: mechanical with hydraulic silencer on rocker bushing. Carburetion: Detroit Lubricator Type L-14, R-14/Model 51.

CHASSIS

[V-8 Series 355B] Wheelbase: 134, 140 inches. Overall length: 207, 213 inches. Front/Rear Tread: 59-7/8/61 inches. Tires: 7 x 17. [Series: 355B Commercial Chassis] W. B.: 156 inches.

[V-12 Series 370B] Wheelbase: 134, 140 inches. Overall length: 207, 213 inches. Front/Rear Tread: 59-7/8/61 inches. Tires: 7.50 x 17. [Series 370B Commercial Chassis] Wheelbase: 156 inches.

[V-16 Series 452B] Wheelbase: 143, 149 inches. Overall length: 216, 222 inches. Front/Rear Tread 59-7/8/61 inches. Tires: 7.50 x 18.

TECHNICAL

[V-8 Series 355B] Selective, synchromesh transmission. Speeds: 3F/1R. Left-hand drive, center controls, right-hand drive optional. Twin disc clutch—selective vacuum-activation. Shaft drive, (torque tube). 3/4 floating rear axle, spiral bevel drive. Overall ratio: 4.36:1, 4.60:1. Mechanical brakes on four wheels, (15-inch drums). Wire wheels standard. Demountable wood optional. Wheels: 17 inches. drop center.

[V-12 Series 370B] Selective, synchromesh transmission. Speeds: 3F/1R. Left-hand drive, Center control, right-hand drive optional. Twin disc clutch—selective vacuum-activation. Shaft drive (torque tube). 3/4 floating rear axle, spiral bevel drive. Overall ratio: 4.60:1, 4.80:1. Mechanical brakes on four wheels, with vacuum assist (15 inch drums). Wire wheels standard. Demountable wood optional. Wheels: 17 inches. Drop center.

[V-16 Series 452B] Selective synchromesh transmission. Speeds: 3F/1R. Left-hand drive, center control, right-hand drive optional. Twin disc-clutch—selective vacuum-activation. Shaft drive (torque tube). 3/4 floating rear axle, spiral bevel drive. Overall ratio: 4.31:1, 4.64:1. Mechanical brakes on four wheels with vacuum assist (16-inch drums.)

Wire wheels standard. Demountable wood optional. Wheels: 18 inches. Drop center.

OPTIONS

[V-8 Series 355B] Tire cover(s) ($5-$20 each). Trunks ($100-$180). Heron or Goddess mascot ($20). Radio (price on application). Heater ($37.50-$47.50). Auxiliary lights ($37.50-$57.50). Wind wings ($25-$47.50). Tonneau shield ($185). Seat covers ($26.50-$73.50). Mirrors ($8-$16 each). Full covers for wire wheels ($10 each). Six wire wheels with fender wells and trunk rack ($130). Five demountable wood wheels ($30). Six demountable wood wheels with wells and rack ($166). Colored fender set ($50).

[V-12 Series 370B] Tire cover(s) ($5-$20 each). Trunks ($100-$180). Heron or Goddess mascot ($20). Radio (price on application). Heater ($37.50-$47.50). Auxiliary lights ($37.50-$57.50). Wind wings ($25-$47.50). Tonneau shield ($185). Seat covers ($26.50-$73.50). Mirrors ($8-$16 each). Full covers for wire wheels ($10 each). Six wire wheels with fender wells and trunk rack ($150). Five demountable wood wheels ($30). Six demountable wood wheels with wells and rack ($186). Colored fender set ($50)

[V-16 Series 452B] Tire covers ($5-$20 each). Trunks ($100-$180). Heron or Goddess ($20). Radio (price on application). Heater ($37.50-$57.50). Wind wings ($25-$47.50). Tonneau shield ($185). Seat covers ($26.50-$73.50). Mirrors ($8-16 each). Full covers for wire wheels ($10 each). Six wire wheels with fender wells and trunk racks ($150). Five demountable wood wheels ($30). Six demountable wood wheels with wells and rack ($186). Colored fender set ($50).

HISTORICAL

Introduced January 1932. Model year sales and production included 2,700 Cadillac V-8s, 1,740 Cadillac V-12s and 300 Cadillac V-16s. The president and general manager of Cadillac was Lawrence P. Fisher. Cadillac's engineering department, justifiably renowned in the industry, came up with Ride Control for 1932.

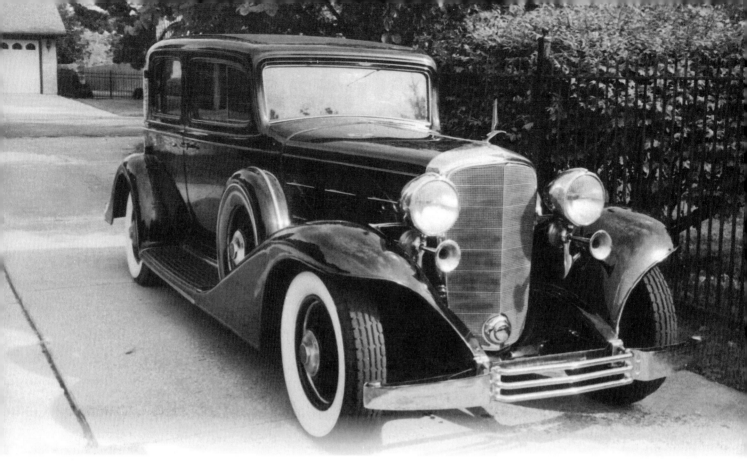

1933

OVERVIEW

In the mid-1920s, Cadillac broke with functional body design and began a period of creating "stylishly functional cars." The 1933 "C" Series cars ushered in the period of styling and streamlining for its own sake. A facelift, simple in execution, but startling in effect, transformed the 1933 Cadillac into a more modern-looking car.

I.D. DATA

[V-8 Series 355C] Serial numbers were not used. Engine numbers were stamped on crankcase near the water inlet on the right-hand side. Starting: 3000001. Ending: 3002100.

[V-8 Series 370C] Serial numbers were not used. Engine numbers were stamped on the right-hand side of the crankcase on the generator drive chain housing. Starting: 4000001. Ending: 4000953.

[V-8 Series 452C] Serial numbers were not used. Engine numbers were stamped on the right-hand side of the crankcase on the generator drive chain housing. Starting: 5000001. Ending: 5000126.

Above: **1933 Cadillac, Series 355-C, V-8 sedan**

SERIES 355-C — V-8

The 1933 appearance revisions started the concept of selling cars on the basis of styling features, as well as the concept of selling new cars on the basis of annual styling changes. The Cadillac bumpers were sectioned and had plain ends with a three-bar center. The grille was made V-shaped and blended into the painted radiator shell. A chrome-plated radiator shell was optional. The radiator filler cap disappeared under the hood on the right side, which was the same side that the oil-level gauge positioned on. After a year's absence, the fender tie-bar returned with a new look. It was sectioned and the center section was hidden behind the grille. Six horizontal doors replaced the vertical hood doors. Deep-skirted front and rear fenders were another new styling touch. The most significant change in body detail was the introduction of the Fisher No-Draft ventilation system. It featured individually controlled ventilation with pivoting vent windows in the front doors and rear quarter or rear door windows. On early-production cars, the front door window had to be lowered to disengage the vent window channel at its front edge. This allowed the vent window to pivot. On later-production units, the sealing channel was attached to the door frame, rather than the window glass. With this arrangement the vent window could be operated independently of the window glass. The windshield and

1933 Cadillac, Series 452-C, Fleetwood seven-passenger limousine

rear quarter windows were stationary. The absence of the windshield-opening mechanism on closed cars allowed room to conceal the windshield wiper motor behind the headboard. The cowl ventilator was baffled and drained in such a way as to be rainproof. The few 1933 chassis changes were minor. The use of controlled freewheeling was discontinued. A vacuum assist was added to the V-8 model's brake system. New shock absorber valves extended the range of the ride control system. At engine unit number 30-3607, the dual-point, four-lobe distributor was replaced by a single-point, eight-lobe unit. Wire-spoke wheels were now standard equipment. Two-passenger rumbleseat models were on a 134-inch wheelbase, while other Cadillac V-8s rode a 140-inch wheelbase.

SERIES 355C—FLEETWOOD—V-8

Eight Fleetwood semi-custom bodies were cataloged for the 1932 long-wheelbase V-8 chassis.

Series 355C-Fisher 134-inch wheelbase

Model Number	Body Type & Seating	Factory Price	Shipping Weight	Production Total
33-8-155	2D Roadster-2/4P	2,795	—	—
33-8-168	2D Convertible Coupe-2/4P	2,845	4,825	—
33-8-178	2D Coupe-2/4P	2,695	4,855	—

Fisher 140-inch wheelbase

Model Number	Body Type & Seating	Factory Price	Shipping Weight	Production Total
33-8-252	4D Sedan-5P	2,995	5,060	—
33-8-256	4D Phaeton-5P	2,895	4,865	—
33-8-259	4D Sedan-5P	2,895	5,000	—
33-8-262	4D Sedan-7P	3,045	5,105	—
33-8-263	4D Imperial Sedan-7P	3,195	5,140	—
33-8-272	2D Coupe-5P	2,895	4,850	—
33-8-273	4D All-Weather Phaeton-5P	3,395	5,110	—

Fleetwood 140-inch wheelbase

Model Number	Body Type & Seating	Factory Price	Shipping Weight	Production Total
5330-S	4D Sedan-5P	3,295	—	—
5375-S	4D Sedan-7P	3,445	—	—
5375	4D Limousine-7P	3,645	—	—
NA	2D Coupe-5P	—	—	—
5312	4D Transformable Town Cabriolet-5/7P	3,995	—	—
5391	4D Transformable Limousine Brougham-7P	4,145	—	—
5325	4D Transformable Town Cabriolet-7P	4,145	—	—
5357	4D Touring-7P	—	—	—
5381	2D Town Coupe-5P	—	—	—
5312-C	4D Collapsible Transformable Town Cabriolet-5/7P	—	—	—
5325-C	4D Collapsible Transformable Town Cabriolet-7P	—	—	—
5375-C	4D Collapsible Limousine-7P	—	—	—
5375-H4	Limousine with 4" extra headroom-7P	—	—	—
5330-FL	4D Imperial Cabriolet-5P	—	—	—
5375-FL	4D Imperial Cabriolet-7P	—	—	—
5364	4D Transformable Town Brougham-5p	—	—	—
5320	4D Transformable Town Cabriolet-7P	—	—	—

SERIES 370-C—V-12

The easiest way to tell the difference between the V-8 and V-12 Cadillac for 1933 is to check the emblems or look under the hood. The radiator filler cap and oil-level gauge were on the left side on V-12s. The V-12 models also had wider tires and a different carburetor made by Detroit Lubricator.

Series 370C-Fisher 134-inch wheelbase

Model Number	Body Type & Seating	Factory Price	Shipping Weight	Production Total
33-12-155	Roadster-2/4P	3,495	—	—
33-12-168	Convertible Coupe-2/4P	3,545	5,125	—
33-12-178	Coupe-2/4P	3,395	5,165	—

Fisher 140-inch wheelbase

Model Number	Body Type & Seating	Factory Price	Shipping Weight	Production Total
33-12-252	Town Sedan-5P	3,695	5,385	—
33-12-256	Phaeton-5P	3,595	—	—
33-12-259	Sedan-5P	3,595	5,335	—
33-12-262	Sedan-7P	3,745	5,440	—
33-12-263	Imperial Sedan-7P	3,895	5,500	—
33-12-272	Coupe-5P	3,595	—	—
33-12-273	All-Weather Phaeton-5P	4,095	5,405	—

Fleetwood 140-inch wheelbase

Model Number	Body Type & Seating	Factory Price	Shipping Weight	Production Total
5430-S	4D Sedan-5P	3,995	5,335	—
5475-S	4D Sedan-7P	4,145	5,440	—
5475	4D Limousine-7P	4,345	5,500	—
NA	2D Coupe-5P	—	—	—
5412	4D Transformable Town Cabriolet-5/7P	4,695	—	—
5425	4D Transformable Town Cabriolet-7P	4,845	—	—
5420	4D Transformable Town Cabriolet-7P	—	—	—
5425-C	4D Collapsible Transformable Town Cabriolet-7P	—	—	—
5430-FL	4D Imperial Cabriolet-5P	—	—	—
5455	4D Imperial Cabriolet (Madame X)-5/7P	—	—	—
5457-A	4D Touring-7P	—	—	—
5464	4D Transformable Town Brougham-7P	—	—	—
5475-H4	4D Limousine with 4" extra headroom-7P	—	—	—
5475-FL	Limousine Cabriolet-7P	—	—	—
5481	2D Town Coupe-5P	—	—	—
5482	4D Sedanette-5P	—	—	—
5485	2D Convertible Coupe-5P	—	—	—

452-C—V-16

Cadillac announced that V-16 production for 1933 would be limited to 400 cars. These were to be serial numbered, with the car number and the owner's name on a gold-finished plate inside the car. Actual production came to just 126 cars. Nearly 70 body styles were suggested, but only half were actually built. In addition, half of the cars produced were the five most conservative five-passenger or seven-passenger sedans. Cadillac V-16s also had a V-shaped radiator shell, deep-skirted fenders and Fisher

No-Draft ventilation. Detail distinctions included a new winged-goddess hood ornament, large, spinner hubcaps, the absence of a crankhole cover in the grille and a distinctive four-bar bumper. The hood side panels carried two vertical doors, plus three stylized horizontal louvers. Front fender valances with vertical louvers were shown in promotional literature and used on mockups. However, "production" cars had three horizontal louvers that matched the hood louvers. Some new styling details were shown on various bodies. Instead of ending at the front of the cowl, some hoods were extended back over the cowl to the windshield. Many four- door bodies sported a rear body panel that swept back over the fuel tank, with a door opening for carrying parcels. At least one open and one closed four-door design offered a built-in trunk. A few styles even retained the "Madame X" look seen on some of the first V16s. Mechanical changes were few. A higher compression ratio was available to utilize improved gasoline. Except on early production cars, the wheel size was reduced from 18 to 17 inches. Beginning with engine unit number 50-24, the starter ring gear was moved from the clutch centerplate to the flywheel, where it was also located on the V-8 and V-12 models.

Series 352C-Fisher 143-inch wheelbase

Model Number	Body Type & Seating	Factory Price	Shipping Weight	Production Total
33-16-168	2D Convertible Coupe-2/4P	—	—	—
33-16-272	2D Coupe-5P	—	—	—

Fleetwood 143-inch wheelbase

Model Number	Body Type & Seating	Factory Price	Shipping Weight	Production Total
5508	2D Convertible Coupe-2/4P	—	—	—
5509	2D Coupe-2/4P	—	—	—

Fleetwood 149-inch wheelbase

Model Number	Body Type & Seating	Factory Price	Shipping Weight	Production Total
5502	2D Roadster-2/4P	—	—	—
5512	4D Town Cabriolet-5/7P	6,850	6,110	—
5513	4D Town Cabriolet-5/7P	—	—	—
5514	4D Town Cabriolet-5/7P	—	—	—
5520	4D Town Cabriolet-7P	—	—	—
5521	4D Town Cabriolet-7P	—	—	—
5524	4D Town Cabriolet-7P	—	—	—
5525	4D Town Cabriolet-7P	6,850	6,270	—
5526	4D Town Cabriolet-7P	—	—	—
5530	4D Imperial Sedan-5P	—	—	—
5530-S	4D Sedan-5P	6,250	6,070	—
5530-FL	4D Imperial Cabriolet-5/7P	—	—	—
5530-SFL	4D Sedan Cabriolet-5P	—	—	—
5530-H4	4D Imperial Sedan-5P	—	—	—
5531	4D Imperial Sedan-5/7P	—	—	—
5531-5	4D Sedan-5/7P	—	—	—
5532	4D Imperial Sedan-5/7P	—	—	—
5532-5	4D Sedan-5/7P	—	—	—
5533	4D Town Imperial-5P	—	—	—
5533-5	4D Town Sedan-5P	—	—	—
5535	2D Convertible Coupe-2/4P	—	—	—
5536	2D Sport Convertible Coupe-2/4P	—	—	—
5540	4D Imperial Cabriolet-5/7P	—	—	—
5540-5	4D Sedan Cabriolet-5/7P	—	—	—
5545	4D Imperial Cabriolet-5/7P	—	—	—
5545-5	4D Sedan Cabriolet-5/7P	—	—	—
5550	4D Full Collapsible Town Cabriolet-7P	—	—	—
5555	4D Imperial Cabriolet-5/7P	—	—	—
5555-C	4D Collapsible Imperial Cabriolet- 5/7P	—	—	—
5557	4D Touring-7P	—	—	—
5558	4D Phaeton-5P	—	—	—
5559	4D Sport Phaeton-5P	—	—	—
5560	4D Sport Phaeton-5P	—	—	—
5561	4D Close Coupled Imperial-5P	—	—	—
5561-5	4D Close Coupled Sedan-5P	—	—	—
5563	4D Sport Imperial-5/7P	—	—	—
5563-5	4D Sport Sedan-5/7P	—	—	—
5564	4D Town Brougham-5/7P	—	—	—
5564-B	4D Town Brougham with canework-5/7P	—	—	—
5565	4D Limousine-7P	—	—	—
5565	4D Sedan-7P	—	—	—
5566	4D Limousine-7P	—	—	—
5566-5	4D Sedan-7P	—	—	—
5573	4D Limousine-7P	—	—	—
5573-5	4D Sedan-7P	—	—	—
5574	4D Imperial Cabriolet-7P	—	—	—
5574-5	4D Sedan-7P	—	—	—
5575	4D Limousine-7P	6,600	6,270	—
5575-5	4D Sedan-7P	6,400	6,200	—
5575-FL	4D Imperial Cabriolet-7P	—	—	—
5575-SFL	4D Sedan Cabriolet-7P	—	—	—
5576	2D Coupe-2/4P	—	—	—
5577	2D Sport Coupe-2/4P	—	—	—
5578	4D All-Weather Sport Phaeton-5P	—	—	—
5579	4D All-Weather Phaeton-5P	8,000	6,110	—
5579-A	4D All-Weather Phaeton-5P	—	—	—
5580	4D Convertible Phaeton-5P	—	—	—
5581	2D Town Coupe-5P	6,250	6,000	—
5583	2D Coupe-2P	—	—	—
5585	2D Convertible Coupe-5P	7,500	5,910	—
5586	2D Convertible Coupe-4P	—	—	—
5590	4D Limousine Brougham-7P	—	—	—
5591	4D Limousine Brougham-7P	6,850	6,300	—
5592	4D Limousine Brougham-7P	—	—	—
5599	2D Aerodynamic Coupe-5P	—	—	—

ENGINE

BASE V-8

L-head. Cast-iron block on aluminum crankcase. Bore and stroke: 3-3/8 x 4-15/16. Displacement: 353 cid. Compression ratio: 5.4:1. Brake hp: 115 at 3000 rpm. Taxable hp: 38.1. Compression pressure: 104 at 1000 rpm. Main bearings: three. Valve lifters: Mechanical. Crankcase capacity: 8 qt. Cooling system capacity: 6.5 gal. Carburetor: Cadillac/Johnson.

OPTIONAL V-8

L-head. Cast-iron block on aluminum crankcase. Bore and stroke: 3-3/8 x 4-15/16. Displacement: 353 cid. Compression ratio: 5.70:1. Brake hp: 115+ at 3000 rpm. Taxable hp: 38.1. Compression pressure: 104 at 1000 rpm. Main bearings: three. Valve lifters: Mechanical. Crankcase capacity: 8 qt. Cooling system capacity: 6.5 gal. Carburetor: Cadillac/Johnson.

V-12

45 degree overhead valve. Twelve cylinders. Cast-iron on aluminum crankcase. Bore and stroke: 3-1/8 x 4 inches. Displacement: 368 cid C.R.: 5.6:1 standard, 5.4:1, 5.1:1 optional Brake horsepower: 135 @ 3400 R.P.M. horsepower: 46.9. Main bearings: four. Valve lifters: mechanical with hydraulic silencer on rocker bushing.

Carburetion: Detroit Lubricator Type L-13, R-13/Model 51.

V-16

45 degree overhead valve. Sixteen cylinders. Cast-iron on aluminum crankcase. Bore and stroke: 3 x 4 inches. Displacement: 452 cid C.R.: 5.7:1 standard, 5.4:1, 5.1:1 optional Brake horsepower: 165 @ 3400 R.P.M. Taxable horsepower: 57.5. Main bearings: five. Valve lifters: mechanical with hydraulic silencer on rocker bushing. Carburetion: Detroit Lubricator Type L-14, R-14/Model 51.

CHASSIS

[Series 355-C] Wheelbase: 134, 140 inches. Overall length: approximately 207- 213 inches. Front/Rear Tread: 59-7/8/61 inches. Tires: 7 x 17. [Semi-Commercial Chassis] Wheelbase: 156 inches.

[Series: 370-C] Wheelbase: 134, 140 inches. Length: approximately 207-213 inches. Front/Rear Tread: 59-7/8/61 inches. Tires: 7.50 x 17. [Semi-commercial chassis] Wheelbase: 156 inches.

[Series 452-C] Wheelbase: 143, 149 inches. Overall length: approximately 216-222 inches. Front/Rear Tread 59-7/8/61 inches. Tires: 7.50 x 17.

TECHNICAL

[Series 355-C] Selective, synchromesh transmission. Speeds: 3F/1R. Left-hand drive, center control, right-hand drive optional. Twin disc clutch. Shaft drive, (torque tube). 3/4 floating rear axle, spiral bevel drive. Overall ratio: 4.36:1, 4.60:1. Mechanical brakes on four wheels with vacuum assist. (15-inch drums.) Wire wheels standard. Demountable wood optional Wheels: 17 inches. Drop center.

[Series: 370-C] Selective, synchromesh transmission. 3F/1R. Left-hand drive, center control, right-hand drive optional. Twin disc clutch. Shaft drive (torque tube). 3/4 floating rear axle, spiral bevel drive. Overall ratio: 4.60:1, 4.80:1. Mechanical brakes on four wheels with vacuum assist. (15-inch drums.) Wire wheels standard. Demountable wood optional. Wheels: 17 inches. Drop center.

[Series 452-C] Selective, synchromesh transmission. Speeds: 3F/1R. Left-hand drive, center controls right-hand drive optional. Twin disc clutch. Shaft drive (torque tube). 3/4 floating rear axle, spiral bevel drive. Overall ratio: 4.31:1, 4.64:1. Mechanical brakes on four wheels with vacuum assist. (15-inch. drums.) Wire wheels standard. Demountable wood option. Wheels: 17 inches. Drop center.

OPTIONS

[Series 355-C] Sidemount cover(s). Wheel discs (chrome $10 each/body color $12.50 each). Radio (Standard $64.50, Imperial $74.50). Heater: Hot air or hot water. Draft deflector for convertible coupe ($35/pair). Luggage sets ($37-$110). Trunks with luggage ($104-$180). Seat covers ($10/seat). Mirrors. Lorraine spotlight ($24.50). Dual Pilot Ray lights ($44.50). Heron radiator ornament ($20). Six wire wheels with fender wells. Five demountable wood wheels. Six demountable wood wheels with fender wells.

[Series 370-C] Sidemount cover(s). Wheel discs (chrome $10 each/body color $12.50 each). Radio (Standard $64.50, Imperial $74.50). Heater, hot air or hot water. Draft deflector for convertible coupe ($35/pair). Luggage sets ($37- 110). Trunks with luggage ($104-$180). Seat Covers ($10/seat). Mirrors. Lorraine spotlight ($24.50). Dual Pilot Ray lights ($44.50). Heron radiator ornament ($20). Six wire wheels with fender wells. Five demountable wood wheels. Six demountable wood wheels with fender wells.

[Series 452-C] Wheel discs. Radio (Standard ($64.50, Imperial $74.50). Heater, hot air or hot water. Luggage sets ($37- $110.06). Trunks with luggage ($104-$180). Mirrors. Lorraine spotlight ($24.50). Dual Pilot Ray lights ($44.50). Goddess radiator ornament (plated gold $50, silver $40). Six wire wheels with fender wells. Five demountable wood wheels. Six demountable wood wheels with fender wells.

HISTORICAL

The 1933 Cadillacs were introduced in January 1933. Lawrence P. Fisher was president and general manager of Cadillac. Total sales for the model year came to 6,655 units. This included 953 V-12s and 126 V-16s. The General Motors exhibit at the "Century of Progress" exhibition in Chicago showcased the prototype of a Cadillac V-16 Aerodynamic Coupe.

1933 Cadillac, Series 370-C, dual cowl phaeton

1934

OVERVIEW

The 1934 Cadillacs were completely restyled and mounted on an entirely new chassis. However, they used the same basic V-8, V-12 and V-16 engines as used in the 1933 models. The new radiator grille slanted towards the rear of the car and had one central divider and five horizontal sections. New teardrop headlights were fitted. On V-8 and V-12 models there were two rows of small, square hood vents with engine call-out badges at the forward end. The V-16 models were on a new 154-inch wheelbase. They had long, horizontal hood vents and front and rear fender moldings. Streamlining was in at Cadillac. New technical features included a "Knee-Action" front suspension, Hotchkiss steering, aluminum pistons, Fisher Turret Tops and dual X-frame chassis construction. Cadillac's "years ahead" image helped sell many extra cars as the Great Depression started winding towards its end.

I.D. DATA

[Model 355-D] Serial numbers were on top surface of frame side bar, right side, just ahead of dash. Same as engine number. Starting: 3100001. Ending: 3108318 (with 1935). Engine numbers were stamped on crankcase near

---

Above: **1934 Cadillac, Series 452-D, Fleetwood seven-passenger town cabriolet**

the water inlet on the right-hand side. Starting: 3100001. Ending: 3108318 (with 1935).

[Model 370-D] Serial numbers were located on top surface of frame side bar, right side, just ahead of dash. Same as engine number. Starting: 4100001. Ending: 4101098 (with 1935). Engine numbers stamped on the right-hand side of the crankcase, on the generator drive chain housing. Starting: 4100001. Ending: 4101098 (with 1935).

[Model 452-D] Serial numbers were on top surface of frame side bar, right side, just ahead of dash. Same as engine number. Starting: 5100001. Ending: 5100150 (with 1935). Engine numbers were stamped on the right-handside of the crankcase, on the generator drive chain housing. Starting: 5100001. Ending: 5100150 (with 1935).

[Fleetwood Body Numbering] Some confusion exists regarding style numbers on 1934-1935 Fleetwood bodies. Under the previous Fleetwood system, V-8s would be 56 or 60 styles, V-12s would be 57 or 61 styles and V-16s would be 58 or 62 styles. This system was followed in promotional literature, in the 1934 Cadillac Master Parts List and in early factory records. However, since the bodies

were identical for all series, Fleetwood stamped all body plates 57 or 60. Master Parts Lists after 1934 used only 57 and 60 style numbers for 1934-1935 Fleetwood bodies. Starting in 1936, V-8 and V-12 style numbers reflected the new 1936 series designations, but V-16s retained the 57 system and 60 styles were no longer offered.

MODEL 355-D — SERIES 10, 20, FLEETWOOD 30 — V-8

Cadillac's 1934 styling emphasized streamlining and the concealment of all chassis features except the wheels. Body construction was improved for better insulation against engine heat and to reduce engine, road and wind noise. The bumpers were of a stylish bi-plane design mounted against telescoping springs. The sloping, V-shaped grille was set into a painted shell. The use of chrome was subdued, but a chrome-plated radiator shell was available as an option. The horns and radiator filler cap were concealed under the hood. Guide brand, teardrop-shaped multi-beam headlights were mounted on streamlined supports attached to the fenders. The parking lamps were mounted in the headlight supports. The airfoil-shaped front fenders sat low over the chassis. The hood sills were high, with the entire fender shape molded into the radiator shell. A curious horizontal crease broke the nose contour of the fenders. Hoods extending nearly to the windshield carried shutter-type louvers in the side panels. The windshields were fixed and steeply sloped. There were three types: 18 degrees straight (or flat) windshield on Fisher bodies, 25 degrees straight windshield on some Fleetwood bodies and 29-1/2 degrees modified V-shaped windshield on other Fleetwood bodies. The cowl vents opened towards the windshield. There was one cowl vent on straight-windshield bodies. Two cowl vents projected through openings in the hood on modified V-windshield bodies. The bodies were two inches lower than those on previous Cadillacs. Moving the hand brake lever to the left of the driver, under the instrument panel, increased front-passenger-compartment space. The rear fenders were airfoil-shaped and carried rear lights that matched the

headlights. On cars with Fisher bodies, the gas tank filler was on the left side, at the rear, of the body. On cars with Fleetwood bodies, the gas filler was in the left rear fender. All bodies featured a beaver tail rear deck that completely covered the chassis. On cars with Fleetwood bodies, the spare tire was concealed inside the rear deck, unless optional in-the-fender sidemounts were ordered. The bodies on the Series 10 and 20 cars were built by Fisher. Bodies on the V-8 Fleetwood Series were shared with the 12s and 16s. In Fisher bodies, the battery was under the front seat, on the right side. Cars with Fleetwood bodies had the battery under the right front fender. The battery had to be removed from underneath these cars.

Series 10-Fisher 128-inch wheelbase

Model Number	Body Type & Seating	Factory Price	Shipping Weight	Production Total
34728	2D Sport Coupe-2/3P	2,395	4,550	—
34718	2D Convertible Coupe-2/4P	2,495	4,515	—
34721	4D Convertible Sedan-5P	2,695	4,750	—
34722	2D Town Coupe-5P	2,545	4,630	—
34709	4D Sedan-5P	2,495	4,715	—
34702	4D Town Sedan-5P	2,545	4,735	—

Series 20 Fisher 136-inch wheelbase

Model Number	Body Type & Seating	Factory Price	Shipping Weight	Production Total
34678	2D Sport Coupe-2/3P	2,595	4,660	—
34668	2D Convertible Coupe-2/4P	2,695	4,625	—
34671	4D Convertible Sedan-5P	2,895	4,860	—
34659	4D Sedan-5P	2,695	4,825	—
34652	4D Town Sedan-5P	2,745	4,815	—
34662	4D Sedan-7P	2,845	4,945	—
34663	4D Imperial Sedan-7P	2,995	4,970	—

Series Fleetwood (30) 146-inch wheelbase vee windshield
Some listings show these as 56-styles.

Model Number	Body Type & Seating	Factory Price	Shipping Weight	Production Total
5702	Roadster-2P	—	—	—
5712-C	Collapsible Town Cabriolet-5P	—	—	—
5712-LB	Town Cabriolet-5P	5,495	5,540	—
5712-MB	Town Cabriolet-5P	—	—	—
5720	Town Cabriolet-7P	—	—	—
5720-C	Collapsible Town Cabriolet-7P	—	—	—
5725-B	Town Cabriolet-7P	—	—	—
5725-LB	Town Cabriolet-7P	5,595	5,650	—
5725-MB	Town Cabriolet-7P	—	—	—
5730	Imperial Sedan-5P	—	—	—
5730-FL	Imperial Cabriolet-5P	4,145	5,500	—
5730-FM	Imperial Brougham-5P	—	—	—
5730-S	Sedan-5P	3,745	5,465	—
5733	Imperial Town Sedan-5P	—	—	—
5733-S	Town Sedan-5P	3,795	5,415	—
5735	Convertible Coupe-2P	4,045	5,115	—
5757	Touring-7P	—	—	—
5759	Sport Phaeton-5P	—	—	—
5775	Imperial Sedan (Limousine)-7P	4,095	5,580	—
5775-6	Limousine-7P	—	—	—
5775-E	Imperial Sedan-7P	—	—	—
5775-FL	Imperial Cabriolet-7P	4,295	5,580	—
5775-FM	Imperial Brougham-7P	—	—	—
5775-H4	Imperial Sedan-7P	—	—	—
5775-S	Sedan-7P	3,895	5,545	—
5775-W	Limousine-7P	—	—	—
5776	Coupe-2P	3,895	5,150	—
5780	Convertible Sedan with divider-5P	4,295	5,465	—
5780-B	Convertible Sedan-5P	—	—	—
5780-5	Convertible Sedan-5P	5,430	—	—
5785	Collapsible Coupe-5P	4,295	5,415	—
5788	Stationary Coupe-5P	—	—	—
5789-A	Victoria Coupe-4P	—	—	—

1934 Cadillac, Series 355-D, five-passenger V-8, touring sedan

5791	Limousine Brougham-7P	5,495	5,580	—
5791-B	Limousine Brougham-7P	—	—	—
5799	Aerodynamic Coupe-5P	4,295	5,430	—

Series Fleetwood (30) 146-inch wheelbase flat windshield

Model Number	Body Type & Seating	Factory Price	Shipping Weight	Production Total
6030-B	Imperial Sedan-5P	—	—	—
6030-FL	Imperial Cabriolet-5P	3,695	5,500	—
6030-FM	Imperial Brougham-5P	—	—	—
6030-S	Sedan-5P	3,295	5,465	—
6033-S	Town Sedan-5P	3,345	5,415	—
6035	Convertible Coupe-2P	—	—	—
6075	Imperial Sedan-7P	3,645	5,580	—
6075-B	Limousine (Special Back)-7P	—	—	—
6075-D	Limousine-7P	—	—	—
6075-E	Limousine-7P	—	—	—
6075-FL	Imperial Cabriolet-7P	3,845	5,580	—
6075-FM	Imperial Brougham-7P	—	—	—
6075-H3	Limousine-7P	—	—	—
6075-H4	Limousine-7P	—	—	—
6075-0	Imperial Sedan-7P	—	—	—
6075-S	Sedan-7P	3,445	5,545	—

MODEL 370-D — V-12

Except for the engine and various emblems, the Cadillac V-12 was much the same car as the Cadillac V-8 model with the 146-inch wheelbase V-8. On V-12s and 16s, the gearshift lever was moved forward to the clutch housing. The V-12 also had larger tires. A Detroit Lubricator carburetor was used on this engine. Fisher No-Draft ventilation was featured. The V-12 lineup was comprised only of Fleetwood straight windshield models and Fleetwood-bodied models with the modified V-type windshield.

Fleetwood 146-inch wheelbase modified V windshield

Model Number	Body Type & Seating	Factory Price	Shipping Weight	Production Total
5702	Roadster-2P	—	—	—
5712-C	Collapsible Town Cabriolet-5P	—	—	—
5712-LB	Town Cabriolet-5P	6,195	5,990	—
5712-MB	Town Cabriolet-5P	—	—	—
5720	Town Cabriolet-7P	—	—	—
5720-C	Collapsible Town Cabriolet-7P	—	—	—
5725-B	Town Cabriolet-7P	—	—	—
5725-LB	Town Cabriolet-7P	6,295	6,040	—
5725-MB	Town Cabriolet-7P	—	—	—
5730	Imperial Sedan-5P	—	—	—
5730-FL	Imperial Cabriolet-5P	4,845	5,765	—
5730-FM	Imperial Brougham-5P	—	—	—
5730-S	Sedan-5P	4,445	5,735	—
5733	Imperial Town Sedan-5P	—	—	—
5733-S	Town Sedan-5P	4,995	5,700	—
5735	Convertible Coupe-2P	4,745	5,485	—
5757	Touring-7P -	—	—	—
5759	Sport Phaeton-5P	—	—	—
5775	Imperial Sedan (Limousine)-7P	4,795	5,790	—
5775-B	Limousine-7P	—	—	—
5775-E	Imperial Sedan-7P	—	—	—
5775-FL	Imperial Cabriolet-7P	4,995	5,790	—
5775-FM	Imperial Brougham-7P	—	—	—
5775-H4	Imperial Sedan-7P	—	—	—
5775-S	Sedan-7P	4,595	5,760	—
5775-W	Limousine-7P	—	—	—
5776	Coupe-2P	4,595	5,520	—
5780	Convertible Sedan with divider-5P	4,995	5,800	—
5780-6	Convertible Sedan-5P	—	—	—
5780-S	Convertible Sedan-5P	—	5,770	—
5785	Collapsible Coupe-5P	4,995	5,685	—

5788	Stationary Coupe-5P	—	5,720	—
5789-A	Victoria Coupe-4P	—	—	—
5791	Limousine Brougham-7P	6,195	6,030	—
5791-B	Limousine Brougham-7P	—	—	—
5799	Aerodynamic Coupe-5P	4,995	5,720	—

Fleetwood 146-inch wheelbase straight windshield
Some listings show these as 61- styles.

Model Number	Body Type & Seating	Factory Price	Shipping Weight	Production Total
6030-B	Imperial Sedan-5P	—	—	—
6030-FL	Imperial Cabriolet-5P	4,395	5,765	—
6030-FM	Imperial Brougham-5P	—	—	—
6030-S	Sedan-5P	3,995	5,735	—
6033-S	Town Sedan-5P	4,045	5,700	—
6035	Convertible Coupe-2P	—	—	—
6075	Imperial Sedan-7P	4,345	5,790	—
6075-B	Limousine (special back)-7P	—	—	—
6075-D	Limousine-7P	—	—	—
6075-E	Limousine-7P	—	—	—
6075-FL	Imperial Cabriolet-7P	4,545	5,790	—
6075-FM	Imperial Brougham-7P	—	—	—
6075-H3	Limousine-7P	—	—	—
6075-H4	Limousine-7P	—	—	—
6075-0	Imperial Sedan-7P	—	—	—
6075-S	Sedan-7P	4,145	5,760	—

MODEL 452-D — V-16

V-16s shared the Fleetwood bodies with the V-8s and V-12s, but they were given a few distinctive styling details. The grille was of an egg-crate design. The headlights were mounted on the radiator shell, rather than on the fenders. The front parking lights were on the fenders, rather than in the headlight supports. Three spears were placed on the hood side panels and front fender skirts. There was no crease across the nose of the front fenders. Chassis changes were the same as on the V-8s and V-12s, with minor differences designed to accommodate the added weight, power and tremendous 154-inch wheelbase. Five wire wheels with disc covers were standard equipment.

Fleetwood 154-inch wheelbase modified V windshield
Some listings show these as 58- styles.

Model Number	Body Type & Seating	Factory Price	Shipping Weight	Production Total
5702	Roadster-2P	—	—	—
5712-C	Collapsible Town Cabriolet-5P	—	—	—
5712-LB	Town Cabriolet-5P	8,850	—	—
5712-MB	Town Cabriolet-5P	—	—	—
5720	Town Cabriolet-7P	—	—	—
5720-C	Collapsible Town Cabriolet-7P	—	—	—
5725-B	Town Cabriolet-7P	—	—	—
5725-LB	Town Cabriolet-7P	8,950	6,390	—
5725-MB	Town Cabriolet-7P	—	—	—
5730	Imperial Sedan-5P	—	—	—
5730-FL	Imperial Cabriolet-5P	7,700	—	—
5730-FM	Imperial Brougham-5P	—	—	—
5730-S	Sedan-5P	7,300	6,100	—
5733	Imperial Town Sedan-5P	—	—	—
5733-S	Town Sedan-5P	7,350	6,085	—
5735	Convertible Coupe-2P	7,600	5,900	—
5757	Touring-7P	—	—	—
5759	Sport Phaeton-5P	—	—	—
5775	Imperial Sedan (Limousine)-7P	7,650	6,210	—
5775-B	Limousine-7P	—	—	—
5775-E	Imperial Sedan-7P	—	—	—
5775-FL	Imperial Cabriolet-7P	7,850	—	—
5775-FM	Imperial Brougham-7P	—	—	—
5775-H4	Imperial Sedan-7P	—	—	—
5775-S	Sedan-7P	7,450	6,190	—
5775-W	Limousine-7P	—	—	—

Model Number	Body Type & Seating	Factory Price	Shipping Weight	Production Total
5776	Coupe-2P	7,450	5,840	—
5780	Convertible Sedan with divider-5P	7,850	6,100	—
5780-B	Convertible Sedan-5P	—	—	—
5780-S	Convertible Sedan-5P	—	—	—
5785	Collapsible Coupe-5P	7,885	—	—
5788	Stationary Coupe-5P	—	—	—
5789-A	Victoria Coupe-4P	—	—	—
5791	Limousine Brougham-7P	8,850	—	—
5791-B	Limousine Brougham-7P	—	—	—
5799	Aerodynamic Coupe-5P	7,850	—	—

Fleetwood 154-inch wheelbase straight windshield
Some listings show these as 62- styles.

Model Number	Body Type & Seating	Factory Price	Shipping Weight	Production Total
6030-B	Imperial Sedan-5P	—	—	—
6030-FL	Imperial Cabriolet-5P	7,050	—	—
6030-FM	Imperial Brougham-5P	—	—	—
6030-S	Sedan-5P	6,650	—	—
6033-S	Town Sedan-5P	6,700	6,085	—
6035	Convertible Coupe-2P	—	—	—
6075	Imperial Sedan-7P	7,000	6,210	—
6075-B	Limousine (special back)-7P	—	—	—
6075-D	Limousine-7P	—	—	—
6075-E	Limousine-7P	—	—	—
6075-FL	Imperial Cabriolet-7P	7,200	—	—
6075-FM	Imperial Brougham-7P	—	—	—
6075-H3	Limousine-7P	—	—	—
6075-H4	Limousine-7P	—	—	—
6075-0	Imperial Sedan-7P	—	—	—
6075-S	Sedan-7P	6,800	6,190	—

ENGINE

BASE V-8

L-head. Cast iron block on aluminum crankcase. Bore and stroke: 3-3/8 x 4-15/16. Displacement: 353 cid. Compression ratio: 6.25:1. Brake hp: 120 at 3000 rpm. Taxable hp: 36.45. Compression pressure: 148 at 1000 rpm. Main bearings: three. Valve lifters: Mechanical. Crankcase capacity: 8 qt. Cooling system capacity: 5 gal. Carburetor: Detroit Lubricator Model 51. Engine changes were few, but horsepower was increased. All Cadillac engines including the V-8 used Lynite aluminum pistons. Compression ratios were increased. Intake ducting to the carburetor air cleaner was extended to the radiator casing, providing cold, dense air rather than the hot air in the engine compartment. The combination of aluminum pistons, cold intake air and higher compression with improved fuels resulted in increased horsepower and engine speeds. Detail changes in the V-8 engine

1934 Cadillac, Series 452-D, Fleetwood five-passenger convertible coupe

included a change to Detroit Lubricator carburetor, use of dual valve springs, discontinuation of the oil filter and discontinuation of the solenoid starter control with starter button on the instrument panel. One V-8 engine change to be appreciated by anyone removing a cylinder head was the change from head studs to cap screws. The change was actually made so that the heads could be turned before lifting, so as to clear the hood shelf. Another change, not necessarily appreciated, was the elimination of provision for hand-cranking the engine.

OPTIONAL V-8

L-head. Cast iron block on aluminum crankcase. Bore and stroke: 3-3/8 x 4-15/16. Displacement: 353 cid. Compression ratio: 5.75:1. Brake hp: 120 at 3000 rpm. Taxable hp: 36.45. Compression pressure: 148 at 1000 rpm. Main bearings: three. Valve lifters: Mechanical. Crankcase capacity: 8 qt. Cooling system capacity: 5 gal. Carburetor: Detroit Lubricator Model 51.

V-12

45 degree, overhead valve. Twelve cylinders. Cast-iron block on aluminum crankcase. Bore and stroke: 3-1/8 x 4 inches. Displacement: 368 cid C.R.: 6.0:1 standard, 5.65:1 optional Brake horsepower: 133 @ 3400 R.P.M. SAE/taxable horsepower: 46.9. Main bearings: four. Valve lifters: mechanical with hydraulic silencer on rocker bushing. Carburetion: Dual Detroit Lubricator, Type R-13, L-13, Model 51.

V-16

45 degree, overhead valve. Sixteen cylinders. Cast-iron block on aluminum crankcase. Bore and stroke: 3 x 4 inches. Displacement: 452 cid C.R.: 6.0:1 standard, 5.57:1 optional Brake horsepower: 169.2 @ 3400 R.P.M. SAE/taxable horsepower: 57.5. Main bearings: five. Valve lifters: mechanical with hydraulic silencer on rocker bushing. Carburetion: Dual Detroit Lubricator, Type R-14, L-14, Model 51.

CHASSIS

[Model 355-D] [Series 10] Wheelbase: 128 inches. Overall length: 205-3/4 or 207-1/2 inches. Front/Rear Tread: 59-3/8/62 inches. Tires: 7 x 17. [Series 20] Wheelbase: 136 inches. Overall length: 213-3/4, 215-1/2 inches. Front/Rear Tread: 59-3/8/62 inches. Tires: 7 x 17. [Series Fleetwood (30)] Wheelbase: 146 inches. Overall length: 227-9/16 inches. Front/Rear Tread: 59-3/8/62 inches. Tires: 7 x 17. Significant changes in Cadillac's chassis resulted in improved riding and handling, plus decreased driver fatigue. The new independent "knee action" front suspension with coil springs and center point steering resulted in greatly reduced unsprung weight. The front shocks were now an integral part of the suspension, the

shock arm being the upper suspension arm. An inverted steering box, mounted on the outside of the frame, was used on Fleetwood-bodied cars. Hotchkiss drive replaced the torque-tube drive. The rear brakes were now operated by pull rods and cables. A new frame of "X" design added to chassis strength and allowed for the reduction in overall vehicle height. A stabilizer bar to control body roll in turns was added at the rear of the chassis. The brake and clutch pedal assembly was relocated from the transmission to the frame. The mufflers on Fleetwood-bodied cars were relocated to the outside of the frame.

[MODEL 370-D] Wheelbase: 146 inches. Overall length: 227-9/16 inches. Front/Rear Tread: 59-3/8/62 inches. Tires: 7.50 x 17.

[MODEL 452-D] Wheelbase: 154 inches. Overall length: 240 inches. Front/Rear Tread: 59-3/8/62 inches. Tires: 7.50 x 17.

TECHNICAL

[Model 355-D] Selective synchromesh transmission. Speeds: 3F/1R. Left-hand drive, center control, emergency brake at left-under panel (right-hand drive optional). Twin disc clutch. Shaft drive, Hotchkiss. 3/4 floating rear axle, spiral bevel drive. Overall ratio: [Series 10, 20] 4.60:1 standard, 4.36, 4.8:1 optional [Series 30] 4.80:1 standard 4.60:1 optional Mechanical brakes with vacuum assist on four wheels. Wire wheels. Wheels: 17 inches. Drop center.

[Model 370-D] Selective, synchromesh transmission. Speeds: 3R/1R. Left-hand drive, center control, emergency brake at left under panel (right-hand drive optional). Twin disc clutch. Shaft drive, Hotchkiss. 3/4 floating rear axle, spiral bevel drive. Overall ratio: 4.80:1 standard, 4.60:1 optional, 5.11:1 optional Mechanical brakes with vacuum assist on four wheels. Wire wheels. Wheels: 17 inches. Drop center.

[Model 452-D] Selective synchromesh transmission. Speeds: 3F/1R. Left-hand drive, center control, emergency brake at left under panel (right-hand drive optional). Twin disc clutch. Shaft drive, Hotchkiss. 3/4 floating rear axle, spiral bevel drive. Overall ratio: 4.64:1 standard, 4.31:1 optional, 4.07:1 optional Mechanical brakes with vacuum assist on four wheels. Wire wheels. Wheels: 17 inches. Drop center.

OPTIONS

[All] Sidemount cover(s) ($20 each). Radio (standard/master) ($64.50/$74.50). Heater ($44.50). Seat covers. Spotlight ($24.50). Flexible steering wheel.

HISTORICAL

The new Cadillacs were introduced in January 1934. Model-year sales and production for 1934-1935 combined included 8,318 Cadillac V-8s, 1,098 Cadillac V-12s and 150 Cadillac V-16s. (with 1935). Lawrence P. Fisher was the president and general manager of Cadillac from the beginning of the calendar year until May 31. Nicholas Dreystadt became general manager on June 1, 1934.

1934 Cadillac, Series 355-D, V-8 coupe

1935

OVERVIEW

Cadillac for 1935 remained virtually unchanged from 1934. The biplane bumpers of 1934 were replaced by more conventional units. One major change was introduced on Fisher bodies—the all-steel Turret Top. Fleetwood bodies did not have the steel top until 1936.

MODEL 355-E— SERIES 10, 20, 30—V-8

For 1934, Fleetwood bodied V-8s on a 146-inch wheelbase were designated Series 30. Fisher-bodied cars continued under the designations Series 10 and Series 20. Having been associated with funeral and ambulance equipment for many years, Cadillac embarked on an extra effort in 1935 to consolidate this business. Three Fleetwood-bodied seven-passenger livery sedans were offered on the V-8 Series 30 chassis. Additionally, a 160-inch wheelbase commercial chassis with V-8 power was offered for hearse and ambulance adaptation.

I.D. DATA

[Model 355-E] Serial numbers were on top surface of frame side bar, right side, just ahead of dash. Same as engine number. Starting: 3100001 (1934-1935). Ending: 3108318. Engine numbers were stamped on crankcase

---

Above: **1935 Cadillac, Series 40, V-12 seven passenger limousine**

---

near the water inlet on the right-hand side. Starting: 3100001 (1934-1935). Ending: 3108318.

[Model 370E] Serial numbers were on top surface of frame side bar, right side, just ahead of dash. Same as engine number. Starting: 4100001 (1934-1935). Ending: 4101098. Engine numbers were stamped on the right-hand side of the crankcase, on the generator drive chain housing. Starting: 4100001 (1934-1935). Ending: 4101098.

[Model 452E] Serial numbers were on top surface of frame side bar, right side, just ahead of dash. Same as engine number. Starting: 5100001 (with 1934). Ending: 5100150. Engine numbers were stamped on the right-hand side of the crankcase, on the generator drive chain housing. Starting: 5100001 (with 1934). Ending: 5100150.

[Fleetwood Body Numbering] Some confusion exists regarding style numbers on 1934-1935 Fleetwood bodies. Under the previous Fleetwood system, V-8s would be 56 or 60 styles, V-12s would be 57 or 61 styles and V-16s would be 58 or 62 styles. This system was followed in promotional literature, in the *1934 Cadillac Master Parts List* and in early factory records. However, since the bodies were identical for all series, Fleetwood stamped all body

plates 57 or 60. Master Parts Lists after 1934 used only 57 and 60 style numbers for 1934-1935 Fleetwood bodies. Starting in 1936, V-8 and V-12 style numbers reflected the new 1936 series designations, but V-16s retained the 57 system and 60 styles were no longer offered.

Series 10 Fisher 128-inch wheelbase

Model Number	Body Type & Seating	Factory Price	Shipping Weight	Production Total
35728	2D Sport Coupe-2/3P	2,345	4,550	—
35718	2D Convertible Coupe-2/4P	2,445	4,515	—
35721	4D Convertible Sedan-5P	2,755	4,750	—
35722	2D Town Coupe-5P	2,495	4,630	—
35709	4D Sedan-5P	2,445	4,715	—
35702	4D Town Sedan-5P	2,495	4,735	—

Series 20 Fisher 136-inch wheelbase

Model Number	Body Type & Seating	Factory Price	Shipping Weight	Production Total
35678	2D Sport Coupe-2/3P	2,545	4,660	—
35668	2D Convertible Coupe-2/4P	2,645	4,625	—
35671	4D Convertible Sedan-5P	2,955	4,860	—
35659	4D Sedan-5P	2,645	4,825	—
35652	4D Town Sedan-5P	2,695	4,815	—
35662	4D Sedan-7P	2,795	4,945	—
35663	4D Imperial Sedan-7P	2,945	4,970	—

Series 30 Fleetwood Livery 146-inch wheelbase

Model Number	Body Type & Seating	Factory Price	Shipping Weight	Production Total
6075-L	4D Livery Limousine-7P	—	—	—
6075-LL	4D Livery Limousine-7P	—	—	—
6075-SL	4D Livery Sedan-7P	—	—	—

Series 30 Fleetwood 146-inch wheelbase vee windshield

Model Number	Body Type & Seating	Factory Price	Shipping Weight	Production Total
fs6075-S	Sedan-7P	3,445	5,545	—

Note: Some listings show these as 56-styles.

MODEL 370-D — SERIES 40 — V-12

The 1935 Cadillac V-12 was essentially the same as the 1934 model, except for new bumper. The gearshift lever in V-12s was moved forward to the clutch housing. It also had larger tires. Fisher No-Draft ventilation was featured. The V-12 lineup was comprised only of Fleetwood models. While designated 370-E models, at least early in the year, the model designation Series 40 was also used to identify these cars.

Series 40 Fleetwood 146-inch wheelbase vee Windshield

Model Number	Body Type & Seating	Factory Price	Shipping Weight	Production Total
5702	Roadster-2P	—	—	—
5712-C	Collapsible Town Cabriolet-5P	—	—	—
5712-LB	Town Cabriolet-5P	6,195	5,990	—
5712-MB	Town Cabriolet-5P	—	—	—
5720	Town Cabriolet-7P	—	—	—
5720-C	Collapsible Town Cabriolet-7P	—	—	—
5725 B	Town Cabriolet-7P	—	—	—
5725-LB	Town Cabriolet-7P	6,295	6,040	—
5725-MB	Town Cabriolet-7P	—	—	—
5730	Imperial Sedan-5P	—	—	—
5730-FL	Imperial Cabriolet-5P	4,845	5,765	—
5730-FM	Imperial Brougham-5P	—	—	—
5730-S	Sedan-5P	4,445	5,735	—
5733	Imperial Town Sedan-5P	—	—	—
5733-S	Town Sedan-5P	4,995	5,700	—
5735	Convertible Coupe-2P	4,745	5,485	—
5757	Touring-7P	—	—	—
5759	Sport Phaeton-5P	—	—	—

5775	Imperial Sedan (Limousine)-7P	4,795	5,790	—
5775-B	Limousine-7P	—	—	—
5775 E	Imperial Sedan-7P	—	—	—
5775-FL	Imperial Cabriolet-7P	4,995	5,790	—
5775-FM	Imperial Brougham-7P	—	—	—
5775-H4	Imperial Sedan-7P	—	—	—
5775 S	Sedan-7P	4,595	5,760	—
5775-W	Limousine-7P	—	—	—
5776	Coupe-2P	4,595	5,520	—
5780	Convertible Sedan with div.-5P	4,995	5,800	—
5780-8	Convertible Sedan-5P	—	—	—
5780-S	Convertible Sedan-5P	—	5770	—
5785	Collapsible Coupe-5P	4,995	5,685	—
5788	Stat. Coupe-5P	—	5,720	—
5789-A	Victoria Coupe-4P	—	—	—
5791	Limousine Brougham-7P	6,195	6,030	—
5791-B	Limousine Brougham-7P	—	—	—
5799	Aero. Coupe-5P	4,995	5,720	—

Series 40 Fleetwood 146-inch wheelbase flat windshield

Model Number	Body Type & Seating	Factory Price	Shipping Weight	Production Total
6030-B	Imperial Sedan-5P	—	—	—
6030-FL	Imperial Cabriolet-5P	4,395	5,765	—
6030-FM	Imperial Brougham-5P	—	—	—
6030-S	Sedan-5P	3,995	5,735	—
6033-S	Town Sedan-5P	4,045	5,700	—
6035	Convertible Coupe-2P	—	—	—
6075	Imperial Sedan-7P	4,345	5,790	—
6075-B	Limousine (spec. back)-7P	—	—	—
6075-D	Limousine-7P	—	—	—
6075-E	Limousine-7P	—	—	—
6075 FL	Imperial Cabriolet-7P	4,545	5,790	—
6075-FM	Imperial Brougham-7P	—	—	—
6075-H3	Limousine-7P	—	—	—
6075-H4	Limousine-7P	—	—	—
6075-0	Imperial Sedan-7P	—	—	—
6075-S	Sedan-7P	4,145	5,760	—

Note: Some listings show these as 61-styles.

MODEL 452-D — SERIES 60 — V-16

The 1935 Cadillac V-16 was essentially the same as the 1934 model, except for new bumpers. The gearshift lever in V-12s was moved forward to the clutch housing. V-16s shared the Fleetwood bodies with the V-8s and V-12s, but they were given a few distinctive styling details. The grille was of egg-crate design. The headlights were mounted on the radiator shell, rather than on the fenders. The front parking lights were on the fenders, rather than

1935 Cadillac, Series 60, Fleetwood V-16 convertible sedan

in the headlight supports. Three spears were placed on the hood side panels and front fender skirts. There was no crease across the nose of the front fenders. Chassis changes were the same as on the V-8s and V-12s, with minor differences designed to accommodate the added weight, power and tremendous 154-inch wheelbase. Five wire wheels with disc covers were standard equipment. While designated 452-E models, at least early in the year, the model designation Series 60 was also used to identify these cars.

Series 60 Fleetwood 154-inch wheelbase vee windshield

Model Number	Body Type & Seating	Factory Price	Shipping Weight	Production Total
5702	Roadster-2P	—		
5712-C	Collapsible Town Cabriolet-5P	—	—	—
5712-LB	Town Cabriolet-5P	8,950	6,100	—
5712-MB	Town Cabriolet-5P	—	—	—
5720	Town Cabriolet-7P	—		
5720-C	Collapsible Town Cabriolet-7P	—	—	—
5725-B	Town Cabriolet-7P	—		
5725 LB	Town Cabriolet-7P	9,050	6,390	—
5725-MB	Town Cabriolet-7P	—	—	—
5730	Imperial Sedan-5P	—		
5730-FL	Imperial Cabriolet-5P	7,800	6,150	—
5730-FM	Imperial Brougham-5P	—		—
5730-S	Sedan-5P	7,400	6,085	—
5733	Imperial Town Sedan-5P		6,140	—
5733-S	Town Sedan-5P	7,450	6,050	—
5735	Convertible Coupe-2P	7,700	5,800	—
5757	Touring-7P	7,700	5,800	—
5759	Sport Phaeton-5P	—	—	
5775	Imperial Sedan (Limousine)-7P	7,750	6,210	—
5775-B	Limousine-7P	—		
5775 E	Imperial Sedan-7P	—		
5775-FL	Imperial Cabriolet-7P	7,950		—
5775 FM	Imperial Brougham-7P	—		
5775-H4	Imperial Sedan-7P	—		
5775-S	Sedan-7P	7,550	6,190	—
5775-W	Limousine-7P	—		
5776	Coupe-2P	7,550	5,840	—
5780	Convertible Sedan with div.-5P	7,950	6,100	—
5780-B	Convertible Sedan-5P	—	—	—
5780-S	Convertible Sedan-5P	—	6,080	—
5785	Collapsible Coupe-5P	—	6,000	—
5788	Stat. Coupe-5P	—		
5789-A	Victoria Coupe-4P	—		
5791	Limousine Brougham-7P	8,950	6,225	—
5791-B	Limousine Brougham-7P	—		—
5799	Aerodynamic Coupe-5P	8,150	6,050	—

Note: Some listings show these as 58- styles.

Series 60 Fleetwood 154-inch wheelbase flat windshield
Some listings show these as 62-styles.

Model Number	Body Type & Seating	Factory Price	Shipping Weight	Production Total
6030-B	Imperial Sedan-5P	—		
6030-FL	Imperial Cabriolet-5P	7,150	—	—
6030-FM	Imperial Brougham-5P		—	—
6030-S	Sedan-5P	6,750	6,050	—
6033-S	Town Sedan-5P	6,800	6,085	—
6035	Convertible Coupe-2P	—		
6075	Imperial Sedan-7P	7,100	6,210	—
6075 B	Limousine (spec. back)-7P	—		
6075-D	Limousine-7P	—		
6075-E	Limousine-7P	—		
6075-FL	Imperial Cabriolet-7P	7,300		—
6075-FM	Imperial Brougham-7P	—		—
6075-H3	Limousine-7P	—		—
6075 H4	Limousine-7P	—		
6075 0	Imperial Sedan-7P	—		—
6075 S	Sedan-7P	6,900	6,190	—

ENGINE

BASE V-8

L-head. Cast iron block on aluminum crankcase. Bore and stroke: 3-3/8 x 4-15/16. Displacement: 353 cid. Compression ratio: 6.25:1. Brake hp: 130 at 3400 rpm. Taxable hp: 36.45. Compression pressure: 148 at 1000 rpm. Main bearings: three. Valve lifters: Mechanical. Crankcase capacity: 8 qt. Cooling system capacity. 5 gal. Carburetor: Detroit Lubricator Model 51.

OPTIONAL V-8

L-head. Cast iron block on aluminum crankcase. Bore and stroke: 3-3/8 x 4-15/16. Displacement: 353 cid. Compression ratio: 5.75:1. Brake hp: 130 at 3400 rpm. Taxable hp: 36.45. Compression pressure: 148 at 1000 rpm. Main bearings: three. Valve lifters: Mechanical. Crankcase capacity: 8 qt. Cooling system capacity. 5 gal. Carburetor: Detroit Lubricator Model 51.

V-12

45 degree, overhead valve. Twelve. Cast iron block on aluminum crankcase. Bore and stroke: 3-1/8 x 4 inches.

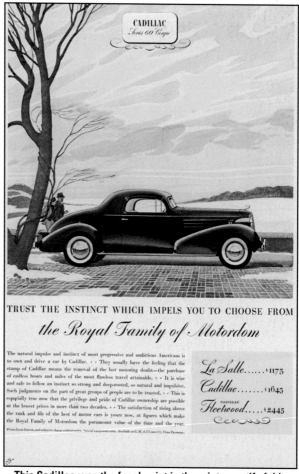

This Cadillac was the focal point in the winter motif of this 1936 ad.

A stable was the setting for this 1937 Cadillac Fleetwood cleanup scene.

Displacement: 368 cid C.R.: 6.0:1 standard, 5.65:1 optional Brake horsepower: 150 @ 3600 r.p.m. SAE/Taxable horsepower: 46.9. Main bearings: four. Valve lifters: mechanical with hydraulic silencer on rocker bushing. Carburetion: Dual Detroit Lubricator, Type R-13, L-13, Model 51.

V-16

45 degree, overhead valve. Sixteen. Cast iron block on aluminum crankcase. Bore and stroke: 3 x 4 inches. Displacement: 452 cid C.R.: 6.0:1 standard Brake horsepower: 185 @ 3800 r.p.m. SAE/Taxable horsepower: 57.5. Main bearings: five. Valve lifters: mechanical with hydraulic silencer on rocker bushing. Carburetion: Dual Detroit Lubricator, Type R-14, L-14, Model 51.

CHASSIS

[Model 355-E] [Series 10] Wheelbase: 128 inches. Overall length: 207-1/2 inches. Front/Rear Tread: 59-3/8/62 inches. Tires: 7 x 17. [Series 20] Wheelbase: 136 inches. Overall length: 215-1/2 inches. Front/Rear Tread:

59-3/8/62 inches. Tires: 7 x 17. [Series 30] W. B.: 146 inches. Overall length: 227-9/16 inches. Front/Rear Tread: 59-3/8/62 inches. Tires: 7 x 17. [Commercial chassis] Wheelbase: 160 inches.

[Model 370-E] Wheelbase 146 inches. Front/Rear Tread: 59-3/8/62 inches. Tires: 7.50 x 17.

[Model 452-E] Wheelbase 154 inches. Overall length: 240 inches. Front/Rear Tread: 59-3/8/62 inches. Tires: 7.50 x 17.

TECHNICAL

[Model 355-E] Selective, synchromesh transmission. Speeds: 3F/1R. Left-hand drive, center control, emergency brake at left under panel (right-hand drive optional). Twin disc clutch. Shaft drive, Hotchkiss. 3/4 floating rear axle, spiral bevel drive. Overall ratio: [Series 10, 20] 4.60:1 standard, 4.36:1, 4.8:1 optional [Series 30] 4.80:1 standard, 4.60:1 optional Mechanical brakes with vacuum assist on four wheels. Wire wheels. Wheels: 17 inches. Drop center.

[Model 370-E] Selective, synchromesh transmission. Speeds: 3F/1R. Left-hand drive, center control, emergency brake at left under panel (right-hand drive optional). Twin disc clutch. Shaft drive, Hotchkiss. 3/4 floating rear axle, spiral bevel drive. Overall ratio: 4.80:1 standard, 4.60:1 optional, 5.11:1 optional. Mechanical brakes with vacuum assist on four wheels. Wire wheels. Wheels: 17 inches. Drop center.

[Model 452-E] Selective, synchromesh transmission. Speeds: 3F/1R. Left-hand drive, center control, emergency brake at left under panel (right-hand drive optional). Twin disc clutch. Shaft drive, Hotchkiss. 3/4 floating rear axle, spiral bevel drive. Overall ratio: 4.64:1 standard 4.31:1 optional, 4.07:1 optional Mechanical brakes with vacuum assist on four wheels. Wire wheels. Wheels: 17 inches. Drop center.

OPTIONS

[All] Sidemount cover(s) ($20 ea.). Radio (standard/master) ($64.50/$74.50). Heater ($44.50). Seat covers. Spotlight ($24.50). Flexible steering wheel.

HISTORICAL

The 1935 Cadillacs were a continuation of the 1934 series introduced in January 1934. Model-year sales and production for 1934-1935 combined included 8,318 Cadillac V-8s, 1,098 Cadillac V-12s and 150 Cadillac V-16s. (with 1935). Nicholas Dreystadt was the general manager of Cadillac from the beginning of the calendar year until May 31.

1936

OVERVIEW

A narrower radiator grille with added horizontal moldings bars characterized the 1936 Cadillac. The bumper guards were also spaced further apart. A new 90-degree L-head V-8 was offered in Cadillacs in three series: "60," "70" and "75." The all-new 60 series models rode a 120-inch wheelbase. All models offered Fisher "Unisteel" turret-top body construction and all Cadillacs, except some with the V-16, had forward-hinged doors. Other updates included hydraulic brakes, an under-the-dash emergency brake, bullet-shaped headlights and pontoon fenders. The 1936 Cadillacs were said to be 500 to 800 pounds lighter than their 1935 counterparts. For the first time since 1914, Cadillacs were identified by model year—"The 1936 Cadillacs."

I.D. DATA

[Series 60] Engine numbers were on top of the crankcase, just behind the fan support. Starting: 6010001. Ending: 6016712.

[Series 70-75] Engine numbers were on top of the crankcase, just behind the fan support. Starting: 3110001. Ending: 3115248.

Above: **1936 Cadillac, Series 60, V-8 coupe**

[Series 80-85] Engine numbers were on the upper left surface of the generator drive chain housing. Starting: 4110001. Ending: 4110901.

[Series 90] Engine numbers were on the upper surface of the generator drive chain housing. Starting: 5110201. Ending: 5110252.

NOTE: Starting in 1936, V-8 and V-12 style numbers reflected the new 1936 series designations, but V-16s retained the 57-system, 60-styles were no longer offered.

SERIES 60—V-8

The Series 60 Cadillac was a new model for 1936. It had more features than a LaSalle, but less than a full-size Cadillac. The concept behind the car was similar to the LaSalle concept with the Cadillac name added. It was smaller, shorter, lighter, less powerful and less expensive than other Cadillac V-8s, but featured full Cadillac build quality. Model selections were limited to three Fisher body styles. The Convertible Coupe had a rumbleseat, but the two-passenger Coupe had only a small folding seat inside for an extra passenger. Both these body styles had a single fenderwell on the side opposite the driver. The V-shaped windshield, the grille and the front fender treatment were the same as seen on the larger V-8s. The engine was the same new V-8 used in the Fleetwood-bodied cars, but with a 3/8-inch smaller bore. The transmission was similar

to that fitted to the LaSalle, but smaller than a regular Cadillac transmission. Many dimensions of this car were smaller than those of other Cadillacs and fit the overall theme of a lower-priced and less pretentious automobile with a quality level equal to that of other Cadillacs.

Series 36-60 Fleetwood 121-inch wheelbase

Model Number	Body Type & Seating	Factory Price	Shipping Weight	Production Total
36-6077	Coupe-2P	1,645	3,830	—
36-6067	Convertible Coupe-2P	1,725	3,940	—
36-6019	Touring Sedan-5P	1,695	4,010	—

SERIES 70 — V-8

The Series 36-70 models represented the bread-and-butter Cadillacs. The LaSalle and the three lower-priced Series 60 models sold better, while the V-12s and V-16s were fancier. However, the four 70 Series V-8 models on the 131-inch wheelbase and the 10 Series 75 models on the 138-inch wheelbase—all with a new 346-cid V-8 under their hood—were the cars that survived and became the primary Cadillac models. Fleetwood bodies featuring a V-type windshield were used on all of these cars. A narrower radiator shell supported the new louver-style "convex-V" grille. The headlights were mounted on the radiator shell and the parking lights were inside the headlights. The front fenders were of a new design, with a crease along their center line. The cowl vent reverted to a forward-opening type. The Touring Sedan and Convertibles Sedan both had a built-in trunk. The Convertible Coupe had a rumble seat and a separate door for the spare tire at the extreme rear of the deck. Closed bodies now had all-steel construction and a turret top. New chassis features included the use of two mufflers in series. The battery was mounted under the left side of the front seat. There was a double universal joint in the steering shaft. A single-plate clutch was used. Cadillac's Ride Control system was discontinued, but a ride stabilizer was added at the front. The 1936 models were the first Cadillacs to feature hydraulic brakes.

1936 Cadillac, Series 60, V-8 convertible coupe

1936 Cadillac, Series 70, Fleetwood touring sedan

Series 36-70 Fleetwood 131-inch wheelbase

Model Number	Body Type & Seating	Factory Price	Shipping Weight	Production Total
36-7057	Coupe-2P	2,595	4,620	—
36-7067	Convertible Coupe-2P	2,695	4,690	—
36-7019	Touring Sedan-5P	2,445	4,670	—
36-7029	Convertible Sedan-5P	2,745	4,710	—

SERIES 75 — V-8

The Series 36-75 models mated the 346-cid V-8 with the 138-inch wheelbase chassis in a pleasing combination that became one of Cadillac's trademark product lines. An assortment of 10 Fleetwood bodies was offered. The Touring Sedans and the Convertible Sedan included a built-in trunk. Other features and characteristics were the same described above for Series 70 models. Commercial cars and the commercial chassis were also available on the V-8 chassis.

Fleetwood Series 36-75 138-inch wheelbase

Model Number	Body Type & Seating	Factory Price	Shipping Weight	Production Total
36-7509	Sedan-5P	2,645	4,805	—
36-7519	Touring Sedan-5P	2,645	4,805	—
36-7509F	Formal Sedan-5P	3,395	4,805	—
36-7529	Convertible Sedan-5P	3,395	5,040	—
36-7539	Town Sedan-5P	3,145	4,840	—
36-7503	Sedan-7P	2,795	4,885	—
36-7513	Imperial Sedan-7P	2,995	5,045	—
36-7523	Touring Sedan-7P	2,795	4,885	—
36-7533	Imperial Touring Sedan-7P	2,995	5,045	—
36-7543	Town Car-7P	4,445	5,115	—

Fleetwood Commercial Cars

Model Number	Body Type & Seating	Factory Price	Shipping Weight	Production Total
36-7503L	Commercial Sedan-7P	2,695	—	—
36-7513L	Commercial Imperial Sedan-7P	2,865	—	—
36-7523L	Commercial Touring Sedan-7P	2,695	—	—
36-7533L	Commercial Imperial Touring Sedan-7P	2,865	—	—

SERIES 80 — V12

The 36-80 line combined the four body styles built on the 131-inch wheelbase with a V-12 engine. This new V-12 was essentially a 1936 V-8 with four more cylinders. It had the same piston displacement as the 1935 V-12, but

performance was greatly improved. Identification with the hood closed was only possible by reading emblems. Dual exhaust pipes were no longer an indication of V-12 models. A crossover pipe from left to right manifold resulted in a single exhaust system with two mufflers mounted in series.

Fleetwood Series 36-80 131-inch wheelbase

Model Number	Body Type & Seating	Factory Price	Shipping Weight	Production Total
36-8057	Coupe-2P	3295	4690	—
36-8067	Convertible Coupe-2P	3395	4800	—
36-8019	Touring Sedan-5P	3145	4945	—
36-8029	Convertible Sedan-5P	3445	4990	—

SERIES 85 — V-12

The 36-85 line combined the 10 body styles built on the 138-inch wheelbase with the V-12 engine. Other features and characteristics were the same described above for Series 80 models. Commercial cars and the commercial chassis were also available on the 138-inch-wheelbase V-12 chassis.

Fleetwood Series 36-85 138-inch wheelbase

Model Number	Body Type & Seating	Factory Price	Shipping Weight	Production Total
36-8509	Sedan-5P	3,345	5,115	—
36-8509F	Formal Sedan-5P	4,095	5,115	—
36-8519	Touring Sedan-5P	3,345	5,115	—
36-8529	Convertible Sedan-5P	4,095	5,230	—
36-8539	Town Sedan-5P	3,845	5,065	—
36-8503	Sedan-7P	3,495	5,195	—
36-8513	Imperial Sedan-7P	3,695	5,230	—
36-8523	Touring Sedan-7P	3,495	5,195	—
36-8533	Imperial Touring Sedan-7P	3,695	5,230	—
36-8543	Town Car-7P	5,145	5,300	—

Fleetwood Commercial Cars

Model Number	Body Type & Seating	Factory Price	Shipping Weight	Production Total
36-8503L	Commercial Sedan-7P	2,695	—	—
36-8513L	Commercial Imperial Sedan-7P	2,865	—	—
36-8523L	Commercial Touring Sedan-7P	2,695	—	—
36-8533L	Commercial Imperial Touring Sedan-7P	2,865	—	—

SERIES 90 — V-16

The 1936 V-16 was a continuation of the 1935 cars. Built to order only, nearly half of the 52 units were seven-passenger limousines. As with V-8 and V-12 lines, Fleetwood bodies for the V-16 now used the all-steel turret top. All body styles had vee windshields. A minor mechanical change involved the use of the "Peak-load" generator.

Fleetwood Series 36-90, 154-inch wheelbase

Model Number	Body Type & Seating	Factory Price	Shipping Weight	Production Total
36-5825LB	Town Cabriolet-7P	6,390	—	—
36-5825C	Town Cabriolet-7P	—	—	—
36-5830FL	Imperial Cabriolet-5P	—	—	—
36-5830S	Sedan-5P	—	—	—
36-5833S	Town Sedan-5P	6,085	—	—
36-5835	Convertible Coupe-2P	—	—	—
36-5875	Imperial Sedan (Limousine)-7P	6,190	—	—
36-5875FL	Imperial Cabriolet-7P	6,210	—	—
36-5875S	Sedan-7P	6,190	—	—
36-5876	Coupe-2P	—	—	—
36-5880	Convertible Sedan with Div.-5P	6,100	—	—
36-5891	Limousine Brougham-7P	—	—	—
36-5899	Aerodynamic Coupe-5P	—	—	—

Note: Some listings show these as 58- styles.

ENGINE

SERIES 60 BASE V-8

L-head. Cast iron block on blocks cast enbloc with crankcase. Bore and stroke: 3-3/8 x 4-1/2. Displacement: 322 cid. Compression ratio: 6.25:1. Brake hp: 125 at 3400 rpm. Taxable hp: 36.45. Compression pressure: 155 at 1000 rpm. Main bearings: three. Valve lifters: Hydraulic. Crankcase capacity: 7 qt. Cooling system capacity. 30 qt. Carburetor: Stromberg EE-25 dual downdraft. Cadillac brought out a completly new V-8 in 1936. Produced in two displacements, it featured a block and crankcase cast in "enbloc" configuration. The water jacket ran the full length of the cylinder bore and a more rigid crankshaft had six counterweights. There were new connecting rods that had the large ends split at an angle. This allowed them to be removed through the top of the engine. Hydraulic valve silencers were used, along with new manifolding and a downdraft carburetor. Suction-type crankcase ventilation was used to take fumes out of the engine through the exhaust system. The lubrication was system was simplified by restricting piping only to the hydraulic lifters. A combination fuel pump and vacuum pump was mounted on the front engine cover. The starter was on the right-hand side of the engine, in front of the bell housing. The generator could be serviced by removing an access panel under the left front fender. The radiator was fitted with a pressure cap.

SERIES 70 BASE V-8; SERIES 75 BASE V-8

L-head. Cast iron block on blocks cast enbloc with crankcase. Bore and stroke: 3-1/2 x 4-1/2. Displacement: 346 cid. Compression ratio: 6.25:1. Brake hp: 135 at 3400 rpm. Taxable hp: 39.20. Compression pressure: 170 at

1936 Cadillac, Series 75, Fleetwood V-8 convertible sedan

1000 rpm. Main bearings: three. Valve lifters: Hydraulic. Crankcase capacity: 7 qt. Cooling system capacity. 29 qt.

Carburetor: Stromberg EE-25 dual downdraft. The 346-cid version of the new V-8 had most of the same features as the 322-cid version and was the version that ultimately survived for many years.

SERIES 80 V-12; SERIES 85 V-12

45 degree, overhead valve. Twelve. Cast iron block on aluminum crankcase. Bore and stroke: 3-1/8 x 4 inches. Displacement: 368 cid C.R.: 6.0:1 std, 5.65:1 optional Brake horsepower: 150 @ 3600 r.p.m. Main bearings: four. Valve lifters: mechanical with hydraulic silencer on rocker bushing. Carburetion: Dual Detroit Lubricator, Type R-13, L-13, Model 51.

SERIES 90 V-16

45 degree, overhead valve. Sixteen. Cast iron block on aluminum crankcase. Bore and stroke: 3 x 4 inches. Displacement: 452 cid C.R.: 6.0:1 std, 5.65:1 optional Brake horsepower: 185 @ 3800 r.p.m. SAE/Taxable horsepower: 57.5. Main bearings: five. Valve lifters: mechanical with hydraulic silencer on rocker bushing. Carburetion: Dual Detroit Lubricator, Type R-14, L 14, Model 51.

CHASSIS

[Series 60] Wheelbase: 121 inches. Overall length: 196 inches. Height: 65-3/4/67-1/2 inches. Front/Rear Tread: 58/59 inches. Tires: 7 x 16.

[Series 70] Wheelbase: 131 inches. Overall length: 206-1/4 inches. Height: 66, 69-1/2 inches. Front/Rear Tread: 60-3/16/60-1/2 inches. Tires: 7.50 x 16.

[Series 75] Wheelbase: 138 inches. Overall length: 213-1/2 inches. Height: 68-13/16 inches. Front/Rear Tread: 60-3/16/62-1/2 inches. Tires: 7.50 x 16. [Series 36-75 Commercial Chassis] Wheelbase: 156 inches.

[Series 80] Wheelbase: 131 inches. Overall length: 206-1/4 inches. Height: 66, 69-1/2 inches. Front/Rear Tread: 60-3/16/60-1/2 inches. Tires: 7.50 x 16. [

[Series 85] Wheelbase: 138 inches. Overall length: 213-1/2 inches. Front/Rear Tread: 60-3/16/62-1/2 inches. Tires: 7.50 x 16. [Series 85 Commericial Chassis] Wheelbase: 156 inches.

[Series 90] Wheelbase: 154 inches. Overall length: 238 inches. Front/Rear Tread: 59-3/8/62 inches. Tires: 7.50 x 17.

TECHNICAL

[Series 60] Selective, synchromesh transmission. Speeds: 3P/1R. Left-hand drive, center control, emergency brake at left under panel (right-hand drive optional). Single disc clutch. Shaft drive, Hotchkiss. Semi-floating rear axle, spiral bevel drive. Hydraulic brakes on four wheels. Disc wheels. Wheels: 16 inches.

[Series 70] Selective, synchromesh transmission. Speeds: 3F/1R. Left-hand drive, center control, emergency brake at left under panel (right-hand drive optional). Single disc clutch. Shaft drive, Hotchkiss. Semi-floating rear axle, spiral bevel drive. Overall ratio: 4.55:1 standard, 4.3:1 optional. Hydraulic brakes on four disc wheels. Wheels: 16 inches.

[Series 75] Selective, synchromesh transmission. Speeds: 3F/1R. Left-hand drive, center control, emergency brake at left under panel (right-hand drive optional). Single disc clutch. Shaft drive, Hotchkiss. Semi-floating rear axle, spiral bevel drive. Overall ratio: 4.6:1 standard, 4.3:1 optional Hydraulic brakes on four disc wheels. Wheels: 16 inches.

[Series 80; Series 85] Selective, synchromesh transmission. Speeds: 3F/1R. Left-hand drive, center control, emergency brake at left under panel (right-hand drive optional). Single disc clutch. Shaft drive, Hotchkiss. Semi-floating rear axle, spiral bevel drive. Overall ratio: 4.6:1 standard, 4.3:1 optional Hydraulic brakes on four wheels. Disc wheels. Wheels: 16 inches.

[Series 90] Selective, synchromesh transmission. Speeds: 3F/1R. Left-hand drive, center control, emergency brake at left under panel (right-hand drive optional). Twin disc clutch. Shaft drive, Hotchkiss. 3/4 floating rear axle, spiral bevel drive. Overall ratio: 4.64:1 std, 4.31:1 opt, 4.07:1 optional Mechanical brakes with vacuum assist on four wheels. Wire wheels. Wheels: 17 inches. Drop center.

OPTIONS

[All] Sidemount cover(s) ($20). Radio (master/standard $89.50/$54.50). Heater ($18.50). Seat covers. Flexible steering wheel ($16). Trim rings ($1.50 each). Wheel discs ($4 each).

HISTORICAL

The 1936 Cadillacs were introduced in October 1935. Model year sales and production included 6,712 of the new Series 60 V-8 models, 5,248 of the Series 70 and Series 75 cars with the larger V-8, 901 of the V-12 models and 52 of the Series 90 Cadillac V-16s. The general manager of Cadillac was again Nicholas Dreystadt. Starting in the 1936 model year, the new-car introductions were done in

the fall of the previous model year, rather than in January 1936. From this point on, annual model-year changes and fall new-model introductions would become regular practices in the American auto industry. A special showing of V-16 Cadillacs was displayed in the General Motors Building in Detroit in April 1936. The cars exhibited in the lobby included an Aerodynamic Coupe, a seven-passenger Sedan, a Convertible Sedan and a Limousine. The four cars represented 8 percent of the total output of Cadillac V-16s.

1936 Cadillac, Series 90, Fleetwood V-16 convertible sedan

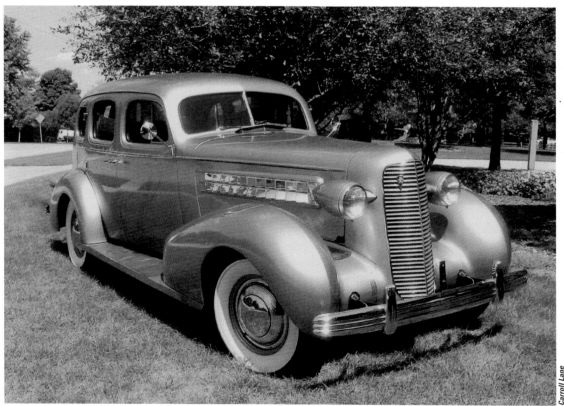

Carroll Lane

1936 Cadillac, Series 60, V-8 sedan

1937

OVERVIEW

For 1937, Cadillac introduced a new egg crate grille that went on to become a company trademark for some time. The 1937 grille had very narrow openings forming a relatively tight mesh. Decorating the "catwalks" on either side of the radiator, near the bottom, were three short horizontal chrome strips. The smaller V-8 models in the 60 and 65 Series had a narrow-mesh vent along the upper edge of the hood side panels. Larger 70 and 75 Series V-8s had four horizontal bars mounted low and towards the rear of the hood side panels. The V-12 models were like the larger V-8s. The V-16 were like the 1934-1936 V-16. The only V-8 used this year was the 346-cid engine.

I.D. DATA

[Series 60] Engine numbers were on the crankcase, just behind the left cylinder group, parallel to the dash. Starting: 6030001. Ending: 6037003.

[Series 65] Engine numbers were on the crankcase, just behind the left cylinder group, parallel to the dash. Starting: 703001. Ending: 7032401.

Above: **1937 Cadillac, Series 75, Fleetwood V-8 sedan**

[Series 70; Series 75] Engine numbers were on the crankcase, just behind the left cylinder group, parallel to the dash. Starting: 3130001. Ending: 3134232.

[Series 85] Engine numbers were on the upper surface of the generator drive chain housing. Starting: 4130001. Ending: 4130478.

[Series 90] Engine numbers were on the upper surface of the generator drive chain housing. Starting: 5130301. Ending: 5130350.

SERIES 60 — V-8

A new Fisher-built body style for the Series 60 line was the Convertible Sedan. Changes included an eggcrate grille, new hood louvers, higher fenders with a lengthwise crease along the top, three horizontal bars on each side of the grille, bumpers carrying the Cadillac emblem, swinging rear quarter windows and true all-steel Fisher Body construction. Series 60 Cadillacs shared many features with the LaSalle, but used the 346-cid V-8. A Series 60 commercial chassis with a 160-3/8-inch wheelbase was offered.

Series 37-60 Fisher 124-inch wheelbase

Model Number	Body Type & Seating	Factory Price	Shipping Weight	Production Total
37-6019	Touring Sedan-5P	1,545	3,845	—
37-6049	Convertible Sedan-5P	1,885	3,885	—
37-6067	Convertible Coupe-2P	1,575	3,745	—
37-6027	Sport Coupe-2P	1,445	3,710	—

SERIES 65 — V-8

The all-new 65 Series offered only one body style. It was a five-passenger touring Fisher Touring Sedan built on the 131-inch wheelbase. This provided Cadillac buyers with a longer, heavier Fisher-bodied car than the Series 60 model at a price below that of a Fleetwood-bodied car.

Series 37-65 Fisher 131-inch wheelbase

Model Number	Body Type & Seating	Factory Price	Shipping Weight	Production Total
37-6519	Touring Sedan-5P	1,945	4,835	—

SERIES 70 — V-8

The Series 70 models again represented the Cadillac best suited for the mass market. These Fleetwood-bodied models were the same as their 1936 counterparts, with only a couple of exceptions. A drip molding now ran from the bottom of the front pillar up and over the doors and rear quarter window. New fenders and bumpers were seen. The headlights were now rigidly attached and could be adjusted by moving the reflectors. The wheel discs incorporated a hubcap. Most models featured a built-in trunk. A die-cast eggcrate grille was used, but the hood louver treatment differed from that used on Fisher-bodied cars. Chrome die-cast strips were used at the rear of the hood side panels. Engine changes included a lighter flywheel, a generator relocated in the "V" of the engine, an oil filter, a new carburetor (with fully-automatic electric choke), an oil-bath air cleaner and a relocated distributor. A new transmission design featured pin-type synchronizers. The shifter rails were relocated to the side of case and the cover was on the bottom of the case extension, integral with the transmission mainshaft.

Series 37-70 Fleetwood 131-inch wheelbase

Model Number	Body Type & Seating	Factory Price	Shipping Weight	Production Total
37-7019	Touring Sedan-5P	2,445	4,420	—
37-7029	Convertible Sedan-5P	2,795	4,460	—
37-7057	Sport Coupe-2P	2,645	4,285	—
37-7067	Convertible Coupe-2P	2,745	4,325	—

SERIES 75 — V-8

The 75 Series Cadillacs were similar to the 70 Series models with a seven-inch longer wheelbase. A seven-passenger Fisher-bodied Special Touring Sedan was offered. It came with or without a division window. These models had the eggcrate hood louvers typical of all Fisher-bodied 1937 Cadillacs. Other models had Fleetwood styling motifs. The Business Car line included eight-passenger versions of these Special Sedans, plus eight-passenger versions of four Fleetwood body styles. The eighth passenger was

1937 Cadillac, Series 70, convertible sedan

Lowell Carlson

seated with two others on the auxiliary seats. A 156-inch wheelbase Commercial Chassis was offered.

Model Number	Body Type & Seating	Factory Price	Shipping Weight	Production Total
37-7523S	Special Touring Sedan-7P	2,445	4,825	—
37-7533S	Special Imperial Touring Sedan-7P	2,645	4,985	—

Series 37-75 Fleetwood 138-inch wheelbase

Model Number	Body Type & Seating	Factory Price	Shipping Weight	Production Total
37-7503	Sedan-7P	—	—	—
37-7509-F	Formal Sedan-5P	3,495	4,745	—
37-7513	Imperial Sedan-7P	—	—	—
37-7519	Touring Sedan-5P	2,645	4,745	—
37-7523	Touring Sedan-7P	2,795	4,825	—
37-7529	Convertible Sedan-5P	3,445	4,980	—
37-7533	Imperial Touring Sedan-7P	2,995	4,985	—
37-7539	Town Sedan-5P	3,145	4,780	—
37-7543	Town Car-7P	4,545	5,055	—
37-7589-A	Coupe-5P	—	—	—
37-7592	Limousine Brougham-7P	—	—	—

Series 37-75 Fisher 138-inch wheelbase Business Cars

Model Number	Body Type & Seating	Factory Price	Shipping Weight	Production Total
37-7523-SL	Special Business Touring Sedan-8P	2,575	4,825	—
37-7533-SL	Special Business Imperial Touring Sedan-8P	2,775	4,985	—

Series 37-75 Fleetwood 138-inch wheelbase Business Cars

Model Number	Body Type & Seating	Factory Price	Shipping Weight	Production Total
37-7503-L	Business Sedan-8P	—	—	—
37-7513-L	Business Imperial Sedan-8P	—	—	—
37-7523-L	Business Touring Sedan-8P	—	—	—
37-7533-L	Business Imperial Sedan-8P	—	—	—

SERIES 85 — V-12

The Cadillac V-12 was essentially a V-8 with a bigger engine. This was the V-12's final model year. The Series 80 with 131-inch wheelbase was dropped. An oil bath air cleaner and pressure radiator cap were new.

Series 37-85 Fleetwood 138-inch wheelbase

Model Number	Body Type & Seating	Factory Price	Shipping Weight	Production Totals
37-8509F	Formal Sedan-5P	4,195	5,050	—
37-8513	Imperial Sedan-7P	3,695	5,165	—
37-8519	Touring Sedan-5P	3,345	5,050	—
37-8523	Touring Sedan-7P	3,495	5,130	—

Model Number	Body Type & Seating	Factory Price	Shipping Weight	Production Totals
37-8529	Convertible Sedan-5P	4,145	5,165	—
37 8533	Imperial Touring Sedan-7P	3,695	5,165	—
37-8539	Town Sedan-5P	3,845	5,000	—
37-8543	Town Car-7P	5,245	5,230	—
37-8511	Touring Coupe-5P	—	—	—
37-8518	Sedan-5P	—	—	—
37-8589A	Coupe-5P	—	—	—
37-8591	Limousine Brougham-7P	—	—	—

Series 37-85 Fisher 138-inch wheelbase Business Cars

Model Number	Body Type & Seating	Factory Price	Shipping Weight	Production Totals
37-8523SL	Special Business Touring Sedan-8P	2,575	4,825	—
37 8533SL	Special Business Imperial Touring Sedan-8P	2,785	4,985	—

Series 37-85 Fleetwood 138-inch wheelbase Business Cars

Model Number	Body Type & Seating	Factory Price	Shipping Weight	Production Totals
37-8503L	Business Sedan-8P	—	—	—
37-8513L	Business Imperial Sedan-8P	—	—	—
37-8523L	Business Touring Sedan-8P	—	—	—
37-8533L	Business Imperial Touring Sedan-8P	—	—	—

SERIES 37-90 — V-16

The 1937 Cadillac V-16 remained essentially the same as the 1934-1936 cars. This was the final model year for the overhead-valve V-16. For the first time, hydraulic brakes (with a vacuum booster on the pedal) were used on these cars. A stabilizer bar was added to the front suspension. A Handy oil filter replaced the Cuno self-cleaning unit. A pressure cap was used on the radiator.

Series 37-90 Fleetwood 154-inch wheelbase

Model Number	Body Type & Seating	Factory Price	Shipping Weight	Production Total
37-5725LB	Imperial Twn Cabriolet-7P	—	—	—
37-5730S	Sedan-5P	—	—	—
37-5730FL	Imperial Cab-5P	—	—	—
37-5733S	Town Sedan-5P	7,350	6,085	—
37 5735	Convertible Coupe-2P	—	—	—
37-5775	Imperial Sedan-7P	7,550	6,190	—
37-5775S	Sedan-7P	7,350	6,190	—
37 5775SF	Sedan-7P	—	—	—
37-5775FL	Imperial Cab-7P	7,950	6,210	—
37-5775H4	Lmousine-7P	—	—	—
37-5776	Coupe-2P	—	—	—
37-5780	Convertible Sedan-5P	7,950	6,100	—
37-5785	Collapsible Coupe-5P	—	—	—
37 5791	Limousine Brougham-7P	—	—	—
37-5799	Aerodynamic Coupe-5P	7,500	—	—

ENGINE

BASE V-8

L-head. Cast iron block on blocks cast enbloc with crankcase. Bore and stroke: 3-1/2 x 4-1/2 inches. Displacement: 346 cid. Compression ratio: 6.25:1. Brake hp: 135 at 3400 rpm. Taxable hp: 39.20. Compression pressure: 155 at 1000 rpm. Main bearings: three. Valve lifters: Hydraulic. Crankcase capacity: 7 qt. Cooling sysytem capacity: 25 qt. Carburetor: Stromberg AA-25 dual downdraft.

OPTIONAL "LOW-COMPRESSION" V-8

L-head. Cast iron block on blocks cast enbloc with crankcase. Bore and stroke: 3-1/2 x 4-1/2 inches. Displacement: 346 cid. Compression ratio: 5.75:1. Brake hp: 135 at 3400 rpm. Taxable hp: 39.20. Main bearings: three. Valve lifters: Hydraulic. Crankcase capacity: 7 qt. Cooling system capacity: 25 qt. Carburetor: Stromberg AA-25 dual downdraft.

V-12

45 degree, overhead valve. Twelve. Cast iron block on aluminum crankcase. Bore and stroke: 3-1/8 x 4 inches. Displacement: 368 cid C.R.: 6.0:1 standard, 5.65:1 optional Brake horsepower: 150 @ 3600 r.p.m. SAE/Taxable horsepower: 46.9. Main bearings: four. Valve lifters: mechanical with hydraulic silencer on rocker bushing. Carburetion: Dual Detroit Lubricator, Type R-13, L-13, Model 51.

V-16

45 degree, overhead valve. Sixteen. Cast iron block on aluminum crankcase. Bore and stroke: 3 x 4 inches. Displacement: 452 cid C.R.: 6.0:1 standard, 5.65:1 optional Brake horsepower: 185 @ 3800 r.pm. SAE/Taxable horsepower: 57.5. Main bearings: five. Valve lifters: mechanical with hydraulic silencer on rocker bushing. Carburetion: Dual Detroit Lubricator, Type R-14, L-14, Model 51.

CHASSIS

[Series 60] Wheelbase: 124 inches. Overall length: 201-1/4 inches Front/Rear Tread: 58/59 inches. Tires: 7.50 x 16.

[Series 60 Commercial Chassis] Wheelbase: 160-3/8 inches. Overall length: 237-7/8 inches. Tires: 7 x 16.

[Series 65] Wheelbase: 131 inches. Overall length: 208-3/16 inches. Front/Rear Tread: 60-3/16/60-1/2 inches Tires: 7.50 x 16.

[Series 70] Wheelbase: 131 inches. Overall length: 208-3/16 inches. Front/Rear Tread: 60-3/16/60-1/2 inches. Tires: 7.50 x 16.

1937 Cadillac, Series 60, coupe

[Series 75] Wheelbase: 138 inches. Overall length: 215-7/8 inches. Front/Rear Tread: 60-3/16/62-1/2 inches. Tires: 7.50 x 16.

[Series 75 Commercial Chassis] Wheelbase: 156 inches. Overall length: 231-1/4 inches. Tires: 7.50 x 16.

[Series 85] Wheelbase: 138 inches. Overall length: 215-7/8 inches. Front/Rear Tread: 60-3/16/61-1/2 inches. Tires: 7.50 x 16.

[Series 90] Wheelbase: 154 inches. Overall length: 238 inches. Front/Rear Tread: 59-3/8/62 inches. Tires: 7.50 x 17.

TECHNICAL

[Series 60] Selective, synchromesh transmission. Speeds: 3F/1R. Left-hand drive, center control, emergency brake at left under panel (right-hand drive optional). Single disc clutch. Shaft drive, Hotchkiss. Hypoid rear axle. Overall ratio: 3.69:1. Hydraulic brakes on four wheels. Disc wheels. Wheels: 16 inches.

[Series 70; Series 75] Selective, synchromesh transmission. Speeds: 3F/1R. Left-hand drive, center control, emergency brake at left under panel (right-hand drive optional). Single disc clutch. Shaft drive, Hotchkiss. Semi-floating rear axle, spiral bevel drive. Overall ratio: 4.3:1. Hydraulic brakes on four wheels. Disc wheels. Wheels: 16 inches.

[Series 85] Selective, synchromesh transmission. Speeds: 3F/1R. Left-hand drive, center control, emergency brake at left under panel (right-hand drive optional). Single disc clutch. Shaft drive, Hotchkiss. Semi-floating rear axle, spiral bevel drive. Overall ratio: 4.6:1. Hydraulic brakes on four wheels. Disc wheels. Wheels: 16 inches.

[Series 90] Selective, synchromesh transmission. Speeds: 3F/1R. Left-hand drive, center control, emergency brake at left under panel (right-hand drive optional). Twin disc clutch. Shaft drive, Hotchkiss. 3/4 floating rear axle, spiral bevel drive. Overall ratio: 4.64:1 standard, 4.31:1 optional, 4.07:1. Hydraulic brakes with vacuum booster on four wheels. Wire wheels with disc cover. Wheels: 17 inches. Drop center.

OPTIONS

[All] Sidemount cover(s) ($15-$17.50). Radio (master/standard) ($79.50/$59.50). Heater ($19.50-$60). Seat covers ($7.50 per seat). Wheel disc ($4 each). Trim rings ($1.50 each). Flexible steering wheel ($15).

HISTORICAL

The 1937 Cadillacs were introduced in November 1936. Model year sales and production included 7,003 of the new Series 60 V-8 models, 4,232 of the Series 70 and Series 75 cars, 478 of the V-12 models and 50 of the Series 90 Cadillac V-16s. The general manager of Cadillac was again Nicholas Dreystadt. Model-year sales of 46,152 cars set a record for Cadillac.

1937 Willy Hartman-bodied Cadillac

1938

OVERVIEW

For 1938, the Series 70 and Fisher-bodied Series 75 Specials were dropped, but a convertible sedan was added to the Series 65 line. The styling bonanza for 1938 was the sensational new Sixty Special Sedan.

I.D. DATA

[All V-8s] Serial numbers were on the left-hand frame side bar, at the rear of the left-hand front motor support. Starting: same as engine number. Ending: Same as engine number. Engine numbers were on crankcase, just behind left cylinder block. Starting: [Series 38-60] 8270001, [Series 38-60S] 6270001, [Series 38-65] 7270001, [Series 38-75] 3270001. Ending: [Series 38-60] 8272052, [Series 38-60S] 6273704, [Series 38-65] 7271476, [Series 38-75] 3271911.

[V-16] Serial numbers were on frame side bar, just ahead of the steering gear. Starting: same as engine number. Ending: same as engine number. Engine numbers were on upper rear left-hand corner of the left-hand cylinder block, parallel with the cylinder head. Starting: 5270001. Ending: 5270315.

Above: **1938 Cadillac, Series 90, Fleetwood V-16 convertible coupe**

Angelo Van Bogart, Jim Kiser, owner

SERIES 60 — V-8

The Series 60 Cadillac was restyled. It now had a squared-off grille made up of horizontal bars extending around the front and sides of the nose. Three sets of four chrome bars decorated the side panel louvers. A front-opening "alligator" style hood was used. The headlights were fixed to the sheet metal between the fenders and the grille.

Fisher Series 38-60, 124-inch wheelbase

Model Number	Body Type & Seating	Factory Price	Shipping Weight	Production Total
38-6127	Coupe-2P	1,695	3,855	—
38-6167	ConvertibleCoupe-2P	1,810	3,845	—
38-6149	ConvertibleSedan-5P	2,215	3,980	—
38-6119	Sedan-5P	1,775	3,940	—

SERIES 60 "SIXTY SPECIAL" — V-8

The Sixty Special had much the same nose as the Series 60 model, with one less bar in the grille assembly. The body itself was entirely new and unique. It was mounted on a double-drop frame and sat three inches lower than the conventional Series 60 Cadillac's body. The 60 Special had no runningboards. The floor was at at normal runningboard height. Large side windows trimmed with chrome frames were flush with the sides of the body. The convertible-shaped top featured a thin roof section and a notched back.

Fisher Series 38-60S, 127-inch wheelbase

Model Number	Body Type & Seating	Factory Price	Shipping Weight	Production Total
38-6019S	Special Sedan-5P	2,085	4,170	—

SERIES 65—V-8

Series 65 (Custom V-8) and Series 75 (Fleetwood) models shared a new front end featuring a massive vertical cellular grille, three sets of horizontal bars on the hood sides, an alligator hood and headlights positioned on the filler piece between the fenders and the hood. Optional sidemount covers were hinged to the fenders. The quarter windows were of sliding, rather than hinged, construction. The rear of the body had rounder corners and more smoothly blended lines. On all Series 65 models, the trunk appeared to be more of an integral part of the body. The bodies featured all-steel construction, except for having wooden main sills.

Fisher Series 38-65, 132-inch wheelbase

Model Number	Body Type & Seating	Factory Price	Shipping Weight	Production Total
38-6519	Sedan-5P	2,285	4,540	—
38-6519-F	Imperial Sedan-5P	2,360	4,580	—
38-6549	ConvertibleSedan-5P	2,600	4,580	—

SERIES 75—V-8

New Series 75 chassis details included a column-mounted gear shift lever, the repositioning of the horns just behind the grille, placing the battery under the right-hand side of the hood and a transverse muffler just behind the fuel tank. The wheels were now made by a different manufacturer and were not interchangeable with the 1937 wheels. Also new was a "Synchro-Flex" flywheel, the use of a hypoid rear axle on all series and deletion of the oil filter. The compression ratio of the V-8 engine used in Series 75 Cadillacs was raised to 6.70:1, necessitating the use of high-octane gasoline.

Fleetwood Series 38-75, 141-inch wheelbase Business Cars

Model Number	Body Type & Seating	Factory Price	Shipping Weight	Production Total
38-7523-L	Business Touring Sedan-7P	3,105	4,945	—
38-7533-L	Business Touring Imperial-7P	3,255	5,105	—

Fleetwood Series 38-75 141-inch wheelbase

Model Number	Body Type & Seating	Factory Price	Shipping Weight	Production Total
38-7557	Coupe-2P	3,275	4,675	—
38-7557-B	Coupe-5P	3,380	4,775	—
38-7567	ConvertibleCoupe-2P	3,380	4,665	—
38-7519	Sedan-5P	3,075	4,865	—
38-7519-F	Imperial Sedan-5P	3,155	4,925	—
38-7559	Formal Sedan-5P	3,990	4,865	—
38-7539	Town Sedan-5P	3,635	4,900	—
38-7529	ConvertibleSedan-5P	3,940	5,110	—
38-7523	Sedan-7P	3,205	4,945	—
38-7533	Imperial Sedan-7P	3,360	5,105	—
38-7533-F	Formal Sedan-7P	3,990	5,105	—
38-7553	Town Car-7P	5,115	5,175	—

SERIES 90—V-16

The 1938 Series 90 Cadillac essentially became a Series 75 model with a V-16 engine. Even though the wheelbase was 13 inches shorter than that previously used with the

1938 Cadillac, Series 90, Fleetwood V-16 convertible sedan

V-16, the bodies were equal or larger in all dimensions. This was accomplished by fitting the nearly flat engine low in the frame and partially behind the line of the firewall. The V-16 models were distinguished from their counterpart V-8s by an eggcrate grille with a coarser pitch, the use of fender lamps, a hood with streamlined louvers on the side panels and all fender skirts. The new V-16 engine was of L-head, short-stroke (square) design. The cylinders were cast enbloc, with a 135-degree "vee." With each block in running balance, the engine was basically a twin eight. Dual accessories included carburetors, oil bath air cleaners, manifolds, distributors, coils, fuel pumps and water pumps. The fuel pumps were interconnected so that either one could supply both carburetors if needed. Only the left-hand distributor contained breaker arms. The two breaker arms were electrically independent, but both operated by a single eight-lobe cam. The right-hand unit acted only to distribute the high-tension voltage to the spark plugs in the right bank. A cross pipe connected both exhaust manifolds and fed into a single down-pipe at the left. The generator was placed low in the vee and was driven by an internal rubber ring in the fan hub acting on a driven wheel on the generator shaft. This arrangement allowed for fan speeds less than engine speed and generator speeds nearly twice engine speed—it lasted only one year.

Fleetwood Series 38-90 141-inch wheelbase

Model Number	Body Type & Seating	Factory Price	Shipping Weight	Production Total
38-9057	Coupe-2P	5,335	4,915	—
38-9057-B	Coupe-5P	5,440	5,015	—
38-9067	ConvertibleCoupe-2P	5,440	4,905	—
38-9019	Sedan-5P	5,135	5,105	—
38-9019 F	Imperial Sedan-5P	5,215	5,165	—
38 9059	Formal Sedan-5P	6,050	5,105	—
38-9039	Town Sedan-5P	5,695	5,140	—
38-9029	ConvertibleSedan-5P	6,000	5,350	—
38-9023	Sedan-7P	5,265	5185	—
38-9033	Imperial Sedan-7P	5,420	5,345	—
38-9033-F	Formal Sedan-7P	6,050	5,345	—
38-9053	Town Car-7P	7,170	5,415	—

ENGINE

SERIES 60 BASE V-8, SERIES 60 SPECIAL BASE V-8, SERIES 65 BASE V-8

L-head. Cast iron block on blocks cast enbloc with crankcase. Bore and stroke: 3-1/2 x 4-1/2. Displacement: 346 cid. Compression ratio: 6.25:1. Brake hp: 135 at 3400 rpm. Taxable hp: 39.20. Compression pressure: 155 at 1000. Main bearings: three. Valve lifters: Hydraulic. Crankcase capacity: 7 qt. Cooling system capacity: (Series 60) 24 qt.; (Series 65) 25 qt. Carburetor: Stromberg AAV-25 dual downdraft.

SERIES 75 BASE V-8

L-head. Cast iron block on blocks cast enbloc with crankcase. Bore and stroke: 3-1/2 x 4-1/2. Displacement: 346 cid. Compression ratio: 6.70:1. Brake hp: 140 at 3400 rpm. Taxable hp: 39.20. Compression pressure: 170 at 1000 rpm. Main bearings: three. Valve lifters: Hydraulic. Crankcase capacity: 7 qt. Cooling system capacity: 25 qt. Carburetor: Stromberg AAV-25 dual downdraft.

SERIES 90 BASE V-16:

135 degree vee L-Head. Sixteen. Cast iron block. Bore and stroke: 3-1/4 x 3-1/4 inches. Displacement: 431 cid C.R.: 7:1. Brake horsepower: 185 @ 3600 r.p.m. SAE/Taxable horsepower: 67.6. Main bearings: nine. Valve lifters: hydraulic. Carburetion: Carter WDO 407s(L)-408s(R).

CHASSIS

[Series 60] Wheelbase: 124 inches. Overall length: 207-5/8 inches. Front/Rear Tread: 58/61 inches. Tires: 7 x 16.

[Series 60S] Wheelbase: 127 inches. Overall length: 207-5/8 inches. Front/Rear Tread: 58/61 inches. Tires: 7 x 16.

[Series 65] Wheelbase: 132 inches. Overall length: 211-3/8 inches. Front/Rear Tread: 60-1/2/62-3/8 inches. Tires: 7 x 16.

1938 Cadillac, Series 90, Fleetwood V-16 convertible coupe

1938 Cadillac, Series 90, Fleetwood V-16 seven-passenger sedan

[Series 75] Wheelbase: 141 inches. Overall length: 220-5/8 inches. Front/Rear Tread: 60-1/2/62- 1/2 inches. Tires: 7.50 x 16.

[Series 60 Commercial Chassis] Wheelbase: 160 inches. [Series 38-65 Commercial Chassis] Wheelbase: 160 inches.

[Series 75 Commercial Chassis] Wheelbase: 161 inches.

[Series 90] Wheelbase: 141 inches. Overall length: 200-5/8 inches. Front/Rear Tread: 60-1/2/62-1/2 inches. Tires: 7.50 x 16.

TECHNICAL

[Series 60, Series 60S, Series 65] Selective synchromesh manual transmission. Speeds: 3F/1R. Left-hand drive, gearshift on column, handbrake at left (right-hand drive optional). Single disc clutch. Shaft drive, Hotchkiss. Semi-floating rear axle. Hypoid gears. Overall ratio: 3.92:1. Hydraulic brakes on four wheels. Disc wheels. Wheels: 16 inch.

[Series 75] Selective synchromesh manual transmission. Speeds: 3F/1R. Left-hand drive, gearshift on column, handbrake at left (right-hand drive optional). Single disc clutch. Shaft drive, Hotchkiss. Semi-floating rear axle. Hypoid gears. Overall ratio: 4.58:1. Hydraulic brakes on four wheels. Disc wheels. Wheels: 16 inch.

[Series 90] Selective synchromesh manual transmission. Speeds: 3F/1R. Left-hand drive, gearshift on column, handbrake at left. Single disc clutch. Shaft drive, Hotchkiss. Semi-floating rear axle. Hypoid gears. Overall ratio: 4.31:1. Hydraulic brakes on four wheels. Disc wheels. Wheels: 16 inch.

OPTIONS

Radio ($95). Radio (master/standard) ($79.50/$65). Heater ($26.50-$42.50). Seat covers ($7.50 per seat). Spotlight ($18.50). Automatic battery filler ($7.50). Flexible steering wheel ($15). Fog lights ($17.50 pair). Wheel discs for V-8s ($4 each). Trim rings for V-8s ($1.50 each).

HISTORICAL

Introduced October 1937. Model-year sales and production included 2,052 Series 60 models, 3,704 Sixty Specials, 1,476 Series 65 models, 1,911 Series 75 models and just 315 Cadillac V-16s. The general manager of Cadillac was again Nicholas Dreystadt. Though Cadillac had not suffered as horrendously as many other automakers during the depths of the Depression, the company was nonetheless hurting. Dreystadt's formula for easing the pain was to streamline operations and cut costs. In 1938, this resulted in the discontinuation of the overhead-vale V-12 and V-16 engines, which were replaced by a new flathead V-16 that generated the same 185 hp as its predecessor, but was a less troublesome engine and more economical to build. The year 1938 also saw Cadillac go to a steering-column-mounted gearshift lever a year before other GM cars and introduce a new Sixty Special V-8 model with a notched back, no running boards and a spunky new look courtesy of a young designer from Harley Earl's staff named Bill Mitchell.

1938 Cadillac, Series 60S, sedan

1938 Cadillac, Series 75, convertible sedan

1939

OVERVIEW

All V-8-powered 1939 Cadillacs had new tri-corner grilles in the fender "catwalks" flanking the regular grille. These cars were completely new in appearance with a V-shaped main grille, larger glass areas, automatic-adjusting rear springs and no running boards. The Cadillac V-8 chassis had a four-inch shorter wheelbase, but interior room was actually increased. A moon-roof-like "Sunshine Top" was available at extra cost. The V-16s were much like the 1938 V-16 models, although the rear license plate holder was not incorporated into the trunk handle. Although basic body shells remain unchanged from 1938, the instrument panel was restyled. There were small changes in the design of the running boards, bumper edges and taillights. Some V-16s shared the same basic body with different seating and roof trim treatments.

I.D. DATA

[All V-8s] Serial numbers were located on the left frame side bar, opposite the steering gear. Starting: same as engine number. Ending: same as engine number. Engine numbers were on the crankcase, just behind the left cylinder block, parallel to the dash. Starting: [Series 39-60S] 6290001,

[Series 39-61] 8290001, [Series 39-75] 3290001. Ending: [Series 39-60S] 6295513, [Series 39-61] 8295913, [Series 39-75] 3292069.

[V-16] Serial numbers were located on the left frame side bar, opposite the steering gear. Starting: same as engine number. Ending: same as engine number. Engine numbers were on the left rear corner on the flat top of the crankcase, parallel to the dash. Starting: 5290001. Ending: 5290138.

SERIES 60 "SIXTY SPECIAL" — V-8

All Cadillac V-8s, including the Sixty Special Sedan, had the same styling motifs, but the detail dimensions differed for each car-line. A new pointed center grille and functional side grilles were made of die-cast metal and had fine-pitch bars. A single die-cast louver was positioned to the rear of each hood side panel. The headlights were once again attached to the radiator casing. Series 60 chassis changes included a tube-and-fin radiator core, sea shell horns under the hood, 10-mm spark plugs and slotted disc wheels. The Cadillac Sixty Special, now bodied by Fleetwood, was offered with optional Sunshine Turret Top or with a center division.

Above: **1939 Cadillac, Series 90, Fleetwood V-16 limousine**

Fleetwood Special Sedan Series 39-60S, 127-inch wheelbase

Model Number	Body Type & Seating	Factory Price	Shipping Weight	Production Total
39-6019S	Touring Sedan-5P	2,195	4,110	—
39 6019S-A	Sunshine Top Touring Sedan-5P	2,245	—	—
39-6019S-F	Center Division Touring Sedan-5P	—	—	—

SERIES 61 — V-8

For 1939, Cadillac's Series 61 line to replace the old Series 60 and Series 65. Like all Cadillac V-8s, it had the new styling motifs. The Sunshine Turret Top and center division options were also available for the Series 61 Sedan. All models were available with or without runningboards. The 61s had concealed door hinges, except for the lower front door hinge, Chrome reveals were seen on all windows. Chassis changes included the tube-and-fin type radiator core, sea shell horns under the hood, 10mm spark plugs, cross-link steering and slotted disc wheels.

Fisher Series 39-61, 126-inch wheelbase

Model Number	Body Type & Seating	Factory Price	Shipping Weight	Production Total
39-6127	Coupe-2P	1,695	3,685	—
39-6167	Convertible Coupe-2P	1,855	3,765	—
39-6129	Convertible Sedan-5P	2,265	3,810	—
39-6119	Touring Sedan-5P	1,765	3,770	—
39-6119-A	Sunshine Top Touring Sedan-5P	1,805	—	—
39-6119-F	Division Window Touring Sedan-5P	—	—	—

SERIES 75 — V-8

The Series 75 Cadillacs also had the new styling motifs, but on a larger chassis. The Series 75 cars also had slightly more horsepower, larger tires and a lower (numerically higher) final gear ratio.

Fleetwood Series 39-75, 141-inch wheelbase Business Cars

Model Number	Body Type & Seating	Factory Price	Shipping Weight	Production Total
39-7523-L	Business Touring Sedan-8P	3,215	4,865	—
39 7533-L	Business Touring Imperial-8P	3,370	5,025	—

Fleetwood Series 39-75, 141-inch wheelbase

Model Number	Body Type & Seating	Factory Price	Shipping Weight	Production Total
39-7557	Coupe-2P	3,395	4,595	—
39 7557-B	Coupe-5P	3,495	4,695	—
39 7567	ConvertibleCoupe-2P	3,495	4,675	—
39-7519	Sedan-5P	3,100	4,785	—
39-7519-F	Imperial Sedan-5P	3,265	4,845	—
39-7559	Formal Sedan-5P	4,115	4,785	—
39-7539	Town Sedan-5P	3,750	4,820	—
39 7529	ConvertibleSedan-5P	4,065	5,030	—
39-7523	Sedan-7P	3,325	4,865	—
39 7533	Imperial Sedan-7P	3,475	5,025	—
39-7533-F	Formal Sedan-7P	4,115	5,025	—
39-7553	Town Car-7P	5,245	5,095	—

SERIES 90 — V-16

The Cadillac V-16 was the same as in 1938, except for a few detail changes. Chrome strips were used along the runningboard edges. The spears on the hood and fender skirts were fully chromed. There was a new instrument panel and minor differences could be detected in the designs of the bumpers and taillights. The generator was relocated high in the "vee" between the cylinders and it was now belt driven.

Fleetwood Series 39-90, 141-inch wheelbase

Model Number	Body Type & Seating	Factory Price	Shipping Weight	Production Total
39-9057	Coupe-2P	5,440	4,915	—
39-9057-B	Coupe-5P	5,545	5,015	—
39-9067	ConvertibleCoupe-2P	5,545	4,995	—
39-9019	Sedan-5P	5,240	5,105	—
39-9019-F	Imperial Sedan-5P	5,315	5,165	—
39-9059	Formal Sedan-5P	6,165	5,105	—
39-9039	Town Sedan-5P	5,800	5,140	—
39-9029	Convertible Sedan-5P	6,110	5,350	—
39-9023	Sedan-7P	5,375	5,185	—
39-9033	Imperial Sedan-7P	5,525	5,345	—
39-9033-F	Formal Sedan-7P	6,165	5,345	—
39-9053	Town Car-7P	7,295	5,415	—

ENGINE

SERIES 60S BASE V-8, SERIES 61 BASE V-8

L-head. Cast iron block on blocks cast enbloc with crankcase. Bore and stroke: 3-1/2 x 4-1/2. Displacement: 346 cid. Compression ratio: 6.25:1. Brake hp: 135 at 3400 rpm. Taxable hp: 39.20. Torque: 250 at 1700 rpm. Main bearings: three. Valve lifters: Hydraulic. Crankcase capacity: 7 qt. Cooling system capacity: 24.5 qt. Carburetor: Stromberg AAV-26 dual downdraft.

SERIES 60S BASE V-8

L-head. Cast iron block on blocks cast enbloc with crankcase. Bore and stroke: 3-1/2 x 4-1/2. Displacement: 346 cid. Compression ratio: 6.70:1. Brake hp: 140 at 3400 rpm. Taxable hp: 39.20. Main bearings: three. Valve lifters: Hydraulic. Crankcase capacity: 7 qt. Cooling system capacity: 24.5 qt. Carburetor: Stromberg AAV-26 dual downdraft.

SERIES 90 BASE V-16

135 degree vee L-head. Sixteen. Cast iron block. Bore and stroke: 3-1/4 x 3-1/4 inches. Displacement: 431 cid. Compression rato: 6.75:1. Brake horsepower: 185 at 3600 rpm. Taxable horsepower: 67.6. Main bearings: nine.

1939 Cadillac, Series 75, Fleetwood convertible

Valve lifters: hydraulic. Carburetion: Carter WDO-407s (L)-408s (R).

CHASSIS

[Series 60S] Wheelbase: 127 inches. Overall length: 214-1/4 inches. Front/Rear Tread: 58/61 inches. Tires: 7 x 16.

[Series 61] Wheelbase: 126 inches. Overall length: 207-1/4 inches. Front/Rear Tread: 58/59 inches. Tires: 7 x 16.

[Series 75] Wheelbase: 141 inches. Overall length: 225-1/8 inches. Front/Rear Tread: 60-1/2/62-1/2 inches. Tires: 7.50 x 16.

[Series 61 Commercial Chassis] Wheelbase: 162-1/4 inches. Overall length: 243-1/2 inches. Tires: 7 x 16.

[Series 75 Commercial Chassis] Wheelbase: 161-3/8 inches. Overall length: 245-3/8 inches. Tires: 7.50 x 16.

[Series 90] Wheelbase: 141 inches. Overall length: 222 inches. Front/Rear Tread: 60- 1/2/62-1/2 inches. Tires: 7.50 x 16.

TECHNICAL

[Series 61, Series 60] Selective synchromesh manual transmission. Speeds: 3F/1R. Left-hand drive, gearshift on column, handbrake at left (right-hand drive optional). Single disc clutch. Shaft drive, Hotchkiss. Semi-floating rear axle. Hypoid gears. Overall ratio: 3.92:1. Hydraulic brakes on four wheels. Slotted disc wheels. Wheels: 16 inch.

[Series 75] Selective synchromesh manual transmission. Speeds: 3F/1R. Left-hand drive, gearshift on column, handbrake at left (right-hand drive optional). Single disc clutch. Shaft drive, Hotchkiss. Semi-floating rear axle. Hypoid gears. Overall ratio: 4.58:1. Hydraulic brakes on four wheels. Slotted disc wheels. Wheels: 16 inch.

[Series 90] Selective synchromesh manual transmission. Speeds: 3F/1R. Left-hand drive, gearshift on column, handbrake at left. Single disc clutch. Shaft drive, Hotchkiss. Semi-floating rear axle. Hypoid gears. Overall ratio: 4.31:1. Hydraulic brakes on four wheels. Disc wheels. Wheels: 16 inch.

HISTORICAL

Introduced October 1938. Model year sales and production were 5,513 Series 60S, 5,913 Series 61, 2,069 Series 75 and 138 Series 90. Once again, Nicholas Dreystadt was general manager of Cadillac.

1939 Cadillac, Series 90, Fleetwood V-16 coupe

1940

OVERVIEW

For 1940, the triangular grilles in the fender "catwalks" on Cadillac V-8s were formed by vertical bars arranged in groups of three. The "ship's prow" front had a grille with multiple horizontal bars, but a vertical center divider. V-16 models continued using the basic 1938 styling, except that the taillights now wrapped around the trailing edge of each rear fender. The 1940 models had sealed-beam headlights, directional signals and concealed door hinges. There was a new Fisher "C" or "Torpedo" body. Variations of the Special Sedan and Town Car were included in the 60S Series, which rode Cadillac's shortest wheelbase. The new Series 62 replaced the Series 61 and had a three-inch longer wheelbase than that 1939 line. There were eight models in a new Series 72 line. These cars were large and luxurious like Series 75 models, but had a shorter wheelbase and lower prices. Only 61 of the Series 90 V-16s were made this year.

I.D. DATA

[All V-8s] Serial numbers were located on the left frame side bar, opposite the steering gear. Starting: same as engine number. Ending: same as engine number. Engine

number location: on the crankcase, just behind the left cylinder block, parallel to the dash. Starting: [Series 40-60S] 632001, [Series 40-62] 832001, [Series 40-72] 7320001, [Series 40-75] 3320001. Ending: [Series 40-60S] 6324600, [Series 40-62] 8325903, [Series 40-72] 7321525, [Series 40-75] 3320956.

[V-16] Serial numbers were located on the left frame side bar, opposite the steering gear. Starting: same as engine number. Ending: same as engine number. Engine numbers were on the upper rear corner of the left cylinder block, parallel to the cylinder head. Starting: 5320001. Ending: 5320061.

SERIES 60 SPECIAL—V-8

The 60 Special series Special Sedan had a clean, smooth look. Its high top and large windows emphasized the glass area. This model was available with the Sunshine TurretTop or with a center division. The 60 Special five-passenger Town Car came in standard, Leatherback and Metalback versions. These cars rode Cadillac's shortest wheelbase and had the least-powerful version of the V-8 under the hood.

Above: **1940 Cadillac, Series 75, convertible coupe**

Alex Lindemann

Fleetwood Series 40-60S, 127-inch wheelbase

Model Number	Body Type & Seating	Factory Price	Shipping Weight	Production Total
40-6019S	Special Sedan-5P	2,090	4,070	—
40-6019S-A	Special Sedan (STT)-5P	—	—	—
40-6019S-F	Special Sedan (Div)-5P	2,230	4,110	—
40-6053S	Town Car-5P	—	—	—
40-6053-Leatherback	Town Car-5P	3,820	4,365	—
40-6053-Metalback	Town Car-5P	3,465	4,365	—

SERIES 62 — V-8

For 1940, Series 61 was replaced by Series 62, featuring the "Projectile" or "Torpedo" bodies. Series 62 models featured a low, sleek body with chrome window reveals, more slant to the windshield and a curved rear window. Runningboards were no-cost options. Convertible coupes and sedans were introduced at midyear. Sealed beam headlights and turn indicators were standard equipment. The engine manifold was set at five degrees to the engine to cancel the rearward tilt of the engine and give balanced fuel distribution.

Fisher Series 40-62, 129-inch wheelbase

Model Number	Body Type & Seating	Factory Price	Shipping Weight	Production Total
40-6219	Touring Sedan-5P	1,745	4,030	—
40-6227C	Coupe-2P	1,685	3,940	—
40-6229	Convertible Sedan-5P	2,195	4,230	—
40-6267	Convertible Coupe-2P	1,795	4,045	—

SERIES 72 — V-8

The one-year-only Series 72 was introduced as a less expensive companion to the Series 75. Series 72 models had the general appearance of the Series 75, but their wheelbase was three inches shorter. One distinction of the 72 was that the rectangular taillights were positioned up high on the sides of the trunk. Recirculating ball steering was tried on Series 72 in 1940, then adopted for all 1941 Cadillacs.

Fleetwood Series 40-72, 138-inch wheelbase

Model Number	Body Type & Seating	Factory Price	Shipping Weight	Production Total
40-7219	Touring Sedan-5P	2,670	4,670	—
40-7219-F	Touring Sedan (Div)-5P	2,790	4,710	—
40-7223	Touring Sedan-7P	2,785	4,700	—
40-7233	Imperial Sedan-7P	2,915	4,740	—
40-7259	Formal Sedan-5P	3,695	4,670	—
40-7233-F	Formal Sedan-7P	3,695	4,780	—

Fleetwood Series 40-72, 138-inch wheelbase Business Cars

Model Number	Body Type & Seating	Factory Price	Shipping Weight	Production Total
40-7223-L	Business Touring Sedan-9P	2,690	4,700	—
40-7233-L	Business Touring Imperial-9P	2,824	4,740	—

SERIES 75 — V-8

A full range of 12 models, including Coupe, Convertible and Convertible Sedan made up the Series 75 car-line. These cars were essentially the same as the V-16 models with a smaller engine. They shared the 141-inch wheelbase with the V-16s.

Fleetwood Series 40-75, 141-inch wheelbase

Model Number	Body Type & Seating	Factory Price	Shipping Weight	Production Total
40-7557	Coupe-2P	3,280	4,785	—
40-7557-B	Coupe-5P	3,380	4,810	—
40-7567	Convertible Coupe-2P	3,380	4,915	—
40-7519	Sedan-5P	2,995	4,900	—
40-7519-F	Imperial Sedan-5P	3,155	4,940	—
40-7559	Formal Sedan-5P	3,995	4,900	—
40-7539	Town Sedan-5P	3635	4,935	—
40-7529	Convertible Sedan-5P	3,945	5,110	—
40-7523	Sedan-7P	3,210	4,930	—
40-7533	Imperial Sedan-7P	3,360	4,70	—
40-7533-F	Formal Sedan-7P	3,995	4,970	—
40-7553	Town Car-7P	5,115	5,195	—

Fleetwood Series 40-75, 141-inch wheelbase Business Cars

Model Number	Body Type & Seating	Factory Price	Shipping Weight	Production Total
40-7523-L	Business Touring Sedan-8P	—	—	—
40-7533-L	Business Touring Imperial-8P	—	—	—

SERIES 90 — V-16

The last Cadillac V-16 was the last non-V-8 Cadillac for more than 40 years to come. Only such detail changes as a new instrument panel and redesigned taillights and bumpers were seen. The introduction of sealed beam headlights and directional signals also distinguished the 1940 models. The basic body shell remained unchanged from 1938. Some models shared the same body, but differed in seating arrangements and interior equipment such as jump seats and division windows.

Fleetwood Series 40-90, 141-inch wheelbase

Model Number	Body Type & Seating	Factory Price	Shipping Weight	Production Total
40-9057	Coupe-2P	5,340	4,915	—
40-9057 B	Coupe-5P	5,440	5,015	—
40-9067	Convertible Coupe-2P	5,440	4,995	—
40-9019	Sedan-5P	5,140	5,190	—
40 9019-F	Imperial Sedan-5P	5,215	5,230	—
40-9059	Formal Sedan-5P	6,055	5,190	—
40-9039	Town Sedan-5P	5,695	5,140	—
40-9029	Convertible Sedan-5P	6,000	5,265	—
40-9023	Sedan-7P	5,270	5,215	—
40 9033	Imperial Sedan-7P	5,420	5,260	—
40-9033-F	Formal Sedan-7P	6,055	5,260	—
40-9053	Town Car-7P	7,175	5,415	—

ENGINE
SERIES 60S BASE V-8, SERIES 62 BASE V-8

1940 Cadillac, Series 62, convertible coupe

Long Island Auto Museum

L-head. Cast iron block on blocks cast enbloc with crankcase. Bore and stroke: 3-1/2 x 4-1/2. Displacement: 346 cid. Compression ratio: 6.25:1. Brake hp: 135 at 3400 rpm. Taxable hp: 39.20. Torque: 250 at 1700 rpm. Main bearings: three. Valve lifters: Hydraulic. Crankcase capacity: 7 qt. Cooling system capacity: 24.5 qt. Carburetor: Stromberg AAV-26 dual downdraft.

SERIES 72 BASE V-8, SERIES 75 BASE V-8

L-head. Cast iron block on blocks cast enbloc with crankcase. Bore and stroke: 3-1/2 x 4-1/2. Displacement: 346 cid. Compression ratio: 6.70:1. Brake hp: 140 at 3400 rpm. Taxable hp: 39.20. Torque: 270 at 1700 rpm. Main bearings: three. Valve lifters: Hydraulic. Crankcase capacity: 7 qt. Cooling system capacity: 24.5 qt. Carburetor: Stromberg AAV-26 dual downdraft.

BASE V-16

135 degree vee L-head. Sixteen. Cast iron block. Bore and stroke: 3-1/4 x 3-1/4 inches. Displacement: 431 cid Compression ratio: 6.75:1. Brake hp: 185 at 3600 rpm. Taxable horsepower: 67.6. Main bearings: nine. Valve lifters: hydraulic. Carburetor : Carter WDO-407s (Left)-408s (Right).

CHASSIS

[Series 60S] Wheelbase: 127 inches. Overall length: 216-7/8 inches. Front/Rear Tread: 58/61 inches. Tires: 7 x 16.

[Series 62S] Wheelbase: 129 inches. Overall length: 216-1/16 inches. Front/Rear Tread: 58/59 inches. Tires: 7 x 16.

[Series 72S] Wheelbase: 138 inches. Overall length: 226-11/16 inches. Front/Rear Tread: 58/62-1/2 inches. Tires: 7.50 x 16.

[Series 75] Wheelbase: 141 inches. Overall length: 228-3/16 inches. Front/Rear Tread: 60-1/2/62-1/2 inches. Tires: 7.50 x 16.

[Series 72 Commercial Chassis] Wheelbase: 165-1/4 inches. Overall length: 253-13/16 inches. Tires: 7.50 x 16.

[Series 75 Commercial Chassis] Wheelbase: 161-3/8 inches. Overall length: 248-11/16 inches. Tires: 7.50 x 16.

1940 Cadillac, Series 75, seven-passsenger touring sedan

1940 Cadillac, Bohman and Schwartz-bodied convertible

David Lyon

[Series 90] Wheelbase: 141 inches. Overall length: 255-11/16 inches. Front/Rear Tread: 60-1/2/62-1/2 inches. Tires: 7.50 x 16.

TECHNICAL

[Series 60S, Series 62] Selective synchromesh manual transmission. Speeds: 3F/1R. Left-hand drive, gearshift on column, handbrake at left (right-hand drive optional). Single disc clutch. Shaft drive, Hotchkiss. Semi-floating rear axle. Hypoid gears. Overall ratio: 3.92:1. Hydraulic brakes on four wheels. Slotted disc wheels. Wheels: 16 inch.

[Series 72] Selective synchromesh manual transmission. Speeds: 3F/1R. Left-hand drive, gearshift on column, handbrake at left (right-hand drive optional). Single disc clutch. Shaft drive, Hotchkiss. Semi-floating rear axle. Hypoid gears. Overall ratio: 4.31:1. Hydraulic brakes on four wheels. Slotted disc wheels. Wheels: 16 inch.

[Series 75] Selective synchromesh manual transmission. Speeds: 3F/1R. Left-hand drive, gearshift on column, handbrake at left (right-hand drive optional). Single disc clutch. Shaft drive, Hotchkiss. Semi-floating rear axle. Hypoid gears. Overall ratio: 4.58:1. Hydraulic brakes on four wheels. Slotted disc wheels. Wheels: 16 inch.

[Series 90] Selective synchromesh manual transmission. Speeds: 3F/1R. Left-hand drive, gearshift on column, handbrake at left. Single disc clutch. Shaft drive, Hotchkiss. Semi-floating rear axle. Hypoid gears. Overall ratio: 4.31:1. Hydraulic brakes on four wheels. Disc wheels. Wheels: 16 inch.

OPTIONS

Radio ($69.50). Heater ($26.50-52.50). Seat covers ($8.25 per seat). Spotlight ($18.50). Automatic battery filler ($7.50). Flexible steering wheel ($15). Fog lights ($14.50 pair). Windshield washer ($6.50). Grille guard. Wheel discs ($4 each). Trim rings ($1.50 each). Drivetrain Options: Hill-Holder (No roll) ($13.50).

HISTORICAL

The 1940 Cadillacs were introduced in October 1939. Model year sales and production included 4,600 Series 60S models, 5,903 Series 62 models, 1,525 Series 721 models, 956 Series 75 models and 61 Series 90 V-16 models. The general manager of Cadillac was still Nicholas Dreystadt. Cadillac was the 15th-ranked American car brand in terms of sales. Gangster Al Capone owned a V-16 seven-passenger Formal Touring Sedan. Actor and singer Eddie Cantor owned a V-16 Town Car. Derham Body Co. produced a V-16 two-passenger Coupe on a leftover 1940 V-16 chassis.

1941

OVERVIEW

Cadillac designers adopted a front-end styling theme that was to be repeated for years to come. The one-piece hood came down lower in front and included the side panels. It extended sideways to the fenders. A single, rectangular panel of louver trim was used on each side of the hood. Access to the engine compartment was improved, to say the least. The rectangular grille was wide and vertical and bulged forward in the middle. Rectangular parking lights were built into the top outer corners of the grille. The headlights were built into the nose of the fenders and provision for built-in accessory fog lights was provided under the headlights. When the extra-cost fog lamps were not ordered, the openings were covered by circular chrome ornaments with a "V" emblem in their center. Three chrome spears decorated the rear section of all four fenders, except on the Sixty Special. Rear wheel shields (fender skirts) were standard on most Cadillac bodies. Only V-8s were offered this year. They came in six different series. The revived Series 61 models filled the gap on the pricing ladder left by the LaSalle. The Series 63 and Series 67 models were new. Following Packard's 1940 lead, air conditioning was introduced by Cadillac. In addition, the no-shift Hydra-Matic Drive that General Motors introduced on 1940 Oldsmobiles made it into Cadillacs.

I.D. DATA

Serial numbers were located on the left frame side bar, opposite the steering gear. Starting: same as engine number. Ending: same as engine number. Engine numbers were on the crankcase, just behind the left cylinder block, parallel to the dash. Starting: [Series 41-60S] 6340001, [41-61] 5340001, [41-62] 8340001, [41-63] 7340001, [41-67] 9340001, [41-75] 3340001. Ending: [Series 41-60S] 6344101, [41-61] 5369258, [41-62] 8364734, [41-63] 7345050, [41-67] 9340922, [41-75] 3342104.

SERIES 60 SPECIAL—V-8

Sixty Special front fenders extended into the front doors. No runningboards were available for cars in this line. The Town Car was no longer offered. The Special Sedan was available with the Sunshine Turret Top or with a divider.

Above: **1941 Cadillac, Series 62, convertible**

Fleetwood Series 41-60S, 126-inch wheelbase

Model Number	Body Type & Seating	Factory Price	Shipping Weight	Production Total
41-6019S	Sedan-5P	2,195	4,230	—
41-6019S-A	Sedan With Sunshine Top-5P	—	—	—
41-6019S-F	Sedan With Division-5P	2,45	4,290	—

| 41-6723 | Touring Sedan-7P | 2,735 | 4,630 | — |
| 41-6733 | Imperial Touring Sedan-7P | 2,890 | 4,705 | — |

SERIES 61 — V-8

The Series 61 Coupe and Touring Sedan were fastback body styles reminiscent of the Aerodynamic Coupes of the 1930s. Both models came in standard or deluxe trim versions. They shared the same wheelbase as the Sixty Specials. The 61s replaced the LaSalle and represented the lowest-priced Cadillac products.

Fisher Series 41-61, 126-inch wheelbase

Model Number	Body Type & Seating	Factory Price	Shipping Weight	Production Total
41-6127	Coupe-5P	1,345	3,985	—
41-6127D	Coupe Deluxe-5P	1,435	4,005	—
41-6109	Touring Sedan-5P	1,445	4,065	—
41-6109 D	Touring Sedan Deluxe-5P	1,535	4,085	—

SERIES 62 — V-8

Series 62 came in the standard body style lineup. This series now included the only Convertible Sedan. It was also the last time that Cadillac would offer that body style. Runningboards were concealed or a no-cost option on all Cadillacs (except the 60 Special and the 75 models). Power tops, electrically-operated compartment dividers, factory-installed air-conditioning and Hydra-Matic Drive were available features. There were four basic body styles in this series and six models. The Coupe and Touring Sedan could be had in standard or deluxe trim, while all open cars had deluxe equipment.

Fisher Series 41-62, 126-inch wheelbase

Model Number	Body Type & Seating	Factory Price	Shipping Weight	Production Total
41-6227	Coupe-2/4P	1,420	3,950	—
41-6227D	Coupe Deluxe-2/4P	1,510	3,970	—
41-6219	Touring Sedan-5P	1,495	4,030	—
41-6219D	Touring Sedan Deluxe-5P	1,535	4,050	—
41-6267D	Convertible Coupe Deluxe-2/4P	1,645	4,055	—
41-6229D	Convertible Sedan Deluxe-5P	1,965	4,230	—

SERIES 63 — V-8

A new Series 63 was offered in one body style. It was based on the new six-window Fisher "B" body and shared the 126-inch wheelbase used for Series 62 models. It had streamlined notch back styling, concealed runningboards and a triple-section rear window. In place of belt moldings below the side windows, this model had a single loop of chrome around all three side windows.

Fisher Series 41-63, 126-inch wheelbase

Model Number	Body Type & Seating	Factory Price	Shipping Weight	Production Total
41-6319	Touring Sedan-5P	1,696	4,140	—

SERIES 67 — V-8

A new Series 67, with Fisher sedan bodies and the Cadillac's longest 139-inch wheelbase replaced the 1940 Series 72.

Fisher Series 41-67, 139-inch wheelbase

Model Number	Body Type & Seating	Factory Price	Shipping Weight	Production Total
41-6719	Touring Sedan-5P	2,595	4,555	—
41-6719-F	Touring Sedan With Division-5P	2,745	4,615	—

SERIES 75 — V-8

Only eight models made up the 1941 Series 75 car-line. Coupes and open models were no longer offered in what was now the top Cadillac series. The 136-inch wheelbase was five inches shorter than that used for the 1940 Series 75 models.

Fleetwood Series 41-75, 136-inch wheelbase

Model Number	Body Type & Seating	Factory Price	Shipping Weight	Production Total
41-7519	Touring Sedan-5P	2,995	4,750	—
41-7519-F	Touring Sedan With Division-5P	3,150	4,810	—
41-7523	Touring Sedan-7P	3,140	4,800	—
41-7533	Touring Imperial-7P	3,295	4,860	—
41-7559	Formal Sedan-5P	3,920	4,900	—
41-7533-F	Formal Sedan-7P	4,045	4,915	—

Business Cars Series 41-75, 136-inch wheelbase

Model Number	Body Type & Seating	Factory Price	Shipping Weight	Production Total
41-7523-L	Business Touring Sedan-9P	2,895	4,750	—
41-7533-L	Business Touring Imperial-9P	3,050	4,810	—

ENGINE

BASE V-8 (ALL)

L-head. Cast iron block on blocks cast enbloc with crankcase. Bore and stroke: 3-1/2 x 4-1/2. Displacement: 346 cid. Compression ratio: 7.25:1. Brake hp: 150 at 3400 rpm. Taxable hp: 39.20. Torque: 283 at 1700. Main bearings: three. Valve lifters: Hydraulic. Crankcase capacity: 7 qt. Cooling system capacity: 24.5 qt. Carburetor: Stromberg AAV-26 dual downdraft or Carter WDO 506-S.

CHASSIS

[Series 60S] Wheelbase: 126 inches. Overall length: 217-3/16 inches. Front/Rear Tread: 59/63 inches. Tires: 7 x 15.

[Series 61] Wheelbase: 126 inches. Overall length: 215 inches. Front/Rear Tread: 59/63 inches. Tires: 7 x 15.

[Series 62] Wheelbase: 126 inches. Overall length: 216 inches. Front/Rear Tread: 59/63 inches. Tires: 7 x 15.

1941 Cadillac, Series 62, convertible

[Series 63] Wheelbase: 126 inches. Overall length: 215 inches. Front/Rear Tread: 59/63 inches. Tires: 7 x 15.

[Series 67] Wheelbase: 139 inches. Overall length: 228 inches. Front/Rear Tread: 58-1/2/62-1/2 inches. Tires: 7.50 x 16.

[Series 75] Wheelbase: 136 inches. Overall length: 226-1/8 inches. Front/Rear Tread: 58-1/2/62-1/2 inches. Tires: 7.50 x 16.

[Series 62 Commercial Chassis] Wheelbase: 163 inches. Overall length: 252-7/8 inches. Tires: 7 x 16.

[Series 75 Commercial Chassis] Wheelbase: 163 inches. Overall length: 252-7/8 inches. Tires: 7.50 x 16.

TECHNICAL

Selective synchromesh manual transmission. Speeds: 3F/1R. Left-hand drive, gearshift on column, handbrake at left (right-hand drive optional except 60S and 67). Single disc clutch. Shaft drive, Hotchkiss. Semi-floating rear axle. Hypoid gears. Overall ratio: [60S, 61, 62, 63] 3.77:1 (3.36:1 optional), [67, 75] 4.27:1 (3.77:1 optional).

Hydraulic brakes on four wheels. Slotted disc wheels. Wheels: 15 inch. (16 inch. on 67 and 75).

OPTIONS

Fender skirts ($17.50 pair). Radio ($69.50). Heater ($59.50-$65). Seat covers ($8.75/seat). Spotlight ($18.50). Fog lights ($14.50). Backup light ($7.50). Windshield washer ($7.50). Wheel discs ($4 each). Trim rings ($1.50 each). Automatic transmission ($125). No-Rol hill-holder ($11.50).

HISTORICAL

The 1941 Cadillacs were introduced in September 1940. Model year sales and production included 4,101 Seriers 60 Special, 29,258 Series 61, 24,734 Series 62, 5,050 Series 63, 922 Series 67 and 2,104 Series 75. Once again, the general manager of Cadillac was Nicholas Dreystadt. By 1941, the final rationalization of Dreystadt's streamlined operations program arrived with the Cadillac V-16 and LaSalle being discontinued. Full attention was then lavished on seven V-8 models mounted riding three different wheelbases and offering some new options. Sales for 1941 approached 60,000 cars, the best in the company's history.

1941 Cadillac, Series 62, convertible sedan

1942

OVERVIEW

Cadillac's 40th anniversary was shortened by the outbreak of World War II. The soon-to-be-rare 1942 Cadillacs sported streamlined "pontoon" fenders. GM's "Aerodynamic" coupes were in vogue. Sales of Cadillacs optional Hydra-Matic Drive doubled and represented nearly 60 percent of the luxury marque's total production. A bright new radiator grille characterized 1942. It was more massive ever before with six bright moldings running nearly the width of the car (which was pretty wide). Up front were overriders topped by Cadillac's trade-mark chrome "bullets." The taillights were redesigned to follow the fender shape.

I.D. DATA

Serial numbers were on the right frame side bar, just behind the engine support bracket. Starting: same as engine number. Ending: same as engine number. Engine numbers were on the right-hand side of the crankcase, just above the water pump. Chrome or polished stainless steel brightwork. Starting: [Series 42A-60S] 6380001, [Series 42A- 61] 5380001, [Series 42A-62] 8380001, [Series 42A-63] 7380001, [Series 42A-67] 9380001, [Series 42A-75] 3380001. Ending: [Series 42A-60S] 6381500,

[Series 42A-61] 5385237, [Series 42A-62] 8384401, [Series 42A-63] 7381500, [Series 42A- 67] 9380520, [Series 42A-75] 3381200. Painted "brightwork": [Series 42B-60S] 6386001, 6386375, [Series 42B-61] 5386001, 5386463, [Series 42B-62] 8386001, 8386560, [Series 42B-63] 7386001, 7386250, [Series 42B-67] 9386001, 9386180, [Series 42B-75] 3386001, 3386327.

SERIES 60 SPECIAL–V-8

For 1942, the Series lineup remained the same as in 1941. The new grille was of a more massive design, with fewer (but heavier) bars. The parking lights were round and new rectangular fog light sockets were included within the grille area. Bullet-shaped tips appeared on the bumper guards. The front fenders were longer and more rounded. They extended onto the doors. The first general styling change on the Sixty Special changed the whole character of the car. It had more bulbous lines and louver bars on the quarters. Numerous short vertical bars decorated the lower section of the fenders. The rear fenders extended forward onto rear doors. The new fenders had heavy moldings along the sides. The Sunshine Turret Top was no longer offered. The Sedan and the Sedan with Division remained. A new fresh-air ventilating system with air ducts leading from the grille replaced the use of cowl ventilators. The hand-brake control was changed from a lever to a tee-

Above: **1942 Cadillac, Series 75, Fleetwood limousine**

shaped pull handle. Radiator shutter control of the engine temperature was replaced by a blocking-type thermostat in the water return fitting on the radiator.

Fleetwood Series 42-60S, 133-inch wheelbase

Model Number	Body Type & Seating	Factory Price	Shipping Weight	Production Total
42-6069	4D Sedan	2,435	4,310	—
42-6069-F	4D Sedan With Division	2,589	4,365	—

SERIES 61 – V-8

Series 61 was down to two fastback models, the Club Coupe and the four-door Sedan. As in 1941, the wheelbase measured 126 inches. These were the most popular Cadillacs in this era.

Fisher Series 42-61, 126-inch wheelbase

Model Number	Body Type & Seating	Factory Price	Shipping Weight	Production Total
42-6107	Club Coupe-5P	1,560	4,035	—
42-6109	4D Sedan	1,647	4,115	—

SERIES 62—V-8

Series 62 came in the standard body style lineup. This series now included the only Convertible. This open car now had rear quarter windows and was called a Convertible Club Coupe instead of just a Convertible Coupe. Runningboards were concealed or a no-cost option. The Series 62 models also used rear fenders that extended forward onto rear doors. These new fenders used the heavy moldings along their sides. There were three basic body styles in this series and five models. The Club Coupe and Sedan could be had in standard or "optional" trim, while the ragtop came only with the "optional" trim. That meant the same as "Deluxe."

Fisher Series 42-62, 129-inch wheelbase

Model Number	Body Type & Seating	Factory Price	Shipping Weight	Production Total
42-6207	Club Coupe-5P	1,667	4,105	—
42-6207D	Optional Club Coupe-5P	1,754	4,125	—
42-6269	4D Sedan	1,754	4,185	—
42-6269D	4D Optional Sedan	1,836	4,205	—

1942 Cadillac, Fleetwood 60 Special sedan

42-6267D	Optional Convertible Club Coupe-5P	2,020	4,365	—

SERIES 63—V-8

The Series 63 four-door sedan was again based on the Fisher six-window "B" body and used the 126-inch wheelbase. It had sleek notch back styling, concealed runningboards and a three-piece rear window with bright division bars. In place of belt moldings below the side windows, this model had a single chrome loop around all three side windows.

Fisher Series 42-63, 126-inch wheelbase

Model Number	Body Type & Seating	Factory Price	Shipping Weight	Production Total
42-6319	4D Sedan	1,882	4,115	—

SERIES 67 — V-8

A new Series 67, with Fisher sedan bodies and the Cadillac's longest 139-inch wheelbase replaced the 1940 Series 72.

Fisher Series 42-67, 139-inch wheelbase

Model Number	Body Type & Seating	Factory Price	Shipping Weight	Production Total
42-6719	Sedan-5P	2,896	4,605	—
42-6719-F	Sedan With Division-5P	3,045	4,665	—
42-6723	Sedan-7P	3,045	4,680	—
42-6733	Imperial-7P	3,204	4,775	—

SERIES 75 — V-8

Series 75 had the new grille but retained the 1941 fender treatment. A detail trim change on the 75s was a rounded nose on the hood louvers. The same eight models made up the 1942 Series 75 car-line. The 136-inch wheelbase was retained.

Fleetwood Series 42-75, 136-inch wheelbase

Model Number	Body Type & Seating	Factory Price	Shipping Weight	Production Total
42-7519	Sedan-5P	3,306	4,750	—
42-7519-F	Sedan With Division-5P	3,459	4,810	—
42-7523	Sedan-7P	3,459	4,800	—
42-7533	Imperial-7P	3,613	4,860	—
42-7559	Formal Sedan-5P	4,330	4,900	—
42-7533-F	Formal Sedan-7P	4,484	4,915	—

Business Cars Series 42-75, 136-inch wheelbase

Model Number	Body Type & Seating	Factory Price	Shipping Weight	Production Total
42-7523-L	Business Sedan-9P	3,152	4,750	—
42-7533-L	Business Imperial-9P	3,306	4,810	—

ENGINE

ALL MODELS BASE V-8

L-head. Cast iron block on blocks cast enbloc with crankcase. Bore and stroke: 3-1/2 x 4-1/2. Displacement: 346 cid. Compression ratio: 7.25:1. Brake hp: 150 at 3400 rpm. Taxable hp: 39.20. Torque: 283 at 1700. Main bearings: three. Valve lifters: Hydraulic. Crankcase capacity: 7 qt. Cooling system capacity: 24.5 qt. Carburetor: Stromberg AAV-26 dual downdraft or Carter WDO 486-S.

CHASSIS

[Series 60S] Wheelbase: 133 inches. Overall length: 224 inches. Front/Rear Tread: 59/63 inches. Tires: 7 x 15.

[Series 61] Wheelbase: 126 inches. Overall length: 215 inches. Front/Rear Tread: 59/63 inches. Tires: 7 x 15.

[Series 62] Wheelbase: 129 inches. Overall length: 220 inches. Front/Rear Tread: 59/63 inches. Tires: 7 x 15.

[Series 63] Wheelbase: 126 inches. Overall length: 215 inches. Front/Rear Tread: 59/63 inches. Tires: 7 x 15.

[Series 67] Wheelbase: 139 inches. Overall length: 228 inches. Front/Rear Tread: 58-1/2/62-1/2 inches. Tires: 7.50 x 16.

[Series 75] Wheelbase: 136 inches. Overall length: 227 inches. Front/Rear Tread: 58-1/2/62-1/2 inches. Tires: 7.50 x 16.

[Series 75 Commercial Chassis] Wheelbase: 163 inches. Overall length: 253-1/32 inches. Tires: 7.50 x 16.

TECHNICAL

[Series 60S, Series 61, Series 62, Series 63] Selective synchromesh manual transmission. Speeds: 3F/1R. Left-hand drive, gearshift on column, handbrake at left (right-hand drive optional on Series 61 and Series 63). Single disc clutch. Shaft drive, Hotchkiss. Semi-floating rear axle. Hypoid gears. Overall ratio: 3.77:1, (3.36:1 optional. Hydraulic brakes on four wheels. Slotted disc wheels. Wheels: 15 inch.

[Series 67, Series 75] Selective synchromesh manual transmission. Speeds: 3F/1R. Left-hand drive, gearshift on column, handbrake at left. Single disc clutch. Shaft drive, Hotchkiss. Semi-floating rear axle. Hypoid gears. Overall ratio: 4.27:1 (3.77:1 optional). Hydraulic brakes on four wheels. Slotted disc wheels. Wheels: 16 inch.

OPTIONS

Radio ($65). Heater ($59.50-$65). Seat covers ($9.75/ seat). Spotlight ($19.50). Fog lights ($24.50). Backup light ($12.50). Windshield washer ($8.25). Wheel discs ($4 each). Trim rings ($1.50 each). Automatic transmission ($135). No-Rol hill-holder ($12.50).

HISTORICAL

The 1942 Cadillacs were introduced in September 1941. Model-year sales and production included 1,875 Series 60

Special models, 5,700 Series 61 models, 4,961 Series 62 models, 1,750 Series 63 models, 700 Series 67 models and 1,527 Series 75 models. Once again, Cadillac's general manager was Nicholas Dreystadt.

1942 Cadillac, Series 62, touring sedan

During World War II, the Cadillac assembly lines turned to M-24 tank engines and transmissions.

1946

OVERVIEW

All 1946 Cadillacs were a continuation of prewar styling and engineering with the unpopular 63 and 67 series being dropped. Features common to each series included dual downdraft carburetors, a Torbend disc clutch, directional signals, knee-action wheels, double ride stabilizers, permanently-lubricated universal joints, ball-bearing steering, a mechanical fuel pump, an oil-bath air cleaner, an intake silencer, an automatic choke, a Synchromesh transmission, sealed-beam lighting, front coil springs, Super-Safe hydraulic brakes, wax-lubricated rear springs, a hypoid rear axle, slotted disc wheels, low-pressure tires, a large luggage compartment and safety plate glass throughout.

I.D. DATA

Cadillac serial numbers matched the engine numbers and were used for all license, insurance and identification purposes. For 1946, they were located on the right-hand side of the engine crankcase, just above the water pump and on the right frame side member, behind the engine support. Numbers 5400001 to 5402975 appeared on Series 61 models. Numbers 8400001 to 8418566 appeared on Series 62 models. Numbers 6400001 to 6405679 appeared

Above: **1946 Cadillac, Series 62, sedan**

on Fleetwood Series 60 Special models. Numbers 3400001 to 640579 appeared on Series 75 models.

SERIES 61 — V-8

Cadillac's lowest-priced Series 61 line was based on the General Motors "B" body, also was used on cars in the Buick 40, Oldsmobile 70 and Pontiac 26 and 28 series. Fastback styling characterized the two available body styles, which saw a late production startup in May 1946. Standard features included small hubcaps, a wider, more massive grille, bullet-shaped front and rear fenders, skirted rear wheel openings and chrome-plated rear fins. The gas filler cap was located under the rear signal light.

Series 61

Model Number	Body/Style Number	Body Type & Seating	Factory Price	Shipping Weight	Production Total
46-61	6107	2D Club Coupe-5P	2,052	4,145	800
46-61	6109	4D Sedan-5P	2,176	4,225	2,200
46-61	—	Chassis only	—	—	1

SERIES 62 — V-8

Series 62 Cadillacs were based on the General Motors C-Body, also used on the Cadillac 60S, Buick 50 and 70 and Oldsmobile 90 series. Notchback styling characterized the racy-looking cars in this line, except for the Club Coupe, which had fastback styling. The Series 62 four-door sedan was the first Cadillac to enter production after World War

II. Styling and technical features were similar to those seen on the lower-priced models, but with a longer chassis with slightly richer interior appointments.

SERIES 62

SERIES 62	Body/Style Number	Body Type & Seating	Factory Price	Shipping Weight	Production Total
46-62	6207	2D Club Coupe-5P	2,284	4,215	2,323
46-62	6267D	2D ConvertibleCoupe-5P	2,556	4,475	1,342
46-62	6269	4D Sedan-5P	2,359	4,295	14,900
46-62	—	Chassis only	—	—	1

SERIES 60 SPECIAL FLEETWOOD — V-8

The Series 60 Special Fleetwood line included only one model, a four-door sedan which was also based on the corporate C-Body. However, each door was made two inches wider, amounting to an overall four-inch extension over the standard Series 62 sedan. For easy identification, there were four slanting louvers on the rear roof pillar and a distinctive type of roof drip molding, which was separate for each door opening.

SERIES 60 SPECIAL FLEETWOOD

Model Number	Body/Style Number	Body Type & Seating	Factory Price	Shipping Weight	Production Total
46-60S	6069	4D Sedan-5P	3,099	4,420	5,700

SERIES 75 FLEETWOOD — V-8

Cadillac's Fleetwood long-wheelbase line used totally distinctive bodies that were not shared with other General Motors divisions They were generally characterized by a prewar appearance and came in five different touring sedan configurations: Sedan with quarter windows, Sedan with auxiliary seats, Business Sedan, Imperial seven-passenger Sedan and Imperial nine-passenger Sedan. The last two models had rear auxilary seats. Standard equipment included large wheel discs, fender skirts, hood, side and lower beltline moldings and stainless steel runningboards.

SERIES 75 FLEETWOOD

Model Number	Body/Style Number	Body Type & Seating	Factory Price	Shipping Weight	Production Total
46-75	7519	4D Sedan-5P	4,298	4,860	150
46-75	7523	4D Sedan-7P	4,475	4,905	225
46-75	7523L	4D Business Sedan-9P	4,153	4,920	22
46-75	7533L	4D Imperial Business Sedan-9P	4,346	4,925	17
46-75	7533	4D Imperial Sedan-7P	4,669	4,925	221
46-75	—	Commercial Chassis	—	—	1,292

ENGINE

L-head. Cast iron block. Displacement: 346-cid. Bore and Stroke: 3-1/2 x 4-1/2 inches. Compression ratio: 7.25:1. Brake hp: 150 at 3600 rpm. Taxable hp: 39.20. Torque: 274 at 1600 rpm. Three main bearings. Hydraulic valve lifters. Crankcase capacity: 7 qt. (Add 1 qt. if new filter installed). Cooling system capacity: 25 qt. (add 1 qt. for heater). Carburetor: Carter WCD two-barrel Models 595-S or 595-SA or Stromberg AAV 26 two-barrel Models 380154 or 380871.

CHASSIS

(Series 61) Wheelbase: 126 inches. Overall length: 215-11/16 inches. Width: 80-7/8 inches. Height: 64-7/8 inches. Front tread: 59 inches. Rear tread: 63 inches. Tires: 7.00 x 15.

(Series 62) Wheelbase: 129 inches. Overall length: 219-3/16 inches. Width: 80-3/4 inches. Height: 63-1/16 inches. Front tread: 59 inches. Rear tread: 63 inches. Tires: 7.00 x 15.

(Series 60S) Wheelbas e: 133 inches. Overall length: 224-3/4 inches. Width: 80-3/4 inches. Height: 63-1/16 inches. Front tread: 59 inches. Rear tread: 63 inches. Tires: 7.00 x 15.

(Series 75) Wheelbase: 136. Overall length: 226-5/16 inches. Width: 82-5/16 inches. Height: 68-1/2 inches. Front tread: 58-1/2 inches. Rear tread: 62-1/2 inches. Tires: 7.50 x 16.

OPTIONS

Hydra-Matic Drive ($176). Large wheel discs ($19). White sidewall disc. Fog lights. Safety spotlight.

HISTORICAL

Division windows between front and rear seats were available on Fleetwood models for limousine use. Commercial chassis were provided for makers of hearses and ambulances. A limited number of dual-cowl phaetons were also constructed on the Cadillac chassis this year. The Classic Car Club of America recognizes all 1946 Series 75 models as Classic cars.

1946 Cadillac, Series 75, limousine

1947

OVERVIEW

A minor styling face-lift characterized 1947 Cadillacs, which now had grilles with five massive horizontal blades instead of the six used the previous year. A new identification feature was a striped field for the V- shaped hood crest. Sombrero style wheelcovers were an attractive new option seen on many Cadillacs. In the logo department, a script-type nameplate replaced the block lettering used on the sides of front fenders in 1946. Upholstery and paint combinations were generally revised and steering wheel horn rings were changed to a semi-circular design. The old style rubber stone shields were replaced with a bright metal type and a new winged trunk ornament was used on all models except the Series 60 Fleetwood Special sedan. Other features were basically unchanged over the previous year's cars.

I.D. DATA

Cadillac serial numbers again matched engine numbers and were used for all license, insurance and identification purposes. They were placed in the same locations as before. Engine serial numbers 5420001 to 5428555 appeared on 1947 Series 61 models. Engine serial numbers 8420001

Above: **1947 Cadillac, Series 62, convertible**

Steven Kriesman

to 8459835 appeared on 1947 Series 62 models. Engine serial numbers 6420001 to 6428500 appeared on 1947 Series 60S models. Engine serial numbers 3420001 to 3425036 appeared on 1947 Series 75 models.

SERIES 61—V-8

The Series 61 models continued to utilize the GM B-Body with fastback styling. Standard features included small hubcaps, a wider, more massive grille, bullet-shaped front and rear fenders, skirted rear wheel openings and chrome-plated rear fins. The gas filler cap was located under the rear signal light.

SERIES 61

Model Number	Body/Style Number	Body Type & Seating	Factory Price	Shipping Weight	Production Total
47-61	6107	2D Club Coupe-5P	2,200	4,080	3,395
47-61	6109	4D Sedan-5P	2,324	4,165	5,160

SERIES 62—V-8

Series 62 Cadillacs were again based on the GM C-Body and had a slightly sleeker appearance than models in the other lines. Notchback styling was seen on all models except the fastback coupe. However it was easy to distinguish this car from a 61 coupe, as the door skins did not flare out above the rocker panels, the side window openings were lower and the reveal moldings circled

each window individually instead of looping around all windows, as on the smaller car. The 62 sedan also had door skins that mated flush with the rocker panels and featured ventipanes on both the front and rear windows. The 62 convertible was the only open-bodied Cadillac available.

SERIES 62

Model Number	Body/Style Number	Body Type & Seating	Factory Price	Shipping Weight	Production Total
47-62	6207	2D Club Coupe-5P	2,446	4,145	7,245
47-62	6267	2D Convertible Coupe-5P	2,902	4,455	6,755
47-62	6269	4D Sedan-5P	2,523	4,235	25,834
47-62	—	Chassis only	—	—	1

SERIES 60 SPECIAL FLEETWOOD—V-8

Two-inch wider doors were again seen on the Series 60 Special Fleetwood line, giving this car a custom look, as compared to standard Series 62 sedans based on the same GM C-Body shell. A heavy upper beltline molding, individual window loop moldings and four slanting louvers on the rear roof pillar were identification features as was the new Fleetwood trunk ornament, which varied from that seen on lower models. Bright metal stone guards were adopted this season and skirted rear fenders were used again.

SERIES 60 SPECIAL—FLEETWOOD—V-8

Model Number	Body/Style Number	Body Type & Seating	Factory Price	Shipping Weight	Production Total
47-60	6069	4D Sedan-5P	3,195	4,370	8,500

SERIES 75 FLEETWOOD —V-8

Unchanged in all but minor details for 1947, the big Fleetwood 75 series continued to use the touring sedan body with a stately prewar appearance. It came in the same five configurations marketed the year before and had the same assortment of standard equipment geared to the luxury class buyer.

SERIES 75 FLEETWOOD

Model Number	Body/Style Number	Body Type & Seating	Factory Price	Shipping Weight	Production Total
47-75	7519	4D Sedan-5P	4,340	4,875	300
47-75	7523	4D Sedan-7P	4,517	4,895	890
47-75	7523L	4D Business Sedan-9P	4,195	4,790	135
47-75	7533L	4D Imperial Business Sedan-9P	4,388	4,800	80
47-75	7533	4D Imperial Sedan-7P	4,711	4,930	1,005
47-75	—	Chassis only	—	—	3
47-75	—	Commercial Chassis	—	—	2,423
47-75	—	Business Chassis	—	—	200

ENGINE

L-head. Cast iron block. Displacement: 346-cid. Bore and Stroke: 3-1/2 x 4-1/2 inches. Compression ratio: 7.25:1. Brake hp: 150 at 3600 rpm. Taxable hp: 39.20. Torque: 274 at 1600 rpm. Three main bearings. Hydraulic valve lifters. Crankcase capacity: 7 qt. (Add 1 qt. if new filter installed). Cooling system capacity: 25 qt. (add 1 qt. for heater). Carburetor: Carter WCD two-barrel Models 595-S or 595-SA or Stromberg AAV 26 two-barrel Models 380154 or 380871.

CHASSIS

(Series 61) Wheelbase: 126 inches. Overall length: 214-1/8 inches. Width: 80-7/8 inches. Height: 68-1/2 inches. Front tread: 59 inches. Rear tread: 63 inches. Tires: 7.00 x 15.

(Series 62) Wheelbase: 129 inches. Overall length: 219-3/16 inches. Width: 80-3/4 inches. Height: 66-11/16 inches. Front tread: 59 inches. Rear tread: 63 inches. Tires: 7.00 x 15.

(Series 60S) Wheelbase: 133 inches. Overall length: 223-3/16 inches. Width: 80-3/4 inches. Height: 66-11/16 inches. Front tread: 59 inches. Rear tread: 63 inches. Tires: 7.00 x 15.

(Series 75) Wheelbase: 136. Overall length: 225-15/16 inches. Width: 82-5/16 inches. Height: 72 inches. Front tread: 58-1/2 inches. Rear tread: 62-1/2 inches. Tires: 7.50 x 16.

OPTIONS

Hydra-Matic Drive ($186). Large wheel discs ($25). White sidewall discs. Fog lights. Safety spotlight. Fender-mounted radio antenna.

HISTORICAL

Division windows between front and rear windows were available on some Fleetwood models for limousine use. Commercial and business chassis were provided to professional carmakers. The Classic Car Club of America recognizes all 1947 Series 75 models as Classic cars.

1947 Cadillac, 60 Special sedan

1948

OVERVIEW

Major design changes marked the short wheelbase Cadillacs for 1948. They featured General Motors' first all-new postwar body with styling advances including tail fins inspired by the Lockheed P-38 fighter plane. There was also an attractive eggcrate grille, which was higher in the middle than on the sides. The front of the car was protected by a heavier and more massive bumper bar that curved around the fenders. The Cadillac crest was centered low in a 'V' above the radiator grille. Chrome headlight rims were used.

I.D. DATA

Cadillac serial numbers again matched engine numbers and were used for all license, insurance and identification purposes. They were placed in the same locations as before. Engine serial numbers 481000001 to 486148663 appeared on 1948 Series 61 models. Engine serial numbers 486200001 to 486252704 appeared on 1948 Series 62 models. Engine serial numbers 486000001 to 486052706 appeared on 1948 Series 60S Fleetwood models. Engine serial numbers 487500001 to 487546088 appeared on 1948 Series 75 Fleetwood models.

Above: **1948 Cadillac, Series 61, Sedanet**

SERIES 61 — V-8

Cars in the 61 series lacked bright metal front fender shields and under-taillight trim. A new dashboard with "rainbow" style instrument cluster and leather grained panels extending to the carpets was seen only this year. Standard features included small hubcaps, a wider, more massive grille, bullet-shaped front and rear fenders, skirted rear wheel openings and chrome-plated rear fins. The gas filler cap was located under the rear signal light.

SERIES 61

Model Number	Body/Style Number	Body Type & Seating	Factory Price	Shipping Weight	Production Total
48-61	6169	4D Sedan-5P	2,833	4,150	5,081
48-61	6107	2D Club Coupe-5P	2,728	4,068	3,521
48-61	—	Chassis only	—	—	1

SERIES 62 — V-8

The Series 62 was now on the same wheelbase as the lowest priced line, making the Club Coupe and Sedan practically identical to similar models in the Series 61 range except for trim and appointments. Distinguishing features included grooved bright metal front fender gravel guards, rocker panel brightwork, chevron style chrome slashes below taillights and richer interior trim. The Convertible Coupe was exclusive to this line.

Model Number	Body/Style Number	Body Type & Seating	Factory Price	Shipping Weight	Production Total
48-62	6269	4D Sedan-5P	2,996	4,179	23,997
48-62	6207	2D Club Coupe-5P	2,912	4,125	4,764
48-62	6267	2D Convertible Coupe-5P	3,442	4,449	5,450
48-62	—	Chassis only	—	—	2

SERIES 60 SPECIAL FLEETWOOD — V-8

The Series 60 Special Fleetwood sedan was again based on an extended General Motors C-Body shell with two-inch wider front and rear doors. The tail fins, built-in rear bumper design and eggcrate grile seen on the lower-priced lines were used. Appearing again, on the rear roof pillar were four slanting chrome slashes. Instead of the standard wide stone shields, the 60 Special had a thinner type that curved upward along the forward contour of the rear fender and incorporated an attractive ribbed insert panel. At the rear of the car, a band of chrome extended across the bottom of the fender skirts and quarter panels. Standard equipment included cloth and leather upholstery combinations and leather grained doors and instrument panel.

SERIES 60 SPECIAL FLEETWOOD

Model Number	Body/Style Number	Body Type & Seating	Factory Price	Shipping Weight	Production Total
48-60S	6069	4D Sedan-5P	3,820	4,356	6,561

SERIES 75 FLEETWOOD — V-8

Consideration was given to the deletion of the long wheelbase line this year, but competitive pressures from Packard in the luxury class market dictated the retention of these models. Again, they featured General Motors old-fashioned "Turret Top" styling, a throwback to the prewar years. Minor revisions on the outside of the cars included a new background for the V-shaped hood emblem and Cadillac script—replacing block lettering—low on the fenders behind the front wheel opening. Buyers ordering fog lights got rectangular parking lights in place of the smaller round style. Stainless steel runningboards were seen once more and the 75s also had the new dashboard treatment, but with burled leather trim.

SERIES 75 FLEETWOOD

Model Number	Body/Style Number	Body Type & Seating	Factory Price	Shipping Weight	Production Total
48-75	7519X	4D Sedan-5P	4,779	4,875	225
48-75	7523X	4D Sedan-7P	4,999	4,878	499
48-75	7523L	4D Business Sedan-9P	4,679	4,780	90
48-75	7533X	4D Imperial Sedan-7P	5,199	4,959	382
48-75	7533L	4D Business Imperial-9P	4,868	4,839	64
48-75	—	Chassis only	—	—	2

ENGINE

L-head. Cast iron block. Displacement: 346-cid. Bore and Stroke: 3-1/2 x 4-1/2 inches. Compression ratio: 7.25:1.

1948 Cadillac, Jacques Saoutchik-bodied convertible

Brake hp: 150 at 3400 rpm. Taxable hp: 39.20. Torque: 283 at 1600 rpm. Three main bearings. Hydraulic valve lifters. Crankcase capacity: 7 qt. (Add 1 qt. if new filter installed). Cooling system capacity: 25 qt. (add 1 qt. for heater). Carburetor: Carter WCD two-barrel Models 595-S or 595-SA or Stromberg AAV 26 two-barrel Models 380154 or 380871.

CHASSIS

(Series 61) Wheelbase: 126 inches. Overall length: 214 inches. Width: 79 inches. Height: 67-1/2 inches. Front tread: 59 inches. Rear tread: 63 inches. Tires: 8.20 x 15.

1948 Cadillac, Series 62, sedan

Tom Jevcak

(Series 62) Wheelbase: 126 inches. Overall length: 214 inches. Width: 79 inches. Height: 67-1/2 inches. Front tread: 59 inches. Rear tread: 63 inches. Tires: 8.20 x 15.

(Series 60S) Wheelbase: 133 inches. Overall length: 225-21/32 inches. Width: 78-3/16 inches. Height: 67-1/2 inches. Front tread: 59 inches. Rear tread: 63 inches. Tires: 8.20 x 15.

(Series 75) Wheelbase: 136-1/4. Overall length: 225-15/16 inches. Width: 82-5/16 inches. Height: 71-13/16 inches. Front tread: 58-1/2 inches. Rear tread: 62-1/2 inches. Tires: 7.50 x 16.

OPTIONS

Hydra-Matic Drive ($174). Whitewall tires. Radio and antenna. Fog lights. Safety spotlight. Rear window defroster.

HISTORICAL

The Classic Car Club of America recognizes all 1948 Series 75 models as Classic cars. The following models were recognized as Milestones by the Milestone Car Society: Series 61 Coupe (Sedanet), Series 62 Coupe (Sedanet), Series 62 Convertible, Series 60S Fleetwood Special Sedan.

1948 Cadillac, Series 62, convertible

1949

OVERVIEW

The big news at Cadillac in 1949 centered on engineering, with the release of a new overhead valve V-8 engine. Only minor appearance changes were seen. They included a more massive grille treatment with grooved extension panels housing the front parking lights. A more conventional dashboard design, featuring a horizontal speedometer, appeared on all Cadillacs this year.

I.D. DATA

Cadillac serial numbers again matched engine numbers. They appeared stamped on a boss at the front right-hand face of the engine block and on the right frame side member behind the engine support. Engine serial numbers 496100000 to 496192552 were used on 1949 Series 61 models. Engine serial numbers 496200000 to 496292554 appeared on 1949 Series 62 models. Engine serial numbers 496000000 to 496088221 appeared on 1949 Series 60S Fleetwood models. Engine serial numbers 497500000 to 497577135 appeared on 1949 Series 75 models.

SERIES 61—V-8

Once again, the Series 61 cars lacked front fender gravel shields and rocker panel moldings. They had plainer interior trim. A larger luggage compartment lid was seen

on all sedans, except early production units. Standard equipment now included twin back-up lights mounted on the deck lid latch panel. Series 61 coupes had chevron slashes below the taillights.

SERIES 61

Model Number	Body/Style Number	Body Type & Seating	Factory Price	Shipping Weight	Production Total
49-61	6169	4D Sedan-5P	2,893	3,915	15,738
49-61	6107	2D Club Coupe-5P	2,788	3,838	6,409
49-61	—	Chassis only	—	—	1

SERIES 62—V-8

The major difference between Series 61 and Series 62 models of similar body style was found in minor trim variations. The higher-priced series again had grooved, front fender stone shields and bright rocker panel moldings. Chevrons below the taillights were no longer seen. The Convertible was an exclusive offering, as was a new pillarless two-door "hardtop convertible" called the Coupe DeVille. A plusher interior was featured and power window lifts were standard on the Series 62 Convertible Coupe and Coupe DeVille, but optional with other body styles. The sedan for export was shipped in completely-knocked-down (CKD) form.

Above: **1949 Cadillac, Series 62, Sedanet**

Elton McFall

1949 Cadillac, Series 62, convertible

SERIES 62

Model Number	Body/Style Number	Body Type & Seating	Factory Price	Shipping Weight	Production Total
49-62	6269	4D Sedan-5P	3,050	3,956	37,617
49-62	6207	2D Club Coupe-5P	2,966	3,862	7,515
49-62	6237	2D Coupe DeVille-5P	3,496	4,033	2,150
49-62	6267X	2D Convertible Coupe-5P	3,497	4,218	8,000
49-62	6269	4D Export Sed	3,050	3,956	360
49-62	—	Chassis only	—	—	1

SERIES 60 SPECIAL FLEETWOOD—V-8

The car with the big doors, the 60 Special Fleetwood sedan, again had four chrome slashes on the rear roof pillar for instant identification. It also had thinner rear fender stone guards with front and rear extensions and a Cadillac script mounted high on the front fenders, above the crease line. The new grille design, with parking light extensions, was seen. Back-up lights and hydraulic window lifts were also standard equipment on this car.

SERIES 60 SPECIAL FLEETWOOD

Model Number	Body/Style Number	Body Type & Seating	Factory Price	Shipping Weight	Production Total
49-60S	6069X	4D Sedan-5P	3,828	4,129	11,399
49-60S	6037X	2D Special Coupe DeVille-5P	—	—	1

SERIES 75 FLEETWOOD — V-8

To accommodate luxury-class buyers, the long-wheelbase Fleetwood models were carried over without any basic changes, except for revisions to the dashboard design that followed those on other models.

SERIES 75 FLEETWOOD

Model Number	Body/Style Number	Body Type & Seating	Factory Price	Shipping Weight	Production Total
49-75	7519X	4D Sedan-5P	4,750	4,579	220
49-75	7523X	4D Sedan-7P	4,970	4,626	595
49-75	7523L	4D Business Sedan-9P	4,650	4,522	35
49-75	7533X	4D Imperial Sedan-7P	5,170	4,648	626
49-75	7533L	4D Business Imperial-9P	4,839	4,573	25
49-75	—	Chassis only	—	—	1
49-75	—	Commercial chassis	—	—	1,861

ENGINE

Overhead valves. Cast iron block. Displacement: 331-cid. Bore and Stroke: 3-13/16 x 3-5/8 inches. Compression ratio: 7.5:1. Brake hp: 160 at 3800 rpm. Taxable hp: 46.5. Torque: 312 at 1800 rpm. Five main bearings. Hydraulic valve lifters. Crankcase capacity: 5 qt. (Add 1 qt. if new filter installed). Cooling system capacity: 18 qt. (add 1 qt. for heater). Carburetor: Carter WCD two-barrel Model 742-S.

CHASSIS

(Series 61) Wheelbase: 122 inches. Overall length: 211-7/8 inches. Width: 80-1/8 inches. Height: 62 inches. Front tread: 59 inches. Rear tread: 63 inches. Tires: 8.00 x 15.

(Series 62) Wheelbase: 126 inches. Overall length: 215-7/8 inches. Width: 80-1/8 inches. Height: 62-11/16 inches. Front tread: 59 inches. Rear tread: 63 inches. Tires: 8.00 x 15.

(Series 60S) Wheelbase: 130 inches. Overall length: 224-7/8 inches. Width: 80-1/8 inches. Height: 62-11/16 inches. Front tread: 59 inches. Rear tread: 63 inches. Tires: 8.00 x 15.

(Series 75) Wheelbase: 146-3/4. Overall length: 236-5/8 inches. Width: 80-1/8 inches. Height: 64-1/16 inches. Front tread: 59 inches. Rear tread: 63 inches. Tires: 8.20 x 15.

OPTIONS

Hydra-Matic Drive ($174). Whitewall tires. Radio and antenna. Heating and ventilating system. Chrome wheel discs. Fog lights. Safety spotlights. Other standard accessories.

HISTORICAL

The one-millionth Cadillac ever produced was a 1949 Coupe DeVille assembled on November 25, 1949. The Milestone Car Society recognized the following 1949 Cadillacs as Milestone Cars: Series 61 Coupe (Sedanet), Series 62 Coupe (Sedanet), Series 62 Convertible, Series 60 Special Fleetwood Sedan.

1949 Cadillac, Series 62, Sedanet

1950

OVERVIEW

Described as "gorgeously beautiful creations" that "embodied all the good and wonderful things a motor car can currently provide," the 1950 Cadillacs were completely restyled. They had a heavier look than the first all-new prewar models of 1948-1949. The hood protruded out further and was underlined by a more massive grille. When buyers chose fog lights, an additional bulb and larger housing were used combining the fog lights with the directional signals. "Turtle-shell" roofs were adapted and one-piece windshields. No longer available was the GM jet-back aerodynamic body. Cadillac styling traditions like the egg-crate grille and tail fin were maintained in slightly-modernized formats. Chrome Cadillac signatures decorated the front fenders. A Cadillac script again appeared on the sides of front fenders. The front and rear fenders now had one continuing feature line flowing from headlight to taillight. The rear fenders ended in swooping tail fins. In front of the rear wheel openings were large, vertical air-intake moldings. Rear fender shields (skirts) were seen on all models. All 1950 Cadillacs were 80-1/8 inches wide and four-door sedan heights ranged from 62 inches to 64-1/16 inches. All Cadillac models were lower than Chevrolets. All Cadillacs had the V-8 engine.

I.D. DATA

Cadillac serial numbers again matched engine numbers and were used for all license, insurance and identification purposes. They were located on a boss on the right-hand face of the engine block and on the right frame side member behind the engine support. Engine serial numbers 506100000 to 5061103853 appeared on 1950 Series 61 models. Engine serial numbers 506200000 to 5062103857 appeared on 1950 Series 62 models. Engine serial numbers 506000000 to 5060103850 appeared on 1950 Series 60 models. Engine serial numbers 507500000 to 507510387 were used on 1950 Series 75 Fleetwood models.

SERIES 61—V-8

Cadillac's cleanest-looking cars were the Series 61 models. They had no rocker sill moldings or rear panel underscrores. A big styling change was a return to marketing this line on a shorter wheelbase than used on the 62s. This led to some styling differences. For example, the Series 61 sedan had no rear ventipanes and featured a wraparound backlight. Only a Club Coupe and a four-door Sedan were offered on the Series 61 chassis. They shared the GM "B" body with Buick and Oldsmobile and

Above: **1950 Cadillac, Series 62, Coupe de Ville**

Tom Jevcak

were four inches shorter than the previous season's "entry-level" Cadillacs. An identifying feature of both cars was the absence of rocker panel moldings and rear quarter panel chrome underscores. While the 61 was Cadillac's least-expensive line, it was not its best-selling series and production peaked at 26,772 units.

SERIES 61

Model Number	Body/Style Number	Body Type & Seating	Factory Price	Shipping Weight	Production Total
50-61	6169	4D Sedan-5P	2,866	3,822	14,619
50-61	6137	2D Club Coupe-5P	2,761	3,829	11,839
50-61	6169	4D Export Sedan-5P	2,866	3,822	312
50-61	—	Chassis only	—	—	2

SERIES 62—V-8

The cars in the Series 62 line included four models with four more inches of wheelbase and overall length than Series 61 models. This line included Cadillac's two sporty models, the Coupe DeVille hardtop and the Convertible Coupe. All 62s could be identified by slightly richer interior appointments and by chrome underscores running the full length of the body at the bottom. The Series 62 four-door Sedan incorporated rear vent windows (called "ventipanes"). Part of the reason for the 62 Series' "sales-leader" status was the fact that this was the first full year for the popular Coupe DeVille. While the four-door Sedan was by far the favorite of buyers, the Coupe DeVille increased showroom traffic. Hydra-Matic Drive was standard in the Series 62.

SERIES 62

Model Number	Body/Style Number	Body Type & Seating	Factory Price	Shipping Weight	Production Total
50-62	6219	4D Sedan-5P	3,234	4,012	41,890
50-62	6237	2D Club Coupe-5P	3,150	3,993	6,434
50-62	6237DX	2D Coupe DeVille-5P	3,523	4,074	4,507
50-62	6267	2D ConvertibleCoupe-5P	3,654	4,316	6,986
50-62	—	Chassis only	—	—	1

SERIES 60 SPECIAL FLEETWOOD—V-8

Though larger than the Series 61 and 62 models, the 1950 Cadillacs 60 Special rode a new wheelbase that was three inches shorter than that used previously. Further identification came from eight vertical louvers on the bottom of the rear fenders, just ahead of the rear wheel openings. The only model in this car-line was a four-door sedan. It looked lower than the Series 62 four-door Sedan because of the extra length. It also had a different rear deck contour. Hydra-Matic Drive and power windows were standard.

SERIES 60 SPECIAL FLEETWOOD

Model Number	Body/Style Number	Body Type & Seating	Factory Price	Shipping Weight	Production Total
50-60S	6019X	4D Sedan-5P	3,797	4,136	13,755

SERIES 75 FLEETWOOD—V-8

Ultimate luxury was available from Cadillac Motor Division in the three Series 75 Fleetwood models, which included the four-door Sedan, Business Sedan (just one was built) and the seven-passenger Imperial Sedan. For the first time since 1941, the Fleetwood "limousine" body had styling lines generally similar to those of other Cadillacs, although it featured six-window styling and a "high-headroom" limousine-type appearance. The Fleetwood 75 was built on a longer-wheelbase chassis and had nearly 20 feet of overall length. Jump seats were provided in all seven-passenger models. Since many of these cars were owned by conservative buyers and driven by professional chauffeurs who preferred a synchromesh gear box, Hydra-Matic Drive was *optional* equipment. Jump seats were used in the seven-passenger sedan and the Imperial limousine. Power windows were standard equipment. Cadillac built the Fleetwood 75 commercial chassis, which was used for ambulances, hearses, station buses and other models built by aftermarket coachmakers.

SERIES 75 FLEETWOOD

Model Number	Body/Style Number	Body Type & Seating	Factory Price	Shipping Weight	Production Total
50-75	7523X	4D Sedan-7P	4,770	4,555	716
50-75	7533X	4D Imperial Sedan-7P	4,959	4,586	743
50-75	7523L	4D Business Sedan-7P	—	—	1
50-75	86	Commercial chassis	—	—	2,052

ENGINE

Overhead valves. Cast iron block. Displacement: 331-cid. Bore and Stroke: 3-13/16 x 3-5/8 inches. Compression ratio: 7.5:1. Brake hp: 160 at 3600 rpm. Taxable hp: 46.5. Torque: 312 at 1800 rpm. Five main bearings. Hydraulic valve lifters. Crankcase capacity: 5 qt. (Add 1 qt. if new filter installed). Cooling system capacity: 17.25 qt. (add 1 qt. for heater). Carburetor: Carter WCD two-barrel Models 682-S or 722-S.

CHASSIS

(Series 61) Wheelbase: 122 inches. Overall length: 211-7/8 inches. Width: 80-1/8 inches. Height: 62 inches. Front tread: 59 inches. Rear tread: 63 inches. Tires: 8.00 x 15.

(Series 62) Wheelbase: 126 inches. Overall length: 215-7/8 inches. Width: 80-1/8 inches. Height: 62-11/16 inches. Front tread: 59 inches. Rear tread: 63 inches. Tires: 8.00 x 15.

(Series 60S) Wheelbase: 130 inches. Overall length: 224-7/8 inches. Width: 80-1/8 inches. Height: 62-11/16 inches. Front tread: 59 inches. Rear tread: 63 inches. Tires: 8.00 x 15.

(Series 75) Wheelbase: 146-3/4. Overall length: 236-5/8 inches. Width: 80-1/8 inches. Height: 64-1/16 inches. Front tread: 59 inches. Rear tread: 63 inches. Tires: 8.20 x 15.

OPTIONS

Hydra-Matic Drive on Series 61 and 75 ($174). Power windows (on specific models). Heating and ventilating system. Radio and antenna. Chrome wheel discs (Sombrero). Windshield washers. Fog lights. White sidewall tires. Other standard accessories.

HISTORICAL

The company would sell an all-time high of over 100,000 cars this year and go on to dominate the segment, throughout the 1950s, while Lincoln struggled and Packard faltered. While the 1950 Cadillacs set the pace for a year of record sales, they were viewed as America's ultimate high-performance machine. No other domestic model came near the same horsepower rating. Sportsman Briggs Cunningham entered a pair of Cadillacs in the French Grand Prix at LeMans. One was a stock-bodied coupe and the other a special-bodied racing machine called "Le Monstre." Both had Cadillac V-8s tuned by Bill Frick and they finished a respectful 10th and 11th overall in the contest. A 1950 Cadillac driven by Tom Deal, of El Paso, Texas, also came in second in the 1950 Carrera-PanAmericana Mexico or Mexican Road Race. Cadillac produced 1,460 Series 75 cars (not counting commercial chassis) and 103,857 other Cadillacs in the model-year. This was an all-time record, as well as the first six-figure-production year. Lush Cadillac ads that included furs and jewels emphasized the tradtional "standard of the automotive world" theme.

A beautiful model, a fur and the crest announce a 1950 Cadillac 60 Special sedan.

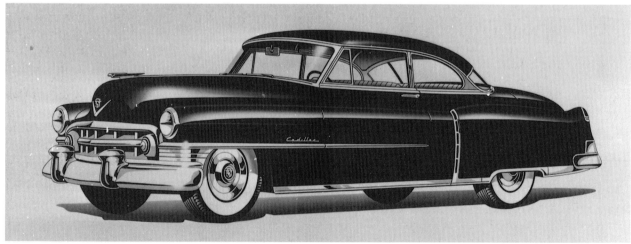

1950 Cadillac, Series 62, coupe

1951

OVERVIEW

A minor facelift and small trim variations were the main Cadillac styling news in 1951. Only a few subtle changes were made. Miniature "ice-cube-tray" grilles were set into the outboard grille extension panels below the headlights. Larger, bullet-shaped bumper guards were used and these rapidly became an automotive icon of the 1950s. The standard equipment list included a hand brake warning light, key-start ignition, a steering column cover, a Delco-Remy generator, a knee-action front suspension, directional signals, a mechanical fuel pump, dual downdraft carburetion, slipper-type pistons, rubber engine mountings, oversize brakes, Super Cushion tires, a one-piece windshield, an intake silencer, an oil-bath air cleaner, equalized engine manifolding, an automatic choke and luxury appointments. On the dashboard, telltale lights were used to monitor oil pressure and the electrical charging rate, instead of gauges. Cadillacs continued to be powered by a powerful engine. Hydra-Matic Drive, still optional on the lowest and highest series, had what Cadillac described as a "major improvement." A driver could change from forward gear to reverse while the

Above: **1951 Cadillac, Series 62, coupe**
Bob Harrington

engine was racing to "rock" out of difficult situations like being stuck in sand or snow.

I.D. DATA

Cadillac serial numbers again matched engine numbers and were used for all license, insurance and identification purposes. They were located on a boss at the front right-hand face of the engine block and on the right frame side member behind the engine support. Engine serial numbers for 1951 Series 61 models began at 51610000000. The ending number for all Cadillac series was 110340 (proceeded by applicable model-year and series code for final unit). Engine serial numbers 516200000 and up appeared on 1951 Series 62 models. Engine serial numbers 516000000 and up appeared on 1951 Series 60S models. Engine serial numbers 517500000 and up appeared on 1951 Series 75 Fleetwood models.

SERIES 61 — V-8

Series 61 models had the same type of trim as in 1950, with the exception of a medallion being added on the rear roof pillar. The same 122-inch wheelbase was used. Due to the long bumper guards (called "Dagmars") the overall length crept upwards, but other measurements were unchanged. Standard equipment included a hand-brake warning light, a steering column cover and an automatic

choke. With sluggish demand, this was to be the price-leader Cadillac series' last year. It was dropped on May 1, 1951. In 1952, the 62 became the base series.

SERIES 61

Model Number	Body/Style Number	Body Type & Seating	Factory Price	Shipping Weight	Production Total
51-61	6169	4D Sedan-5P	2,917	3,827	2,300
51-51	6137	2D Club Coupe-5P	2,810	3,829	2,400

SERIES 62 — V-8

Once again in 1951, the 62 had a four-inch longer stance and four-inch longer length than the 61. The cars in this series had full-length chrome underscores on the rocker panels, the rear fender skirts and the lower rear body quarters. The sedan had a conventional back window (called a "backlight") and featured rear ventipanes. A new Coupe DeVille chrome script was seen on the rear roof pillar of the hardtop and distinguished it from the plainer Club Coupe. The script clearly distinguished the more luxurious DeVille from the plainer club coupe, a distinction not emphasized in 1950. The Coupe DeVille, like the Convertible Coupe, was an exclusive Series 62 offering. Hydra-Matic drive was regular equipment on all Series 62 models (with a new type dial) and power windows were standard in the Convertible and Coupe DeVille. Only slightly more than 6,000 convertibles were built, while Coupe DeVille production shot up to over 10,000 units.

SERIES 62

Model Number	Body/Style Number	Body Type & Seating	Factory Price	Shipping Weight	Production Total
51-62	6219	4D Sedan-5P	3,528	4,102	54,596
51-62	6219	4D Export Sedan-5P	—	—	756
51-62	6237	2D Club Coupe-5P	3,436	3,993	10,132
51-62	6237DX	2D Coupe DeVille-5P	3,843	4,074	10,241
51-62	6267	2D ConvertibleCoupe-5P	3,987	4,316	6,117
51-62	126	Chassis only	—	—	2

SERIES 60 SPECIAL FLEETWOOD — V-8

The 60 Special Fleetwood sedan was facelifted to conform with the minor changes in other models. Eight vertical chrome louvers on the forward edge of the rear fenders continued to identify this car. All 1951 Cadillacs with full wheel discs featured a new type design lacking the popular Sombrero look. Hydra-Matic and power windows were standard on Sixty Specials. Despite a substantial price increase, the 60 Special also enjoyed a production increase to 18,631 units for the model year. Part of the 60 Special's popularity rise in 1951 may have been due to a combination of social changes and a well-timed advertising program. This was the start of the two-car-family era in America and many 1951 Cadillac ads were designed to sell cars to upscale homemakers.

SERIES 60 SPECIAL FLEETWOOD

Model Number	Body/Style Number	Body Type & Seating	Factory Price	Shipping Weight	Production Total
51-60	6019	4D Sedan-5P	4,142	4,136	18,631

SERIES 75 FLEETWOOD — V-8

The Series 75 Fleetwood models were also facelifted to conform to the minor changes seen in other lines. Jump seats were used in both the seven-passenger sedan and Imperial limousine. Hydra-Matic drive was optional and hydraulic window lifts were standard. The same assortment of large Fleetwood 75 series sedans also returned in 1951. They had a 146-3/4-inch wheelbase and 236-1/4-inch overall length. Business Sedans were built in limited numbers on a special order basis. The Business Sedans became funeral cars, commercial limousines and taxis. The chassis-only were used to build ambulances, funeral vehicles and station buses.

SERIES 75 FLEETWOOD

Model Number	Body/Style Number	Body Type & Seating	Factory Price	Shipping Weight	Production Total
51-75	7523X	4D Sedan-8P	5,200	4,555	1,090
51-75	7533X	4D Imperial Sedan-8P	5,405	4,586	1,085
51-75	7523L	4D Business Sedan-8P	—	—	30
51-75	86	Commercial chassis	—	—	2,960

ENGINE

Overhead valves. Cast iron block. Displacement: 331-cid. Bore and Stroke: 3-13/16 x 3-5/8 inches. Compression ratio: 7.5:1. Brake hp: 160 at 3800 rpm. Taxable hp: 46.5. Torque: 312 at 1800 rpm. Five main bearings. Hydraulic valve lifters. Crankcase capacity: 5 qt. (Add 1 qt. if new filter installed). Cooling system capacity: 18 qt. (add 1 qt. for heater). Carburetor: Carter WCD two-barrel Model 845-S or Rochester BB two-barrel Model 7004200.

CHASSIS

(Series 61) Wheelbase: 122 inches. Overall length: 211-1/2 inches. Width: 80-1/8 inches. Height: 62 inches. Front tread: 59 inches. Rear tread: 63 inches. Tires: 8.00 x 15.

(Series 62) Wheelbase: 126 inches. Overall length: 215-1/2 inches. Width: 80-1/8 inches. Height: 62-11/16 inches. Front tread: 59 inches. Rear tread: 63 inches. Tires: 8.00 x 15.

(Series 60S) Wheelbase: 130 inches. Overall length: 224-1/2 inches. Width: 80-1/8 inches. Height: 62-11/16 inches. Front tread: 59 inches. Rear tread: 63 inches. Tires: 8.00 x 15.

(Series 75) Wheelbase: 146-3/4. Overall length: 236-1/4 inches. Width: 80-1/8 inches. Height: 64-1/16 inches. Front tread: 59 inches. Rear tread: 63 inches. Tires: 8.20 x 15.

OPTIONS

Hydra-Matic Drive on Series 61 and 75 ($186). Power windows (specific models). Heating and ventilating system. Radio and antenna. Chrome wheel discs. Windshield washers. Fog lights. White sidewall tires (availability limited).

HISTORICAL

Cadillac retained its position as America's No. 1 luxury carmaker in 1951. The approximately 1,700 Cadillac dealers across the country sold 1.9 percent of all American cars and 4.6 percent of all General Motors cars. At the end of 1951, with National Production Agency controls having been tightened up, Cadillac had a backlog of 88,000 unfilled new-car orders. By December 31, 1951, the company had recorded its second-best year in history. Calendar-year production was 103,266 cars, compared to 110,535 the previous season. However, Cadillac's market share rose to 1.93 percent in 1951. Cadillac also built 3.9 percent of all convertibles made in the U.S. and four percent of all two-door hardtops. On a model-year basis, the total included 2,205 Fleetwoods, 110,340 Cadillacs and 2,960 Fleetwood 75 commercial chassis. All of these production totals were records for Cadillac. The Series 61 line was discontinued in the middle of the year. On November 27, 1951, the 300,000th Cadillac overhead-valve V-8 was produced. In sports-car circles, the powerful Cadillac V-8 wound up under the bonnet of the Cadillac-Allard made by Englishman Sydney J. Allard. Cadillac got some military orders to make up for lost car sales. It produced Walker Bulldog light tanks, as well as spare parts for Cadillac-built World War II-era M-24 tanks that were still being used by the U.S. Army. During calendar-year 1951, Cadillac installed 100,702 Hydra-Matic Drive units and built its 448,229th Hydra-Matic transmission.

1951 Cadillac, Series 62, convertible

1951 Cadillac, Series 75, limousine

1952

OVERVIEW

Cadillac observed its 50th birthday in 1952 and the new cars introduced on January 22, 1952 were called "Golden Anniversary" models. Small styling changes, but bigger engineering improvements were the order of the day. The overhead-valve V-8 got a four-barrel carburetor, a new free-flowing intake manifold, larger exhaust valves and dual-exhaust manifolds. A new type of Hydra-Matic transmission with two drive positions was standard in all models except Fleetwood 75s. One drive position was for operation on open roads and the other was for use for driving on congested city streets or in mountains. The first went through three gear ratios and the other went through four. Saginaw power steering was a new option. The hydraulic assist took over when three or more pounds of "pull" were exerted on the steering wheel. Ads said power steering eliminated up to 75 percent of normal steering effort. Also new was a 12-volt electrical system. A special Golden Anniversary show car was the prototype for the limited-production 1953 Eldorado. Its features included gold trim, an aircraft-type crash pad, jet-like rear fender air scoops and dual exhaust openings in the rear bumper, a specially-designed vertical-pillar windshield housing and

Above: **1952 Cadillac, Series 75, Limousine**

Pepper Red leather upholstery. A second 1952 show car seen this year was the Townsman, a gussied-up version of the 60 Special sedan that also had links to the 50-years celebration. Finished in glistening Nubian Black lacquer, the Townsman was crowned with a soft, gold-hued top of linen-grained, coated fabric mounted over felt padding. Framing the golden top were moldings of highly polished stainless steel. Crested emblems of gold metallic thread were woven into the Jacquard cloth interior on which the Cadillac crest was reproduced in a rich Deauville (golden beige) nylon. It took a good eye to spot design revisions made to the production-type Cadillacs for 1952. Instead of miniature egg-crate grilles below the headlights, there were now solid trim plates with small, winged emblems in the same position. The V-shaped hood and deck emblems were done as gold castings to commemorate the 50th anniversary. At the rear, the directional and back-up lights were built into the taillights. Cadillacs got four mufflers and tailpipes that exited through slits in the rear bumper.

I.D. DATA

Serial numbers and engine numbers were again one and the same. They appeared on the right-hand side of the crankcase above the water pump and on the right frame side bar behind the engine support. The first two symbols were "52" for 1952. The next two symbols indicated the series as

follows: "62," "60S," or "75." The remaining digits represented the consecutive unit number and began with 00000 for all series. All series had the same ending number.

SERIES 62 — V-8

With the 61 Series dropped, the Cadillac 62 became the base car line. It contained the same four body styles as in 1951. The 62s could be identified by the Cadillac crest over a broad "V" on the trunk lid. The Series 62 sedan was also characterized by a distinct, higher rear deck lid contour. This provided additional luggage space. The sedan was five inches shorter than other body styles. The Coupe DeVille again had a script nameplate on the rear roof pillar. New standard equipment included a self-winding clock, dual-range Hydra-Matic Drive, improved direction signal indicators, glare-proof mirrors, stannate treated pistons, four-barrel carburetion and all other features seen the previous year. Hydraulic window lifts remained as regular equipment on the Series 62 Convertible and the Coupe DeVille.

SERIES 62

Model Number	Body/Style Number	Body Type & Seating	Factory Price	Shipping Weight	Production Total
52-62	6219	4D Sedan-5P	3,636	4,151	42,625
52-62	6237	2D Club Coupe-5P	3,542	4,174	10,065
52-62	6237DX	2D Coupe DeVille-5P	3,962	4,205	11,165
52-62	6267X	2D Convertible Coupe-5P	4,110	4,419	6,400

SERIES SIXTY SPECIAL FLEETWOOD — V-8

A "Sixty-Special" script on the trunk identified the 1952 model of the same name. It had the same general styling changes seen in other lines, plus minor trim and appointment variations. For example, the word "Fleetwood" appeared on the rear deck lid (instead of a Cadillac crest). Eight vertical rear fender louvers were seen again. Hydra-Matic Drive and hydraulically-operated power window lifts were standard. A steep increase was put into effect and production tapered off somewhat.

SERIES SIXTY SPECIAL FLEETWOOD

Model Number	Body/Style Number	Body Type & Seating	Factory Price	Shipping Weight	Production Total
52-60	6019	4D Sedan-5P	4,720	4,258	16,110

SERIES 75 FLEETWOOD — V-8

Styling changes for the big Fleetwood 75 series conformed to the year's "Golden Anniversary" theme. There were two models, both using the extra-long General Motors "D" body shell. The seven-passenger sedan and the limousine had jump seats and the limousine had a division window separating the driver and passenger compartments. Equipment features were the same as before and no business sedans were built.

SERIES 75 FLEETWOOD

Model Number	Body/Style Number	Body Type & Seating	Factory Price	Shipping Weight	Production Total
52-75	7523X	4D Sedan-8P	5,361	4,699	1,400
52-75	7533X	4D Imperial Sedan-8P	5,572	4,734	800
52-76	86	Commercial chassis	—	—	1,694

ENGINE

Overhead valves. Cast iron block. Displacement: 331-cid. Bore and Stroke: 3-13/16 x 3-5/8 inches. Compression ratio: 7.5:1. Brake hp: 190 at 4000 rpm. Taxable hp: 46.5. Torque: 322 at 2400 rpm. Five main bearings. Hydraulic valve lifters. Crankcase capacity: 5 qt. (Add 1 qt. if new filter installed). Cooling system capacity: 18 qt. (add 1 qt. for heater). Carburetor: Carter WFCB four-barrel Model 896-S or Rochester 4GC four-barrel Model 7004500.

CHASSIS

(Series 62) Wheelbase: 126 inches. Overall length: 215-1/2 inches. Width: 80-1/8 inches. Height: 62-11/16 inches. Front tread: 59 inches. Rear tread: 63 inches. Tires: 8.00 x 15.

(Series 60S) Wheelbase: 130 inches. Overall length: 224-1/2 inches. Width: 80-1/8 inches. Height: 62-11/16 inches. Front tread: 59 inches. Rear tread: 63 inches. Tires: 8.00 x 15.

(Series 75) Wheelbase: 146-3/4. Overall length: 236-1/4 inches. Width: 80-1/8 inches. Height: 64-1/16 inches. Front tread: 59 inches. Rear tread: 63 inches. Tires: 8.20 x 15.

OPTIONS

Hydra-Matic Drive on Series 75 ($186). Wheel discs ($28). Windshield washer ($11). Oil filter ($11). Fog lights ($37). License frames ($4). Outside mirror ($6). Vanity mirror ($2). E-Z-Eye glass ($46). Heater and blower ($114). Push-button radio and rear speaker ($112). Signal-seeking radio and rear speaker ($129). Power steering ($198). Autronic Eye headlight beam control ($53). White sidewall tires Series 62 and 60S ($34). Automatic window regulators ($139). Wheel trim rings ($11).

HISTORICAL

Cadillac had a successful anniversary season, anchoring its hold on the top position in luxury-car sales. Its calendar-year output dropped six percent to 96,850 cars, but that had to be measured against an eight and one-half percent drop for that segment of the market in total. Cadillac's 35.9 percent share of the luxury market was a half-percent gain. Model-year production included 2,200 Fleetwood 75 cars, 1,694 Fleetwood 75 commercial chassis and 90,715 other Cadillacs. Cadillac promoted the 1952 model as a "Cadillac Among Cadillacs" with a lineup that climaxed 50 years of progress. The 1,300,000th Cadillac of all time was built.

1953

OVERVIEW

When it announced its 1953 models, Cadillac led the American automobile industry in power with its 210-hp V-8. "The year 1953 marks the beginning of Cadillac's second half-century of progress in the automotive world," said an advertisement for the Sixty Special. "The new 1953 Cadillacs, now on display, represent one of the greatest strides forward in Cadillac history. Numerous changes in styling have made them unbelievably beautiful . . . and gorgeous new interiors, together with a wonderful new Cadillac Air Conditioner, offer unprecedented luxury and comfort." Most collectors consider 1953 styling and technical changes were minor. On April 16, 1953, Cadillac announced that Hydra-Matic Drive would be standard in all models but a fire in the Livonia, Michigan, transmission plant on August 12, 1953, forced Cadillac to stop building cars. About 80 percent of its workforce was laid off for three weeks. On September 8, all 10,000 Cadillac assembly line employees began building Cadillacs with Buick Dynaflow transmissions. Production of such cars amounted to some 19,000 vehicles. Cadillac produced its 100,000th car of the year on December 1, 1953. On December 10, 1953, Cadillac changed over to 1954

Above: **1953 Cadillac, Series 62, sedan**

Al Larson

production. Despite Korean War production controls and the limited number built after the transmission plant fire, 1953 was still a Cadillac high note.

I.D. DATA

Serial numbers and engine numbers were again one and the same. They appeared on the right-hand side of the crankcase above the water pump and on the right frame side bar behind the engine support. The first two symbols were "53" for 1953. The next two symbols indicated the series as follows: "62," "60," or "75." The remaining digits represented the consecutive unit number and began with 00000 for all series. All series had the same ending number, which would be misinterpreted if listed.

SERIES 62—V-8

The front grille was redesigned and had a heavier integral bumper and bumper guards. These new "Dagmars" were gigantic. And smaller versions protected the rear bumper. The parking lights were mounted directly under the headlights, in ribbed panels that matched the wraparound grille extensions. The headlights had chrome-plated "eyebrow" type doors. At the rear was a one-piece window without division bars. The winged Golden Anniversary emblems used in 1952 were gone. New wheel covers appeared. They had a fuller outer edge and a dished

center with the Cadillac medallion. Series 62 models were identified by non-louvered rear fenders, the use of thin bright metal underscores on the bottom rear of the cars only and the decoration of both hood and deck lid with Cadillac crests and V-shaped ornaments. Series 62 sedan bodies were five inches shorter than the other body styles. A Coupe DeVille roof pillar script was seen again on the luxury hardtop. Other standard equipment on 1953 Cadillacs included "Knee-Action" independent front suspension, a one-piece windshield, oversize brakes, an automatic choke, a glare-proof mirror, a self-winding clock, a four-barrel carburetor, oil bath air cleaner and a mechanical fuel pump. Options included power steering, fog lights, E-Z-Eye tinted glass, air conditioning (introduced in April), wire wheels, a radio and white sidewall tires. The other body styles in this series were the Sedan, the Hardtop Coupe, the Coupe DeVille Hardtop Coupe and the regular Series 62 Convertible. All remained on a 126-inch wheelbase with the sedan measuring 215-13/16 inches end-to-end and the two-doors being five inches longer. Non-Eldorado prices started at $3,571 and ranged to $4,144 for the convertible. The Eldorado in the showroom did help sales, especially in the case of the convertibles. The 62s had a narrow body bumper strip on the front fender and door and the V-with-Cadillac-crest trunk lid treatment. The Coupe DeVille wore its name on each chrome-plated rear roof pillar.

SERIES 62

Model Number	Body/Style Number	Body Type & Seating	Factory Price	Shipping Weight	Production Total
53-62	6219(X)	4D Sedan-5P	3,666	4,201	47,316
53-62	6219(X)	4D Export Sedan-5P	3,666	4,201	324
53-62	6237(X)	2D Coupe-5P	3,571	4,189	14,353
53-62	6237DX	2D Coupe DeVille-5P	3,995	4,252	14,550
53-62	6267X	2D Convertible Coupe-5P	4,144	4,476	8,367
53-62	62	Chassis only	—	—	4

SERIES 62 ELDORADO SPECIAL—V-8

The Eldorado luxury convertible was added to the line as a one-model sub-series of the 62 lineup. A full assortment of Deluxe accessories, including wire wheels, were standard on this specialty car, which introduced the wraparound windshield for production models. The limited-edition Eldorado convertible had additional styling updates including a lowered wraparound windshield, cut-down door sills and a flush-fitting metal tonneau cover that hid the lowered convertible top entirely. Laced wire wheels were standard equipment along with just about every option you could fit on one car, except air conditioning. No wonder it cost $7,750 and only 532 were built. Like Chevrolet's Corvette, the Cadillac Eldorado was a dream car brought to life. As such, it was never intended as a volume-production model, but rather as a publicity-getter that would pull the curious into Cadillac showrooms where salesmen could pounce on them and sell them a more practical Cadillac. It was the "Let's-go-see-the-

dream-car-down-the-street," approach to automotive marketing. There was no special Eldorado V-8 in 1953. The enriched ragtop used the same improved 331-cid V-8 the other Cadillacs relied on. This engine did have an 8.25:1 compression ratio that helped it crank up 210 hp at 4150 rpm, a bit more than in 1952. The four-barrel carburetors used were a Carter WFCB or a Rochester 4GC. An improved dual-range Hydra-Matic Drive was again standard in 62s and 60 Specials—at least before the Hydra-Matic fire. It was smoother, quieter and more efficient than the 1952 version.

SERIES 62SX ELDORADO SPECIAL

Model Number	Body/Style Number	Body Type & Seating	Factory Price	Shipping Weight	Production Total
53-62	6267SX	2D SportConvertible Coupe-5P	7,750	4,799	532

SERIES SIXTY SPECIAL FLEETWOOD—V-8

A unique decoration on the Sixty Special was a wide rocker sill molding. The traditional (for this car) rear fender hash marks and the Fleetwood signature on the trunk lid were other identifiers. Narrow body bumper strips decorated the front fenders and doors of this 130-inch-wheelbase model, too. An even 20,000 examples rolled out the factory gates, which was a nice 25 percent jump for the season. The Sixty Special had particularly wide doors.

SERIES SIXTY SPECIAL FLEETWOOD

Model Number	Body/Style Number	Body Type & Seating	Factory Price	Shipping Weight	Production Total
53-60	6019X	4D Sedan-5P	4,305	4,337	20,000

SERIES 75 FLEETWOOD—V-8

The Fleetwood 75 series again offered a large limousine with a glass dividing partition and jump seats and a large sedan with jump seats only. Both long-wheelbase models were now called 8-passenger, rather than 7-passenger, cars. The Limousine was known as the Imperial Sedan, a name that dated back to the World War I era, when the previously-used term Berline lost favor due to its Germanic roots. The older term was derived from the city of Berlin, in Germany. The prices of both Fleetwood 75s were raised to include Hydra-Matic Drive. Styling facelifts on the cars in the 75 Fleetwood line conformed to those seen on other models. Appearance features and equipment were about the same as in previous years.

SERIES 75 FLEETWOOD

Model Number	Body/Style Number	Body Type & Seating	Factory Price	Shipping Weight	Production Total
53-75	7523X	4D Sedan-8P	5,604	4,801	1,435
53-75	7533X	4D Imperial Sedan-8P	5,818	4,853	765
53-86	8680S	Commercial chassis	—	—	2,005

ENGINE

Overhead valves. Cast iron block. Displacement: 331-cid. Bore and Stroke: 3-13/16 x 3-5/8 inches. Compression

ratio: 8.25:1. Brake hp: 210 at 4150 rpm. Taxable hp: 46.5. Torque: 330 at 2700 rpm. Five main bearings. Hydraulic valve lifters. Crankcase capacity: 5 qt. (Add 1 qt. if new filter installed). Cooling system capacity: 19.75 qt. (add 1 qt. for heater). Carburetor: (Hydra-Matic) Carter WFCB four-barrel Model 2005-S or Rochester 4GC four-barrel Model 7005100; (Dynaflow) Carter WFCB four-barrel Model 2088-S or Model 2119-S or Rochester 4GC four-barrel Model 7006215.

CHASSIS

(Series 62) Wheelbase: 126 inches. Overall length: (Model 6219) 215-1/2, (Other models) 220-13/16 inches. Width: 80-7/64 inches. Height: 62-11/16 inches. Front tread: 59-1/8 inches. Rear tread: 63-7/64 inches. Tires: 8.00 x 15. Dual exhaust system standard. Rear axle ratio: 3.07:1.

(Series 60S) Wheelbase: 130 inches. Overall length: 224-13/16 inches. Width: 80-7/64 inches. Height: 62-11/16 inches. Front tread: 59-1/8 inches. Rear tread: 63-7/64 inches. Tires: 8.00 x 15. Dual exhaust system standard. Rear axle ratio: 3.07:1.

(Series 75) Wheelbase: 146-3/4. Overall length: 236-1/4 inches. Width: 80-7/64 inches. Height: 64-1/16 inches. Front tread: 59-1/8 inches. Rear tread: 63-7/64 inches. Tires: 8.20 x 15. Dual exhaust system standard. Rear axle ratio: 3.77:1.

OPTIONS

Hydra-Matic Drive on Series 75 ($186). Hydraulic window lifts optional on some Series 62 models. Heating and ventilation system ($199). Power steering ($177). Signal-seeking radio with preselector and antenna ($132).

Remote control signal-seeking radio with preselector and antenna ($214). Five white sidewall tires ($48 exchange). Tinted E-Z-Eye glass ($46). Autronic Eye automatic headlight beam control ($53). Chrome wire wheels ($325). Air conditioning ($620). 8.20 x 15 tires (except standard on convertibles and Series 75 models). Other standard GM accessories.

HISTORICAL

Calendar-year production of 103,538 cars (102,500 with automatic transmission) was insufficient to fulfill all customer orders and Cadillac ended the year with a backlog. Model-year production had been the highest since 1951, with 2,201 Fleetwood 75 sedans and Imperial sedans, 2,005 Fleetwood 75 commercial chassis and 109,657 other Cadillacs produced. Cadillac reported that 95 percent of those cars had power steering and 10 percent had air conditioning. The futuristic Cadillac LeMans show car convertible was displayed this year and would heavily influence the 1954 Eldorado styling. It had a special 270-hp V-8 with dual four-barrel carburetors and a fiberglass body. Also, 28,000 Cadillacs were built with Buick Dynaflow transmissions after GM's Hydra-Matic plant burned to the ground. Cadillac introduced two dream cars at the General Motors Motorama on January 16, 1953. The first, the Orléans, previewed many 1954-1956 Cadillac styling features, such as the Panoramic windshield. The Orléans looked like a closed-bodied Eldorado. The Cadillac Le Mans was a precursor of the 1957-1958 Eldorado. This fiberglass-bodied two-seat convertible had 1954 Cadillac-style fenders, a low Panoramic windshield, open wheel housings and "turbine-fin" wheels. Cadillac built three slightly different Le Mans two-seaters.

1953 Cadillac, Eldorado convertible

1954

OVERVIEW

Cadillac pitched its 1954 model as "The Dream Car of twenty-five million!" An ad showing the year's non-DeVille hardtop coupe pointed out that "research among motorists indicates that literally tens of millions of people dream of owning this car." In the 1950s, heavyweight champion Sugar Ray Robinson and others, such as Marilyn Monroe and Frank Sinatra, were often seen driving Cadillac Eldorado convertibles. The 1954 Cadillac had the marque's first major restyling in four years. The headlights were mounted higher, with body-color sheet metal between them and the grille. The Cadillac front bumper had an inverted "gull-wing" appearance with trademark "Dagmar" type bumper guards tapered to a point and a chromed, horizontal grille blade connected them. Cadillac got a new-for-1954 feature, the Panoramic, wraparound-style windshield. A fashion hit on two-door hardtop models was a new "Florentine" rear window pillar that curved backwards towards the bottom. Cadillac's new rear-end styling featured new vertical bumper extensions housing round dual-exhaust openings. As Cadillac fought to maintain its edge in the luxury-car horsepower race, engineers pushed the envelope up to 230 hp still using the

Above: **1954 Cadillac, Series 62, Coupe de Ville**

same 8.25:1 compression ratio. Four-barrel carburetors made by either Carter or Rochester were used in mixed production. Hydra-Matic Drive was standard and Cadillac added power steering and windshield washers at no extra cost. All series were poised on three-inch longer wheelbases.

I.D. DATA

Serial numbers and engine numbers were again one and the same. They appeared on the right-hand side of the crankcase above the water pump and on the right frame side bar behind the engine support. The first two symbols were "54" for 1954. The next two symbols indicated series as follows: "62," "60," or "75." The remaining digits represented the consecutive unit number and began with 00000 for each series. All series had the same ending number, which would be misinterpreted if listed.

SERIES 62—V-8

The Series 62 chassis had a brand new, longer wheelbase. Series 62 identification features were the same as in the past. One identifying feature of this line was the lack of rear fender louvers. V-shaped ornaments and crests were used on the hood and deck and there were full-length body underscores in bright metal. On the Coupe DeVille, the model name was presented in a gold-colored script

on the rear window sill. In some catalog artwork, the Coupe DeVille was shown with body side moldings that extended about six inches further back on the doors than on the regular coupe, but this was incorrect. Both cars used the same molding running across the front fender and door and stopping about seven inches short of the rear door break line. The Coupe DeVille did have wider sill moldings. The Series 62 four-door sedan was seven inches shorter than other cars in this model range. There was an "export" version of the four-door sedan, but that was only a variation for overseas buyers. One chassis-only was sold and a Sedan DeVille (four-door hardtop) was built as a one-off creation. A special Eldorado coupe was also made for the president of Reynolds Aluminum Company.

SERIES 62

Model Number	Body/Style Number	Body Type & Seating	Factory Price	Shipping Weight	Production Total
54-62	6219(X)	4D Sedan-5P	3,933	4,330	33,845
54-82	8219(X)	4D Export Sedan-5P	3,933	4,330	408
54-62	6219SX	4D Sedan DeVille-5P	—	—	1
54-62	6237(X)	2D Coupe-5P	3,838	4,347	17,460
54-62	6237DX	2D Coupe DeVille-5P	4,261	4,409	17,170
54-62	6267X	2D Convertible Coupe-5P	4,404	4,598	6,310
54-62	62	Chassis only	—	—	1

SERIES 62SX ELDORADO SPECIAL–V-8

The 1954 Eldorado had golden identifying crests centered directly behind the air-slot fenderbreaks and wide, fluted beauty panels to decorate the lower rear bodysides. These panels were made of extruded aluminum and also appeared on a unique, one-of-a-kind Eldorado coupe built for the president of the Reynolds Aluminum Co. Also included on the production convertible were monogram plates on the doors, wire wheels and custom interior trimmings with the Cadillac crest embossed on the seat bolsters. Automatic windshield washers, power steering, 12-volt electrical system and aluminum alloy pistons made the long standard equipment list this year. The Eldorado as only available in Aztec Red, Azure Blue, Alpine White or Apollo Gold. The price was high and production was low.

ELDORADO SPECIAL

Model Number	Body/Style Number	Body Type & Seating	Factory Price	Shipping Weight	Production Total
54-62	6267SX	2D Sport Convertible Coupe-5P	5,738	4,809	2,150

SERIES SIXTY SPECIAL FLEETWOOD—V-8

The Sixty Special sedan had luxurious Fleetwood style interior appointments and its famous eight louvers ahead of each rear wheel opening. The Cadillac crest was positioned above the front "V," but the rear one had a Fleetwood script above it. A series of Cadillac advertisements that appeared this year pictured Cadillac 60 Special owners at balls, operas, grand hotels and mansions. Headlines such as "The one car that fits the occasion!" or "Where a Man is at his Best" or "You Could Guess What Car They Came In," made it clear that the 60 Special was — as another

ad stated — "Worth Its Price in Prestige." Wheelbase measurements returned to 133 inches for the first time since 1949. Also seen were a panoramic (wraparound) windshield, a new grille, longer more sweeping fenders and all other 1954-style appearance innovations. Cadillac's newly-expanded equipment list applied to the 60S sedan, too.

SERIES SIXTY SPECIAL FLEETWOOD

Model Number	Body/Style Number	Body Type & Seating	Factory Price	Shipping Weight	Production Total
54-60	6019X	4D Sedan-5P	4,683	4,490	16,200

SERIES 75 FLEETWOOD—V-8

The big Fleetwood "high headroom" job came as an eight-passenger Limousine with driver's partition or an eight-passenger Sedan without partition, both having jump seats. V-shaped ornaments appeared on the hood and deck lid with a Fleetwood script in the latter location. Wheelbase increased to 149.8 inches. Styling changes conformed with those seen on other lines.

SERIES 75 FLEETWOOD

Model Number	Body/Style Number	Body Type & Seating	Factory Price	Shipping Weight	Production Total
54-75	7523X	4D Sedan-8P	5,875	5,031	889
54-75	7533X	4D Imperial Sedan-8P	6,090	5,093	611
54-86	8680	Commercial chassis	—	—	1,635

ENGINE

Overhead valves. Cast iron block. Displacement: 331-cid. Bore and Stroke: 3-13/16 x 3-5/8 inches. Compression ratio: 8.25:1. Brake hp: 230 at 4400 rpm. Taxable hp: 46.5. Torque: 330 at 2700 rpm. Five main bearings. Hydraulic valve lifters. Crankcase capacity: 5 qt. (Add 1 qt. if new filter installed). Cooling system capacity: 19.75 qt. (add 1 qt. for heater). Carburetor: Carter WFCB four-barrel Models 2143-S, 2109-S or 2110-S or Rochester 4GC four-barrel Model 7006963 (with air conditioning) or Model 7006962 (without air conditioning).

CHASSIS

(Series 62) Wheelbase: 129 inches. Overall length: (Model 6219) 216.4 inches. Width: 79.6 inches. Height: 64.1 inches. Front tread: 60 inches. Rear tread: 63.1 inches. Tires: (Eldorado) 8.20 x 15, (Others) 8.00 x 15. Dual exhaust system standard. Rear axle ratio: 3.07:1

(Series 60S) Wheelbase: 133 inches. Overall length: 227.4 inches. Width: 79.6 inches. Height: 64.1 inches. Front tread: 60 inches. Rear tread: 63.1 inches. Tires: 8.00 x 15. Dual exhaust system standard. Rear axle ratio: 3.07:1.

(Series 75) Wheelbase: 149.8. Overall length: 237.2 inches. Width: 79.6 inches. Height: 66.2 inches. Front

tread: 60 inches. Rear tread: 63.2 inches. Tires: 8.20 x 15. Dual exhaust system standard. Rear axle ratio: 3.07:1.

OPTIONS

Hydra-Matic drive on Series 75 ($186). Power brakes ($48). Radio ($120). Heater ($129). Air-conditioning ($620). Power operated window and seat ($124). Chrome wire wheels ($325). White sidewall tires ($49 exchange). E-Z-Eye tinted glass. Autronic Eye automatic headlight dimmer. Vertical front seat adjuster. Horizontal front seat adjuster (standard on Coupe DeVille, convertible, Eldorado, Series 60S and Series 75). Optional tires (Series 60 and 62 except 6267S) 8.20 x 15 whitewall. Dual exhaust system standard. Rear axle ratios: (standard) 3.07:1, (standard with air conditioning, optional without) 3.36:1. Other standard GM options and accessories.

HISTORICAL

Assembly of Cadillac 1954 models began January 4, 1954, after a 25-day halt for changeover to new production specifications. Between the start of 1954 model assembly on January 4 and the changeover to 1955 models on October 4, Cadillac built 1,500 Fleetwood 75 cars, 1,635 Fleetwood 75 commercial chassis and 96,680 other models. On September 7, the 1,500,000th Cadillac was put together. Cadillac presented three dream cars at the 1954 GM Motorama. The El Camino Coupe, the LaEspada Roadster and the Park Avenue four-door luxury Sedan all contributed styling, design and engineering elements to future models.

1954 Cadillac, Eldorado convertible

Kris Kandler Owner: Everett Lindsay

1955

OVERVIEW

GM's entry in the fine-car field prospered in 1955. Weekly, monthly and quarterly sales and production records were snapped throughout the season and Cadillac ruled the luxury-car niche with a 44.8 percent market share. Chrysler Imperial (20.9 percent) and Buick Limited (20.6 percent) were far behind, while Lincoln (8.6 percent) and Packard (5.1 percent) were literally "out of the race." Cadillacs featured longer, lower bodies. Power steering was standard. The 1955 grille had the parking lights moved back into the ribbed panels directly below the headlights. Described as "super-powered" cars, the '55s came with up to 270 hp as an option. The familiar 331-cid V-8 now had a 9.0:1 compression ratio and produced 250 hp at 4600 rpm. The base V-8 had one carburetor and the "Eldorado" V-8 had two. The latter was an optional "Power Package" for other 1955 Cadillacs. The Eldorado sport convertible also featured chrome body belt moldings, a distinctive rear fender design with twin round taillights halfway up the fenders and flatter, pointed tail fins.

Above: **1955 Cadillac, Series 62, Coupe de Ville**

I.D. DATA

Serial numbers and engine numbers were the same again and were found in the same locations. The first two symbols were "55" to designate 1955 model production. The next two symbols indicated the series as follows: "62," "60," or "75." The remaining digits represented the consecutive unit number and began at 00000 for each series. All series had the same ending number, which would be misinterpreted if listed.

SERIES 62 — V-8

Models in the Series 62 range shared the new grille with wider spaces between the blades and the parking lights below the headlights. On 62s (as well as 60 Specials), the body side moldings now extended a little further back on the body, meeting the vertical air-vent moldings on the cars' rear quarters at right angles. On most models, these vertical moldings no longer ran downwards, from the right angle where they intersected, to the body sills. Such trim accentuated a character line in the sheet metal. The "Florentine Curve" rear window treatment was adopted for sedans. Three chrome moldings bordered the rear license plate on either side and deck lid decorations consisted of a V-shaped ornament and a Cadillac crest. The Coupe DeVille had a golden script nameplate at the upper body belt just forward of the rear window pillar. Tubeless tires

were a new feature throughout the line. As usual, Cadillac had the same arrangement of body types in each line. There were only fractional changes in body measurements. On all Series 62 models, the Cadillac name was seen in script on the front fender. Chrome beauty panels highlighted the body sills, fender skirts and rear quarter panels of all models, except the Eldorado convertible, which was quite distinctive this season. *Motor Trend* magazine reported fuel consumption figures of 12.9 miles per gallon (stop-and-go) for a Series 62 sedan with the standard 250-hp V-8.

SERIES 62

Model Number	Body/Style Number	Body Type & Seating	Factory Price	Shipping Weight	Production Total
55-62	6219(X)	4D Sedan-6P	3,977	4,375	44,904
55-62	6219(X)	4D Export Sedan-6P	3,977	4,375	396
55-62	6237(X)	2D Hardtop Coupe-6P	3,882	4,364	27,879
55-62	6237DX	2D Coupe DeVille-6P	4,305	4,428	33,300
55-62	6267X	2D Convertible Coupe-6P	4,448	4,631	8,150
55-62	62	Chassis only	—	—	7

SERIES 62SX ELDORADO — V-8

While other Cadillacs retained the blunt, rounded P-38-style tail fins of the past, the 1955 Eldorado Special Sport Convertible had new sharp-edged, "blade" type tail fins that came to a pointy angle at the rear, then dropped down to meet the dual round tail and back-up lights nestled in pods below each fin. The Eldorado's rear wheel openings were enlarged and only thin chrome moldings decorated them. The wheel openings carried no fender skirts, so that viewers could see the special, finned "Sabre" wheels. There were no rocker panel moldings or rear quarter extensions on this ragtop. The Eldorado's shelf-like rear bumper jutted out further than those of other models and it had "jet pod" exhaust outlets on either end. Blade-style bumper guards surrounded the license plate recess on the trunk-latching panel, which was decorated with three vertical moldings on each side. On the trunk was a large chrome "V" and the Eldorado name in script. The Eldorado was available only in four colors. Standard equipment on the Eldorado included customized interior and rear-end styling, a 270-hp V-8 with two four-barrel carburetors, a radio and antenna, a heater, power brakes, a power seat, power windows, whitewall tires, a metal tonneau cover, custom trim and ornamentation, individual circular tail and rear directional lights and saber-spoke wheels.

ELDORADO SPECIAL

Model Number	Body/Style Number	Body Type & Seating	Factory Price	Shipping Weight	Production Total
55-62	6267SX	2D Sport Convertible Coupe-5P	6,286	4,809	3,950

SERIES SIXTY SPECIAL FLEETWOOD — V-8

Cadillac must have made maximum profits on sales of 60 Specials, because this year it increased the number of chrome hash marks on the car's rear quarters. It now had 12 of the chrome ornaments to make it look even fancier. As on Series 62 models, the body side rub-rail moldings formed a right angle with the vertical trim on either the rear doors or rear fenders. A Fleetwood script decorated the rear deck. The special "glamour" upholstery used in the 60S was similar to the combination used in the Series 62 Coupe DeVille. It featured metallic-thread fabric with genuine leather trim. Standard equipment included an automatic choke, full-pressure lubrication, a 12-volt electrical system, a hypoid semi-floating rear axle, wheel discs and push-button automatic windshield washers. The advertising campaign, showing 60 Special owners in grand ballrooms and boardrooms, continued. "Styling the Whole World Admires" said one ad depicting a gold car. "Brings Out The Best In a Man!" was the pitch in another. This year, Cadillac managed to build over 2,000 more of these "small" Fleetwoods. The advertising must have helped sales a bit.

SERIES SIXTY SPECIAL FLEETWOOD

Model Number	Body/Style Number	Body Type & Seating	Factory Price	Shipping Weight	Production Total
55-60	6019X	4D Sedan-6P	4,728	4,545	18,300

SERIES 75 FLEETWOOD — V-8

The trim on long-wheelbase Fleetwood models was distinctive from that used on other lines and looked like that used on earlier Cadillacs. Most likely, it didn't pay to manufacture new moldings for such low-volume cars that were purchased by wealthy, conservative buyers who probably didn't care much for change anyway. A horizontal rub molding ran from the front parking light housings to the trailing edge of the front door and stopped. A full-length vertical air slot-style fenderbreak molding was placed directly behind the rear gap of the back doors. The two moldings did not meet at right angles. Other styling alterations, such as grille design changes, conformed to the new 1955 theme. A Fleetwood script appeared on the deck lid. The high-headroom appearance was seen again. Both models continued to feature auxiliary seats for extra passenger-carrying capacity. The Imperial Sedan-Limousine had a hydraulically-operated glass driver's partition.

SERIES 75 FLEETWOOD

Model Number	Body/Style Number	Body Type & Seating	Factory Price	Shipping Weight	Production Total
55-75	7523X	4D Sedan-8P	6,187	5,020	1,075
55-75	7533X	4D Imperial Sedan-8P	6,402	5,113	841
55-86	8680S	Commercial chassis	—	—	1,975

ENGINE
CADILLAC BASE V-8

Overhead valve. Cast iron block. Displacement: 331-cid. Bore and stroke: 3.81 x 3.63 inches. Compression ratio: 9.0:1. Brake hp: 250 at 4600 rpm. Five main bearings.

Hydraulic valve lifters. Carburetors: Carter WCFB four-barrel Models 2355S, 2354S, 2185S, 2186S, 2266S, 2267S and 2255, also Rochester 4GC four-barrel (less air conditioning) Model 7007970, (with air conditioning) Model 7007971.

ELDORADO BASE V-8; CADILLAC OPTIONAL V-8

The Eldorado engine had the following changes from the above specifications: Brake hp: 270 at 4800 rpm. Carburetors: Two Rochester 4GC four-barrels (front) Model 7007240, (rear, less air conditioning) Model 7007240, (rear, with air conditioning) Model 7007241.

CHASSIS

(Series 62) Wheelbase: 129 inches. Overall length: 216.3 inches. Width: 79.8 inches. Height: 64.1 inches. Front tread: 60 inches. Rear tread: 63.1 inches. Tires: (Eldorado) 8.20 x 15 whitewall, (Others) 8.00 x 15. Dual exhaust system standard. Rear axle ratio: 3.36:1.

(Series 60S) Wheelbase: 133 inches. Overall length: 227.3 inches. Width: 79.8 inches. Height: 64.1 inches. Front tread: 60 inches. Rear tread: 63.1 inches. Tires: 8.00 x 15. Dual exhaust system standard. Rear axle ratio: 3.36:1.

(Series 75) Wheelbase: 149.8. Overall length: 237.1 inches. Width: 79.8 inches. Height: 66.2 inches. Front tread: 60 inches. Rear tread: 63.2 inches. Tires: 8.20 x 15 six-ply. Dual exhaust system standard. Rear axle ratio: 3.36:1.

OPTIONS

Radio and antenna ($132). Heating and ventilation system ($129). Power brakes ($48). Four-way adjustable power seat ($70). Vertically adjustable power seat ($54). Power windows ($108). Air conditioning ($620). White sidewall tires. E-Z-Eye safety glass. Autronic Eye automatic headlight dimmer. Other standard GM options and accessories available. The 270-hp Eldorado engine was available as an optional "Power Package" in other models for $161 extra 3.07:1 rear axle ratio.

HISTORICAL

By the time the 1955 model assembly lines stopped in September, an unparalleled company total of 2,000 Fleetwood 75 eight-passenger sedans and limos, 1,975 Fleetwood 75 commercial chassis and 140,778 Cadillac 62s and 60 Specials were counted up for the calendar-year. In July 1954, Cadillac announced that it had purchased 6-1/2 acres of land to add to a 14-acre parcel it already owned across from its Detroit plant. In March 1955, it was reported that Cadillac would begin production of an ultra-plush 1956 model that would "make people forget about the Rolls-Royce." Initially expected to sell for about $8,500, annual output of 1,000 units was projected for this Eldorado Brougham hardtop sedan. Cadillac also decided to revive the LaSalle name in 1955—at least on a Motorama dream car in roadster and four-door hardtop versions. The Park Avenue sedan became the predecessor to the Eldorado Brougham and it appeared at the New York Motorama on January 19, 1955. It was built in less than 74 days. Another show car seen this year was the Celebrity hardtop coupe. The 1955 Eldorado is a certified Milestone Car.

1955 Cadillac, Series 62, coupe

1956

OVERVIEW

Cadillac did some heavy advertising in 1956 to bring new customers into Cadillac showrooms. Headlining 1956 changes were a 305-hp V-8, a brand-new Hydra-Matic transmission and two entirely new body styles. A new aluminum grille came with either gold or satin-finish and had the parking lights set into the bumper. On the driver's side of the grille was a Cadillac script. A larger displacement V-8 had a higher compression ratio and more power even in standard four-barrel form. The Eldorado came with a special version carrying two four-barrel carburetors (optional in other Cadillac and Fleetwood models). Cadillac's new "Controlled Coupling" Hydra-Matic Drive was said to be smoother and more durable. GM claimed it spent $35 million developing it.

I.D. DATA

Serial numbers and engine numbers were the same again and were found in the same locations. The first two symbols were "56" to designate 1956 model production. The next two symbols indicated the series as follows: "62," "60" or "75." The remaining digits represented the consecutive unit number and began at 00000 for each series. All series had the same ending number, which would be misinterpreted if listed.

SERIES 62—V-8

Cars in the 62 Series were on the same wheelbase as the 1955 versions, but about two inches shorter. The annual "beauty treatment" consisted of a new grille with a finer-textured insert and parking lights in the bumper, below the wing guards. Buyers were given a choice of a standard satin finish grille or optional gold finish, both selections decorated with Cadillac script on the left-hand side. The 62s had narrow, horizontal moldings on the guide-missile-shaped "projectile" bulges on the rear quarter panels. Behind these moldings were nine short vertical moldings that curved over the sculptured projectiles. The Coupe DeVille had a model nameplate and crest medallion on the front fenders, while other models—except for a new pillarless four-door Sedan DeVille—had the Cadillac crest only. As usual, the standard four-door 62 sedan was seven inches than the other cars in the same series.

Above: **1956 Cadillac, Series 62, Coupe de Ville**

SERIES 62

Model Number	Body/Style Number	Body Type & Seating	Factory Price	Shipping Weight	Production Total
56-62	6219(X)	4D Sedan-6P	4,241	4,430	26,222
56-62	6219(X)	4D Export Sedan-6P	4,241	4,430	444
56-62	6239DX	4D SedanDeVille-6P	4,698	4,550	41,732
56-62	6237(X)	2D Hardtop Coupe-6P	4,146	4,420	26,649

56-62	6237DX	2D Coupe DeVille-6P	4,569	4,445	25,086
56-62	6267X	2D ConvertibleCoupe-6P	4,711	4,645	8,300
56-62	62	Chassis only	—	—	19

SERIES 62SX/SERIES 62DX ELDORADO — V-8

Two additional models were now in the Eldorado sub-series. The Eldorado Seville two-door hardtop and Eldorado Convertible Biarritz were both priced the same. These cars had the blade-style tail fins instead of the smooth, rounded "slip stream" fins used on other Cadillacs and Fleetwoods. The special rear-end treatment introduced on the 1955 Eldorado was seen on both the hardtop and ragtop. Both shared a new twin-fin hood ornament and a ribbed chrome saddle molding that extended from the windshield to the rear window along the body belt line. The rear quarter panel moldings were thin and ran to the taillights. There were no vertical "rib" moldings. With their jet-pod bumpers, both Eldorados were fractionally longer than other 62s. Eldorados carried the Fleetwood name above the "V" emblem on the trunk. An Eldorado script appeared, with a fender crest on the luxury convertible, which also featured a twin-fin hood ornament.

ELDORADO (SUB-SERIES)

Model Number	Body/Style Number	Body Type & Seating	Factory Price	Shipping Weight	Production Total
56-62	6237DX	2D Hardtop Coupe Sev-6P	6,501	4,665	3,900
56-62	6267SX	2D Convertible Biarritz-6P	6,501	4,880	2,150

SERIES SIXTY SPECIAL FLEETWOOD—V-8

Model Number	Body/Style Number	Body Type & Seating	Factory Price	Shipping Weight	Production Total
56-62	6019X	4D Sedan-6P	6,019	4,992	17,000

SERIES 75 FLEETWOOD — V-8

Side trim on the long wheelbase Fleetwood models was about the same as 1955, except for the addition of exhaust extension moldings on the rear fender. This trim ran along a tapering conical flare from above the wheel housing to the rear bumper. A Fleetwood script appeared on the deck lid and limousine styling was seen again. Both models had auxiliary seats and the Imperial sedan again featured a glass driver's partition. The Fleetwood 75s retained the same wheelbase, but shrunk almost two inches in length due to bumper design changes. Models included a big jump-seat Sedans, an Imperial Limousine with division-window and a commercial chassis for hearse and ambulance builders.

SERIES 75 FLEETWOOD

Model Number	Body/Style Number	Body Type & Seating	Factory Price	Shipping Weight	Production Total
56-75	7523X	4D Sedan-8P	6,558	5,050	1,095
56-75	7533X	4D Imperial Sedan-8P	6,773	5,130	955
56-86	8680S	Commercial chassis	—	—	2,025

ENGINE

CADILLAC BASE V-8

Overhead valves. Cast iron block. Displacement: 365-cid. Bore and Stroke: 4.00 x 3.63 inches. Compression ratio: 9.75:1. Brake hp: 285 at 4600 rpm. Taxable hp: 51.2. Torque: 400 at 2800 rpm. Five main bearings. Hydraulic valve lifters. Crankcase capacity: 5 qt. (Add 1 qt. if new filter installed). Cooling system capacity: 17.5 qt. (add 2 qt. for heater). Carburetor: Carter WFCB four-barrel Models 2370S.

ELDORADO BASE V-8 ; CADILLAC OPTIONAL V-8

Overhead valves. Cast iron block. Displacement: 365-cid. Bore and Stroke: 4.00 x 3.63 inches. Compression ratio: 9.75:1. Brake hp: 305 at 4700 rpm. Taxable hp: 51.2. Torque: 400 at 3200 rpm. Five main bearings. Hydraulic valve lifters. Crankcase capacity: 5 qt. (Add 1 qt. if new filter installed). Cooling system capacity: 17.5 qt. (add 2 qt. for heater). Carburetor: Two Carter WFCB four-barrel Models 2371. Carburetor: Carter WFCB four-barrel Models

CHASSIS

(Series 62) Wheelbase: 129 inches. Overall length: 214.9 inches. Width: 80.1 inches. Height: 64.1 inches. Front tread: 60 inches. Rear tread: 63.2 inches. Tires: (Eldorado) 8.20 x 15 whitewall, (Others) 8.00 x 15. Dual exhaust system standard.

(Series 60S) Wheelbase: 133 inches. Overall length: 225.9 inches. Width: 80.1 inches. Height: 64.1 inches. Front tread: 60 inches. Rear tread: 63.2 inches. Tires: 8.00 x 15. Dual exhaust system standard.

(Series 75) Wheelbase: 149.8. Overall length: 235.7 inches. Width: 80.1 inches. Height: 66.2 inches. Front tread: 60 inches. Rear tread: 63.2 inches. Tires: 8.20 x 15 six-ply black sidewall. Dual exhaust system standard.

OPTIONS

Air conditioning. White sidewall tires. E-Z-Eye safety glass. Autronic Eye automatic headlight dimmer. Signal-seeking radio with preselector and antenna. Power window lifts (specific models). Gold finish grille. Two-way posture power seat ($81). Six-way power seat ($97). Other standard GM accessories available. (Note: Posture power adjustable seat on convertible, DeVilles and Series 60S only. Six-way seat on 62 coupe and sedan and standard for Eldorado). The 305-hp Eldorado engine was available in other models at extra cost.

HISTORICAL

"More owners of competitive make cars switched to Cadillac during the '56 model-year than ever before," said the Ward's 1957 Automotive Yearbook. "These buyers were largely responsible for the enormously successful '56 Cadillac automobile, which set records and sales and production." In all, the division turned out 154,631 cars, surpassing record-year 1955 by 10 percent. This was a very impressive performance in a year in which the bulk of U.S. automakers experienced a "leveling-off" period from 1955's all-time industry highs. The Cadillac Series 62 Sedan DeVille four-door hardtop and Eldorado Seville two-door hardtop were introduced to the public almost a month earlier than other models, on October 24, 1955. The remaining cars in the line were introduced the following month on November 18. Cadillac moved from 10th to 9th position in the American sales race. In 1956, five dream cars were exhibited in the GM Motorama. The Castilian had an "Old Spain" theme. The Gala or Wedding Car—a silver Series 62 Sedan DeVille with pearlescent white leather trim—was the second car. The Maharani, was a specially-appointed Sixty-Special with built-in kitchen sink and the Palomino was a specially-appointed Series 62 convertible with calfskin upholstery and Western-motif interior. The Eldorado Brougham Town Car was a fiberglass-bodied dream machine. This year's deliveries included the one-millionth Cadillac ever built.

1956 Cadillac, Series 62, convertible

1956 Cadillac, Fleetwood 60 Special, sedan

1956 Cadillac, Sedan de Ville, four-door hardtop

1956 Cadillac, Series 62, Coupe de Ville

1957

OVERVIEW

"Car-of-the-future" styling made the 1957 Cadillac stand out. It had a redesigned lower body and a restyled front end that included rubber bumper guard tips and dual, circular parking lights set into a lower bumper section. Hooded headlights were lifted directly from the 1954 Park Avenue show car, as were larger front wheel openings, curved roof lines and notched-back roof pillars. There was new trim on the sides of the bodies and a new, Eldorado-inspired dual taillight grouping. Underlying the new ground-hugging appearance was a tubular-center X-frame with greater torsional rigidity. By using different center frame sections, the wheelbases and overall lengths of specific Cadillac body styles were altered. There were 10 body styles and center posts were eliminated on all models except the Series 75 seven-passenger Sedan. A four-barrel V-8 was standard in most models, but a V-8 with dual four-barrel carburetors came in Eldorados. The base engine had a redesigned carburetor and larger combustion chambers.

I.D. DATA

Serial numbers and engine numbers were again the same. They appeared on a boss on the front right-hand face of the engine block, on the lubrication plate on the left front door pillar (1953-1957) and on the right frame side member behind the engine support. The first pair of symbols were "57" to designate the 1957 model-year. The next two symbols indicated series as follows: "62," "60," "70," and "75." The immediately following numbers, beginning at 00000 for each series, indicated the production sequence in consecutive order. Ending numbers were the same for all series since the engines were installed in mixed production fashion.

SERIES 62 — V-8

In the 62 lineup, including the Eldorado sub-series, three different overall measurements appeared on cars with matching wheelbases. The Sedan DeVille was bigger than "standard" models and the Eldorado Coupe Seville and Biarritz convertible were larger still. Identifying the "standard" 62 models were vertical bright metal moldings, just forward of the rear wheel openings, highlighted by seven horizontal windsplits. At the upper end this fenderbreak trim joined a horizontal molding that ran along a conical flare extending forward from the taillights. A crest medallion was seen on the forward angled rear fins. Coupe DeVilles and Sedan DeVilles had special nameplates on the front fenders. The export sedan was

shipped in completely-knocked-down (CKD) form for assembly by local labor in foreign countries.

SERIES 62

Model Number	Body/Style Number	Body Type & Seating	Factory Price	Shipping Weight	Production Total
57-62	6239(X)	4D Hardtop Sedan-6P	4,713	4,595	32,342
57-62	6239(X)	4D Export Sedan-6P	4,713	4,595	384
57-62	6239DX	4D DeVille Hardtop-6P	5,188	4,655	23,808
57-62	6237(X)	2D Hardtop Coupe-6P	4,609	4,565	25,120
57-62	6237DX	2D Coupe DeVille-6P	5,048	4,620	23,813
57-62	6267X	2D Convertible Coupe-6P	5,225	4,730	9,000
57-62	62	Chassis only	—	—	1

ELDORADO SPECIAL SERIES 62—V-8

Eldorados were further distinguished by the model name above a V-shaped rear deck ornament and on the front fenders. A three-section built-in front bumper was another exclusive trait of the ultra-luxury cars, which came with a long list of standard accessories. The rear fender and deck contour was sleekly rounded and the wheel housing was trimmed with broad, sculptured stainless steel beauty panels with chrome beauty panels below them. Also seen were pointed, "shark" style tail fins pointing towards the back of the car. The fins ran to a single round taillight. In the center of the rear was a V-shaped emblem with the Eldorado name above it. Below this was a chrome license-plate recess surrounded by rolled-under body-color body panels. The chrome bumpers swept around each rear body corner and incorporated two pods on either side. One pod held the round back-up light lens and the other was an exit for the exhaust pipe on each side of the car. The Eldorado Seville was a two-door hardtop and the Eldorado Biarritz was a convertible. It was possible to special order an Eldorado Sedan DeVille, but only four customers did. The Eldorado Seville and Biarritz shared the Series 62 wheelbase, but were longer with their larger rear bumper.

SERIES 62 ELDORADO SPECIALS

Model Number	Body/Style Number	Body Type & Seating	Factory Price	Shipping Weight	Production Total
57-62	6237SDX	2D Hardtop Coupe Sev-6P	7,286	4,810	2,100
57-62	6267SX	2D Biarritz Convertible-6P	7,286	4,930	1,800
57-62	6239SX	4D Sedan Seville-6P	—	—	4

SERIES SIXTY SPECIAL FLEETWOOD—V-8

The 60S Fleetwood long-deck four-door hardtop sedan featured a wide, ribbed bright metal fairing extending from the lower rear half of the door to the back bumper. A Fleetwood nameplate appeared on the rear deck lid, which also housed the back-up lights on this car. The Fleetwood Sixty Special was now a long-deck four-door hardtop, rather than a sedan. "Cadillac" in script appeared on the front fenders, although the deck lid still carried the Fleetwood name above the V-emblem. A bright, ribbed beauty panel decorated a section of the rear doors and the entire lower rear body quarters. The rectangular back-up

lights were built into the rear deck lid. As had been the case for several years, this model appeared in many of Cadillac's color advertisements.

SERIES SIXTY SPECIAL FLEETWOOD

Model Number	Body/Style Number	Body Type & Seating	Factory Price	Shipping Weight	Production Total
57-60	6039	4D Hardtop Sedan-6P	5,539	4,755	24,000

SERIES 70 ELDORADO BROUGHAM—V-8

Announced in December of 1956 and released around March of 1957, the Eldorado Brougham was a hand-built, limited-edition four-door Hardtop Sedan derived from the ultra-luxurious Park Avenue and Orleans show cars of 1953-1954. Designed by Ed Glowacke, the Brougham was the "Rolls-Royce" of Cadillacs and featured America's first completely pillarless four-door body styling. The Brougham was further distinguished by a brushed stainless steel roof, the first appearance of quad headlights and totally unique trim. The exterior ornamentation included wide, ribbed lower rear quarter beauty panels (extending along the full rocker sills) and a rectangularly sculptured side body "cove" highlighted by five horizontal windsplits on the rear doors. Tail-end styling treatments followed the Eldorado theme and "suicide" type mounting was used for the rear doors. Standard equipment included all possible accessories such as a 325-hp dual four-barrel V-8, air-suspension, low-profile tires with thin whitewalls, an automatic trunk lid opener, an automatic "memory" seat, Cruise Control, a high-pressure cooling system, polarized sun visors, a Signal-Seeking twin speaker radio, a silver magnetized glovebox, an Autronic-Eye automatic headlight dimmer, a drum-type electric clock, power windows, forged aluminum wheels and air conditioning. Buyers of Broughams had a choice of 44 full leather interior trim combinations and could select Mouton, Karakul or lambskin carpeting. Planned to be sold at about $8,500, the final price turned out to be $13,074. The Eldorado Brougham was GM's competition for the Lincoln-Continental Mark II. The Brougham's dual quad headlights were illegal in some states during 1957. The Brougham air suspension system proved unreliable and Cadillac later released a kit to convert cars to rear coil-spring suspension. Broughams with air suspension are rarer and more valuable today. The Brougham is a certified Milestone Car.

SERIES 70 ELDORADO BROUGHAM

Model Number	Body/Style Number	Body Type & Seating	Factory Price	Shipping Weight	Production Total
57-70	7059X	4D Hardtop Sedan-6P	13,074	5,315	400

SERIES 75 FLEETWOOD—V-8

Long wheelbase Cadillacs came in Fleetwood limousine or nine-passenger sedan configurations, both with auxiliary seats. Side trim was the same as on Series 62 models,

except that no Cadillac crest was used on the rear fins. For the first time ever, the big Fleetwood 75 sedans and limos were not the priciest Cadillacs. The seven-passenger sedan was a bit less expensive than the Imperial limousine, which had a divider. Production of the two models was 1,010 and 890 units, respectively. In addition, Cadillac did construct 2,169 Fleetwood 75 chassis for custom-made models, mostly Superior-Cadillac ambulances and funeral cars.

SERIES 75 FLEETWOOD

Model Number	Body/Style Number	Body Type & Seating	Factory Price	Shipping Weight	Production Total
57-75	7523X	4D Sedan-9P	7,348	5,340	1,010
57-75	7533X	4D Imperial Sedan-9P	7,586	5,390	890
57-86	8680S	Commercial chassis	—	—	2,169

ENGINE

CADILLAC (EXCEPT ELDORADO) BASE V-8

Overhead valves. Cast iron block. Displacement: 365-cid. Bore and Stroke: 4.00 x 3.625 inches. Compression ratio: 10.0:1. Brake hp: 300 at 4800 rpm. Taxable hp: 51.2. Torque: 400 at 3200 rpm. Five main bearings. Hydraulic valve lifters. Crankcase capacity: 5 qt. (Add 1 qt. if new filter installed). Cooling system capacity: 19.5 qt. (add 2 qt. for heater). Dual exhaust. Carburetor: Rochester four-barrel Model 7015701 or Carter WFCB four-barrel Model 2370-S.

ELDORADO BASE V-8

Overhead valves. Cast iron block. Displacement: 365-cid. Bore and Stroke: 4.00 x 3.625 inches. Compression ratio: 10.0:1. Brake hp: 325 at 4800 rpm. Taxable hp: 51.2. Torque: 400 at 3200 rpm. Five main bearings. Hydraulic valve lifters. Crankcase capacity: 5 qt. (Add 1 qt. if new filter installed). Cooling system capacity: 19.5 qt. (add 2 qt. for heater). Dual exhaust. Carburetor: Two Carter four barrels (front) Model 2584S; (rear) Model 2583S. Carburetor: Carter WFCB four-barrel Models 2370-S. The 325-hp Eldorado Brougham engine was available as an option on the Eldorado Seville and Biarritz only. In normal installations the front carburetor was changed to a Carter Model 258-S. When air conditioning was installed, the front carburetor was the same model used on the Brougham, which came with air conditioning as standard equipment.

CHASSIS

(Series 62) Wheelbase: 129 inches. Overall length: 215.9 inches. Width: 80 inches. Height: 61 inches. Front tread: 61 inches. Rear tread: 61 inches. Tires: (Eldorado) 8.20 x 15 whitewall, (Others) 8.00 x 15. Dual exhaust system standard.

(Series 60S) Wheelbase: 133 inches. Overall length: 224.4 inches. Width: 80 inches. Height: 61 inches. Front tread: 61 inches. Rear tread: 61 inches. Tires: 8.00 x 15. Dual exhaust system standard.

(Series 75) Wheelbase: 149.8. Overall length: 236.2 inches. Width: 80 inches. Height: 63.7 inches. Front tread: 61 inches. Rear tread: 61 inches. Tires: 8.20 x 15 six-ply black sidewall. Dual exhaust system standard.

OPTIONS

Hydra-Matic drive, power steering and power brakes were standard in all Cadillacs. Many models (designated by non-bracketed "X" suffix in charts above) also had standard power window lifts. Fore- and-Aft power seats were standard on the same models. Six-Way power seats were regularly featured on Eldorados and Sixty Specials. Air conditioning, radios, heaters, etc, were optional on most other models (standard in Brougham) along with regular GM factory-and-dealer-installed extras.

HISTORICAL

Cadillac's 1957 model-year started November 12, 1956 and saw the assembly of 146,840 cars. Calendar-year output of 153,236 was up nine percent from 1956 and only 98 cars short of the all-time record set in 1955. Cadillac ranked ninth in the U.S. industry. In May, Cadillac demonstrated the air suspension system it would introduce in 1958. Ball joint suspension was a new GM technical feature. GM design chief Harley J. Earl stated that the company's future car designs were going to be more in tune with the public. The 1957 models began a three-year binge of wild new Cadillac styling.

1957 Cadillac, Eldorado Seville, two-door hardtop

1957 Cadillac, Eldorado Biarritz, convertible

1958

OVERVIEW

Cadillacs for 1958 were basically carryover models with a facelift on all models but the Brougham. There was a new grille featuring multiple round "cleats" at the intersection of horizontal and vertical members. The grille insert was wider and the bumper guards were positioned lower to the parking lights. New dual headlights were seen throughout all lines and small chrome fins decorated the front fenders. The tailfins were less pronounced and trim items were revised.

I.D. DATA

Serial numbers now used a three symbol prefix. The first pair of numerical symbols "58" designated the 1958 model-year. A one-letter alphabetical code (included as part of model number in charts below) indicated model and series. Each prefix was followed by the consecutive unit number, which started at 000001 and up. The serial number was located at the front of the left-hand frame side bar. Engine serial numbers again matched and were found on the center left-hand side of the block above the oil pan.

Above: **1958 Cadillac, Series 62, four-door hardtop**

SERIES 62—V-8

The word Cadillac appeared, in block letters, on the fins of Series 62 base models. On the sides of the cars there were five longer horizontal windsplits ahead of the unskirted rear wheel housings. Front fender horizontal moldings with crests were placed above the windsplits, at the trailing edge. There was no rocker sill trim. The Convertible, Coupe DeVille and Sedan DeVille used solid metal trim on the lower half of the conical projectile flares on the rear quarters, while Series 62 Cadillacs had a thin ridge molding in the same location. All new was an extended-deck Series 62 sedan, which was 8.5 inches longer than other models.

SERIES 62

Model Number	Body/Style Number	Body Type & Seating	Factory Price	Shipping Weight	Production Total
58K-82	6239(X)	4D Hardtop Sedan-6P	4,891	4,675	13,335
58K-62	6239(X)	4D Export Sedan-6P	4,891	4,675	204
58N-62	6239E(X)	4D Ext Sedan-6P	5,079	4,770	20,952
58L-62	6239EDX	4D SedanDeVille-6P	5,497	4,855	23,989
58G-62	6237(X)	2D Hardtop Coupe-6P	4,784	4,630	18,736
58J-62	6237DX	2D Coupe DeVille-6P	5,231	4,705	18,414
58F-62	6267X	2D ConvertibleCoupe-6P	5,454	4,845	7,825
58-62	62	Chassis only	—	—	1

SERIES 62 ELDORADO SPECIAL—V-8

On Series 62 Eldorados, a V-shaped ornament and a model identification script were mounted to the rear deck lid. The two luxury Cadillacs also had 10 vertical

chevron slashes ahead of the open rear wheel housings and crest medallions on the flanks of tailfins. Broad, sculptured beauty panels decorated the lower rear quarters on Eldorados and extended around the wheel opening to stretch along the body sills.

SERIES 62 ELDORADO SPECIAL

Model Number	Body Style Number	Body Type & Seating	Factory Price	Shipping Weight	Production Total
58H-62	6237SDX	2D Hardtop Coupe Sev-6P	7,500	4,910	855
58E-62	6267SX	2D Biarritz Convertible-6P	7,00	5,070	815
58-62	6267SSX	2D SpecialEldorado Coupe-6P	—	—	1

SERIES SIXTY SPECIAL FLEETWOOD—V-8

The Sixty Special was distinctive and rich looking this year. Broad, ribbed stainless steel fairings decorated the entire rear quarter panel, below the conical flare. Even the fender skirts featured this type of trim, which extended fully forward along the body sills. A "Sixty Special" script appeared on the sides of the tail fins and a "Fleetwood" script nameplate adorned the rear deck lid. Standard equipment included Hydra-Matic Drive, power brakes, power steering, power windows and a Fore-and-Aft power front seat.

SERIES SIXTY SPECIAL FLEETWOOD

Model Number	Body/Style Number	Body Type & Seating	Factory Price	Shipping Weight	Production Total
58M-60	6039X	4D Hardtop Sedan-6P	6,232	4,930	12,900

SERIES 70 FLEETWOOD ELDORADO BROUGHAM—V-8

The major change for the Eldorado Brougham was seen inside the car. The interior upper door panels were now finished in leather instead of the metal finish used in 1957. New wheel covers also appeared. Forty-four trim combinations were available, along with 15 special monotone paint colors. This was the last year for domestic production of the hand-built Brougham at Cadillac's Detroit factory, as future manufacturing of the special bodies was to be transferred to Pininfarina, of Turin, Italy.

SERIES 70 FLEETWOOD ELDORADO BROUGHAM

Model Number	Body/Style Number	Body Type & Seating	Factory Price	Shipping Weight	Production Total
58P-70	7059X	4D Hardtop Sedan-6P	13,074	5,315	304

SERIES 75 FLEETWOOD—V-8

The limousine and nine-passenger long-wheelbase sedans were available once again, both with auxiliary seats. They carried the same basic side trim as Series 62 models.

SERIES 75 FLEETWOOD

Model Number	Body/Style Number	Body Type & Seating	Factory Price	Shipping Weight	Production Total
58R-75	7523X	4D Sedan-9P	8,460	5,360	802
58S-75	4533X	4D Imperial Sedan-9P	8,675	5,475	730
58-86	8680S	Commercial chassis	—	—	1,915

ENGINE

CADILLAC (EXCEPT ELDORADO) BASE V-8

Overhead valve. Cast iron block. Displacement: 365-cid. Bore and Stroke: 4.00 x 3.625 inches. Compression ratio: 10.25:1. Brake hp: 310 at 4800 rpm. Taxable hp: 51.2. Torque: 405 at 3100 rpm. Five main bearings. Hydraulic valve lifters. Crankcase capacity: 5 qt. (Add 1 qt. if new filter installed). Cooling system capacity: (Series 75) 22 qt.; (Series 60 and Series 62) 19.5 qt. (add 1 qt. for heater). Dual exhaust. Carburetor: Carter AFB four-barrel (without air conditioning) Model 2696S; (with air conditioning) Model 2697S-2802S. Alternate carburetor: Rochester 4GC (early production without air conditioning) Model 7012010; (late production without air conditioning) Model 7012910; (early production with air conditioning) Model 7012011; (late production with air conditioning) Model 7012811.

ELDORADO BASE V-8

Overhead valve. Cast iron block. Displacement: 365-cid. Bore and Stroke: 4.00 x 3.625 inches. Compression ratio: 10.25:1. Brake hp: 335 at 4800 rpm. Taxable hp: 51.2. Torque: 405 at 3400 rpm. Five main bearings. Hydraulic valve lifters. Crankcase capacity: 5 qt. (Add 1 qt. if new filter installed). Cooling system capacity: (Series 75) 22 qt.; (Series 60 and Series 62) 19.5 qt. (add 1 qt. for heater). Dual exhaust. Carburetion: Rochester 2GC Triple Power Pack (front carburetor with or without air conditioning) Model 7012201 used in early production and Model 7012901 used in late production; (center carburetor without air conditioning) Model 7012202 used in early production and Model 7012902 used in late production; (center carburetor with air conditioning) Model 7012205 used in early production and Model 7012905 used in late production; (rear carburetor with or without air conditioning) Model 7012203 used in early production and Model 7012903 used in late production.

CHASSIS

(Series 62) Wheelbase: 129.5 inches. Overall length: (58K) 216.8 inches, (58G, 58J and 58F) 221.8 inches, (58N and 58L) 225.3 inches, (58M) 225.3 inches, (58H and 58E) 223.4 inches. Width: 80 inches. Height: 59.1 inches. Front tread: 61 inches. Rear tread: 61 inches. Tires: (Eldorado) 8.20 x 15 whitewall, (Others) 8.00 x 15. Dual exhaust system standard.

(Series 60S) Wheelbase: 133 inches. Overall length: 224.4 inches. Width: 80 inches. Height: 59.1 inches. Front tread: 61 inches. Rear tread: 61 inches. Tires: 8.00 x 15. Dual exhaust system standard.

(Series 70S) Wheelbase: 126 inches. Overall length: 216.3 inches. Width: 80 inches. Front tread: 61 inches. Rear tread: 61 inches. Tires: 8.40 x 15 high-speed thin whitewall. Dual exhaust system standard.

(Series 75) Wheelbase: 149.7. Overall length: 237.1 inches. Width: 80 inches. Height: 61.6 inches. Front tread: 61 inches. Rear tread: 61 inches. Tires: 8.20 x 15 six-ply black sidewall. Dual exhaust system standard.

OPTIONS

Radio with antenna and rear speaker ($164). Radio with rear speaker and remote-control on Series 75 only ($246). Automatic heating system for Series 75 ($179), for other models ($129). Posture seat adjuster ($81). Six-Way seat adjuster ($103). Power window regulators ($108). E-Z-Eye Glass ($46). Fog lights ($41). Automatic headlight beam control ($48). Five sabre spoke wheels ($350). White sidewall 8.20 x 15 four-ply tires ($55). Gold finish grille on Eldorado (no charge), on other models ($27).

Four-door door guards ($7). Two-door door guards ($4). Remote control trunk lock ($43). License plate frame ($8). Air conditioning ($474). Series 75 air conditioner ($625). Eldorado engine in lower models ($134). Air suspension ($214). Electric door locks on coupes ($35), on sedans ($57). Local dealer options: Utility kit ($15). Monogram ($12). Blue Coral waxing ($25). Undercoating ($5). Lubrication agreement ($34).

HISTORICAL

Cadillac's 1958 model-year started November 13, 1957 and saw the assembly of 121,786 cars or 2.9 percent of total U.S. auto production. A total of 122,545 new-car registrations went to Cadillac. From the standpoint of market penetration, Cadillac established all-time records in 1958, both in price group and in the industry. The division captured 59 percent of all fine-car sales, compared to 47 percent in 1957. On February 21, 1958, it was announced that Cadillac had spent $20 million converting the former Hudson Motor Car Co. plant on the east side of Detroit to the fabrication of sheet metal parts. Five special Eldorado Biarritz convertibles were built with completely automatic top riser mechanisms and metal tonneaus. These cars had four-place bucket seating and custom leather interior trims. The 1958 Eldorado Brougham is a certified Milestone Car.

1958 Cadillac, Series 62, Coupe de Ville

1959

OVERVIEW

No single automotive design better characterizes the American automobile industry's late-1950s flamboyance than the 1959 Cadillac. All models incorporated large tailfins, twin bullet taillights, a choice of two distinctive roof lines and roof-pillar configurations, new jewel-like radiator grille patterns and matching deck-latch-lid beauty panels. A total of 13 cars were offered. Also available was a bare chassis for commercial-vehicle builders and an "export" version of the six-window Sedan that was shipped in CKD (Completely Knocked Down) form, to other countries for local assembly. Series 62 models, Eldorados and Sixty Specials shared a 130-inch wheelbase. Heights dropped more than three inches. Cadillac stroked the overhead-valve V-8 engine's displacement to 390 cubic inches and the compression ratio rose again. The Tri-Power Eldorado version was good for 345 hp and could be added to the other cars as an option. Other Cadillac selling points included Hydra-Matic Drive, a tubular-center X-frame and Magic-Mirror acrylic lacquer finish.

Above: **1959 Cadillac, Series 62, convertible**

I.D. DATA

The engine serial number system adopted in 1958 was used again with numbers in the same locations. The first pair of symbols changed to "59" to designate the 1959 model-year. The third symbol (a letter listed as a Body/Style Number suffix in charts below) identified model and series. Consecutive unit numbers began at 000001 and up.

SERIES 6200—V-8

The former Series 62 line was now commonly called the 6200 Series and was actually comprised of three sub-series, all with similar wheelbases and lengths. The five base models were identifiable by their straight body rub moldings, running from front wheel openings to back bumpers, with crest medallions below the tip of the spear. A one-deck jeweled rear grille insert was seen. Standard equipment included power brakes, power steering, automatic transmission, dual back-up lights, windshield washers, two-speed electric windshield wipers, full wheel discs, an outside rearview mirror, a vanity mirror and an oil filter. The Convertible also had power windows and a two-way power seat. Plain fender skirts covered the rear wheels. Series 62 Sedans were available in four-window (4W) and six-window (6W) configurations.

SERIES 6200

Model Number	Body/Style Number	Body Type & Seating	Factory Price	Shipping Weight	Production
59-62	6229K	4D 6W Sedan-6P	5,080	4,835	23,461
59-62	6229K	4D Export 6W Sedan-6P	5,080	4,835	60
59-62	6239A	4D 4W Sedan-6P	5,080	4,770	14,138
59-62	6237G	2D Hardtop Coupe-6P	4,892	4,690	21,947
59-62	6267F	2D Convertible Coupe-6P	5,455	4,855	11,130

DEVILLE SUB-SERIES 6300 — V-8

The DeVille models, two sedans and a coupe, had script nameplates on the rear fenders. This eliminated the need to use Cadillac crest medallions on the front fenders. Otherwise, these cars were trimmed like 6200s. Standard equipment included power brakes, power steering, automatic transmission, dual back-up lights, windshield washers, two-speed electric windshield wipers, full wheel discs, an outside rearview mirror, a vanity mirror, an oil filter, power windows and two-way power seats.

DEVILLE SUB-SERIES 6300

Model Number	Body/Style Number	Body Type & Seating	Factory Price	Shipping Weight	Production
59-63	6329L	4D 6W Sedan-6P	5,498	4,850	19,158
59-63	6339B	4D 4W Sedan-6P	5,498	4,825	12,308
59-63	6337J	2D Coupe-6P	5,252	4,720	21,924

SUB-SERIES 6400/6900 ELDORADO/BROUGHAM — V-8

As if to cause confusion, the 6400 Eldorado sub-series included two 6400 models (the Seville and Biarritz) and one 6900 model (the Brougham). All were characterized by a three-deck, jeweled, rear grille insert, but other trim and equipment features varied. The Seville and Biarritz had the Eldorado model name spelled out behind the front wheel openings and featured broad, full-length body sill highlights that curved over the rear fender profile and back along the upper beltline region. Standard equipment included power brakes, power steering, automatic transmission, two-speed electric windshield wipers, full wheel discs, an outside rearview mirror, a vanity mirror, an oil filter, power windows, two-way power seats, fog lights, a 345-hp V-8, a remote-control deck-lid release, a six-way power seat, air suspension, electric door locks and license frames. The Brougham was now an Italian-bodied, limited-production car. A vertical crest medallion with Brougham script plate appeared on the front fenders and a single, thin molding ran from front to rear along the mid-sides of the body. Styling predicted the 1960 themes used on other Cadillacs. The Brougham included cruise control, an Autronic Eye, air conditioning and E-Z-Eye glass.

SUB-SERIES 6400/6900 ELDORADO/BROUGHAM

Model Number	Body/Style Number	Body Type & Seating	Factory Price	Shipping Weight	Production
59-64	6437H	2D Seville Hardtop-6P	7,401	4,855	975
59-64	6467E	2D Biarritz Convertible-6P	7,401	5,060	1,320
59-69	6929P	4D Brougham Hardtop-6P	13,075	—	99

SERIES SIXTY SPECIAL FLEETWOOD — V-8

On the Fleetwood 60 Special lettering was used on the front fenders and on the trim strip crossing the bottom of the deck lid. A rear-facing, bullet-shaped, scoop decorated the rear doors and fenders and was trimmed by a similarly shaped body rub molding. Pillared, six-window styling was seen and rear wheels were skirted. Standard equipment included power brakes, power steering, automatic transmission, full wheel discs, power windows, two-way power seats, fog lights, a 345-hp V-8, a remote-control deck-lid release, a radio with an antenna and rear speaker, power vent windows, a six-way power seat, air suspension, electric door locks, license plate frames, power vent windows and dual outside rearview mirrors.

SERIES SIXTY SPECIAL FLEETWOOD

Model Number	Body/Style Number	Body Type & Seating	Factory Price	Shipping Weight	Production
59-60	6029M	4D Hardtop Sedan-6P	6,233	4,890	2,250

SERIES 6700 FLEETWOOD 75 — V-8

The long wheelbase Fleetwoods were still called Seventy-Fives, although a new numerical series designation was in official use. Production models again were a nine-passenger sedan and Imperial Sedan/Limousine with auxiliary jump seats. Fleetwood lettering appeared on the rear deck lid trim strip. Single side trim moldings extended from the front wheel housing to the rear of the car. Standard equipment included power brakes, power steering, automatic transmission, dual back-up lights, power windows, two-way power seats, a heater, fog lights, a 345-hp V-8, a radio with an antenna and rear speaker, power vent windows, a six-way power seat, air suspension, electric door locks, power vent windows and dual outside rearview mirrors.

SERIES 6700 FLEETWOOD 75

Model Number	Body/Style Number	Body Type & Seating	Factory Price	Shipping Weight	Production
59-67	6723R	4D Sedan-9P	9,533	5,490	710
59-67	6733S	4D Imperial Sedan-9P	9,748	5,570	690
59-68	6890	Commercial chassis	—	—	2,102

ENGINE

CADILLAC (EXCEPT ELDORADO) BASE V-8

Overhead valve. Cast iron block. Displacement: 390-cid. Bore and Stroke: 4.00 x 3.875 inches. Compression ratio: 10.5:1. Brake hp: 325 at 4800 rpm. Taxable hp: 51.2. Torque: 430 at 3100 rpm. Five main bearings. Hydraulic valve lifters. Crankcase capacity: 5 qt. (Add 1 qt. if new filter installed). Cooling system capacity: (Series 60 and Series 62) 18.5 qt. without heater; 19.5 qt. with heater; (Series 67) 18.5 qt. without heater; 20.75 qt. with heater; (Series 69) 19.5 qt. with heater only. Dual exhaust. Carburetor: Carter AFB four-barrel (without air conditioning) Model 2814S; (with air conditioning) Model 2815S. Alternate

carburetor: Rochester 4GC (without air conditioning) Model 7013030; (with air conditioning) Model 7013031.

ELDORADO BASE V-8

Overhead valve. Cast iron block. Displacement: 390-cid. Bore and Stroke: 4.00 x 3.875 inches. Compression ratio: 10.5:1. Brake hp: 345 at 4800 rpm. Taxable hp: 51.2. Torque: 435 at 34000. Five main bearings. Hydraulic valve lifters. Crankcase capacity: 5 qt. (Add 1 qt. if new filter installed). Cooling system capacity: (Series 63) 18.5 qt. without heater; 19.5 qt. with heater. Dual exhaust. Carburetion: Rochester 2GC Triple Power Pack (front carburetor with or without air conditioning) Model 7013033; (center carburetor without air conditioning) Model 7013034; (center carburetor with air conditioning) Model 7013037 used in early production; (rear carburetor with or without air conditioning) Model 7013035.

CHASSIS

(Series 62) Wheelbase: 130 inches. Overall length: 225 inches. Width: 80.2 inches. Height: 54.3 inches. Front tread: 61 inches. Rear tread: 61 inches. Tires: 8.00 x 15. Dual exhaust system standard.

(Series 62 Eldorado) Wheelbase: 130 inches. Overall length: 225 inches. Width: 80.2 inches. Front tread: 61 inches. Rear tread: 61 inches. Tires: 8.20 x 15. Dual exhaust system standard.

(Series 60S) Wheelbase: 130 inches. Overall length: 225 inches. Width: 81.1 inches. Height: 56.2 inches. Front tread: 61 inches. Rear tread: 61 inches. Tires: 8.00 x 15. Dual exhaust system standard.

(Series 75) Wheelbase: 149.75. Overall length: 244.8 inches. Width: 80.2 inches. Height: 59.3 inches. Front tread: 61 inches. Rear tread: 61 inches. Tires: 8.20 x 15 six-ply black sidewall. Dual exhaust system standard.

OPTIONS

Radio with rear speaker ($165). Radio with rear speaker and remote-control ($247). Automatic heating system on Series 75 ($179), on other models ($129). Six-Way power seat on 6200s, except convertible ($188). Six-Way power seat on 6300-6400 and 6200 convertible ($89). Power window regulators ($73). Power vent regulators ($73). Air conditioning, on Series 75 ($624), on other models ($474). Air suspension ($215). Autronic Eye ($55). Cruise Control ($97). Electric door locks on two-doors ($46), on four-doors ($70). E-Z-Eye glass ($52). Fog lights ($46). White sidewall tires 8.20 x 15 four-ply ($57 exchange), 8.20 x 15 six-ply ($65 exchange). Door guards on four-doors ($7), on two-doors ($4). Remote control trunk lock ($59). License plate frame ($8). Local options: Utility kit ($15), Monogram ($12). Acrylic Lustre finish ($20). Undercoating ($25). Radio foot switch ($10). Gas cap lock ($4). Pair of rugs for front ($8), for rear ($5). Note: Bucket seats were a no-cost option on the Biarritz convertible. The 345-hp Eldorado V-8 was optional on all other Cadillacs.

HISTORICAL

Flat-top roof styling was used on four-window sedans. The Eldorado Brougham was a distinctive model that was built by hand at Italian designer Pinin Farina's shop in Turin. Only 99 examples of the $13,074 four-door hardtop Brougham were created. The 1959s sold well, despite a steel strike that forced the Cadillac factory to close down. Model-year production was 142,272, an increase from 1958, but lower than in 1956 and 1957. Executives asserted an all-time divisional record could have been set if the strike had not occurred. June, deliveries to U.S. customers had hit 77,134—the highest ever for any Cadillac model year.

1959 Cadillac, Series 62, six-window hardtop

1960

OVERVIEW

The 1960 Cadillacs exhibited a smoother, more subtle rendition of the styling theme introduced one year earlier. General changes included a full-width grille, the elimination of pointed front bumper guards, increased restraint in the application of chrome trim, lower tail fins with oval-shaped nacelles that enclosed stacked taillights and back-up lights and front-fender-mounted directional indicator lights.

I.D. DATA

The VIN was stamped on the top left-hand frame support next to the radiator support and took the form * 60F100001 *. The same number is stamped on the top surface of the engine block ahead of the left-hand valve cover. The first two symbols indicate model-year: 60=1960. The third symbol identifies the body style: A=Series 62 four-window Sedan, B=Sedan DeVille four-window sedan, E=Eldorado Biarritz Convertible, F=Series 62 Convertible, G=Series 62 Coupe, H=Eldorado Seville, J=Coupe DeVille, K=Series 62 six-windows Sedan, L=Sedan DeVille six-window sedan, M=Fleetwood Sixty Special, P=Eldorado Brougham, R=Fleetwood 75 Series Sedan, S=Fleetwood 75 Limousine, Z=Commercial Chassis. The last six symbols are the sequential production number. The Fisher Body Style Number plate is attached to the cowl under the hood on the left and identifies the year, series and body style as follows: 60-6239=Series 62 four-window Sedan, 60-6339=Sedan DeVille four-window sedan, 60-6467=Eldorado Biarritz Convertible, 60-6267=Series 62 Convertible, 60-6237=Series 62 Coupe, 60-6437=Eldorado Seville, 60-6237=Coupe DeVille, 60-6229=Series 62 six-windows Sedan, 60-6329=Sedan DeVille six-windows Sedan, 60-6029=Fleetwood Sixty Special, 60-6929=Eldorado Brougham six-windows Sedan, 60-6723=Fleetwood 75 Series Sedan, 60-6733=Fleetwood 75 Limousine, 60-6890=Commercial Chassis. Note: Cadillac used the term "Sedan" to identify its four-door hardtop models. The Fisher Body Style Number plate also carries the paint code. The 1960 paint codes were: 10=Ebony Black, 12=Olympic White, 14=Platinum Gray, 16=Aleutian Gray, 22=Hampton Blue, 24=Pelham Blue, 26=York Blue, 29=Arroyo Turquoise, 32=Inverness Green, 36=Glencoe Green, 44=Beaumont Beige, 45=Palomino, 46=Fawn, 48=Persian Sand, 50=Pompeian Red, 94=Luserne Blue, 96=Carrara Green, 97=Champagne, 98=Sienna Rose and 99=Heather.

Above: **1960 Cadillac, Fleetwood 60 Special, "sedan" (four-door hardtop)**

SERIES 6200—V-8

The 1960 Cadillacs exhibited a smoother, more subtle rendition of the styling theme introduced one year earlier. General changes included a full-width grille, the elimination of pointed front bumper guards, increased restraint in the application of chrome trim, lower tail fins with oval-shaped nacelles that enclosed stacked taillights and back-up lights and front-fender-mounted directional indicator lights. Series 6200 base models had plain fender skirts, thin three-quarter length bodyside spears and Cadillac crests and lettering on short horizontal front fender bars mounted just behind the headlights. Four-window (4W) and six-window (6W) Sedans were offered again. The former featured a one-piece wraparound backlight and flat-top roof, while the latter had a sloping rear window and roofline. Standard equipment on 6200 models included power brakes, power steering, automatic transmission, dual back-up lights, windshield washers and dual speed wipers, wheel discs, outside rearview mirror and oil filter. Added extras on convertibles included power windows and two-way power seats. Technical highlights were comprised of finned rear drums, a vacuum-operated automatic-releasing floor controlled parking brake and tubular X-frame construction. Interiors were done in Fawn, Blue or Gray Cortina Cord or Turquoise, Green, Persian Sand or Black Caspian cloth with Florentine vinyl bolsters. Convertibles were upholstered in Florentine leather single or two-tone combinations or monochromatic Cardiff leather combinations.

SERIES 6200

Model Number	Body/Style Number	Body Type & Seating	Factory Price	Shipping Weight	Production Total
60-62K	6229K	4D 6W Sedan-6P	5,080	4,805	26,824
60-62K	6229K	4D Export 6W Sedan-6P	5,080	4,805	36
60-62A	6239A	4D 4W Sedan-6P	5,080	4,775	9,984
60-62G	6237G	2D Hardtop Coupe-6P	4,892	4,670	19,978
60-62F	6267F	2D Convertible-6P	5,455	4,850	14,000
60-62( )	62	Chassis only	—	—	2

DEVILLE SUB-SERIES 6300—V-8

Models in the DeVille sub-series were trimmed much like 6200s, but there was no bar medallion on the front fenders and special script nameplates appeared on the rear fenders. Standard equipment included all base model features, plus power windows and two-way power seat. Interiors were done in Chadwick cloth or optional Cambray cloth-and-leather combinations.

DEVILLE SUB-SERIES 6300

Model Number	Body/Style Number	Body Type & Seating	Factory Price	Shipping Weight	Production Total
60-63L	6329L	4D 6W Sedan-6P	5,498	4,835	22,579
60-63B	6339B	4D 4W Sedan-6P	5,498	4,815	9,225
60-63J	6337J	2D Hardtop Coupe-6P	5,252	4,705	21,585

ELDORADO / BROUGHAM SUB-SERIES 6400 / 6900—V-8

External variations on the Seville two-door hardtop and Biarritz convertible coupe took the form of bright body highlights that extended across the lower edge of fender skirts and Eldorado lettering on the sides of front fenders, just behind the headlights. Standard equipment was the same as on 6300 models plus heater, fog lights, Eldorado engine, remote-control trunk lock, radio with antenna and rear speaker, power vent windows, six-way power seat, air suspension, electric door locks, license frames, and five whitewall tires. A textured vinyl fabric top was offered on the Eldorado Seville and interior trim choices included cloth and leather combinations. The Brougham continued as an Italian-bodied four-door hardtop with special Brougham nameplates above the grille. It did not sport Eldorado front fender letters or body sill highlights, but had a distinctive squared-off roofline with rear ventipanes. A fin-like crease, or "skeg," ran from behind the front wheel opening to the rear of the car on the extreme lower body sides and there were special vertical crest medallions on the trailing edge of rear fenders. Cruise control, a Guide-Matic headlight dimmer, air conditioning and E-Z-Eye glass were regular equipment.

ELDORADO/BROUGHAM SUB-SERIES 6400/6900

Model Number	Body/Style Number	Body Type & Seating	Factory Price	Shipping Weight	Production Total
60-64H	6437H	2D Seville Hardtop Coupe-6P	7,401	4,855	1,075
60-64E	6467E	2D Biarritz Convertible-6P	7,401	5,060	1,285
60-69P	6929P	4D Brougham-6P	13,075	—	101

SERIES SIXTY SPECIAL FLEETWOOD—V-8

The Sixty Special Fleetwood sedan had the same standard equipment as the 6200 convertible and all 6300 models. This car was outwardly distinguished by a Fleetwood script on the rear deck, nine vertical bright metal louvers on the rear fenders, vertical crest medallions on the front fenders and wide full-length bright metal sill underscores, which extended to the fender skirts and lower rear quarter panels.

1960 Cadillac, Series 62, Coupe de Ville

Model Number	Body/Style Number	Body Type & Seating	Factory Price	Shipping Weight	Production Total
60-60M	6029M	4D Hardtop Sedan-6P	6,233	4,880	11,800

SERIES 6700 FLEETWOOD SEVENTY-FIVE — V-8

The long wheelbase sedan and limousine had auxiliary jump seats, high-headroom formal six-window styling, broad ribbed roof edge beauty panels and trim generally similar to 6200 Cadillacs in other regards. The limousine passenger compartment was trimmed in either Bradford cloth or Bedford cloth, both in combinations with wool. Florentine leather upholstery was used in the chauffeur's compartment.

SERIES 6700 FLEETWOOD SEVENTY-FIVE

Model Number	Body/Style Number	Body Type & Seating	Factory Price	Shipping Weight	Production Total
60-67R	6723R	4D Sedan-9P	9,533	5,475	718
60-67S	6733S	4D Limousine-9P	9,748	5,560	832
60-68	6890	Commercial chassis	—	—	2,160

ENGINE

BASE CADILLAC V-8

Overhead valve. Cast-iron block. Displacement: 390-cid. Bore and Stroke: 4.00 x 3.875 inches. Compression ratio: 10.5:1. Brake hp: 325 at 4800 rpm. Taxable hp: 51.2. Torque: 430 at 3100 rpm. Five main bearings. Hydraulic valve lifters. Crankcase capacity: 5 qt. (Add 1 qt. if new filter installed). Cooling system capacity: (without heater) 18.5 qt.; (with heater) 19.25 qt.; (with air conditioning) 19.75 qt. Dual exhaust. Carburetor: Carter four-barrel (without air conditioning) Model 2951S; (with air conditioning) Model 2952S. Alternate carburetor: Rochester 4GC (without air conditioning) Model 7013030; (with air conditioning) Model 7013031.

ELDORADO / BROUGHAM BASE V-8

Overhead valve. Cast-iron block. Displacement: 390-cid. Bore and Stroke: 4.00 x 3.875 inches. Compression ratio: 10.5:1. Brake hp: 345 at 4800 rpm. Taxable hp: 51.2. Torque: 435 at 34000. Five main bearings. Hydraulic valve lifters. Crankcase capacity: 5 qt. (Add 1 qt. if new filter installed). Cooling system capacity: (without heater) 18.5 qt.; (with heater) 19.25 qt.; (with air conditioning) 19.75 qt. Dual exhaust. Rochester 2GC Triple Power Pack Carburetion: (front carburetor with or without air conditioning) Model 7013033; (center carburetor without air conditioning) Model 7013034; (center carburetor with air conditioning) Model 7013037 used in early production; (rear carburetor with or without air conditioning) Model 7013035.

CHASSIS

(Series 62) Wheelbase: 130.0 inches. Overall length: 225.0 inches. Width: 79.9 inches. Front tread: 61 inches. Rear tread: 61 inches. Tires: 8.00 x 15.

(Series 60S) Wheelbase: 130 inches. Overall length: 225 inches. Width: 79.9 inches. Front tread: 61 inches. Rear tread: 61 inches. Tires: 8.00 x 15. Dual exhaust system standard.

(Series 75) Wheelbase: 149.8. Overall length: 244.8 inches. Width: 79.9 inches. Front tread: 61 inches. Rear tread: 61 inches. Tires: 8.20 x 15 six-ply black sidewall. Dual exhaust system standard.

OPTIONS

Air conditioning on Series 62 or 60 ($474), on Series 75 ($624). Air suspension on non-Eldorados ($215), standard on Eldorado Autronic Eye ($46). Cruise control ($97). Door guards on two-door ($4), on four-door ($7). Electric door locks on two-door ($46), on four-door ($70), standard on Eldorado. E-Z-Eye glass ($52). Fog lights ($43). Automatic heating system on Series 62 or

1960 Cadillac tailfin area

60 ($129), on Series 75 ($279). License plate frame ($6). Six-Way power seat ($85 to $113) depending on style number. Power window regulators ($118). Power vent windows ($73). Radio with rear speaker ($165), with rear speaker and remote-control ($247). Remote control trunk lock ($59). White sidewall tires, size 8.20 x 15 four-ply ($57 exchange), size 8.20 x 15 six-ply ($64). Antifreeze -20 degrees ($8), -40 degrees ($9). Accessory Group "A" included whitewalls, heater, radio and E-Z-Eye glass for $402 extra and air suspension, Cruise control and Eldorado engine at regular prices. Accessory Group "B" included air conditioner, whitewalls, heater, radio and E-Z-Eye glass at $876 extra and six-way power seat, power vent windows and power windows at regular prices. Gas and oil delivery charge was $7 and district warehousing and handling charges averaged $15. Note: Eldorado standard equipment features specified above are those not previously mentioned in text. Consult both sources for complete list. The 345-hp Eldorado V-8 with three two-barrel carburetors was $134.40 extra for any other Cadillac model.

HISTORICAL

The 1960 Cadillac line was officially introduced on October 2, 1959. Cadillac turned out a total of 142,184 cars in the 1960 model-year, which represented 2.4 percent of passenger-car output in the United States. Calendar-year production came to a record 158,941 units for a 2.37 percent market share. The company's factory in Detroit hummed along all year at maximum capacity, trying to make up lost ground after the 1959 steel strike. Sales for the entire year were a new high of 151,954 cars. That outdid the record of 143,611 set in 1955. The overall increase ran at about seven percent for the season.

1960 Cadillac, Series 62, convertible

1960 Cadillac, Eldorado Biarritz, convertible

1961

OVERVIEW

Cadillacs were moderately restyled and re-engineered for 1961. A new styling motif was characterized by a crisp, clean look with sculpted side panels and a roof line with sharper angles. The new grille slanted back towards both the bumper and the hood lip, along the horizontal plane and sat between dual headlights. New forward slanting front roof pillars with non-wraparound windshield glass were seen. The revised backlight treatment had crisp, angular lines with thin pillars on some models and heavier, semi-blind-quarter roof posts on others. A new short-deck sedan was available in the 6300 lineup. Despite a slightly reduced wheelbase, the cars had more headroom and legroom, wider doors, better shock absorbers and an improved suspension system. The wraparound windshield was redesigned and overlapping windshield wipers were incorporated to enlarge the sweep area by 15 percent. A new steering wheel had a reduced 16-inch diameter. The DeVille models were retained as the 6300 sub-series (technically part of the Sixty-Two line). The Eldorado Seville and Brougham were dropped. This moved the Eldorado Biarritz convertible into the DeVille sub-series.

Above: **1961 Cadillac, Series 62, convertible**

SERIES 6200—V-8

Standard equipment on base 6200 models included power brakes, power steering, automatic transmission: dual back-up lights, windshield washer and dual speed wipers, wheel discs, plain fender skirts, outside rearview mirror, vanity mirror, and oil filter. Rubberized front and rear coil springs replaced the trouble-prone air suspension system. Wheelbases were decreased. Four-barrel induction systems were the sole power choice and dual exhaust were no longer available. Series designation trim appeared on the front fenders.

I.D. DATA

The VIN was stamped on the top left-hand frame support next to the radiator support and took the form *61F100001*. The same number is stamped on the top surface of the engine block ahead of the left-hand valve cover. The first two symbols indicate model-year: 61=1961. The third symbol identifies the body style: A=Series 62 four-window Sedan, B=Sedan DeVille four-window sedan, C=Series 62 short-deck Sedan, E=Eldorado Biarritz Convertible, F=Series 62 Convertible, G=Series 62 Coupe, J=Coupe DeVille, K=Series 62 six-windows Sedan, L=Sedan DeVille six-windows Sedan, M=Fleetwood Sixty Special, R=Fleetwood 75 Series nine-passenger Sedan, S=Fleetwood 75 Imperial Limousine, Z=Commercial

Chassis. The last six symbols are the sequential production number. The Fisher Body Style Number plate is attached to the cowl under the hood on the left and identifies the year, series and body style as follows: 61-6299=Series 62 short-deck Sedan, 61-6239=Series 62 four-window Sedan, 61-6339=Sedan DeVille four-window sedan, 61-6367=Eldorado Biarritz Convertible, 61-6267=Series 62 Convertible, 61-6237=Series 62 Coupe, 61-6337=Coupe DeVille, 61-6229=Series 62 six-windows Sedan, 61-6329=Sedan DeVille six-windows Sedan, 61-6039=Fleetwood Sixty Special, 61-6723=Fleetwood 75 Series Sedan, 61-6733=Fleetwood 75 Limousine, 61-6890=Commercial Chassis. Note: Cadillac used the term "Sedan" to identify its four-door hardtop models. The Fisher Body Style Number plate also carries the paint code. The 1961 paint codes were: 10=Ebony Black, 12=Olympic White, 14=Platinum Gray, 16=Aleutian Gray, 22=Bristol Blue, 24=Dresden Blue, 26=York Blue, 29=San Remo Turquoise, 32=Concord Green, 36=Granada Green, 44=Laredo Tan, 46=Tunis Beige, 48=Fontana Rose, 50=Pompeian Red, 94=Nautilus Blue, 96=Jade Green, 97=Aspen Gold, 98=Topaz and 99=Shell Pear. Convertible top colors were: 1=White, 2=Black, 4=Light Gold, 5=Medium Blue, 6=Light Sandalwood, 7=Medium Pink and 8=Light Blue.

SERIES 6200

Model Number	Body/Style Number	Body Type & Seating	Factory Price	Shipping Weight	Production Total
61-62A	6239A	4D 4W Sedan-6P	5,080	4,660	4,700
61-62K	6229K	4D 6W Sedan-6P	5,080	4,680	26,216
61-62G	6237G	2D Hardtop Coupe-6P	5,892	4,560	16,005
61-62F	6267F	2D Convertible-6P	5,455	4,720	15,500

SERIES 62 DEVILLE 6300 SUB-SERIES—V-8

DeVille models featured front fender designation scripts and a lower body 'skeg' trimmed with a thin three-quarter length spear molding running from behind the front wheel opening to the rear of the car. Standard equipment was the same used on 6200 models plus two-way power seat and power windows. The Biarritz convertible also had power vent windows, six-way power bench seat (or bucket seats) and remote-control trunk lock. The new short-deck four-door hardtop appeared in mid-season, often referred to as the Town Sedan.

SERIES 62 DEVILLE 6300 SUB-SERIES

Model Number	Body/Style Number	Body Type & Seating	Factory Price	Shipping Weight	Production Total
61-63B	6339B	4D 4W Sedan-6P	5,498	4,715	4,847
61-63L	6329L	4D 6W Sedan-6P	5,498	4,710	26,415
61-63C	6399C	4D Town Sedan-6P	5,498	4,670	3,756
61-63J	6337J	2D Hardtop Coupe-6P	5,252	4,595	20,156

SERIES 62 ELDORADO 6300 MODEL

Model Number	Body/Style Number	Body Type & Seating	Factory Price	Shipping Weight	Production Total
61-63E	6367E	2D Biarritz Convertible-6P	6,477	4,805	1,450

SERIES SIXTY SPECIAL FLEETWOOD—V-8

The Sixty Special Fleetwood sedan featured semi-blind-quarter four-door hardtop styling with an angular roofline that approximated a raised convertible top. Six chevron slashes appeared on the rear fender sides at the trailing edge. A model nameplate was seen on the front fender. Standard equipment was the same as used on 6300 models including power seats and windows.

SERIES SIXTY SPECIAL FLEETWOOD

Model Number	Body/Style Number	Body Type & Seating	Factory Price	Shipping Weight	Production Total
61-60M	6039M	4D Hardtop Sedan-6P	6,233	4,770	15,500

SERIES 6700 FLEETWOOD 75—V-8

The limousine and big sedan for 1961 sported the all-new styling motifs. Standard equipment was the same as used on 6300 models including power seats and windows.

SERIES 6700 FLEETWOOD 75

Model Number	Body/Style Number	Body Type & Seating	Factory Price	Shipping Weight	Production Total
61-67R	6723R	4D Sedan-9P	9,533	5,390	699
61-67S	6733S	4D Imperial Sedan-9P	9,748	5,420	926
61-68	6890	Commercial chassis	—	—	2,204

ENGINE

Overhead valve. Cast-iron block. Displacement: 390-cid. Bore and Stroke: 4.00 x 3.875 inches. Compression ratio: 10.5:1. Brake hp: 325 at 4800 rpm. Taxable hp: 51.2. Torque: 430 at 3100 rpm. Five main bearings. Hydraulic valve lifters. Crankcase capacity: 5 qt. (Add 1 qt. if new filter installed). Cooling system capacity: (all without heater) 18.25 qt.; (Series 60 and Series 62 with heater) 19.25 qt.; (Series 75 with heater only) 20.75 qt. Single exhaust with crossover. Carburetor: Carter four-barrel (without air conditioning) Model 3177S; (with air conditioning) Model 3178S. Alternate carburetor: Rochester four-barrel (without air conditioning) Model 7019030; (with air conditioning) Model 7019031.

1961 Cadillac, Series 62, coupe

CHASSIS

Wheelbase: (Series 75) 149.8 inches, [Commercial chassis] 156 inches, (All others) 129.5 inches. Overall length: (Series 75) 242.3 inches, (Town Sedan) 215 inches, (All others) 222 inches. Single exhaust only. Tires: (Eldorado and Series 75) 8.20 x 15, (All others) 8 x 15.

(Series 62, Series 63) Wheelbase: 129.5 inches. Overall length: 222.0 inches (Town Sedan 215 inches). Width: 79.8 inches. Front tread: 61 inches. Rear tread: 61 inches. Tires: Eldorado 8.20 x 15, Others 8.00 x 15.

(Series 60S) Wheelbase: 129.5 inches. Overall length: 222 inches. Width: 79.8 inches. Front tread: 61 inches. Rear tread: 61 inches. Tires: 8.00 x 15.

(Series 75) Wheelbase: 149.8. Overall length: 242.3 inches. Width: 80.6 inches. Front tread: 61 inches. Rear tread: 61 inches. Tires: 8.20 x 15 six-ply black sidewall.

(Commercial chassis) Wheelbase: 156 inches.

OPTIONS

Air conditioning Series 62 or 60 ($474), Series 75 ($624). Autronic Eye ($46). Cruise control ($97). Door guards on two-door ($4), on four-door ($7). Electric door locks on two-door ($46), on four-door ($70). E-Z-Eye glass ($52). Pair of fog lights ($43). Automatic heating system on Series 62 or 60 ($129), on Series 75 ($179). License plate frame ($6). Six-Way power seat ($85-$113). Power windows ($85). Power vent windows ($73). Radio with rear speaker ($16), with remote-control ($247). Remote control trunk lock ($59). Five white sidewall tires size 8.20 x 15 four-ply ($58 exchange) standard on Eldorado, size 8.20 x 15 six-ply for Series 75 ($64 exchange). Permanent anti-freeze -20 degrees ($8), -40 degrees ($9). Limited-slip differential ($53.70). Accessory groups A and B included mostly the same features as 1960 at the combined total of individual prices listed above. All 1961 Cadillacs were built in Detroit, Michigan.

HISTORICAL

The 1961 Cadillac line was officially introduced on October 3, 1960. Cadillac turned out a total of 138,379 cars in the 1961 model year, which represented 2.6 percent of passenger-car output in the United States. Calendar-year production came to 148,298 units for a 2.69 percent market share. Cadillac production dropped 6.7 percent on a calendar-year basis, but its market share registered the highest percentage for any year in the company's history, except 1958. The Detroit factory averaged 87 percent of 1960's record production total. The company's retail sales number was 143,790 units, only 5.4 percent below the record set in 1960.

1961 Cadillac, Series 62, Sedan de Ville

1961 Cadillacs, Fleetwood 60 Special sedan (left) and Series 62 coupe (right)

1962

OVERVIEW

A mild facelift characterized Cadillac styling trends for 1962. Changes were mainly evolutionary, although a classic new roof design gave the car an entirely new silhouette. A flatter grille with a thicker horizontal center bar and more delicate cross-hatched insert appeared. Ribbed chrome trim panels were now replaced with cornering lights and front fender model and series identification badges were eliminated. More massive front bumper end pieces appeared and housed rectangular parking lights. The taillights were now housed in vertical nacelles designed with an angled peak at the center. The tail fins were lower and lacked chrome trim. The taillights had a "set-jewel" look. Engineering updates included a new three-way braking system and a front cornering light. The automatic trunk lock now operated mechanically, rather than electrically.

I.D. DATA

The VIN was stamped on the top left-hand frame support next to the radiator support and took the form * 62F100001 *. The same number is stamped on the top surface of the engine block ahead of the left-hand valve cover. The first

Above: **1962 Cadillac, Series 62, convertible**

Angelo Van Bogart

two symbols indicate model-year: 62=1962. The third symbol identifies the body style: A=Series 62 four-window Sedan, B=Sedan DeVille four-window sedan, C=Series 62 short-deck Sedan, D= DeVille Park Avenue Sedan, E=Eldorado Biarritz Convertible, F=Series 62 Convertible, G=Series 62 Coupe, J=Coupe DeVille, K=Series 62 six-windows Sedan, L=Sedan DeVille six-windows Sedan, M=Fleetwood Sixty Special, N=Series 62 four-window sedan, R=Fleetwood 75 Series nine-passenger Sedan, S=Fleetwood 75 Imperial Limousine, Z=Commercial Chassis. The last six symbols are the sequential production number. The Fisher Body Style Number plate is attached to the cowl under the hood on the left and identifies the year, series and body style as follows: 62-6289=Series 62 short-deck Town Sedan, 62-6239=Series 62 four-window Sedan, 62-6339=Sedan DeVille four-window sedan, 62-6367=Eldorado Biarritz Convertible, 62-6268=Series 62 Convertible, 62-6247=Series 62 Coupe, 62-6347=Coupe DeVille, 62-6229=Series 62 six-windows Sedan, 62-6329=Sedan DeVille six-windows Sedan, 62-6389 Series 62 four-window Park Avenue Sedan, 62-6039=Fleetwood Sixty Special, 62-6723=Fleetwood 75 Series Sedan, 62-6733=Fleetwood 75 Limousine, 62-6890=Commercial Chassis. Note: Cadillac used the term "Sedan" to identify its four-door hardtop models. The Fisher Body Style Number plate also carries the paint code. The 1962

paint codes were: 1=White, 2=Black, 3=Concord Blue, 4=Sandalwood, 5=Metallic Saddle Tan (Bronze), 8=Pink (Heather), 9=Red, 10=Ebony Black, 12=Olympic White, 14=Nevada Silver, 16=Aleutian Gray, 22=Newport Blue, 24=Avalon Blue, 26=York Blue, 29=Turquoise, 32=Sage, 36=Granada Green, 44=Sandalwood, 45=Maize, 46=Driftwood Beige, 48=Laurel, 50=Pompeian Red, 52=Burgundy, 61=Silver Fire Frost, 64=Gold Fire Frost, 94=Neptune Blue, 96=Pinehurst Green, 97=Victorian Gold, 98=Bronze and 99=Heather. Convertible top colors were: 1=White, 2=Black, 4=Light Gold, 5=Medium Blue, 6=Sandalwood, 7=Medium Pink and 8=Light Blue.

SERIES 62 — V-8

On Series 6200 models a vertically-ribbed rear beauty panel appeared on the deck lid latch panel. A Cadillac script also appeared on the lower left side of the radiator grille. The short-deck Town Sedan was switched to the base 6200 lineup, while a similar model was still part of the DeVille sub-series. Standard equipment on 6200 models included power brakes, power steering, automatic transmission, dual back-up lights, windshield washers, dual-speed wipers, wheel discs, fender skirts, a remote-control outside rearview mirror, a left-hand vanity mirror, an oil filter, five tubeless black sidewall tires, a heater and defroster and front cornering lights.

SERIES 6200

Model Number	Body/Style Number	Body Type & Seating	Factory Price	Shipping Weight	Production Total
62-62A	6239A	4D 4W Sedan-6P	5,213	4,645	17,314
62-62K	6229K	4D 6W Sedan-6P	5,213	4,640	16,730
62-62C	6289C	4D Town Sedan-6P	5,213	4,590	2,600
62-62G	6237G	2D Hardtop Coupe-6P	5,025	4,530	16,833
62-62F	6268F	2D Convertible-6P	5,588	4,630	16,800

SERIES 62 DEVILLE 6300 SUB-SERIES — V-8

The DeVille lineup was much more of a separate series this year and some historical sources list it as such. Others list it as a 6200 sub-series. The latter system is utilized here. The new model for 1962 was a variation of Town Sedan, introduced the previous season, with a new Style Number and name. It was now Body Style 6389D and referred to as the Park Avenue four-window sedan. DeVilles were trimmed similar to base 6200 models. They had all of the same standard equipment, plus two-way power seats and power windows. The Style Number 6367E Biarritz Convertible also featured power vent windows, white sidewall tires and a six-way power bench seat. Buyers could substitute bucket seats, in place of the last item, at no cost.

SERIES 6200 DEVILLE 6300 SUB-SERIES

Model Number	Body/Style Number	Body Type & Seating	Factory Price	Shipping Weight	Production Total
62-63B	6339B	4D 4W Sedan-6P	5,631	4,675	27,378
62-63L	6329L	4D 6W Sedan-6P	5,631	4,660	16,230
62-63D	6389D	4D Park Ave Sedan-6P	5,631	4,655	2,600
62-63J	6347J	2D Hardtop Coupe-6P	5,385	4,595	25,675

SERIES 62 ELDORADO 6300 MODEL

Model Number	Body/Style Number	Body Type & Seating	Factory Price	Shipping Weight	Production Total
62-63E	6367E	2D Biarritz Convertible-6P	6,610	4,620	1,450

SERIES SIXTY SPECIAL FLEETWOOD — V-8

The Sixty Special Fleetwood sedan stood apart in a crowd. It had chevron slash moldings on the rear roof pillar and a distinctly cross-hatched rear deck latch panel grille. Standard equipment comprised all features found on closed cars in the 6300 DeVille sub-series.

SERIES SIXTY SPECIAL FLEETWOOD

Model Number	Body/Style Number	Body Type & Seating	Factory Price	Shipping Weight	Production Total
62-60W	6039	4D Hardtop Sedan-6P	6,366	4,710	13,350

SERIES 6700 FLEETWOOD 75 — V-8

The limousine and big sedan for 1962 sported the new styling motifs. Standard equipment was the same used on Sixty Special Fleetwoods. A distinctive high-headroom look was again seen.

SERIES 6700 FLEETWOOD 75

Model Number	Body/Style Number	Body Type & Seating	Factory Price	Shipping Weight	Production Total
62-67R	6723R	4D Sedan-9P	9,722	5,325	696
62-67S	6733S	4D Limousine-9P	9,937	5,390	904
62-68	8890	Commercial chassis	—	—	2,280

ENGINE

Overhead valve. Cast-iron block. Displacement: 390-cid. Bore and Stroke: 4.00 x 3.875 inches. Compression ratio: 10.5:1. Brake hp: 325 at 4800 rpm. Taxable hp: 51.2. Torque: 430 at 3100 rpm. Five main bearings. Hydraulic valve lifters. Crankcase capacity: 4 qt. (Add 1 qt. if new filter installed). Cooling system capacity: (Series 60, Series 62 and Series 63 with heater only) 19.33 qt.; (Series 67 with heater only) 20.89 qt. Single exhaust with crossover. Carburetor: Carter four-barrel (without air conditioning)

1961 Cadillac, Series 62, convertible

Model 3351S; (with air conditioning) Model 3352S. Alternate carburetor: Rochester four-barrel (without air conditioning) Model 7019030; (with air conditioning) Model 7019031.

CHASSIS

(Series 62, Series 63) Wheelbase: 129.5 inches. Overall length: 222.0 inches (Town Sedan 215 inches). Width: 79.9 inches. Front tread: 61 inches. Rear tread: 61 inches. Tires: Eldorado 8.20 x 15, Others 8.00 x 15.

(Series 60S) Wheelbase: 129.5 inches. Overall length: 222 inches. Width: 79.9 inches. Front tread: 61 inches. Rear tread: 61 inches. Tires: 8.00 x 15.

(Series 75) Wheelbase: 149.8. Overall length: 242.3 inches. Width: 80.6 inches. Front tread: 61 inches. Rear tread: 61 inches. Tires: 8.20 x 15 six-ply black sidewall.

(Commercial chassis) Wheelbase: 156 inches.

OPTIONS

Air conditioning on Series 62 or 60 ($474), on Series 75 ($624). Air suspension on non-Eldorados ($215), standard on Eldorado. Autronic Eye ($46). Cruise control ($97). Door guards on two-door ($4), on four-door ($7). Electric door locks on two-door ($46), on four-door ($70), standard on Eldorado. E-Z-Eye glass ($52). Fog lights ($43). Automatic heating system on Series 62 or 60 ($129), on Series 75 ($279). License plate frame ($6). Six-Way power seat ($85-$113) depending on style number. Power window regulators ($118). Power vent windows ($73). Radio with rear speaker ($165), with rear speaker and remote-control ($247). Remote-control trunk lock ($59). White sidewall tires size 8.20 x 15 four-ply ($57 exchange), size 8.20 x 15 six-ply ($64). Antifreeze - 20 degrees ($8), -40 degrees ($9). Accessory Group "A" included whitewalls, heater, radio and E-Z-Eye glass for $402 extra and air suspension, cruise control and Eldorado engine at regular prices. Accessory Group "B" included air conditioner, whitewalls, heater, radio and E-Z-Eye glass at $876 extra and six-way power seat, power vent windows and power windows at regular prices. Gas and oil delivery charge was $7 and district warehousing and handling charges averaged $15. Bucket seats were available for 6267F, 6339B, 6347J or 6389D as an option ($108). All 1962 Cadillacs were built in Detroit, Michigan.

HISTORICAL

This was the 60th anniversary year for Cadillac. Dealer introductions of new models took place on September 22, 1961. The automaker produced 160,840 Cadillacs during the model-year, all equipped with the new dual-safety braking system and 59.4 percent sold with air conditioning. Calendar-year output was 158,528 units, which equated to a 2.28 percent share of the market. Dealer sales of 1962 models hit a record of 155,457, an increase of 8.1 percent over 1961. An advertisement for the 1962 Cadillac flashed back to a slogan used by the company 60 years earlier: "Craftsmanship a creed . . . accuracy a law!" On December 7, 1962, Cadillac announced plans for a new engineering building and expanded manufacturing and assembly operations to be built over the next two years at a cost of $55 million.

1962 Cadillac, Series 62, convertible

1963

OVERVIEW

The 1963 Cadillacs were essentially the same as the previous models. Minor exterior changes imparted a bolder and longer look. The hood and deck lid were redesigned. The front fenders projected 4-5/8 inches further forward than in 1962, while the tail fins were trimmed to provide a lower profile. The roof line for some models was shortened and smaller rear windows with a formal look were used. Bodyside sculpturing was entirely eliminated. The slightly V-shaped radiator grille was taller. A total of 143 options, including bucket seats with wool, leather or nylon upholstery fabrics, set an all-time record for interior choices. The instrument panel revealed a new gauge cluster and the dashboard and doors featured wood paneling. A four-way tilting driver's seat was standard. More than 70 engineering changes were made. Cadillac's array of models was reduced to 12 with the discontinuation of the Series 62 short-deck sedan.

I.D. DATA

The VIN was stamped on the top left frame support next to the radiator support and took the form * 63F100001 *. The same number is stamped on the surface of the engine

block ahead of the left-hand valve cover. The first two symbols indicate model-year: 63=1963. The third symbol identifies the body style: B=Sedan DeVille four-window sedan, D=DeVille Park Avenue Sedan, E=Eldorado Biarritz Convertible, F=Series 62 Convertible, G=Series 62 Coupe, J=Coupe DeVille, K=Series 62 six-windows Sedan, L=Sedan DeVille six-windows Sedan, M=Fleetwood Sixty Special, N=Series 62 four-window sedan, R=Fleetwood 75 Series nine-passenger Sedan, S=Fleetwood 75 Imperial Limousine, Z=Commercial Chassis. The last six symbols are the sequential production number. The Fisher Body Style Number plate is attached to the cowl and identifies the year, series and body style as follows: 63-6239=Series 62 four-window Sedan, 63-6229=Series 62 six-window sedan, 63-6339=Sedan DeVille four-window sedan, 63-6367=Eldorado Biarritz Convertible, 63-6267=Series 62 Convertible, 63-6257=Series 62 Coupe, 63-6357=Coupe DeVille, 63-6329=Sedan DeVille six-windows Sedan, 63-6389 Series 62 four-window Park Avenue Sedan, 63-6039=Fleetwood Sixty Special, 63-6723=Fleetwood 75 Series Sedan, 63-6733=Fleetwood 75 Limousine, 63-6890=Commercial Chassis. Note: Cadillac used the term "Sedan" to identify its four-door hardtop models. The Fisher Body Style Number plate also carries the paint code. The 1963 paint codes were: 10=Ebony Black, 12=Aspen White, 14=Nevada Silver, 16=Cardiff Gray,

Above: **1963 Cadillac, Series 62, convertible (bottom) and Series 75, limousine (top)**

22=Benton Blue, 24=Basque Blue, 26=Somerset Blue, 29=Turino Turquoise, 32=Basildon Green, 36=Brewster Green, 44=Bahama Sand, 46=Fawn, 47=Palomino, 48=Briar Rose, 50=Matador Red, 52=Royal Maroon, 92=Silver Frost, 94=Frost Aquamarine, 96=Frost Green, 97=Frost Gold and 98=Frost Red. Convertible top colors were: 1=White, 2=Black, 4=Light Gold, 5=Medium Blue, 6=Light Sandalwood, 7=Medium Pink, 8=Light Blue and 9=Silver Blue.

SERIES 62—V-8

Standard equipment for cars in the 62 series (6200 models) included power brakes, power steering, automatic transmission, dual back-up lights, windshield washers, dual-speed windshield wipers, full wheel discs, remote-control outside rearview mirrors, a left-hand vanity mirror, an oil filter, five tubeless black sidewall tires, a heater and defroster and cornering lights. Convertibles were equipped with two-way power seats and power windows.

SERIES 62 (6200 MODELS)

Model Number	Body/Style Number	Body Type & Seating	Factory Price	Shipping Weight	Production Total
63-62K	6229K	4D 6W Sedan-6P	5,214	4,610	12,929
63-62G	6257G	2D Coupe-6P	5,026	4,505	16,786
63-62N	6239N	4D 4W Sedan-6P	5,214	4,595	16,980
63-62F	6267F	2D Convertible-6P	5,590	4,544	17,600
63-62	6200	Chassis only	—	—	3

SERIES 62—DEVILLE 6300 SUB-SERIES—V-8

The 6300 DeVille line shared Series 62 styling revisions, but incorporated a DeVille signature script above the lower belt line molding, near the rear of the body. Standard features on DeVilles were the same as on closed body 6200 models, plus two-way power seats and power windows. The Park Avenue was a short-deck DeVille sedan. All Sedan DeVilles were pillarless four-door hardtops.

SERIES 62 DEVILLE 6300 SUB-SERIES

Model Number	Body/Style Number	Body Type & Seating	Factory Price	Shipping Weight	Production Total
63-63L	6329L	4D 6W Sedan-6P	5,633	4,650	15,146
63-63J	6357J	2D Coupe DeVille-6P	5,386	4,520	31,749
63-63B	6339B	4D 4W Sedan-6P	5,633	4,065	30,579
63-63D	6389D	4D Park Ave. Sedan-6P	5,633	4,590	1,575

SERIES 62—DEVILLE 6300 ELDORADO BIARRITZ—V-8

The Eldorado Biarritz convertible had special styling with untrimmed bodysides, full-length stainless steel underscores and a rectangular grid pattern rear decorative grille. Power vent windows, white sidewall tires and a six-way power seat (in bench-seat models) were standard in Eldorados.

SERIES 62 ELDORADO BIARRITZ 6300 MODEL

Model Number	Body/Style Number	Body Type & Seating	Factory Price	Shipping Weight	Production Total
63-63E	6367E	2D SportConvertible-6P	6,609	4,640	1,825

SERIES SIXTY SPECIAL FLEETWOOD—V-8

The Sixty Special Fleetwood sedan was again distinguished by chevron slashes of bright metal on the sides of the roof "'C" pillars. Full-length bright metal underscores, clean side styling, a rear end quadrant pattern grille and Cadillac crest medallions also were seen. Standard equipment included all normal 6300 sub-series features, plus power ventipanes.

SERIES SIXTY SPECIAL FLEETWOOD

Model Number	Body/Style Number	Body Type & Seating	Factory Price	Shipping Weight	Production Total
63-60M	6039M	4D Hardtop Sedan-6P	6,366	4,690	14,000

SERIES 6700—FLEETWOOD 75—V-8

Cadillac's extra-long nine-passenger cars were the only pillared four-door sedans in the line. Standard equipment

1963 Cadillac, Fleetwood 60 Special, "sedan" (four-door hardtop)

was the same as on base 6300 models and Series 62 convertibles. Trimmings included a full-length lower belt line molding of a simple, but elegant, design. Convertible top-like roof lines and windshields with forward "dog leg" style pillars were 1962 carryovers seen exclusively on this line.

SERIES 6700 FLEETWOOD 75

Model Number	Body/Style Number	Body Type & Seating	Factory Price	Shipping Weight	Production Total
63-67R	6723R	4D Sedan-9P	9,724	5,240	680
63-67S	6733S	4D Limousine-9P	9,939	5,300	795
63-68	6890	Commercial chassis	—	—	2,527

ENGINE

Overhead valve. Cast-iron block. Displacement: 390-cid. Bore and Stroke: 4.00 x 3.875 inches. Compression ratio: 10.5:1. Brake hp: 325 at 4800 rpm. Taxable hp: 51.2. Torque: 430 at 3100 rpm. Five main bearings. Hydraulic valve lifters. Crankcase capacity: 4 qt. (Add 1 qt. if new filter installed). Cooling system capacity: 17.25 qt. Single exhaust with crossover. Carburetor: Rochester 4GC four-barrel (without air conditioning) Model 7019030; (with air conditioning) Model 7019031. Although neither engine displacement or horsepower output changed, the 1963 Cadillac V-8 was completely redesigned. Quieter, smoother and more efficient, the new engine was one inch lower, four inches narrower and 1-1/4 inches shorter than the 1962 V-8. It also weighed about 82 less pounds, due to the use of aluminum accessory drives.

CHASSIS

(Series 62, Series 63) Wheelbase: 129.5 inches. Overall length: 223.0 inches (Park Ave. 215 inches). Width: 79.7 inches. Height: 54.8 inches. Front tread: 61 inches. Rear tread: 61 inches. Tires: Eldorado 8.20 x 15, Others 8.00 x 15. Rear axle ratio: 2.94:1.

(Series 60S) Wheelbase: 129.5 inches. Overall length: 223 inches. Width: 79.7 inches. Height: 56.6 inches. Front tread: 61 inches. Rear tread: 61 inches. Tires: 8.00 x 15. Rear axle ratio: 2.94:1.

(Series 75) Wheelbase: 149.8. Overall length: 243.3 inches. Width: 79.9 inches. Height: 59.0 inches. Front tread: 61 inches. Rear tread: 61 inches. Tires: 8.20 x 15 six ply black sidewall. Rear axle ratio: 3.38:1.
(Commercial chassis) Wheelbase: 156 inches.

OPTIONS

Air conditioner for Series 60-62 ($474). Air conditioner for Series 75 ($624). Automatic headlight control ($45). Bucket seats in styles 6267F, 6339B, 6357J, or 6389D with leather upholstery required ($188). Controlled differential ($54). Cruise control ($97). Door guards for two-door styles ($4), for four-door styles ($7). Electric door locks for two-door styles ($46), for four-door styles ($70). E-Z-Eye Glass ($52). Leather upholstery for styles 6339B, 6357J, 6389D, or 6039M ($134). License plate frame ($6). Padded roof for style 6357J ($91), for style 6039M ($134). Six-way power seat ($85-$113 depending on body style). Power window regulators as an option ($118). Power ventipanes as an option ($73). Radio with rear seat speaker ($165). Radio with rear seat speaker and remote-control ($247). AM/FM radio ($191). Front seat belts in Series 60-62 models ($22). Rear seat belts in same models ($22). Adjustable steering wheel ($48). Remote control trunk lock ($53). Five white sidewall tires, 8.20 x 15 four-ply on Series 60-62, standard on Eldorado ($57 exchange). Five white sidewall tires, 8.20 x 15 six-ply on Series 75 models ($64 exchange).

HISTORICAL

Dealer introductions of new models took place on October 5, 1962. The automaker produced 163,174 Cadillacs during the model-year. Calendar-year output was 164,735 units, which equated to a 2.15 percent share of the market. Dealer sales hit 163,077, a 4.9 percent gain over the record 1962 total. Cadillac's new-for-1963 V-8 was the first major redesign of its V-8 since that power plant's introduction as a 331-cid engine in 1949. "Take a look at the best-liked Cadillac of all time!" suggested a 1963 Sedan De Ville advertisement.

In 1963, the Cadillac Fleetwood 60 Special was a chauffeur favorite.

1964

OVERVIEW

It was time for a minor facelift this year. A bi-angular grille formed a V-shape along both its vertical and horizontal planes. The main horizontal grille bar was now carried around the bodysides. Outer grille extension panels again housed the parking and cornering lights. It was the 17th consecutive year for Cadillac tail fins, with a new, fine-blade design carrying on this tradition. Performance improvements, including a larger V-8, were the dominant changes for the model run. The new engine had a larger bore, a larger stroke and more total cubic inches. Cadillac said it brought performance gains mainly in the 20-50-mph range. A new feature was a Comfort Control system that brought Cadillac buyers a completely-automatic heating and air conditioning system controlled by a dial-in thermostat on the dashboard.

I.D. DATA

The VIN was stamped on the top left frame support next to the radiator support and took the form * 64F100001 *. The same number is stamped on the top the engine block ahead of the left-hand valve cover. The first two symbols indicate model-year: 64=1964. The third symbol identifies

---

Above: **1964 Cadillac, Series 62, two-door hardtop coupe**

the body style: B=Sedan DeVille four-window sedan, E=Eldorado Convertible, F=Series 62 DeVille Convertible, G=Series 62 Coupe, J=Coupe DeVille, K=Series 62 six-windows Sedan, L=Sedan DeVille six-windows Sedan, M=Fleetwood Sixty Special, N=Series 62 four-window sedan, R=Fleetwood 75 Series nine-passenger Sedan, S=Fleetwood 75 Imperial Limousine, Z=Commercial Chassis. The last six symbols are the sequential production number. The Fisher Body Style Number plate is attached to the cowl under the hood on the left and identifies the year, series and body style as follows: 64-6239=Series 62 four-window Sedan, 64-6229=Series 62 six-window sedan, 64-6339=Sedan DeVille four-window sedan, 64-6367=Eldorado Convertible, 64-6267=Series 62 Convertible, 64-6257=Series 62 Coupe, 64-6357=Coupe DeVille, 64-6329=Sedan DeVille six-windows Sedan, 64-6039=Fleetwood Sixty Special, 64-6723=Fleetwood 75 Series Sedan, 64-6733=Fleetwood 75 Limousine, 64-6890=Commercial Chassis. Note: Cadillac used the term "Sedan" to identify its four-door hardtop models. The Fisher Body Style Number plate also carries the paint code. The 1964 paint codes were: 10=Ebony Black, 12=Aspen White, 14=Nevada Silver, 16=Cardiff Gray, 22=Beacon Blue, 24=Spruce Blue, 26=Somerset Blue, 29=Turino Turquoise, 32=Seacrest Green, 34=Lime, 36=Nile Green, 44=Bahama Sand, 46=Sierra Gold, 47=Palomino,

50=Matador Red, 52=Royal Maroon, 92=Firemist Blue, 94= Firemist Aquamarine, 96= Firemist Green, 97= Firemist Saddle and 98= Firemist Red. Convertible top colors were: 1=White, 2=Black, 3=Aquamarine, 4=Light Lime, 6=Sandalwood, 8=Light Blue and 9=Silver Blue.

SERIES 62 — V-8

Standard equipment for cars in the 62 series (6200 models) again included power brakes, power steering, automatic transmission, dual back-up lights, windshield washers, dual-speed windshield wipers, full wheel discs, remote-control outside rearview mirrors, a left-hand vanity mirror, an oil filter, five tubeless black sidewall tires, a heater and defroster and cornering lights. Convertibles were again equipped with two-way power seats and power windows. Introduced as an industry first was Comfort Control, a completely automatic heating and air conditioning system controlled by a dial thermostat on the instrument panel.

SERIES 62 (6200 MODELS)

Model Number	Body/Style Number	Body Type & Seating	Factory Price	Shipping Weight	Production Total
64-62K	6229K	4D 6W Sedan-6P	5,236	4,575	9,243
64-62N	6239N	4D 4W Sedan-6P	5,236	4,550	13,670
64-62G	6257G	2D Coupe-6P	5,048	4,475	12,166

SERIES 62 — DEVILLE 6300 SUB-SERIES — V-8

Styling changes for new DeVilles followed the Series 62 pattern. Standard features on DeVilles were the same as on closed body 6200 models, plus two-way power seats and power windows. Performance gains from the new engine showed best in the lower range, at 20 to 50 mph traffic driving speeds. A new standard technical feature was Turbo-Hydra-Matic transmission, also used in Eldorado convertibles and Sixty Special sedans. A DeVille script, above the lower belt molding at the rear, was continued as an identifier.

SERIES 62 DEVILLE 6300 SUB-SERIES

Model Number	Body/Style Number	Body Type & Seating	Factory Price	Shipping Weight	Production Total
64-63L	6329L	4D 6W Sedan-6P	5,655	4,600	14,627
64-63B	6339B	4D 4W Sedan-6P	5,655	4,575	39,674
64-63J	6357J	2D Hardtop Coupe-6P	5,408	4,495	38,195
64-63F	6267F	2D Convertible-6P	5,612	4,545	17,900

SERIES 62 — DEVILLE 6300 ELDORADO — V-8

The Eldorado convertible, had special styling with untrimmed bodysides, full-length stainless steel underscores and a rectangular grid pattern rear decorative grille. Power vent windows, white sidewall tires and a six-way power seat (in bench-seat models) were standard in Eldorados.

SERIES 62 ELDORADO 6300 MODEL

Model Number	Body/Style Number	Body Type & Seating	Factory Price	Shipping Weight	Production Total
64-63P	6367P	2D Sport Convertible-6P	6,630	4,605	1,870

SERIES SIXTY SPECIAL FLEETWOOD — V-8

The Sixty Special Fleetwood sedan had the new styling features combined with carryover trim. Standard equipment included all normal 6300 sub-series features, plus power ventipanes.

SERIES SIXTY SPECIAL FLEETWOOD

Model Number	Body/Style Number	Body Type & Seating	Factory Price	Shipping Weight	Production Total
64-60M	6039M	4D Hardtop Sedan-6P	6,388	4,680	14,550

SERIES 6700 — FLEETWOOD 75 — V-8

This Fleetwood 75 series featured the same limousine-type styling seen in 1963, combined with a new frontal treatment, angular taillights and revised rear sheet metal. The back fenders swept rearward in a straighter and higher line. The fins began with a more pronounced kickup and housed new notch-shaped taillight lenses.

SERIES 6700 FLEETWOOD 75

Model Number	Body/Style Number	Body Type & Seating	Factory Price	Shipping Weight	Production Total
63-67R	6723R	4D Sedan-6P	9,746	5,215	617
63-67S	6733S	4D Limousine-9P	9,960	5,300	808
63-67Z	6890Z	Commercial chassis	—	—	2,527

ENGINE

Overhead valve. Cast-iron block. Displacement: 429-cid. Bore and Stroke: 4.13 x 4.00 inches. Compression ratio: 10.5:1. Brake hp: 340 at 4600 rpm. Taxable hp: 54.6. Torque: 480 at 3000 rpm. Five main bearings. Hydraulic valve lifters. Crankcase capacity: 4 qt. (Add 1 qt. if new filter installed). Cooling system capacity: 17.25 qt. Single exhaust with crossover. Carburetor: Carter AFB four-barrel Model 3655S. Alternate carburetor: Rochester 4GC four-barrel.

CHASSIS

(Series 62, Series 63) Wheelbase: 129.5 inches. Overall length: 223.5 inches (Park Ave. 215 inches). Width: 79.5 inches. Height: 54.8 inches. Front tread: 61 inches. Rear tread: 61 inches. Tires: Eldorado 8.20 x 15, Others 8.00 x 15. Rear axle ratio: 2.94:1.

(Series 60S) Wheelbase: 129.5 inches. Overall length: 223.5 inches. Width: 79.5 inches. Height: 56.6 inches. Front tread: 61 inches. Rear tread: 61 inches. Tires: 8.00 x 15. Rear axle ratio: 2.94:1.

(Series 75) Wheelbase: 149.8. Overall length: 243.8 inches. Width: 79.8 inches. Height: 59.0 inches. Front tread: 61 inches. Rear tread: 61 inches. Tires: 8.20 x 15 six-ply black sidewall. Rear axle ratio: 3.36:1.

(Commercial chassis) Wheelbase: 156 inches.

OPTIONS

Air conditioner for Series 60-62 ($474). Air conditioner for Series 75 ($624). Automatic headlight control ($45). Bucket seats in styles 6267F, 6339B, 6357J, or 6389D with leather upholstery required ($188). Controlled differential ($54). Cruise control ($97). Door guards for two-door styles ($4), for four-door styles ($7). Electric door locks for two-door styles ($46), for four-door styles ($70). E-Z-Eye Glass ($52). Leather upholstery for styles 6339B, 6357J, 6389D, or 6039M ($134). License plate frame ($6). Padded roof for style 6357J ($91), for style 6039M ($134). Six-way power seat ($85-$113 depending on body style). Power window regulators as an option ($118). Power ventipanes as an option ($73). Radio with rear seat speaker ($165). Radio with rear seat speaker and remote-control ($247). AM/FM radio ($191). Front seat belts in Series 60-62 models ($22). Rear seat belts in same models ($22). Adjustable steering wheel ($48). Remote control trunk lock ($53). Five white sidewall tires, 8.20 x 15 four-ply on Series 60-62, standard on Eldorado ($57 exchange). Five white sidewall tires, 8.20 x 15 six-ply on Series 75 models ($64 exchange). All 1964 Cadillacs were built in Detroit, Michigan.

HISTORICAL

Dealer introductions of new models took place on October 3, 1963. The automaker produced 165,959 Cadillacs during the model year or 2.1 percent of total industry output of 1964 models. Calendar-year output was 154,603 units, which equated to a two-percent share of the market. Dealer sales hit 151,740, a seven-percent gain over 1963. Cadillac's 1963 V-8 was the first major redesign since that power plant's introduction as a 331-cid engine in 1949. The Clark Avenue factory had closed down on July 8, 1964 to allow workers to put the finishing touches on the 471,000-sq.-ft. expansion. When it re-opened on August 24, Cadillac was poised to soon build its 3 millionth car, but a United Auto Workers Union strike shut the plant down again on September 25.

1964 Cadillac, De Ville convertible

1964 Cadillac, De Ville convertible

1965

OVERVIEW

A broader, unified grille and vertically-mounted headlights were among 1965 styling changes. The Cadillac tail fin was said to be gone but symmetrical rear fender forms tapered to thin edges, top and bottom, giving a traditional visual impression. Curved side windows with frameless glass were new and convertibles had tempered glass backlights. The standard wheelbase pillared sedan returned. Perimeter frame construction allowed repositioning of engines six inches forward in the frame, lowering the transmission hump and increasing interior room.

I.D. DATA

The VIN was stamped on the top left-hand frame support next to the radiator support and took the form *65F100001 *. The same number is stamped on the top surface of the engine block ahead of the left-hand valve cover. The first two symbols indicate model-year: 65=1965. The third symbol identifies the body style: B=Sedan DeVille four-window sedan, E=Eldorado Convertible, F=DeVille Convertible, G=Calais Coupe, J=Coupe DeVille, K=Calais Sedan, L=Sedan DeVille, M=Fleetwood Sixty Special (Includes Fleetwood Brougham option),

N=Calais Hardtop Sedan, R=Fleetwood 75 Sedan, S=Fleetwood 75 Limousine, Z=Commercial Chassis. The last six symbols are the sequential production number. The Fisher Body Style Number plate is attached to the cowl under the hood on the left and identifies the year, series and body style as follows: 65-68239=Calais Hardtop Sedan, 65-68257=Calais Coupe, 65-68269=Calais Sedan, 65-68339=Sedan DeVille Hardtop, 65-68357=Coupe DeVille, 65-68367=DeVille Convertible, 65-68369=Sedan DeVille, 65-68069=Sixty Special (Including Brougham option), 65-68467=Eldorado Convertible, 65-69723=Fleetwood 75 Sedan, 65-69733=Fleetwood 75 Limousine and 65-69890=Commercial Chassis. The Fisher Body Style Number plate also carries the paint code. The 1965 paint codes were: 10=Sable Black, 12=Aspen White, 16=Starlight Silver, 18=Ascot Gray, 20=Hampton Blue, 24=Tahoe Blue, 26=Ensign Blue, 30=Cascade Green, 36=Inverness Green, 40=Cape Ivory, 42=Sandalwood, 44=Sierra Gold, 46=Samoan Bronze, 48=Matador Red, 49=Claret Maroon, 90=Peacock Firemist, 52=Royal Maroon, 92=Sheffield Firemist, 96=Jade Firemist, 97=Saddle Firemist and 98=Crimson Firemist. Convertible top colors were: 1=White, 2=Black, 3=Blue, 5=Brown and 6=Sandalwood.

Above: **1965 Cadillac, Calais four-door hardtop**

CALAIS SERIES—V-8

The Calais series replaced the Sixty-Two line for 1965. Standard Calais equipment was comprised of power brakes, power steering, automatic transmission, dual back-up lights, windshield washers, dual-speed windshield wipers, full-wheel discs, a remote-controlled outside rearview mirror, a visor-vanity mirror, oil filter, five tubeless black sidewall tires, a heater and defroster, lights for the luggage, glove and rear passenger compartments, cornering lights and front- and rear-seat safety belts.

CALAIS SERIES 682

Model Number	Body/Style Number	Body Type & Seating	Factory Price	Shipping Weight	Production Total
65-682	68257-G	2D Hardtop Coupe-6P	5,059	4,435	12,515
65-682	68239-N	4D Hardtop Sedan-6P	5,247	4,500	13,975
65-682	68269-K	4D Sedan-6P	5,247	4,490	7,721

DEVILLE SERIES—V-8

DeVilles kept their rear fender signature scripts for distinctions of trim. One auto writer described this feature as "Tiffany-like." Standard equipment matched that found in Calais models, plus power window lifts. Vinyl roofs for Coupe DeVilles and Sedan DeVilles came in four different colors.

DEVILLE SERIES 683

Model Number	Body/Style Number	Body Type & Seating	Factory Price	Shipping Weight	Production Total
65-683	68367-F	2D Convertible-6P	5,639	4,690	19,200
65-683	68357-J	2D Hardtop Coupe-6P	5,419	4,480	43,345
65-683	68339-B	4D Hardtop Sedan-6P	5,666	4,560	45,535
65-683	68369-L	4D Sedan-6P	5,666	4,555	15,000

FLEETWOOD SIXTY SPECIAL SUB-SERIES—V-8

Poised on a new 133-inch wheelbase, the Sixty Special sedan wore Fleetwood crests on the hood and deck. All features found in lower priced Cadillacs were standard, as well as power ventipanes, glare-proof rearview mirror and automatic level control. Like Calais and DeVilles, the Fleetwood Sixty Special had an improved Turbo-Hydra-Matic transmission with a variable stator. The $150 Fleetwood Brougham trim option included a more richly-appointed interior.

FLEETWOOD SIXTY SPECIAL SUB-SERIES 680

Model Number	Body/Style Number	Body Type & Seating	Factory Price	Shipping Weight	Production Total
65-680	68069-M	4D Sedan-6P	6,479	4,670	18,100

FLEETWOOD ELDORADO SUB-SERIES—V-8

Under a new model arrangement, the Eldorado became a one-car Fleetwood sub-series. Fleetwood hood and deck lid crests were the main difference in outer trim. Additional standard equipment, over that found in Sixty Specials, included white sidewall tires and a six-way power seat for cars with regular bench seating.

FLEETWOOD ELDORADO SUB-SERIES 684

Model Number	Body/Style Number	Body Type & Seating	Factory Price	Shipping Weight	Production Total
65-684	68467-E	2D Eldorado Convertible-6P	6,754	4,660	2,125

FLEETWOOD 75 SUB-SERIES—V-8

Cadillac's longest, heaviest, richest and highest-priced models were, again, more traditionally engineered than the other lines. The new perimeter frame was not used and neither was the improved automatic transmission. In addition, automatic level control was not featured. The annual styling facelift did not affect these tradition-bound luxury cars. They came with all power controls found in Eldorados and added courtesy and map lights to the standard equipment list. Sales of commercial chassis earned an increase of 30 units, while Limousine deliveries tapered slightly downward and the popularity of the nine-passenger Sedan declined.

FLEETWOOD 75 SUB-SERIES 697

Model Number	Body/Style Number	Body Type & Seating	Factory Price	Shipping Weight	Production Total
65-697	69723-R	4D Sedan-9P	9,746	5,190	455
65-697	69733-S	4D Limousine-9P	9,960	5,260	795

FLEETWOOD 75 SUB-SERIES 698

Model Number	Body/Style Number	Body Type & Seating	Factory Price	Shipping Weight	Production Total
65-698	69890-Z	Commercial chassis	—	—	2,669

ENGINE

Overhead valve. Cast-iron block. Displacement: 429-cid. Bore and Stroke: 4.13 x 4.00 inches. Compression ratio: 10.5:1. Brake hp: 340 at 4600 rpm. Taxable hp: 54.6. Torque: 480 at 3000 rpm. Five main bearings. Hydraulic valve lifters. Crankcase capacity: 4 qt. (Add 1 qt. if new filter installed). Cooling system capacity: 17.25 qt. Single exhaust with crossover. Carburetor: Carter AFB four-barrel Model 3903S. Alternate carburetor: Rochester 4GC four-barrel.

CHASSIS

Wheelbase: (commercial chassis) 156 inches, (Series 75) 149.8 inches, (Series 60 Special) 133 inches, (all other series) 129.5 inches. Overall length: (Series 75) 243.8 inches, (Series 60 Special) 227.5 inches, (all other series) 224 inches. Front tread: (all series) 62.5 inches. Rear tread: (all series) 62.5 inches. Automatic level control standard where indicated in text. A new engine mounting system and patented quiet exhaust were used. Tires: (Series 75) 8.20 x 15, (Eldorado) 9 x 15, (all others) 8 x 15.

(Series 6800) Wheelbase: 129.5 inches. Overall length: 224.0 inches. Width: 79.9 inches. Height: 55.6 inches. Front tread: 62.5 inches. Rear tread: 62.5 inches. Tires: 8.00 x 15 (Eldorado 9.00 x 15).

(Series 6900) Wheelbase: 149.8. Overall length: 243.8 inches. Width: 79.9 inches. Height: 59.0 inches. Front tread: 61 inches. Rear tread: 61 inches. Tires: 8.20 x 15.

(Commercial chassis) Wheelbase: 156 inches.

OPTIONS

Air conditioner, except 75 series models ($495). Air conditioner, 75 series model ($624). Bucket seats with console in F-J-B models with leather upholstery ($188). Controlled differential ($54). Cruise control ($97). Door guards on two-door models ($4), on four-door models ($7). Fleetwood Brougham option on M model ($199). Soft Ray tinted glass ($52). Delete-option heater and defroster on 75 series models ($135 credit), on other models ($97 credit). Leather upholstery on J-B-L-M models ($141). License plate frame ($6). Padded roof on J model ($124), on B or L models ($140). Left-hand four-way power bucket seat on F-J-B models ($54). Power door locks on G-F-J-E models ($46), on N-K-B-L-M models ($70). Power headlight control on R-S models ($46), on other models ($51). Six-way power front seat on G-N-K models ($113), on F-J-B-L-M models ($85). Power window regulators on G-N-K models ($119). Power vent window regulator option ($73). Radio with rear speaker ($165). Radio with rear speaker and remote-control ($246). AM/FM radio ($191). Rear seat belts ($18). Front seat belt delete option ($17 credit). Adjustable steering wheel, except on R-S models ($91). Remote control trunk lock, except on R-S models ($53). Twilight Sentinel, except on E-R-S models ($57). Five white sidewall tires, 9 x 15 size with four-ply construction, except E-R-S models ($57 exchange). Five white sidewall tires, 9 x 15 size with six-ply construction on R-S models only ($64 exchange).

HISTORICAL

Dealer introductions of 1965 models took place on September 24, 1964. The automaker produced 181,435 Cadillacs during the model-year or 2.1 percent of total industry output of 1965 models. Calendar-year output was 195,595 units, which equated to a 2.10 share of the market. Dealer sales hit 189,024. Cadillac's three-millionth car, a 1965 Fleetwood Brougham, was produced on November 4, 1964. Cadillac's new engineering center was dedicated. A United Auto Workers (UAW) walkout closed Cadillac's newly expanded Clark Avenue (Detroit) factory from September 25, 1964, through the following December and created a decline in production and sales for the 1964 calendar-year and 1965 model-year.

Late model 1964 De Ville convertible (left) and 1962 Coupe de Ville (right) join the new Sedan de Ville in this 1965 Cadillac "family portrait" ad.

1966

OVERVIEW

For 1966, Cadillac offered 12 models in three series, Calais, DeVille and Fleetwood. A new model was the Fleetwood Brougham, which was formerly merchandised as an option package for the Fleetwood Sixty-Special. Cadillac "firsts" seen this season included variable-ratio power steering and optional front seats with carbon cloth heating pads built into cushions and seat backs. Comfort and convenience innovations were headrests, reclining bucket seats for the front passenger and an AM/FM stereo system. Engineering improvements made to the Series 75 perimeter frame increased ride and handling ease. Newly designed piston and oil rings were adopted and new engine and body mountings were employed. All models, except the Series 75 seven-passenger Sedan and Limousine were mildly facelifted.

I.D. DATA

The VIN was stamped on the top surface of the right-hand frame side rail toward the front coil-spring suspension and may be covered by a rubber splash shield. The number was also stamped on the rear portion of the engine block, behind the left-hand cylinder bank. It took the form *

Above: **1966 Cadillac, Fleetwood Eldorado, convertible**

N6100001 *. The first symbol indicates model: B=Sedan DeVille Hardtop, D=Fleetwood Sedan, E=Eldorado Convertible, F=DeVille Convertible, G=Calais Coupe, J=Coupe DeVille, K=Calais Sedan, L=Sedan DeVille six-windows Sedan, M=Fleetwood Sixty Special Sedan, N=Calais Hardtop Sedan, P=Fleetwood Brougham Sedan, R=Fleetwood 75 Sedan, S=Fleetwood 75 Limousine, Z=Commercial Chassis. The second symbol indicates model-year: 6=1966. The last six symbols are the sequential production number. The Fisher Body Style Number plate is attached to the cowl under the hood on the left and identifies the year, series and body style as follows: 66-68239=Calais Hardtop Sedan, 66-68257=Calais Coupe, 66-68269=Calais Sedan, 66-68339=Sedan DeVille Hardtop, 66-68357=Coupe DeVille, 66-68367=DeVille Convertible, 66-68369=Sedan DeVille, 66-68069=Sixty Special, 66169=Fleetwood Brougham Sedan, 66-68467=Eldorado Convertible, 66-69723=Fleetwood 75 Sedan, 66-69733=Fleetwood 75 Limousine and 66-69890=Commercial Chassis. The Fisher Body Style Number plate also carries the paint code. The 1966 paint codes were: 10=Sable Black, 12=Strathmore White, 16=Starlight Silver, 18=Summitt Gray, 20=Mist Blue, 24=Marlin Blue, 26=Nocturne Blue, 30=Cascade Green, 36=Inverness Green, 40=Cape Ivory, 42=Sandalwood, 44=Antique Gold, 46=Autumn Rust, 48=Flamenco Red,

49=Claret Maroon, 90=Cobalt Firemist, 96=Tropical Green Firemist, 97=Florentine Firemist and 98=Ember Firemist. Convertible top colors were: 1=White, 2=Black, 3=Blue, 5=Brown and 6=Sandalwood.

CALAIS — SERIES 682 — V-8

A Cadillac crest and V-shaped molding trimmed the hood of Calais. Separate, rectangular side marker lights replaced the integral grille extension designs. There was generally less chrome on Calais (and other Cadillac models) this year. Standard Calais equipment included power brakes, power steering, automatic transmission, dual back-up lights, dual-speed windshield wipers, full-wheel discs, a remote-controlled outside rearview mirror, a visor-vanity mirror, oil filter, five tubeless black sidewall tires, a heater and defroster, lights for the luggage, glove and rear passenger compartments, cornering lights and front- and rear-seat safety belts.

CALAIS SERIES 682

Model Number	Body/Style Number	Body Type & Seating	Factory Price	Shipping Weight	Production Total
66-682	68269-K	4D Sedan-6P	5,171	4,460	4,575
66-682	68239-N	4D Hardtop Sedan-6P	5,171	4,465	13,025
66-682	68257-G	2D Hardtop Coupe-6P	4,986	4,390	11,080

DEVILLE — SERIES 683 — V-8

Following the general styling theme found on Calais models, the DeVille series was again distinguished with Tiffany-like script above the rear tip of the horizontal body rub moldings. Cadillac crests and V-shaped moldings, front and rear, were DeVille identifiers. Standard equipment matched that found in Calais models, plus power window lifts. Vinyl roofs were available for Coupe DeVilles and Sedan DeVilles.

DEVILLE SERIES 683

Model Number	Body/Style Number	Body Type & Seating	Factory Price	Shipping Weight	Production Total
66-683	68369-L	4D Sedan-6P	5,581	4,535	11,860
66-683	68339-B	4D Hardtop Sedan-6P	5,581	4,515	60,550
66-683	68357-J	2D Coupe DeVille-6P	5,339	4,460	50,580
66-683	68367-F	2D Convertible Coupe-6P	5,555	4,445	19,200

FLEETWOOD SIXTY SPECIAL — SUB-SERIES 680/681 — V-8

Models in this range were characterized by traditional standard equipment additions and by emblems containing a Cadillac shield encircled by a laurel wreath, which appeared on the hood and center of the deck. Fleetwood designations, in block letters, were also found at the right-hand side of the deck. The Brougham had the wreath-style medallions on the roof pillar, along with Tiffany script in the same location to identify this extra-rich model.

FLEETWOOD SIXTY SPECIAL SUB-SERIES 680/681

Model Number	Body/Style Number	Body Type & Seating	Factory Price	Shipping Weight	Production Total
66-680	68069-M	4D Sedan-6P	6,378	4,615	5,445
66-681	68169-P	4D Brougham-6P	6,695	4,616	13,630

FLEETWOOD ELDORADO — SUB-SERIES 684 — V-8

Fleetwood-type trim was seen again on the Eldorado. Equipment additions included white sidewall tires and a six-way power front bench seat. It was the last season that conventional engineering characterized this model.

FLEETWOOD ELDORADO SUB-SERIES 684

Model Number	Body/Style Number	Body Type & Seating	Factory Price	Shipping Weight	Production Total
66-684	68567-E	2D Eldorado Convertible-6P	6,631	4,500	2,250

FLEETWOOD SEVENTY-FIVE — SERIES 697/698 — V-8

Fleetwood exterior trim and Fleetwood interior appointments enriched the cars in Cadillac's high-dollar lineup. The first major restyling since 1959 was carried out for 1966. A new perimeter-type frame was used. The new look brought the appearance of the big sedan and the limousine so up-to-date that it matched the visual impression of other Cadillacs. A big jump in sales for both regular-production 75s resulted.

FLEETWOOD 75 SUB-SERIES 697

Model Number	Body/Style Number	Body Type & Seating	Factory Price	Shipping Weight	Production Total
66-697	69723-R	4D Sedan-9P	10,312	5,320	980
66-697	69733-S	4D Limousine-9P	10,521	5,435	1,037

FLEETWOOD 75 SUB-SERIES 698

Model Number	Body/Style Number	Body Type & Seating	Factory Price	Shipping Weight	Production Total
66-698	69890-Z	Commercial chassis	—	—	2,463

ENGINE

Overhead valve. Cast-iron block. Displacement: 429-cid. Bore and Stroke: 4.13 x 4.00 inches. Compression ratio: 10.5:1. Brake hp: 340 at 4600 rpm. Taxable hp: 54.6. Torque: 480 at 3000 rpm. Five main bearings. Hydraulic valve lifters. Crankcase capacity: 4 qt. (Add 1 qt. if new filter installed). Cooling system capacity: 18 qt. Single exhaust with crossover. Carburetor: Carter AFB four-barrel: (Fleetwood, Calais and DeVille) Model 4168S; (Fleetwood 75 limousine) 4169S; (Fleetwood Eldorado) 4171S. Alternate carburetor: Rochester 4GC four-barrel (Fleetwood, Calais and DeVille) Model 7026030.

CHASSIS

(Calais, DeVille, Eldorado) Wheelbase: 129.5 inches. Overall length: 224.2 inches. Front tread: 62.5 inches. Rear tread: 62.5 inches. Automatic level control standard where indicated in text. Tires: (Eldorado) 9.00 x 15, (all others) 8.00 x 15.

(Fleetwood Brougham, Fleetwood 60 Special) Wheelbase: 133 inches. Overall length: 227.7 inches. Front tread: 62.5 inches. Rear tread: 62.5 inches. Automatic level control standard where indicated in text. Tires: 8.00 x 15.

(Fleetwood 75) Wheelbase: 149.8 inches. Overall length: 244.5 inches. Front tread: 62.5 inches. Rear tread: 62.5 inches. Automatic level control standard where indicated in text. Tires: 8.20 x 15.

(Commercial Chassis) Wheelbase: 156 inches. Front tread: 62.5 inches. Rear tread: 62.5 inches. Automatic level control standard where indicated in text. Tires: 9.00 x 15.

OPTIONS

Air conditioner, except 75 series models ($495). Air conditioner, 75 series model ($624). Bucket seats with console in F-J-B models with leather upholstery ($188). Controlled differential ($54). Cruise control ($97). Door guards on two-door models ($4), on four-door models ($7). Fleetwood Brougham option on M model ($199). Soft Ray tinted glass ($52). Delete option heater and defroster on 75 series models ($135 credit), on other models ($97 credit). Leather upholstery on J-B-L-M models ($141). License plate frame ($6). Padded roof on J model ($124), on B or L models ($140). Left-hand four-way power bucket seat on F-J-B models ($54). Power door locks on G-F-J-E models ($46), on N-K-B-LM models ($70). Power headlight control on R-S models ($46), on other models ($51). Six-way power front seat on G-N-K models ($113), on F-J-B-L-M models ($85). Power window regulators on G-N-K models ($119). Power vent window regulator option ($73). Radio with rear speaker ($165). Radio with rear speaker and remote-control ($246). AM/FM radio ($191). Rear seat belts ($18). Front seat belt delete option ($17 credit). Adjustable steering wheel except on R-S models ($91). Remote control trunk lock, except on R-S models ($53). Twilight Sentinel, except on E-R-S models ($57). Five white sidewall tires, 9 x 15 size with four-ply construction, except E-R-S models ($57 exchange). Five white sidewall tires, 9 x 15 size with six-ply construction on R-S models only ($64 exchange). A new seat warmer sold for $60.20. The recliner seat with headrest was $64.20 extra and was available only in F-J-B-H models with Eldorado bench seats or optional bucket seats. Headrests were a separate $40.15 option for all Cadillacs. All 1966 Cadillacs were built in Detroit, Michigan.

HISTORICAL

The 1966 models were introduced October 14, 1965. This was the best year ever with model-year production hitting 196,675 cars or 2.3 percent of the industry total. That made it the best year in Cadillac history and the second year running for increases, despite a downturn in the overall U.S. car market. Calendar-year production (including 1967 models built in 1966) included 198,797 regular Cadillacs and 6,204 Eldorados. Cadillac dealer sales for the calendar-year were 198,789 for a 2.4 percent market share. A record of 5,570 one-week builds was marked December 5 and a record one-day output of 1,017 cars was achieved October 27. A new assembly line was set up to manufacture front-wheel-drive 1967 Eldorados.

1966 Cadillac, De Ville convertible

1967

OVERVIEW

The 1967 Cadillac Eldorado was a completely new front-wheel-drive six-passenger coupe. It was described as a "sports-styled" automobile and the first car to combine front-wheel-drive, variable-ratio power steering and automatic level control. It replaced the Eldorado Convertible in the Fleetwood series and used the standard Cadillac V-8. Regular 1967 Cadillacs featured a redesigned side panel contour that created a longer look and more sculptured appearance. The coupe roof structure was restyled after the Florentine show car and had a more formal look. Technical improvements included a revised engine valve train, a different carburetor, a Mylar printed-circuit instrument panel, re-tuned body mounts and a new engine fan with clutch for quieter operation. A squarer-cornered radiator grille insert had a cross-hatch pattern that appeared both above the bumper and through a horizontal slot cut into it. Rear-end styling revisions were highlighted by metal-divided taillights and a painted lower bumper section. The new front grille had a forward angle and blades that seemed to emphasize its vertical members. Rectangular parking lights were housed at the outer ends.

Above: **1967 Cadillac, Fleetwood Brougham**

I.D. DATA

The VIN was stamped on the top surface of the right-hand frame side rail toward the front coil-spring suspension and may be covered by a rubber splash shield. The number was also stamped on the rear portion of the engine block, behind the left-hand cylinder bank. It took the form * N7100001 *. The first symbol indicates model: B=Sedan DeVille Hardtop, F=DeVille Convertible, G=Calais Coupe, H=Fleetwood Eldorado, J=Coupe DeVille, K=Calais Sedan, L=Sedan DeVille six-windows Sedan, M=Fleetwood Sixty Special Sedan, N=Calais Hardtop Sedan, P=Fleetwood Brougham Sedan, R=Fleetwood 75 Sedan, S=Fleetwood 75 Limousine, Z=Commercial Chassis. The second symbol indicates model-year: 7=1967. The last six symbols are the sequential production number. The Fisher Body Style Number plate is attached to the cowl under the hood on the left and identifies the year, series and body style as follows: 67-68249=Calais Hardtop Sedan, 67-68247=Calais Coupe, 67-68269=Calais Sedan, 67-68349=Sedan DeVille Hardtop, 67-68347=Coupe DeVille,67-68367=DeVille Convertible,67-68369=Sedan DeVille, 67-68069=Sixty Special, 67169=Fleetwood Brougham Sedan, 67-68367=Eldorado Convertible, 67-69723=Fleetwood 75 Sedan, 67-69733=Fleetwood 75 Limousine and 67-69890=Commercial Chassis. The Fisher Body Style Number plate also carries the

paint code. The 1967 paint codes were: 10=Sable Black, 12=Grecian White, 16=Regal Silver, 18=Summit Gray, 20=Venetian Blue, 24=Marina Blue, 26=Admiralty Blue, 30=Pinecrest Green, 36=Sherwood Green, 40=Persian Ivory, 42=Sudan Beige, 43=Baroque Gold, 44=Doeskin, 48=Flamenco Red, 49=Regent Maroon, 90=Atlantis Blue Firemist, 92=Crystal Firemist, 96=Tropical Green Firemist, 97=Olympic Bronze Firemist and 98=Ember Firemist. Convertible top colors were: 1=White, 2=Black, 3=Dark Blue, 5=Dark Brown and 6=Sandalwood.

CALAIS—SERIES 682—V-8

Standard Calais equipment included automatic transmission, power brakes, power steering, a heater and defroster, reflectors, full wheel discs, three-speed windshield wipers and washers, a left-hand remote-control outside rearview mirror, an inside non-glare rearview mirror, a visor-vanity mirror, a cigarette lighter, an electric clock, cornering lights, lights for the rear compartment, glovebox and luggage compartment, interior courtesy lights and all standard GM safety features. Also included at base price were Automatic Climate Controls, a rear cigarette lighter (except coupes), a padded dashboard, a Hazard Warning system and front and rear seat belts with outboard retractors.

CALAIS SERIES 682

Model Number	Body/Style Number	Body Type & Seating	Factory Price	Shipping Weight	Production Total
67-682	68269-K	4D Sedan-6P	5,215	4,520	2,865
67-682	68249-N	4D Hardtop Sedan-6P	5,215	4,550	9,880
67-682	68247-G	2D Coupe-6P	5,040	4,445	9,085

DEVILLE—SERIES 683—V-8

Minor trim variations and slightly richer interiors separated DeVilles from Calais. For example, a Tiffany-style chrome signature script was again found above the bodyside molding on the rear fenders. DeVille equipment lists were comprised of all the same features found on Calais models, plus power-operated window regulators, rear cigarette lighters in all styles and two-way power front seats. An innovative slide-out fuse box and safety front seat back lock for two-door models were additional Cadillac advances for the 1967 model-year.

DEVILLE SERIES 683

Model Number	Body/Style Number	Body Type & Seating	Factory Price	Shipping Weight	Production Total
67-683	68369-L	4D Sedan-6P	5,625	4,675	8,800
67-683	68349-B	4D Hardtop Sedan-6P	5,625	4,550	59,902
67-683	68347-J	2D Coupe DeVille-6P	5,392	4,505	52,905
67-683	68367-F	2D Convertible-6P	5,608	4,500	18,200

FLEETWOOD SIXTY SPECIAL—SUB-SERIES 680/681—V-8

Full-length bright metal body underscores, Fleetwood wreath and crest emblems for the hood, trunk and roof pillars, the lack of horizontal lower body rub moldings and Fleetwood block letters on the lower front fenders and passenger side of the deck lid characterized the new Sixty Special. The Brougham featured a padded Cordova vinyl top with a model identification script attached to the roof "C" pillars. Added to the list of DeVille equipment were Automatic Level Control suspension and power-operated ventipanes. The Brougham also included lighted fold-down trays, adjustable reading lights and carpeted fold-down footrests.

FLEETWOOD SIXTY SPECIAL SUB-SERIES 680/681

Model Number	Body/Style Number	Body Type & Seating	Factory Price	Shipping Weight	Production Total
67-680	68069-M	4D Sedan-6P	6,423	4,685	3,550
67-681	68169-P	4D Brougham-6P	6,739	4,735	12,750

1967 Cadillac Hardtop Sedan de Ville

FLEETWOOD SEVENTY-FIVE—SUB-SERIES 697/698—V-8

The year's new styling was beautifully rendered on the Cadillac long wheelbase models, which had extra-long rear fenders and an extended "greenhouse" with a formal, high-headroom look. Fleetwood wreath and crest emblems decorated the hood and the trunk and there were Fleetwood block letters at the right side of the deck lid. A simple horizontal body rub molding, lengthened to fit the elongated sheet metal, trimmed the sides of these elegant machines. Standard equipment included all found in DeVilles, plus Automatic Level Control, air conditioning, carpeted fold-down foot rests, and 8.20 x 15, four-ply 8PR blackwall tires.

FLEETWOOD SEVENTY-FIVE SUB-SERIES 697/698

Model Number	Body/Style Number	Body Type & Seating	Factory Price	Shipping Weight	Production Total
67-697	69723-R	4D Sedan-6P	10,360	5,335	835
67-697	69733-S	4D Limousine-6P	10,571	5,450	965
67-698	69890-Z	Commercial chassis	—	—	2,333

ENGINE

FLEETWOOD ELDORADO — SUB-SERIES 693—V-8

Built off the Oldsmobile Toronado platform and sharing the same basic body shell, the all-new Eldorado was shorter and lower than even the smallest Cadillacs, but could provide full six-passenger seating because of its drive train layout. Concealed, horizontally-mounted headlights were featured. The Cadillac V-8 was fitted to the platform with changes in the oil pan, exhaust manifolds, accessory and drive belt layout and engine mount system. It had dual exhaust, but a single outlet muffler and tailpipe arrangement. An improved fresh-air system eliminated the need for front ventipanes. The rear windows slid back into the roof structure. The Eldorado shared 1967 Cadillac technical changes such as Mylar- backed circuitry, a bigger power brake booster, a slide-out fuse box and braided rayon brake hoses. However, it was the only model in the line to offer the front disc brake option. The typical assortment of Fleetwood extra equipment was standard on Eldorados as well.

1967 Cadillac, convertible De Ville

1967 Cadillac, Fleetwood Brougham

FLEETWOOD ELDORADO SUB-SERIES 693

Model Number	Body/Style Number	Body Type & Seating	Factory Price	Shipping Weight	Production Total
67-693	69347-H	2D Hardtop Coupe-6P	6,277	4,590	17,930

CHASSIS

(Eldorado) Wheelbase: 120 inches. Overall length: 221 inches. Front tread: 63.5 inches. Rear tread: 63.0 inches. Tires: 9.00 x 15.

(Calais, DeVille) Wheelbase: 129.5 inches. Overall length: 224.0 inches. Front tread: 62.5 inches. Rear tread: 62.5 inches. Tires: 9.00 x 15.

(Fleetwood Brougham, Fleetwood 60 Special) Wheelbase: 133 inches. Overall length: 227.5 inches. Front tread: 62.5 inches. Rear tread: 62.5 inches. Tires: 9.00 x 15.

(Fleetwood 75) Wheelbase: 149.8 inches. Overall length: 244.5 inches. Front tread: 62.5 inches. Rear tread: 62.5 inches. Tires: 8.20 x 15.

(Commercial Chassis) Wheelbase: 156 inches. Front tread: 62.5 inches. Rear tread: 62.5 inches.

OPTIONS

Auxiliary horn ($12). Automatic level control option on models G-N-K-F-J-B-L ($79). Automatic Climate Control except R and S models ($516). Bucket seats with console on models F-J-B-H with leather upholstery required ($184). Firemist finish ($132). Cruise control ($95). Rear window defogger on models G-N-K-J-B-L-M-P ($27). Front disc brakes on Eldorado only ($105). Door guards on model G-F-J-H ($5), on models N-K-B-L-M-P-R-S ($8). Expanded vinyl upholstery on models G-N-K ($42). Soft Ray glass ($51). Guide-Matic headlight control ($50). Headrests ($53). Leather upholstery, models J-B-L-M-P ($138), model H ($158). License frame, single ($6), pair ($12). Padded roof, models J-H ($132), models B-L ($137). Power door locks, two- door ($47), four-door ($68). Power door locks for Fleetwood 75 models ($116). Power ventipanes, except models H-M-P, power windows required ($72). Rear quarter power ventipanes on Eldorado only ($63). Power windows on Calais models ($116). AM radio ($162). AM/FM radio

($188). AM/FM stereo, except Fleetwood 75 models ($288). AM radio rear controls on Fleetwood 75 models ($242). Reclining front seat with headrests on models F-J-B-H with bucket seats or Eldorado bench seats required ($84). Four-way left-hand power bucket seat on models F-J-B-H ($53). Six-way power front seat on models G-N-K ($111), models F-J-B-L-H-M-P-R ($83). Rear center seat belt ($11). Front shoulder straps ($32). Tilt- telescope steering wheel ($90). Remote control trunk lock ($52). Twilight Sentinel on Eldorado ($37), other models ($32). White sidewall tires, size 9 x 15 four-ply 8PR-5 except nine- passenger models ($56 exchange). White sidewall tires, size 8.20 x 15, four-ply 8PR-5 on nine-passenger models ($64 exchange). A 3.21:1 rear axle gear ratio was standard on Series Seventy-Five and Eldorado, optional on other models. A controlled differential was $40.15 extra on all models except Eldorados. An air injection reactor was $34.13 extra on all Cadillacs and required on all cars built for California sale. Closed positive crankcase ventilators were $4 extra on all Cadillacs and required on all cars built for California sale. All 1967 Cadillacs and Eldorados were built in Detroit, Michigan.

HISTORICAL

Dealer introduction date for 1967 Cadillacs and Eldorados was October 6, 1966. A third successive year of record production and sales was marked by Cadillac Division in 1967. Model-year production included 182,070 Cadillacs and 17,930 Eldorados for a third-time-in-a-row record total of 200,000 cars. This gave Cadillac a 2.6 percent share of total U.S. automobile production. This was the first year that Cadillac and Eldorado model-year output was totaled separately, but even the regular Cadillac had a larger 2.4 percent share of the market, indicating that the attention-getting "Eldo" was helping to build showroom traffic and sell other Cadillacs. Calendar-year production included 192,339 regular Cadillacs and 20,822 Eldorados. The total of 213,161 units was good for a 2.88 percent market share. Cadillac dealer sales for the calendar-year were 188,313 Cadillacs (2.5 percent market share) and 19,799 Eldorados (0.3 percent market share). A record of 5,570 one-week builds was marked December 5 and a record one-day output of 1,017 cars was achieved October 27. Cadillac sales for a single month passed the 20,000-unit level for the first time in the company's history and set an all-time high of 22,072 cars in October 1966.

Cadillac was proud to announce its Fleetwood Eldorado in 1967.

1967 Cadillac, Fleetwood Eldorado

1968

OVERVIEW

Cadillac was not about to alter its popular product in any major way, so the same basic styling and engineering continued into the 1968 model year, with a number of refinements. New grilles were added. They had an insert with a finer mesh and step-down outer section, which held the rectangular parking lights just a little higher than before. Rear-end styling was modestly altered. An obvious change was a 6-1/2 inch longer hood, designed to accommodate recessed windshield wipers. An enlarged engine offered more cubic inches and torque than any other American V-8 and put out 375 hp. Of 20 exterior paint color combinations, 14 were totally new. On the inside enriched appointments included molded inner door panels and a selection of 147 upholstery combinations, 76 in cloth, 67 in leather and four in vinyl. It was the second year for the front-wheel-drive Fleetwood Eldorado Coupe. It had new front parking lights, a longer hood and a larger V-8.

I.D. DATA

The VIN was now stamped on a steel plate riveted to the top surface of the instrument panel and visible through the lower left-hand corner of the windshield. The number was also stamped on the rear portion of the engine block, behind the left-hand cylinder bank. It took the form * N8100001 *. The first symbol indicates model: B=Sedan DeVille Hardtop, F=DeVille Convertible, G=Calais Coupe, H=Fleetwood Eldorado, J=Coupe DeVille, L=Sedan DeVille six-windows Sedan, M=Fleetwood Sixty Special Sedan, N=Calais Hardtop Sedan, P=Fleetwood Brougham Sedan, R=Fleetwood 75 Sedan, S=Fleetwood 75 Limousine, Z=Commercial Chassis. The second symbol indicates model-year: 8=1968. The last six symbols are the sequential production number starting with 100001. The Fisher Body Style Number plate is attached to the cowl under the hood on the left and identifies the year, series and body style as follows: 68-68249=Calais Hardtop Sedan, 68-68247=Calais Coupe, 68-68349=Sedan DeVille Hardtop Sedan, 68-68347=Coupe DeVille, 68-68367=DeVille Convertible, 68-68369=Sedan DeVille, 68-68069=Sixty Special, 68169=Fleetwood Brougham Sedan, 68-69347=Eldorado Hardtop Coupe (front-wheel drive), 68-69723=Fleetwood 75 Sedan, 68-69733=Fleetwood 75 Limousine and 68-69890=Commercial chassis. The Fisher Body Style Number plate also carries the paint code. The 1968 paint codes were: 10=Satin Black, 12=Grecian White, 16=Regal Silver, 18=Summit Gray, 20=Arctic Blue, 24=Normandy Blue, 26=Emperor Blue, 30=Silver

Above: **1968 Cadillac, Fleetwood Eldorado**

Pine Green, 36=Ivanhoe Green, 40=Kashmir Ivory, 42=Sudan Beige, 43=Baroque Gold, 44=Chestnut Brown, 48=San Mateo Red, 49=Regent Maroon, 90=Spectre Blue Firemist, 94=Topaz Gold Firemist, 96=Monterey Green Firemist, 97=Rosewood Firemist and 98=Madeira Plum Firemist. Convertible top colors were: 1=White, 2=Black, 3=Dark Blue, 4=Dark Brown and 5=Sandalwood. Roof panel colors were: 1=White, 2=Black, 3=Dark Blue, 4=Dark Brown and 5=Sandalwood.

CALAIS—SERIES 682—V-8

The Calais four-door pillared sedan was dropped. Standard features for the two remaining styles included Turbo-Hydra-Matic, power steering, power brakes, power windows, a heater and defroster, center arm rests, an electric clock, dual back-up lights, cornering lights, front and rear side marker lights, a Light Group, a Mirror Group, a padded instrument panel, seat belts, a trip odometer, an ignition key warning buzzer, recessed three-speed windshield wipers and washers and five black sidewall tires.

CALAIS SERIES 682

Model Number	Body/Style Number	Body Type & Seating	Factory Price	Shipping Weight	Production Total
68-682	68247-G	2D Coupe-6P	5,315	4,570	8,165
68-682	68249-N	4D Hardtop Sedan-6P	5,491	4,640	10,025

DEVILLE—SERIES 683—V-8

On paper, it seemed that the main distinctions of cars in the DeVille lineup were the installation of a power-operated front seat with horizontal adjustment and the addition of illuminated door panel reflectors. There were, however, richer appointments inside and out, including the traditional rear fender Tiffany-like script and plusher upholstery trims. In addition, twice as many body styles were provided in DeVille level finish.

DEVILLE SERIES 683

Model Number	Body/Style Number	Body Type & Seating	Factory Price	Shipping Weight	Production Total
68-683	68369-L	4D Sedan-6P	5,785	4,680	9,850
68-683	68349-B	4D Hardtop Sedan-6P	5,785	4,675	72,662
68-683	68347-J	2D Coupe DeVille-6P	5,552	4,595	63,935
68-683	68367-F	2D Convertible DeVille-6P	5,736	4,600	18,025

FLEETWOOD SIXTY SPECIAL—SUB-SERIES 680/681—V-8

Features distinguishing 1968 Sixty Specials, in addition to a longer wheelbase, were Fleetwood wreath and crest emblems decorating the hood and the trunk and Fleetwood block letters at the right side of the deck lid. A simple horizontal body rub molding, lengthened to fit the elongated sheet metal, trimmed the body sides. Extra items of standard equipment included Automatic Level Control, front and rear power operated ventipanes and,

1968 Cadillac, convertible De Ville

1968 Cadillac, convertible De Ville

on Broughams, an adjustable reading light, a padded roof with special scripts and emblems and carpeted folding foot rests.

FLEETWOOD SIXTY-SPECIALS SUB-SERIES 680/681

Model Number	Body/Style Number	Body Type & Seating	Factory Price	Shipping Weight	Production Total
68-680	68069-M	4D Sedan-6P	6,583	4,795	3,300
68-681	68169-P	4D Brougham-6P	6,899	4,805	15,300

FLEETWOOD SEVENTY-FIVE — SUB-SERIES 697/698 — V-8

Again marked by simple extra-long body rub moldings, a formal high-headroom look (with doors cut into roof) and Fleetwood-type wreath and crest emblems, the nine-passenger models had the longest Cadillac production car wheelbase. Standard features of these models included power front ventipanes, Automatic Level Control, a right-hand manually-operated outside rearview mirror, 8.20 x 15-8PR black sidewall tires and Automatic Climate Control air conditioning as standard equipment.

FLEETWOOD SEVENTY-FIVE SUB-SERIES 697/698

Model Number	Body/Style Number	Body Type & Seating	Factory Price	Shipping Weight	Production Total
68-697	69723-R	4D Sedan-9P	10,629	5,300	805
68-697	69733-S	4D Limousine-9P	10,768	5,385	995
68-698	69890-Z	Commercial chassis	—	—	2,413

FLEETWOOD ELDORADO — SUB-SERIES 693 — V-8

The 1968 Eldorado had the front parking lights located to the leading edge of the fenders, where they were now mounted vertically. On the rear fenders, small round safety lights were now affixed. The design of the lens for the front cornering lights (formerly vertically ribbed) was modified. The new 472-cid V-8, with 525 pound-feet of torque, made it possible to spin the front-driven wheels on

smooth, dry surfaces. Spring rates were slightly lowered to give a more cushiony ride. Interior trimmings included diamond-pattern cloth-and-vinyl upholstery or Deauville cloth upholstery with vinyl bolsters in four color choices or genuine leather. Removed from the rear roof pillar, but not the hood and deck lid, were the familiar wreath and crest-style Fleetwood emblems. Regular equipment on the luxury sports-type car included all Fleetwood standards plus power rear quarter ventipanes, power front disc brakes, retractable headlight covers and Rosewood pattern dash panel appliques.

FLEETWOOD ELDORADO SUB-SERIES 693

Model Number	Body/Style Number	Body Type & Seating	Factory Price	Shipping Weight	Production Total
68-693	69347-H	2D Hardtop Coupe-6P	6,605	4,580	24,528

ENGINE

Overhead valve. Cast-iron block. Displacement: 472-cid. Bore and Stroke: 4.30 x 4.06 inches. Compression ratio: 10.5:1. Brake hp: 375 at 4400 rpm. Taxable hp: 59.2. Torque: 525 at 3000 rpm. Five main bearings. Hydraulic valve lifters. Crankcase capacity: (Eldorado) 5 qt.; (other models) 4 qt. (Add 1 qt. if new filter installed). Cooling system capacity: (Series 75) 24.8 qt.; (Eldorado) 20 qt.); (All Cadillacs other series) 21.3 qt. Dual exhaust on Eldorado, single exhaust system with crossover on other models. Carburetor: Rochester 4MV Quadrajet four-barrel: (Calais, DeVille and Fleetwood) Model 7028230; (Eldorado) Model 7028234. The new engine featured a metal temperature-monitoring device; an air-injection emissions control system; an integral air conditioning system (still optional); a cast crankshaft and cast connecting rods; an integral water crossover pipe with

thermostatic passages; engine bearings with more surface area and a 15-plate battery.

CHASSIS

(Eldorado) Wheelbase: 120 inches. Overall length: 221 inches. Overall width: 80.0 inches. Overall height: 53.3 inches. Front tread: 63.5 inches. Rear tread: 63.0 inches. Tires: 9.00 x 15.

(Calais) Wheelbase: 129.5 inches. Overall length: 224.7 inches. Overall width: 79.9 inches. Overall height: 54.3 inches. Front tread: 62.5 inches. Rear tread: 62.5 inches. Tires: 9.00 x 15.

(DeVille) Wheelbase: 129.5 inches. Overall length: 224.7 inches. Overall width: 79.9 inches. Overall height: 55.6 inches. Front tread: 62.5 inches. Rear tread: 62.5 inches. Tires: 9.00 x 15.

(Fleetwood Brougham, Fleetwood 60 Special) Wheelbase: 133 inches. Overall length: 228.2 inches. Overall width: 79.9 inches. Front tread: 62.5 inches. Rear tread: 62.5 inches. Tires: 9.00 x 15.

(Fleetwood 75) Wheelbase: 149.8 inches. Overall length: 244.5 inches. Front tread: 62.5 inches. Rear tread: 62.5 inches. Tires: 8.20 x 15.

(Commercial Chassis) Wheelbase: 156 inches. Front tread: 62.5 inches. Rear tread: 62.5 inches.

OPTIONS

Auxiliary horn ($16). Automatic level control option on models G-N-K-F-J-B-L ($79). Automatic Climate Control, except R and S models ($516). Bucket seats with console on models F-H with leather upholstery required ($184). Firemist finish ($132). Cruise control ($95). Rear window defogger on models G-N-K-J-B-L-M-P ($27). Front disc brakes on Eldorado only ($105). Door guards on model G-F-J-H ($5), on models N-K-B-L-M-P-R-S ($8). Expanded vinyl upholstery on models G-N-K ($42). Soft Ray glass ($51). GuideMatic headlight control ($51). Headrests ($53). Leather upholstery, models J-B-L-M-P ($138), model H ($158). License frame, single ($6), pair ($13). Padded roof, models J-H ($132), models B-L ($137). Power door locks, two-door ($47), four-door ($68). Power door locks for Fleetwood 75 models

($116). Power ventipanes, except models H-M-P, power windows required ($72). Rear quarter power ventipanes on Eldorado only ($63). Power windows on Calais models ($116). AM radio ($162). AM/FM radio ($188). AM/FM stereo, except Fleetwood 75 models ($288). AM radio rear controls on Fleetwood 75 models ($242). Reclining front seat with headrests on models F-H with bucket seats or Eldorado bench seats required ($84). Four-way left-hand power bucket seat on models F-J-B-H ($53). Six-way power front seat on models G-N-K ($111), models F-J-B-L-H-M-P-R ($83). Rear center seat belt ($11). Front shoulder straps ($32). Tilt-telescope steering wheel ($90). Remote control trunk lock ($52). Twilight Sentinel on Eldorado ($37), other models ($32). White sidewall tires, size 9 x 15, four-ply 8PR- 5, except nine-passenger models ($56 exchange). White sidewall tires, size 8.20 x 15, four-ply 8PR-5 on nine-passenger models ($63 exchange). Four new items of optional equipment were: Twin front and rear floor mats for all models except H-R-S ($17). One-piece front and rear floor mats for Eldorado ($20). Twin front floor mats for Fleetwood 75 models ($10) and front seat warmer for all models except Fleetwood 75s, which came instead with rear seat warmer only, both at ($95). Optional axle ratio data not available. Air injector reactor and closed positive crankcase ventilation standard. Controlled differential was now $52.65 extra on all models except Eldorado. All 1968 Cadillacs and Eldorados were built in Detroit, Michigan.

HISTORICAL

Dealer introduction date for 1968 Cadillacs and Eldorados was September 21, 1967. A fourth successive yearly sales record was set this year despite a 21-day United Auto Workers (UAW) shutdown at Fisher Body Fleetwood plant in Detroit (November 1967). Production was down 1.1 percent, due to the same strike. Model-year production included 205,475 Cadillacs and 24,528 Eldorados for a fourth-time-in-a-row record of 230,003 total cars. This gave Cadillac a 2.7 percent share of total U.S. automobile production. The regular Cadillac held its 2.4 percent share of the total market, while the Edorado's percentage increased from 0.2 to 0.3. Calendar-year production included 187,768 regular Cadillacs and 23,136 Eldorados. The total of 210,904 units was good for a 2.39 percent market share. Cadillac dealer sales for the calendar-year were 186,067 Cadillacs (2.2 percent market share) and 22,616 Eldorados (0.2 percent market share).

1969

OVERVIEW

Although its overall size and character was largely unchanged, the 1969 Cadillac was restyled in the Eldorado image. An Eldorado-like front fender treatment evolved and helped to emphasize a stronger horizontal design line. The rear quarters of the body were extended to give the car a longer look. There was also an all-new grille with dual horizontal headlights positioned in the outboard step-down areas of the grille. The 1969 Eldorado had a new texture in the grille and stationary headlights.

I.D. DATA

The VIN was stamped on a steel plate riveted to the top surface of the instrument panel and visible through the lower left-hand corner of the windshield. The number was also stamped on the rear portion of the engine block, behind the left-hand cylinder bank. It took the form * B9100001 *. The first symbol indicates model: B=Sedan DeVille Hardtop, F=DeVille Convertible, G=Calais Coupe, H=Fleetwood Eldorado, J=Coupe DeVille, L=Sedan DeVille six-windows Sedan, M=Fleetwood Sixty Special Sedan, N=Calais Hardtop Sedan, P=Fleetwood Brougham Sedan, R=Fleetwood 75 Sedan, S=Fleetwood

Above: **1969 Cadillac, Sedan de Ville**

75 Limousine, Z=Commercial Chassis. The second symbol indicates model-year: 9=1969. The last six symbols are the sequential production number. The Fisher Body Style Number plate is attached to the cowl under the hood on the left and identifies the year, series and body style as follows: 69-68249=Calais Hardtop Sedan, 69-68247=Calais Coupe, 69-68349=Sedan DeVille Hardtop Sedan, 69-68347=Coupe DeVille, 69-68367=DeVille Convertible, 69-68369=Sedan DeVille, 69-68069=Sixty Special, 69169=Fleetwood Brougham Sedan, 69-69347=Eldorado Hardtop Coupe (front-wheel drive), 69-69723=Fleetwood 75 Sedan, 69-69733=Fleetwood 75 Limousine and 69-69890=Commercial Chassis. The last six symbols are the sequential production number starting with 100001. The Fisher Body Style Number plate also carries the paint code. The 1969 paint codes were: 10=Sable Black, 12=Cotillion White, 16=Patina Silver, 18=Phantom Gray, 24=Astral Blue, 26=Athenian Blue, 28=Persian Aqua, 30=Palmetto Green, 36=Rampur Green, 40=Colonial Yellow, 42=Cameo Beige, 44=Shalimar Gold, 46=Cordovan, 47=Wisteria, 48=San Mateo Red, 49=Empire Maroon, 90=Sapphire Blue Firemist, 94=Chalice Gold Firemist, 96=Biscay Aqua Firemist, 97=Nutmeg Brown Firemist and 99=Chateau Mauve Firemist. Convertible top colors were: J=White, B=Black, L=Dark Blue, M=Light Flax and N=Ark Cordovan.

Roof panel colors were: J=White, K=Black, L=Dark Blue, M=Light Flax, N=Dark Cordovan and R=Medium Gold.

CALAIS—SERIES 682—V-8

Calais models came with all GM safety features plus a V-8, Turbo-Hydra-Matic transmission, variable-ratio power steering, dual power brakes, power windows, a center front arm rest, an electric clock, two front cigarette lighters, twin front and rear ashtrays, a complete set of interior and exterior courtesy, safety and warning lights, a Mirror Group, concealed three-speed windshield washers and wipers and five black sidewall tires. All regular Cadillac models had a squarer roof line and sculptured rear deck and bumper treatments.

CALAIS SERIES 682

Model Number	Body/Style Number	Body Type & Seating	Factory Price	Shipping Weight	Production Total
69-682	68249-N	4D Hardtop Sedan-6P	5,660	4,630	6,825
69-682	68247-G	2D Hardtop Coupe-6P	5,484	4,555	5,600

DEVILLE SERIES—SERIES 683—V-8

DeVilles had all of the features used in Calais, plus a rear center arm rest, dual rear cigarette lighters and two-way power-operated horizontal front seat adjusters. A model identification signature script sat above the horizontal bodyside rub molding, towards the back of the rear fenders.

DEVILLE SERIES 683

Model Number	Body/Style Number	Body Type & Seating	Factory price	Shipping Weight	Production Total
69-683	68369-L	4D Sedan DeVille-6P	5,954	4,640	7,890
69-683	68347-J	2D Coupe DeVille-6P	5,721	4,595	65,755
69-683	68349-B	4D Sedan DeVille-6P	5,954	4,660	72,958
69-683	68367-F	2D Convertible DeVille-6P	5,905	4,590	16,445

FLEETWOOD SIXTY SPECIAL—SUB-SERIES 680/681—V-8

Fleetwood models had all standard features of DeVilles, except the Limousine had no front center arm rest. Extra regular equipment included Automatic Level Control. The Brougham included adjustable reading lights and a Dual Comfort front seat. External identification was provided with bright metal underscores, Fleetwood emblems and lettering and a padded Brougham roof. The wheelbase for Sixty Specials was again 3-1/2 inches longer than that of other models. Interior appointments were enriched.

FLEETWOOD SIXTY SPECIAL SUB-SERIES 680/681

Model Number	Body/Style Number	Body Type & Seating	Factory Price	Shipping Weight	Production Total
69-680	68069-M	4D Sedan-6P	6,779	4,765	2,545
69-681	68169-P	4D Brougham-6P	7,110	4,770	17,300

FLEETWOOD SEVENTY-FIVE—SUB-SERIES 697/698—V-8

Stretched bodies and trim, Fleetwood emblems and embellishments, doors cut into a formal, high headroom roof and generally higher appointment and trim levels continued to mark Cadillac's most luxurious line. All DeVille equipment plus Automatic Level Control, Automatic Climate Control, a rear window defogger, four rear ashtrays and 8.20 x 15 four-ply blackwall tires were standard.

FLEETWOOD SEVENTY-FIVE SUB-SERIES 697/698

Model Number	Body/Style Number	Body Type & Seating	Factory Price	Shipping Weight	Production Total
69-697	69723-R	4D Sedan-6P	10,841	5,430	880
69-697	69733-S	4D Limousine-9P	10,979	5,555	1,156
69-698	69890-Z	Commercial chassis	—	—	2,550

FLEETWOOD ELDORADO —SUB-SERIES 693—V-8

The front-wheel-drive Eldorado continued to be offered as a single model. It was a six-passenger, two-door hardtop on a short-wheelbase platform. There was a new cross-hatch grille that was separated from the headlights. The dual headlights were now part of the body design and were fully exposed and stationary. Standard equipment included power-operated rear quarter vent windows.

FLEETWOOD ELDORADO SUB-SERIES 693

Model Number	Body/Style Number	Body Type & Seating	Factory Price	Shipping Weight	Production Total
69-693	69347-H	2D Hardtop Coupe-6P	6,711	4,550	23,333

ENGINE

Overhead valve. Cast-iron block. Displacement: 472-cid. Bore and Stroke: 4.30 x 4.06 inches. Compression ratio: 10.5:1. Brake hp: 375 at 4400 rpm. Taxable hp: 59.2. Torque: 525 at 3000 rpm. Five main bearings. Hydraulic valve lifters. Crankcase capacity: (Eldorado) 5 qt.; (other models) 4 qt. (Add 1 qt. if new filter installed). Cooling system capacity: (Series 75) 24.8 qt.; (Eldorado) 21.8 qt. with visual capacity tank; (All Cadillacs other series) 21.3 qt. Dual exhaust on Eldorado, single exhaust system with crossover on other models. Carburetor: Rochester 4MV Quadrajet four-barrel Model (Calais, DeVille and Fleetwood) Model 7028230; (Eldorado) Model 7028234. On 1969-1974 Cadillacs, the air conditioning must be turned off before making hot idle speed adjustments. In addition, disconnect the hose at the vacuum release cylinder and close the hot idle compensator by pressing finger or eraser end of a pencil on the compensator.

CHASSIS

(Eldorado) Wheelbase: 120 inches. Overall length: 221 inches. Overall width: 79.9 inches. Overall height: 53.7 inches. Front tread: 63.5 inches. Rear tread: 63.0 inches. Tires: 9.00 x 15.

(Calais) Wheelbase: 129.5 inches. Overall length: 224.7 inches. Overall width: 79.9 inches. Overall height: 54.4 inches. Front tread: 62.5 inches. Rear tread: 62.5 inches. Tires: 9.00 x 15.

(DeVille) Wheelbase: 129.5 inches. Overall length: 224.7 inches. Overall width: 79.9 inches. Overall height: 54.4 inches. Front tread: 62.5 inches. Rear tread: 62.5 inches. Tires: 9.00 x 15.

(Fleetwood Brougham, Fleetwood 60 Special) Wheelbase: 133 inches. Overall length: 228.5 inches. Overall width: 79.9 inches. Overall height: 56.6 inches. Front tread: 62.5 inches. Rear tread: 62.5 inches. Tires: 9.00 x 15.

(Fleetwood 75) Wheelbase: 149.8 inches. Overall length: 244.5 inches. Front tread: 62.5 inches. Rear tread: 62.5 inches. Tires: 8.20 x 15.

(Commercial Chassis) Wheelbase: 156 inches. Front tread: 62.5 inches. Rear tread: 62.5 inches.

OPTIONS

Automatic Climate Control option ($516). Automatic level control, models G-N-F-J-B-L ($79). Bucket seats with console, model H with leather upholstery required ($184). Firemist paint ($132). Cruise control ($95). Rear window defogger, models G-N-H-J-B-L-M-P ($26). Door guards, models G-F-J-H ($5), models N-B-L-M-

1969 Cadillac, Calais, Hardtop sedan

1969 Cadillac, Coupe de Ville

1969 Cadillac, Fleetwood Brougham

P-R-S ($8). Dual comfort seat, standard in Brougham, optional models F-J-B-M ($105). Twin front and rear floor mats, all models except H-R-S ($17). One-piece front and rear floor mats, model H ($20). Twin front floor mats, models R-S ($10). Soft Ray tinted glass ($53). Guide-Matic headlight control ($51). Head restraints ($18). Note: Head restraints mandatory after January 1, 1969. Leather upholstery, models J-B-L-M-P ($138), model H ($158). License frame, single ($6), dual ($13). Power door locks, includes electric seat back release, models G-F-J-H ($68), models N-B-L-M-P ($68), models R-S ($116). AM radio ($162). AM/FM radio ($188). AM/FM stereo radio, except models R-S ($288). AM rear-control radio models R-S ($242). Four-way left-hand bucket seat, model H ($53). Six-way power seat adjuster: front seat, models G-N ($116), front seat models F-J-B-L-H-M-R with bench seat only ($90), models F- J-B-M-P for right-hand Dual Comfort seat, Code Y accessories required, ($116). Front seat warmer, available all models except rear seat only in models R-S ($95). Front shoulder belts ($32). Tilt and telescope steering wheel ($95). Trumpet horn ($16). Remote control trunk lock ($32). Twilight Sentinel, Eldorado ($37), other models ($32). Expanded vinyl roof in standard production colors, models G-N ($42). Vinyl roof, models J-B-L ($153). Padded vinyl roof, model H ($158). Whitewall tires, size 9 x 15 four-ply, except models R-S ($57 exchange). Whitewall tires, size 8.20 x 15 four-ply, models R-S only ($63 exchange). Whitewall tires, heavy-duty high mileage type for Eldorado ($83 exchange). Controlled differential was $52.65 extra on all models except Eldorado. All Cadillacs and Eldorados were built in Detroit, Michigan.

HISTORICAL

Dealer introduction date for 1969 Cadillacs and Eldorados was September 26, 1968. A fifth successive yearly sales record was set and calendar-year deliveries went over 250,000 cars for the first time in company history. Post-strike sales of regular Cadillacs in calendar-year 1969 rose 26.7 percent, while the Eldorado gained 17.6 percent. Model-year production included 199,904 Cadillacs and 23,333 Eldorados for a total of 223,237 cars. This gave Cadillac a 2.6 percent share of U.S. automobile production. The regular Cadillac held a 2.3 percent share of the total market, while the Eldorado's percentage remained at 0.3. Calendar-year production included 239,584 regular Cadillacs and 27,214 Eldorados. Production of the Eldorado body for 1969 was transferred from the Fleetwood plant in Detroit to the Fisher Body plant in Euclid, Ohio. The total of 266,798 units was good for a 3.25 percent market share. Cadillac dealer sales for the calendar-year were 227,027 Cadillacs (2.68 percent market share) and 25,497 Eldorados (0.30 percent market share).

1969 Cadillac, Fleetwood Brougham

1970

OVERVIEW

A relatively minor restyling marked the 1970 Cadillacs. A facelift included a grille with 13 vertical blades set against a delicately cross-hatched rectangular opening. The bright metal headlight surrounds were bordered with body color to give them a more refined look. Narrow, vertical "V-shaped" taillights were seen again. The taillights no longer had smaller V-shaped bottom lenses pointing downward below the bumper. The Cadillac full wheel discs and winged crest fender tip emblems were of a new design.

I.D. DATA

The VIN was stamped on a steel plate riveted to the top surface of the instrument panel and visible through the lower left-hand corner of the windshield. The number was also stamped on the rear portion of the engine block, behind the left-hand cylinder bank. It took the form * B0100001 *. The first symbol indicates model: B=Sedan DeVille Hardtop, F=DeVille Convertible, G=Calais Coupe, H=Fleetwood Eldorado, J=Coupe DeVille, L=Sedan DeVille, M=Fleetwood Sixty Special Sedan, N=Calais Hardtop Sedan, P=Fleetwood Brougham Sedan, R=Fleetwood 75 Sedan, S=Fleetwood 75 Limousine, Z=Commercial Chassis. The second symbol indicates model-year: 0=1970.

Above: **11970 Cadillac, convertible De Ville**

William Refakis

The last six symbols are the sequential production number. The Fisher Body Style Number plate is attached to the cowl under the hood on the left and identifies the year, series and body style as follows: 70-68247=Calais Coupe, 70-68249=Calais Hardtop Sedan, 70-68347=Coupe DeVille, 70-68349=Sedan DeVille Hardtop Sedan, 70-68367=DeVille Convertible, 70-68369=Sedan DeVille (pillared sedan), 70-69347=Fleetwood Eldorado Hardtop Coupe (front-wheel drive), 70-68309=Fleetwood Sixty Special, 70-69169=Fleetwood Brougham Sedan, 70-69723=Fleetwood 75 Limousine With Auxiliary Seat, 70-69733=Fleetwood 75 Limousine With Division Window and 70-69890=Commercial chassis. The last six symbols are the sequential production number starting with 100001. The Fisher Body Style Number plate also carries the paint code. The 1970 paint codes were: 11=Cotillion White, 14=Patina Silver, 18=Phantom Gray, 19=Sable Black, 24=Corinthian Blue, 29=Condor Blue, 34=Adriatic Turquoise, 42=Lanai Green, 49=Glenmore Green, 54=Byzantine Gold, 59=Bayberry, 64=Sauterne, 69=Dark Walnut, 74=San Mateo Red, 79=Monarch Burgundy, 90=Spartacus Blue Firemist, 93=Lucerne Aqua Firemist, 94=Regency Bronze Firemist, 95=Cinnamon Firemist, 96=Nottingham Green Firemist, 97=Briarwood Firemist, 99=Chateau Mauve Firemist. Convertible top colors were: B=Black, C=Blue, J=White, M=Beige and

N=Bayberry. Vinyl roof colors were: J=White, K=Black, L=Blue, M=Beige, N=Bayberry, P=Mauve and R=Brown.

CALAIS — SERIES 682—V-8

A Calais signature script was placed above the rear end of the horizontal lower belt molding, just ahead of the chromed taillight dividers. Standard equipment included Turbo-Hydra-Matic transmission, power steering, front disc brakes, power windows, center front armrest, electric clock, two front cigarette lighters, twin front and rear ashtrays, complete interior and exterior courtesy lights, safety, warning and convenience lights, outside remote-control left-hand mirror, visor vanity mirror and L78-15 bias-belted fiberglass blackwall tires.

CALAIS SERIES 682

Model Number	Body/Style Number	Body Type & Seating	Factory Price	Shipping Weight	Production Total
70-682	68249-N	4D Hardtop Sedan-6P	5,813	4,680	5,187
70-682	68247-G	2D Hardtop Coupe-6P	5,637	4,620	4,724

DEVILLE SERIES — SERIES 683—V-8

DeVilles had all of the same features as Calais models, plus dual rear cigarette lighters, two-way horizontal control front seat adjustment and rear center armrest in all models, except convertibles. Exterior distinction came from a DeVille script above the rear end of the belt molding and from the use of long, rectangular back-up light lenses set into the lower rear bumper as opposed to the smaller, square lenses used on the Calais. A new feature seen this year was a body color border around the edge of the vinyl top covering, when this option was ordered. This treatment had first been seen on 1969 Fleetwoods. The Sedan DeVille and DeVille convertible were in their last season.

DEVILLE SERIES 683

Model Number	Body/Style Number	Body Type & Seating	Factory Price	Shipping Weight	Production Total
70-683	68370-L	4D Sedan-6P	6,118	4,690	7,230
70-683	68349-B	4D Hardtop DeVille-6P	6,118	4,725	83,274
70-683	68347-J	2D Coupe DeVille-6P	5,884	4,650	76,043
70-683	68367-F	2D Convertible DeVille-6P	6,068	4,660	15,172

FLEETWOOD SIXTY SPECIAL—SUB-SERIES 680/681—V-8

The Fleetwood models had all the equipment ordered in DeVilles plus Automatic Level Control. The Brougham also came standard with adjustable reading lights, Dual Comfort front seat with two-way power adjustment (left side) and a padded vinyl top. Distinguishing Sixty Specials externally were bright metal wheelhouse moldings, wide full-length rocker panels with rear extensions and block lettering, denoting the series, positioned in back of the front wheel opening. At the end of the 1970 model run, the standard Sixty Special Sedan was dropped. A

noticeable trim change was the use of a thin, horizontal beltline molding on all 1970 Sixty Specials.

FLEETWOOD SIXTY SPECIAL SUB-SERIES 680/681

Model Number	Body/Style Number	Body Type & Seating	Factory Price	Shipping Weight	Production Total
70-680	68070-M	4D Sedan-6P	6,953	4,830	1,738
70-681	68170-P	4D Brougham-6P	7,284	4,835	16,913

FLEETWOOD SEVENTY-FIVE—SUB-SERIES 697/698—V-8

Special equipment found on the big Cadillac sedan and limousine included Automatic Level Control, rear window defogger, four rear ashtrays and a manual right-hand outside rearview mirror. Separate Climate Control systems were provided for front and rear compartments. Fleetwood wreath crests appeared at the extreme edge of the rear fenders, above the belt molding, on both models. The doors on the limousine were cut into the roof and a fixed driver's partition with adjustable glass compartment divider was inside. The front compartment was trimmed in genuine leather, the rear in one of five combinations. Three of these were the more standard Divan cloth trims, while Decordo cloth or Dumbarton cloth with leather were available.

FLEETWOOD ELDORADO —SUB-SERIES 693 —V-8

A new, 500-cid/ 400-hp V-8 was the big news for the Eldorado this year. A special "8.2-Litre" badge was placed on the left-hand side of the redesigned grille to announce the industry's biggest power plant. The grille itself again had a cross-hatched insert, but horizontal blades were set upon it, emphasizing the V-shape of the front. Thinner vertical taillights were used, giving a more rakish look. The winged-V emblems used at the front of the fenders on other Cadillacs were added to the Eldorado front parking light lenses. Bright rocker panel trim, with front and rear extensions, was used. There was also Eldorado

By 1970, Cadillac was a symbol of financial success and achievement.

1970 Cadillac convertible De Ville

block lettering at the lower front fender, behind the wheel housing.

Model Number	Body/Style Number	Body Type & Seating	Factory Price	Shipping Weight	Production Total
70-693	69347-H	2D Hardtop Coupe-6P	6903	4630	23,842

ENGINE

CADILLAC BASE V-8

Overhead valve. Cast-iron block. Displacement: 472-cid. Bore and Stroke: 4.30 x 4.06 inches. Compression ratio: 10.0:1. Brake hp: 375 at 4400 rpm. Taxable hp: 59.2. Torque: 525 at 3000 rpm. Five main bearings. Hydraulic valve lifters. Crankcase capacity: 4 qt. (Add 1 qt. if new filter installed). Cooling system capacity: (Series 75) 24.8 qt.; (All Cadillacs other series except Eldorado) 21.3 qt. Single exhaust system with crossover. Carburetor: Rochester 4MV Quadrajet four-barrel: Model 7028230.

ELDORADO BASE V-8

Overhead valve. Cast-iron block. Displacement: 500-cid. Bore and Stroke: 4.30 x 4.30 inches. Compression ratio: 10.0:1. Brake hp: 400 at 4400 rpm. Taxable hp: 59.2. Torque: 550 at 3000 rpm. Five main bearings. Hydraulic valve lifters. Crankcase capacity: 5 qt. (Add 1 qt. if new filter installed). Cooling system capacity: 21.8 qt. with visual capacity tank. Dual exhaust. Carburetor: Rochester 4MV Quadrajet four-barrel Model 7028230.

CHASSIS

(Eldorado) Wheelbase: 120 inches. Overall length: 221 inches. Overall width: 80.0 inches. Overall height: 53.7 inches. Front tread: 63.7 inches. Rear tread: 63.0 inches. Tires: L78 x 15.

(Calais) Wheelbase: 129.5 inches. Overall length: 225.0 inches. Overall width: 79.8 inches. Overall height: 56.2 inches. Front tread: 63.0 inches. Rear tread: 63.0 inches. Tires: L78 x 15.

(DeVille) Wheelbase: 129.5 inches. Overall length: 225.0 inches. Overall width: 79.8 inches. Overall height: 56.2 inches. Front tread: 63.0 inches. Rear tread: 63.0 inches. Tires: L78 x 15.

(Fleetwood Brougham, Fleetwood 60 Special) Wheelbase: 133 inches. Overall length: 228.5 inches. Overall width: 79.8 inches. Overall height: 56.8 inches. Front tread: 63.0 inches. Rear tread: 63.0 inches. Tires: L78 x 15.

(Fleetwood 75) Wheelbase: 149.8 inches. Overall length: 244.5 inches. Front tread: 63.0 inches. Rear tread: 63.0 inches. Tires: L78 x 15.

(Commercial Chassis) Wheelbase: 156 inches. Front tread: 63.0 inches. Rear tread: 63.0 inches.

OPTIONS

Automatic Climate Control ($516). Automatic Level Control on models G-N-F-J-B-L ($79). Bucket seats with console in Eldorado with leather upholstery required ($184). Bucket seats in Eldorado, with cloth upholstery, as SPO ($292). Special carpets with matching instrument carpet panels in all models, except H-R-S, as SPO ($32), in Eldorados, as SPO ($37). Cloth front compartment in limousine, as SPO ($126). Firemist paint, as SPO ($205).

Special paint, except Firemist, as SPO ($179). Dual Comfort front seat in model L, as SPO with standard cloth upholstery ($184). Dual Comfort front seat in model L as SPO with production leather upholstery ($316). Vinyl padded roof in models R-S as SPO ($758). Vinyl padded roof with Landau bows in models R-S, as SPO ($2,131). Vinyl padded blind quarter roof in models R-S without Landau bows, as SPO ($2,026). NOTE: The term "SPO" means "Special Production Option." Cruise control ($95). Rear window defogger ($26-$37). Door edge guards ($6-$10). Dual Comfort seat with-standard Brougham trim in models F-J-B-M ($105). Soft Ray glass ($53). Guide-Matic headlight control ($51). Leather upholstery ($156-$184). License frame(s) in all models ($6-$13). Floor and trunk mats ($11-$20). Power door locks in standard wheelbase models ($68), in limousines ($116). Signal seeking radio AM/FM with rear control ($289), without rear control ($222), with stereo, except models R-S ($322). AM/FM radio ($188). Power seats, Eldorado left-hand four-way bucket ($53), six-way front ($90-$116), six-way left-hand front with Dual-Comfort ($90-$116). Shoulder belts ($32). Tilt and telescope steering wheel ($95). Electric powered sunroof in models B-H-J-L-P with vinyl top required and six-way seat recommended ($626). Trumpet horn ($15). Remote control trunk lock ($53). Twilight Sentinel ($37). Expanded vinyl upholstery in models G-N ($42). Vinyl roof in models J-B-L ($153), in Eldorado ($158). White sidewall L78-15 tires models

R-S ($46), all other models except commercial ($40). Controlled differential, except Eldorado ($53).

HISTORICAL

A total of 214,903 Cadillacs were built in the 1970 model-year, setting an all-time divisional record and representing a strong (for Cadillac) 2.8 percent of total U.S. production. Additionally, 23,842 Eldorados were produced in the same time period, raising the divison's total share of industry output to 3.1 percent. Calendar-year sales totals were off the mark due to a major GM strike. They peaked at just 152,859 units, including 137,365 Caddys and 15,494 Eldorados. The strike had kept Cadillac from realizing its second best sales year in company history as dealer deliveries dropped nearly 100,000 units below the record of 252,524 sold the previous calendar-year. Sales of the new Cadillac line began September 18, 1969. The optional Trackmaster skid control system was made available for the Eldorado, subsequent to initial model introductions. Despite the poor sales performance, Cadillac Motor Division opened a new luxury-car showroom on Park Avenue in New York City in February and started work on a new engine parts plant in Livonia, Michigan. A new multi-million dollar emissions controls laboratory was announced for construction in Detroit. This was also the first year the company built Cadillacs outside Detroit with construction of 1971 DeVille models commencing at a Linden, N. J. factory in the fall of 1970. In December, Cadillac built its 3,500,000th postwar automobile!

1970 Cadillac, Fleetwood Eldorado

1971

OVERVIEW

The nine basic Cadillac models were completely restyled for 1971. They had pairs of individually housed squarish headlights set wider apart. The V-shaped grille had an egg-crate style insert and was protected by massive vertical guards framing a rectangular license plate indentation. A wide hood with full-length windsplits, a prominent center crease and hidden windshield wipers were seen. A Cadillac crest decorated the nose and new indicator lights appeared atop each front fender. A horizontal beltline molding ran from behind the front wheel housing almost to the rear, stopping where an elliptical bulge in the body came to a point. The rear wheel openings were again enclosed with fender skirts. The front-wheel-drive Eldorado took on a more classic appearance and a new convertible was added to the Eldorado lineup. The overall length of the cars increased by six inches and styling revisions included sculptured front and rear fender treatments and new body side sheet metal. Both the 472-cid Cadillac V-8 and the 500-cid Eldorado V-8 were revised to operated on both leaded or low-lead fuels.

Above: **1971 Cadillac, Coupe De Ville**

Tom Jevcak

I.D. DATA

The VIN was stamped on a steel plate riveted to the top of the instrument panel and visible through the lower left corner of the windshield. The number was also stamped on a pad on the upper rear portion of the engine block, behind the intake manifold. The numbering system was changed this year and the new system was used only in 1971. The VIN took the form * 682491Q100001 *. The first symbol indicates make: 6=Cadillac Motor Division. The second and third symbols indicate series or car line: 82=Calais, 83=DeVille, 81=Fleetwood 60 Special, 97=Fleetwood 75, 93=Fleetwood Eldorado and 98=Commercial Chassis. The third and fourth symbols indicated body style as follows: 49=four-door Hardtop Sedan, 47=two-door Hardtop Coupe, 69=Fleetwood four-door Sedan, 23=Fleetwood limousine, 67=two-door Convertible and 90=Commercial chassis. The last six symbols are the sequential production number starting with 100001. The Fisher Body Style Number plate also carries the paint code. The 1970 paint codes were: 11=Cotillion White, 13=Grenoble Silver, 16=Oxford Gray, 19=Sable Black, 24=Zodiac Blue, 29=Brittany Blue, 34=Adriatic Turquoise, 44=Cypress Green, 49=Sylvan Green, 50=Casablanca Yellow, 55=Duchess Gold, 64=Desert Beige, 69=Clove, 74=Cambridge Red, 89=Empire Maroon Firemist, 90=Bavarian Blue

Firemist, 92=Pewter Firemist, 94=Chalice Gold Firemist, 95=Almond Firemist, 96=Sausalito Green Firemist and 99=Primrose Firemist. Vinyl roof colors were: J=White, K=Black, L=Blue, M=Aqua, N=Bayberry, N=Green, P=Gold, R=Brown and S=Light Beige. Convertible top colors were: A=White, B=Black, C=Blue, E=Light Beige, N=Green and R=Brown.

CALAIS—SERIES 682—V-8

Calais models had the series name written in chrome scripts on the front fenders and the right side of the deck lid. The taillights were of the same general shape as a year earlier, but were no longer divided by a chrome bar. Long, horizontal back-up lights were set into the bumper, on either side of a deeply recessed license plate housing. Standard Calais equipment included Turbo-Hydra-Matic transmission, power steering, dual power brakes with front discs, power windows, a center front armrest, an electric clock, twin front cigarette lighters, twin front and rear ashtrays, complete interior and exterior lighting (courtesy, safety, warning and convenience lights), a remote-control left-hand outside rearview mirror, a visor-vanity mirror, L78-15 bias-belted tires and a 472-cid four-barrel V-8 engine.

CALAIS SERIES 682

Model Number	Body/Style Number	Body Type & Seating	Factory Price	Shipping Weight	Production Total
71-682	68249-N	4D Hardtop Sedan-6P	6,075	4,715	3,569
71-682	68247-G	2D Hardtop Coupe-6P	5,899	4,635	3,360

DEVILLE SERIES—SERIES 683—V-8

DeVilles came with all of the equipment that was standard on Calais models, plus dual rear cigarette lighters, a two-way horizontal front seat adjuster and rear center armrests on all styles, except the DeVille. To set them apart visually, the DeVilles had thin, bright metal rocker panel strips and a signature script on each front fender bearing the series name. The bottoms of the rear fenders were decorated with a bright metal beauty panel that was wider than the rocker strips and blended into the molding running along the bottom of the fender skirt. As on Calais, the lower beltline molding ended on the elliptical rear fender bulge, where thin rectangular side markers were placed above and below the chrome strip. Only two body styles remained in this series.

DEVILLE SERIES 683

Model Number	Body/Style Number	Body Type & Seating	Factory Price	Shipping Weight	Production Total
71-683	68349-B	4D Hardtop Sedan DeVille-6P	6,498	4,730	69,345
71-683	68347-J	2D Coupe DeVille-6P	6,264	4,685	66,081

1971 Cadillac, Calais Sedan (four-door hardtop)

FLEETWOOD SIXTY SPECIAL—SUB-SERIES 681—V-8

The Sixty Special was now a one-model line including only the Brougham sedan. It came with standard extras such as Automotive Level Control, adjustable reading lights, a two-way adjustable Dual Comfort front seat and a padded vinyl roof. New exterior styling was seen, along with several new trim features. The windows were cut nearly into the roof in semi-limousine fashion and had softly rounded corners. Vertically-angled rectangular coach lights were a common option incorporated into the rear roof pillar. A broad rocker panel trim plate, with rear extension, was used. The Fleetwood name was block lettered on the front fenders, behind the wheel opening and on the right-hand side of the rear deck lid. The new window styling included a wide pillar separating the front and rear door glass.

FLEETWOOD SIXTY SPECIAL
SUB-SERIES 681

Model Number	Body/Style Number	Body Type & Seating	Factory Price	Shipping Weight	Production Total
71-681	68170-P	4D Brougham-6P	7,763	4,910	15,200

FLEETWOOD SEVENTY-FIVE—SUB-SERIES 697/698—V-8

The long-wheelbase Fleetwoods came with everything found on DeVilles (except for a front center armrest in the limousine) plus Automatic Level Control, Automatic Climate Control, rear window defogger, four rear ashtrays and a manual right-hand outside rearview mirror. Externally these cars had the new Cadillac styling and window treatments similar to those described for the Sixty Special. The rear roof pillar could be custom finished in several different ways including triangular "coach" windows or vinyl "covered blind quarter" looks. Ornamentation included the traditional Fleetwood laurel wreath crests and lettering, plus thin horizontal belt moldings. No rocker sill strips, panels or extension moldings were used. Of course, the limousine had the doors cut into the roof, special upholstery appointments and a driver's partition with adjustable division window.

1971 Cadillac, 60 Special Brougham

FLEETWOOD SEVENTY-FIVE SUB-SERIES 697/698

Model Number	Body/Style Number	Body Type & Seating	Factory Price	Shipping Weight	Production Total
71-697	69723-R	4D Sedan-6P	11,869	5,335	752
71-697	69733-S	4D Lmousine-9P	12,008	5,475	848
71-698	69890-Z	Commercial chassis	—	—	2,014

FLEETWOOD ELDORADO — SUB-SERIES 693 — V-8

The second generation of front-wheel-drive Eldorados appeared this year, including a new convertible. Used again was the big 500-cid V-8, but with a lower compression ratio and 35 fewer horsepower. Rear coil springs were another new technical feature. The Eldorado wheelbase was stretched more than six inches, too. Body styling was heavily sculptured. A vertically-textured, rectangular grille was new. The front fenders had a chiseled cut-off look and a vertical windsplit, that harkened back to the early 1950s, appeared just behind the doors. Fender skirts were new for Eldorados and added to the car's old-fashioned, classical image, as did the revival of convertible styling in this line. Trim features included twin vertical front bumper guards, Fleetwood wreaths on the hood and deck, an Eldorado script on the lower front fenders, short horizontal beltline moldings on the front fenders and doors, rocker sill beauty panels and a stand-up hood ornament. Narrow "coach" windows were cut into the rear roof pillars of the Eldorado coupe. Rear end treatments for the new body included an extended trunk lid appearance, an extra large backlight and a massive rear bumper with a flat in-and-out look that housed vertical wraparound taillights. Standard on the sporty luxury series included all DeVille equipment, less rear armrests, plus Automatic Level Control and front-wheel-drive technology.

FLEETWOOD ELDORADO SUB-SERIES 693

Model Number	Body/Style Number	Body Type & Seating	Factory Price	Shipping Weight	Production Total
71-693	69367-E	2D ConvertibleCoupe-6P	7,751	4,690	6,800
71-693	69347-H	2D Hardtop SportCoupe-6P	7,383	4,650	20,568

ENGINE

CADILLAC (EXCEPT ELDORADO) BASE V-8

Overhead valve. Cast-iron block. Displacement: 472-cid. Bore and Stroke: 4.30 x 4.06 inches. Compression ratio: 8.8:1. Brake hp: 345 at 4400 rpm. Net brake hp: 220 at 4000 rpm. Taxable hp: 59.2. Torque: 500 at 2800 rpm. Net torque: 380 at 2400 rpm. Five main bearings. Hydraulic valve lifters. Crankcase capacity: 4 qt. (Add 1 qt. if new filter installed). Cooling system capacity: (Series 75) 24.8 qt.; (All Cadillacs other series except Eldorado) 21.3 qt. Single exhaust system with crossover. Carburetor: Rochester 4MV Quadrajet four-barrel: Model 7028230.

ELDORADO BASE V-8

Overhead valve. Cast-iron block. Displacement: 500-cid. Bore and Stroke: 4.30 x 4.30 inches. Compression ratio: 9.0:1. Brake hp: 365 at 4400 rpm. Taxable hp: 59.2. Net brake hp: 235 at 3800 rpm. Torque: 535 at 2800 rpm. Net torque: 410 at 2400 rpm. Five main bearings. Hydraulic valve lifters. Crankcase capacity: 5 qt. (Add 1 qt. if new filter installed). Cooling system capacity: 21.8 qt. with visual capacity tank. Single exhaust system with crossover. Carburetor: Rochester 4MV Quadrajet four-barrel Model 7028230.

CHASSIS

(Eldorado) Wheelbase: 127 inches. Overall length: 222.0 inches. Overall width: 79.8 inches. Overall height: 53.9 inches. Front tread: 63.7 inches. Rear tread: 63.0 inches. Tires: L78 x 15.

(Calais) Wheelbase: 130.0 inches. Overall length: 225.8 inches. Overall width: 80.0 inches. Overall height: 56.2 inches. Front tread: 63.0 inches. Rear tread: 63.0 inches. Tires: L78 x 15.

(DeVille) Wheelbase: 130.0 inches. Overall length: 225.8 inches. Overall width: 80.0 inches. Overall height: 56.2 inches. Front tread: 63.0 inches. Rear tread: 63.0 inches. Tires: L78 x 15.

(Fleetwood Brougham, Fleetwood Sixty Special) Wheelbase: 133 inches. Overall length: 228.8 inches. Overall width: 80.0 inches. Overall height: 56.8 inches. Front tread: 63.0 inches. Rear tread: 63.0 inches. Tires: L78 x 15.

(Fleetwood 75) Wheelbase: 151.5 inches. Overall length: 247.3 inches. Front tread: 63.0 inches. Rear tread: 63.0 inches. Tires: L78 x 15.

(Commercial Chassis) Wheelbase: 156 inches. Front tread: 63.0 inches. Rear tread: 63.0 inches.

OPTIONS

Automatic Climate Control ($537). Automatic Level Control for Calais and DeVille ($79.) Cruise control ($95). Rear window defogger in Eldorado ($37), in other models ($32). Eldorado grid-type rear window defogger

($63). Door edge guards in two-door ($6), in four-door ($10). Power door locks for 75 ($118), other models ($71). Power door locks with electric seat back release in coupes and convertibles ($71). DeVille, Dual Comfort front seat ($105). Front and rear floor mats, twin type in 75 ($10), one-piece type in Eldorado ($20), twin type in other models ($17). Soft Ray tinted glass ($59). Guide-Matic ($51). Lamp monitors ($50). License frames, one ($6), pair ($12). Remote control right mirror ($26). Brougham and 75 opera lights ($53). Firemist paint ($132). Radios, AM/FM push-button ($138), AM/FM signal-seeking stereo ($328), AM/FM with tape ($416), AM/FM stereo signal-seeking with rear control in 75 ($421). DeVille vinyl roof ($156). Eldorado padded vinyl roof ($161). DeVille and Brougham six-way seat ($92). Six-way seat in DeVille/Brougham/Calais, with passenger Dual-Comfort in DeVille/Brougham ($118). Shoulder belts in convertible front seat or rear seat all models ($32). Tilt and Telescope steering wheel ($95). DeVille/Eldorado/Brougham sunroof with vinyl or padded roof mandatory ($626). Trumpet horn in Eldorado coupe ($16). Remote control trunk lock ($58). Trunk mat ($8). Twilight Sentinel ($41). Expanded vinyl Calais upholstery ($42). Expanded leather upholstery, in DeVille/Brougham ($174), in Eldorado coupe ($184). White sidewall L78-15 tires, in 75 ($49), in others ($42). Controlled differential, except Eldorado ($58). Trackmaster for Eldorado only ($211).

HISTORICAL

Cadillac Motor Division's model-year production totals were curtailed by labor disputes and peaked at 188,537 units, which included 161,169 Cadillacs and 27,368 Eldorados. Of these, 135,283 Cadillacs and all of the Eldorados were built in Detroit, while 25,886 DeVilles were put together in Linden, N.J. Calendar-year production was a different story, with 236,496 Cadillacs and 40,064 Eldorados being constructed. That totaled 276,563 vehicles for a 3.22 percent share of total U.S. production, the company's highest calendar-year output in history. U.S. dealer sales were higher at 266,798 cars marking the fifth straight year of record gains. The new models were introduced September 29, 1970. Hints of a down-sized Cadillac line were heard.

1971 Cadillac, Fleetwood 75 limousine

1971 Cadillac, Fleetwood Eldorado convertible

1972

OVERVIEW

Cadillac Motor Division marked its 70th anniversary in 1972 and the cars were little changed from 1971. This was a year in which General Motors kept busy with the task of re-engineering its cars to conform to new fuel and safety standards established by Federal Government mandate. There was little time to pay attention to altering appearances and few styling changes were seen in the latest Cadillacs. A modest frontal revision placed more emphasis on horizontal grille blades. The parking lights were moved from the bumper to between the square-bezeled headlights, now set wider apart. V-shaped emblems made a return appearance on the hood and deck lid. A number of equipment changes were seen.

I.D. DATA

The GM serial numbering system changed slightly this year to incorporate an alphabetical series code and a new alphabetical code designating engine type. The 13-symbol serial number was again located on top of the instrument panel, where it was visible through the windshield. The number was also stamped on a pad on the rear upper portion of the cylinder block, behind the intake manifold

Above: **1972 Cadillac, Fleetwood 75 limousine**

and on the left side of the transmission case (without the model identity symbol). The number took the form * 6C47R2Q100001 *. The first symbol 6=Cadillac Motor Division. The second symbol was a letter identifying the series as follows: B=Brougham, C=Calais, D=DeVille, F= Fleetwood 75, L=Eldorado and Z=Commercial Chassis. The third and fourth symbols togetherer indicated body style: 23=four-door Limousine with auxiliary seat, 33=four-door Limousine with center divider, 47=two-door Hardtop Coupe, 49=four-door Hardtop Sedan, 67=two-door Convertible, 69=four-door pillared Sedan and 90=Commercial chassis. The fifth symbol was a letter identifying the engine: R = 472-cid V-8, S = 500-cid Eldorado V-8. The sixth symbol was a number identifying model-year: 2=1972. The seventh symbol was a letter designating the manufacturing point as follows: Q=Detroit, Michigan and E=Linden, New Jersey. The next group of numbers was the sequential production code starting with 100001. The Fisher Body tag on the cowl, under the hood includes additional information. The top left stamping is the Body Style Code (ST) and takes the form 72 68347 where "72" indicates model-year and the last five symbols indicate the body type matching the codes in the specifications tables below. Other stampings on the tag indicate the plant code, the sequential production number, the trim code, the paint code and the

Modular Seat Code. Paint codes for 1972 Cadillacs are: 11=Cotillion White, 14=Contessa Pewter, 18=Mayfair Gray, 19=Sable Black, 24=Zodiac Blue, 29=Brittany Blue, 34=Adriatic Turquoise, 44=Sumatra Green, 49=Brewster Green, 50=Willow, 54=Promenade Gold, 59=Stratford Covert, 64=Tawny Beige, 69=Cognac, 73=Cambridge Red, 90=Ice Blue Firemist, 92=St. Moritz Blue Firemist, 93=Palomino Firemist, 94=Patrician Covert Firemist, 96=Balmoral Green Firemist and 99=Russet Firemist. Convertible top colors were: A=White, B=Black, C=Blue, E=Light Beige and M=Covert. Vinyl roof colors were: J=White, K=Black, L=Blue, M=Covert, N=Green, R=Brown and S=Beige.

CALAIS—SERIES C/SERIES 682—V-8

Calais standard equipment started with all regulation safety devices, plus variable-ratio power steering, dual power brakes with front discs, automatic transmission, power windows, all courtesy and warning lights, a new bumper impact system, three-speed windshield wipers, windshield washers, a visor-vanity mirror, two front cigar lighters, an automatic parking brake release, a front center armrest, passenger assist straps, side marker lights, cornering lights, a 472-cid four-barrel V-8, flow-through ventilation and five L78-15 black sidewall bias-belted tires. Externally, the Calais was identified by a front fender model script, thin horizontal belt moldings, fender skirts, full wheel covers and a script on the right side of the trunk.

CALAIS SERIES C/CALAIS SERIES 682

Model Number	New Body Style No.	Body Type & Seating	Factory Price	Shipping Weight	Production Total
68249	C49	4D Hardtop Sedan-6P	5,938	4,698	3,875
68247	C47	2D Hardtop Coupe-6P	5,771	4,642	3,900

NOTE: Both the old and new Body Style codes are shown for 1972 models. Research indicates that the old type Body/Style Number was still found on the vehicle data plate below the hood. The new style was used for the VIN on the instrument panel viewable through the windshield. Starting in 1973, the new form of code was used exclusively.

DEVILLE—SERIES D/SERIES 683—V-8

DeVille standard equipment included all found on Calais plus rocker panel moldings, a rear center armrest and twin rear cigarette lighters. Of course, the rocker panel trim helped in identifying the cars, but there was also new DeVille signature script affixed to the sides of the rear roof pillars.

DEVILLE SERIES D/DEVILLE SERIES 683

Model Number	New Body Style No.	Body Type & Seating	Factory Price	Shipping Weight	Production Total
68349	D49	4D Sedan DeVille-6P	6,390	4,762	99,531
68347	D47	2D Coupe DeVille-6P	6,168	4,682	95,280

FLEETWOOD SIXTY SPECIAL—SUB-SERIES B/681—V-8

Fleetwood models had all DeVille features plus Automatic Level Control and, on the Brougham, a Dual Comfort front seat, a rear seat reading light, carpeted footrests and a padded vinyl roof with rear window chrome molding. As the only Cadillacs on the 133-inch wheelbase, the

1972 Cadillac, Fleetwood Eldorado convertible

1972 Cadillac, Fleetwood 60 Special brougham

Broughams were identified by their large, rounded-corner, four-window styling. The Broughams also had Fleetwood front fender lettering and laurel wreath hood and deck badges. Many Broughams that were sold were equipped with the coach light option and bright body underscores with rear quarter panel extensions.

FLEETWOOD SIXTY SPECIAL SUB-SERIES B/681

Model Number	New Body Style No.	Body Type & Seating	Factory Price	Shipping Weight	Production Total
68169	B69	4D Brougham-6P	7,637	4,858	20,750

FLEETWOOD SEVENTY-FIVE—SUB-SERIES F/697—V-8

Fleetwood 75s had all DeVille equipment (less a front seat armrest on the Limousine) plus Automatic Level Control, carpeted footrests, fixed-ratio power steering, a remote-control right-hand outside rearview mirror, a rear window defogger and Automatic Climate Control. The big Series 75 Sedan included folding auxiliary seats. The Limousine had the doors cut into the roof, the traditional partition and a glass divider. Trim included bright body underscores with rear extensions, horizontal thin belt moldings, Fleetwood front fender lettering and laurel wreath badges for the hood and deck lid. Several optional rear roof treatments were available.

FLEETWOOD SEVENTY-FIVE SUB-SERIES F/697

Model Number	New Body Style No.	Body Type & Seating	Factory Price	Shipping Weight	Production Total
69723	F23	4D Sedan-6/9P	11,948	5,620	995
69733	F33	4D Lmousine-9P	12,080	5,742	960
69890	F90	Commercial chassis	—	—	2,462

FLEETWOOD ELDORADO — SUB-SERIES L/693—V-8

The 1972 Eldorados had a vertically-textured grille. The Cadillac name was engraved on the left side of the upper grille surround and an Eldorado script appeared above the cornering lights on the lower front fender tips. The 8.2-Litre badges were moved to the sides of the body, below the belt molding and behind the front wheel openings. New full wheel covers with concentric rings were seen. Eight colors of Sierra grain leather were supplied as convertible upholstery selections. Standard equipment included the detuned 1972 version of the 500-cid V-8, a front-wheel-drive chassis layout, Automatic Level Control, a front center armrest only and coach windows on the hardtop coupe.

FLEETWOOD ELDORADO SUB-SERIES L/693

Old Body Style No.	New Body Style No.	Body Type & Seating	Factory Price	Shipping Weight	Production Total
69367	L67	2D Convertible-6P	7,681	4,966	7,975
69347	L47	2D Hardtop Coupe-6P	7,360	4,880	32,099

ENGINE

CADILLAC (EXCEPT ELDORADO) BASE V-8

Overhead valve. Cast-iron block. Displacement: 472-cid. Bore and Stroke: 4.30 x 4.06 inches. Compression ratio: 8.5:1. Gross hp: 345 at 4400 rpm. Net brake hp: 220 at 4000 rpm. Taxable hp: 59.2. Torque: 365 at 2400 rpm. Five main bearings. Hydraulic valve lifters. Crankcase capacity: 4 qt. (Add 1 qt. if new filter installed). Cooling system capacity: (Series 75) 24.8 qt.; (All Cadillacs other series except Eldorado) 21.3 qt. with heater only; 21.8 qt. with air conditioning. Single exhaust system with crossover. Carburetor: Rochester Quadrajet four-barrel.

ELDORADO BASE V-8

Overhead valve. Cast-iron block. Displacement: 500-cid. Bore and Stroke: 4.30 x 4.30 inches. Compression ratio: 8.5:1. Brake hp: 365 at 4400 rpm. Taxable hp: 59.2. Net brake hp: 235 at 3800 rpm. Torque: 385 at 2400. Five main bearings. Hydraulic valve lifters. Crankcase capacity: 5 qt. (Add 1 qt. if new filter installed). Cooling system capacity: 21.3 qt. with heater only; 21.8 qt. with air conditioning. Single exhaust system with crossover. Carburetor: Rochester Quadrajet four-barrel (Eldorado Special).

CHASSIS

(Eldorado) Wheelbase: 126.3 inches. Overall length: 222.7 inches. Overall width: 79.84 inches. Overall height: 53.9 inches. Front tread: 63.7 inches. Rear tread: 63.0 inches. Tires: L78 x 15.

1972 Cadillac, Fleetwood 75 sedan

(Calais) Wheelbase: 130.0 inches. Overall length: 226.9 inches. Overall width: 79.78 inches. Overall height: 54.1 inches. Front tread: 63.0 inches. Rear tread: 63.0 inches. Tires: L78 x 15.

(DeVille) Wheelbase: 130.0 inches. Overall length: 226.9 inches. Overall width: 79.78 inches. Overall height: 54.1 inches. Front tread: 63.0 inches. Rear tread: 63.0 inches. Tires: L78 x 15.

(Fleetwood Brougham) Wheelbase: 133 inches. Overall length: 229.9 inches. Overall width: 79.78 inches. Overall height: 55.5 inches. Front tread: 63.0 inches. Rear tread: 63.0 inches. Tires: L78 x 15.

(Fleetwood 75) Wheelbase: 151.5 inches. Overall length: 248.4 inches. Front tread: 63.0 inches. Rear tread: 63.0 inches. Tires: L78 x 15.

(Commercial Chassis) Wheelbase: 156 inches. Front tread: 63.0 inches. Rear tread: 63.0 inches.

OPTIONS

Automatic Climate Control ($523). Automatic Level Control ($77). Rear window defoggers, grid type in Eldorado convertible ($62), standard type in Eldorado coupe ($36), standard type in all others, except regular equipment in 75 ($31). Door edge guards, two-door ($6), four-door ($9). Power door locks, in two-doors, includes automatic seat back release ($69), in 75 ($115), in other four-doors ($69). Dual Comfort seat in DeVille and Eldorado ($103). Front and rear twin rubber floor mats ($16). Front and rear one-piece rubber floor mats for Eldorados ($19). Front and rear twin rubber floor mats for 75 ($10). Soft Ray tinted glass ($57). Convertible hard boot ($40). Auxiliary horn ($15). Bumper impact strips ($24). One license frame ($6), two ($11). Remote control right-hand outside rearview mirror, standard on 75 ($26). Roof pillar coach lights on Brougham and 75 ($51). Firemist paint ($128). AM/FM radios, regular ($183), stereo signal-seeking ($320), stereo signal-seeking with rear control in 75 only ($410), stereo with tape player ($406). Full vinyl padded top for DeVilles, including "halo" on Coupe DeVille ($152). Full vinyl Eldorado padded top ($157). Custom Cabriolet Eldorado Coupe roof ($360). Power seat options ($89-$115 depending on model and use of Dual Comfort seats). Twin front shoulder harness in convertible ($31). Tilt & Telescope steering wheel ($92). DeVille Brougham/Eldorado Coupe sunroof, with vinyl top mandatory ($610). Sunroof with Eldorado Coupe Custom Cabriolet treatment ($1,005). White sidewall tires, on 75 ($47), others ($41). Remote control trunk lock ($56). Trunk mat ($8). Twilight Sentinel ($40). Expanded vinyl Calais upholstery ($41). Expanded leather DeVille/Brougham upholstery ($169). Expanded leather Eldorado Coupe upholstery ($179). Cruise Control ($92). Controlled differential ($56). Eighty-amp generator ($41). Heavy-duty cooling system ($56). Exhaust emissions system, required on all cars built for California sale ($15). Trackmaster ($205). Trailer towing package, Eldorado ($62), all others ($92).

HISTORICAL

The 1972 introductions took place in September 23, 1971 with production continuing until July 7, 1972. Model-year production came to 225,251 Cadillacs and 40,074 Eldorados. The Cadillac held a 2.6 percent share of total industry output and the Eldorado added another half a percent for a 3.1 percent total piece of the pie. Some 191,571 Cadillacs and all of the Eldorados were built in Detroit and 36,142 DeVilles were made in Linden, N.J. Calendar-year production included 233,456 Cadillacs and 43,795 Eldorados. The total of 277,251 vehicles was an all-time record for Cadillac. *Ward's Automotive Yearbook* predicted the "not-so-spectacular increase in production and sales last year might hasten a Cadillac decision of coming out with a small sports-oriented car approximating the size of a Mercedes-Benz."

1972 Cadillac, Fleetwood 75 sedan with 1911 Cadillac Thirty limousine

1973

OVERVIEW

New energy-absorbing bumpers were seen with Cadillac styling refinements. The wider Cadillac grille had an intricate eggcrate design. Larger, vertical rectangles housed the parking lights between wide-spaced headlights, which had square bezels, but round lenses. The bumpers ran across the front of the cars and wrapped around each end. Vertical bumper guards were spaced apart, outboard of the grille. The rear bumper was wider, flatter with an upper section housing an angled license plate recess. Vertically "veed" border outline moldings paralleled the fender edge shape at the rear bodysides. Single, rectangular rear side marker lights were placed over and under the rear tip of the thin beltline trim. A Cadillac script was seen on the front fender sides, below the belt molding and behind the wheel opening. The front-wheel-drive Eldorados were restyled. A new eggcrate grille was seen. The front bumper had an angular look, with wide vertical guards. The parking lights wrapped around the body corners. A thin rub molding ran from behind the forward wheel housing and stretched nearly to the round, rear side marker lights, which had wreath-and-crest ornamentation. Gone were the vertical rear fender breaks (along with the windsplit trim), but

Above: **1973 Cadillac, Fleetwood Eldorado coupe**
Phil Hall

fender skirts were used. An Eldorado script was seen behind the front wheel openings. The rear bumper was flatter and straighter. Heavy chrome taillight housings were deleted. They slanted slightly forward, at the same angle as the fender line.

I.D. DATA

The 13-symbol serial number was located on top of the instrument panel, where it was visible through the windshield. The number was also stamped on a pad on the rear upper portion of the cylinder block, behind the intake manifold. The number took the form * 6C47R3Q100001 *. The first symbol 6=Cadillac Motor Division. The second symbol was a letter identifying the series as follows: B=Brougham, C=Calais, D=DeVille, F= Fleetwood 75, L=Eldorado and Z=Commercial Chassis. The third and fourth symbols togetherer indicated body style: 23=four-door Limousine with auxiliary seat, 33=four-door Limousine with center divider, 47=two-door Hardtop Coupe, 49=four-door Hardtop Sedan, 67=two-door Convertible, 69=four-door pillared Sedan and 90=Commercial chassis. The fifth symbol was a letter identifying the engine: R = 472-cid V-8, S = 500-cid Eldorado V-8. The sixth symbol was a number identifying model-year: 3=1973. The seventh symbol was a letter designating the manufacturing point as follows:

Q=Detroit, Michigan and E=Linden, New Jersey. The next group of numbers was the sequential production code starting with 100001. The Fisher Body tag on the cowl, under the hood includes additional information. The top left stamping is the Body Style Code (ST) and takes the form 73 6C47 where "73" indicates model-year and the last four symbols indicate the body type matching the codes in the specifications tables below. Other stampings on the tag indicate the plant code, the sequential production number, the trim code, the paint code and the Modular Seat Code. Paint codes for 1973 Cadillacs are: 11=Cotillion White, 13=Georgian Silver, 18=Park Avenue Gray, 19=Sable Black, 24=Antigua Blue, 29=Diplomat Blue, 39=Gargency Teal, 44=Sage, 49=Forest Green, 54=Renaissance Gold, 63=Laredo Tan, 64=Mirage Taupe, 68=Burnt Sienna, 72=Dynasty Red, 81=Harvest Yellow, 90=Shadow Taupe Firemist, 92=St. Topez Blue Firemist, 94=Phoenix Gold, 95=Oceanic Teal Firemist, 96=Viridian Green Firemist and 99=Saturn Bronze Firemist. Convertible top colors were: A=White, B=Black, C=Blue, E=Light Beige and M=Medium Maize. Vinyl roof colors were: J=White, K=Black, L=Blue, M=Medium Maize, N=Green, P=Taupe, S=Light Beige and X=Brown.

CALAIS—SERIES C—V-8

Once again, standard equipment on the Calais included all regulation safety devices, variable-ratio power steering, dual power brakes with front discs, automatic transmission, power windows, all courtesy and warning lights, a new bumper impact system, three-speed windshield wipers, windshield washers, a visor-vanity mirror, two front cigar lighters, an automatic parking brake release, a front center armrest, passenger assist straps, side marker lights, cornering lights, a 472-cid four-barrel V-8, flow-through ventilation and five L78-15 black sidewall bias-belted tires. Externally, the Calais was identified by a model name script, thin horizontal belt moldings, fender skirts, full wheel covers and a script on the right side of the trunk.

CALAIS SERIES 6C

Model Number	Body/Style Number	Body Type & Seating	Factory Price	Shipping Weight	Production Total
6C	C47	2D Hardtop Coupe-6P	5,886	4,900	4,202
6C	C49	4D Hardtop Sedan-6P	6,038	4,953	3,798

DEVILLE—SERIES 6D—V-8

Bright body underscores with rear extensions distinguished the DeVille externally. There were also DeVille signatures on the rear roof pillars. Equipment specifications were comparable to 1972. The DeVille was actually a Calais with added trim, richer appointments, rear armrest and standard power seat.

DEVILLE SERIES 6D

Model Number	Body/Style Number	Body Type & Seating	Factory Price	Shipping Weight	Production Total
6D	D47	2D Coupe DeVille-6P	6,268	4,925	112,849
6D	D49	4D SedanDeVille-6P	6,500	4,985	103,394

Phil Hall

In 1973, Cadillac displayed its legendary heritage in sales literature.

FLEETWOOD SIXTY SPECIAL BROUGHAM— SERIES 6B — V-8

Standard equipment on the Brougham included most DeVille features (the Sixty Special had different bright body underscores), plus Automatic Level Control, a Dual-Comfort front seat, rear reading lights, a new front reading light, a padded vinyl roof with rear chrome moldings and carpeted, rear compartment footrests. Four-window, round-cornered roof styling, with extra wide center pillars, was seen again. Tires with pencil thin whitewall bands were used.

FLEETWOOD SIXTY SPECIAL BROUGHAM
SERIES 6B

Model Number	Body/Style Number	Body Type & Seating	Factory Price	Shipping Weight	Production Total
6B	B69	4D Sedan-6/9P	7,765	5,102	24,800

FLEETWOOD SEVENTY-FIVE—SERIES 6F—V-8

The long-wheelbase, high-dollar Fleetwoods were immense automobiles with low-cut, extra-large rounded corner side window treatments and rather large coach windows cut into the rear roof pillars. These Fleetwoods had the annual Cadillac styling changes, plus a thin, horizontal bodyside molding, front fender nameplates, full-length body underscores with rear extensions and Fleetwood-style laurel wreath badge ornamentation. Standard equipment included a rear seat window defogger, Automatic Climate Control and a remote-control right-hand outside rearview mirror. Bumper impact strips were standard on 75s and optional on other Cadillacs.

FLEETWOOD SEVENTY-FIVE SERIES 6F

Model Number	Body/Style Number	Body Type & Seating	Factory Price	Shipping Weight	Production Total
6F	F23	4D Sedan-6P	11,948	5,620	1,017
6F	F33	4D Limousine-9P	12,080	5,742	1,043
6F	F90	Commercial chassis	—	—	2,212

FLEETWOOD ELDORADO— SERIES 6L—V-8

The 1973 Eldorado had a more neo-Classic look. There were changes in grille styling, lighting, side moldings and ornamentation. The sheet metal was better protected with the license plate area moved up and out of the bumper impact region. Incorporated in the wreath and crest decorations on the rear quarter panels were reflex and side-marker lights. Standard equipment included the 500-cid V-8, a front-wheel-drive chassis layout, Automatic Level Control, coach windows on the hardtop coupe and a new energy-absorbing bumper system.

FLEETWOOD ELDORADO SERIES 6L

Model Number	Body/Style Number	Body Type & Seating	Factory Price	Shipping Weight	Production Total
6L	L47	2D Hardtop Coupe-6P	7,360	5,094	42,136
6L	L67	2D Convertible-6P	7,681	5,131	9,315

ENGINE

CADILLAC (EXCEPT ELDORADO) BASE V-8

Overhead valve. Cast-iron block. Displacement: 472-cid. Bore and Stroke: 4.30 x 4.06 inches. Compression ratio: 8.5:1. Gross hp: 345 at 4400 rpm. Net brake hp: 220 at 4000 rpm. Taxable hp: 59.2. Net torque: 385 at 2400 rpm. Five main bearings. Hydraulic valve lifters. Crankcase capacity: 4 qt. (Add 1 qt. if new filter installed). Cooling system capacity: (Series 75 with air conditioning) 26.8 qt.; (All Cadillacs other series) 21.3 qt. with heater only; 23.8 qt. with air conditioning. Single exhaust system with crossover. Carburetor: Rochester Quadrajet four-barrel.

ELDORADO BASE V-8

Overhead valve. Cast-iron block. Displacement: 500-cid. Bore and Stroke: 4.30 x 4.30 inches. Compression ratio: 8.5:1. Net brake hp: 365 at 4400 rpm. Taxable hp: 59.2. Net brake hp: 235 at 3800 rpm. Net torque: 385 at 2400 rpm. Five main bearings. Hydraulic valve lifters. Crankcase capacity: 5 qt. (Add 1 qt. if new filter installed). Cooling system capacity: 21.3 qt. with heater only; 23.8 qt. with air conditioning. Single exhaust system with crossover. Carburetor: Rochester Quadrajet four-barrel (Eldorado Special).

CHASSIS

(Eldorado) Wheelbase: 126.3 inches. Overall length: 222.0 inches. Overall width: 79.8 inches. Overall height: 53.9 inches. Front tread: 63.7 inches. Rear tread: 63.0 inches. Tires: L78 x 15.

(Calais) Wheelbase: 130.0 inches. Overall length: 228.5 inches. Overall width: 79.8 inches. Overall height: 54.1 inches. Front tread: 63.0 inches. Rear tread: 63.0 inches. Tires: L78 x 15.

(DeVille) Wheelbase: 130.0 inches. Overall length: 228.5 inches. Overall width: 79.8 inches. Overall height: 54.1 inches. Front tread: 63.0 inches. Rear tread: 63.0 inches. Tires: L78 x 15.

1973 Cadillac, Coupe De Ville

(Fleetwood Brougham) Wheelbase: 133 inches. Overall length: 231.5 inches. Overall width: 79. 8 inches. Overall height: 55.5 inches. Front tread: 63.0 inches. Rear tread: 63.0 inches. Tires: L78 x 15.

(Fleetwood 75) Wheelbase: 151.5 inches. Overall length: 250.0 inches. Overall height: 57.8 inches. Front tread: 63.0 inches. Rear tread: 63.0 inches. Tires: L78 x 15.

(Commercial Chassis) Wheelbase: 157.5 inches. Front tread: 63.0 inches. Rear tread: 63.0 inches.

OPTIONS

Automatic Climate Control ($523). Automatic Level Control ($77). Rear window defoggers, grid type in Eldorado convertible ($62), standard type in Eldorado coupe ($36), standard type in all others, except regular equipment in 75 ($31). Door edge guards, two-door ($6), four-door ($9). Power door locks, in two-doors, includes automatic seat back release ($69), in 75 ($115), in other four-doors ($69). Dual Comfort seat in DeVille and Eldorado ($103). Front and rear twin rubber floor mats ($16). Front and rear one-piece rubber floor mats for Eldorados ($19). Front and rear twin rubber floor mats for 75 ($10). Soft Ray tinted glass ($57). Convertible hard boot ($40). Auxiliary horn ($15). Bumper impact strips ($24). One license frame ($6), two ($11). Remote control right-hand outside rearview mirror, standard on 75 ($26). Roof pillar coach lights on Brougham and 75 ($51). Firemist paint ($128). AM/FM radios, regular ($183), stereo signal-seeking ($320), stereo signal-seeking with rear control in 75 only ($410), stereo with tape player ($406). Full vinyl padded top for DeVilles, including "halo" on Coupe DeVille ($152). Full vinyl Eldorado padded top ($157). Custom Cabriolet Eldorado Coupe roof ($360). Power seat options ($89-$115 depending on model and use of Dual Comfort seats). Twin front shoulder harness in convertible ($31). Tilt & Telescope steering wheel ($92). DeVille Brougham/Eldorado Coupe sunroof, with vinyl top mandatory ($610). Sunroof with Eldorado Coupe Custom Cabriolet treatment ($1,005). White sidewall tires, on 75 ($47), others ($41). Remote control trunk lock ($56). Trunk mat ($8). Twilight Sentinel ($40). Expanded vinyl Calais upholstery ($41). Expanded leather DeVille/Brougham upholstery ($169). Expanded leather Eldorado Coupe upholstery ($179). Steel- belted radial ply tires, size L78-15 with Space Saver spare, for all models except 75 ($156). Lighted right-hand visor vanity mirror ($430). Theft deterrent system ($80), Brougham d'Elegance Group ($750). Deluxe robe and pillow ($85). Left-hand remote-control thermometer mirror ($15). Cruise Control ($92). Controlled differential ($56). Eighty-amp generator ($41). Heavy-duty cooling system ($56). Exhaust emissions system, required on all cars built for California sale ($15). Trackmaster ($205). Trailer towing package, Eldorado ($62), all others ($92).

HISTORICAL

Dealer introductions were held September 21, 1972. Model-year production hit a record 304,839 Cadillacs. This total included 253,388 rear-wheel-drive Cadillacs and 51,451 front-wheel-drive Eldorados. This represented 3.1 percent of all cars made in the United States with one half of a percent being Eldorados. All of the Eldorados and 213,478 of the Cadillacs were built in Detroit. An additional 39,910 DeVilles were built in Linden, N.J. Calendar-year production included 252,767 Cadillacs and 54,931 Eldorados. Sales by franchised Cadillac dealers totaled 238,905 Cadillacs and 50,328 Eldorados for the model-year (289,233 cars in all). A new all-time monthly sales record of 33,347 units was set in October 1973. The five-millionth Cadillac, a blue Sedan DeVille, was built June 27, 1973. A Cotillion white Eldorado convertible paced the Indianapolis 500.

1973 Cadillac, Fleetwood 75 limousine

Phil Hall

1974

OVERVIEW

Major restyling marked the "Gas Crunch" era Cadillacs of 1974. The full-size models had a modified version of its "colonnade" roof styling on two-door models, but continued full hardtop styling on the four-door DeVille models. The roofs had a limousine-like look with heavy pillars and deep-cut glass areas. A wide egg-crate grille was used. Dual round headlights were mounted close together in square bezels. Further outboard were double-deck wraparound parking lights. Shorter, vertical grille guards appeared in about the same position as before. The thin beltline molding was positioned lower by several inches. The rear end had vertical bumper ends with the taillights built in. Both bumpers protruded further from the body. Coupes sported wide "coach" windows giving a thick center pillar look. A new grille for Eldorados had a finer cross-hatched grille insert. It also had a brushed aluminum top header bar, providing a neo-classical appearance.

I.D. DATA

The 13-symbol serial number was located on top of the instrument panel, where it was visible through the

Above: **1974 Cadillac, Fleetwood Eldorado convertible**
Bill and Helen Page

windshield. The number was also stamped on a pad on the rear upper portion of the cylinder block, behind the intake manifold. The number took the form * 6C47R4Q100001 *. The first symbol 6=Cadillac Motor Division. The second symbol was a letter identifying the series as follows: B=Brougham, C=Calais, D=DeVille, F= Fleetwood 75, L=Eldorado and Z=Commercial Chassis. The third and fourth symbols togetherer indicated body style: 23=four-door Limousine with auxiliary seat, 33=four-door Limousine with center divider, 47=two-door Hardtop Coupe, 49=four-door Hardtop Sedan, 67=two-door Convertible, 69=four-door pillared Sedan and 90=Commercial chassis. The fifth symbol was a letter identifying the engine: R=472-cid V-8, S=500-cid Eldorado V-8. The sixth symbol was a number identifying model-year: 4=1974. The seventh symbol was a letter designating the manufacturing point as follows: Q=Detroit, Michigan and E=Linden, New Jersey. The next group of numbers was the sequential production code starting with 100001. The Fisher Body tag on the cowl, under the hood includes additional information. The top left stamping is the Body Style Code (ST) and takes the form 74 6C47 where "74" indicates model-year and the last four symbols indicate the body type matching the codes in the specifications tables below. Other stampings on the tag indicate the plant code, the sequential production number, the trim code, the

paint code and the Modular Seat Code. Paint codes for 1974 Cadillacs are: 11=Cotillion White, 13=Georgian Silver, 18=Deauville, 19=Sable Black, 24=Antigua Blue, 29=Diplomat Blue, 30=Lido Green, 34=Mandarin Orange, 38=Pueblo Beige, 44=Jasper Green, 49=Pinehurst Green, 54=Promenade Green, 57=Apollo Yellow, 59=Canyon Amber, 63=Conestoga Tan, 69=Chesterfield Brown, 71=Andeas Copper, 72=Dynasty Red, 92=Regal Blue Firemist, 94=Victorian Amber Firemist, 95=Pharoah Gold Firemist, 96=Persian Lime Firemist, 98=Terra Cotta Firemist and 99=Cranberry Firemist. Convertible top colors were: A=White, B=Black, C=Blue, M=Maize, Q=Amber, S=Sandalwood and T=Terra Cotta. Vinyl roof colors were: C=Dark Blue, J=White, K=Black, M=Maize, N=Green, Q=Amber, S=Sandalwood, T=Terra Cotta, U=Beige, V=Light Green, X=Brown, Y=Orange and Z=Medium Blue.

CALAIS — SERIES 6C — V-8

Standard equipment for the Cadillac Calais included variable-ratio power steering, dual power brakes, front disc brakes, automatic transmission, power windows, all courtesy and warning lights, three-speed windshield wipers, electric windshield washers, a visor-vanity mirror, two front cigar lighters, front and rear armrests, a remote-control left-hand outside rearview mirror, assist straps, side and cornering lights, an automatic parking brake release, a front center armrest, a litter container, flow-through ventilation, L78-15/B blackwall bias-belted tires and a 472-cid four-barrel V-8.

CALAIS SERIES 6C

Model Number	Body/Style Number	Body Type & Seating	Factory Price	Shipping Weight	Production Total
6C	C49	4D Hardtop Sedan-6P	7,545	4,979	2,324
6C	C47	2D Hardtop Coupe-6P	7,371	4,900	4,449

DEVILLE — SERIES 60 — V-8

DeVilles again had all Calais equipment, plus rocker moldings, rear cigar lighters and a power front seat adjuster. A DeVille script nameplate replaced the Calais signature above the rear tip of the lower belt molding.

1974 Cadillac, Coupe De Ville

New options included a DeVille d'Elegance luxury appointments package and a fully-padded vinyl Cabriolet roof treatment. Ingredients of the former package were velour upholstery, Deluxe padded doors, front seat back storage pockets, deep-pile carpeting, floor mats, a see-through standup hood ornament and vinyl tape accent stripes. The Cabriolet group incorporated a landau style top with a bright metal forward divider strip.

DEVILLE SERIES 6D

Model Number	Body/Style Number	Body Type & Seating	Factory Price	Shipping Weight	Production Total
6D	D49	4D Sedan DeVille-6P	8,100	5,032	60,419
6D	D47	2D Coupe DeVille-6P	7,867	4,924	112,201

FLEETWOOD BROUGHAM — SERIES 6B — V-8

The 1974 Fleetwood Sixty Special Brougham came with all DeVille standard equipment plus Automatic Level Control, a Dual Comfort front seat, front and rear reading lights, a padded vinyl roof with chrome rear window moldings, carpeted footrests and L78-15/B white sidewall tires of bias-belted construction. Fleetwood ornamentation, nameplates and round-corner, four-window roof styling were seen again. The Brougham d'Elegance option package was available again, including the same type of appointments outlined for the DeVille d'Elegance, but at nearly twice the price. Even more ostentatious was the Talisman option group with four-place seating in Medici crushed velour armchair-style seats, full-length center consoles with a writing set in front and a rear vanity, a reclining front passenger seat, special Turbine wheel discs, deep-pile carpeting, floor mats, and special "Fleetwood Talisman" scripts on the roof panels. Even more luxurious was the leather-trim Talisman package, an option that cost only $100 less than a brand new 1974 Ford Pinto two-door sedan.

FLEETWOOD BROUGHAM SERIES 6B

Model Number	Body/Style Number	Body Type & Seating	Factory Price	Shipping Weight	Production Total
6B	B69	4D Sedan-6P	9,537	5,143	18,250

1974 Cadillac, Sedan De Ville

FLEETWOOD SEVENTY-FIVE—SERIES 6F—V-8

Standard equipment on 1974 Fleetwood Seventy-Five models included all DeVille features, plus Automatic Level Control, carpeted footrests, an Automatic Climate Control system, a trailering package and a remote-control right-hand outside rearview mirror. Black sidewall L78-15/D tires (optional on other Cadillacs) were used. Also found on all of the big Fleetwoods were new, gray-and-white bumper impact strips, which cost extra on other models. A series script appeared on the front fenders, behind the wheelhousings and coach windows appeared in the rear roof pillar. Twilight Sentinel was now featured on all 75s at regular prices. This was a system that automatically turned the headlights on and off, with a secondary delayed-shutoff feature.

FLEETWOOD SEVENTY-FIVE SERIES 6F

Model Number	Body/Style Number	Body Type & Seating	Factory Price	Shipping Weight	Production Total
6F	F23	4D Sedan-6P	13,120	5,719	895
6F	F33	4D Limousine-9P	13,254	5,883	1,005
6F	F90	Commercial chassis	—	—	2,265

FLEETWOOD ELDORADO— SERIES 6L —V-8

A Cadillac signature was engraved on the left side of the Fleetwood Eldorado model's roof header. The rear fender line looked squarer than in 1973 and a bumper/taillight arrangement that telescoped upon impact was used. A curved instrument panel another new-for-1974 feature. The Eldorado's standard equipment list included all DeVille features, plus L78-15/B whitewall bias-belted tires, coach windows on the coupe and the big 500-cid V-8. Expanded leather interiors were standard in America's only production luxury convertible.

FLEETWOOD ELDORADO SERIES 6L

Model Number	Body/Style Number	Body Type & Seating	Factory Price	Shipping Weight	Production Total
6L	L47	2D Hardtop Coupe-6P	9,110	4,960	32,812
6L	L67	2D Convertible-6P	9,437	5,019	7,600

ENGINE

CADILLAC (EXCEPT ELDORADO) BASE V-8

Overhead valve. Cast-iron block. Displacement: 472-cid. Bore and Stroke: 4.30 x 4.06 inches. Compression ratio: 8.25:1. Net brake hp: 205 at 3600 rpm. Taxable hp: 59.2. Net torque: 365 at 2000 rpm. Five main bearings. Hydraulic valve lifters. Crankcase capacity: 4 qt. (Add 1 qt. if new filter installed). Cooling system capacity: (Series 75 with air conditioning) 26.8 qt.; (All Cadillacs other series) 21.3 qt. with heater only; 23.8 qt. with air conditioning. Single exhaust system with crossover. Carburetor: Four-barrel. VIN Code: R. Built by Cadillac.

ELDORADO BASE V-8

Overhead valve. Cast-iron block. Displacement: 500-cid. Bore and Stroke: 4.30 x 4.30 inches. Compression ratio: 8.25:1. Net brake hp: 210 at 3600 rpm. Taxable hp: 59.2. Net torque: 380 at 2000 rpm. Five main bearings. Hydraulic valve lifters. Crankcase capacity: 5 qt. (Add 1 qt. if new filter installed). Cooling system capacity: 21.3 qt. with heater only; 23.8 qt. with air conditioning. Single exhaust system with crossover. Carburetor: Four barrel. VIN Code: S. Built by Cadillac.

CHASSIS

(Eldorado) Wheelbase: 126.3 inches. Overall length: 224.1 inches. Overall width: 79.8 inches. Overall height: 54.1 inches. Front tread: 63.7 inches. Rear tread: 63.0 inches. Tires: L78 x 15.

(Calais) Wheelbase: 130.0 inches. Overall length: 230.7 inches. Overall width: 79.8 inches. Overall height: 53.9 inches. Front tread: 63.0 inches. Rear tread: 63.0 inches. Tires: L78 x 15.

(DeVille) Wheelbase: 130.0 inches. Overall length: 230.7 inches. Overall width: 79.8 inches. Overall height: 53.9 inches. Front tread: 63.0 inches. Rear tread: 63.0 inches. Tires: L78 x 15.

(Fleetwood Brougham) Wheelbase: 133 inches. Overall length: 233.7 inches. Overall width: 79.8 inches. Overall height: 55.6 inches. Front tread: 63.0 inches. Rear tread: 63.0 inches. Tires: L78 x 15.

(Fleetwood 75) Wheelbase: 151.5 inches. Overall length: 250.0 inches. Overall height: 57.8 inches. Front tread: 63.0 inches. Rear tread: 63.0 inches. Tires: L78 x 15.

(Commercial Chassis) Wheelbase: 157.5 inches. Front tread: 63.0 inches. Rear tread: 63.0 inches.

OPTIONS

Automatic Climate Control, standard in 75 ($523). Airbag restraint system, except 75 and Eldorado convertible ($225). Automatic Level Control on Calais/DeVille ($77). Brougham d'Elegance group ($750). Cruise Control ($95). Coupe DeVille Custom Cabriolet, with sunroof ($640), without sunroof ($220). Eldorado Custom Cabriolet Coupe, with sunroof ($1,005), without sunroof ($385). Rear window defogger, except 75 and convertible ($64). Deluxe robe and pillow ($85). DeVille d'Elegance group, in Sedan DeVille ($355), in Coupe DeVille ($300). Door edge guards, two-door ($6), four-door ($10). Power door locks, two-door including seat back release ($69), four-door, except 75 ($69), 75 sedan and limousine ($115). Dual Comfort front seat in DeVille, Eldorado, 75 sedan ($108).

Fleetwood Brougham Talisman group ($1,800). Fleetwood Brougham Talisman group with leather trim ($2,450). Front/rear twin floor mats in all except Eldorado/75 ($17). Eldorado front and rear one-piece floor mats ($20). Twin rubber front floor mats in 75 ($11). Soft Ray tinted glass ($57). Guide-Matic headlight control ($49). Trumpet horn ($15). Bumper impact strips, standard on 75 ($24). Lamp monitors ($48). License frame ($6). Illuminated vanity mirror ($43). Right-hand remote-control outside rearview mirror, standard in 75 ($27). Opera lights on Brougham 75 ($52). Firemist paint ($132). Special Firemist paint ($200). Special non-Firemist paint ($174). Radios (all with power antenna), AM/FM push-button ($203), AM/FM with tape ($426), AM/FM signal-seeking ($340), AM/FM stereo with rear control in 75 ($430). Fully-padded vinyl roofs, on DeVille/Calais ($152), Eldorado coupe ($157), 75 ($741). Six-way power seat in Calais ($120), in DeVille/Fleetwood, except limousine ($89), passenger seat only, with Dual-Comfort ($120), driver's seat only, with Dual-Comfort ($89). Convertible shoulder harness ($33). Tilt & Telescope steering ($94). Sunroof, DeVille/Brougham/Eldorado coupe ($610). Theft deterrent system ($80). Left-hand remote-control thermometer mirror ($15). Tires, L78-15/D whitewall, on 75 ($47), others ($41), LR78-15/B whitewall steel belted radial on 75 ($162), on Calais ($156), on DeVille with Space Saver spare ($156), L78-15/B blackwall bias belted with Space Saver spare ($35), whitewall ($63). Eldorado convertible top boot ($40). Trailering package, standard on 75 ($65). Remote control trunk lock ($60). Trunk mat ($80). Twilight Sentinel, standard in 75 ($42). Expanded vinyl upholstery in DeVille/Brougham ($184). Expanded leather upholstery in Eldorado coupe ($195). Special wheel discs, except Eldorado ($40). Controlled cycle windshield wipers ($25). Controlled differential, except Eldorado ($56). Emissions test, required in California ($20). High altitude performance package ($16). High energy electronic ignition ($77). Trackmaster skid control ($214).

HISTORICAL

Model introductions took place on September 16, 1973. Model-year production hit 242,330 cars including 201,918 Cadillacs and 40,412 Eldorado. Calendar-year production of 230,649 units included 192,729 Cadillacs and 37,920 Eldorados. Cadillac dealers delivered 187,162 Cadillacs (2.5 percent market share) and 36,682 (0.5 percent market share) Eldorados. All U.S. auto sales were off this season, as a side effect of the Arab oil embargo and Cadillac sales dropped 19.1 percent. However, other automakers fared even worse and, as a result of this, Cadillac's lower production was still sufficient to generate a greater market share. Cadillac dealers actually set monthly sales records in May, July and August.

1974 Cadillac, Sedan De Ville

1975

OVERVIEW

All 1975 Cadillacs received a new appearance with the first use of rectangular headlight lenses. A technological advance was GM's heavily-promoted "Efficiency System" that improved gas mileage and driveability, while still meeting tougher new emissions standards. Cadillac became the first U.S. automaker (since Chrysler in 1958) to offer electronic fuel injection. This feature was made optional on all models beginning in February 1975. Biggest news was the Seville's introduction, a small Cadillac that was promoted as having "Rolls-Royce" quality. It was scheduled for introduction May 1, 1975, and arrived right on deadline.

I.D. DATA

The 13-symbol serial number was located on top of the instrument panel, where it was visible through the windshield. The number was also stamped on a pad on the rear upper portion of the cylinder block, behind the intake manifold. The number took the form * 6C47R5Q100001 *. The first symbol 6=Cadillac Motor Division. The second symbol was a letter identifying the series as follows: B=Brougham, C=Calais, D=DeVille, F= Fleetwood 75,

Above: **1975 Cadillac, Fleetwood Eldorado, convertible)**

L=Eldorado and Z=Commercial Chassis. The third and fourth symbols toget indicated body style: 23=four-door Limousine with auxiliary seat, 33=four-door Limousine with center divider, 47=two-door Hardtop Coupe, 49=four-door Hardtop Sedan, 67=two-door Convertible, 69=four-door pillared Sedan and 90=Commercial chassis. The fifth symbol was a letter identifying the engine: S=500-cid V-8. The sixth symbol was a number identifying model-year: 5=1975. The seventh symbol was a letter designating the manufacturing point as follows: Q=Detroit, Michigan and E=Linden, New Jersey. The next group of numbers was the sequential production code starting with 100001. The Fisher Body tag on the cowl, under the hood includes additional information. The top left stamping is the Body Style Code (ST) and takes the form 75 6C47 where "75" indicates model-year and the last four symbols indicate the body type matching the codes in the specifications tables below. Other stampings on the tag indicate the plant code, the sequential production number, the trim code, the paint code and the Modular Seat Code. Paint codes for 1975 Cadillacs are: 11=Cotillion White, 13=Georgian Silver, 15=Vapour Gray, 19=Sable Black, 24=Jennifer Blue, 29=Monarch Blue, 30=Lido Green, 32=Medium Blue Green Firemist, 34=Mandarin Orange, 36=Firethorn Metallic Firemist, 38=Pueblo Beige, 44=Jasper Green, 49=Inverarary Green,

52=Bombay Yellow, 54=Tarragon Gold, 65=Knickerbocker Tan, 69=Roan Brown, 77=Roxena Red, 78=Rosewood, 92=Gossamer Blue Firemist, 94=Light Blue Green Firemist, 97=Cameo Rose, 98=Emberust Firemist and 99=Carise Firemist. Convertible top colors were: A=White, B=Black, C=Dark Blue, E=Yellow, G=Graystone, H=Dark Red, S=Sandalwood and Y=Orange. Vinyl roof colors were: C=Dark Blue, D=Silver Blue Metallic, E=Yellow, F=Firethorn, G=Graystone, H=Dark Red, K=Black, L=Light Rosewood Metallic, N=Medium Green, P=Silver Metallic, R=Dark Blue Metallic, S=Sandalwood, U=Beige Metallic, V=Silver Green Metallic, X=Dark Brown and Y=Orange Metallic.

SEVILLE—SERIES 6S—V-8

The Seville was introduced as a down-sized 1976 Cadillac in April 1975 and appeared in dealer showrooms the first day of May. It was based on the GM "X" car platform used for the Chevrolet Nova and its derivatives such as Oldsmobile Omega, Pontiac Ventura and Buick Apollo. The exterior panels were exclusive to Cadillac. Included at a base price of $12,479 were padded vinyl roof, air conditioning, Automatic Level Control, power seats, windows, and door locks, AM/FM stereo, leather or cloth upholstery, Tilt & Telescope steering wheel, chimes and GR78-15/B steel-belted radial whitewall tires. Sevilles came only as four-door sedans. Square headlights, wraparound cornering lights and an eggcrate grille with narrow vertical center division bar were seen. The base power plant was a 350-cid Oldsmobile product with electronic fuel injection.

SEVILLE SERIES 6S

Model Number	Body/Style Number	Body Type & Seating	Factory Price	Shipping Weight	Production Total
6S	6S69	4D Sedan-6P	12,479	4,232	16,355

CALAIS— SERIES 6C —V-8

Styling changes for 1975 brought dual, square headlight lenses flanked by rectangular cornering lights wrapping around the body. A new cross-hatched grille appeared. Calais coupes and sedans had triangular 'coach' windows in their 'C' pillars. Standard equipment was about the same as in 1974, plus front fender light monitors, power door locks, high-energy ignition, steel-belted radial tires and catalytic converter. Once again, substantial midyear price increases were seen. Also, all cars offered at the beginning of the model run were equipped with 500-cid V-8s and electronic fuel injection became optional in March 1975.

CALAIS SERIES 6C

Model Number	Body/Style Number	Body Type & Seating	Factory Price	Shipping Weight	Production Total
6C	C49	4D Hardtop Sedan-6P	8,377	5,087	2,500
6C	C47	2D Hardtop Coupe-6P	8,184	5,003	5,800

DEVILLE— SERIES 6D—V-8

Chrome underscores, DeVille series rear fender nameplates and richer interiors identified Coupe and Sedan DeVille models. They both had slim, triangular rear quarter windows and power front seat adjusters. Luxury level options, including d'Elegance and Cabriolet packages were available again.

DEVILLE SERIES 6D

Model Number	Body/Style Number	Body Type & Seating	Factory Price	Shipping Weight	Production Total
6D	D49	4D Hardtop Sedan-6P	8,801	5,146	63,352
6D	D47	2D Hardtop Coupe-6P	8,600	5,049	110,218

FLEETWOOD BROUGHAM— SERIES 6B —V-8

The Sixty Special designation was retired this year. Identification features for Broughams included front fender script, Fleetwood decorative touches and the traditional extra equipment such as padded top, automatic leveling, dual-comfort seats and reading lights. Talisman and d'Elegance option groups were available again. Size was unchanged from 1974.

FLEETWOOD BROUGHAM SERIES 6B

Model Number	Body/Style Number	Body Type & Seating	Factory Price	Shipping Weight	Production Total
6B	B69	4D Sedan-6P	10,414	5,242	18,755

FLEETWOOD SEVENTY-FIVE—SERIES 6F—V-8

Both long wheelbase Cadillacs came with two separate climate control systems, automatic leveling air shocks, folding jump seats, rear window defogger, trailering equipment and remote-control right-hand outside rearview mirrors. The limousine had a leather front chauffeur's compartment and glass partition window. Script identification nameplates were worn on the front fenders, behind the wheel opening. Fleetwood decorative trim was seen. New triangular rear quarter windows, of much slimmer design than before, were seen.

FLEETWOOD SEVENTY-FIVE SERIES 6F

Model Number	Body/Style Number	Body Type & Seating	Factory Price	Shipping Weight	Production Total
6F	F23	4D Sedan-9P	14,218	5,720	876
6F	F23	4D Limousine-9P	14,557	5,862	795
6F	F90	Commercial chassis	—	—	1,328

FLEETWOOD ELDORADO— SERIES 6L—V-8

The Eldorado lost its rear fender skirts this season and saw a major face lift, as well. Square headlights were new. Wraparound cornering lights were gone, being replaced by a narrow, rectangular type, housed in the front fender tips. The parking lights and directionals were placed in the bumper ends. Larger rear quarter windows appeared on the coupe and a new cross-hatch grille was used on both styles. The rear fender wells were enlarged, causing the horizontal belt molding to end just ahead of the wheel opening. On the coupes, Fleetwood ornaments decorated

the roof "C" pillar. Front-wheel-drive technology was retained.

FLEETWOOD ELDORADO SERIES 6L

Model Number	Body/Style Number	Body Type & Seating	Factory Price	Shipping Weight	Production Total
6L	L47	2D Hardtop Coupe-6P	9,935	5,108	35,802
6L	L67	2D Convertible-6P	10,354	5,167	8,950

ENGINE

SEVILLE BASE V-8
Overhead valve. Cast-iron block. Displacement: 350-cid. Bore and Stroke: 4.057 x 3.385 inches. Compression ratio: 8.0:1. Net brake hp: 180 at 4400 rpm. Net torque: 360 at 2000. Hydraulic valve lifters. Crankcase capacity: 4 qt. Cooling system capacity: (with heater and air conditioner) 18.9 qt. Induction: Fuel-injection. VIN Code: R. Built by Oldsmobile exclusively for Cadillac. Due to midyear release in May 1975 this engine does not show up in many references until 1976.

CADILLAC (EXCEPT DEVILLE) BASE V-8
Overhead valve. Cast-iron block. Displacement: 500-cid. Bore and Stroke: 4.30 x 4.30 inches. Compression ratio: 8.5:1. Net brake hp: 190 at 3800 rpm. Taxable hp: 59.2. Net torque: 360 at 2000 rpm. Five main bearings. Hydraulic valve lifters. Crankcase capacity: 5 qt. (Add 1 qt. if new filter installed). Cooling system capacity: (Series 75 with heater and air conditioner) 25.8 qt.; (Others except Seville with heater and air conditioner) 23 qt. Carburetor: Four barrel. VIN Code: S. Built by Cadillac.

CHASSIS

(Seville) Wheelbase: 114.3 inches. Overall length: 204.0 inches. Overall width: 71.8 inches. Overall height: 54.7 inches. Tires: GR78 x 15.

(Eldorado) Wheelbase: 126.3 inches. Overall length: 224.1 inches. Overall width: 79.8 inches. Overall height: 54.1 inches. Front tread: 63.7 inches. Rear tread: 63.0 inches. Tires: L78 x 15.

(Calais) Wheelbase: 130.0 inches. Overall length: 230.7 inches. Overall width: 79.8 inches. Overall height: 53.8 inches. Front tread: 63.0 inches. Rear tread: 63.0 inches. Tires: L78 x 15.

(DeVille) Wheelbase: 130.0 inches. Overall length: 230.7 inches. Overall width: 79.8 inches. Overall height: 54.3 inches. Front tread: 63.0 inches. Rear tread: 63.0 inches. Tires: L78 x 15.

(Fleetwood Brougham) Wheelbase: 133 inches. Overall length: 233.7 inches. Overall width: 79.8 inches. Overall height: 55.3 inches. Front tread: 63.0 inches. Rear tread: 63.0 inches. Tires: L78 x 15.

(Fleetwood 75) Wheelbase: 151.5 inches. Overall length: 250.0 inches. Overall height: 57.8 inches. Front tread: 63.0 inches. Rear tread: 63.0 inches. Tires: L78 x 15.

(Commercial Chassis) Wheelbase: 157.5 inches. Front tread: 63.0 inches. Rear tread: 63.0 inches.

1975 Cadillac, Calais sedan

OPTIONS

Talisman Brougham ($1,788). Astro roof ($843). Sunroof ($668). Rear window defroster, standard on 75 ($73). Automatic Level Control ($84). Cruise control ($100). Eldorado reclining seat ($188). Air cushion restraints ($300). Coupe DeVille Cabriolet without sunroof ($236). Eldorado Cabriolet Coupe, without sunroof ($413). Brougham d'Elegance Group ($784). DeVille d'Elegance Group ($350). Dual Comfort six-way passenger seat ($125). AM/FM stereo with tape ($229). Padded roof on 75 ($745). Controlled differential ($60). Trackmaster ($250). Fuel injection ($600).

HISTORICAL

The Seville was introduced to the press on April 22, 1975, and went on sale May 1, 1975. Model-year production was 264,731 cars. This figure included 8,300 Calais, 173,570 DeVilles, 18,755 Fleetwoods, 2,999 Series 75, 16,355 Sevilles and 44,752 Eldorados. Cadillac's Michigan factory built all of the Sevilles and Eldorados and 173,390 other units. An additional 30,234 Cadillacs were built in the Linden, N.J., assembly plant. Cadillac's model-year numbers were 9.2 percent higher than the 1974 total and close to the first and second best years in the company's history. Calendar-year output included 36,826 Sevilles, 194,044 Cadillacs and 47,534 Eldorados for a total of 47,534 cars. Cadillac dealers sold 26,531 Sevilles, 194,600 Cadillacs and 45,918 Eldorados in the calendar-year. These cars represented a 3.8 percent share of the total market. Lower axle ratios were used for fuel mileage improvements, except on limousines.

1975 Cadillac, Fleetwood 60 Special, sedan

1975 Cadillac, Coupe De Ville

1976

OVERVIEW

Even though 1976 was a year of refinement rather than major body or engineering change at Cadillac, it signaled the end of several eras. GM's last convertible was in its final season. This would be the final year for the low-rung Calais (after a dozen years in the lineup) and for the traditional mammoth Cadillac. Full-size Cadillacs retained the ample 1975 dimensions, but the international-size Seville (introduced in mid 1975) was 27 inches shorter, eight inches narrower and 1,000 pounds lighter than a Sedan DeVille. New grilles on all models carried on the traditional Cadillac crosshatch theme. They had crosshatching within crosshatching. Cornering lights were used on Calais, DeVille, Brougham, nine-passenger and limousine models. Cadillacs also got new horizontal chrome trim and the taillights gained a new bold look. Standard wheel discs kept the three-dimensional Cadillac crest on the hub (except on Eldorados). Cadillac's 10 models came in four size categories: Family (Calais/DeVille), Personal (Eldorado), International (Seville) and Executive (Fleetwood Brougham and Seventy Five). Full-size Cadillacs stretched as long in wheelbase as 133 inches and 233.7 inches, overall (limousines, 151.5 and 252.2

Above:**1976 Cadillac, Fleetwood Eldorado, convertible**

inches, respectively). The big Cadillacs still carried the monstrous 500-cid V-8. The smaller Seville was powered by a more reasonably-sized 350-cid V-8 with electronic fuel injection. (Fuel injection was optional in all models except the Fleetwood Seventy-Five.) Vinyl roofs now were integral padded elk grain material, except on Seville and Seventy Five models, which had cross-grain padded vinyl. New trims for full-size models included sporty plaids, plush velours, knits and 11 distinctive genuine leathers. Calais and DeVille coupes had a new vinyl roof and its top molding served as continuation of the door belt molding. All full-size Cadillacs except Eldorado included a Controlled (limited-slip) Differential for extra traction. All had light monitors atop each front fender to show status of front and rear lights. All could have optional illuminated entry and theft-deterrent systems. The new Freedom battery never needed water. All models but the Eldorado offered new-look turbine-vaned and wire wheel covers. A new option locked doors when the lever was shifted to "Drive." Three full-size special editions with new refinements were offered this year: d'Elegance, Talisman and Cabriolet. New options included a push-button Weather Band (exclusive to Cadillac) built into the AM/FM stereo signal-seeking radio, loose-pillow style seats for d'Elegance packages, plus power passenger and manual driver seat back recliners for 50/50 front seats.

The 13-symbol serial number was located on top of the instrument panel, where it was visible through the windshield. The number was also stamped on a pad on the rear upper portion of the cylinder block, behind the intake manifold. The number took the form * 6B47R6Q100001 *. The first symbol 6=Cadillac Motor Division. The second symbol was a letter identifying the series as follows: B=Brougham, C=Calais, D=DeVille, F= Fleetwood 75, L=Eldorado, S=Seville and Z=Commercial Chassis. The third and fourth symbols together indicated body style: 23=four-door Limousine with auxiliary seat, 33=four-door Limousine with center divider, 47=two-door Hardtop Coupe, 49=four-door Hardtop Sedan, 67=two-door Convertible, 69=four-door pillared Sedan and 90=Commercial chassis. The fifth symbol was a letter identifying the engine: R=350-cid V-8, S=500-cid V-8. The sixth symbol was a number identifying model-year: 6=1976. The seventh symbol was a letter designating the manufacturing point as follows: Q=Detroit, Michigan, and E=Linden, New Jersey. The next group of numbers was the sequential production code starting with 100001. The Fisher Body tag on the cowl, under the hood includes additional information. The top left stamping is the Body Style Code (ST) and takes the form 76 6KS47 where "76" indicates model-year and the last four symbols indicate the body type matching the codes in the specifications tables below. Other stampings on the tag indicate the plant code, the sequential production number, the trim code, the paint code and the Modular Seat Code. Paint codes for 1975 Cadillacs are: 11=Cotillion White, 13=Georgian Silver, 16=Academy Gray, 19=Sable Black, 28=Innsbruck Blue, 29=Commodore Blue, 32=Dunbarton Green, 36=Firethorn, 37=Claret Red, 38=Pueblo Beige, 39=Kingswood Green, 50=Calumet Cream, 52=Phoenician Ivory, 67=Brentwood Brown, 69=Chesterfield Brown, 90=Crystal Blue Firemist, 91=Amberlite Firemist, 93=Greenbrier Firemist, 94=Galloway Green Firemist, 95=Florentine Gold Firemist, 96=Emberglow Firemist. Vinyl roofs came in C=Dark Blue Metallic, D=Silver Blue Metallic, F=Firethorn Metallic, J=White, K=Black, M=Mahogany Metallic, P=Silver Metallic, R=Dark Blue Green Metallic, T=Buckskin, V=Ivory and X=Dark Brown Metallic. Convertible top colors were A=White, B=Black, C=Dark Blue, F=Firethorn, R=Dark Blue Green, T=Buckskin and V=Ivory.

SEVILLE—SERIES 6K—V-8

Described as "among the most fully equipped cars in the world," the Seville debuted in May 1975 and changed little for its first complete model-year. Marketed against Mercedes, the international-size, contemporary styled four-door sedan offered near-European ride/handling qualities, along with respectable fuel mileage. Seville could hit 60 mph in 11 seconds or less, top 110 mph and cruise gently on the highway. The computer-designed chassis was actually derived from Chevrolet's Nova, but Cadillac did an extensive reworking of the X-body, with exclusive body panels and mounted a vinyl top. The Seville's front end was unmistakably Cadillac. A horizontal crosshatch grille was arranged in three rows, divided into two sections by a vertical center bar. Quad rectangular headlights sat above twin rectangular parking/signal lights and alongside large wraparound cornering lights. A Seville nameplate was fairly low on the front fender, behind the wheel opening. Up front, a stand-up wreath/crest hood ornament. Large wraparound taillights (far different from full-size models) and full wheel openings complemented the formal profile. Body preparation included two primers, four finish coats and an additional lacquer coat. New zincrometal was used in key areas to fight rust. All told, Seville was described as having an "uncluttered" look, less glitzy than other luxury cars had become. Measuring about two feet shorter than full-size domestic luxury cars, the new breed of Cadillac sold well.

1976 Cadillac, Seville, sedan

SEVILLE SERIES 6S

Model Number	Body/Style Number	Body Type & Seating	Factory Price	Shipping Weight	Production Total
6K	S69	4D Sedan-6P	12,479	4,232	43,772

CALAIS—SERIES 6C—V-8

For its final outing, the Cadillac Calais displayed the same front-end look as the more expensive DeVille, with a Cadillac "V" and crest at the hood front. Interiors came in Morgan Plaid in four possible color combinations or in expanded vinyl in Antique Light Buckskin or Black. Standard features included an AM/FM radio with automatic power antenna, an Automatic Climate Control system, a digital clock, tinted glass, light monitors and power door locks. Sedans had small coach windows on the rear pillar, but Coupes had much larger, squarish rear quarter windows. The rear fenders held script nameplates. Electronic fuel injection had become optional on the 500-cid V-8 in March 1975, but the carbureted version continued as standard equipment.

CALAIS SERIES 6C

Model Number	Body/Style Number	Body Type & Seating	Factory Price	Shipping Weight	Production Total
6C	C49	4D Hardtop Sedan-6P	8,825	5,083	1,700
6C	C47	2D Hardtop Coupe-6P	8,,629	4,989	4,500

DEVILLE—SERIES 6C—V-8

Coupe DeVille, a name that had been around for over two decades, was advertised as "America's favorite luxury car." The mid-1970s edition had a vinyl cabriolet roof with chrome accent strip at the leading edge and a squarish quarter window (considerably larger than most such windows at this time). The Sedan DeVille continued the pillarless hardtop that had been part of the GM tradition for years, but would soon be doomed to extinction. Sedans also featured narrow sail-shaped fixed windows in the roof quarter panels. The DeVille's crosshatch grille was dominated by a framed set of vertical bars. An upper horizontal bar above the grille mesh held a Cadillac script at the side and swept down alongside the grille, then outward to wrap around the fenders just above the bumpers. Quad rectangular headlights met wraparound cornering lights. Set into traditional tall housings at the rear fender tips were vertical inward- and outward-facing side lights. Horizontal taillights were below the deck lid, back-up lights in toward the license plate housing. Script nameplates were on rear quarter panels, just above the bodyside molding. New Magnan ribbed knit upholstery came in six colors, Merlin Plaid or Manhattan velour. Eleven leather combinations were available. The special-edition Coupe DeVille d'Elegance now carried standard opera lights behind the quarter windows, which were optional on other DeVille Coupes. The hood on cars with the d'Elegance option omitted the customary "V" and crest, substituting a distinctive stand-up see-through

1976 Cadillac, Fleetwood 75, limousine

ornament along the chrome windsplit. Styling highlights included dual accent stripes on front and sides of hood, door surfaces and rear deck (in choice of eight colors). Interiors contained new loose-pillow style 50/50 seats in two-toned Magnan ribbed knit cloth (four colors). A "DeVille d'Elegance" script was on the instrument panel and sail panels of the Coupe only). The package also included wide brushed-chrome lower door moldings and bodyside moldings with colored vinyl inserts to match the vinyl roof color. A decorative Cadillac crest was added on the sail panels. Cabriolet roofs had been available on Coupe DeVille since 1974.

DEVILLE SERIES 6D

Model Number	Body/Style Number	Body Type & Seating	Factory Price	Shipping Weight	Production Total
6D	D49	4D Hardtop Sedan-6P	9,265	5,127	67,677
6D	D47	2D Hardtop Coupe-6P	9,067	5,025	114,482

FLEETWOOD SIXTY SPECIAL BROUGHAM—SERIES 6C—V-8

For the last time, the luxurious Brougham would carry on the Sixty Special name, riding a lengthy 133-inch wheelbase—three inches longer than a Sedan DeVille. New "Fleetwood" plaques replaced script nameplates on both the Brougham and the long-wheelbase Fleetwood Seventy-Five models. A stand-up "jewel-like" wreath-and-crest hood ornament was now standard on both. Basic styling was similar to DeVille, including the large chrome housings at rear fender tips that held inward- and outward-facing red lenses. The deck lid held a wreath-and-crest emblem rather than Calais/DeVille's "V" and crest. Modest Fleetwood nameplates on front fenders (behind the wheel openings, below the bodyside molding) and deck lid corner were in block letters, colored to match the body. Broughams could have premium wheel covers with Fleetwood wreath/crest and black centers. Two luxury option packages were offered again. The Brougham d'Elegance option was changed for 1976 to include contoured loose-pillow style seats trimmed in soft Mansion brushed-knit fabric (five colors available), with 50/50 Dual Comfort front seats, seat back pockets,

extra-dense pile carpeting, "Brougham d'Elegance" script on the instrument panel and wide brushed-chrome lower door moldings. The roof was thickly padded in elk grain vinyl with roller perimeter around the backlight, rich French seam and bright chrome belt moldings. Also in the package were turbine-vaned wheel discs, opera lights and Brougham d'Elegance scripts on the sail panels. The Fleetwood Talisman option package included 40/40 front seats with a six-way power adjuster and power passenger recliner. The Talisman package also included special interior trim, a console with a lighted compartment, a stand-up wreath-and-crest hood ornament, a padded elk grain vinyl roof, turbine-vaned wheel discs and Fleetwood Talisman identification on the sail panels.

FLEETWOOD BROUGHAM SERIES 6B

Model Number	Body/Style Number	Body Type & Seating	Factory Price	Shipping Weight	Production Total
6B	B69	4D Sedan-6P	10,935	5,213	24,500

FLEETWOOD SEVENTY-FIVE LIMOUSINE— SERIES 6D—V-8

This would be the final year for the Cadillac limousine and nine-passenger sedan, a style that appeared in 1971. Like the Fleetwood Brougham, they gained a new grille pattern, plus revised cornering lights with horizontal chrome trim. Fleetwood 75s remained the only American-built vehicles that were designed and built strictly as a limousine. The Fleetwoods had two separate automatic climate control systems. Interior choices were Medici crushed velour fabric in Black or Dark Blue or Light Gray Magnan knit. Full-width folding seats held three extra passengers. Passengers used a control panel to turn on reading lights, operate the radio, or raise/lower the limousine's center partition. Fixed quarter windows behind the rear doors were larger than those on Sedan DeVille. Electronic fuel injection was optional on the 500-cid (8.2-liter) V-8 engine.

FLEETWOOD SEVENTY-FIVE SERIES 6F

Model Number	Body/Style Number	Body Type & Seating	Factory Price	Shipping Weight	Production Total
6F	F23	4D Sedan-9P	14,889	5,746	981
6F	F23	4D Limousine-9P	15,239	5,889	834
6F	F90	Commercial chassis	—	—	1,328

ELDORADO—SERIES 6E—V-8

Cadillac's personal-luxury coupe had lost its rear skirts in a major 1975 restyle. This year brought no drastic changes, but some styling refinements. The Cadillac script signature was now on the hood (driver's side) rather than on the grille itself. Though similar to the 1975 version, this year's crosshatch grille was dominated by vertical bars, peaked forward at the center. It also reached a bit higher than the quad rectangular headlights. New amber-lensed parking lights rested down in the bumper. Amber-lensed cornering lights sat back on front fenders. Massive vertical

extensions of the outboard bumper protrusions stood at front fender tips. Eldorado script was on rear fenders and deck lid. Wide, simple new taillights were continuous red slots within wide bezel frames, below the deck lid and above the bumper. Additional red lenses, facing both side and rear, sat in the massive vertical chrome fender extensions. Distinctively-shaped opera windows sloped down and forward at the base, following the dip in the quarter panel. The big 500-cid V-8 powered Eldorados once again, but in a weakened, de-tuned state due to more rigorous emissions standards. New wheel covers had a black center hub area with bright metal raised wreath and crest. Eldorado's simulated wood dash insert displayed a carved gunstock pattern. Power disc brakes were standard, as was a padded vinyl "half" roof. So was the Astroroof that debuted in 1975, with tinted panel for power sunroof, along with sunshade and metal slider. The front-wheel-drive Eldorado's rear suspension included upper and lower control arms, helical-coil springs and automatic level control. A chain drive connected the torque converter section to the gear portion of the automatic transmission. A Custom Biarritz option arrived late in the model-year. It included thick padding on the rear roof area, a limousine-style backlight, opera lights, chrome moldings along fender line and Sierra Grain pillow-soft leather seats. The Eldorado held the dubious record of being the world's biggest car with front-wheel drive. The coupe got far less attention than the convertible, simply because this was the final year for any GM ragtop. The Eldorado convertibles gained considerable media coverage and the covetous attention of speculators hoping to make a profit.

FLEETWOOD ELDORADO - SERIES 6L

Model Number	Body/Style Number	Body Type & Seating	Factory Price	Shipping Weight	Production Total
6L	L47	2D Hardtop Coupe-6P	10,586	5,085	35,184
6L	L67	2D Convertible-6P	11,049	5,153	14,000

ENGINE

SEVILLE BASE V-8

Overhead valve. Cast-iron block. Displacement: 350 cid (5.7 liters). Bore and Stroke: 4.057 x 3.385 inches. Compression ratio: 8.0:1. Net brake hp: 180 at 4400 rpm. Taxable hp: 52.6. Net torque: 275 at 2000 rpm. Five main bearings. Hydraulic valve lifters. Crankcase capacity: 4 qt. Cooling system capacity: (with heater and air conditioner) 18.9 qt. Induction: Electronic fuel injection (speed-density; port injected). VIN Code: R. Built by Oldsmobile exclusively for Cadillac.

CADILLAC (EXCEPT SEVILLE) BASE V-8

Overhead valve. Cast-iron block. Displacement: 500 cid (8.2 liters). Bore and Stroke: 4.300 x 4.304 inches.

Compression ratio: 8.5:1. Net brake hp: 190 at 3600 rpm. Taxable hp: 59.2. Net torque: 360 at 2000 rpm. Five main bearings. Hydraulic valve lifters. Crankcase capacity: 5 qt. (Add 1 qt. if new filter installed). Cooling system capacity: (Series 75 with heater and air conditioner) 25.8 qt.; (Others except Seville with heater and air conditioner) 23 qt. Carburetor: Rochester four barrel Model M4ME. VIN Code: S. Built by Cadillac.

CADILLAC (EXCEPT SEVILLE) OPTIONAL V-8
Overhead valve. Cast-iron block. Displacement: 500 cid (8.2 liters). Bore and Stroke: 4.300 x 4.304 inches. Compression ratio: 8.5:1. Net brake hp: 215 at 3600 rpm. Taxable hp: 59.2. Net torque: 400 at 2000 rpm. Five main bearings. Hydraulic valve lifters. Crankcase capacity: 5 qt. (Add 1 qt. if new filter installed). Cooling system capacity: (Series 75 with heater and air conditioner) 25.8 qt.; (Others except Seville with heater and air conditioner) 23 qt. Induction: Fuel injection. VIN Code: S. Built by Cadillac

CHASSIS
(Seville) Wheelbase: 114.3 inches. Overall length: 204.0 inches. Overall width: 71.8 inches. Overall height: 54.7 inches. Front tread: 61.3 inches. Rear tread: 59.0 inches. Tires: GR78 x 15.

(Eldorado) Wheelbase: 126.3 inches. Overall length: 224.1 inches. Overall width: 79.8 inches. Overall height: 54.1 inches. Front tread: 63.7 inches. Rear tread: 63.6 inches. Tires: LR78 x 15B.

(Calais) Wheelbase: 130.0 inches. Overall length: 230.7 inches. Overall width: 79.8 inches. Overall height: 53.8 inches. Front tread: 61.7 inches. Rear tread: 60.7 inches. Tires: LR78 x 15B.

(DeVille) Wheelbase: 130.0 inches. Overall length: 230.7 inches. Overall width: 79.8 inches. Overall height: 53.8 inches. Front tread: 61.7 inches. Rear tread: 60.7 inches. Tires: LR78 x 15B.

(Fleetwood Brougham) Wheelbase: 133 inches. Overall length: 233.7 inches. Overall width: 79. 8 inches. Overall height: 55.3 inches. Front tread: 61.7 inches. Rear tread: 60.7 inches. Tires: LR78 x 15B.

1976 Cadillac, Fleetwood Eldorado, convertible

(Fleetwood 75) Wheelbase: 151.5 inches. Overall length: 250.0 inches. Overall height: 57.8 inches. Front tread: 61.7 inches. Rear tread: 60.7 inches. Tires: LR78 x 15D.

(Commercial Chassis) Wheelbase: 157-1/2 inches. Front tread: 61.7 inches. Rear tread: 60.7 inches.

TECHNICAL

Transmission: Three-speed Turbo-Hydra-Matic standard on all models, column shift (400 series except Eldorado, 425 series). Gear ratios: (1st) 2.48:1, (2nd) 1.48:1, (3rd) 1:1, (Reverse) 2.07:1 or 2.09:1. Standard axle (final drive) ratio: (Seville) 2.56:1, (limousine) 3.15:1, (others) 2.73:1. Optional: (Seville) 3.08:1, (Eldorado) 3.07:1, (others) 3.15:1. Hypoid rear axle except (Seville) Salisbury type. Steering: variable-ratio power assisted. Front suspension: (Seville) unequal length upper/lower control arms, coil springs, stabilizer bar; (Eldorado) upper/lower control arms, torsion bars, (others) upper/lower control arms, coil springs, rod-and-link stabilizer bar. Rear suspension: (Seville) multiple leaf spring, (others) four-link drive, coil springs, automatic level control on all except Calais and DeVille. Body construction: (full-size) separate body and perimeter frame. Wheels: (Seville) 15 x 6 JJ, (others) 15 x 6 JK. Brakes: front ventilated disc, rear drum except Eldorado four-wheel disc, power booster on all. HEI electronic ignition. Fuel tank: (Seville) 21 gallons, (others) 27.5 gallons.

OPTIONS

Brougham d'Elegance ($885). Coupe DeVille Cabriolet ($329), with Astroroof ($1288), with sunroof ($1104). DeVille d'Elegance ($650). Eldorado Cabriolet ($432), with Astroroof ($1391), with sunroof ($1207). Fleetwood Talisman: Brougham ($1813). Astroroof for full vinyl roof ($885) except Limousines. Astroroof (painted): Calais/ DeVille/Brougham/Eldorado ($985). Sunroof for full vinyl roof ($701) except Limousines. Sunroof for painted roof ($800) except Limousine/Seville. Cruise control ($104). Controlled-cycle wipers ($28). Rear defogger, grid-type ($77) except Iimousines. Six-way dual comfort power passenger seat: DeVille/Brougham/Eldorado ($131). Six-way power front lounge seat: Calais ($'31), Limousine ($98). Power passenger 50/50 seat with recliner: DeVille/Brougham/Eldorado ($221). Manual driver's 50/50 seat back recliner ($65) except Calais/Limousine. Power passenger seat back recliner: Seville($90). Tilt/ telescope steering wheel ($102). Automatic door locks ($100). Illuminated entry system ($52). Fuel monitor ($26). Theft deterrent system ($114). Track master ($263) except Seville/Eldorado. Remote trunk lock ($68) except Seville. Opera lights: Calais/DeVille coupe, Brougham, Limousine ($58). Twilight Sentinel ($47). Guidematic headlight control ($54). Trumpet horn ($19) except

Seville. Remote-control right mirror ($30). Thermometer on left mirror ($18) except Seville. Lighted vanity mirror, passenger ($44- $60). AM/FM stereo radio with tape player: Calais/DeVille/Limousine ($239), others ($93). Signal-seeking AM/FM stereo radio ($147). Signal-seeking AM/FM stereo radio with weather band: Calais/ DeVille/Limousine ($209), others ($61). Signal-seeking AM/FM stereo radio with rear control: Limousine ($275). Firemist paint ($146). Padded vinyl roof: Calais/DeVille ($163). Eldorado ($170), Limousine ($819). Hard boot (two-piece) convertible ($63). Accent stripes: Calais/ DeVille ($42). Door edge guards ($7-$11). License frame: each ($7). Expanded vinyl upholstery: Calais ($47). Dual comfort 50/50 front seat: DeVille/Eldorado ($185). Dual comfort 60/40 front seat: DeVille ($123). Leather upholstery ($220-$235) except Calais/Limousine. Front shoulder belts: Eldorado convertible ($36). Air cushion restraint system: Calais/DeVille/Brougham/Eldorado coupe (Not available). Carpeted rubber floor mats, front/ rear ($38-$47), except Limousine, front ($26). Trunk mat ($10). Turbine-vaned wheel covers ($45), Not available on Eldorado. Wire wheel covers: ($167) except Eldorado, on d'Elegance/Talisman ($122). Stowaway spare tire (NC) except Limousine. Fuel-injected V-8 engine ($647) except Iimousine. Heavy-duty cooling system ($40). 80-amp alternator ($45). California emission equipment ($50). Limited-slip differential ($61 and not available on Eldorado). Trailering package ($85, except Iimousine/ Seville). Automatic level control: Calais/DeVille ($92).

HISTORICAL

The 1976 Cadillacs were introduced September 12, 1975, and in showrooms by September 18, 1975. Model-year production was 309,139 cars, which set a record. Calendar-year production was 312,845. Calendar-year sales by U.S. dealers was 304,485 units for a 3.5 percent share of the industry total. This compared to 267,049 (3.8 percent) in 1975. Model-year sales by U.S. dealers was 299,579 units. This year beat the all-time record (set in 1973) for sales and production, with 309,139 Cadillacs built. Seville was the shining star of the sales rise. At $13,000, the Seville was the most costly standard domestic production car built by the Big Four automakers. It also offered a foretaste of what was coming soon as General Motors down-sized all its models. All Sevilles and Eldorados, were built in Detroit, but 42,570 vehicles emerged from the Linden, New Jersey, plant. Full-size standard Cadillacs continued to sell well, defying the market conditions. Exactly 14,000 Eldorado convertibles were built in their final season (compared to just 8,950 in 1975). Cadillac promoted them as the "Last of a magnificent breed." The actual "last" American convertible was driven off the line at Cadillac's Clark Avenue plant in Detroit, on April 21, 1976, by general manager Edward C. Kennard and manufacturing

manager Bud Brawner. Passengers for this major media event included several production workers and Detroit Mayor Coleman Young. Just 60 years before, the first Cadillac to use the name "convertible" had appeared. Cadillac produced 200 identical "final" convertibles. These were dubbed "Bicentennial Cadillacs" by Mr. Kennard. The one and only last example was kept for the company's collection. All 200 were White with White top, White wheel covers and White leather upholstery with red piping, dash and carpeting. A dash plaque confirmed the fact that each of these cars was one of the last convertibles—at least until the ragtop re-emerged once again in the early 1980s. Speculation sent prices up. The original $11,049 sticker price meant little as some "collectors" quickly began to snap up open Eldorados at prices approaching $20,000. Before too long, prices fell almost as swiftly. Within months, various conversion manufacturers were slicing metal roofs off Cadillac coupes to create custom convertibles. The next regular production ragtop would be Chrysler's LeBaron in 1982. In most recent years over 2,000 Fleetwood commercial chassis had been produced annually, for conversion to hearses and ambulances. Most of those conversions were done by Superior, Miller-Meteor, or Hess & Eisenhardt. Stretch limousines were built on Cadillac chassis by Moloney (in Illinois) and Wisco (in Michigan). There were also other specialty firms involved in the "professional" car business.

1976 Cadillac, Sedan De Ville

1977

OVERVIEW

Cadillac's 75th anniversary year arrived with a shock to traditionalists, as full-size models endured an eye-opening downsizing. The new C-bodied DeVille, Brougham and limousine were 8 to 12 inches shorter, 3-1/2 inches narrower and an average of 950 pounds lighter than their massive predecessors. Only the Eldorado carried on in its mammoth form for a while longer. The Seville, which entered life in 1975 with contemporary dimensions, was mostly unchanged. Even the commercial chassis shrunk. It went from 157.5 to 144.5 inches in wheelbase, requiring funeral car and ambulance suppliers to create some new bodies. All models except the Seville carried a new lighter, smaller 425-cid (7.0-liter) V-8 engine. The huge 500 V-8 was gone. Electronic fuel injection was optional in DeVille, Brougham and Eldorado models. A standard Turbo-Hydra-Matic transmission fed power to low-ratio drive axles. Four-wheel disc brakes were standard on the Seville, Eldorado and Brougham. Carryover special editions included the Coupe DeVille, Sedan DeVille d'Elegance and Brougham d'Elegance. One new special edition joined the lineup: the Eldorado Custom Biarritz. All sedans now had pillars and framed door glass. With

the Calais gone, the DeVille took over as the cheapest Cadillac. All models had a new two-spoke steering wheel—but the spokes were wide. A new door design offered better hold-open qualities. The wheels and tires were now match-mounted for a smooth ride.

I.D. DATA

The 13-symbol serial number was located on top of the instrument panel, where it was visible through the windshield. The number was also stamped on a pad on the rear upper portion of the cylinder block, behind the intake manifold. The number took the form * 6B47R6Q100001 *. The first symbol 6=Cadillac Motor Division. The second symbol was a letter identifying the series as follows: B=Brougham, D=DeVille, F=Fleetwood Limousine, L=Eldorado, S=Seville and Z=Commercial Chassis. The third and fourth symbols indicated body style: 23=four-door Limousine with auxiliary seat, 33=four-door Limousine with center divider, 47=two-door Hardtop Coupe, 69=four-door pillared Sedan and 90=Commercial chassis. The fifth symbol was a letter identifying the engine: R=350-cid V-8, S=425-cid V-8, T=425-cid V-8. The sixth symbol was a number identifying model-year: 7=1977. The seventh symbol was a letter designating the manufacturing point as follows: Q=Detroit, Michigan and E=Linden, New Jersey. The next group of numbers

---

Above: **1977 Cadillac, Coupe De Ville**

Maurice Hanson

was the sequential production code starting with 100001. The Fisher Body tag on the cowl, under the hood, includes additional information. The top left stamping is the Body Style Code (ST) and takes the form 77 6CD47 where "77" indicates model year and the last four symbols indicate the body type matching the codes in the specifications tables below. Other stampings on the tag indicate the plant code, the sequential production number, the trim code, the paint code and the Modular Seat Code. Paint codes for 1977 Cadillacs are: 11=Cotillion White, 13=Georgian Silver, 16=Academy Gray, 19=Sable Black, 24=Jennifer Blue, 29=Hudson Bay Blue, 40=Seamist Green, 49=Edinburgh Green, 50=Naples Yellow, 54=Sovereign Gold, 61=Sonora Tan, 67=Saffron, 69=Demitasse Brown, 74=Bimini Beige, 77=Crimson, 79=Maderia Maroon, 90=Cerulean Blue Firemist, 94=Thyme Green Firemist, 95=Buckskin Firemist, 96=Frost Orange Firemist, 98=Damson Plum Firemist, 99=Desert Rose Firemist. Vinyl roof colors were: 11T=White, 13T=Silver, 19T=Black, 28T=Dark Blue, 44T=Medium Green, 49T=Dark Green, 50T=Yellow, 54T=Gold, 61T=Light Buckskin, 69T=Dark Brown, 74T=Pastel Red Beige, 79T=Claret, 90T=Silver Blue, 95T=Buckskin, 96T=Light Orange and 98T=Dark Red.

SEVILLE—SERIES 6S—V-8

The Seville had been the first production American car to offer a 350-cid electronic-fuel-injected engine as standard and it returned for 1977. Sensors fed engine data back to an on-board analog computer under the dash, which in turn signaled the eight injectors how to meter the fuel charge from the constant-supply fuel rail. Added this year were standard four-wheel power disc brakes, a retuned suspension system and Butyl rubber body mounts. The Seville entered the model year wearing a new vertical grille, rectangular quad headlights and new amber parking/signal lights. A total of 21 body colors were offered plus 16 color-coordinated Tuxedo Grain padded vinyl tops. Most customers chose vinyl. A new scan button on the AM/FM signal-seeking stereo radio allowed sampling of each station for six seconds. The Seville front end was similar to that of full-size Cadillacs, but the grille used only three horizontal divider bars and many vertical bars, forming vertical "holes." Four amber-lensed parking/signal lights sat below the quad rectangular headlights, with large cornering lights on fender sides. Cadillac's crest was on the rear roof pillar and a Seville nameplate was on the front fenders between the door and wheels. Wire wheel covers were optional. Standard upholstery was smooth Dover cloth in Claret, Black, Light Gray, Dark Blue, Medium Sage Green, Light Yellow-Gold, Light Buckskin or Medium Saffron. Optional was Sierra Grain leather in 10 colors. Standard fittings included power windows and door locks, a tilt/telescope steering wheel, individual rear reading lights, and a new seat/shoulder belt combination.

Body finishing used extensive hand work. Large-diameter Pliacell-R shock absorbers were the same as those on the Cadillac Limousine. Bolts were epoxy-encapsulated to prevent loosening.

SEVILLE - SERIES 6S

Model Number	Body/Style Number	Body Type & Seating	Factory Price	Shipping Weight	Production Total
S	69	4D Sedan-6P	13,359	4,192	45,060

Note 1: In addition to total shown, 1,152 Sevilles were built in Canada.

DEVILLE—SERIES 6D—V-8

The new-generation Fleetwood/DeVille was, in Cadillac's words, "engineered from the ground up, to make more efficient use of space." That meant a new body, new chassis, new suspension and new engine, in an integrated design. DeVilles gave more rear leg/headroom. Broughams were just as spacious as before. DeVilles (and Fleetwoods) wore a new horizontal crosshatch grille with four horizontal and nine vertical divider bars, peaking forward at the center, topped by a Cadillac script nameplate at the side of the wide upper bar. Small vertical parking/signal lights just outside the grille, quad rectangular headlights reaching all the way out to fender edges and large cornering lenses at the side, were all the same height as the grille. That combination gave the whole front end a wide, uniform appearance that flowed into the bodysides. All that was topped off by a stand-up crest hood ornament. In sum, it carried on the traditional Cadillac look. Bodies had full rear wheel openings and vertical taillights. New bumpers had dual rubber strip protective inserts. The new instrument panel had a "central control area" that allowed both driver and passenger to reach air conditioning, radio and accessory controls. Options included wire wheel discs, opera lights and accent stripes. Standard DeVille/Fleetwood equipment included light monitors, power windows and door locks, Soft-Ray tinted glass, three-speed wiper/washers, six-way power driver's seat, center armrests, a visor-vanity mirror and Turbo-Hydra-Matic transmission. Cadillac's automatic climate control system was redesigned so it operated only when necessary. The standard AM/FM radio included an automatic power antenna. The DeVille d'Elegance special edition added pillow-style 50/50 Dual Comfort seats in Medici crushed velour cloth in Claret, Medium Saffron, Dark Blue or Light Buckskin. The Coupe DeVille Cabriolet roof option came in 13 coordinated colors, with a Cadillac crest on the sail panel and bright roof moldings.

DEVILLE — SERIES 6D

Model Number	Body/Style Number	Body Type & Seating	Factory Price	Shipping Weight	Production Total
D	49	4D Hardtop Sedan-6P	9,864	4,222	95,421
D	47	2D Hardtop Coupe-6P	9,654	4,186	138,750

FLEETWOOD BROUGHAM—SERIES 6B—V-8

Billed as a car "for very special people," the shrunken Brougham had a distinctively tapered center side pillar that leaned slightly backward, as well as a custom-trimmed small back window. The rocker panel moldings were wider, too. Fleetwood block lettering appeared on the front fenders (just ahead of the door) and deck lid. Otherwise, it looked much like DeVille's sedan in the new down-sized form. The Fleetwood's new engine was a 425-cid (7.0-liter) V-8. Four-wheel disc brakes were standard, along with Automatic Level Control. The wheelbase was now identical to that of the DeVille. Broughams displayed a distinctive roof treatment in Tuxedo Grain vinyl, with opera lights, carpeted rear footrests and one-piece wall-to-wall carpeting. New Florentine velour upholstery fabric came in Medium Saffron, Light Gray, Dark Blue, Medium Sage Green, Light Yellow-Gold, Light Buckskin or Claret. Smooth-finish Dover fabric was offered in Black, Dark Blue, Light Buckskin or Claret. Standard 50/50 front seats had individual pull-down armrests and a six-way power adjustment for the driver (two-way for the passenger). The AM/FM stereo radio included a signal-seeking scanner and was available with 23-channel CB transceiver. The Brougham d'Elegance option included special contoured pillow-style seats trimmed in Florentine velour cloth (in Light Gray, Dark Blue, Light Buckskin or Claret). Included were three roof-mounted assist straps, turbine-vaned wheel discs, a d'Elegance script on each sail panel and distinctive accent striping. The Fleetwood Talisman was dropped.

FLEETWOOD BROUGHAM - SERIES 6B

Model Number	Body/Style Number	Body Type & Seating	Factory Price	Shipping Weight	Production Total
B	69	4D Sedan-6P	10,935	5,213	24,500

FLEETWOOD LIMOUSINE—SERIES 6F—V-8

Newly-designed Fleetwood and Fleetwood Formal Limousines continued to serve as "flagships of the Cadillac fleet," but in sharply shrunken form. The contemporary edition was over a foot shorter and 900 pounds lighter than last year's counterpart. Large door openings allowed easy entry/exit. Automatic Climate Control could be operated from front or rear. A Dual Accessory Panel let passengers operate the power windows and radio and set the temperature. The new wheel covers could be matched

1977 Cadillac, Fleetwood Eldorado, coupe

to any color. Both outside mirrors were remote-controlled. Upholstery choices included Dark Blue Florentine velour or Light Gray or Black Dover cloth. Formal Limousines had Black leather up front, plus a glass partition. Opera lights were standard. Only 1,299 commercial chassis were turned out this year.

FLEETWOOD SEVENTY-FIVE - SERIES 6F

Model Number	Body/Style Number	Body Type & Seating	Factory Price	Shipping Weight	Production Total
F	F23	4D Sedan-8P	18,193	4,738	1,582
F	F33	4D Limousine-7P	18,858	4,806	1,032

FLEETWOOD COMMERCIAL CHASSIS — SERIES 6Z

Model Number	Body/Style Number	Body Type & Seating	Factory Price	Shipping Weight	Production Total
Z	90	Commercial Chassis	NA	NA	1,299

ELDORADO—SERIES 6L—V-8

Unlike the other full-size Cadillacs, the Eldorado continued in its previous large-size format. A brushed chrome molding reached across the new coordinated horizontal-style grille and headlights. This year's grille pattern featured more thin vertical bars and stood on a line with the tops of the headlight. Individual "Eldorado" block letters sat on the hood front, above the grille. The rear fenders held new rectangular side marker lights, while new vertical taillights were formed into the bumper tips. The power-assisted four-wheel disc brakes had cooling fins. In a modified automatic climate control, the compressor ran only when needed. The $1,760 Biarritz option (introduced during the 1976 model-year) included a special fully-padded elk grain cabriolet roof, formal quarter and rear windows with French seams and opera lights. A script nameplate stood to the rear of quarter windows. Sierra Grain leather covered contoured pillow seats.

ELDORADO - SERIES 6L

Model Number	Body/Style Number	Body Type & Seating	Factory Price	Shipping Weight	Production Total
L	47	2D Coupe-6P	11,187	4,955	47,344

ENGINE

SEVILLE BASE V-8

Overhead valve. Cast-iron block. Displacement: 350 cid (5.7 liters). Bore and Stroke: 4.057 x 3.385 inches. Compression ratio: 8.0:1. Net brake hp: 180 at 4400 rpm. Taxable hp: 52.6. Net torque: 275 at 2000 rpm. Five main bearings. Hydraulic valve lifters. Induction: Electronic fuel injection (speed-density; port injected). VIN Code: R. Built by Oldsmobile exclusively for Cadillac.

CADILLAC (EXCEPT SEVILLE) BASE V-8

Overhead valve. Cast-iron block. Displacement: 425 cid (7.0 liters). Bore and Stroke: 4.082 x 4.06 inches. Compression ratio: 8.2:1. Net brake hp: 180 at 4000 rpm. Taxable hp: 53.31. Net torque: 320 at 2000 rpm. Five main

bearings. Hydraulic valve lifters. Carburetor: Four barrel. VIN Code: S. Built by Cadillac

DE VILLE, BROUGHAM, ELDORADO OPTIONAL V-8

Overhead valve. Cast-iron block. Displacement: 425 cid (7.0 liters). Bore and Stroke: 4.082 x 4.06 inches. Compression ratio: 8.2:1. Net brake hp: 195 at 3800 rpm. Taxable hp: 53.31. Net torque: 320 at 2400 rpm. Five main bearings. Hydraulic valve lifters. Induction: Electronic fuel-injection. VIN Code: T. Built by Cadillac

CHASSIS

(Seville) Wheelbase: 114.3 inches. Overall length: 204.0 inches. Overall width: 71.8 inches. Overall height: 54.6 inches. Front tread: 61.3 inches. Rear tread: 59.0 inches. Tires: GR78 x 15 steel-belted radial with wide white sidewall.

(Eldorado) Wheelbase: 126.3 inches. Overall length: 224.0 inches. Overall width: 79.8 inches. Overall height: 54.2 inches. Front tread: 63.7 inches. Rear tread: 63.6 inches. Tires: GR78 x 15B.

(DeVille, Brougham) Wheelbase: 121.5 inches. Overall length: 221.2 inches. Overall width: 76.48 inches. Overall height: 55.3 inches. Front tread: 61.7 inches. Rear tread: 60.7 inches. Tires: (DeVille) GR78 x 15 steel-belted radial with wide white sidewall; (Brougham) GR78 x 15-D steel-belted radial with wide white sidewall.

(Fleetwood 75) Wheelbase: 144.5 inches. Overall length: 244.2 inches. Overall width: 76.48 inches. Overall height: 56.9 inches. Front tread: 61.7 inches. Rear tread: 60.7 inches. Tires: HR78 x 15-D steel-belted radial with wide white sidewall.

TECHNICAL

Transmission: Turbo-Hydra-Matic transmission standard on all models, column shift. Gear ratios: (1st) 2.48:1, (2nd) 1.48:1, (3rd) 1:1, (Reverse) 2.07:1. Standard axle (final drive) ratio: (Seville) 2.56:1, with 3.08:1 optional (standard high altitude), (DeVille/Brougham) 2.28:1, with 3.08:1 optional, (Limousine) 3.08:1. Hypoid rear axle, except (Seville), Salisbury type. Steering: variable-ratio, power-assisted. Front suspension: independent coil spring, link-type stabilizer except (Eldorado) same as 1976. Rear suspension: (Seville) Hotchkiss leaf spring, link-type stabilizer, (DeVille/Fleetwood) four-link drive, coil springs, (Eldorado) same as 1976. Automatic level control, except DeVille. Body construction: (DeVille/Fleetwood) ladder type frame. Brakes: front disc, rear drum except Brougham/Eldorado/Seville, four-wheel disc. HEI electronic ignition. Fuel tank, (Seville) 21 gallons, (DeVille/Fleetwood) 24 gallons, (Eldorado) 27.5 gallons.

OPTIONS

Astroroof for full vinyl roof ($938) except Limousines. Astroroof (painted): DeVille/Seville/Eldorado ($1043). Sunroof for full vinyl roof ($742) except Limousine. Sunroof (painted roof): DeVille/Seville/Eldorado ($846). Cruise control ($111). Controlled-cycle wipers ($30). Rear defogger, grid-type ($83). Six-way dual comfort power seat adjuster, passenger ($107-$138) except Limousine. Six-way power driver's seat adjuster: Limousine ($99). Power passenger 50/50 seat with six-way adjuster ($197-$248) except Limousine. Driver's 50/50 seat recliner ($110) except Limousine. Power passenger seat back recliner, notchback seat: DeVille ($110). Tilt/telescope steering wheel ($109). Automatic door locks ($101). Illuminated entry system ($56). Fuel monitor ($28). Theft deterrent system ($123). Trunk lid release and power pull-down ($61-$73). Opera lights: DeVille ($60). Twilight Sentinel ($51). Guidematic headlight control ($58). Trumpet horn ($20) except Seville. Remote-control right mirror ($32). Lighted thermometer on left mirror ($26). Lighted vanity mirror ($47). AM/FM stereo radio with tape player: DeVille/Iimousine ($254), others ($100). AM/FM stereo radio with digital display: DeVille/Limousine ($254). AM/FM stereo radio with CB: DeVille/Limousine ($386), others ($230). Signal seeking/scan AM/FM stereo radio ($156). Seek/scan AM/FM stereo radio with rear control: Limousine ($326). Firemist paint ($153). Vinyl roof: DeVille ($179), Eldorado ($186). Bumper: DeVille/Brougham/Limousine ($8). Accent stripes: DeVille/Brougham ($45). Door edge guards ($8-$12). License frame: each ($7). Dual Comfort 50/50 front seats: DeVille/Eldorado ($187). Leather seats ($235-$252). Two-tone 50/50 dual comfort front seats: Eldorado ($471). Twin floor mats ($13-$28) except Eldorado. Floor mats, one-piece: Eldorado front ($31), rear ($19). Trunk mat ($10). Turbine-vaned wheel covers ($49), Not available on Eldorado. Wire wheel covers: Brougham ($129), others ($176) except Eldorado Brougham d'Elegance ($885). Coupe DeVille Cabriolet ($348), with Astroroof ($1365),

1977 Cadillac Seville, sedan

with sunroof ($1169). DeVille d'Elegance ($650). Eldorado Cabriolet ($457), with Astroroof ($1474), with sunroof ($1278). Eldorado Custom Biarritz ($1760), with Astroroof ($2777), with sunroof ($2581). Fuel-injected V-8 engine: DeVille/Brougham/Eldorado ($702). Heavy-duty cooling system ($43). 80-amp alternator ($47). California emission equipment ($70). Limited-slip differential ($61), Not available on Eldorado. High-altitude package. ($22). Trailering package: Seville($43), others ($90) except Limousine. Automatic level control: DeVille ($100).

HISTORICAL

Introduced on September 23, 1976. Model-year production was 358,487 for a 3.9 percent share of the industry total. Calendar-year production was 369,254. Calendar-year sales by U.S. dealers: 335,785 for a 3.7 percent market share. Model-year sales were 328,129. The new smaller Cadillacs were selling well, at least at the beginning. Total sales of 328,129 Cadillacs scored 9.5 percent over the 1976 record. Model-year production also beat the 1976 score by 16 percent. Rumors early in the year suggested that Cadillacs might be "upsized" within a couple of years, but that wasn't likely with Corporate Average Fuel Economy (CAFE) requirements. Conversion companies stepped up production of "stretch" limousines. Moloney Coachbuilders (in Illinois) offered a 40-inch stretch Brougham for under $15,000 (plus the cost of the car). Phaeton Coach Corp. of Dallas and the California-based American Custom Coachworks, did similar work and created custom convertibles based on the Coupe DeVille. Convertibles, Inc. of Ohio turned out ragtop Eldorado conversions.

John McCans

1977 Cadillac, Sedan De Ville

1978

OVERVIEW

Subtle exterior changes dominated the year, as wheelbases and dimensions were virtually identical to 1977. The DeVille, Brougham, Limousine and Eldorado had a bolder horizontal crosshatch grille. All models but the Eldorado had new rear bumper ends with vertical taillights and a three-dimensional crest insignia. Most Broughams, all California Cadillacs and the fuel-injected DeVille sedan sported aluminum hoods. Passenger compartments had seven new interior colors and three new body cloths, including Random velour. Of the 21 body colors, 17 were new and all but two of those were exclusive to Cadillac. Signal-seeking AM/FM stereo radios were now standard on all Cadillacs. For the first time, chromed Dunlop wire wheels from the British firm were offered as options on DeVille, Brougham and Seville models. New electronic level control (standard on all models except the DeVille) used a height sensor to signal a motor-driven compressor that automatically adjusted for changing loads. DeVille and Brougham body mounts were retuned for a smoother, quieter ride. Four new special editions were offered: Seville Elegante, Phaeton Coupe (or Sedan) DeVille and revised Eldorado Custom Biarritz. An available Oldsmobile-built

Above: **1978 Cadillac, Fleetwood Eldorado, coupe**
Dr. Robert Newbrough

diesel V-8 engine for Seville was announced during the model-year, at the Chicago Auto Show. All Cadillacs except Seville carried a standard 425-cid V-8. Cadillac boasted that owning one had always "expressed success" and proclaimed "...calling something 'the Cadillac of its field' is one of the finest compliments you can pay a product."

I.D. DATA

The 13-symbol serial number was located on top of the instrument panel, where it was visible through the windshield. The number was also stamped on a pad on the rear upper portion of the cylinder block, behind the intake manifold. The number took the form * 6B69T8Q100001 *. The first symbol 6=Cadillac Motor Division. The second symbol was a letter identifying the series as follows: B=Brougham, D=DeVille, F=Fleetwood Limousine, L=Eldorado, S=Seville and Z=Commercial Chassis. The third and fourth symbols indicated body style: 23=four-door Limousine with auxiliary seat, 33=four-door Limousine with center divider, 47=two-door Hardtop Coupe, 69=four-door pillared Sedan and 90=Commercial chassis. The fifth symbol was a letter identifying the engine: B=350-cid V-8 with electronic fuel injection, N=350-cid diesel V-8, S=425-cid four-barrel V-8, T=425-cid V-8 with electronic fuel injection.

The sixth symbol was a number identifying model-year: 8=1978. The seventh symbol was a letter designating the manufacturing point as follows: Q=Detroit, Michigan and E=Linden, New Jersey. The next group of numbers was the sequential production code starting with 100001. The Fisher Body tag on the cowl, under the hood includes additional information. The top left stamping is the Body Style Code (ST) and takes the form 78 6CD47 where "78" indicates model-year and the last four symbols indicate the body type matching the codes in the specifications tables below. Other stampings on the tag indicate the plant code, the sequential production number, the trim code, the paint code and the Modular Seat Code. Paint codes for 1978 Cadillacs are: 11=Cotillion White, 15=Platinum Poly, 16=Pewter Poly, 19=Sable Black, 21=Columbia Blue, 22=Sterling Blue Poly, 28=Commodore Blue Poly, 40=Seamist Green, 49=Blackwatch Green Poly, 54=Colonial Yellow, 62=Arizona Beige, 64=Demitasse Brown Poly, 69=Ruidoso Saddle Poly, 74=Mulberry Poly, 80=Carmine Red, 90=Medium Blue Firemist Poly, 94=Basil Green Firemist Poly, 95=Aztec Gold Firemist Poly, 96=Western Saddle Firemist Poly, 98=Autumn Haze Firemist Poly and 99=Canyon Copper Firemist Poly. Vinyl roof colors were: A=Medium Blue Metallic, C=Dark Blue Metalic, D=Light Blue Metallic, E=Light Yellow, G=Medium Gold Metallic, J=White, K=Black, L=Dark Camel Metallic, N=Medium Green Metallic, P=Silver Metallic, R=Dark Green Metallic, T=Light Beige, U=Medium Saddle Metallic, W=Medium Beige Metallic, X=Dark Brown Metallic and Y=Dark Mulberry Metallic.

SEVILLE—SERIES 6S—V-8

Seville displayed new bumper guards, an engraved chrome insignia on the taillights and a painted accent stripe that extended across the deck lid to give a wider, lower appearance. The lower bumper rub strips were body-colored. The Seville's grille had vertical slots in four rows, with the pattern repeated in two openings on the bumper, alongside the license plate. Amber parking and signal lights sat below the quad rectangular headlights, with amber and clear cornering lights on the fender sides. A Seville script was behind the front wheels and a Cadillac script was at the back of rear fenders, just ahead of the angled wraparound taillights. Once again, the electronically fuel-injected 350-cid V-8 engine was standard, with an on-board analog computer and new Electronic Spark Selection that altered spark advance to meet varying conditions. The intake manifold was lightweight aluminum. Oldsmobile's 350-cid diesel V-8 became available in midyear and was first offered only in seven major cities. Electronic load leveling was new this year. Buyers could choose either a matching metal roof or Tuxedo Grain padded vinyl top. Sevilles came in 15 standard body colors plus six Firemist options. The

vinyl roof came in 16 colors, including metallics. Options included real wire wheels as well as wire wheel covers, plus opera lights, a sunroof, a 40-channel CB transceiver, electronically-tuned radios and tape player combinations. A new trip computer option offered 11 digital displays, including average speed and miles per gallon, miles to destination, estimated arrival time, engine speed, coolant temp and voltage. The Seville Elegante was offered in two duo-tone body finishes: Platinum and Sable Black, or Western Saddle Firemist and Ruidoso Brown. Both had a painted metal top. The second color began just above the beltline. Real wire wheels (not covers) had long-laced spokes. Full-length brushed chrome moldings had etched black grooving. An "Elegante" script and crest were on the pillar behind the rear doors. The seats used perforated leather inserts (Antique Gray or Antique Medium Saddle) and soft, suede-like trim. Compartments were provided for a telephone, tapes and personal items. Only 5,000 or so Elegantes were built this year.

SEVILLE - SERIES 6S

Model Number	Body/Style Number	Body Type & Seating	Factory Price	Shipping Weight	Production Total
S	69	4D Sedan-5P	14267	4179	56,985

DEVILLE—SERIES 6D—V-8

Several styling refinements were seen on the 1978 DeVille and Fleetwood models. A Cadillac script was above the grille's header bar (mounted on the body), on the driver's side. A new solid-colored wreath-and-crest ornament decorated the hood. New, extra-slim vertical taillights in tall chrome bumper tips had thin back-up lights inset in the middle and built-in side marker lights. The DeVille's padded vinyl roof had a custom-trimmed backlight. Under the hood was the 425-cid (7.0-liter) V-8 introduced the year before. Six-way power driver's seat controls were now in the door armrest. The Coupe and Sedan DeVille also had automatic climate control, power windows and much more. A sunroof, wire wheel discs and 50/50 Dual Comfort seats were available. Nine interior color selections were offered in new Random velour or Hampton woven cloth. Up to a dozen Sierra Grain

1978 Cadillac, Fleetwood Eldorado, coupe

leather choices came with color-coordinated carpeting. Options included a custom-trimmed padded vinyl top, rear deck accent stripes, color-keyed bodyside moldings, chrome wire wheels, electronic leveling and chrome accent moldings. Coupe DeVilles could have the Cabriolet roof package, including a chrome accent strip to highlight the elk grain vinyl top, Cadillac crests and a French seam around the back windows. A DeVille d'Elegance special edition featured pillow-style 50/50 Dual Comfort seats in new Random velour (Antique Dark Green, Light Beige, Light Blue or Dark Mulberry). The upper doors and front seat back assist straps wore matching Random velour. High-pile carpeting extended part way up the doors. The glove box door held a "DeVille d'Elegance" insignia, as did the pillar behind rear side windows. The hood, door and deck lid were striped. Other extras: opera lights, three roof-mounted assist straps and door-pull handles. The d'Elegance trim package came in 21 body colors. Phaeton packages that featured a simulated convertible top (down to authentic-looking welts and stitching). Offered in Cotillion White, Platinum or Arizona Beige (with contrasting top colors), these were identified by "Phaeton" nameplates on back fenders and wire wheels.

DEVILLE SERIES 6D

Model Number	Body/Style Number	Body Type & Seating	Factory Price	Shipping Weight	Production Total
D	47	2D Coupe-6P	10,444	4,163	117,750
D	69	4D Sedan-6P	10,668	4,236	88,951

FLEETWOOD BROUGHAM—SERIES 6B—V-8

The Fleetwood Brougham had a distinctive tapered-roof-pillar design between the front and rear doors. Broughams also featured four-wheel disc brakes. New this year was the restyled grille and back bumper, plus a weight-saving aluminum hood. Brushed chrome moldings held new wreath-and-crest ornamentation. The elk grain vinyl roof held opera lights just behind the back doors. Brougham interiors included individual reading lights. The standard engine was the 425-cid (7.0-liter) V-8. Oversized steel-belted radial tires rode match-mounted wheels. New standard equipment included electronic leveling control. Joining the option list were seven new interior colors, rear deck accent stripes, color-keyed bodyside moldings and chrome accent moldings. Available chrome wire wheels showed the Cadillac insignia on a hexagonal center hub. An electronic-tuning stereo radio with digital readout was available with an 8-track tape player. The familiar Astroroof was available too. The Brougham d'Elegance package added contoured pillow-styled seats trimmed in Florentine velour (in five Antique colors), with velour trim in doors, pull straps and seat back assist straps. Medium Saddle leather was also available on the 50/50 Dual Comfort front seats. A "Brougham d'Elegance"

insignia was on the glove box door. Also included were three above-door passenger assist grips.

FLEETWOOD BROUGHAM - SERIES 6B

Model Number	Body/Style Number	Body Type & Seating	Factory Price	Shipping Weight	Production Total
B	69	4D Sedan-6P	12,292	4,314	36,800

FLEETWOOD LIMOUSINE—SERIES 6F—V-8

The two Fleetwood Limousines were the "Flagships of the Cadillac fleet." They carried styling alterations similar to other Fleetwoods. New electronic leveling control was standard. The six-way power driver's seat controls were now in the door armrest. Standard Limousines sat eight. The seven-passenger Formal Limousine had a standard divided 45/45 front seat with black leather seating, plus a sliding glass partition. Both models had two additional fold-down seats. Florentine velour upholstery was offered in Light Gray, Black or Dark Blue. The Automatic Climate Control System could be operated by driver or passengers. A Dual Accessory Control Panel also let passengers operate the power windows—a logical decision, to be sure. A padded elk grain vinyl roof was standard. Not many Formal Limousines were built as the standard variety. Chrome landau bars were available by special order.

FLEETWOOD LIMOUSINE - SERIES 6F

Model Number	Body/Style Number	Body Type & Seating	Factory Price	Shipping Weight	Production Total
F	23	4D Sedan-8P	19,642	4,772	848
F	33	4D Fml Limousine-7P	20,363	4,858	682

FLEETWOOD COMMERCIAL CHASSIS — SERIES 6Z

Model Number	Body/Style Number	Body Type & Seating	Factory Price	Shipping Weight	Production Total
Z	90	Commercial Chassis	NA	NA	852

ELDORADO—SERIES 6L—V-8

The 1978 Eldorado received no major changes, other than a revised crosshatch pattern in the grille. It dominated by heavier horizontal bars. Also noteworthy on the outside was the padded elk grain vinyl top. The four-row peaked checkerboard grille was flanked by quad rectangular headlights. Amber parking lights sat low on the bumper. The grille pattern was repeated between license plate and bumper guards, below the protruding protective strip. Massive chrome vertical bumper ends extended upward to form housings for auxiliary lights, forming a huge bright extension of fender tips. Eldorado block letters stood above the upper grille bar, which tapered outward above the headlights. The standard engine was the 425-cid (7.0-liter) V-8. It was available with the choice of a carburetor or fuel injection. Eldorados had four-wheel disc brakes, front-wheel drive, electronic level control, automatic climate control, power windows and door locks, cornering lights, a six-way power seat, three-speed windshield wipers, a Freedom battery, light monitors, a trip odometer, wide white sidewall steel-belted radial tires, Soft-Ray

tinted glass, and a stowaway spare tire. Options included a 40-channel CB, an 8-track tape player, an Astroroof and a sunroof. The Eldorado Biarritz now sported a convertible-like padded vinyl top, unique script, accent stripes and distinctive chrome body moldings. The Cabriolet roof accented the Eldorado's distinctively-shaped quarter windows, which tapered downward at the front and sported a vinyl-insert molding across the fully-padded elk grain vinyl top. Black-accented brushed stainless steel belt moldings stretched from the rear to the hood, terminating in a spearlike design at the front. Special stripes accented the front fenders, doors and rear quarter panels. All had opera lights, a remote-control passenger-side mirror and color-coordinated wheel discs.

ELDORADO

Model Number	Body/Style Number	Body Type & Seating	Factory Price	Shipping Weight	Production Total
L	47	2D Coupe-6P	11,921	4,906	46,816

ENGINE

SEVILLE BASE V-8

Overhead valve. Cast-iron block. Displacement: 350 cid (5.7 liters). Bore and Stroke: 4.057 x 3.385 inches. Compression ratio: 8.0:1. Net brake hp: 170 at 4400 rpm. Taxable hp: 52.6. Net torque: 270 at 2000 rpm. Five main bearings. Hydraulic valve lifters. Induction: Electronic fuel injection. VIN Code: B. Built by Cadillac.

CADILLAC (EXCEPT SEVILLE) BASE V-8

Overhead valve. Cast-iron block. Displacement: 425 cid (7.0 liters). Bore and Stroke: 4.082 x 4.06 inches. Compression ratio: 8.2:1. Net brake hp: 180 at 4000 rpm. Taxable hp: 53.31. Net torque: 320 at 2000 rpm. Five main bearings. Hydraulic valve lifters. Carburetor: Four barrel. VIN Code: S. Built by Cadillac.

DE VILLE, BROUGHAM, ELDORADO OPTIONAL V-8

Overhead valve. Cast-iron block. Displacement: 425 cid (7.0 liters). Bore and Stroke: 4.082 x 4.06 inches. Compression ratio: 8.2:1. Net brake hp: 195 at 3800 rpm. Taxable hp: 53.31. Net torque: 320 at 2400 rpm. Five main bearings. Hydraulic valve lifters. Induction: Electronic fuel-injection. VIN Code: T. Built by Cadillac.

DE VILLE, BROUGHAM, ELDORADO OPTIONAL V-8

Overhead valve. Cast-iron block. Displacement: 350 cid (5.7 liters). Bore and Stroke: 4.057 x 3.385 inches. Compression ratio: 22.5:1. Net brake hp: 120 at 3600 rpm. Taxable hp: 52.6. Net torque: 220 at 1600 rpm. Five main bearings. Hydraulic valve lifters. Induction: Electronic fuel injection. VIN Code: N. Built by Oldsmobile.

CHASSIS

(Seville) Wheelbase: 114.3 inches. Overall length: 204.0 inches. Overall width: 71.8 inches. Overall height: 54.6 inches. Front tread: 61.3 inches. Rear tread: 59.0 inches. Tires: GR78 x 15 steel-belted radial with wide white sidewall.

(Eldorado) Wheelbase: 126.3 inches. Overall length: 224.0 inches. Overall width: 79.8 inches. Overall height: 54.2 inches. Front tread: 63.7 inches. Rear tread: 63.6 inches. Tires: LR78 x 15B steel-belted radial with wide white sidewall.

(DeVille, Brougham) Wheelbase: 121.5 inches. Overall length: 221.2 inches. Overall width: 76.48 inches. Overall height: 55.3 inches. Front tread: 61.7 inches. Rear tread: 60.7 inches. Tires: (DeVille) GR78 x 15-B steel-belted radial with wide white sidewall; (Brougham) HR78 x 15-B steel-belted radial with wide white sidewall.

(Fleetwood 75) Wheelbase: 144.5 inches. Overall length: 244.2 inches. Overall width: 76.48 inches. Overall height: 56.9 inches. Front tread: 61.7 inches. Rear tread: 60.7 inches. Tires: HR78 x 15-D steel-belted radial with wide white sidewall.

TECHNICAL

Transmission: Turbo-Hydra-Matic transmission standard on all models, column shift. Gear ratios: (1st) 2.48:1, (2nd) 1.48:1, (3rd) 1:1, (Reverse) 2.07:1. Standard axle ratio: (Seville) 2.56:1 except high-alt. 3.08:1, (DeVille/Brougham) 2.28:1, with 3.08:1 available, (Limo) 3.08:1, (Eldorado) 2.73:1 except high-altitude 3.07:1. Hypoid rear axle except (Seville) Salisbury type, (Eldorado) spiral bevel. Steering/Suspension: same as 1977. Brakes: front disc, rear drum except Eldorado/Seville/Brougham, four-wheel disc. HEI electronic ignition. Fuel tank: (Seville) 21 gallon, (Eldorado) 27 gallon, (others) 25.3 gallons.

Phil Hall

1978 Cadillac, Coupe de Ville

OPTIONS

Astroroof with full vinyl roof ($995) except Iimousine. Astroroof (painted): DeVille/Seville/Eldorado ($1106). Sunroof with full vinyl roof ($795) except Iimousine. Sunroof (painted roof): DeVille/Seville/Eldorado ($906). Cruise control ($122). Trip computer: Seville ($875). Controlled-cycle wipers ($32). Rear defogger, grid-type ($94). Six-way Dual Comfort power passenger seat adjuster ($118-$150). Power 50/50 seat recliner ($116). Power 50/50 passenger seat recliner ($210-$262). Power passenger seat back recliner, notchback seat: DeVille ($116). Tilt/telescope steering wheel ($121). Automatic door locks ($114). Illuminated entry system ($59). Fuel monitor ($29). Theft deterrent system ($130). Trunk lid release and power pull-down ($80) except Seville. Trunk lid power pull-down: Seville($67). Opera lights: DeVille/Seville($63). Twilight Sentinel ($54). Guidematic headlight control ($62). Trumpet horn ($21) except Seville. Remote-control right mirror ($34). Lighted thermometer on left mirror ($27). Lighted vanity mirror, passenger ($50). AM/FM stereo radio with digital display, ($106), with tape player ($106), with CB ($281), with tape and CB ($427). Seek/scan AM/FM stereo radio with tape player and digital display: Seville/Brougham ($225). Seek/scan AM/FM stereo radio with rear control: Limousine ($203). Firemist paint ($163). Padded vinyl roof: DeVille/Seville($215-$222). Front bumper reinforcement ($9) except Seville/Eldorado. Chrome accent molding: DeVille/Brougham ($85-$100). Accent stripes: DeVille/Brougham ($53). Door edge guards ($11- $18). License frame: each ($9). Dual Comfort 50/50 front seats: DeVille/Eldorado ($198). Leather seating area ($295-$315), Eldorado with two-tone paint and 50/50 dual comfort front seats ($556). Carpeted rubber front floor mats ($31-$34). Rear carpeted rubber front floor mats ($15-$21). Trunk mat ($12). Turbine-vaned wheel covers ($54), Not available on Eldorado. Locking wire wheels ($541-$595). Locking wire wheel covers ($179-$233). Stowaway spare tire: Limousine (NC). Fuel-injected V-8 engine: DeVille/Brougham/Seville ($744). Heavy-duty cooling system ($47). 80-amp. alternator ($51). Engine block heater ($20). California emission equipment ($75). Limited-slip differential ($67), not available on Eldorado. High-altitude package. ($33). Electronic level control: DeVille ($140). Brougham d'Elegance: cloth ($938), leather ($1,270). DeVille Cabriolet ($369). DeVille Cabriolet with Astroroof ($1,450). DeVille Cabriolet with sunroof ($1,250). DeVille d'Elegance ($689). DeVille Custom Phaeton ($1,929). Eldorado Cabriolet ($484). Eldorado Cabriolet with Astroroof ($1,565). Eldorado Cabriolet with sunroof ($1,365). Eldorado Custom Biarritz ($1,865), with Astroroof ($2,946), with sunroof ($2,746). Eldorado Custom Biarritz Classic ($2,466), with Astroroof ($3,547), with sunroof ($3,347). Seville Elegante ($2,600), Elegante with Astroroof ($3,706), Elegante with sunroof ($3,506).

HISTORICAL

Introduced on September 29, 1977. Model-year production was 349,684 for a 3.9 percent share of the industry total and the second highest Cadillac total ever. Calendar-year production was 350,761. Calendar-year sales by U.S. dealers were 350,813, giving Cadillac a 3.8 percent market share. Model-year sales by U.S. dealers hit 347,221. Record sales greeted Cadillac for the third year in a row. The model-year total beat 1977's mark by six percent. The new Seville diesel (engine built by Oldsmobile) sold only about 2,800 copies, barely half the early prediction. Buyers snapped up the last of the large Eldorados before the down-sized 1979 version arrived. A three-month shutdown of the Linden, New Jersey, plant to tool up for the new E-body 1979 Eldorado, Toronado and Riviera models, contributed to a loss in calendar-year production of DeVilles this year. Cadillac asserted that the company "consistently leads all U.S. Iuxury car makes in repeat ownership." The ads suggested, "Once you own a Cadillac, it is difficult to accept anything less."

1978 Cadillac, Sedan De Ville

1978 Cadillac, Seville sedan

1979

OVERVIEW

Apart from a daringly down-sized E-body Eldorado, the year 1979 brought few stunning announcements from Cadillac. A new electronic-tuning AM/FM stereo radio with signal seeker and scanner included digital display of time and station frequencies. A new convex remote-control right-hand mirror that increased the field of view was standard on Broughams and Limousines, but optional on DeVilles. The lap belts were of the new "free-wheeling" style and chimes gently warned passengers to buckle up. A new dome light had dual spotlight-type map lights. Sevilles and Eldorados could have an optional Trip Computer with a digital display that showed average speed, miles yet to travel, engine speed, arrival time and elapsed trip time. DeVilles, Fleetwood Broughams and Limousines were powered by a 425-cid (7.0-liter) V-8 with a four-barrel carburetor, but a fuel-injected version of the big V-8 was again available. Oldsmobile's diesel V-8, first offered only in Sevilles and Eldorados, could go under the hoods of DeVilles and Broughams by year's end.

I.D. DATA

The 13-symbol serial number was located on top of the instrument panel, where it was visible through the wind-

Above: **1979 Cadillac, Eldorado coupe**

shield. The number was also stamped on a pad on the rear upper portion of the cylinder block, behind the intake manifold. The number took the form * 6D37S9E100001 *. The first symbol 6=Cadillac Motor Division. The second symbol was a letter identifying the series as follows: B=Brougham, D=DeVille, F=Fleetwood Limousine, L=Eldorado, S=Seville and Z=Commercial Chassis. The third and fourth symbols indicated body style: 23=four-door Limousine with auxiliary seat, 33=four-door Limousine with center divider, 47=two-door Hardtop Coupe, 57=two-door Coupe, 69=four-door pillared Sedan and 90=Commercial chassis. The fifth symbol was a letter identifying the engine: B=350-cid V-8 with electronic fuel injection, N=350-cid diesel V-8, S=425-cid four-barrel V-8, T=425-cid V-8 with electronic fuel injection. The sixth symbol was a number identifying model-year: 9=1979. The seventh symbol was a letter designating the manufacturing point as follows: C=Southgate, California, E=Linden, New Jersey and 9=Detroit, Michigan. The next group of numbers was the sequential production code starting with 100001. The Fisher Body tag on the cowl, under the hood includes additional information. The top left stamping is the Body Style Code (ST) and takes the form 79 6CD47 where "79" indicates model-year and the last four symbols indicate the body type matching the codes in the specifications tables below. Other stampings

on the tag indicate the plant code, the sequential production number, the trim code, the paint code and the Modular Seat Code. Paint codes for 1979 Cadillacs are: 11=Cotillion White, 15=Platinum Poly, 19=Sable Black, 22=Sterling Blue Iridescent, 29=Crater Lake Blue Iridescent, 49=Blackwatch Green Iridescent, 54=Colonial Yellow, 62=Laramie Beige, 68=Burnished Gold, 69=Post Road Brown Iridescent, 76=Red Cedar Iridescent, 89=Norfolk Gray, 90=Slate Firemist Poly, 91=Pottery Gold Firemist, 92=Biscayne Aqua Firemist, 93=Cedar Firemist, 94=Basil Green Firemist, 95=Cerulean Blue Firemist, 96=Western Saddle Firemist Poly. Vinyl roof colors were: B=Silver Blue Metallic, C=Dark Blue Metalic, D=Light Blue Metallic, E=Light Yellow, G=Light Gold Metallic, H=Light Gray, J=White, K=Black, M=Dark Aqua Metalic, N=Medium Green Metallic, P=Silver Metallic, R=Dark Green Metallic, S=Slate Gray Metallic, T=Light Beige, U=Medium Saddle Metallic, X=Dark Brown Metallic and Y=Light Cedar Metallic.

SEVILLE—SERIES 6K—V-8

Carried over with only modest trim changes, Sevilles got a retuned suspension to improve their ride, plus new body mounts. Nameplates moved from the upper right of the grille to the upper left and that grille had a tighter pattern than before. The grille's pattern of vertical crosshatch slots was repeated in twin insets in the front bumper. The standard engine remained the 350-cid (5.7-liter) V-8 with electronic fuel injection. It was now rated at 170 hp. The diesel version introduced at midyear was offered again. Sevilles destined for California received the three-way catalytic converter with closed-loop electronic controls, previously used only on other GM models. Options included the new digital trip computer and signal-seeking radios. Cadillac's catalog claimed that Seville had been chosen "one of the 10 most beautifully designed production cars of the last 50 years." The special edition Elegante came in two-tone Slate Firemist and Sable Black. The Elegante was identified by a Cadillac wreath-and-crest as well as script nameplate. Standard equipment included chrome-plated wire wheels with long-laced spokes. The seating areas and door panels had perforated leather inserts with suede-like vinyl trim. A leather-trimmed steering wheel was provided. The Elegante's price tag was $2,735.

SEVILLE — SERIES 6S

Model Number	Body/Style Number	Body Type & Seating	Factory Price	Shipping Weight	Production Total
S	69	4D Sedan-5P	15,646	4,180	53,487

DEVILLE—SERIES 6C—V-8

Appearance changes for the DeVille and Fleetwood models included restyled taillights and a revised front-end look, plus new interior trim. This year's grille had many more horizontal and vertical bars in its simple crosshatch pattern and was designed to accentuate the traditional Cadillac front end look. A "Cadillac" script returned on the driver's side of the wide upper grille bar. A thin molding above the grille extended outward, over the headlights, to wrap around each fender. Quad rectangular headlights were mounted outside the twin, vertically-positioned rectangular parking lights. The crosshatch grille pattern repeated itself in twin Cadillac-style rectangular openings in the bumper, on either side of the license plate. The front fenders held large cornering lights with clear and amber lenses. New brushed-chrome wheel covers showed the Cadillac crest on a black background. Also new were seat belt chimes, a standard AM/FM stereo radio with digital display, a dome light with dual spotlight-type map lamps and optional electrically-controlled outside mirrors. DeVille interiors were upholstered in Durand knit cloth available in six colors or in genuine leather. Standard fittings included power door locks and windows, a six-way power seat and automatic climate control. The standard 425-cid (7.0-liter) V-8 had new EGR riser tubes. A fuel-injected, 195-hp 7.0-liter V-8 was optional. The Olds-built 350-cid diesel V-8 became optional in midyear. Special-edition DeVilles included a Custom Phaeton Coupe and Custom Phaeton Sedan, both offering styling touches intended to remind observers of "classic" convertibles. Their features included brushed chrome moldings with flush-mounted opera lights and the Cadillac crest, reduced-size quarter windows, a sporty convertible-like roof, a "Phaeton" script on each rear quarter panel, wire wheel discs, accent striping, 45/55 Dual Comfort front seats with leather seating and a leather-trimmed steering wheel. Also on the option list was the DeVille d'Elegance, which featured soft Venetian velour upholstery, in a choice of four colors, on pillow-style 50/50 seats. It also had Tangier carpeting, special door-pull handles and a "DeVille d'Elegance" script on the glove box door and exterior. The Coupe d'Elegance had opera lights and sedans had three roof mounted assist straps. The Coupe DeVille also came with a Cabriolet roof treatment, which included a chrome crossover roof molding and an elk grain vinyl roof. A French seam surrounded the back window on this model and a Cadillac script-and-crest symbol identified the Cabriolet model.

DEVILLE—SERIES 6D

Model Number	Body/Style Number	Body Type & Seating	Factory Price	Shipping Weight	Production Total
D	47	2D Coupe-6P	11,139	4,143	121,890
D	69	4D Sedan-6P	11,493	4,212	93,211

FLEETWOOD BROUGHAM—SERIES 6C—V-8

Brougham sedans had the same new front-end look and restyled taillights as the less costly DeVille and the same engine choices. New brushed-chrome wheel covers displayed the Cadillac wreath-and-crest symbol on a dark red background. Dual comfort 45/55 front seats held three

people. Upholstery was new Slate Gray Dante knit cloth. Broughams came with four-wheel disc brakes, rather than the DeVille's disc/drum combination. The They also had a few distinctive styling touches to separate them from DeVilles. The pillars between the front and rear doors tapered inward toward the belt line. Wide rocker panel moldings continued behind the rear wheels, stretching to the back bumper. Cars with the Brougham d'Elegance package carried new pillow-style seats in Dante and Roma knits, plus plush Tangier carpeting. Three roof-mounted assist straps, a choice of standard or turbine-vaned wheel covers, accent striping and a "d'Elegance" nameplate directly behind the rear side windows completed the package. Leather seating areas were also offered.

FLEETWOOD BROUGHAM — SERIES 6B

Model Number	Body/Style Number	Body Type & Seating	Factory Price	Shipping Weight	Production Total
B	69	4D Sedan-6P	13,446	4,250	42,200

FLEETWOOD LIMOUSINE—SERIES 6D—V-8

About 2,000 Limousines, offered in standard or Formal form, found buyers each year. Both had the same new crosshatch grille as the Fleetwood Brougham, along with new simulated woodgrain interior accents, a lower profile and revised two-spoke steering wheel. Fleetwood remained the only American-built chassis for use in "professional" cars used for funeral vehicles and for ambulances. The basic Limousine seated eight, the Formal edition, seven. Both were powered by the 425-cid (7.0-liter) V-8, which had to haul over 4,800 pounds of car. All Limousines included two fold-down auxiliary seats. There was a dual accessory control panel for climate control and power windows, along with new optional rear seat controls for the radio.

FLEETWOOD LIMOUSINE — SERIES 6F

Model Number	Body/Style Number	Body Type & Seating	Factory Price	Shipping Weight	Production Total
F	23	4D Sedan-8P	20,987	4,782	Note 1
F	33	4D Fml Limousine-7P	21,735	4,866	Note 1

FLEETWOOD COMMERCIAL CHASSIS — SERIES 6Z

Model Number	Body/Style Number	Body Type & Seating	Factory Price	Shipping Weight	Production Total
Z	90	Commercial Chassis	NA	NA	864

Note 1: Total limousine production was 2,025.

ELDORADO—SERIES 6E—V-8

Two years after other full-size Cadillacs were down-sized, the personal-luxury coupe received similar treatment. The front-wheel-drive Eldorado shrunk drastically in its form. It lost some 1,150 pounds in weight and 20 inches in overall length. The wheelbase was over a foot shorter at 114 inches. The width was narrower by more than 8 inches. Despite the new proportions, head room and leg room managed to grow in both front and rear. As before, Eldorados included standard four-wheel disc brakes, while

independent rear suspension was a new feature. The new space-efficient design also featured electronic level control. The Eldorado's upright rectangular rear side windows also brought back the look of the recently-abandoned pillarless hardtop. Wide, squarish, closed in rear quarters also helped give the Eldorado a distinctive appearance. Steel-belted whitewall radial tires rode match-mounted wheels. A new flush-mounted windshield reduced wind noise. The standard dual outside mirrors were remote-controlled (right mirror convex). New permanently-sealed wheel bearings never needed lubrication. The Eldorado's boxy-looking crosshatch grille had rectangular openings and extended down into a portion of the bumper (not in two separate sections as on other full-size Cadillacs). Quad rectangular headlights sat above the horizontal park/signal lights. There were wide cornering lights on the forward portion of the front fenders. An Eldorado script was on the trailing segment of the front fenders, as well as on the deck lid. The optional Cabriolet roof was offered with or without padding. The base power plant was now the Seville's fuel-injected 350-cid (5.7-liter) gasoline V-8. For the first time, the Olds-built 5.7-liter diesel V-8 was an Eldorado option. The fancy Eldorado Biarritz had a number of exclusive accents, including a Cabriolet roof treatment with new brushed stainless steel front roof cap and padded vinyl at the rear.

1979 Cadillac, Eldorado coupe

Model Number	Body/Style Number	Body Type & Seating	Factory Price	Shipping Weight	Production Total
L	57	2D Coupe-4P	14,240	3,792	67,436

ENGINE

SEVILLE, ELDORADO BASE V-8

Overhead valve. Cast-iron block. Displacement: 350 cid (5.7 liters). Bore and Stroke: 4.057 x 3.385 inches. Compression ratio: 8.0:1. Net brake hp: 170 at 4400 rpm. Taxable hp: 52.6. Net torque: 270 at 2000 rpm. Five main bearings. Hydraulic valve lifters. Induction: Electronic fuel injection. VIN Code: B. Built by Cadillac.

DEVILLE, BROUGHAM, FLEETWOOD BASE V-8

Overhead valve. Cast-iron block. Displacement: 425 cid (7.0 liters). Bore and Stroke: 4.082 x 4.06 inches. Compression ratio: 8.2:1. Net brake hp: 180 at 4000 rpm. Taxable hp: 53.31. Net torque: 320 at 2000 rpm. Five main bearings. Hydraulic valve lifters. Carburetor: Four barrel. VIN Code: S. Built by Cadillac.

DEVILLE, BROUGHAM OPTIONAL V-8

Overhead valve. Cast-iron block. Displacement: 425 cid (7.0 liters). Bore and Stroke: 4.082 x 4.06 inches. Compression ratio: 8.2:1. Net brake hp: 195 at 3800 rpm. Taxable hp: 53.31. Net torque: 320 at 2400 rpm. Five main bearings. Hydraulic valve lifters. Induction: Electronic fuel-injection. VIN Code: T. Built by Cadillac.

DEVILLE, BROUGHAM, ELDORADO OPTIONAL DIESEL V-8

Overhead valve. Cast-iron block. Displacement: 350 cid (5.7 liters). Bore and Stroke: 4.057 x 3.385 inches. Compression ratio: 22.5:1. Net brake hp: 125 at 3600 rpm. Taxable hp: 52.6. Net torque: 225 at 1600 rpm. Five main bearings. Hydraulic valve lifters. Induction: Electronic fuel injection. VIN Code: N. Built by Oldsmobile.

CHASSIS

(Seville) Wheelbase: 114.3 inches. Overall length: 204.0 inches. Overall width: 71.8 inches. Overall height: 54.6 inches. Front tread: 61.3 inches. Rear tread: 59.0 inches. Tires: GR78 x 15-B steel-belted radial with wide white sidewall.

(Eldorado) Wheelbase: 113.9 inches. Overall length: 204.0 inches. Overall width: 71.4 inches. Overall height: 54.2 inches. Front tread: 59.3 inches. Rear tread: 60.5 inches. Tires: P20575R15 steel-belted radial with wide white sidewall.

(DeVille) Wheelbase: 121.5 inches. Overall length: 221.2 inches. Overall width: 76.48 inches. Overall height: 54.4 inches. Front tread: 61.7 inches. Rear tread: 60.7 inches. Tires: (DeVille) GR78 x 15-B steel-belted radial with wide white sidewall.

(Fleetwood Brougham) Wheelbase: 121.5 inches. Overall length: 221.2 inches. Overall width: 76.48 inches. Overall height: 56.7 inches. Front tread: 61.7 inches. Rear tread: 60.7 inches. Tires: (DeVille) GR78 x 15-B steel-belted radial with wide white sidewall; (Brougham) HR78 x 15-B steel-belted radial with wide white sidewall.

(Fleetwood 75) Wheelbase: 144.5 inches. Overall length: 244.2 inches. Overall width: 76.48 inches. Overall height: 56.9 inches. Front tread: 61.7 inches. Rear tread: 60.7 inches. Tires: HR78 x 15-D steel-belted radial with wide white sidewall.

TECHNICAL

Transmission: Three-speed Turbo-Hydra-Matic transmission standard on all models, column shift. Eldorado/Seville gear ratios: (1st) 2.74:1, (2nd) 1.57:1, (3rd) 1:1, (Reverse) 2.07:1. Other models: (1st) 2.48:1, (2nd) 1.48:1, (3rd) 1:1, (Reverse) 2.07:1. Standard axle ratio: (Seville) 2.24:1, (Eldorado) 2.19:1, (DeVille/Brougham) 2.28:1, (Limousine) 3.08:1. Steering: recirculating ball. Front suspension: (Eldorado) independent transverse torsion bars, link stabilizer bar, (others) independent with ball joints and coil springs, stabilizer bar. Rear suspension: (Eldorado) independent trailing arm, (Seville) Hotchkiss 56 inches. leaf springs, five leaves, link stabilizer, (others) four link coil springs, link stabilizer. Electronic level control (except DeVille). Brakes: front disc, rear drum except Brougham/Seville/Eldorado, four-wheel disc. HEI electronic ignition. Fuel tank: (Seville/Eldorado) 19.6 gallons, (others) 25 gallons.

OPTIONS

Astroroof (with full vinyl roof): DeVille/Fleetwood/Seville($998). Astroroof (painted): DeVille/Seville/Eldorado ($1163). Sunroof (full vinyl roof): DeVille/

1979 Cadillac, Seville sedan

Fleetwood/Seville($798). Sunroof (painted roof): DeVille/Seville/Eldorado ($953). Cruise control ($137). Controlled-cycle wipers: DeVille/Limousine ($38). Rear defogger, grid-type ($101). Six-way Dual Comfort power passenger seat adjuster ($125-$160). Power driver's seat recliner ($122). Power passenger seat recliner with six-way adjuster ($221-$280). Power passenger seat back recliner, bench seat: DeVille ($122). Tilt/telescope steering wheel ($130). Automatic door locks ($121). Illuminated entry system: DeVille/Limousine ($62). Fuel monitor ($31). Trip computer: Seville ($920). Theft deterrent system ($137). Trunk lid release and power pull-down: DeVille/Limousine ($85). Opera lights: DeVille/Seville($66). Twilight Sentinel: DeVille/Limousine ($56). Guidematic headlight control ($91). Trumpet horn ($22). Remote-control right mirror: DeVille ($40). Electric remote left mirror with thermometer ($90). Lighted thermometer on left mirror ($28). Lighted vanity mirror, passenger ($52). Electronic tuning seek/scan AM/FM stereo radio with 8-track tape player ($195), with 8-track and CB ($480), with cassette ($225), with CB ($380). Electronic tuning seek/scan AM/FM stereo radio with 8-track player, rear control: Limousine ($398). Two-tone paint, partial Firemist ($361). Firemist paint ($171). Padded vinyl roof: DeVille ($225). Front bumper reinforcement ($9). Chrome accent molding: DeVille ($90-$105). Accent stripes: DeVille/Fleetwood ($56). Door edge guards ($13-$20). License frame: each ($10). Dual comfort front seats: DeVille ($208). Leather seating area ($330-$350). Carpeted rubber front floor mats ($33-$36), rear ($16). Trunk mat ($13). Turbine-vaned wheel covers ($59), not available on Eldorado. Aluminum wheels ($350), Not available on Eldorado. Locking wire wheels: DeVille/Seville/Fleetwood ($570-$628). Locking wire wheel covers ($189-$292). 425-cid V-8 Fl engine: DeVille/Fleetwood ($783). 5.7-liter diesel V-8 engine: Seville/

Eldorado ($287), DeVille/Brougham, later in model-year ($849). Heavy-duty cooling system ($49). 80-amp alternator ($54). Engine block heater ($21). California emission equipment ($83-$150). California fuel economy equipment: DeVille/Fleetwood ($65). Limited slip differential ($70), not available on Eldorado. High altitude package. ($35). Electronic level control: DeVille ($160). Trailering package ($49-$103). Brougham d'Elegance: cloth ($987), leather ($1,344). DeVille Cabriolet ($384). DeVille Cabriolet with Astroroof ($1,522). DeVille Cabriolet with sunroof ($1,312). DeVille d'Elegance ($725). DeVille Custom Phaeton ($2,029). Eldorado Cabriolet ($350). Eldorado Cabriolet with Astroroof ($1,488). Eldorado Cabriolet with sunroof ($1,278). Eldorado Biarritz: leather seating ($2,600), cloth ($2,250). Eldorado Biarritz with Astroroof: leather seating ($3,738), cloth ($3,388). Seville Elegante ($2,735). Seville Elegante with Astroroof ($3,873). Seville Elegante with sunroof ($3,663).

HISTORICAL

The 1979 Cadillacs were introduced on September 28, 1978. Model-year production was 381,113 for a 4.1 percent share and a new record. Calendar-year production was 345,794. Calendar-year sales by U.S. dealers was 314,034, which amounted to a 3.8 percent market share. Model-year sales by U.S. dealers was 328,815. DeVilles this year were built at South Gate, California. The DeVille Phaeton's simulated convertible top didn't satisfy real ragtop fans who could afford one of the re-manufactured versions. One such conversion by Hess & Eisenhardt, called "Le Cabriolet," was marketed through Cadillac dealers. Cadillac had high expectations for diesel power, but that phenomenon was destined to evaporate in the next half-dozen years.

1979 Cadillac, Hess and Eisenhardt-bodied "Le Cabriolet" convertible

1980

OVERVIEW

"Through the years," boasted the 1980 full-line catalog, "Cadillac has earned for itself an exclusive place...a solitary niche...in the pantheon of the world's truly fine automobiles." Readers were even reminded how Cadillac had twice won the DeWar trophy in the early years of the 20th century, first for its use of interchangeable parts and, later, for pioneering the electric self-starter. This year brought a restyled Brougham and DeVille, both with a more formal roof line that gave more space in back. They shared a new grille that was supposed to boost aerodynamic efficiency, too. Suspension refinements included low-friction ball joints and larger bushings, plus new low-rolling-resistance tires. New options included a three-channel garage door opener and heated outside rearview mirrors. On the engine roster, the 368-cid (6.0-liter) V-8 with a four-barrel carburetor was standard on Fleetwood Brougham, DeVille and Limousine models. A digital fuel-injected (DFI) V-8 with computerized self-diagnostic features was standard on the Eldorado and a no-cost option for the Seville. The Seville's standard 5.7-liter diesel V-8, manufactured by Oldsmobile, was also available under the hood of Eldorado, DeVille and Fleetwood Brougham models. Later, a 4.1-liter Buick V-6

was added—the first such offering ever on a Cadillac, and the first engine other than a V-8 to power a Cadillac in six decades.

I.D. DATA

The 13-symbol serial number was located on top of the instrument panel, where it was visible through the windshield. The first symbol 6=Cadillac Motor Division. The second symbol was a letter identifying the series as follows: B=Fleetwood Brougham, D=DeVille, F=Fleetwood Limousine, L=Eldorado, S=Seville and Z=Commercial Chassis. The third and fourth symbols indicated body style: 23=four-door Limousine with auxiliary seat, 33=four-door Limousine with center divider, 47=two-door Hardtop Coupe, 57=two-door Coupe, 69=four-door pillared Sedan and 90=Commercial chassis. The fifth symbol was a letter identifying the engine: See engine listings below. The sixth symbol was a letter identifying model-year: A=1980. The seventh symbol was a letter designating the manufacturing point as follows: A=Lakewood, Ga., B=Baltimore, Md., D=Doraville, Ga., J=Janesville, Wis., K=Leeds, Mo., L=Van Nuys, Calif., N= Norwood, Ohio, R=Arlington, Tex., S=St. Louis, Mo., T=Tarrytown, N.Y., W=Willow Run, Mich., Y=Wilmington, Del., Z= Fremont, Calif., 1=Oshawa, Ontario, Canada and 6=Oklahoma City, Okla. Note:

Above: **1980 Cadillac, Fleetwood Eldorado, coupe**
Phil Hall

Cadillacs were not built at all General Motors assembly plants. The next group of numbers was the sequential production code starting with 100001. The Fisher Body tag on the cowl, under the hood includes additional information. Paint colors for 1980 Cadillacs are: Cotillion White, Platinum, Sable Black, Steel Blue, Superior Blue, Twilight Blue, Canyon Rock, Princess Green, Blackwatch Green, Colonial Yellow, Flax, Sandstone, Columbian Brown, Bordeaux Red, Saxony Red, and Norfolk Gray. At extra cost, buyers could have any of five Firemist colors: Azure Blue, Desert Sand, Victoria Plum, Sheffield Gray and Western Saddle.

SEVILLE—SERIES 6S—V-8

Billed in the full-line catalog as "quite possibly the most distinctive car in the world today…and the most advanced," the all new Seville was dramatic. A total redesign gave buyers more interior space and trunk volume, along with the radical body shape. The humped deck lid began almost horizontal, but hit a distinctive horizontal crease before tapering down to wide taillights. Small lenses were inset into the new one-piece, high-strength back bumper: two at the rear and two at the sides. On the deck lid were Cadillac's wreath-and-crest, plus the Seville script. Both emblems were repeated on the back roof pillar. The Seville script was also on front fenders, just below the thin bodyside molding. Chrome rocker moldings were tall and strong. Designed by Wayne Cady, the bustleback body and long hood suggested more than a nodding acquaintance with the impressive old razor-edge styling used on the Hooper and Vanden Plas Rolls-Royce in the 1950s. Not everyone loved Seville's bustleback shape, with sloping rear end and "boot" trunk, but it drew considerable attention. Wheelbase was 114 inches, length almost 205 inches, overall dimensions not much different than the 1979 edition. Running gear and front-drive chassis were shared with the other luxury E-body coupes: Eldorado, Buick Riviera and Oldsmobile Toronado. But Seville hardly resembled its mechanical mates. Up front, the squared off look was similar to earlier Sevilles. The front end was lower and the car weighed 300 pounds less than before. The new, yet traditional grille consisted of narrow vertical bars and a wide horizontal header bar with "Cadillac" script at the side, plus a stand up wreath-and-crest at the hood front. The windshield sat at a sharp angle. Seville was also described as an "electronic wonder." The new version was viewed as a "test" for other GM vehicles. Among other details, Seville was the first to offer a diesel as "standard" power plant (except in California). The optional engine was a 6.0-liter gasoline V-8 with single-point fuel injection (heavy on digital electronics), which gave better cold start performance and lower emissions. Front wheel drive kept the floor flat, adding more room. Sevilles had a new four-wheel independent suspension and disc brakes all around.

All models had electronic level control, new electronic climate control, electrically-controlled outside mirrors (heated, with lighted thermometer), and cruise control. The full-length beltline molding swept downward aft of the back door, into the bustle-shaped back end and the upper color tapered to a point at the base of the humped deck lid. Chrome-plated "Elegante" script was on the sail panels. The new simulated teak woodgrain instrument panel, with driver only controls on the left was said to have the look of Butterfly Walnut. Ads referred to "The Beauty of Being First" and dubbed Seville the car "that looks like no other car." William L. Mitchell, who retired as GM's design vice-president in 1977, was responsible for Seville.

SEVILLE (DIESEL V-8)—SERIES S

Model Number	Body/Style Number	Body Type & Seating	Factory Price	Shipping Weight	Production Total
S	69	4D Sedan-5P	19,662	3,911	39,344

DEVILLE—SERIES 6D—V-8

Aerodynamic alterations gave DeVilles a more streamlined profile this year. The new, traditional-style "isolated" grille was made up of narrow vertical bars, peaked forward at the center. A Cadillac script was on the side of the heavy upper header. New flush-mount quad rectangular headlights stood above new amber-lensed horizontal parking/signal

CIMARRON '84
THIS ONE'S GOT THE TOUCH.

The Cadillac touch. It's Electronic Fuel Injection, matched by a tenacious Touring Suspension that comes to grips with the road. It's leather-faced front bucket seats with lumbar support behind a leather-trimmed steering wheel that lets you know you're in control. It's new grille and taillight styling. Laser-accurate quality fits. It's Cimarron '84, with something no other car in its class has. The Cadillac touch.

BEST OF ALL…IT'S A CADILLAC.
Let's Get It Together…Buckle Up.

The 1980s brought a small edition of Cadillac, the 1984 Cimarron.

lights. Matching cornering lights consisted of a large rectangular lens over a small horizontal one, one followed the line of the headlights, the other wrapped around in line with the signal lights. Wheel openings showed a squared-off, formal look. The rear roof pillar held a Cadillac "V" and crest, plus script nameplate. New wheel covers displayed Cadillac's crest on a dark red background. DeVilles came in 21 body colors. Both DeVille and Brougham had a stiffer roof profile this year, with a sharpened crease line running the full length of the side. Deck lids also had a higher profile, with beveled rear surface. The new roofline added two inches of legroom in the back seat. Base engine was the 368-cid (6.0-liter) carbureted V-8, with 5.7-liter diesel available. Coupe DeVille was also offered with a dramatic Cabriolet roof that featured a chrome crossover roof molding. That came in 15 colors of elk grain vinyl, with French seam surrounding the back window. DeVilles d'Elegance had textured Venetian velour upholstery in any of four colors, plus Tampico carpeting, special door pull handles and "DeVille d'Elegance" script on the glove compartment. The body held accent stripes and another nameplate. Opera lights were standard on the coupe.

DEVILLE Series 6D-V-8

Model Number	Body/Style Number	Body Type& Seating	Factory Price	Shipping Weight	Production Total
D	47	2D Coupe-6P	12,401	4,048	55,490
D	69	4D Sedan-6P	12,770	4,084	49,188

FLEETWOOD BROUGHAM—SERIES 6B—V-8
Noticeable immediately on the "King of Cadillacs" was an exclusive new limousine-style, closed-in back window. Center pillars held new electroluminiscent opera lights, just above the beltline. New wheel covers with silver-colored vaned inserts contained the Cadillac wreath-and-crest on a dark red background. New body trim included a distinctive wide rocker molding that continued onto the rear quarter panels. The familiar tall chrome rear fender caps held integral marker lights, around the corner from the vertical taillights. The hood held a stand-up wreath-and-crest ornament. Brougham also had chrome belt moldings. Standard equipment included a Twilight Sentinel that turned headlights on/off, illuminated entry system, six-way power Dual Comfort front seats, adjustable rear reading lights, large door pull handles and tilt/telescope steering wheel. Brougham interiors had new biscuit sculptured seats with bolsters, with an embroidered Cadillac wreath on front and rear arm rests. Upholstery was Heather knit with Raphael inserts, in Slate Gray, Dark Blue, Dark Green, Saddle, Light Beige or Dark Claret. Leather seating was optional in ten shades. At midyear, a Brougham coupe joined the sedan. Its cabriolet-style roof contained a coach window, plus a chrome molding across the top. Opera lights shined from each sail panel. Brougham d'Elegance emphasized the privacy window

treatment, with the rear quarter panel wrapping around to the small Limousine-like back window. Inside and on the sail panel was a d'Elegance script nameplate. Standard pillow-style 50/50 Dual Comfort seats combined Heather and Raphael knits. Leather was also available at a higher cost.

FLEETWOOD BROUGHAM

Model Number	Body/Style Number	Body Type & Seating	Factory Price	Shipping Weight	Production Total
B	47	2D Coupe-6P	14,971	4,025	2,300
B	69	4D Sedan-6P	14,927	4,092	29,659

FLEETWOOD LIMOUSINE/COMMERCIAL CHASSIS—SERIES 6F/6Z—V-8
Once again, the big Fleetwoods came in Limousine and Formal Limousine form, with dual accessory control panels. Interiors of the basic Limousine were upholstered in dark blue Heather cloth. Formal Limousines carried black leather upholstery up front and either black or slate gray in back. All had two fold-down auxiliary seats. Opera lights were now on the rear roof panels, behind the quarter windows. Deeply concave wheel covers had red inserts and Cadillac's wreath-and-crest.

FLEETWOOD LIMOUSINE

Model Number	Body/Style Number	Body Type & Seating	Factory Price	Shipping Weight	Production Total
F	23	4D Sedan-8P	22,586	4,629	Note 1
F	33	4D Fml Limousine-7P	23,388	4,718	Note 1

FLEETWOOD COMMERCIAL CHASSIS

Model Number	Body/Style Number	Body Type & Seating	Factory Price	Shipping Weight	Production Total
Z	90	Commercial Chassis	NA	NA	750

Note 1: Total limousine production, 1,612.

ELDORADO—SERIES 6L—V-8
Downsized the year before, Eldorado entered 1980 with few significant changes beyond a bolder crosshatch grille pattern, dominated by vertical bars. Its upper horizontal bar, with Cadillac script peaked forward and upward. Quad rectangular headlights sat above amber-lensed parking/signal lights, with wide horizontal cornering lights on the fenders. An Eldorado script was behind the front wheel openings, just above the bodyside molding. Wide rocker panel moldings stretched all the way, front to rear. Atop the hood was a Cadillac wreath-and-crest. New two-tone paint schemes were offered. Multi-slot

1980 Cadillac, Fleetwood Brougham

style wheel covers were standard. So was Heather knit-cloth pillow-type front upholstery, offered in six colors for the Dual Comfort 50/45 front seats (for two people). Customers could also select from 10 leather possibilities. The instrument panel featured simulated teak woodgrain. Eldorado enjoyed an improved EPA fuel mileage rating as a result of the 6.0-liter V-8 with electronic fuel injection. A new MPG Sentinel was available with the DFI engine, which also offered new on-board computer diagnostics. New Electronic Climate Control offered digital accuracy. An optional Cabriolet roof of textured elk grain vinyl came in 15 colors, including matching Firemist shades. The optional theft-deterrent system now disabled the starter motor. Eldorado Biarritz rode cast aluminum wheels and carried a number of unique styling accents, including an exclusive brushed stainless steel front roof section. The wide chrome molding crossing over that roof continued all the way to the front fenders. Biarritz script and opera lights enhanced the rear roof pillars and the model also featured accent stripes. Inside, the tufted pillow-style interior came in seven leather choices or slate gray Heather knit fabric. The steering wheel was leather-trimmed. Biarritz carried a price tag of $18,003, compared to $15,509 for a base Eldorado.

ELDORADO

Model Number	Body/Style Number	Body Type & Seating	Factory Price	Shipping Weight	Production Total
L	57	2D Coupe-4P	15,509	3,806	52,683

ENGINE

ALL CADILLAC MODELS EXCEPT LIMOUSINES OPTIONAL V-6 (LATE 1980)

Overhead valve. Cast-iron block. Displacement: 252 cid (4.1 liters). Bore and Stroke: 3.97 x 3.40 inches. Compression ratio: 8.0:1. Net brake hp: 125 at 3800 rpm. Taxable hp: 37.7. Net torque: 210 lbs.-ft. at 2000 rpm. Four main bearings. Hydraulic valve lifters. Induction: Electronic fuel injection. VIN Code: 4. Built by Buick.

SEVILLE BASE DIESEL V-8; DEVILLE, BROUGHAM, ELDORADO OPTIONAL DIESEL V-8

Overhead valve. Cast-iron block . Displacement: 350 cid (5.7 liters). Bore and Stroke: 4.057 x 3.385 inches. Compression ratio: 22.5:1. Net brake hp: 105 at 3200 rpm. Taxable hp: 52.6. Net torque: 205 lbs.-ft. at 1600 rpm. Five main bearings. Hydraulic valve lifters. Induction: Electronic fuel injection. VIN Code: N. Built by Oldsmobile.

DEVILLE, BROUGHAM, FLEETWOOD BASE V-8

Overhead valve. Cast-iron block . Displacement: 368 cid (6.0 liters). Bore and Stroke: 3.80 x 4.06 inches. Compression ratio: 8.2:1. Net brake hp: 150 at 3800 rpm.

Taxable hp: 46.20. Net torque: 265 lbs.-ft. at 1600 rpm. Five main bearings. Hydraulic valve lifters. Carburetion: Four-barrel. VIN Code: 6. Built by Cadillac.

ELDORADO BASE V-8; SEVILLE OPTIONAL V-8

Overhead valve. Cast-iron block. Displacement: 368 cid (6.0 liters). Bore and Stroke: 3.80 x 4.06 inches. Compression ratio: 8.2:1. Net brake hp: 145 at 3600 rpm. Taxable hp: 46.20. Net torque: 270 lbs.-ft. at 2000 rpm. Five main bearings. Hydraulic valve lifters. Induction: Digital fuel-injection. VIN Code: 9. Built by Cadillac.

ELDORADO BASE V-8 (CALIFORNIA)

Overhead valve. Cast-iron block. Displacement: 350 cid (5.7 liters). Bore and Stroke: 4.057 x 3.385 inches. Compression ratio: 8.0:1. Net brake hp: 160 at 4400 rpm. Taxable hp: 52.6. Net torque: 265 lbs.-ft. at 1600 rpm. Five main bearings. Hydraulic valve lifters. Induction: Electronic fuel injection. VIN Code: 8. Built by Cadillac.

CHASSIS

(Seville) Wheelbase: 114.0 inches. Overall length: 204.8 inches. Overall width: 71.4 inches. Overall height: 54.3 inches. Front tread: 61.3 inches. Rear tread: 60.6 inches. Tires: P20575R15 steel-belted radial with wide white sidewall.

(Eldorado) Wheelbase: 113.9 inches. Overall length: 204.5 inches. Overall width: 71.5 inches. Overall height: 54.2 inches. Front tread: 59.3 inches. Rear tread: 60.6 inches. Tires: P20575R15 steel-belted radial with wide white sidewall.

(DeVille) Wheelbase: 121.4 inches. Overall length: 221.0 inches. Overall width: 76.48 inches. Overall height: 55.6 inches. Front tread: 61.7 inches. Rear tread: 60.7 inches. Tires: P21575R15 steel-belted radial with wide white sidewall.

(Brougham) Wheelbase: 121.4 inches. Overall length: 221.0 inches. Overall width: 76.48 inches. Overall height: 56.7 inches. Front tread: 61.7 inches. Rear tread: 60.7 inches. Tires: P21575R15 steel-belted radial with wide white sidewall.

(Fleetwood 75) Wheelbase: 144.5 inches. Overall length: 244.1 inches. Overall width: 76.48 inches. Overall height: 56.9 inches. Front tread: 61.7 inches. Rear tread: 60.7 inches. Tires: P21575R15 steel-belted radial with wide white sidewall.

TECHNICAL

Transmission: Turbo-Hydra-Matic transmission standard on all models: column shift. Gear ratios for DeVille/

Brougham with V8-368: (1st) 2.48:1, (2nd) 1.48:1, (3rd) 1:1, (Reverse) 2.07:1. Other models: (1st) 2.74:1, (2nd) 1.57:1, (3rd) 1:1, (Reverse) 2.07:1. Standard final drive ratio: (Seville) 2.41:1, (DeVille/Brougham) 2.28:1, (Limousine) 3.08:1, (Eldorado) 2.19:1. Hypoid drive axle. Steering: recirculating ball, power assisted. Front suspension: (Seville/Eldorado) independent torsion bars, link-type stabilizer bar, (others) coil springs and link-type stabilizer bar. Rear suspension: (Seville/Eldorado) independent trailing arm, coil springs, electronic level control, (others) four-link drive coil springs, electronic level control available (except Limousine). Brakes: front disc, rear drum except Seville/Eldorado four-wheel disc. Fuel tank: (Seville) 23 gallons, (others) 20.6 gallons, except Limousines, 25 gallons (available on DeVille/Brougham). Unleaded fuel only.

OPTIONS

Astroroof ($1,058), Not available on Limousine. Cruise control ($147). Controlled-cycle wipers: DeVille/Limousine ($43). Rear defogger, grid-type ($170). Six-way Dual Comfort power passenger seat adjuster: DeVille ($395), Eldorado ($171). Power driver's seat recliner ($130). Power passenger seat back recliner: Brougham ($71). Notchback passenger seat back recliner: DeVille ($130). Tilt/telescope steering wheel ($142). Automatic door locks ($129). Illuminated entry system: DeVille/Limousine ($67). Garage door opener ($125). Theft deterrent system ($153). Trunk lid release and power pull-down: DeVille ($92). Opera lights: DeVille ($71). Twilight Sentinel: DeVille/Limousine ($62). Guidematic headlight control ($72). Front light monitor ($35). Trumpet horn ($26). Electric remote-control left mirror with thermometer ($97). Lighted thermometer on left mirror ($30). Lighted vanity mirrors, pair ($112). Electronic-tuning seek/scan AM/FM stereo radio with 8-track tape player ($195), with 8-track and CB ($480), with cassette ($225): with CB ($380), with cassette and CB ($510). Electronic-tuning seek/scan AM/FM stereo radio with 8-track player rear control: Limousine ($398). Two-tone paint: DeVille/Brougham ($293). Two-tone paint, partial Firemist: DeVille/Brougham ($394). Firemist paint ($201). Padded vinyl roof: DeVille ($240). Accent stripes: DeVille ($61). Door edge guards ($16-$24). License frame: each ($11). Leather seating area ($435-$595). Carpeted rubber front floor mats ($35-$38), rear ($19). Trunk mat ($15). Turbine-vaned wheel covers: DeVille ($63). Cast aluminum wheels: Eldorado ($376), no charge on diesel Seville. Locking wire wheels: DeVille/Brougham ($755). Locking wire wheel covers ($262-$320), no charge on Seville. Puncture sealing tires ($105). 6.0-liter Fl V-8 engine: Seville ($266 credit). 5.7-liter diesel V-8 engine: Eldorado ($266), DeVille/Fleetwood ($924). Heavy-duty cooling system ($59).

100-amp alternator ($41-$59). Engine block heater ($22). California emission equipment ($83-$250). Limited-slip differential ($86) except Seville/Eldorado. Sport handling package: Seville/Eldorado ($95). Heavy-duty suspension: DeVille/Brougham ($270). Electronic level control: DeVille/Brougham ($169). Trailering package ($100-$118). Brougham d'Elegance: cloth ($1,062), leather ($1,525). Coupe DeVille Cabriolet ($350). DeVille d'Elegance ($1,005). Eldorado Cabriolet ($363). Eldorado Biarritz: leather seating ($2,937), cloth ($2,494). Seville Elegante ($,2934).

HISTORICAL

Introduced on October 11, 1979. Model-year production was 231,028 for a 3.4 percent share of the industry total. Calendar-year production was 203,992. Calendar-year sales by U.S. dealers was 213,002 for a 3.2 percent market share. Model-year sales by U.S. dealers was 238,999. This was not a top-notch year for Cadillac, as sales plummeted over 27 percent. Production fell even further for the model-year, down 39.4 percent. The reason evidently was a interest in compact, fuel-efficient models. Cadillac had reduced the size of the standard gasoline engine from its prior 425-cid displacement down to a mere 368-cid (6.0-liters). Buick's V-6 became optional late in the year. The division also sped production of the subcompact J-bodied Cimarron, originally intended for introduction in 1985. Cadillac had problems meeting the emissions control standards of the California Air Resources Board, long stricter than the rest of the country. The "standard" diesel on the new Seville wasn't offered in California. A new assembly plant for production of lightweight V-6 engines was announced at Livonia, Michigan. No Cadillacs were built at the Linden, New Jersey. Convertible conversions continued to be turned out by Hess & Eisenhardt in Cincinnati, which claimed to be the largest producer of Cadillac ragtops. The company's 1980 brochure displayed a Coupe DeVille conversion.

1980 Cadillac, Coupe De Ville

1981

OVERVIEW

The biggest news for 1981 was a 1982 model: the new subcompact Cimarron, introduced in the spring (more on that in the 1982 listing). Second biggest was the new variable-displacement gasoline engine, developed by the Eaton Corporation and standard in all models but Seville. Depending on driving conditions, the innovative V-8-6-4 engine ran on four, six, or eight cylinders, switching back and forth as needed. The object, of course, was to conserve fuel in the wake of rising gasoline prices. A microprocessor determined which cylinders weren't necessary at the moment. Then it signaled a solenoid-actuated blocker plate, which shifted to permit the rocker arm to pivot at a different point than usual. Therefore, selected intake and exhaust valves would remain closed rather than operate normally. Valve lifters and push rods traveled up-and-down in the normal manner, but unneeded valve pairs stood idle. When running on four, displacement grew back to eight as soon as the driver stepped on the gas to pass, demanding maximum power—an assurance to those who might wonder if a four-cylinder Cadillac power plant was good enough. The system had been tested (and "proven") in over a half-million miles of driving. Cadillac

Above: **1981 Cadillac, Fleetwood Brougham, sedan**

Phil Hall

claimed that the "perceived sensation" during displacement changes was "slight," because no shifting was involved. Expanded self-diagnostics now displayed 45 separate function codes for mechanics to investigate. Imaginative but complex, the V-8-6-4 brought more trouble than ease to many owners and didn't last long in the overall lineup. On another level, Buick's 252-cid (4.1-liter) V-6 engine, introduced late in the 1980 model-year, continued for a full season as an economy option. Cadillacs now carried an on-board digital computer capable of making 300,000 decisions per second. To improve emissions, the new Computer Command Control module used seven sensors to monitor exhaust, engine speed, manifold air pressure and coolant temperature, then adjusted the air/fuel mixture. "Answering Today's Needs with Tomorrow's Technology" was the logical theme of the full-line catalog. Though technically impressive, 1981 was not a year of significant change beyond some new grilles and other cosmetic alterations.

I.D. DATA

A new 17-symbol serial number was located on top of the instrument panel, where it was visible through the windshield. The first symbol 1=U.S.-built vehicle. The second symbol 2=General Motors. The third symbol 6=Cadillac Motor Division. The fourth symbol indicated type of

restraint system: A=manual belts, B=automatic belts, C=airbag. The fifth symbol identified the series as follows: B=Fleetwood Brougham, D=DeVille, F=Fleetwood Limousine, L=Eldorado and S=SeVille. The sixth and seventh symbols indicated body style: 23=four-door Limousine with auxiliary seat, 33=four-door Limousine with center divider, 47=two-door Hardtop Coupe, 57=two-door Coupe and 69=four-door pillared Sedan. The eighth symbol indicated the engine (See engine listings below). The ninth symbol was a check digit. The 10th symbol was a letter indicating model year: B=1981. The 11th symbol indicated the manufacturing plant as follows: A=Lakewood, Ga., B=Baltimore, Md., D=Doraville, Ga., J=Janesville, Wis., K=Leeds, Mo., L=Van Nuys, Calif., N=Norwood, Ohio, R=Arlington, Tex., S=St. Louis, Mo., T=Tarrytown, N.Y., W=Willow Run, Mich., Y=Wilmington, Del., Z=Fremont, Calif., 1=Oshawa, Ontario, Canada and 6=Oklahoma City, Okla. Note: Cadillacs were not built at all General Motors assembly plants. The next group of numbers was the sequential production code starting with 100001. The Fisher Body tag on the cowl, under the hood includes additional information. Cadillac colors for 1981 were: 11=Cotillion White, 16=Sterling Silver Poly, 19=Sable Black, 21=Steel Blue Poly, 22=Superior Blue Poly, 29=Twilight Blue Poly, 31=Neptune Aqua Poly, 32=Pepper Green Poly, 35=Waxberry Yellow, 36=Sierra Gold Poly, 44=Seaspray Green, 55=Burnished Oak Poly, 61=Sandstone, 69=Briarwood Brown Poly, 76=Bordeaux Red Poly, 78=Saxony Red, 89=Norfolk Gray, 90=Azure Blue Firemist Poly, 91=Desert Sand Firemist Poly, 92=Victoria Plum Firemist Poly, 94=Sheffied Gray Firemist Poly, 96=Jadestone Firemist Poly, 97=Doeskin Firemist Poly, 99=Mulberry Gray Firemist Poly. Cadillac vinyl roof colors were: 11T=White, 19T=Black, 16T=Silver Poly, 21T=Light Blue Poly, 29T=Dark Blue Poly, 35T=Pastel Waxberry, 36T=Light Waxberry Poly, 44T=Pastel Jadestone, 55T=Dark Doeskin Poly, 69T=Dark Sandstone Poly, 76T=Dark Claret Poly, 78T=Carmine, 90T=Light Blue Poly, 91T=Tan Poly, 92T=Claret Poly, 94T=Medium Silver Gray Poly, 96T=Medium Jadestone Poly, 97T=Doeskin Poly.

SEVILLE — SERIES 6S — V-8

Though basically unchanged for 1980, Seville got a few new touches, including restyled (optional) wire wheel covers. Base engine was the Olds-built diesel V-8, now with roller cam followers on the valve lifters. That made Seville the only car around with a standard V-8 diesel. Also new: an improved water detection/removal system for the fuel tank. New component labeling procedures were supposed to prevent theft. New options: Several radio and tape systems of advanced design, a memory system for the power driver's seat and the modulated-

displacement V-8-6-4 engine that was standard in other Cadillacs. A Buick-built 252-cid V-6 with four-barrel carburetor was also available this year. Both gasoline engines brought buyers a credit of several hundred dollars. Hoods displayed a burnished wreath-and-crest ornament over the vertical-style grille with its large header bar and engine compartments had a new light. Cast aluminum wheels were standard. One-piece bumpers had built-in guards. A Touring Suspension became optional during the 1981 model-year. Seville Elegantes had been easy to spot with their bold "French Curve" molding separating two-tone body colors. This year, base Sevilles gained the full-length accent moldings that had formerly been an Elegante exclusive. The pricey Elegante package included tucked seating areas and steering wheel in Sierra Grain leather, 40/40 Dual Comfort seats, leather-topped console, Tampico carpeting, "Elegante" script on glove box and body, cross-laced wire wheel covers, and chrome side moldings.

SEVILLE — SERIES 6S - V-6

Model Number	Body/Style Number	Body Type & Seating	Factory Price	Shipping Weight	Production Total
6S	69	4D Sedan-5P	20,598	3,688	Note 1

SEVILLE — SERIES 6S - DIESEL V-8

Model Number	Body/Style Number	Body Type & Seating	Factory Price	Shipping Weight	Production Total
6S	69	4D Sedan-5P	21,088	4,028	Note 1

Note 1: Seville production was 28,636.

DEVILLE — SERIES 6C — V-8

Standard engine for DeVille and Fleetwood Brougham was the "modulated displacement" 368-cid (6.0-liter) V-8-6-4, with digital fuel injection. Optional was a 252-cid (4.1-liter) V-6, provided by Buick. That V-6 had Computer Command Control and a knock sensor to adjust spark advance, as well as diagnostics. The Olds diesel V-8 was also offered. Externally, DeVilles and Fleetwoods carried a new forward-peaked grille with heavy wide upper header bar (Cadillac script again at the side) over an undivided tight crosshatch pattern. Quad headlights sat above quad amber parking/signal lights, with wraparound clear/amber cornering lights. Standard wheel covers displayed a Cadillac crest on dark red background. New standard Electronic Climate Control offered digital accuracy. Standard equipment also included a six-way power passenger seat, power windows and low-fuel warning.

DEVILLE — SERIES D - V-6

Model Number	Body/Style Number	Body Type & Seating	Factory Price	Shipping Weight	Production Total
6D	47	2D Coupe-6P	13,285	3,801	Note 2
6D	69	4D Sedan-6P	13,682	3,852	Note 2
DEVILLE—SERIES D-V-8-6-4					
6D	47	2D Coupe-6P	13,450	4,016	Note 2
6D	69	4D Sedan-6P	13,847	4,067	Note 2

Note 2: The production totals for DeVilles and Fleetwood Broughams were combined. See notes 3 and 4 below.

FLEETWOOD BROUGHAM—SERIES 6C—V-8

Billed again as the "Cadillac of Cadillacs," the Brougham came in Coupe and Sedan form with a grille and front-end look that matched that of the DeVille. The Coupe had an elk grain vinyl Cabriolet roof treatment with flush-looking, small size rear quarter windows and broad sail panels. The roof on both the Coupe and the Sedan had a chrome crossover roof molding at the front of the vinyl portion, stretching across the top and sides. Both had small, limousine-style rear windows. Options included an Astroroof and a leather-trimmed steering wheel. A stand-up wreath-and-crest ornament adorned the hood. The standard wheel covers were varied chrome with wreath-and-crest on a dark red background. Three power trains were offered: the standard fuel-injected V-8-6-4, a Buick V-6 with automatic overdrive transmission and a diesel V-8. Standard equipment included Twilight Sentinel (which automatically turned the headlights on and off), illuminated entry, a tilt/telescope steering wheel, six-way driver and passenger seats and electroluminiscent opera lights. The Coupe's Dual Comfort front seat held three people and its rear seat featured adjustable reading lights. The standard interior upholstery were Heather knit with Raphael inserts and was available in six colors. New door panels displayed an embroidered "Fleetwood" script. Nine varieties of tucked leather seating were also offered. The Brougham d'Elegance had chrome wheel covers with body-colored vanes and the Cadillac wreath-and-crest on an emblem in a dark red background, a "d'Elegance" script and body accent striping.

FLEETWOOD BROUGHAM—
SERIES B-V-6

Model Number	Body/Style Number	Body Type & Seating	Factory Price	Shipping Weight	Production Total
6B	47	2D Coupe-6P	15,777	3,854	Note 3
6B	69	4D Sedan-6P	16,190	3,884	Note 4

FLEETWOOD BROUGHAM
SERIES B-V-8-6-4

Model Number	Body/Style Number	Body Type & Seating	Factory Price	Shipping Weight	Production Total
6B	47	2D Coupe-6P	15,942	4,069	Note 3
6B	69	4D Sedan-6P	16,355	4,115	Note 4

Note 3: Combined production of DeVille and Fleetwood Brougham Coupes was 62,724.
Note 4: Combined production of DeVille and Fleetwood Brougham Sedans was 86,991.

FLEETWOOD LIMOUSINE—SERIES 6D—V-8-6-4

Differing mainly in dimensions from DeVille and Fleetwood Brougham models, the Fleetwood Limousine carried the new crosshatch grille. The Limousines could not have the diesel engine option. Both standard and Formal Limousine models included a dual accessory panel so rear passengers could adjust the climate control system and power windows. The seven-passenger formal edition held a sliding glass partition. Standard Limousines held eight passengers. The Limousine upholstery was done in

Dark Blue Heather cloth or Black in the rear. All carried two fold-down auxiliary seats.

FLEETWOOD LIMOUSINE--
SERIES F - V-8-6-4

Model Number	Body/Style Number	Body Type & Seating	Factory Price	Shipping Weight	Production Total
6F	23	4D Sedan-8P	24,464	4,629	Note 5
6F	33	4D Fml Limousine-7P	25,323	4,717	Note 5

FLEETWOOD COMMERCIAL CHASSIS --SERIES Z - V-8-6-4

Model Number	Body/Style Number	Body Type & Seating	Factory Price	Shipping Weight	Production Total
6Z	90	Commercial Chassis	NA	NA	NA

Note 5: Combined limousine and commercial chassis production was 1,200.

ELDORADO—SERIES 6E—V-8

Up front, Eldorado's new grille had a tiny crosshatch pattern below the wide, brushed-chrome finished, peaked upper bar. Quad rectangular headlights sat above amber-lensed quad parking/signal lights. Horizontal-style clear/amber cornering lights sat a short distance back on the fenders. Like the Seville, the Eldorado also added a front air dam below the bumper. The wheel covers had big red medallions. Inside, Eldorados sported a new center console, woodgrain appliqués on the door panels and simulated teakwood dashboard trim. Standard equipment this year included dual-spot map lights/courtesy lights, seat belt chimes, light monitors, an electric trunk release and power pull-down, a compact spare tire, dual remote-control rearview mirrors, a six-way power driver's seat, an electronic-tuning signal-seeking stereo radio, an MPG Sentinel, Twilight Sentinel, much more. Eldorados featured four-wheel independent suspension, four-wheel disc brakes and electronic level control. On the option list was a Touring Suspension that included larger tires. New Dual Comfort 45/45 seats held the driver and front passenger. New door handles were seen, too. The standard engine was the new 368-cid V-8-6-4 with on-board computer diagnostics. Two options were offered: Buick's 4.1-liter V-6 with three-speed automatic transmission (a four-speed overdrive automatic transmission was used with the V-8-6-4 engine) or the Oldsmobile diesel V-8. Major body components now carried labels conforming to

1981 Cadillac, Fleetwood Brougham, coupe

vehicle identification numbers, in an attempt to prevent thefts.

ELDORADO – SERIES L - V-6

Model Number	Body/Style Number	Body Type & Seating	Factory Price	Shipping Weight	Production Total
6L	57	2D Coupe-5P	17,385	3,615	Note 6

ELDORADO – SERIES L - V-8-6-4

Model Number	Body/Style Number	Body Type & Seating	Factory Price	Shipping Weight	Production Total
6L	57	2D Coupe-5P	17,550	3,822	Note 6

Note 6: Eldorado production was 60,643.

ENGINE

OPTIONAL V-6 (ALL CADILLACS EXCEPT LIMOUSINES)

Overhead valve. Cast-iron block and head. Displacement: 252-cid (4.1-liters). Bore and stroke: 3.965 x 3.40 inches. Compression ratio: 8.0:1. Brake horsepower: 125 at 3800 rpm. Torque: 210 Ibs.-ft. at 2000 rpm. Four main bearings. Hydraulic valve lifters. Carburetor: four-barrel. Built by Buick. VIN Code: 4.

SEVILLE BASE DIESEL V-8; DEVILLE, BROUGHAM, ELDORADO OPTIONAL DIESEL V-8

Overhead valve. Cast-iron block . Displacement: 350 cid (5.7 liters). Bore and Stroke: 4.057 x 3.385 inches. Compression ratio: 22.5:1. Net brake hp: 105 at 3200 rpm. Taxable hp: 52.6. Net torque: 200 lbs.-ft. at 1600 rpm. Five main bearings. Hydraulic valve lifters. Induction: Electronic fuel injection. VIN Code: N. Built by Oldsmobile.

DEVILLE, BROUGHAM, ELDORADO BASE V-8-6-4*, SEVILLE OPTIONAL V-8-6-4*

Overhead valve. Cast-iron block . Displacement: 368 cid (6.0 liters). Bore and Stroke: 3.80 x 4.06 inches. Compression ratio: 8.2:1. Net brake hp: 140 at 3800 rpm. Taxable hp: 46.20. Net torque: 265 lbs.-ft. at 1400 rpm. Five main bearings. Hydraulic valve lifters. Induction: Digital fuel injection. VIN Code: 9. Built by Cadillac.

* Also called Variable Displacement V-8

FLEETWOOD COMMERCIAL CHASSIS V-8

Overhead valve. Cast-iron block. Displacement: 368 cid (6.0 liters). Bore and Stroke: 3.80 x 4.06 inches. Compression ratio: 8.2:1. Net brake hp: 150 at 3800 rpm. Taxable hp: 46.20. Net torque: 265 at 1600 rpm. Five main bearings. Hydraulic valve lifters. Carburetion: Four-barrel. VIN Code: 6. Built by Cadillac.

CHASSIS

(Seville) Wheelbase: 114.0 inches. Overall length: 204.8 inches. Overall width: 71.5 inches. Overall height: 54.3 inches. Front tread: 59.3 inches. Rear tread: 60.6 inches.

Tires: P20575R15 steel-belted radial with wide white sidewall.

(Eldorado) Wheelbase: 113.9 inches. Overall length: 204.5 inches. Overall width: 71.5 inches. Overall height: 54.2 inches. Front tread: 59.3 inches. Rear tread: 60.6 inches. Tires: P20575R15 steel-belted radial with wide white sidewall.

(DeVille) Wheelbase: 121.4 inches. Overall length: 221.0 inches. Overall width: 76.48 inches. Overall height: 54.6 inches. Front tread: 61.7 inches. Rear tread: 60.7 inches. Tires: P21575R15 steel-belted radial with wide white sidewall.

(Brougham) Wheelbase: 121.4 inches. Overall length: 221.0 inches. Overall width: 76.48 inches. Overall height: 56.7 inches. Front tread: 61.7 inches. Rear tread: 60.7 inches. Tires: P21575R15 steel-belted radial with wide white sidewall.

(Fleetwood 75) Wheelbase: 144.5 inches. Overall length: 244.1 inches. Overall width: 76.48 inches. Overall height: 56.9 inches. Front tread: 61.7 inches. Rear tread: 60.7 inches. Tires: HR7815-D steel-belted radial with wide white sidewall.

TECHNICAL

Transmission: Turbo-Hydra-Matic transmission standard on all models, column shift. Gear ratios for DeVille/Brougham/Limousine V8-368: (1st) 2.48:1, (2nd) 1.48:1, (3rd) 1:1, (Reverse) 2.07:1. Other three-speed models: (1st) 2.74:1, (2nd) 1.57:1, (3rd) 1:1, (Reverse) 2.07:1. Four-speed automatic in DeVille/Brougham with V-6: (1st) 2.74:1, (2nd) 1.57:1, (3rd) 1:1, (4th) 0.67:1, (Reverse) 2.07:1. Standard final drive ratio: (Seville/Eldorado) 2.41:1 except with V-6, 2.93:1, (DeVille/Brougham) 2.41:1 except with V- 6, 3.23:1, (Limousines) 3.08:1. Steering: recirculating ball (power assisted). Suspension: same as 1980. Brakes: front disc, rear drum except Seville/ Eldorado, four-wheel disc. Fuel tank: (Seville/Eldorado) 22.8 gallons with diesel, 20.3 gallons with V-8-6-4, 21.1 gallons with V-6. (DeVille/Brougham) 24.6 gallons, 27 gallons with diesel and 25 gallons with the V-6. (Limousines) 24.6 gallons

OPTIONS

Astroroof ($1,058), not available on Limousine. Controlled-cycle wiper system: DeVille/Limousine ($45). Rear defogger, grid-type ($134-$175). Automatic door locks ($129). Garage door opener ($125). Illuminated entry system ($67). Digital instrument cluster: Seville/ Eldorado ($200). Dual Comfort front seats with six-way power passenger seat adjuster: DeVille ($395).

Memory driver's seat ($169). Six-way power passenger seat: Eldorado ($172). Power driver's seat recliner ($130). Power passenger's seat recliner: Brougham ($71). Power passenger seat recliner with six- way power seat: Eldorado ($302). Notchback passenger seat recliner: DeVille ($130). Leather trimmed steering wheel ($79). Tilt/telescope steering wheel ($147). Power trunk lid release and pull down: DeVille/Limousine ($96). Theft deterrent system ($157). Twilight Sentinel: DeVille/ Limousine ($65). Guidematic headlight control ($78). Opera lights: DeVille/Eldorado ($72). Trumpet horn ($28). Thermometer on left mirror ($35). Electric remote mirrors with thermometer on left: Limousine ($99). Twin lighted vanity mirrors ($116). Electronic tuning seek/scan AM/FM stereo radio with 8-track tape player ($195), with 8-track and CB ($480), with cassette ($281), with cassette and CB ($547). Rear-control electronic-tuning radio with 8-track: Limousine ($398). Full padded vinyl roof: DeVille ($240). Two-tone paint: Seville Firemist ($520), DeVille/ Eldorado ($293), partial Firemist: DeVille/Eldorado ($394). Firemist paint ($208). Accent striping: DeVille ($61). Door edge guards ($16-$24). License frames, each ($11). Front console: Eldorado/Seville ($151). Leather seating area ($439-$595). Automatic lap/shoulder belts: DeVille sedan ($150). Carpeted rubber floor mats: front ($35-$38), rear ($20). Trunk mat ($16). Cast aluminum wheels: Eldorado ($376), Seville (NC). Locking wire wheels: DeVille/Brougham ($755). Turbine-vaned wheel covers: DeVille ($63). Locking wire wheel covers ($266-$328). Puncture-sealing tires ($106). 4.1-liter gas V-6 engine ($165 credit), Seville ($490 credit). V-8-6-4 gas engine: Seville ($325 credit). 5.7-liter diesel V-8 engine ($325-$351), not available on the Limousine. California emission equipment ($46-$182). Engine block heater ($22). 100 amp alternator ($41). Heavy-duty cooling ($59). Limited slip differential: DeVille/Brougham/ Limousine ($86). Electronic level control: DeVille/ Brougham ($173). Heavy-duty ride package: DeVille/ Brougham sedan ($270). Touring suspension: Eldorado/ Seville ($95). Trailering package. ($59-$100). Brougham d'Elegance: cloth seating ($1,066), leather ($1,536). DeVille d'Elegance ($1,005). Coupe DeVille Cabriolet ($363). Eldorado Biarritz ($2,937). Eldorado Cabriolet ($363). Seville Elegante ($2,734). Appearance value package, DeVille ($802).

HISTORICAL

Introduced September 25, 1980. Model-year production: 253,591 (including 13,402 1982 Cimarrons built during the 1981 model-year). The total included 30,440 cars with V-6 engines and 42,200 diesels. Calendar-year production: 259,135. Calendar-year sales by U.S. dealers: 230,665 for a 3.7 percent market share. Model-year sales by U.S. dealers was 226,427 (including 8,790 Cimarrons built before September 1981). "Cadillac is class," the full-line catalog declared, a theme that had been used for decades. "Class" seemed to take many forms by the 1980s. In addition to the customary funeral/ambulance adaptations and stretch Limousines from various manufacturers, two conversions came from Wisco Corporation (in Michigan): a Renaissance Coupe DeVille and a Seville Caballero.

1981 Cadillac, Sedan De Ville

1982

OVERVIEW

"Best of all...it's a Cadillac," declared the 1982 full-line catalog. Perhaps so, but longtime Cadillac fans must have been startled by the company's latest offering: the four-cylinder Cimarron, with a manual floor shift. Introduced several years earlier than originally planned, this drastically different breed of luxury car was intended to give Cadillac a toehold in the rising market for smaller, fuel-efficient designs. On other Cadillacs, a 249-cid (4.1-liter) HT-4100 V-8 engine with Digital Fuel Injection (DFI) became standard. This engine was coupled to an overdrive automatic transmission. The Oldsmobile-built diesel 5.7-liter V-8 was also available. So was a Buick-built 4.1-liter V-6, which was offered as a credit option. A new Fuel Data Panel (standard with the HT-4100 engine) displayed instantaneous miles per gallon and average miles per gallon, estimated driving range and amount of fuel used. Electronic Climate Control had a new outside temperature display, available by touching a button. The HT-4100 V-8 engine had an aluminum block for light weight and chrome-plated valve covers for looks. During manufacture, it received individually balanced components and automatic in-process gauging

Above: **1980 Cadillac, Fleetwood Eldorado, coupe**
Tom Glatch

and had to pass a 78-step "stress test" before installation. Features added to improve fuel economy included fast-burn compact combustion chambers, digital fuel injection and bearings designed for low-drag lubricants. Standard with the HT-4100 engine was a four-speed overdrive automatic transmission that helped to further improve gas mileage. EPA estimates reached 26 highway/17 city for Fleetwoods and DeVilles and 27 highway for Sevilles and Eldorados. A Fuel Data Panel computed average miles per gallon on the road. On-board computer diagnostics warned of engine problems and helped the mechanic locate the trouble quickly. The digital fuel injection included automatic altitude compensation, determined by a microprocessor, plus constant idle speed. The HT-4100 replaced the troublesome V-8-6-4 variable-displacement engine and boosted both gas mileage and sales. That new engine was installed in some 90 percent of Sevilles, DeVilles and Eldorados.

I.D. DATA

The 17-symbol serial number was located on top of the instrument panel, where it was visible through the windshield. The first symbol   1=U.S.-built vehicle. The second symbol 2=General Motors. The third symbol 6=Cadillac Motor Division. The fourth symbol indicated

type of restraint system: A=manual belts or B=automatic belts. The fifth symbol identified the series as follows: B=Fleetwood Brougham, D=DeVille, F=Fleetwood Limousine, G=Cimarron, L=Eldorado and S=Seville. The sixth and seventh symbols indicated body style: 23=four-door Limousine with auxiliary seat, 33=four-door Limousine with center divider, 47=two-door Hardtop Coupe, 57=two-door Coupe and 69=four-door pillared Sedan. The eighth symbol indicated the engine (See engine listings below). The ninth symbol was a check digit. The 10th symbol was a letter indicating model year: C=1982. The 11th symbol indicates the GM assembly plant: A=Lakewood, Ga., B=Baltimore, Md., C=Southgate, Calif., D=Doraville, Ga., E=Linden, N.J., F=Flint, Mich., G=Framingham, Mass., H=Flint, Mich. (Buick), J=Janesville, Wis., K=Leeds, Mo., L=Van Nuys, Calif., M=Lansing, Mich., N= Norwood, Ohio, P=Pontiac, Mich., R=Arlington, Tex., S=St. Louis, Mo., T=Tarrytown, N.Y., V=Pontiac, Mich. (GMC), W=Willow Run, Mich., X=Fairfax, Kan., Y=Wilmington, Del., Z=Fremont, Calif., 1=Oshawa, Ontario, Canada, 2=Moraine, Ohio, 2=Ste. Therese, Quebec, Canada, 3=Detroit (Chevrolet), Mich., 3=St. Eustache, Quebec, Canada, 4=Orion, Mich., 4=Scarborough, Ontario, Canada, 5=Bowling Green, Ken., 5=London, Ontario, Canada, 6=Oklahoma City, Okla., 7=Lordstown, Ohio, 8=Shreveport, La., 8=Fujisawa, Japan and 9=Detroit, Mich. (Cadillac). Note: Cadillacs were not built at all GM assembly plants. The next group of numbers was the sequential production code starting with 100001. The Fisher Body tag on the cowl, under the hood includes additional information.

CIMARRON—SERIES 6G—FOUR

After decades of success in manufacturing large luxury cars, Cadillac turned to a small luxury car in an attempt to rival BMWs, Audis, Volvos, Saabs, some Mercedes and other small high-class imports. The Cimarron came with a standard 112-cid (1.8-liter) four-cylinder engine and a four-speed overdrive manual shift with a floor shifter. A three-speed Turbo-Hydra-Matic transmission also was available. This was Cadillac's first four-cylinder engine since 1914 and its first "stick shift" since 1953. Most customers had never driven a Cadillac without some form of Hydra-Matic Drive. The Cimarron was billed as "...a new kind of Cadillac for a new kind of Cadillac owner." Initially billed as the "Cimarron by Cadillac" rather than a straight out Cadillac. The body carried a Cadillac emblem in the grille center and on the taillights, but no script identification. Five people fit into the car's body-contoured leather seats with lumbar support. Deep-pile Trianon carpeting lined the floors. Even the trunk was carpeted. A tachometer, oil pressure gauge and voltmeter filled the dashboard. The Cimarron rode on an exclusive

Cadillac-tuned touring suspension with MacPherson struts up front and a semi-independent rear suspension, plus front and rear stabilizer bars. The Cimarron's aircraft-type aluminum alloy wheels held match-mounted steel-belted radial tires. Sharing the same J-body as Chevrolet's Cavalier and the similarly derivative Pontiac J2000, the Cimarron didn't quite manage a truly separate identity, but offered a long list of standard features. The Cimarron's front end carried a finely-meshed crosshatch horizontal chrome grille and quad rectangular tungsten-halogen headlights. At the rear were horizontal taillights. The wheels had small slots. The full-width back seat could hold three passengers. The initially short option list included a Vista Vent roof and vacuum-type cruise control.

CIMARRON—SERIES 6G
FOUR-CYLINDER

Model Number	Body/Style Number	Body Type & Seating	Factory Price	Shipping Weight	Production Total
G	69	4D Sedan-5P	12,181	2,524	25,968

SEVILLE—SERIES 6K—V-8

"With styling imitated but never equaled, Seville is an American standard for the world." So claimed Cadillac in its full-line catalog for 1982. Little change was evident this year, but there was a new standard power plant under the hood: the lightweight HT-4100 aluminum-block V-8. The idea of a standard diesel engine hadn't lasted long. Seville's chassis carried new shock absorbers and rear springs, along with the familiar four-wheel independent suspension and electronic level control. Optional wire wheel covers had a locking device and aluminum alloy wheels were available at no extra cost. A full Cabriolet roof became available in Black, White or Dark Blue diamond-grain vinyl. That option gave Seville the look of a convertible sedan—at least from a distance. The available Touring suspension included P225/70R15 steel-belted radial tires, large-diameter front and rear stabilizer bars, altered power steering that gave more feedback, stiffer front torsion bar and rear spring rates and increased shock absorber valving. The limited-edition Elegante, with a package price of $3,095, used a sweeping two-tone French curve to accent the burnished and bright full-length bodyside moldings. Sail panels carried the "Elegante" script nameplate.

SEVILLE—SERIES 6S-V-6

Model Number	Body/Style Number	Body Type & Seating	Factory Price	Shipping Weight	Production Total
6S	69	4D Sedan-6P	23,269	----	Note 1

SEVILLE—SERIES 6S- V-6/V-8

Model Number	Body/Style Number	Body Type & Seating	Factory Price	Shipping Weight	Production Total
6S	69	4D Sedan-6P	23,269	----	Note 1

Note 1: Seville production was 119,998

DEVILLE—SERIES 6C—V-8

DeVilles were powered by the new HT-4100 Digital Fuel Injection V-8 with automatic overdrive transmission. The

dashboard in this model contained a new standard Fuel Data Panel to help determine the most fuel-efficient driving route. Push buttons could display outside temperature or average trip mileage or amount of fuel used. This year's new grille was made up of thin vertical bars, sectioned by two horizontal bars. The wide upper horizontal header, finished in brushed chrome and running full width, held the customary Cadillac script. Quad rectangular headlights stood directly above rectangular amber-lensed parking/signal lights. Cornering lights with clear and amber lenses wrapped around the fender sides. DeVilles displayed a wreath-and-crest stand-up hood ornament. The DeVille d'Elegance had pillow-style seats in Venetian velour cloth, in four colors, plus opera lights and accent striping. Sedan versions added three roof-mounted passenger assist straps. d'Elegance editions were identified by script on the roof sail panels.

DEVILLE —SERIES 6D- V-6

Model Number	Body/Style Number	Body Type & Seating	Factory Price	Shipping Weight	Production Total
D	47	2D Coupe-6P	15,084	----	Note 2
D	69	4D Sedan-6P	15,534	----	Note 2

DEVILLE —SERIES 6D- V-8

Model Number	Body/Style Number	Body Type & Seating	Factory Price	Shipping Weight	Production Total
D	47	2D Coupe-6P	15,249	3,783	Note 2
D	69	4D Sedan-6P	15,699	3,839	Note 2

Note 2: The production totals for DeVilles and Fleetwood Broughams were combined. See notes 3 and 4 below.

FLEETWOOD BROUGHAM—SERIES 6D—V-8

Priced nearly $3,000 higher than last year, the Fleetwood Brougham Coupes and Sedans looked similar to their DeVille "cousins" from the front. They used the same new three-row grille made up of narrow vertical bars. Standard equipment included a stand-up wreath-and-crest hood ornament, Twilight Sentinel, an illuminated entry system, controlled-cycle wipers, tilt/telescope steering wheel and a six-way power-operated front seat. The 55/45 Dual Comfort type front seats held three people and were trimmed in exclusive Fleetwood design, using Heather knit with Raphael cloth inserts. Eight colors of leather were also available. The coupe carried a distinctive elk

1982 Cadillac, Fleetwood Brougham, coupe

grain vinyl Cabriolet roof with large quarter windows and electroluminiscent opera lights. A chrome crossover molding highlighted its forward edge. Sedans had a small (Limousine-style) back window and full elk grain vinyl roof, with Cadillac's wreath-and-crest insignia on the rear roof (sail) panels. A Brougham nameplate stood at the back of rear fenders. Color-keyed, vaned wheel covers were new. Genuine wire wheels were an option. The Brougham d'Elegance offered tufted upholstery in cloth or leather, with 50/50 Dual Comfort seats, special trim, identifying scripts and special wheel covers to match the body color.

FLEETWOOD BROUGHAM – SERIES 6B - V-6

Model Number	Body/Style Number	Body Type & Seating	Factory Price	Shipping Weight	Production Total
B	47	2D Coupe-6P	17,931	----	Note 3
B	69	4D Sedan-6P	18,402	----	Note 4

FLEETWOOD BROUGHAM-- SERIES 6B - V-8

Model Number	Body/Style Number	Body Type & Seating	Factory Price	Shipping Weight	Production Total
B	47	2D Coupe-6P	18,096	3,825	Note 3
B	69	4D Sedan-6P	18,567	3,866	Note 4

Note 3: Combined production of DeVille and Fleetwood Brougham Coupes was 50,130.

Note 4: Combined production of DeVille and Fleetwood Brougham Sedans was 86,020.

FLEETWOOD LIMOUSINE—SERIES 6D—V-8-6-4

While the innovative (but flawed) variable-displacement V-8-6-4 engine no longer powered other Cadillacs, it remained active under limousine hoods for several more years. Fleetwood's standard limo seated eight. For an extra thousand dollars or so, the Formal Limousine held seven, with a sliding glass partition between compartments. A second control panel let passengers adjust the temperature and use the power windows. Heather cloth interior came in black or dark gray-blue. Front compartment of the Formal Limousine was black, with black leather in seating areas.

FLEETWOOD LIMOUSINE—
SERIES F-V-8-6-4

Model Number	Body/Style Number	Body Type & Seating	Factory Price	Shipping Weight	Production Total
F	23	4D Sedan-8P	27,961	4,628	Note 5
F	33	4D Formal Limousine-7P	28,941	4,718	Note 5

FLEETWOOD COMMERCIAL CHASSIS—SERIES Z-V-8-6-4

Model Number	Body/Style Number	Body Type & Seating	Factory Price	Shipping Weight	Production Total
Z	90	Commercial Chassis	N/A	N/A	N/A

Note 5: Combined limousine and commercial chassis production was 1,450.

ELDORADO—SERIES 6E—V-8

While the Eldorado's front-end appearance was similar to that of the DeVille and Fleetwood, the personal-luxury coupe was most noted for its handsome profile. It had a short deck lid, an upright rectangular quarter window and a bodyside molding that turned upward in a square corner just behind that quarter window. This year's vertical-style grille contained three narrow horizontal bars. The bumpers held new black rub strips with white centers, while revised taillights displayed Cadillac's crest insignia.

The Eldorado's full cabriolet roof option, appearing during the model-year, offered the look (almost) of a convertible top. Base power plant was the new HT-4100 DFI V-8 with overdrive automatic transmission. Buick's V-6 was also available. Eldorados continued with four-wheel independent suspension and four-wheel disc brakes. The Dual Comfort 45/50 seats held three people, with six-way power adjustment for the driver. Heather cloth upholstery with Dundee cloth inserts came in five colors and leather trim came in eight colors. The Eldorado Biarritz carried a brushed stainless steel roof cap, wire wheel covers, opera lights and a "Biarritz" script on the sail panels. The interiors offered five different colors of genuine leather trim for the seating areas, plus a leather-trimmed steering wheel, Tampico carpeting and rear quarter reading lights.

ELDORADO—SERIES L-V-6/V-8

Model Number	Body/Style Number	Body Type & Seating	Factory Price	Shipping Weight	Production Total
6E	LS7	2D Coupe-6P	18,551	----	Note 6

ELDORADO—SERIES L-V-6/V-8

Model Number	Body/Style Number	Body Type & Seating	Factory Price	Shipping Weight	Production Total
6E	LS7	2D Coupe-6P	18,716	3,637	Note 6

Note 6: Eldorado production was 52,018.

ENGINE

CIMARRON BASE FOUR

Inline. Overhead valve. Four-cylinder. Cast-iron block and head. Displacement: 112-cid (1.8-liters). Bore and stroke: 3.50 x 2.91 inches. Compression ratio: 9.0:1. Brake horsepower: 88 at 5100 rpm. Torque: 100 lbs.-ft. at 2800 rpm. Five main bearings. Hydraulic valve lifters. Carburetor: two-barrel. VIN Code: G.

SEVILLE, ELDORADO, DEVILLE, BROUGHAM -- OPTIONAL V-6

Overhead valve. Cast-iron block and head. Displacement: 252-cid (4.1-liters). Bore and stroke: 3.965 x 3.40 inches. Compression ratio: 8.0:1. Brake horsepower: 125 at 3800 rpm. Torque: 210 lbs.-ft. at 2000 rpm. Four main bearings. Hydraulic valve lifters. Carburetor: four-barrel. Built by Buick. VIN Code: 4.

SEVILLE, ELDORADO, DEVILLE, BROUGHAM -- BASE HT4100 V-8

Overhead valve. Aluminum block with cast iron liners. Displacement: 249 cid (4.1 liters). Bore and Stroke: 3.465 x 3.307 inches. Compression ratio: 8.5:1. Net brake hp: 125 at 4200 rpm. Taxable hp: 39.2. Net torque: 190 lbs. ft. at 2000 rpm. Five main bearings. Hydraulic valve lifters. Induction: Digital fuel injection. VIN Code: 8. Built by Cadillac.

SEVILLE, ELDORADO

Overhead valve. Cast-iron block . Displacement: 350 cid (5.7 liters). Bore and Stroke: 4.057 x 3.385 inches. Compression ratio: 21.6:1. Net brake hp: 105 at 3200 rpm. Taxable hp: 52.6. Net torque: 200 at 1600 rpm. Five main bearings. Hydraulic valve lifters. Induction: Electronic fuel injection. VIN Code: N. Built by Oldsmobile.

DEVILLE, BROUGHAM-- OPTIONAL DIESEL V-8 CADILLAC LIMOUSINE-- BASE V-8-6-4 "VARIABLE-DISPLACEMENT" V-8

Overhead valve. Cast-iron block . Displacement: 368 cid (6.0 liters). Bore and Stroke: 3.80 x 4.06 inches. Compression ratio: 8.2:1. Net brake hp: 140 at 3800 rpm. Taxable hp: 46.20. Net torque: 200 lbs.-ft. at 1400 rpm. Five main bearings. Hydraulic valve lifters. Induction: Digital fuel injection. VIN Code: 9. Built by Cadillac.

FLEETWOOD COMMERCIAL CHASSIS V-8

Overhead valve. Cast-iron block . Displacement: 368 cid (6.0 liters). Bore and Stroke: 3.80 x 4.06 inches. Compression ratio: 8.2:1. Net brake hp: 150 at 3800 rpm. Taxable hp: 46.20. Net torque: 265 lbs.-ft. at 1600 rpm.

CHASSIS

(Cimarron) Wheelbase: 101.2 inches. Overall length: 173.0 inches. Overall width: 66.3 inches. Overall height: 52.0 inches. Front tread: 55.4 inches. Rear tread: 55.2 inches. Tires: P19570R13 steel-belted radial with wide white sidewall.

(Seville) Wheelbase: 114.0 inches. Overall length: 204.8 inches. Overall width: 71.5 inches. Overall height: 54.3 inches. Front tread: 59.3 inches. Rear tread: 60.6 inches. Tires: P20575R15 steel-belted radial with wide white sidewall.

(Eldorado) Wheelbase: 113.9 inches. Overall length: 204.5 inches. Overall width: 71.5 inches. Overall height: 54.2 inches. Front tread: 59.3 inches. Rear tread: 60.6 inches. Tires: P20575R15 steel-belted radial with wide white sidewall.

(DeVille) Wheelbase: 121.4 inches. Overall length: 221.0 inches. Overall width: 76.48 inches. Overall height: 54.6 inches. Front tread: 61.7 inches. Rear tread: 60.7 inches. Tires: P21575R15 steel-belted radial with wide white sidewall.

(Brougham) Wheelbase: 121.4 inches. Overall length: 221.0 inches. Overall width: 76.48 inches. Overall height: 56.7 inches. Front tread: 61.7 inches. Rear tread: 60.7 inches. Tires: P21575R15 steel-belted radial with wide white sidewall.

(Fleetwood 75) Wheelbase: 144.5 inches. Overall length: 244.1 inches. Overall width: 76.48 inches. Overall height: 56.9 inches. Front tread: 61.7 inches. Rear tread: 60.7 inches. Tires: HR7815-D steel-belted radial with wide white sidewall.

TECHNICAL

Transmission: Four-speed, floor shift manual transmission standard on Cimarron. Manual gear ratios: (1st) 3.53:1, (2nd) 1.95:1, (3rd) 1.24:1, (4th) 0.81:1, (Reverse) 3.42:1. Turbo-Hydra-matic (THM125C) optional on Cimarron with floor selector: (1st) 2.84:1, (2nd) 1.60:1, (3rd) 1:1, (Reverse) 2.07:1. Three-speed Turbo-Hydra-Matic (THM350C) standard on DeVille/Brougham diesel: (1st) 2.52:1, (2nd) 1.52:1, (3rd) 1:1, (Reverse) 1.94:1. Turbo-Hydra-Matic (THM400) standard on Limousines: (1st) 2.48:1, (2nd) 1.48:1, (3rd) 1:1, (Reverse) 2.07:1. Four-speed overdrive automatic standard on others (THM325-4L on Eldorado/Seville, THM200-4R on DeVille/Brougham): (1st) 2.74:1, (2nd) 1.57:1, (3rd) 1:1, (4th) 0.67:1, (Reverse) 2.07:1. All automatics except Limousine had torque converter clutch. Standard final drive ratio: (Cimarron) 3.65:1 except with automatic 3.18:1, (Seville/Eldorado) 3.15:1 except diesel, 2.93:1, (DeVille/Brougham) 3.42:1 except 2.93:1 with diesel, 2.41:1 with diesel and three-speed transmission, 3.23:1 with V-6, (Limousine) 3.08:1. Steering: (Cimarron) rack and pinion, (others) recirculating ball, power assist. Front suspension: (Cimarron) MacPherson struts, anti-roll bar, (Seville/Eldorado) torsion bar and link stabilizer bar, (others) coil springs and link stabilizer bar. Rear suspension: (Cimarron) semi-independent trailing arm, coil springs, anti-roll bar, (Seville/Eldorado) independent trailing arm, coil springs, electronic level control, (others) four-link, coil springs, electronic level control standard on Limousine and available on DeVille/Brougham. Brakes: front disc, rear drum except Seville/Eldorado, four-wheel disc. Fuel tank: (Cimarron) 14.0 gallons, (Seville/Eldorado) 20.3 gallons except 22.8 with diesel, 21.1 with V-6, (DeVille/Brougham) 24.5 gallons except 26 with diesel, (Limousines) 24.5 gallons.

OPTIONS
CIMARRON

Vista Vent with rear tilt ($261). Cruise control, vacuum-type ($145-$155). Power windows ($216). Power door locks ($12). Power trunk release ($29). Tilt steering ($88). Six-way power driver's seat ($183), both seats ($366). Twin lighted vanity mirrors ($92). AM/FM stereo radio with cassette ($153). AM/FM radio with cassette and CB ($560). Delete radio ($151 credit). Door edge guards ($22). License frame ($12). Deck lid luggage rack ($98). Carpeted rubber floor mats: front ($38), rear ($22). Trunk mat ($18). White sidewall tires ($55). California emission

equipment ($46). Engine block heater ($17). Heavy-duty battery ($22). 100-amp alternator ($48). Heavy duty radiator ($37). Three-speed automatic transmission ($370).

SEVILLE / DEVILLE / FLEETWOOD BROUGHAM / LIMOUSINE / ELDORADO

Astroroof ($1,195), not available on Limousine. Electronic cruise control ($175). Controlled-cycle wiper system: DeVille/limo ($53). Rear defogger with heated outside mirrors ($150-$198). Automatic door locks ($145). Remote-locking fuel filler door ($56). Garage door opener ($140). Illuminated entry system ($76). Digital instrument cluster: Seville/Eldorado ($229). Dual Comfort front seats with six-way power passenger seat adjuster ($413). Memory driver's seat ($180). Six-way power passenger seat: Eldorado/Seville ($197). Power driver's seat recliner ($150), passenger seat recliner, DeVille ($150). Power passenger seat recliner with six-way power seat: Eldorado ($347), Seville ($282). Leather-trimmed steering wheel rim ($95). Tilt/telescope steering wheel ($169). Power trunk lid release and pull-down: DeVille/Limousine ($112). Theft deterrent system ($179). Twilight Sentinel: DeVille/Limousine ($76). Guidematic headlight control ($93). Opera lights: DeVille/Eldorado ($85). Trumpet horn ($35) except Seville. Electric remote-control outside mirrors ($98). Electric remote mirrors with thermometer on left: Limousine ($114). Twin lighted vanity mirrors ($136). Electronic-tuning seek/scan AM/FM stereo radio with 8-track tape player ($225), with 8-track and CB ($515), with cassette and symphony sound system ($290). Elect-tuning radio with 8-track and rear control: Limousine ($430). Triband antenna ($45). Fully padded vinyl roof: DeVille sed ($267). Two-tone paint: Seville ($590), DeVille/Eldorado ($335), partial Firemist, DeVille/Eldorado ($450). Firemist paint ($229). Accent striping: DeVille ($74). Bodyside molding ($61). Door edge guards ($18-$27). License frame ($13). Leather seating area ($498-$680). Carpeted rubber floor mats: front ($41-$43), rear ($24). Trunk mat ($20). Aluminum wheels: Eldorado ($429), Seville (NC). Locking wire wheels: DeVille/Brougham ($860). Turbine-vaned wheel covers: DeVille ($75). Wire wheel covers ($298-$375). Puncture-sealing tires ($130- $175). 4.1-liter V-6 engine ($165 credit). 5.7-liter diesel V-8 engine ($179-$351), not available Limousine. Altitude emissions package for diesel or 4.1 V-8 (NC). Engine block heater in Limousine ($26). 100-amp alternator ($48). Limited-slip differential for DeVille/Brougham/Limousine ($106). Electronic level control for DeVille/Brougham ($198). Heavy-duty ride package for DeVille/Brougham ($310). FE2 touring suspension for Eldorado/Seville ($109). Brougham d'Elegance cloth seating ($1,195). Brougham d'Elegance leather seating ($1,730). DeVille d'Elegance ($1,115).

DeVille Cabriolet ($398). Eldorado Biarritz ($3,335). Eldorado Cabriolet ($398). Eldorado Touring Coupe ($1950). Seville Elegante ($3,095).

HISTORICAL

Introduced September 24, 1981, except that the "1982" Cimarron was introduced on May 21, 1981. Model-year production was 235,584 (including later '82 Cimarrons). The total also included 17,650 V-6 Cadillacs and 19,912 diesels. Only 1,017 Sevilles and 3,453 Eldorados had a V-6. Calendar-year production was 246,602. Calendar-year sales by U.S. dealers was 249,295 for a 4.3 percent share of the market. Model-year sales by U.S. dealers was 237,032, also a 4.3 percent market share. In Cadillac's 80th anniversary year, it was the only GM division to show a sales increase, though not a gigantic one. A depressed economy typically affects luxury-car buyers the least. The new Cimarron sold only one-third of the predicted output and Seville sales also fell below expectations. Heavy dealer orders or the new models in September 1982 caused officials to add a second shift to the Livonia Engine Plant operation. Cadillac had considered selling the new HT-4100 4.1-liter engine to other GM divisions. Until a lightweight V-6 engine could be developed, Cadillac planned to use Buick's 251-cid (4.1-liter) V-6 in the new Cimarron, which was built in South Gate, California. But that would not happen. Cadillac's Corporate Average Fuel Economy (CAFE) rating zoomed up to 22.1 miles per gallon this year, from only 18.7 m.p.h. in 1981, largely due to the improved efficiency of the new 4.1 V-8.

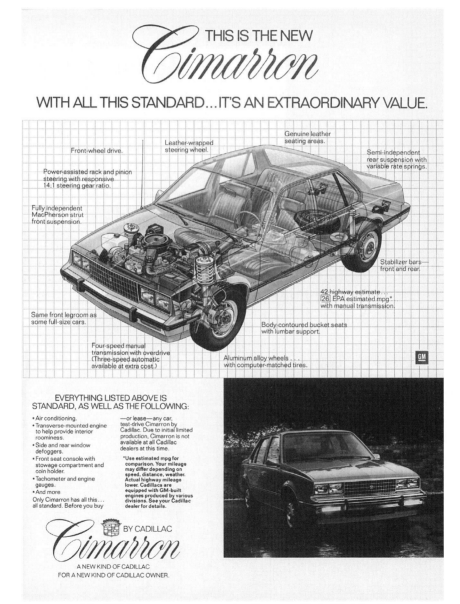

The 1982 Cimarron was promoted as "…a new kind of Cadillac."

1983

OVERVIEW

The 1983 Cadillacs heralded a new line of electronic fuel-injected (EFI) engines. The EFI engine lineup even included the 2.0-liter four that powered Cimarrons. Once again, the HT-4100 V-8 was Cadillac's standard engine (except on Cimarrons and limousines). It now had 10 more horsepower. A four-speed overdrive automatic transmission was standard. The 5.7-liter diesel was available. A new Freedom II battery gave better cold-cranking performance. The curious, undependable, variable-displacement V-8-6-4 engine was consigned only to limousine applications. Added to the Eldorado and Seville option lists was a Delco-GM/Bose Symphony Sound System with four amplifiers and speakers in separate enclosures billed as the "industry's most advanced stereo." Sound was automatically balanced for all passengers. Acoustics were based on window location and shape, upholstery, carpeting and position of driver and passengers. The system included an AM/FM stereo radio and integral cassette player with Dolby tape noise reduction and full-time loudness control. The system was tested with an "acoustically-sensitive" robot.

Above: **1980 Cadillac, Fleetwood Eldorado, coupe**

I.D. DATA

The 17-symbol serial number was located on top of the instrument panel, where it was visible through the windshield. The first symbol 1=U.S.-built vehicle. The second symbol 2=General Motors. The third symbol 6=Cadillac Motor Division. The fourth symbol indicated type of restraint system: A=manual belts or B=automatic belts. The fifth symbol identified the series as follows: B=Fleetwood Brougham, D=DeVille, F=Fleetwood Limousine, G=Cimarron, L=Eldorado and S=Seville. The sixth and seventh symbols indicated body style: 23=four-door Limousine with auxiliary seat, 33=four-door Limousine with center divider, 47=two-door Hardtop Coupe, 57=two-door Coupe and 69=four-door pillared sedan. The eighth symbol indicated the engine (See engine listings below). The ninth symbol was a check digit. The 10th symbol was a letter indicating model year: D=1983. The 11th symbol indicates the GM assembly plant: A=Lakewood, Ga., B=Baltimore, Md., C=Southgate, Calif., D=Doraville, Ga., E=Linden, N.J., F=Flint, Mich., G=Framingham, Mass., H=Flint, Mich. (Buick), J=Janesville, Wis., K=Leeds, Mo., L=Van Nuys, Calif., M=Lansing, Mich., N= Norwood, Ohio, P=Pontiac, Mich., R=Arlington, Tex., S=St. Louis, Mo., T=Tarrytown, N.Y., V=Pontiac, Mich. (GMC), W=Willow Run, Mich., X=Fairfax, Kan., Y=Wilmington, Del., Z= Fremont, Calif., 1=Oshawa, Ontario, Canada,

2=Moraine, Ohio, 2=Ste. Therese, Quebec, Canada, 3=Detroit (Chevrolet), Mich., 3=St. Eustache, Quebec, Canada, PQ, 4=Orion, Mich., 4=Scarborough, Ontario, Canada, 5=Bowling Green, Ken., 5=London, Ontario, Canada, 6=Oklahoma City, Okla., 7=Lordstown, Ohio, 8=Shreveport, La., 8=Fujisawa, Japan and 9=Detroit, Mich. (Cadillac). Note: Cadillacs were not built at all GM assembly plants. The next group of numbers was the sequential production code starting with 100001. The Fisher Body tag on the cowl, under the hood includes additional information.

CIMARRON—SERIES 6G—FOUR

A new fuel-injected 2.0-liter engine with five-speed gear box promised better starting and gas mileage for Cadillac's smallest car. A new front end placed standard tungsten-halogen foglights alongside the license plate, while a lower valance panel helped to separate Cimarron from its related (and much cheaper) J-body relatives. The grille had a finer mesh pattern than before, made up of thin vertical bars all the way across, divided into three sections by two subdued horizontal bars. Quad rectangular headlights and amber parking/signal lights were inset below the bumper rub strips. The hood medallion was new and new aluminum alloy wheels contained bigger slots. Performance got a boost from the increased displacement and higher compression, along with the bigger engine's "swirl" intake ports and revised camshaft. That extra gear in the transmission didn't hurt either. It delivered a higher first-gear ratio for quicker takeoffs, plus closer ratios overall for smoother shift transitions. Ratios in the optional three-speed automatic transmission were changed too. Cimarrons had power rack-and-pinion steering with a leather-trimmed steering wheel. Cimarron drivers enjoyed dual electric remote-control mirrors and the front passenger had a visor-vanity mirror. In the trunk was a compact spare tire. The Cimarron came in 10 colors, accented by dual color paint stripes. Three colors were Cimarron exclusives: Antique Saddle, Midnight Sand Gray and Garnet.

CIMARRON— SERIES G-FOUR

Model Number	Body/Style No.	Body Type & Seating	Factory Price	Shipping Weight	Production Total
G	69	4D Sedan-5P	12,215	2,639	19,194

SEVILLE—SERIES 6S—V-8

With price tags starting at $21,440, the Seville came well equipped with—among other niceties—reminder chimes, electronic climate control with outside temperature display, automatic trunk locking (and release), side defoggers, rear reading lights, overhead assist handles and an automatic power antenna for the electronically-tuned radio. Also standard were an underhood light, light monitors, power windows and door locks, twin remote-control mirrors, cornering lights and four-wheel power disc brakes. The

Seville's appearance changed little from 1982, except that this year's grille had a bit less of a vertical look and carried a Cadillac script. The front end held clear park/signal light lenses. A new premium sound system was available, using Dolby tape noise reduction. The 4.1-liter aluminum-block V-8 received a horsepower and torque boost in its second year, to improve a power-loss problem. Third-gear acceleration rate was also revised. The 5.7-liter diesel included an engine block heater to improve cold-weather startups. The Seville Elegante again came in two-tone color combinations with French curve side styling using chrome bodyside moldings. There was an "'Elegante" script on the side panels and accent striping. Sierra Grain tucked leather seating areas were color-coordinated to match the body color and to complement the leather-trimmed steering wheel. The front console was leather-topped. Wire wheel covers were standard.

SEVILLE—SERIES S-V-8

Model Number	Body/Style No.	Body Type & Seating	Factory Price	Shipping Weight	Production Total
S	69	4D Sedan-6P	21,440	3,844	30,430

DEVILLE—SERIES 6D—V-8

Few changes were evident in the bodies of DeVille or Fleetwood Coupe and Sedan models, although the exhaust system was modified. The refined new grille was similar to the 1982 style, with narrow vertical bars separated into three rows. The "Cadillac" script was moved from the upper horizontal bar to the side of the grille, leaving the upper bar bare. Distinctive taillights carried on Cadillac's traditional style. On the hood was a stand-up hood ornament. On the deck lid was Cadillac's "V" and crest logo. Horsepower rose by 10 on the HT-4100 Digital Fuel Injected 4.1-liter V-8. The miserly (if troublesome) 5.7-liter diesel was available on DeVille and Fleetwood Brougham models.

DEVILLE — SERIES D - V-8

Model Number	Body/Style No.	Body Type & Seating	Factory Price	Shipping Weight	Production Total
D	47	2D Coupe-6P	15,970	3,935	Note 1
D	69	4D Sedan-6P	16,441	3,993	Note 1

Note 1: The production totals for DeVilles and Fleetwood Broughams were combined. See notes 2 and 3 below.

FLEETWOOD BROUGHAM—SERIES 6B—V-8

Offered in Coupe and Sedan models, the Fleetwood Brougham displayed a front end similar to DeVille's with a stand-up wreath-and-crest hood ornament. The Sedan had a limousine-style rear window, while the Coupe's standard Cabriolet vinyl roof featured "privacy size" quarter windows (similar to DeVille's Cabriolet option). The Brougham d'Elegance option, offered on both the Coupe and the Sedan, featured Heather cloth upholstery in a choice of four colors, or leather in six choices, plus special trim, deluxe carpeting, deluxe floor mats and wheel

covers that matched the body color. The package also included "d'Elegance" identifying scripts, both inside and outside the car.

FLEETWOOD BROUGHAM – SERIES B - V-8

Model Number	Body/Style No.	Body Type & Seating	Factory Price	Shipping Weight	Production Total
B	47	2D Coupe-6P	18,688	3,986	Note 2
B	69	4D Sedan-6P	19,182	4,029	Note 3

Note 2: Combined production of DeVille and Fleetwood Brougham Coupes was 65,670.
Note 3: Combined production of DeVille and Fleetwood Brougham Sedans was 109,004.

FLEETWOOD LIMOUSINE—SERIES 6F—V-8-6-4

Luxurious as ever, the Fleetwood limousines saw no evident change this year. The sole available power plant was again the V-8-6-4 variable displacement engine, which was offered only in Limousines. The big Fleetwoods remained the only domestic, mass-produced limousine, though production was modest at only a 1,000 units. Seven or eight passengers rode in comfort and style, enjoying plentiful chrome, and such extras as opera lights.

FLEETWOOD LIMOUSINE—SERIES F-V-8-6-4

Model Number	Body/Style No.	Body Type & Seating	Factory Price	Shipping Weight	Production Total
F	23	4D Sedan-8P	29,223	4,765	Note 4
F	33	4D Fml. Limousine-7P	30,349	4,852	Note 4

FLEETWOOD COMMERCIAL CHASSIS – SERIES Z - V-8-6-4

Model Number	Body/Style No.	Body Type & Seating	Factory Price	Shipping Weight	Production Total
Z	90	Commercial Chassis	N/A	N/A	N/A

Note 4: Total limousine production, 1,000.

ELDORADO—SERIES 6L—V-8

Like other Cadillacs, the Eldorado saw no major body changes this year, although the automatic transmission and cruise control system were recalibrated to boost performance. The standard engine was the HT-4100 4.1-liter V-8 with its complex (yet reliable) fuel-injection system. A 5.7-liter diesel was optional. Prices began at $19,334 (suggested retail), which included plenty of standard equipment. The grille was similar to that of the DeVille and Fleetwood models, with a "Cadillac" script at the driver's side in the center row. The front fender tips held no lights, so the quad rectangular headlights and horizontal-style parking/signal lights had a recessed look. The cornering lights were in horizontal housings back on the front fenders. Heather cloth upholstery with Rocaille cloth inserts came in four colors. Buyers could choose from 10 leather choices. Options included a digital instrument cluster with readouts for fuel level, speed and fuel range (metric or nonmetric). Touring Coupes had a Touring suspension, large-diameter stabilizer bars, larger P225/70R15 steel-belted radial tires and a special cloisonné hood medallion. Reclining saddle leather-faced front bucket seats offered lumbar and lateral support and included a console. The Eldorado Biarritz "dream machine" included a brushed stainless steel roof cap, wire wheel covers, and "Biarritz" scripts on the sail panels.

ELDORADO (V-8)

Model Number	Body/Style No.	Body Type & Seating	Factory Price	Shipping Weight	Production Total
6E	L57	2D Coupe-6P	19,334	3,748	67,416

ENGINE

CIMARRON BASE FOUR-CYLINDER (I4)

Inline. OHV. Four cylinder. Cast-iron block and head. Displacement: 121-cid (2.0-liters). Bore & stroke: 3.50 x 3.15 inches. Compression ratio: 9.3:1. Brake horsepower: 88 at 4000 rpm. Torque: 110 lbs.-ft. at 2400 rpm. Five main bearings. Hydraulic valve lifters. Throttle-body fuel injection. VIN Code: P.

SEVILLE, DEVILLE, BROUGHAM, ELDORADO— BASE V-8

Overhead valve. Aluminum block with cast iron liners. Displacement: 249 cid (4.1 liters). Bore and Stroke: 3.47 x 3.31 inches. Compression ratio: 8.5:1. Net brake hp: 135 at 4400 rpm. Taxable hp: 39.2. Net torque: 200 lbs.-ft. at 2000 rpm. Five main bearings. Hydraulic valve lifters. Induction: Digital fuel injection. VIN Code: 8. Built by Cadillac.

SEVILLE, DEVILLE, BROUGHAM, ELDORADO— OPTIONAL DIESEL V-8

Overhead valve. Cast-iron block. Displacement: 350 cid (5.7 liters). Bore and Stroke: 4.057 x 3.385 inches. Compression ratio: 22.5:1. Net brake hp: 105 at 3200 rpm. Taxable hp: 52.6. Net torque: 200 lbs.-ft. at 1600 rpm. Five main bearings. Hydraulic valve lifters. Induction: Electronic fuel injection. VIN Code: N. Built by Oldsmobile.

FLEETWOOD LIMOUSINE, FLEETWOOD COMMERCIAL CHASSIS—BASE V-8-6-4

Overhead valve. Cast-iron block. Displacement: 368 cid (6.0 liters). Bore and Stroke: 3.80 x 4.06 inches.

1983 Cadillac, Fleetwood Brougham coupe

Compression ratio: 8.2:1. Net brake hp: 140 at 3800 rpm. Taxable hp: 46.20. Net torque: 200 lbs.-ft. at 1400 rpm. Five main bearings. Hydraulic valve lifters. Induction: Digital fuel injection. VIN Code: 9. Built by Cadillac.

FLEETWOOD COMMERCIAL CHASSIS—OPTIONAL V-8

Overhead valve. Cast-iron block . Displacement: 368 cid (6.0 liters). Bore and Stroke: 3.80 x 4.06 inches. Compression ratio: 8.2:1. Net brake hp: 150 at 3800 rpm. Taxable hp: 46.20. Net torque: 265 lbs.-ft. at 1600 rpm. Five main bearings. Hydraulic valve lifters. Carburetion: Four-barrel. VIN Code: 6. Built by Cadillac.

CHASSIS

(Cimarron) Wheelbase: 101.2 inches. Overall length: 173.1 inches. Overall width: 66.5 inches. Overall height: 52.0 inches. Front tread: 55.4 inches. Rear tread: 55.2 inches. Tires: P19570R13 steel-belted radial with wide white sidewall.

(Seville) Wheelbase: 114.0 inches. Overall length: 204.8 inches. Overall width: 71.5 inches. Overall height: 54.3 inches. Front tread: 59.3 inches. Rear tread: 60.6 inches. Tires: P20575R15 steel-belted radial with wide white sidewall.

(Eldorado) Wheelbase: 114.0 inches. Overall length: 204.5 inches. Overall width: 71.5 inches. Overall height: 54.3 inches. Front tread: 59.3 inches. Rear tread: 60.6 inches. Tires: P20575R15 steel-belted radial with wide white sidewall.

(DeVille) Wheelbase: 121.5 inches. Overall length: 221.0 inches. Overall width: 76.5 inches. Overall height: 54.6 inches. Front tread: 61.7 inches. Rear tread: 60.7 inches. Tires: P21575R15 steel-belted radial with wide white sidewall.

(Brougham) Wheelbase: 121.5 inches. Overall length: 221.0 inches. Overall width: 76.5 inches. Overall height: 55.6 inches. Front tread: 61.7 inches. Rear tread: 60.7 inches. Tires: P21575R15 steel-belted radial with wide white sidewall.

(Fleetwood 75) Wheelbase: 144.5 inches. Overall length: 244.3 inches. Overall width: 76.5 inches. Overall height: 56.9 inches. Front tread: 61.7 inches. Rear tread: 60.7 inches. Tires: HR7815-D steel-belted radial with wide white sidewall.

TECHNICAL

Transmission: Five-speed manual transmission standard on Cimarron. Manual gear ratios: (1st) 3.92:1, (2nd) 2.15:1, (3rd) 1.33:1, (4th) 0.92:1, (5th) 0.74:1, (Reverse) 3.50:1. Optional Cimarron three-speed Turbo-Hydra-Matic (THM125C) gear ratios: (1st) 2.84:1, (2nd) 1.80:1, (3rd) 1:1, (Reverse) 2.07:1. Three-speed (THM400) automatic standard on limousine: (1st) 2.48:1, (2nd) 1.48:1, (3rd) 1:1, (Reverse) 2.08:1. Four-speed overdrive automatic standard on all others: (1st) 2.74:1, (2nd) 1.57:1, (3rd) 1:1, (4th) 0.67:1, (Reverse) 2.07:1. Standard final drive ratio: (Cimarron) 3.83:1 with 5-spd. 3.18:1 with auto. (Seville/Eldorado) 3.15:1, with diesel 2.93:1. (DeVille/Brougham) 3.42:1, with diesel 2.93:1. (Limousines) 3.08:1. Steering, Suspension and Brakes: same as 1982. Fuel tank: (Cimarron) 13.6 gallons. (Seville/Eldorado) 20.3 gallons, with diesel, 22.8 gallons. (DeVille/Brougham/Limousine) 24.5 gallons, with diesel, 26 gallons.

OPTIONS

SEVILLE / DEVILLE / FLEETWOOD BROUGHAM / LIMOUSINE / ELDORADO

Astroroof ($1225), not available on Limousine. Electronic cruise control ($185). Controlled-cycle wiper system for DeVille/Limousine ($60). Rear defogger with heated outside mirrors ($160-$210). Automatic door locks ($157). Remote-locking fuel filler door ($59). Garage door opener ($140). Illuminated entry system ($76), not on Brougham). Digital instrument cluster for Seville/Eldorado ($238). Dual comfort front seats for DeVille ($225). Memory driver's seat ($185, except Iimousine). Six-way power passenger seat for DeVille/Eldorado/Seville ($210). Power driver's seat recliner ($155, except Iimousine). Power passenger seat recliner for DeVille ($155). Power passenger seat recliner for Brougham ($90). Power passenger seat recliner with six-way power seat for DeVille/Eldorado ($365). Power passenger seat recliner with six-way power seat for Seville($300). Leather-trimmed steering wheel ($99). Tilt/telescope steering wheel ($179, but standard on formal Limousine). Power trunk lid release and pull-down for DeVille/Limousine ($120). Theft deterrent system ($185). Twilight Sentinel ($79). Guidematic headlight control ($93). Opera lights for DeVille/Eldorado ($88). Trumpet horn ($38, except

1983 Cadillac, Sedan DeVille

Seville). Electric remote mirrors with thermometer on left for Limousine ($99). Electric remote-control outside mirrors ($99, except Iimousine). Twin lighted vanity mirrors ($140). Electronic-tuning seek/scan AM/FM stereo radio with 8-track or cassette tape player ($299), with cassette and CB ($577) with cassette and Bose symphony sound system, Eldorado/Seville ($895). Electronic tuning radio with 8-track and rear control for Limousine ($475). Extended-range rear speakers ($25 with standard radio). Triband antenna ($50). Full padded vinyl roof for DeVille sedan ($280). Two-tone paint for Seville ($600). Two-tone paint for DeVille/Eldorado ($345). Firemist paint on DeVille/Eldorado ($465). Firemist paint ($235). Accent striping DeVille ($77). Bodyside molding for Eldorado Touring coupe ($64). Door edge guards ($19-$29). License frames, each ($14) except Seville. Leather seating area ($515-$680). Carpeted rubber floor mats front ($43-$45), rear ($25). Trunk mat ($21). Aluminum wheels for Eldorado/Seville ($429). Locking wire wheels for DeVille/Brougham ($860). Turbine-vaned wheel covers for DeVille ($77). Turbine-vaned wheel covers for Eldorado/Seville ($389). Locking wire wheel covers ($310-$389, except Limousine). White-letter tires for Eldorado touring coupe ($100). Puncture sealing tires ($135-$180). 5.7-liter diesel V-8 engine except Limousine. California emission equipment ($75), except diesel ($215). Engine block heater for Limousine, ($27). 100-amp alternator ($50). Electronic level control for DeVille/Brougham ($203). Heavy-duty ride package for DeVille/Brougham ($319). FE2 touring suspension for Eldorado/Seville ($115). Seville Elegante ($3,879). Brougham d'Elegance: cloth seating ($1,250), leather ($1,800). DeVille d'Elegance ($1,150). Cabriolet roof for DeVille/Eldorado coupe ($415). Full cabriolet roof for Eldorado/Seville ($995). Eldorado Biarritz ($3,395). Eldorado Touring Coupe ($1,975).

CIMARRON

Astroroof ($915). Vista Vent with rear tilt ($295). Cruise control, vacuum-type ($170). Power windows ($255). Power door locks ($170). Power trunk release ($40). Garage door opener ($165), retainer ($25). Tilt steering wheel ($99). Six-way power driver's seat ($210). Both seats with six-way power ($420). Twilight Sentinel ($79). Twin lighted vanity mirrors ($95). AM/FM stereo radio with cassette ($203). Delete radio ($151 credit). Power antenna ($55). Door edge guards ($25). License frame ($12). Deck lid luggage rack ($98). Carpeted rubber floor mats: front ($38), rear ($22). Trunk mat ($18). White sidewall tires ($55). California emission equipment ($75). Engine block

heater ($18). Heavy-duty battery ($25). H.D. radiator ($40). Three-speed automatic transmission ($320).

HISTORICAL

Introduced on September 23, 1982. Model-year production was 292,714 units, which came to 5.1 percent of the industry total. The total included 5,223 diesels. Calendar-year production: 309,811. Calendar-year sales by U.S. dealers was 300,337. Model-year sales by U.S. dealers was 290,138 for a 4.5 percent market share. Sales rose by over 22 percent for the 1983 model-year, suggesting that Cadillac's appeal to luxury-minded buyers hadn't waned. Cadillac General Manager Robert D. Burger told reporters the company was "confident about the future of the luxury car business" since research by 1982 suggested a "long-term fundamental shift toward luxury cars...that hold their value." Research also showed that Cadillac buyers were considerably older (median age about 60) than car buyers in general—a fact that could become a problem in future years. The popularity of the HT-4100 4.1-liter V-8 brought speculation that a transverse-mounted version would be planned for the 1984 Eldorado. Buyers liked them, so they were expected to remain in the lineup.

1983 Cadillac, Fleetwood Brougham sedan

1983 Cadillac, Fleetwood Eldorado Biarritz, coupe

1984

OVERVIEW

This was more a year of waiting than one of major changes. All Cadillac engines were now fuel injected. All models but the Cimarron and Fleetwood Limousine carried the HT-4100 (4.1-liter V-8 with aluminum alloy block and digital fuel injection). This year, that 249-cid engine gained a new exhaust system and catalytic converter, plus revised calibration settings, to meet high-altitude emissions standards. New features on DeVille, Fleetwood Brougham and Fleetwood Limousines included a goldtone horizontally-winged Cadillac crest ornament on the front parking and turn signal lenses, new car-colored bodyside moldings, a new goldtone vertically-winged Cadillac crest, gold tone accents on the taillight lenses and standard electronic level control. Diesel engine identification plaques were now placed on the left rear of the deck lid. Faster-warming glow plugs went into the optional 5.7-liter diesel V-8, for improved cold start ups. A modified optional theft-deterrent system could detect any object on the driver's seat that weighed 40 pounds or more.

Above: **1984 Cadillac, Cimarron sedan**
Phil Hall

I.D. DATA

The 17-symbol serial number was located on top of the instrument panel, where it was visible through the windshield. The first symbol 1=U.S.-built vehicle. The second symbol 2=General Motors. The third symbol 6=Cadillac Motor Division. The fourth symbol indicated type of restraint system A=manual belts. The fifth symbol identified the series as follows: F=Fleetwood Limousine, G=Cimarron, L=Eldorado, M=DeVille (rear-wheel drive), S=Seville, W=Fleetwood Brougham (rear-wheel drive). The sixth and seventh symbols indicated body style: 23=four-door Limousine with auxiliary seat, 33=four-door Limousine with center divider, 47=two-door Hardtop Coupe, 57=two-door Coupe, 67=two-door Convertible and 69=four-door pillared Sedan. The eighth symbol indicated the engine (See engine listings below). The ninth symbol was a check digit. The 10th symbol was a letter indicating model year: E=1984. The 11th symbol indicates the GM assembly plant: A=Lakewood, Ga., B=Baltimore, Md., D=Doraville, Ga., E=Linden, N.J., F=Flint, Mich., G=Framingham, Mass., H=Flint, Mich. (Buick), J=Janesville, Wis., K=Leeds, Mo., L=Van Nuys, Calif., M=Lansing, Mich., N= Norwood, Ohio, P=Pontiac, Mich., R=Arlington, Tex., S=St. Louis, Mo., T=Tarrytown, N.Y., U=Hamtrack, Mich., V=Pontiac, Mich. (GMC), W=Willow Run, Mich., X=Fairfax, Kan., Y=Wilmington,

Del., 1=Wentzville, Mo., 1=Oshawa, Ontario, Canada, 2=Moraine, Ohio, 2=Ste. Therese, Quebec, Canada, 3=Kawasaki, Japan, 3=Detroit (Chevrolet), Mich., 3=St. Eustache, Quebec, Canada, 4=Orion, Mich., 4=Scarborough, Ontario, Canada, 5=Bowling Green, Ken., 5=London, Ontario, Canada, 6=Oklahoma City, Okla., 7=Lordstown, Ohio, 8=Shreveport, La., 8=Fujisawa, Japan, 9=Detroit, Mich. (Cadillac) and 9=Oshawa No.1, Ontario, Canada. Note: Cadillacs were not built at all GM assembly plants. The next group of numbers was the sequential production code starting with 100001. The Fisher Body tag on the cowl, under the hood includes additional information.

CIMARRON—SERIES 6G—FOUR

Cimarron's new crosshatch grille had a bolder look, but kept the Cadillac script at its lower left-hand corner. The new front end was evidently designed with a V-6 in mind, though none was offered, yet. The fuel-injected 2.0-liter four remained standard. It could be had with a five-speed manual gear box or an optional three-speed automatic transmission. Three new stripe insert colors (white, red, orange) were offered for the bumper rub strips, end caps and bodyside moldings and gold striping was used with the Cimarron d'Oro option. The fog lights introduced in 1983 continued as standard equipment. A new rear-end lighting arrangement used horizontal upper red stop and taillights accented with flush-mounted winged Cadillac crest ornaments. New amber turn signal lights and more dominant white back-up lights sat below the red tail and stop lights. Interiors were now available in combinations of leather and cloth. The push-button heating and ventilation controls now had accent lights. A 24-position click-stop temperature control lever allowed more precise settings. Optional cruise control now included acceleration/deceleration capabilities. The special edition Cimarron d'Oro, introduced during 1983, was available again with distinctive Sable Black body finish. Gold tone accents replaced all the body chrome. In an effort to attract younger motorists to the Black-and-Gold version of the small Cadillac, radio commercials played an upbeat jingle promoting the "Cimarron touch."

CIMARRON - SERIES G - FOUR

Model Number	Body/Style No.	Body Type & Seating	Factory Price	Shipping Weight	Production Total
G	69	4D Sedan-5P	12,614	2,639	21,898

SEVILLE—SERIES 6S—V-8

Restyled taillights and new body-colored side moldings gave the bustleback front-wheel-drive Seville a slightly different look for 1984. Its horizontal taillights were modified to include a clear outer lens and a red inner lens. This year's grille had fine vertical accents and a bright "Cadillac" script nameplate in the lower left corner. The traditional Cadillac stand-up wreath-and-crest hood ornament stood on a tapered hood center molding. The Seville had new low-gloss black finished door trim bezels, instrument panel bezels and air conditioning outlets. New tufted multi-button cloth or leather-and-vinyl trim were the upholstery choices for base models. New options included aluminum alloy wheels with center hubcaps and exposed chrome lug nuts. A Delco/Bose stereo was again available and other sound systems were improved. The Seville's lengthy standard equipment included a manual seat back recliner, overhead assist handles, door-pull straps, four-wheel power disc brakes, air conditioning, power windows, bumper guards, rub strips and P205/75R15 steel-belted radial whitewall tires. The limited-edition Elegante could be ordered in a single color instead of only two-tone combinations. The $3,879 package included a leather-trimmed steering wheel, leather 40/40 Dual Comfort front seats, six-way power seat adjustment with recliners, chrome side moldings, wire wheel covers and deluxe floor mats.

SEVILLE – SERIES S - V-8

Model Number	Body/Style No.	Body Type & Seating	Factory Price	Shipping Weight	Production Total
S	69	4D Sedan-6P	22,468	3,844	39,997

DEVILLE—SERIES 6M—V-8

New front-wheel-drive versions of the DeVille were anticipated, but their introduction was delayed because of quality-control questions. As a result, the rear-drive Coupe and Sedan returned in 1984. Body side moldings were now color-keyed to the body finish. The taillight lenses held goldtone Cadillac wing crests. All DeVille models now had electronic level control. The standard fuel injected 249-cid (4.1-liter) V-8 engine fed into a revised exhaust system with a monolithic catalytic converter. The electronic controls were modified to meet stricter emissions standards in high-altitude regions. The diesel V-8 remained on the options list, except in California because of that state's more stringent emissions regulations. Standard equipment included power brakes, power steering, electronic level control, automatic climate-control air conditioning, a signal-seeking stereo radio with a power antenna, power windows, a six-way power seat, a remote-control left-hand outside rearview mirror, a right-hand visor-vanity mirror, and a stowaway spare tire. The all-new front-wheel-drive DeVille made its first appearance during the 1984 model year, but was considered an early 1985 model.

DEVILLE—SERIES M-V-8

Model Number	Body/Style No.	Body Type & Seating	Factory Price	Shipping Weight	Production Total
M	47	2D Coupe-6P	17,140	3,935	Note 1
M	69	4D Sedan-6P	17,625	3,993	Note 1

Note 1: The production totals for DeVilles and Fleetwood Broughams were combined. See notes 2 and 3 below.

FLEETWOOD BROUGHAM—SERIES 6W—V-8

New front-wheel-drive versions of the Fleetwood Brougham were also anticipated, but didn't arrive due to quality-control questions. As a result, the rear-drive Coupe and Sedan returned in 1984. Fleetwood Brougham sedans had a more closed-in back window, plus bright belt and hood moldings, large rocker moldings and wheel covers that were also used on Limousines. Electro-luminescent opera lights were standard. The coupe had a stylish roof with a custom Cabriolet vinyl top enclosing a distinctive rear quarter window. Standard equipment was the same as on the DeVille coupe, plus four-wheel power disc brakes, a remote-control right-hand rearview mirror and 45/55 dual-comfort front seats.

FLEETWOOD BROUGHAM — SERIES W - V-8

Model Number	Body/Style No.	Body Type & Seating	Factory Price	Shipping Weight	Production Total
W	47	2D Coupe-6P	19,942	3,986	Note 2
W	69	4D Sedan-6P	20,451	4,029	Note 3

Note 2: Combined production of DeVille and Fleetwood Brougham Coupes was 50,840.
Note 3: Combined production of DeVille and Fleetwood Brougham Sedans was 107,920.

FLEETWOOD LIMOUSINE—SERIES 6F—V-8

Limousines carried the same standard equipment as DeVille, plus accent striping, opera lights and HR78 x 15-D tires. Only the formal Limousine had the six-way power seat. Fleetwood Limousines still used the variable-displacement 6.0-liter V-8-6-4 engine.

FLEETWOOD LIMOUSINE — SERIES F - V-8

Model Number	Body/Style No.	Body Type & Seating	Factory Price	Shipping Weight	Production Total
F	23	4D Sedan-8P	30,454	4,765	Note 4
F	33	4D Fml Limousine-7P	31,512	4,852	Note 4

Note 4: Total limousine production, 1,839.

ELDORADO—SERIES 6L—V-8

For the first time since the famed 1976 Eldorado ragtop, Cadillac offered a convertible, the posh new Biarritz. Its rear side windows raised and lowered automatically with the power top and it contained a glass back window. Reinforced frame rails and crossmember braces and a bolstered body structure added the necessary strength and rigidity to support a roofless body. Convertibles had specific wide bright door and fender accent moldings, deck lid accent striping, a "Biarritz" script nameplate and wire wheel covers. Also standard were a special Biarritz multi-button tufted seat design, a leather-wrapped steering wheel rim and Cadillac's theft deterrent system. The revived Biarritz Convertible carried a hefty opening

price tag: $31,286. That was nearly triple the cost of a 1976 Eldorado ragtop when it was new. Eldorado Coupes started at a more modest $20,342. The Eldorado's grille this year was vertically accented with a bright "Cadillac" script nameplate in the lower left corner. Rectangular headlights sat above clear park/signal lights. Appearance changes included new car-colored bodyside moldings, plus new low-gloss Black finish on the door trim bezels, instrument panel bezels and air conditioning outlets. Base Eldorados had a new leather seat trim design. Other additions included an improved theft prevention system, new dashboard bezels, suspension refinements, improved stereo performance and a new glow-plug system in the optional diesel V-8 engine. Coupes had a Cabriolet vinyl top with glass rear window, brushed stainless steel roof cover and opera lights. Extended-range rear speakers became standard, except on the Delco/Bose sound system.

Eldorado—Series L—V-8

Model Number	Body Style No.	Body Type & Seating	Factory Price	Shipping Weight	Production Total
L	57	2D Coupe-6P	20,342	3,748	74,506
L	67	2D Convertible-6P	31,286	3,300	—

ENGINE

CIMARRON BASE FOUR

Inline. OHV. Four-cylinder. Cast-iron block and head. Displacement:121-cid (2.0-liters). Bore & stroke: 3.50 x 3.15 inches. Compression ratio: 9.3:1. Brake horsepower: 88 at 4800 rpm. Torque: 110 lb.-ft. at 2400 rpm. Five main bearings. Hydraulic valve lifters. Throttle-body fuel injection. VIN Code: P.

SEVILLE, DEVILLE, FLEETWOOD BROUGHAM, ELDORADO--BASE V-8

Overhead valve. Aluminum block with cast iron liners. Displacement: 249 cid (4.1 liters). Bore and Stroke: 3.47 x 3.31 inches. Compression ratio: 8.5:1. Net brake hp: 135 at 4400 rpm. Taxable hp: 39.2. Net torque: 200 at 2000 rpm. Five main bearings. Hydraulic valve lifters. Induction: Digital fuel injection. VIN Code: 8. Built by Cadillac.

1984 Cadillac, Coupe DeVille

SEVILLE, DEVILLE, FLEETWOOD BROUGHAM, ELDORADO--OPTIONAL DIESEL V-8

Overhead valve. Cast-iron block . Displacement: 350 cid (5.7 liters). Bore and Stroke: 4.057 x 3.385 inches. Compression ratio: 22.5:1. Net brake hp: 105 at 3200 rpm. Taxable hp: 52.6. Net torque: 200 at 1600 rpm. Five main bearings. Hydraulic valve lifters. Induction: Electronic fuel injection. VIN Code: N. Built by Oldsmobile.

FLEETWOOD LIMOUSINE, FLEETWOOD COMMERCIAL CHASSIS BASE V-8-6-4

Overhead valve. Cast-iron block. Displacement: 368 cid (6.0 liters). Bore and Stroke: 3.80 x 4.06 inches. Compression ratio: 8.2:1. Net brake hp: 140 at 3800 rpm. Taxable hp: 46.20. Net torque: 200 at 1400 rpm. Five main bearings. Hydraulic valve lifters. Induction: Digital fuel injection. VIN Code: 9. Built by Cadillac.

CHASSIS

(Cimarron) Wheelbase: 101.2 inches. Overall length: 173.1 inches. Overall width: 65.0 inches. Overall height: 52.0 inches. Front tread: 55.4 inches. Rear tread: 55.2 inches. Tires: P19570R13 steel-belted radial with wide white sidewall.

(Seville) Wheelbase: 114.0 inches. Overall length: 204.8 inches. Overall width: 70.9 inches. Overall height: 54.3 inches. Front tread: 59.3 inches. Rear tread: 60.6 inches. Tires: P20575R15 steel-belted radial with wide white sidewall.

(Eldorado) Wheelbase: 114.0 inches. Overall length: 204.5 inches. Overall width: 70.6 inches. Overall height: 54.3 inches. Front tread: 59.3 inches. Rear tread: 60.6 inches. Tires: P20575R15 steel-belted radial with wide white sidewall.

(DeVille) Wheelbase: 121.5 inches. Overall length: 221.0 inches. Overall width: 75.3-75.4 inches. Overall height: 54.6-55.6 inches. Front tread: 61.7 inches. Rear tread: 60.7 inches. Tires: P21575R15 steel-belted radial with wide white sidewall.

(Brougham) Wheelbase: 121.5 inches. Overall length: 221.0 inches. Overall width: 75.3-75.4 inches. Overall height: 54.6-55.6 inches. Front tread: 61.7 inches. Rear tread: 60.7 inches. Tires: P21575R15 steel-belted radial with wide white sidewall.

(Fleetwood 75) Wheelbase: 144.5 inches. Overall length: 244.3 inches. Overall width: 75.3 inches. Overall height: 56.9 inches. Front tread: 61.7 inches. Rear tread: 60.7 inches. Tires: HR7815-D steel-belted radial with wide white sidewall.

TECHNICAL

Transmission: Five-speed, floor shift manual transmission standard on Cimarron, Turbo-Hydra-Matic optional, gear ratios same as 1983. Three-speed automatic standard on Limousine, four-speed overdrive automatic on others, ratios same as 1983. Standard final drive ratio: (Cimarron) 3.83:1 with 5-spd, 3.18:1 with automatic transmission, (Seville/Eldorado) 3.15:1 except with diesel, 2.93:1, (DeVille/Brougham) 3.42:1 except with diesel, 2.93:1. Steering: (Cimarron) power rack and pinion, (others) power recirculating ball. Suspension and brakes, same as 1983. Fuel tank: (Cimarron) 13.6 gallons, (Seville/Eldorado) 20.3 gallons except with diesel, 22.8, (DeVille/Brougham) 24.5 gallons except with diesel, 26.0.

OPTIONS

DEVILLE / FLEETWOOD BROUGHAM / LIMOUSINE / ELDORADO / SEVILLE

Astroroof ($1,225, but not available on Limousine). Electronic cruise control ($185). Controlled-cycle wiper system for DeVille/Limousine ($60). Rear defogger with heated outside mirrors ($165-$215). Automatic door locks ($162). Remote-locking fuel filler door ($59). Garage door opener ($140, except convertible). Illuminated entry system ($76, but standard on Brougham). Digital instrument cluster for Seville/Eldorado ($238). Dual comfort front seats for DeVille ($225). Memory driver's seat ($205, except standard in Limousine and convertible). Six-way power passenger seat for DeVille/Eldorado/Seville ($215-$225). Power driver's seat recliner ($155, except standard in Limousine). Power passenger seat recliner for DeVille ($155). Power passenger seat recliner for Brougham ($90). Power passenger seat recliner with six-way power seat for DeVille/Eldorado/Seville($315-$380). Leather-trimmed steering wheel ($99). Tilt/telescope steering wheel ($184, but standard on formal Limousine). Power trunk lid release and pull-down for DeVille/Limousine ($120). Theft deterrent system ($190). Twilight Sentinel ($79). Guidematic headlight control ($93). Opera lights for DeVille/Eldorado ($88). Trumpet horn ($38, except Seville). Electric remote mirrors with thermometer on left for Limousine ($101). Electric remote-control outside mirrors ($101, except Limousine). Twin lighted vanity mirrors ($140). Electronic-tuning seek/scan AM/FM stereo radio with clock and cassette player ($299). Electronic-tuning seek/scan AM/FM stereo radio with clock, cassette and CB ($577, except in Eldorado and Seville). Electronic-tuning seek/scan AM/FM stereo radio with clock, cassette, CB and Delco-GM/Bose sound system in Eldorado and Seville ($895). CB radio for Eldorado/Seville ($278). Rear-control ET radio with cassette for Limousine ($475). Triband antenna ($50). Full padded vinyl roof for DeVille sedan ($285). Two-tone paint for Seville ($600).

Two-tone paint for DeVille/Eldorado ($345). Firemist paint for DeVille/Eldorado ($465). Firemist paint ($235). Accent striping for DeVille ($77). Bodyside molding for Eldorado Touring coupe ($64). Door edge guards ($19-$29). License frames, each ($14). Leather seating area ($515-$680). Carpeted rubber floor mats for front ($43-$45), for rear ($25). Trunk mat ($21). Aluminum wheels for Eldorado/Seville($429). Locking wire wheels for DeVille/Brougham ($860). Turbine-vaned wheel covers for DeVille ($77). Locking wire wheel covers ($315-$394, except Limousine). White-letter tires for Eldorado touring coupe ($100). Puncture-sealing tires ($135-$180, except Limousine). 5.7-liter diesel V-8 engine (NC), except not available in Limousine. California emission equipment ($99). Engine block heater ($18-$45). Heavy-duty battery ($40). 100-amp alternator ($50). Limited slip differential for Limousine ($120). Heavy-duty ride package for DeVille/Brougham ($319). FE2 touring suspension for Eldorado/Seville($115). Seville Elegante ($3,879). Brougham d'Elegance cloth seating ($1,250), leather ($1,800). DeVille d'Elegance ($1,150). Cabriolet roof for DeVille/Eldorado coupe ($420). Full cabriolet roof for Eldorado/Seville ($995). Eldorado Biarritz ($3,395). Eldorado Touring Coupe ($1,975).

CIMARRON

Vista Vent with rear tilt ($300). Electronic cruise control ($175). Power windows ($260). Power door locks ($175). Power trunk release ($40). Garage door opener ($165), retainer ($25). Tilt steering wheel ($104). Six-way power driver's seat ($215), both seats ($430). Twilight Sentinel ($79). Twin lighted vanity mirrors ($95). Seek/scan AM/FM stereo radio with cassette ($203). Delete radio ($151 credit). Power antenna ($60). Door edge guards ($25). License frame ($12). Decklid luggage rack ($100). Cloth upholstery ($100 credit). Carpeted rubber floor mats for front ($38), rear ($22). Trunk mat ($18). Whitewall

tires ($55). California emission equipment ($99). Engine block heater ($18-$45). Heavy-duty battery ($26). H.D. radiator ($40). Three-speed automatic transmission ($320). Cimarron d'Oro ($350).

HISTORICAL

Introduced September 22, 1983. Model-year production was 300,300 (not including early 1985 DeVille/Fleetwoods). The total includes 2,465 diesels. Calendar-year production was 328,534. Calendar-year sales by U.S. dealers was 320,017 for a 4.0 percent market share. Model-year sales by U.S. dealers was 327,587 (including 46,356 early '85 front-drives). Sales rose 13 percent for the model-year, but Cadillac's market share declined. Figures are a bit distorted, since both front- and rear-drive DeVille and Fleetwood Brougham models were sold at the same time. All GM divisions experienced a drop in market share. Rising demand, though, kept plants working overtime during 1984. The Cimarron continued to be Cadillac's weakest seller. Best performers in terms of increased sales were the big Cadillacs: DeVille and Fleetwood Brougham. Research indicated that over three-fourths of Cimarron buyers had never bought a Cadillac before and that many of them had previously owned an import. Late in 1983, a modern new plant at Orion Township in Michigan started producing the new front-wheel-drive DeVille, which was scheduled to be introduced in 1985. Also, Cadillac became part of General Motor's new Buick-Oldsmobile-Cadillac group. Cadillac's new Eldorado convertible was actually a conversion done by ASC Corp. in Lansing, Michigan, after the car was assembled as a coupe in New Jersey. The work included reinforcing the inner rocker panels and radiator support cross rods and adding many body braces. Front and rear anti-roll bars and tougher suspension components were also added. All told, the convertible weighed 179 pounds more than the coupe from which it evolved.

1984 Cadillac, Fleetwood Brougham d'Elegance, sedan

Phil Hall

1984 Cadillac, Sedan De Ville

Phil Hall

1985

OVERVIEW

Front-wheel drive now became the rule at Cadillac, as in nearly all other makes. Two grand old names, DeVille and Fleetwood, made the switch this year. All Cadillacs except the subcompact Cimarron (and carryover rear-wheel-drive Fleetwood Brougham) now carried a transverse-mounted, fuel-injected 4.1-liter V-8 engine with a die-cast aluminum engine block. Two safety improvements arrived this year: anti-lacerative windshield glass (with inner layer of two-part plastic) on Seville's Elegante, plus a high-mount stop light on all DeVilles and Fleetwoods. That stop light would become required on all cars for 1986.

I.D. DATA

The 17-symbol serial number was located on top of the instrument panel, where it was visible through the windshield. The numbering system changed this year. The first symbol 1=U.S.-built vehicle. The second symbol G=General Motors. The third symbol 6=Cadillac. The fourth symbol indicated carline/the fifth symbol indicated series as follows: C/B= front-wheel-drive Fleetwood, C/D=front-wheel-drive DeVille, C/H=front-wheel-drive Fleetwood Limousine, D/W=rear-wheel-drive Fleetwood Brougham, E/L=Eldorado, J/G=Cimarron and K/S=Seville. The sixth

Above: **1985 Cadillac, Fleetwood Eldorado Biarritz convertible**
Socrates Gregoriadis

and seventh symbols indicated body stytle and restraint system: 23=four-door six-window sedan with auxiliary seat (Limousine), 33=four-door six-window sedan with auxiliary seat and partition window(Limousine). 47=two-door notchback special Coupe, 57=two-door notchback special Coupe, 67=two-door convertible, 69=four-door four-window notchback sedan. The eighth symbol identified the engine (See engine listings below). The ninth symbol was a check digit. The 10th symbol was a number indicating model year: F=1985. The 11th symbol indicates the GM assembly plant: A=Lakewood, Ga., B=Baltimore, Md., D=Doraville, Ga., E=Linden, N.J., F=Flint, Mich., G=Framingham, Mass., H=Flint, Mich. (Buick), J=Janesville, Wis., K=Leeds, Mo., L=Van Nuys, Calif., M=Lansing, Mich., N= Norwood, Ohio, P=Pontiac, Mich., R=Arlington, Texas, S=St. Louis, Mo., T=Tarrytown, N.Y., U=Hamtrack, Mich., V=Pontiac, Mich. (GMC), W=Willow Run, Mich., X=Fairfax, Kan., Y=Wilmington, Dela., 1=Wentzville, Mo., 1=Oshawa, Ontario, Canada, 2=Moraine, Ohio, 2=Ste. Therese, Canada, 3=Kawasaki, Japan, 3=Detroit (Chevrolet), Mich., 3=St. Eustach, PQ, 4=Orion, Mich., 4=Scarborough, Ontario, Canada, 5=Bowling Green, Ken., 5=London, Ontario, Canada, 6=Oklahoma City, Okla., 7=Lordstown, Ohio, 8=Shreveport, La., 8=Fujisawa, Japan, 9=Detroit, Mich. (Cadillac) and 9=Oshawa No.1, Ontario, Canada.

Note: Cadillacs were not built at all GM assembly plants. The next group of numbers was the sequential production code starting with 100001. The Fisher Body tag on the cowl, under the hood includes additional information.

CIMARRON—SERIES 6J/G—FOUR

Cadillac's compact received a major revision for 1985, but went on sale a little later than usual. Production of the 1984 models was extended into autumn 1985 to take advantage of the existing Corporate Average Fuel Economy standards, which were to grow more stringent for the coming year. An optional V-6 engine finally arrived for midyear models and delivered a much-needed performance boost. The new 173-cid (2.8-liter) high-output V-6 with fuel injection was built by Chevrolet. Cimarron sales continued sluggish, but style and performance alterations were made to try to draw some younger customers. Prices began just under $13,000, well under other Cadillac prices, but a good deal higher than Chevrolet's Cavalier and the other J-bodied GM models. The stabilizer bars grew longer this year and the front springs became stiffer. Outside, the Cimarron's front end grew by almost five inches. Styled aluminum wheels were available for the first time, as an option. The standard transmission was a five-speed manual gear box. A three-speed automatic transmission or four-speed manual gearbox was optional. Standard equipment included air conditioning, an AM/FM stereo radio with power antenna, power brakes and steering, power door locks, halogen headlights and foglights), a leather-wrapped tilt steering wheel, tachometer, power windows and power trunk release. All that and more helped to justify Cimarron's hefty price tag. Cimarron d'Oro added fine-line gold accent stripes on beltline, hood center and rub strips, gold accented grille and wheels, foglight covers, lower bodyside accent moldings, saddle leather seats, plus gold-tinted hood ornament, steering wheel spokes and horn pad emblem. d'Oro bodies were either red or white, with plaques on front fender and dash.

CIMARRON —SERIES J/G—FOUR

Model Number	Body/Style No.	Body Type & Seating	Factory Price	Shipping Weight	Production Total
6J/G	69	4D Sedan-5P	12,962	2,630	Note 1

CIMARRON — SERIES J/G — V-6

Model Number	Body/Style No.	Body Type & Seating	Factory Price	Shipping Weight	Production Total
6J/G	69	4D Sedan-5P	13,522	----	Note 1

Note 1: Cimarron production was 19,890.

SEVILLE—SERIES 6K/S—V-8

For its final season in this form, the current front-drive Seville sedan changed little. The standard engine remained the fuel-injected 250-cid (4.1-liter) V-8 with a four-speed overdrive automatic transmission. Buyers could also choose a diesel V-8, but not many did. New to the options list were aluminum alloy wheels with a radial fin design and gray accents. Both spoke and non-spoke versions were available. The Seville Elegante had a new "Inner Shield" windshield with a two-section plastic layer intended to prevent cuts from splintered glass in an accident. The Elegante interior featured standard leather seats that were color-coordinated with the car body color. Late in the model-year, a Commemorative Edition package was announced.

SEVILLE—SERIES K/S-V-8

Model Number	Body/Style No.	Body Type & Seating	Factory Price	Shipping Weight	Production Total
6K/S	69	4D Sedan-6P	23,729	3,688	39,755

DEVILLE—SERIES 6C/D—V-8

A dramatically different front-wheel-drive C-body Coupe DeVille hit the market late in March of 1984. It was considered to be an early 1985 models. The Grand Old Cadillacs lost two feet in length and about 600 pounds of weight. Their front-wheel-drive chassis layout was also used by Buick Electra and Oldsmobile Ninety-Eight. Though not exactly small, both were a far cry from the DeVilles and Fleetwoods of prior eras. Arriving in the fall was a new Fleetwood coupe with a formal Cabriolet vinyl roof and opera lights, as well as wire wheel covers. Both Coupe and Sedan models held up to six passengers. A transverse-mounted 249-cid (4.1-liter) V-8 engine with throttle-body fuel injection was standard, 4.3-liter V-6 diesel a no-charge option. Cadillac's was the only transverse-mounted V-8 available in the world. Oldsmobile's diesel V-8 engine also was available. Inside the automatic transmission, the torque converter clutch was computer-controlled and operated by silicone fluid. All models included the Retained Power Accessory System, which permitted use of power windows and trunk release for 10 minutes after shutting off the engine. A third brake light was now mounted on the rear panel shelf.

DEVILLE (FRONT-WHEEL-DRIVE)—SERIES C/D-V-8

Model Number	Body/Style No.	Body Type & Seating	Factory Price	Shipping Weight	Production Total
6C/D	47	2D Coupe-6P	18,355	3,330	Note 2
6C/D	69	4D Sedan-6P	18,947	3,327	Note 2

Note 2: The production totals for DeVilles and Fleetwoods were combined. See notes 3 and 4 below.

1985 Cadillac, Coupe DeVille

FLEETWOOD—SERIES 6C/B—V-8

Fleetwood coupes and sedans carried the same standard equipment as the DeVilles, along with wire wheel covers, opera lights, Dual Comfort front seats and a limousine-style back window. Powertrains were the same as DeVille's. This was the final year for Fleetwood as a separate model. In 1986, it would become a DeVille option package.

FLEETWOOD
(FRONT-WHEEL-DRIVE)
– SERIES C/B - V-8

Model Number	Body/Style No.	Body Type & Seating	Factory Price	Shipping Weight	Production Total
6C/B	47	2D Coupe-6P	21,495	3,267	Note 3
6C/B	69	4D Sedan-6P	21,466	3,364	Note 4

Note 3: Combined production of DeVille and Fleetwood Brougham Coupes was 37,485.
Note 4: Total DeVille/Fleetwood four-door sedan production, 114,278.

For the model-year, 42,911 Fleetwoods and 108,852 DeVilles were produced.

These figures do not include 45,330 DeVille/Fleetwood produced as early 1985 models (9,390 two-doors and 35,940 four-doors).

FLEETWOOD SEVENTY-FIVE LIMOUSINE— SERIES 6C/H—V-8

Like the Fleetwood sedan, the Seventy-Five Limousine switched to front-wheel drive. The rear-wheel drive version was dropped. To create the new limousine, a C-car platform (same as DeVille/Fleetwood) and Coupe body were stretched almost two feet. Even so, the modern edition was more than two feet shorter than the old rear-wheel drive version and weighed 1,200 pounds less. The power train was the same as used in the DeVille/Fleetwood: a transverse-mounted 4.1-liter V-8 and four-speed overdrive automatic. The rear control panels let

1985 Cadillac, Fleetwood Eldorado coupe

passengers unlock the back doors and adjust the climate and control and stereo. The basic Limousine still carried eight passengers. A seven-passenger formal version appeared later in the model year. Fleetwood Seventy-Five limousines had power-operated mirrors, but other standard equipment was similar to that of Fleetwood sedans. Aluminum alloy wheels were made standard on Limousines.

FLEETWOOD LIMOUSINE – SERIES C/H -V-8

Model Number	Body/Style No.	Body Type & Seating	Factory Price	Shipping Weight	Production Total
6C/H	23	4D Limousine-8P	32,640	3,543	Note 5
6C/H	33	4D Fml Limousine-7P	NA	3,642	Note 5

Note 5: Total limousine production was 405 units.

FLEETWOOD BROUGHAM—SERIES 6D/W—V-8

The Brougham was the last surviving rear-wheel-drive Cadillac. It was changed little for 1985 and faced potential extinction, in spite of the fact that its sales were increasing. (In the end, this traditional rear-wheel-drive car lingered on for several more years while other Cadillacs, including Limousines, went to front-wheel drive and shrunk). Large on the inside and outside, the Fleetwood Brougham continued to attract traditional luxury-car buyers. The Brougham Coupe was dropped from the lineup in midyear. Sedans came with a standard full vinyl roof, while the Brougham Coupe included a standard Cabriolet vinyl top with unique rear quarter window. The standard engine was the 4.1-liter V-8, diesel V-8 optional at no charge.

FLEETWOOD BROUGHAM (REAR-DRIVE)—SERIES D/W-V-8

Model Number	Body/Style No.	Body Type & Seating	Factory Price	Shipping Weight	Production Total
6D/W	47	2D Coupe-6P	21,219	3,873	8,336
6D/W	69	4D Sedan-6P	21,835	3,915	52,960

ELDORADO—SERIES 6E/L—V-8

Few changes were evident on the luxury front-wheel-drive personal Coupe and Convertible. The Biarritz Convertible, introduced for 1984, could now get an optional electric defogger for its glass back window. New spoked aluminum alloy road wheels joined the option list. The standard engine remained the 4.1-liter V-8 with throttle-body fuel injection. It was hooked to a four-speed overdrive automatic transmission. A big diesel V-8 also was available (at extra cost) in the Coupe. The Eldorado Biarritz Coupe had a Cabriolet vinyl roof with a brushed steel cap, accent moldings and opera lights. Eldorado Convertibles were similarly decked out. Eldorados with the Touring Coupe package had a stiffer suspension, as well as black-out and body-color trim. This would be the ragtop's final season, since the Eldorado was slated to switch to a new body for 1986.

ELDORADO—SERIES E/L--V-8

Model Number	Body/Style No.	Body Type & Seating	Factory Price	Shipping Weight	Production Total
6E/L	57	2D Coupe-6P	21,355	3,623	74,101
6E/L	67	2D Convertible-6P	32,105	3,804	2,300

ENGINE

CIMARRON BASE FOUR

Inline. Overhead valve. Four-cylinder. Cast iron block and head. Displacement: 121-cid (2.0-liters). Bore & stroke: 3.50 x 3.15 inches. Compression ratio: 9.3:1. Brake horsepower: 88 at 4800 rpm. Torque: 110 lb.-ft. at 2400 rpm. Five main bearings. Hydraulic valve lifters. Fuel injection. VIN Code P.

CIMARRON OPTIONAL V-6

Overhead-valve V-6. Cast iron block and head. Displacement: 173-cid (2.8-liters). Bore & stroke: 3.50 x 2.99 inches. Compression ratio: 8.9:1. Brake horsepower: 125 at 4800 rpm. Torque: 155 lb.-ft. at 3600 rpm. Four main bearings. Hydraulic valve lifters. Multi-point fuel injection. VIN code: W. Chevrolet-built.

DEVILLE, FLEETWOOD OPTIONAL DIESEL V-6

Overhead valve V-8. Cast iron block and head. Displacement: 262-cid (4.3-liters). Bore & stroke: 4.06 x 3.39 inches. Compression ratio: 21.6:1. Brake horsepower: 85 at 3600 rpm. Torque: 165 lb.-ft. at 1600 rpm. Four main bearings. Hydraulic valve lifters. Fuel injection. VIN code: T.

SEVILLE, BROUGHAM, ELDORADO BASE V-8

Overhead valve. Alumnium block with cast iron liners. Displacement: 249 cid (4.1 liters). Bore and Stroke: 3.47 x 3.31 inches. Compression ratio: 8.5:1. Net brake hp: 135 at 4400 rpm. Taxable hp: 39.2. Net torque: 200 at 2200 rpm. Five main bearings. Hydraulic valve lifters. Induction: Digital fuel injection. VIN Code: 8. Built by Cadillac.

DEVILLE, FLEETWOOD BASE V-8

Overhead valve. Alumnium block with cast iron liners. Displacement: 249 cid (4.1 liters). Bore and Stroke: 3.47 x 3.31 inches. Compression ratio: 8.5:1. Net brake hp: 125 at 4200 rpm. Taxable hp: 39.2. Net torque: 190 at 2200 rpm. Five main bearings. Hydraulic valve lifters. Induction: Digital fuel injection. VIN Code: 8. Built by Cadillac.

SEVILLE, DEVILLE, BROUGHAM, ELDORADO OPTIONAL DIESEL V-8

Overhead valve. Cast iron block. Displacement: 350 cid (5.7 liters). Bore and Stroke: 4.057 x 3.385 inches. Compression ratio: 22.7:1. Net brake hp: 105 at 3200 rpm. Taxable hp: 52.6. Net torque: 200 at 1600 rpm. Five main bearings. Hydraulic valve lifters. Induction: Electronic fuel injection. VIN Code: N. Built by Oldsmobile.

CHASSIS

(Cimarron) Wheelbase: 101.2 inches. Overall length: 173.9 inches. Overall width: 65.1 inches. Overall height: 52.0 inches. Front tread: 55.4 inches. Rear tread: 55.2 inches. Tires: P19570R13 steel-belted radial with wide white sidewall.

(Seville) Wheelbase: 114.0 inches. Overall length: 204.8 inches. Overall width: 70.9 inches. Overall height: 54.3 inches. Front tread: 59.3 inches. Rear tread: 60.6 inches. Tires: P20575R14 steel-belted radial with wide white sidewall.

(Eldorado) Wheelbase: 114.0 inches. Overall length: 204.5 inches. Overall width: 70.6 inches. Overall height: 54.3 inches. Front tread: 59.3 inches. Rear tread: 60.6 inches. Tires: P20575R14 steel-belted radial with wide white sidewall.

(DeVille) Wheelbase: 110.8 inches. Overall length: 195.0 inches. Overall width: 71.7 inches. Overall height: 55.0 inches. Front tread: 61.7 inches. Rear tread: 59.8 inches. Tires: P20575R14 steel-belted radial with wide white sidewall.

(Fleetwood) Wheelbase: 110.8 inches. Overall length: 195.0 inches. Overall width: 71.7 inches. Overall height: 55.0 inches. Front tread: 61.7 inches. Rear tread: 59.8 inches. Tires: P20575R14 steel-belted radial with wide white sidewall.

(Brougham) Wheelbase: 121.5 inches. Overall length: 221.0 inches. Overall width: 76.6 inches. Overall height: 54.6 inches. Front tread: 61.7 inches. Rear tread: 60.7 inches. Tires: P21575R15 steel-belted radial with wide white sidewall.

(Fleetwood 75) Wheelbase: 134.4 inches. Overall length: 218.6 inches. Overall width: 75.3 inches. Overall height: 55.0 inches. Front tread: 61.7 inches. Rear tread: 60.7 inches. Tires: HR7815-D steel-belted radial with wide white sidewall.

TECHNICAL

Transmission: Five-speed, floor shift manual transmission standard on Cimarron four: gear ratios: (1st) 3.92:1, (2nd) 2.15:1, (3rd) 1.33:1, (4th) 0.92:1, (5th) 0.74:1, (Reverse) 3.50:1. Four-speed manual transmission standard on Cimarron V-6: (1st) 3.31:1, (2nd) 1.95:1, (3rd) 1.95:1, (4th) 0.90:1, (Reverse) 3.42:1. Cimarron three-speed Turbo-Hydra-Matic (THM125C) ratios: (1st) 2.84:1,

(2nd) 1.60:1, (3rd) 1:1, (Reverse) 2.07:1. Four-speed overdrive automatic transmission (THM440-T4) standard on DeVille/Fleetwood: (1st) 2.92:1, (2nd) 1.57:1, (3rd) 1:1, (4th) 0.67:1, (Reverse) 2.38:1. Four-speed overdrive automatic transmission standard on Eldorado/Seville(THM325-4L) and Brougham (THM200-4R): (1st) 2.74:1, (2nd) 1.57:1, (3rd) 1:1, (4th) 0.67:1, (Reverse) 2.07:1. Standard final drive ratio: (Cimarron) 3.83:1 with five-speed, 3.18:1 with automatic transmission, (Seville/Eldorado) 3.15:1 except with diesel, 2.93:1, (DeVille/Fleetwood) 2.97:1 except with diesel, 3.06:1, (Brougham) 3.42:1 except diesel, 2.93:1, (Limousine) 2.97:1. Steering: (Cimarron/ DeVille/ Fleetwood) rack-and-pinion, (others) recirculating ball. Front suspension: (Cimarron) Touring, with MacPherson struts, (DeVille/Fleetwood) MacPherson struts, lower control arms, coil springs and stabilizer bar, (Eldorado/Seville) torsion bars, upper/lower control arms, stabilizer bar, (Brougham) upper/lower control arms, coil springs, stabilizer bar. Rear suspension: (Cimarron) semi- independent, trailing arms, coil springs, stabilizer bar, (DeVille/Fleetwood) independent struts, coil springs, stabilizer bar, electronic level control, (Eldorado/Seville) independent with semi-trailing arms, coil springs, stabilizer bar and electronic level control, (Brougham) four-link rigid axle, coil springs, electronic level control. Brakes: front disc, rear drum except Eldorado/Seville has four-wheel discs. Disc diameter: (Eldorado/Seville) 10.4 inches, (DeVille/Fleetwood) 10.25 inches, (Brougham) 11.7 inches. Drum diameter: (DeVille/Fleetwood) 8.9 inches, (Brougham) 11.0 inches. Fuel tank: (Cimarron) 13.6 gallons, (Seville/Eldorado) 20.3 gallons except diesel, 22.8, (DeVille/Fleetwood) 18.0 gallons, (Brougham) 24.5 gallons

OPTIONS

DEVILLE / FLEETWOOD BROUGHAM / ELDORADO / SEVILLE

Astroroof ($1225), Not available on Limousine. Electronic cruise control $185). Controlled-cycle wiper system for DeVille/Fleetwood ($60). Rear defogger with heated outside mirrors ($165-$215). Automatic door locks ($162). Remote-locking fuel filler door ($59). Garage door opener ($140). Economy illuminated entry system ($76, but standard on Brougham). Dual comfort 55/45 front seats for DeVille ($235). Memory driver's seat ($205-$225, except standard in Limousine and convertible. Six-way power passenger seat ($225, except standard in Brougham). Power driver's seat back recliner, except in Fleetwood ($155). Power driver's seat back recliner in Fleetwood ($90, but not available in Limousines). Power passenger seat back recliner for DeVille ($155). Power passenger seat back recliner for Brougham, Fleetwood ($90). Power passenger seat recliner with six-way power seat, except Limousine or Brougham ($315-$380).

Leather-trimmed steering wheel ($99). Tilt/telescope steering wheel ($184). Power trunk lid release and pull-down for DeVille/Fleetwood ($80-$120). Power trunk lid release only, in DeVille or Limousine ($40). Theft deterrent system ($190). Twilight Sentinel ($79). Dimming Sentinel ($93-$128). Opera lights for Eldorado ($88). Trumpet horn, except Seville ($38). Electric remote-control outside rearview mirrors, except Limousine ($101). Twin lighted visor-vanity mirrors ($140). Automatic day/night mirror ($80). Electronic-tuning seek/scan AM/FM stereo radio with cassette player ($299). Electronic-tuning seek/scan AM/FM stereo radio with cassette and Delco-GM/Bose sound system, except in Brougham ($895). Electronic-tuning AM/FM stereo radio with cassette and CB for Brougham ($577). CB radio, except in Brougham ($278). Electronic-tuning radio with cassette and rear control for Limousine ($475). Triband radio antenna ($50). Two-tone paint for Seville ($600). Two-tone paint for Eldorado ($345). Two-tone partial Firemist paint for Eldorado ($465). Firemist or Pearlmist paint ($235). Deck lid and bodyside accent striping for DeVille ($52). Bodyside molding for Eldorado Touring coupe ($64). Door edge guards ($19-$29). License frames, each ($14). Front license bracket, except Deville (no charge). Leather seating area ($515-$680). Carpeted rubber floor mats for front ($43-$45). Carpeted floor mats for rear ($25). Trunk mat ($26). Aluminum wheels for Eldorado/Seville/DeVille ($429). Aluminum wheels for Fleetwoods ($114, but standard on Limousine. Spoked aluminum alloy wheels on Eldorado or Seville($835). Spoked aluminumwheels on Biarritz Elegante or convertible ($441). Locking wire wheels on Brougham ($860). Locking wire wheel covers, except Fleetwoods ($315-$394). P225/70R15 white-letter tires for Eldorado Touring Coupe ($100). Puncture-sealing tires, except on Limousines ($135-$180). 4.3-liter diesel V-6 engine for DeVille or Fleetwood (NC). 5.7-liter diesel V-8 engine for Eldorado/Seville/Brougham (NC). California emission equipment ($99). Engine block heater ($45). Heavy-duty battery ($40). 100-amp alternator for Eldorado, Seville or Brougham ($50). Heavy-duty ride package for Brougham ($116). FE2 touring suspension

1985 Cadillac, Fleetwood Eldorado Biarritz convertible

for Eldorado or Seville ($115). FE2 touring package including aluminum wheels, P215/65R15 Eagle GT tires, a leather-wrapped steering wheel and a revised suspension, for DeVille ($695). FE2 touring package including aluminum wheels, P215/65R15 Eagle GT tires, a leather-wrapped steering wheel and a revised suspension, Fleetwood ($375). Seville Elegante ($3,879). Brougham or Fleetwood d'Elegance with cloth seating ($1,250). Brougham or Fleetwood d'Elegance with leather seating ($1,800). Cabriolet roof for DeVille coupe ($498), Cabriolet roof for Eldorado ($420). Full cabriolet roof for Eldorado, Seville ($995). Eldorado Biarritz ($3,395). Eldorado Touring Coupe ($1,975).

CIMARRON

Vista Vent with rear tilt ($310). Digital instrument cluster ($238). Garage door opener ($165). Six-way power passenger seat ($225). Twilight Sentinel ($85). Twin lighted visor-vanity mirrors ($95). Seek/scan AM/FM stereo radio with cassette ($223). Delete radio ($151 credit). Lower bodyside accent moldings ($450). Door edge guards ($25). License frame, rear ($15). Deck lid luggage rack ($130). Cloth upholstery ($100 credit). Carpeted rubber floor mats for front ($38). Carpeted rubber floor mats for rear ($22). Trunk mat ($26). Aluminum wheels, 14 inches. ($40). P195/70R13 steel-belted radial white side wall tires ($55). P205/60R14 steel-belted radial Eagle GT ($94). P205/60R14 steel-belted radial OWL tires ($171). Cimarron d'Oro ($975). 173-cid (2.8-liter) V-6 engine ($560). California emission equipment ($99). Engine block heater ($20). Heavy-duty battery ($26). Delco/Bilstein suspension ($100, but required with V-6).

HISTORICAL

The Fleetwood and DeVille models were introduced April 5, 1984. The Eldorado and Seville models were introduced October 2, 1984. The new Cimarron was introduced on November 8, 1984. Model-year production was 394,840 (including 45,330 early-1985 front-wheel-drive DeVilles and Fleetwoods). That total included 11,968 V-6 engines and 1,088 diesel engines. Calendar-year production was 322,765. Calendar-year sales by U.S. dealers was 298,762 for a 3.6 percent market share. Model-year sales by U.S. dealers was 310,942 (not including 46,356 front-drive DeVille/Fleetwoods sold as early-1985 models). The delayed arrival of the new front-wheel-drive DeVille and Fleetwood was due to shortages of the Type 440 four-speed automatic transaxle produced at GM's Hydra-Matic Division. Production delays meant both rear-wheel-drive and front-wheel-drive DeVilles were offered to the public, at the same time, for a while during 1984. A strike at GM of Canada affected supplies to over 30 General Motors plants in the U.S., including Cadillac plants.

A 1985 Cadillac Sedan DeVille weathers the chill in a factory starting test.

1986

OVERVIEW

All-new Eldorado and Seville models entered the lineup for 1986. They featured an onboard diagnostics system and electronic instruments. There was no Eldorado convertible. Also gone was the front-wheel-drive Fleetwood (which had really been a fancy DeVille). Anti-lock braking was a new option on Fleetwood and DeVille models. All Cadillacs, except the big Brougham, were now front-wheel-drive cars. The Brougham would hang on for another year with a 5.0-liter V-8 under its hood. Luxury touches promoted in the full-line catalog ranged from golden ignition keys to elegant option packages designed to deliver "the feeling of uncompromising excellence." Diesel engines departed from the Cadillac options list. In addition to a lack of interest in them, the diesels had unimpressive reliability record. The HT-4100 V-8 now had stainless steel exhaust manifolds. Floor consoles contained an ashtray that opened at a finger's touch. And to keep up with the times, a cellular telephone ("discreetly" positioned in fold-down arm rest) joined the options list. To attract buyers who preferred good handling to a cushy ride, DeVilles could also get a Touring Coupe or Touring Sedan option with a stiffer suspension and related extras.

Above: **1986 Cadillac, Sedan De Ville**

I.D. DATA

The 17-symbol serial number was located on top of the instrument panel, where it was visible through the windshield. The first symbol 1=U.S.-built vehicle. The second symbol G=General Motors. The third symbol 6=Cadillac. The fourth symbol indicated carline/the fifth symbol indicated series as follows: C/D=front-wheel-drive DeVille, C/H=front-wheel-drive Fleetwood Limousine, D/W=rear-wheel-drive Fleetwood Brougham, E/L=Eldorado, J/G=Cimarron and K/S=Seville. The sixth and seventh symbols incated body stytle and restraint system: 23=four-door six-window sedan with auxiliary seat (Limousine), 33=four-door six-window sedan with auxiliary seat and partition window(Limousine), 47=two-door notchback special Coupe, 57=two-door notchback special Coupe, 69=four-door four-window notchback sedan. The eighth symbol identified the engine (See engine listings below). The ninth symbol was a check digit. The 10th symbol was a number indicating model year: G=1986. The 11th symbol indicates the GM assembly plant: J=Janesville, Wis. (Cimarron), 4=Orion, Mich. (DeVille), 9=Detroit (Cadillac). The next group of numbers was the sequential production code starting with 100001. The Fisher Body tag on the cowl, under the hood includes additional information.

CIMARRON—SERIES 6J/G—FOUR/V-6

Cimarron entered a new year sporting new wraparound taillights at the restyled rear end. Inside was new leather trim on the shift boot and knob (manual shift) and a redesigned console. A premium Delco-Bose sound system was now optional and suspension components were revised. Cadillac's smallest model had been extensively reworked as a midyear 1985 entry with new front-end styling (more evidently Cadillac) and new optional electronic instrument cluster. Most important, though, was the V-6 option, giving the car a much needed performance boost. The Gen II (second generation) 2.8-liter V-6 with multi-port fuel injection came from Chevrolet. The standard engine continued to be a 2.0-liter four with a five-speed (Getrag-designed) manual gear box. The 2.8 could have four-speed manual transmission or three-speed automatic transmission. Even with the V-6 available, the Cimarron still wasn't selling strongly. It enjoyed only a modest increase for 1985. To improve handling there was an optional Delco/Bilstein suspension with gas-charged front struts and rear shocks, plus stiffer front spring rates and a thicker front stabilizer bar. That suspension was required with the V-6 engine. Cimarron used a fine-patterned crosshatch grille with a "Cadillac" script at the driver's side, plus recessed quad rectangular headlights. Wide parking/signal lights were inset below the bumper rub strips, with foglights below them flanking the air dam. A "Cimarron" script appeared on the front doors. Yellow Beige Chamois was a new Cimarron color. Twenty dual-color accent stripes were available. Also revised this year was the d'Oro option package. Offered with a Red or White body, the package included: gold custom fine-line accent stripes on the belt line, on the rub strips and on the hood center. It also had a gold-accented grille, gold-accented fog light covers, gold-accented lower bodyside accent moldings, d'Oro plaques on the front fenders and dash, a gold-tinted lay-down hood ornament, a gold-tinted steering wheel spokes and a special horn pad emblem. The d'Oro also had grooved, body-colored lower body accent moldings.

CIMARRON – SERIES 6J/G - FOUR

Model Number	Body/Style No.	Body Type & Seating	Factory Price	Shipping Weight	Production Total
J/G	69	4D Sedan-5P	13,128	2,514	Note 1

CIMARRON – SERIES J/G - V-6

Model Number	Body/Style No.	Body Type & Seating	Factory Price	Shipping Weight	Production Total
J/G	69	4D Sedan-5P	13,838	2,601	Note 1

Note 1: Cimarron production was 24,534.

SEVILLE—SERIES 6K/S—V-8

A brand new Seville rode the same new platform as Eldorado. It was seven inches shorter and 375 pounds lighter than before. Gone was the striking razor-edge styling of 1980-85, which was replaced by a body not much different from the Eldorado's. The standard engine was the Cadillac 4.1-liter V-8 hooked to four-speed overdrive automatic transaxle. The Seville's vertical grille had a fine-mesh crosshatch pattern. The clear rear lenses of the horizontal side marker lights were angled to match the wheel openings. Wide, clear parking and signal lights were inset into the bumper area. The standard clearcoat finish had a new two-tone paint treatment. New front bucket seats were upholstered in Royal Prima cloth and had Sierra Grain leather seating areas. The front console included a fold-down arm rest and storage compartments, while American walnut highlighted the instrument panel, console and steering wheel. A cellular phone with a removable handset was stored in a locking storage compartment with a hidden mike between the sun visors. A "driver information center" in the digital instrument cluster displayed electronic readouts for outside temperature, fuel economy and engine data (including a tachometer reading). The Elegante was upholstered in Mayfair cloth with Sierra Grain leather seating areas. It had a package price price that started at $3,595.

SEVILLE—SERIES 6K/S-V-8

Model Number	Body/Style No.	Body Type & Seating	Factory Price	Shipping Weight	Production Total
K/S	69	4D Sedan-5P	26,756	3,371	19,098

DEVILLE—SERIES 6C/D—V-8

Front-wheel-drive Cadillacs came in Coupe and Sedan form. The standard engine was a transversely-mounted 4.1-liter V-8 with four-speed overdrive automatic transmission. The six-passenger interior sported a new seat trim design, while a closed-in, limousine-style back window was standard. The DeVille grille used many thin vertical bars, along with three horizontal bars and a "Cadillac" script at the lower corner. The wraparound cornering lights contained a small amber lens and large clear lens. Wide rectangular parking lights were set into the bumper, below the protective gray rub strips. "Coupe DeVille" or "Sedan DeVille" script identification was at the back of the quarter panels. Wide, bright rocker moldings ran the length of the car. The Coupe DeVille's assist handles were moved from the front seat backs to the door lock pillars. The door panels and dash sported cherry woodgrain trim. The optional aluminum alloy wheels

1986 Cadillac, Touring Sedan

had flush new hubcaps. Anti-lock braking (ABS) was an important new option that would gradually find its way onto other models in the years ahead. Developed along with a German firm (called Teves), the ABS used sensors at each wheel to determine when a wheel was about to lock. A 4.3-liter diesel was no longer offered. The 4.1-liter V-8 gained a little horsepower. DeVilles could be had with an optional Touring Package that included handling components and a "more aggressive, no-nonsense" look. Starting in February 1986, the Touring Package was upgraded to include a larger-diameter exhaust pipe, a higher shift point between first and second gear and five more horsepower. The Touring Package was available on either the Coupe or Sedan. It also included color keyed dual remote-control mirrors, a leather-wrapped steering wheel, gray leather seats, gray interior trim and removable quarter window louvers on the Coupe. A "Touring Coupe" or "Touring Sedan" signature went on the back windows. Rather than the whole package, buyers could opt for the Touring Suspension alone. A fine-grain formal Cabriolet roof highlighted the closed-in rear window. A Fleetwood d'Elegance option added walnut wood instrument panel and door trim plates along with deluxe carpeted floor mats, a leather-trimmed steering wheel and d'Elegance identification.

DEVILLE—SERIES 6C/D—V-8

Series No.	Body/Style No.	Body Type & Seating	Factory Price	Shipping Weight	Production Total
C/D	47	2D Coupe-6P	19,669	3,239	36,350
C/D	69	4D Sedan-6P	19,990	3,298	129,857

Note 2: With the Fleetwood option the base prices were $23,443 for the Coupe and $23,764 for the Sedan.

FLEETWOOD SEVENTY-FIVE LIMOUSINE—SERIES 6C/H—V-8

Traditionalists may have scoffed, but the modern front-wheel-drive, unibody Fleetwood Limousine still carried eight passengers in a style that appealed to "Seventy-Five" buyers a generation earlier. Under the hood was a transverse-mounted HT-4100 (4.1-liter) V-8 with digital fuel injection at the chassis and independent four-wheel suspension. Electronic instruments became standard and passengers could take advantage of an optional cellular phone with overhead mike. Cherry grain trim replaced the former walnut woodgrain trim on the instrument

1986 Cadillac, Fleetwood 75 limousine

panel and door trim plates. Automatic door locking prevented the doors from opening with the Limousine in gear. Oddly, the stretched Limousines were created from coupes, rather than sedans. The extra doors were added in the process of stretching the wheelbase from the normal 110.8 inches to 134.4 inches. The Limousines came in six body colors, plus one Firemist shade and Black Cherry Pearlmist.

FLEETWOOD SEVENTY-FIVE LIMOUSINE—SERIES 6C/H-V-8

Model Number	Body/Style No.	Body Type & Seating	Factory Price	Shipping Weight	Production Total
C/H	23	4D Limousine-8P	33,895	3,358	Note 3
C/H	33	4D Fml Limousine-7P	35,895	3,657	Note 3

Note 3: Total limousine production, 1,000.

FLEETWOOD BROUGHAM—SERIES 6D/W—V-8

Cadillac's traditional rear-wheel-drive sedan was now powered by Oldsmobile's 5.0-liter V-8 hooked to a four-speed overdrive automatic transmission. Standard features included a limousine-like closed-in back window, a standard full-length vinyl roof, plus a long list of Cadillac equipment. The Brougham Coupe was dropped soon before the model-year began and the sedan didn't appear until February 1986, so 1985 models remained on sale through the end of the year. At 121.5 inches, the Brougham's wheelbase was the longest of any production automobile other than the stretched (but limited-production) front drive Fleetwood. Broughams came in a dozen standard colors, plus five optional Firemist hues. Bright moldings ran from the front fender tips to below the window line and back around the rear quarters. Broughams also carried large full-length rocker moldings and electroluminescent opera lights.

FLEETWOOD BROUGHAM—SERIES 6D/W—V-8

Model Number	Body/Style No.	Body Type & Seating	Factory Price	Shipping Weight	Production Total
D/W	69	4D Sedan-6P	21,265	3,945	49,115

ELDORADO—SERIES 6E/L—V-8

A down-sized E-body Eldorado was designed, according to Cadillac, for "sporty elegance and sheer driving pleasure." The Eldorado had a transverse-mounted V-8 under its hood. Like the similar Seville, the new Eldorado was more than 16 inches shorter than its predecessor. The Eldorado's side marker lights were set into the body side moldings at the front and rear, with an "Eldorado" script just ahead of each front wheel. A wreath-and-crest insignia was on the wide rear pillar. At the rear were vertical taillights, with vertical rectangular back-up lights alongside the license plate. Along with the altered body came the demise of the Eldorado convertible (for the second time in a decade). Flush composite headlights held both the high-beam and low-beam bulbs. The fully independent suspension used a fiberglass transverse single leaf spring in the back. A new digital instrument cluster included a

tachometer and engine gauges in a "driver information center." The Eldorado Biarritz package included a formal Cabriolet vinyl roof, opera lights, wide body side accent moldings, two-tone paint and wire wheel covers. Inside luxuries included leather upholstery, Tampico carpeting, deluxe floor mats, walnut wood appliqués, dual power front reclining bucket seats with power lumbar support, a six-way power passenger seat and front seat back pockets. American walnut trim was seen on the steering wheel, console, door trim panels and instrument panel. An optional Touring suspension package with P215/60R15 Goodyear Eagle GT high-performance tires, a rear stabilizer bar, a stiffer front stabilizer bar and specially-tuned components offered a firmer, better-controlled ride, but included no special graphics or ornamentation.

ELDORADO—SERIES 6E/L–V-8

Model Number	Body/Style No.	Body Type & Seating	Factory Price	Shipping Weight	Production Total
E/L	57	2D Coupe-5P	24,251	3,291	21,342

ENGINE

CIMARRON BASE FOUR

Inline. OHV. Four-cylinder. Cast iron block and head. Displacement: 121-cid (2.0-liters). Bore and stroke: 3.50 x 3.15 inches. Compression ratio: 9.3:1. Brake hp: 88 at 4800 rpm. Torque: 110 lb.-ft. at 2400 rpm. Five main bearings. Hydraulic valve lifters. Fuel injection. VIN Code: P.

CIMARRON OPTIONAL V-6

Overhead-valve V-6. Cast iron block and head. Displacement: 173-cid (2.8-liters). Bore and stroke: 3.50 x 2.99 inches. Compression ratio: 8.5:1. Brake hp: 125 at 4800 rpm. Torque: 155 lb.-ft. at 3600 rpm. Four main bearings. Hydraulic valve lifters. Fuel injection. Chevrolet built. VIN Code: W.

SEVILLE, DEVILLE, FLEETWOOD, LIMOUSINE, ELDORADO BASE V-8

Overhead valve. Aluminum block with cast iron liners. Displacement: 249 cid (4.1 liters). Bore and Stroke: 3.47 x 3.31 inches. Compression ratio: 8.5:1. Net brake hp: 130 at 4200 rpm. Taxable hp: 39.2. Net torque: 200 at 2200 rpm. Five main bearings. Hydraulic valve lifters. Induction: Digital fuel injection. VIN Code: 8. Built by Cadillac.

BROUGHAM BASE V-8

Overhead valve. Cast iron block. Displacement: 307 cid (5.0 liters). Bore and Stroke: 3.80 x 3.39 inches. Compression ratio: 8.0:1. Net brake hp: 140 at 3200 rpm. Taxable hp: 46.20. Net torque: 346 at 2000 rpm. Five main bearings. Hydraulic valve lifters. Carburetion: Four-barrel. VIN Code: Y.

1986 Cadillac, Fleetwood Eldorado, coupe

CHASSIS

(Cimarron) Wheelbase: 101.2 inches. Overall length: 177.9 inches. Overall width: 65.0 inches. Overall height: 52.0 inches. Front tread: 55.4 inches. Rear tread: 55.2 inches. Tires: P19570R13 steel-belted radial with wide white sidewall.

(Seville) Wheelbase: 108.0 inches. Overall length: 188.2 inches. Overall width: 71.3 inches. Overall height: 53.7 inches. Front tread: 59.9 inches. Rear tread: 59.9 inches. Tires: P20570R14 steel-belted radial with wide white sidewall.

(Eldorado) Wheelbase: 108.0 inches. Overall length: 188.2 inches. Overall width: 71.3 inches. Overall height: 53.7 inches. Front tread: 59.9 inches. Rear tread: 59.9 inches. Tires: P20570R14 steel-belted radial with wide white sidewall.

(DeVille) Wheelbase: 110.0 inches. Overall length: 195.0 inches. Overall width: 71.7 inches. Overall height: 55.0 inches. Front tread: 61.7 inches. Rear tread: 59.8 inches. Tires: P20575R14 steel-belted radial with wide white sidewall.

(Brougham) Wheelbase: 121.5 inches. Overall length: 221.0 inches. Overall width: 75.3 inches. Overall height: 56.7 inches. Front tread: 61.7 inches. Rear tread: 60.7 inches. Tires: P21575R15 steel-belted radial with wide white sidewall.

(Fleetwood Limousine) Wheelbase: 134.4 inches. Overall length: 218.6 inches. Overall width: 75.3 inches. Overall height: 55.0 inches. Front tread: 60.3 inches. Rear tread: 60.7 inches. Tires: P21575R15 steel-belted radial with wide white sidewall.

TECHNICAL

Transmission: Five-speed, floor shift manual transmission standard on Cimarron four, four-speed manual transmission with V-6. Cimarron optional three-speed Turbo-Hydra-Matic transmission (THM125C) gear ratios: (1st) 2.84:1, (2nd) 1.60:1, (3rd) 1:1, (Reverse) 2.07:1. Four-speed overdrive automatic transmission

(THM200-4R) standard on Brougham: (1st) 2.74:1, (2nd) 1.57:1, (3rd) 1:1, (4th) 0.67:1, (Reverse) 2.07:1. Four-speed (THM440-T4) automatic transmission on other models: (1st) 2.92:1, (2nd) 1.57:1, (3rd) 1:1, (4th) 0.70:1, (Reverse) 2.38:1. Standard final drive ratio: (Cimarron) Not available, (Seville/Eldorado) 2.97:1, (DeVille/Fleetwood) 2.97:1, (Brougham) 2.73:1. Steering: power rack-and-pinion except Brougham, recirculating ball. Front suspension: same as 1985 except (Eldorado/Seville) MacPherson struts with dual path mounts, coil springs and stabilizer bar. Rear suspension: same as 1985 except (Eldorado/Seville) independent with transverse leaf spring, struts, electronic level control. Brakes: front disc, rear drum except Eldorado/Seville, four-wheel discs. Fuel tank: (Cimarron) 13.6 gallons, (Brougham) 20.7 gallons, (others) 18.0 gallons.

OPTIONS

DEVILLE / BROUGHAM / SEVENTY-FIVE / ELDORADO / SEVILLE OPTIONS

Astroroof ($1,255, but not available on Limousine). Electronic cruise control for DeVille/Brougham/Limousine ($195). Controlled-cycle wiper system for DeVille/Brougham/Limousine ($60). Rear defogger with heated outside mirrors ($170). Automatic door locks ($170, except Limousine). Remote fuel filler door release ($60). Garage door opener ($140-$165). Illuminated entry system ($80). Digital instrument cluster for DeVille ($238). Cellular telephone for DeVille ($2,850). Cellular telephone provision kit ($395). Six-way power passenger seat for dual comfort seats in DeVille ($235). Two-position memory seat for DeVille ($235). Two-position memory seat for Brougham ($215). Six-way power passenger seat for Eldorado/Seville/Brougham ($235). Power driver's seat recliner for DeVille/Brougham ($95-$160). Power passenger seat recliner for DeVille/Brougham ($95-$395). Power passenger seat recliner with six-way power seat for Eldorado/Seville($330). Leather-trimmed steering wheel: DeVille/Brougham/Limousine ($105). Tilt/telescope steering wheel for DeVille/Brougham/Limousine ($195). Power trunk lid release for DeVille/Brougham/Limousine ($40). Trunk release and pull-down ($80-$120). Theft deterrent system ($200). Twilight Sentinel for DeVille/Brougham/Limousine ($85). Dimming Sentinel headlight control ($130, except Brougham). Guidematic headlight control for Brougham ($95). Rear reading lights for Brougham ($33). Trumpet horn: DeVille/Brougham/Limousine ($45). Electric remote-control outside mirrors for DeVille/Brougham ($101). Twin lighted vanity mirrors ($140). Automatic day/night mirror ($80). Electronic tuning AM/FM stereo radio with cassette for Brougham ($299). Electronic tuning AM/FM stereo radio with cassette with cassette and CB for Brougham ($577). ET AM/FM stereo radio with cassette

and graphic equalizer ($319, except Brougham). ET radio with cassette and rear control for Limousine ($475). ET AM/FM stereo radio with cassette and Delco-GM/Bose music system ($895, except Brougham/Limousine). CB radio for DeVille ($278). Power triband antenna for DeVille/Brougham ($55). Firemist or Pearlmist paint ($240). Two-tone Seville paint ($600). Deck lid and bodyside accent striping for DeVille/Brougham ($55). Accent moldings for Eldorado ($75). Color-keyed door edge guards ($19-$29). License frames, each ($15). Front license bracket for Eldorado (NC). Dual comfort seats for DeVille ($245). Leather seating area, except Limousine ($400-$550). Leather seating area in Limousine ($940). Carpeted front floor mats ($45). Carpeted rear floor mats ($25). Trunk mat ($26). Wire wheels for Brougham ($860- $940). Aluminum alloy wheels for DeVille ($115-$435), Seville Elegante (NC). Wire wheel covers for Eldorado/Seville($190). Wire wheel covers for DeVille/Brougham ($320-$400). Turbine-vaned wheel covers for Brougham ($80). Puncture-sealing tires ($145-$190, except Limousine). P215/65R15 white sidewall tires for DeVille ($66). P215/60R15 steel-belted-radial black sidewall tires for Seville (NC). P215/60R15 steel-belted-radial white sidewall tires for Seville/Eldorado ($66). Engine block heater ($45). Heavy-duty battery ($40). Electronic level control for Brougham ($203). F72 heavy-duty ride suspension package including electronic level control for Brougham ($323). FE2 touring suspension package for DeVille ($695). FE2 touring suspension package with Fleetwood package ($375). FE2 touring suspension package for Eldorado ($200). FE2 touring suspension with 15-inch aluminum alloy wheels, P215/60R15 Goodyear Eagle GT hi-performance black sidewall tires, rear stabilizer bar and stiffer front stabilizer bar for Eldorado/Seville ($155). Fleetwood package, cloth seats ($3,150), leather ($3,700). Fleetwood d'Elegancepackage with cloth seating ($4,445). Fleetwood d'Elegance package with leather seating ($4,995). DeVille Touring Coupe or Touring Sedan package ($2,880). Brougham d'Elegance package with cloth seats ($1,950). Fleetwood d'Elegance package with leather seating ($2,500). Eldorado Biarritz with cloth seating ($3,095). Eldorado Biarritz with leather seating ($3,495). Seville Elegante with cloth seating ($3,595). Seville Elegante with leather ($3,995). Black cambric cloth roof for DeVille ($925). Formal cabriolet roof for DeVille coupe ($698). Security option package for DeVille/Limousine ($290). Security option package for Seville/Eldorado ($460). Security option package for Brougham ($380).

CIMARRON OPTIONS

Vista Vent ($310). Garage door opener transmitter ($165). Garage door opener retainer ($25). Digital instrument cluster ($238). Twilight Sentinel ($85). Twin lighted

visor-vanity mirrors ($95). Electronic-tuning seek/scan AM/FM stereo radio with cassette ($223). Electronic-tuning seek/scan AM/FM stereo radio with cassette and Delco-GM/Bose music system ($895). Delete radio ($151 credit). Lower bodyside accent moldings ($450). Door edge guards ($25). Rear license frame ($15). Deck lid luggage rack ($130). Cloth seat trim ($100 credit). Carpeted rubber floor mats front ($38). Carpeted rubber floor mats rear ($22). Trunk mat ($26). 14-inch aluminum alloy wheels ($40). P195/70R13 steel-belted radial white sidewall tires ($55). P205/60R14 steel-belted radial black sidewall tires ($94). P205/60R14 steel-belted radial raised white-letter tires ($171). P205/60R14 steel-belted radial raised white-letter tires with d'Oro ($77). 173-cid (2.8-liter) EFI V-6 engine ($610). Four-speed manual transmission ($75 credit). Three-speed automatic transmission ($390). California emission equipment ($99). High-altitude emissions package (NC). Engine block heater ($20). Heavy-duty battery ($26). Heavy-duty radiator ($45). Delco/Bilstein suspension system, with V-6 only ($100). Cimarron d'Oro package ($975).

HISTORICAL

Most 1986 Cadillacs were introduced on September 26, 1985. The all-new Eldorado and Seville were added to the line on November 14, 1985 and the all-new Fleetwood Brougham was introduced on February 13, 1986. Model-year production was 281,296 units, including 3,628 with a four-cylinder engine and 20,906 with V-6. This gave Cadillac a 3.6 percent share of the industry total. Calendar-year production was 319,031. Calendar-year sales by U.S. dealers was 304,057. Model-year sales by U.S. dealers was 300,053 for a 3.8 percent market share. Cadillac sales dropped a bit for the second year in a row,

barely edging over 300,000. That was enough to retain dominance among makers of luxury cars. The E-body Eldorado entered production at the new Hamtramck, Michigan, plant in late 1985, but delays kept output below peak levels. As a result, Eldorado and Seville sales dropped by half. The rear-wheel-drive Fleetwood Brougham enjoyed a comeback of sorts, due to low gasoline prices and its upgraded V-8 engine. Front-wheel-drive DeVilles and Fleetwoods also gained in sales for the second year. Cimarron sales rose as well, but not by much. Cadillac clung to hopes that Cimarron would gain strength against new imports such as Acura Legend.

1986 Cadillac symbol

1986 Cadillac, Fleetwood Eldorado Biarritz, coupe

1987

OVERVIEW

The 1987 Cadillacs, energized by what was regarded as "The new spirit of Cadillac," as well as the introduction of the Allante, featured engineering, convenience and styling refinements. A major effort was made to provide the 1987 Cadillacs with enhanced security features. All major body components were now tagged with the car's individual vehicle identification number. Cadillac's door-into-roof design was regarded as "an inherent security feature that helps reduce access through otherwise vulnerable window weatherstripping." All models except the Cimarron were also offered with a theft-deterrent system using the underhood horn as an alarm and the front door lock cylinders and electric door locks to activate itself. The historic nature of the Allante's debut was established by Cadillac general manager John O. Grettenberger, who called it "General Motors' new passenger car flagship."

I.D. DATA

The 17-symbol serial number was located on top of the instrument panel, where it was visible through the windshield. The first symbol 1=U.S.-built vehicle. The second symbol G=General Motors. The third symbol 6=Cadillac.

Above: **1987 Cadillac, Cimarron, sedan**

The fourth symbol indicated carline/the fifth symbol indicated series as follows: C/B=Fleetwood d'Elegance, C/D= DeVille, C/H= Limousine, D/W= Brougham, E/L=Eldorado, J/G=Cimarron, K/S=Seville and V/R=Allante. The sixth symbol incated body stytle: 1=two-door Coupe/Sedan GM/Fisher Style Nos. 11, 27, 37, 47, 57 or 97, 3=two-door Convertible GM/Fisher Style No. 67, 5=four-door Sedan GM/Fisher style nos. 19, 23, 33 or 69. The seventh symbol indicates the type of restaint system: 1=manual belts or 4=automatic belts. The eighth symbol identified the engine : W=2.8L V-6, Y=5.0L V-8, 1=2.0L L4, 7=4.1L V-8, 8=4.1L V-8 and 9=5.0L V-8. The ninth symbol was a check digit. The 10th symbol was a number indicating model year: H=1987. The 11th symbol indicates the GM assembly plant: J=Janesville, Wis. (Cimarron), U=Hamtramck, Mich. (Allante), 4=Orion, Mich. (DeVille), 9=Detroit (Cadillac). The next group of numbers was the sequential production code starting with 100001. The Fisher Body tag on the cowl, under the hood includes additional information.

CIMARRON - SERIES 6J/G - V-6

The 2.8-liter V-6 and MG 582 five-speed manual transmission were standard on the 1987 Cimarron. Design revisions raised the engine's compression ratio to 8.9:1 from 8.5:1. Driving characteristics were enhanced through

changes in the Cimarron's front suspension bushings and stabilizer bar. Lower engine mounts were also used, as was a lightweight master cylinder. All Cimarrons had composite tungsten headlights that had previously been included in the d'Oro package. This option which was no longer offered. New cashmere cloth and leather seating areas were now offered as an option.

Cimarron—SERIES 6J/G- Four/V-6

Model Number	Body/Style No.	Body Type & Seating	Factory Price	Shipping Weight	Production Total
J/G	5	4D Sedan-5P	15,032	2,604	Note 1

Cimarron (Four/V-6)

Model Number	Body/Style No.	Body Type & Seating	Factory Price	Shipping Weight	Production Total
J/G	5	4D Sedan-5P	NA	2,715	Note 1

Note 1: Total Cimarron production was 14,561.

DEVILLE - SERIES 6C/D - V-8 AND FLEETWOOD D'ELEGANCE - SERIES 6C/D - V-8

Both Cadillacs had new deflected-disc front-strut valving, a new two-piece front-strut mount, new shear-type rear-strut mounts and new hydro-elastic engine mounts. The result of these changes was a smoother and quieter ride. The rear brake drums and master cylinder were also revised to provide less pedal travel and improved modulation. Exterior changes included a rear quarter and bumper extension, new taillights that added 1.5 inches to overall length and dual-stacked red reflex appliqués centered between the taillights and the license plate opening. Front-end changes for 1987 included a restyled grille, new composite headlights and new hood header molding. New front side markers, cornering lights and reflex lights were also used. Nine new exterior colors were introduced. Selected models were also offered with a new Cabriolet top. The DeVille Touring Coupe and Touring Sedan models were equipped with the ride-and-handling package, plus a front air dam, front fog lights, specific rocker panel moldings, specific body side accent moldings, a rear deck lid spoiler, leather seating areas, removable vertical louvers for the Coupe quarter windows, a leather-wrapped steering wheel, leather-wrapped lever knobs and a leather-wrapped gearshift lever.

DeVille—SERIES 6C/D—V-8

Model Number	Body/Style No.	Body Type & Seating	Factory Price	Shipping Weight	Production Total
C/D	1	2D Coupe-6P	21,316	3,312	Note 2
C/D	5	4D Sedan-6P	21,659	3,370	Note 2

Note 2: Total front-wheel-drive Cadillac (DeVille, Fleetwood D'Elegance, Sixty Special and Limousine) production was 162,798.

FLEETWOOD D'ELEGANCE-SERIES 6C/B -V-8

New-for-1987 was the Fleetwood Sixty Special which rode a Fleetwood chassis with a five-inch-longer wheelbase. This gave it more seating room than the related DeVille and Fleetwood D'Elegance models.

Fleetwood D'Elegance—SERIES 6C/B - V-8

Model Number	Body/Style No.	Body Type & Seating	Factory Price	Shipping Weight	Production Total
C/B	5	4D Sedan-6P	26,104	3,421	Note 2

Note 2: Total front-wheel-drive Cadillac (DeVille, Fleetwood D'Elegance, Sixty Special and Limousine) production was 162,798.

FLEETWOOD SIXTY-SPECIAL - SERIES 6C/S - V-8

New-for-1987 was the Fleetwood Sixty Special which rode a Fleetwood chassis with a five-inch-longer wheelbase. This gave it more seating room than the related DeVille and Fleetwood D'Elegance models.

Fleetwood Sixty Special—SERIES 6C/S-V-8

Series No.	Body/Style No.	Body Type & Seating	Factory Price	Shipping Weight	Production Total
C/S	5	4D Sedan-6P	34,850	3,408	Note 2

Note 2: Total front-wheel-drive Cadillac (DeVille, Fleetwood D'Elegance, Sixty Special and Limousine) production was 162,798.

FLEETWOOD SEVENTY FIVE LIMOUSINE-SERIES 6C/H-V-8

Both front and rear styling of the limousine and formal limousine were revised for 1987. A new grille, a header molding and composite headlights with wrap-around bezel and cornering lights were used. The rear styling now featured elongated quarter extensions against which the taillights, bumper and bumper trim fascia fit flush. Also new was a grooved six-inch wide rocker molding made of a stainless steel/aluminum composite with a single-rib accent groove. New hydro-elastic engine mounts were used to further isolate powertrain vibration.

Fleetwood 75—SERIES 6C/H - V-8

Model Number	Body/Style No.	Body Type & Seating	Factory Price	Shipping Weight	Production Total
C/H	5	4D Limousine-8P	36,510	3,678	Note 2/3
C/H	5	4D Formal Limousine-7P	36,580	3,798	Note 2/3

Note 2: Total front-wheel-drive Cadillac (DeVille, Fleetwood D'Elegance, Sixty Special and Limousine) production was 162,798.
Note 3: Total limousine production was 302.

BROUGHAM - SERIES 6D/W - V-8

During 1986, sales of the Brougham increased by more than 30 percent. One result was a major effort to further improve its overall interior, exterior and mechanical features. A new cross-hatch grille, a revised header molding and new park and turn signal lights were introduced. Red reflex lenses were added to the rear panel and a "Cadillac" script replaced the "Fleetwood" script on the deck lid. A "Brougham" script replaced "Fleetwood Brougham" on the quarter panels. The upgraded d'Elegance version blended the features of the 1986 model with the changes found in the 1987 Brougham. A new tri-color saddle interior combination was used on both models. The Brougham's parking light and taillight surrounds were changed from gold to silver.

1987 Cadillac, Allante' convertible

Brougham (V-8)

Model Number	Body/Style No.	Body Type & Seating	Factory Price	Shipping Weight	Production Total
6D	W69	4D Sedan-6P	22,637	4,046	65,504

ELDORADO - SERIES 6E/L - V-8

The 20th anniversary version of the Eldorado featured changes in its suspension and engine damping. The use of deflected-disc strut valves on cars with the Touring suspension provided a more comfortable ride and better road manners. New hydro-elastic engine mounts were also used. New vehicle-sensitive rear seat belts were used on all Eldorados. A new cashmere-cloth-and-leather interior trim was offered. Twelve new exterior colors (for a total of 19) were introduced. For the first time, Cadillac offered the Cabriolet top as an option for the base Eldorado. The Biarritz had a redesigned Cabriolet top.

Eldorado (V-8)

Model Number	Body/Style No.	Body Type & Seating	Factory Price	Shipping Weight	Production Total
6E	L57	2D Coupe-6P	23,740	3,360	17,775

SEVILLE - SERIES 6K/S - V-8

The Seville shared the Eldorado's new features and design changes. New rear electric door locks allowing the driver to lock all doors after opening one rear door without returning to the front door was a welcome feature. The Seville had a standard dual-tone finish. Cars with the Elegante option came with special two-color mid-tone finish. A monotone finish was available for both models. The base Seville was also available with the mid-tone finish.

Seville (V-8)

Model Number	Body/Style No.	Body Type & Seating	Factory Price	Shipping Weight	Production Total
6K	S69	4D Sedan-6P	26,326	3,420	18,578

ALLANTE - SERIES 6V/R - V-8

The ultra-luxurious Allante's body and interior were built by Pininfarina in Turin, Italy. The finished bodies were flown to GM's Detroit-Hamtramck assembly plant where the power plant and suspension were installed. Each completed car was driven for 25 miles for an individual evaluation. The front-wheel-drive Allante was powered by a specially-tuned version of Cadillac's 4.1-liter V-

8. It used special magnesium rocker arm covers and an aluminum oil pan. The Allante chassis was intended for use on a convertible. Its all-independent suspension featured MacPherson struts and coil springs in front. The rear suspension combined MacPherson struts and a composite transverse leaf spring. Also found on the Allante was a new Bosch II anti-lock braking system. Only two interior options were available: a choice of two leather colors and a cellular telephone. The Allante interior was available in either Burgundy or natural Saddle leather. The Allante seats were manufactured by Recaro and featured a 10-way memory system. The Allante's exterior design, characterized by a wedge-shaped profile, was aerodynamic and had a 0.34 coefficient of drag. Cadillac General Manager John Grettenberger remarked that "Allante owners will find that even with the top down they will be able to carry on a conversation in normal tones." Sergio Pininfarina reported his work with Cadillac was "the realization of a lifelong dream."

Allante (V-8)

Model Number	Body/Style No.	Body Type & Seating	Factory Price	Shipping Weight	Production Total
6V	R67	2D Convertible-2P	54,700	3,494	3,366

ENGINE

CIMARRON OPTIONAL V-6

Overhead-valve V-6. Cast iron block and head. Displacement: 173-cid (2.8-liters). Bore and stroke: 3.50 x 2.99 inches. Compression ratio: 8.5:1. Brake hp: 125 at 4800 rpm. Torque: 155 lb.-ft. at 3600 rpm. Four main bearings. Hydraulic valve lifters. Fuel injection. Chevrolet built. VIN Code: W.

DEVILLE, FLEETWOOD, SEVILLE, ELDORADO BASE V-8

Overhead valve. Aluminum block with cast iron liners. Displacement: 249 cid (4.1 liters). Bore and Stroke: 3.47 x 3.31 inches. Compression ratio: 8.5:1. Net brake hp: 130 at 4200 rpm. Taxable hp: 39.2. Net torque: 200 at 2200 rpm. Five main bearings. Hydraulic valve lifters. Induction: Digital fuel injection. VIN Code: 8. Built by Cadillac.

1987 Cadillac, Sedan de Ville

ALLANTE BASE V-8

Overhead valve. Aluminum block with cast iron liners. Displacement: 249 cid (4.1 liters). Bore and Stroke: 3.47 x 3.31 inches. Compression ratio: 8.5:1. Net brake hp: 170 at 4300 rpm. Taxable hp: 39.2. Net torque: 235 at 3200 rpm. Five main bearings. Roller hydraulic valve lifters. Induction: Sequential multi-port fuel injection. VIN Code: 7. Built by Cadillac.

BROUGHAM BASE V-8

Overhead valve. Cast iron block. Displacement: 307 cid (5.0 liters). Bore and Stroke: 3.80 x 3.39 inches. Compression ratio: 8.0:1. Net brake hp: 140 at 3200 rpm. Taxable hp: 46.20. Net torque: 346 at 2000 rpm. Five main bearings. Hydraulic valve lifters. Carburetion: Four-barrel. VIN Code: Y. Built by Oldsmobile.

DEVILLE, FLEETWOOD, SEVILLE, ELDORADO OPTIONAL V-8

Overhead valve. Cast iron block. Displacement: 307 cid (5.0 liters). Taxable hp: 46.20. Bore and Stroke: 3.80 x 3.39 inches. Five main bearings. Hydraulic valve lifters. Carburetion: Four-barrel. VIN Code: 9. Built by Oldsmobile.

CHASSIS

(Cimarron) Wheelbase: 101.2 inches. Overall Length: 177.8 inches. Height: 52.1 inches. Width: 65.0 inches. Front Tread: 55.4 inches. Rear Tread: 55.2 inches. Standard Tires: P195/70R14.

(DeVille) Wheelbase: 110.8 inches. Overall Length: 196.5 inches. Height: 55.0 inches. Width: 71.7 inches. Front Tread: 60.3 inches. Rear Tread: 59.8 inches. Standard Tires: (Coupe DeVille) Michelin P205/70R14, (Sedan DeVille) P205/70R14.

(Fleetwood d'Elegance) Wheelbase: 110.8 inches. Overall Length: 196.5 inches. Height: 55.0 inches. Width: 71.7 inches. Front Tread: 60.3 inches. Rear Tread: 59.8 inches. Standard Tires: Michelin P205/70R14.

(Sixty Special) Wheelbase: 115.8 inches. Overall Length: 201.5 inches. Height: 55.0 inches. Width: 71.7 inches. Front Tread: 60.3 inches. Rear Tread: 59.8 inches. Standard Tires: P205/70R14.

(Seville) Wheelbase: 108.0 inches. Overall Length: 188.2 inches. Height: 53.7 inches. Width: 70.9 inches. Front Tread: 59.9 inches. Rear Tread: 59.9 inches. Standard Tires: P205/70R14. (Touring) Goodyear Eagle GT4 P215/65R15.

(Eldorado) Wheelbase: 108.0 inches. Overall Length: 188.2 inches. Height: 53.7 inches. Width: 71.3 inches. Front Tread: 59.9 inches. Rear Tread: 59.9 inches. Standard Tires: P205/70R14. (Touring) Goodyear Eagle GT4 P215/65R15.

(Allante) Wheelbase: 99.4 inches. Overall Length: 178.6 inches. Height: 52.2 inches. Width: 73.4 inches. Front Tread: 60.4 inches. Rear Tread: 60.4 inches. Standard Tires: Goodyear Eagle VL P225/55VR16.

(Brougham) Wheelbase: 121.5 inches. Overall Length: 221.0 inches. Height: 56.7 inches. Width: 75.3 inches. Front Tread: 61.7 inches. Rear Tread: 60.7 inches. Standard Tires: Michelin P225/75R15.

(Fleetwood Seventy Five) Wheelbase: 134.4 inches. Overall Length: 220.0 inches. Height: 55.0 inches. Width: 71.7 inches. Front Tread: 60.3 inches. Rear Tread: 59.8 inches. Standard Tires: P205/70R14.

TECHNICAL

Transmission: (Cimarron) Muncie-Getrag five-speed manual, (DeVille, Fleetwood, Eldorado, Seville) THM 440-T4 four-speed automatic (includes overdrive and viscous converter clutch), (Allante) THM F7 four-speed automatic (includes overdrive, viscous converter clutch and electronic shift control), (Brougham) THM 200-4R TCC four-speed automatic (includes overdrive and torque converter clutch). Steering: All models except Brougham: power-assisted rack and pinion. Brougham: power-assisted recirculating ball. Ratios: DeVille, Fleetwood: 19.1:1, Seville, Eldorado: 16.5:1, Touring: 15.6:1, Allante: 15.6:1, Brougham: 15-13:1. Front Suspension: (All

1987 Cadillac, Coupe de Ville

1987 Cadillac, Touring Sedan

models except Brougham) Independent MacPherson strut with coil springs, strut-type shock absorbers (integral-in strut and electronic variable on Allante) and stabilizer bar, (Brougham) Independent with short/long arms, coil springs, direct acting shock absorbers and link-type stabilizer bar. Rear suspension: (All models except Brougham): fully independent with coil springs. Automatic level control and strut-type superlift shock absorbers on all models except Cimarron, Allante and Brougham. Allante: integral-in strut electronic variable shock absorbers with no rear stabilizer, Brougham: four-link, coil springs with automatic level control and direct acting shock absorbers. Brakes: Cimarron, Brougham, Fleetwood: power front discs, rear drum, Seville, Allante and Eldorado: power disc, front and rear. Body Construction: (All models except Brougham): integral body-frame, Brougham: separate body on frame. Fuel Tank: (Cimarron) 13.6 gallons, (DeVille, Fleetwood) 18.0 gallons, (Eldorado, Seville) 18.8 gallons, (Allante) 22 gallons, (Brougham) 25 gallons.

OPTIONS

CIMARRON OPTIONS

Garage door opener. Vista Vent sun roof. Leather seating areas. Cashmere cloth seating areas. Six-way power seat. Visor-vanity mirrors. Delco-GM Bose symphony sound system. Delco AM/FM stereo with electronically-tuned receiver and cassette player. Electronic instrument cluster. Aluminum alloy wheels. Door edge guards. Floor mats. Deck lid luggage rack. Heavy-duty battery. 13- inch narrow-stripe white sidewall tires.

DEVILLE OPTIONS

Cellular telephone. Automatic day/night mirror. Controlled-cycle wiper system. Rear window defogger. Dimming sentinel. Automatic door locks. Garage door opener. Illuminated entry system. Electrically-powered mirrors. Power driver seat recliner. Six-way power seat adjuster. Dual comfort 45/55 seats. Tilt-and-telescope steering wheel. Trumpet horn. Trunk lid release and power pull down. Twilight Sentinel. Visor-vanity mirrors. Delco-GM Bose symphony sound system. Delco AM stereo/FM stereo electronically-tuned receiver with cassette player. Universal citizens band transceiver. Cambria cloth texture roof treatment. Two-tone paint. formal cabriolet roof. Digital instrument cluster. Full Cabriolet roof. Wire wheel discs. Aluminum alloy wheels. Accent striping. Door edge guards. Fuel filler door remote release. Leather seating areas. Firemist paint. Pearlmist paint. Reversible front and rear floor mats. Leather-trimmed steering wheel. Theft deterrent system. Trunk mat. Ride-and-handling package. Anti-lock braking system. Heavy-duty battery. Engine block heater. Puncture-sealing tires (not available with ride-and-handling package). Aluminum alloy wheels.

1987 Cadillac, Fleetwood d'Elegance, sedan

Performance enhancement package (included in Touring Coupe and Touring Sedan packages, but may also be ordered separately and contains re-tuned suspension, l5-inch aluminum alloy wheels, Eagle GT P215/65R15 black sidewall tires, 32mm front and 18mm rear stabilizer bars and faster steering ratio). Performance enhancement package (included in Touring Coupe and Touring Sedan packages, but may also be ordered separately and includes the same as previous but substitutes Eagle GT white sidewall tires).

FLEETWOOD D'ELEGANCE AND SIXTY SPECIAL OPTIONS

Cellular telephone. Memory seat. Automatic day/night mirror. Controlled-cycle windshield wiper system. Rear window defogger. Dimming sentinel. Automatic door locks. Garage door opener. Illuminated entry system. Electrically- powered mirrors. Power driver seat recliner. Six-way power seat adjuster. Dual comfort 45/55 seats. Tilt-and-telescope steering wheel. Trumpet horn. Trunk lid release and power pull down. Twilight Sentinel. Visor-vanity mirrors. Delco-GM Bose Symphony sound system. Delco AM stereo/FM stereo system including electronically-tuned receiver with cassette player. Universal citizens band transceiver. Cambria cloth texture roof treatment. Two-tone paint. Formal Cabriolet roof. Digital instrument cluster. Wire wheel discs. Aluminum alloy wheels. Accent striping. door edge guards. Fuel filler door remote release. Leather seating areas. Firemist paint. Pearlmist paint. Reversible front and rear floor mats. Leather-trimmed steering wheel. Theft deterrent system. Trunk mat. Ride-and-handling package. Anti-lock braking system (standard on Sixty Special). Heavy-duty battery. Engine block heater. Puncture sealing tires (not available with ride-and-handling package).

ELDORADO OPTIONS

Cellular telephone. Automatic day/night mirror. Astroroof. Controlled-cycle windshield wiper system. Rear window defogger. Dimming sentinel. Automatic door locks. Garage door opener. Illuminated entry system. Electrically powered mirrors. Power driver seat recliner. Delco-GM Bose symphony sound system. Delco AM stereo/FM stereo Electronically-tuned receiver with cassette player. Universal citizens band transceiver. Two-tone paint. Door

edge guards. Fuel filler door remote release. Firemist paint. Pearlmist paint. Theft deterrent system. Trunk mat. Touring suspension. Heavy-duty battery. Engine block heater. Puncture-sealing tires (not available with Touring suspension). Cabriolet roof. Wire wheel discs. Wide brushed and bright body side accent molding. Touring Suspension (consists of 15-inch aluminum alloy wheels, Eagle GT P215/60R15 tires, rear stabilizer bar, stiffer front stabilizer bar, turned suspension components and engine block heater). Eldorado Biarritz (includes power recliners and power lumbar support adjusters for front bucket seats, six-way power seat adjuster for front bucket seats, front seat back pockets and leather-trimmed headrests. Other features include American walnut instrument panel, console and door trim plates, two-tone paint, cabriolet padded roof with opera lights, closed-in rear window, wire wheel discs, Mayfair cloth and Sierra combination seating areas, accent molding, Biarritz identification, deluxe Tampico carpeting and floor mats.)

SEVILLE OPTIONS

Cellular telephone. Automatic day/night mirror. Astroroof. Controlled-cycle windshield wiper system. Rear window defogger. Dimming sentinel. Automatic door locks. Garage door opener. Illuminated entry system. Electrically-powered mirrors. Power driver seat recliner. Delco-GM Bose symphony sound system. Delco AM/FM stereo electronically-tuned receiver with cassette player. Universal citizens band transceiver. Two-tone paint. Door edge guards. Fuel filler door remote release. Firemist paint. Pearlmist paint. Mid-tone paint treatment. Theft deterrent system. Trunk mat. Touring Suspension. Heavy-duty battery. Engine block heater. Puncture-seating tires (not available with Touring Suspension). Cabriolet roof. Wire wheel discs. Wide brushed and bright body side accent molding. Seville Touring option (includes Touring Suspension, 15-inch aluminum alloy wheels, Eagle GT P215/60R15 tires, rear stabilizer bar, stiffer front stabilizer bar, turned suspension components and engine block heater. Seville Elegante (includes power recliners and power lumbar support adjusters for front bucket seats, six-way power seat adjuster for front bucket seats, front seat back pockets and leather-trimmed headrests. Other features consist of mid-tone paint treatment, wire wheel discs, special interior with Mayfair cloth and Sierra grain leather and American walnut door trim plates).

BROUGHAM OPTIONS

Memory seat. Automatic day/night mirror. Twilight Sentinel. Astroroof. Automatic door locks. Guidematic headlight control. Six-way power front seat. Adjustable rear seat reading lights. Rear window defogger. Garage door opener. Electrically-powered exterior mirrors. Power front seat recliner. Tilt-and-telescope steering wheel. Visor-vanity lighted mirrors. Delco electronically-tuned receiver with cassette tape. Remote locking fuel filler door. Theft deterrent system. Security option package. Wire wheels. Wire wheel discs. Accent striping. Door edge guards. Floor mats. Leather seating areas. Firemist paint. Leather-trimmed steering wheel. Electronic level control. Trailering package. Heavy-duty battery. Engine block heater. Puncture-sealing tires. Brougham d'Elegance package includes six-way front power seat adjuster, trunk lid release, controlled-cycle windshield wipers, adjustable rear seat reading lights, manual passenger front seat recliner, three roof-mounted assist handles, dual comfort 50/50 front seats, multi-button seat trim, accent striping, "Brougham d'Elegance" turbine vane wheel discs, "d'Elegance" embroidery on doors, "d'Elegance identification" and deluxe Tampico floor carpeting and mats.

HISTORICAL

Total Cadillac model-year output was 282,562. In 1987, Cadillac became the first automobile manufacturer to use multiplexed wiring to control lighting on a production automobile, the Allante. On January 7, 1987, Cadillac was the only General Motors car division with responsibilities for engineering and manufacturing in addition to its marketing and sales activities. As a result, Cadillac had its own staff of engineers, designers, manufacturing personnel and marketing groups. Cadillac General Manager John O. Grettenberger assumed responsibilities for engineering and manufacturing. Robert L. Dorn, previously acting director of the former B-O-C Detroit Product team, became general director of operations for Cadillac.

1987 Cadillac, Fleetwood 60 Special, sedan

1987 Cadillac, Fleetwood 75 limousine

1988

OVERVIEW

The 1988 Cadillac line featured a new 4.5-liter V-8 for the Seville, Eldorado, Fleetwood and DeVille models. The Eldorado was extensively redesigned and detail changes were evident in the Allante, Brougham and Cimarron. The acceleration of Cadillacs with the new V-8 was better than any comparable Cadillac of the last decade. The Allante offered a new analog instrument option as well as new colors. The Seville was given a new front end look and was available with anti-lock brakes. It also had improved fuel economy. The Eldorado's sheet metal, except for the roof, was all new. Both the Fleetwood Sixty Special and d'Elegance models had added standard equipment features. The best selling of all Cadillac's models, the DeVille Coupe and Sedan also had their standard equipment list extended. The traditional Brougham Sedan was changed only in minor details while the Cimarron, in its last year of production, had its list of standard features expanded.

I.D. DATA

The 17-symbol serial number was located on top of the instrument panel, where it was visible through the windshield. The first symbol 1=U.S.-built vehicle. The second

Above: **1988 Cadillac, Cimarron, sedan**

Phil Hall

symbol G=General Motors. The third symbol 6=Cadillac. The fourth symbol indicated carline/the fifth symbol indicated series as follows: C/B=Fleetwood D'Elegance, C/D= DeVille, C/S= Fleetwood Sixty Special, D/W=Brougham, E/L=Eldorado, J/G=Cimarron, K/S=Seville and V/R=Allante. The sixth symbol incated body stytle: 1=two-door Coupe/Sedan GM/Fisher Style Nos. 11, 27, 37, 47, 57 or 97, 3=two-door Convertible GM/Fisher Style No. 67, 5=four-door Sedan GM/Fisher style nos. 19, 23, 33 or 69. The seventh symbol indicates the type of restaint system: 1=manual belts, 3=Manual belts with driver's air bag, 4=automatic belts. The eighth symbol identified the engine: W=2.8L V-6, Y=5.0L V-8, 5=4.5L V-8, 7=4.1L V-8 and 9=5.0L V-8. The ninth symbol was a check digit. The 10th symbol was a number indicating model year: J=1988. The 11th symbol indicates the GM assembly plant: J=Janesville, Wis. (Cimarron), U=Hamtramck, Mich. (Allante), 4=Orion, Mich. (DeVille), 9=Detroit (Cadillac). The next group of numbers was the sequential production code starting with 100001. The Fisher Body tag on the cowl, under the hood includes additional information.

CIMARRON - SERIES 6J/G - V-6

In its final year of production, the Cimarron was refined with the addition of a speed-density fuel control system,

cross-groove drive axles with the standard five-speed transmission and larger standard all-season and optional high-performance tires. Additional changes for 1988 included a new variable-displacement air conditioning compressor, new standard body-color lower grooved molding, improved corrosion protection and three new exterior and interior colors. Another 1987 option made standard for 1988 in addition to the 14-inch alloy wheels and lower body side molding was a heavy-duty battery. Use of the 14-inch alloy wheels in place of the 13-inch wheels of 1987 also resulted in a re-tuning of the rear shock absorber valving. For 1988, the Cimarron's fuel-injected V-6 was equipped with a speed-density fuel control system. A new V-5 variable displacement air conditioning compressor was also adopted. The use of double-side galvanized steel was expanded to include the doors in 1988.

CIMARRON — SERIES 6J/G - V-6

Model Number	Body/Style No.	Body Type & Seating	Factory Price	Shipping Weight	Production Total
J/G	5	4D Sedan-5P	16,071	2,756	6,454

DEVILLE - SERIES 6C/D - V-8

The DeVille's new V-8 was nearly 20 percent more powerful and 10 percent larger than the unit it replaced. Yet its fuel economy was virtually unchanged from the 1987 level. The larger V-8 also now had roller lifters and low-friction pistons. The DeVille had a revised suspension, new engine mount rates, revised heater/air conditioner components and an electronic cruise control system. Now standard for the DeVille was the tilt-telescope steering wheel, cruise control, Dual Comfort front seat, controlled-cycle windshield wiper system, power trunk release and heavy-duty battery. The DeVille's THM 440 automatic transmission now had computer-controlled electronic torque management to prevent overstressing the driveline components. Six new exterior colors were introduced for the DeVille. A "4.5-liter" engine identification plaque was added to the deck lid. The arm rest switchplate was changed from cherrywood to black. Among the numerous electronic changes found in the 1988 DeVille were a higher resolution internal speed sensor and a new under-dash relay center.

1988 Cadillac, Allante' convertible

DEVILLE - SERIES 6C/D - V-8

Series No.	Body/Style No.	Body Type & Seating	Factory Price	Shipping Weight	Production Total
C/D	1	2D Coupe	23,049	3,437	26,420
C/D	5	4D Sedan	23,404	3,397	Note 1

Note 1: Total combined production, of DeVille, Fleetwood d'Elegance and Fleetwood Sixty Special four-door Sedans was 126,093.

FLEETWOOD d'ELEGANCE - SERIES 6C/B - V-8

The Fleetwood d'Elegance shared all of the electrical and mechanical refinements of the DeVille. It also gained 10 previously optional items as standard equipment. These consisted of tilt-telescope steering wheel, cruise control, controlled-cycle windshield wipers, a power trunk pulldown, an illuminated entry system, Twilight Sentinel, illuminated visor-vanity mirrors, a trunk mat and a heavy-duty battery. Only minimal exterior changes took place for 1988. Two new interior colors and six new exterior colors were available.

FLEETWOOD D'ELEGANCE — SERIES 6C/B - V-8

Model Number	Body/Style No.	Body Type & Seating	Factory Price	Shipping Weight	Production Total
C/B	5	4D Sedan	28,024	3,463	Note 1

Note 1: Total combined production, of DeVille, Fleetwood d'Elegance and Fleetwood Sixty Special four-door Sedans was 126,093.

FLEETWOOD SIXTY SPECIAL - SERIES 6C/S - V-8

The Fleetwood Sixty Special continued to offer a longer wheelbase than the d'Elegance model with which it shared the same refinements and features for 1988.

FLEETWOOD SIXTY SPECIAL — SERIES 6C/S — V-8

Model Number	Body/Style No.	Body Type & Seating	Factory Price	Shipping Weight	Production Total
C/S	5	4D Sedan	34,750	3,547	Note 1

Note 1: Total combined production, of DeVille, Fleetwood d'Elegance and Fleetwood Sixty Special four-door Sedans was 126,093.

BROUGHAM - SERIES 6D/W - V-8

The Brougham's 5.0-liter V-8 received a new electronic spark control system for 1988, as well as a numerically higher axle ratio. Additional improvements included new three-point rear seat belts with integral shoulder belts, new light switch lens with ISO-light symbol and the availability of five new exterior and three new interior colors. Options made standard for 1988 included a 25-gallon fuel tank (in place of a 20.7-gallon unit), a tilt-telescope steering wheel, a heavy-duty battery and larger, puncture-sealing tires.

1988 Cadillac, Sedan DeVille

Two new valve option packages for the base Brougham were introduced for 1988. A new optional formal vinyl roof was offered with new llama-grained vinyl top material, a colored vinyl-top drip molding, a material-covered vinyl-top center pillar appliqué (with opera light), rear door quarter window closeout trim and new a garnish molding around the backlight.

BROUGHAM – SERIES 6D/W–V-8

Model Number	Body/Style No.	Body Type & Seating	Factory Price	Shipping Weight	Production Total
D/W	5	4D Sedan	23,846	4,156	53,130

ELDORADO - SERIES 6E/L - V-8

Cadillac called for "more distinctive styling," and the Eldorado was given a major restyling for 1988. Major exterior sheet metal panels—including the front fenders, hood, C-pillar, rear quarters and rear deck—were all new, as were the grille and taillights. The result was a longer, crisper, more tailored appearance. The traditional Eldorado grille had a bolder, more open pattern and the hood was set off by a raised power dome and a new header molding. The side-view was enhanced by the extension of the rear fender line forward into the C-pillar, which was a long time Eldorado trademark. The new rear fender extensions and rear bumper were contoured into a redesigned end panel that, along with a new taillight design, also gave the 1988 model a classic Eldorado appearance. The Eldorado had the new 4.5-liter V-8 engine with an engine identification plaque on the deck lid. Both the Eldorado and Eldorado Biarritz had new design pin stripes. A restyled full vinyl roof was available for the Eldorado. The Biarritz had a revised formal cabriolet roof as standard equipment. Interior changes for 1988 consisted of a redesigned rear seat frame with added cushion suspension system. A new upholstery design featuring horizontal stripes was also used. Two new interior colors, Antelope and Beechwood, were added to complement the new exterior choices. New self-storing pull-swing door handles along with new-design wider headrests were also found in the 1988 Eldorado.

ELDORADO – SERIES E/L – V-8

Model Number	Body/Style No.	Body Type & Seating	Factory Price	Shipping Weight	Production Total
E/L	1	2D Coupe	24,891	3,399	33,210

SEVILLE-SERIES 6K/S-V-8

Like the Eldorado, the 1988 Seville had a new look from the windshield forward. It also shared the Eldorado's new choice of colors and interior revisions, along with its design and engineering advances. Newly available for the Seville was the electronically-controlled Teves anti-lock braking system. The Seville's suspension was refined for 1988 to improve the ride characteristics of the base-suspension models. The touring suspension was also returned for improved roadability. Among the detail changes for 1988 was a more reliable control unit for the electric engine cooling fan (which was also used in the Seville and Eldorado).

SEVILLE – SERIES 6K/S

Model Number	Body/Style No.	Body Type & Seating	Factory Price	Shipping Weight	Production Total
K/S	5	4D Sedan	27,627	3,449	22,968

ALLANTE - SERIES 6V/R - V-8

The Allante entered its first full year of production after being introduced in March 1987. Its styling, power train and features were essentially unchanged for 1988. A number of running changes did take place. These included a reconfiguring of the headrests and the inclusion of a power deck lid pull down as standard equipment. A new option for 1988 was a European-style analog instrument panel that could be ordered in lieu of the standard electronic cluster at no extra charge.

ALLANTE – SERIES V/R – V-8

Model Number	Body/Style No.	Body Type & Seating	Factory Price	Shipping Weight	Production Total
V/R	3	2D Convertible	56,533	3,489	2,569

ENGINE

CIMARRON BASE V-6

Overhead valve. Cast iron block. Displacement: 173-cid (2.8 liters). Bore and stroke: 3.50 x 2.99 inches. Compression ratio: 8.9:1. Brake horsepower: 125 at 4500 rpm. Torque: 160 lb.-ft. @ 3600 rpm. Hydraulic valve lifters. Multi-port fuel injection. VIN Code: W.

DEVILLE, FLEETWOOD, SEVILLE, ELDORADO BASE V-8

Overhead valve. Aluminum block with cast iron liners. Displacement: 273 cid (4.5 liters). Bore and Stroke: 3.62 x 3.31 inches. Compression ratio: 9.0:1. Net brake hp: 155 at 4000 rpm. Taxable hp: 42.00. Net torque: 240 at 2800 rpm. Five main bearings. Roller hydraulic valve lifters. Induction: Digital fuel injection. VIN Code: 5. Built by Cadillac.

1988 Cadillac, Fleetwood d'Elegance, sedan

ALLANTE BASE V-8

Overhead valve. Aluminum block with cast iron liners. Displacement: 249 cid (4.1 liters). Bore and Stroke: 3.47 x 3.31 inches. Compression ratio: 8.5:1. Net brake hp: 170 at 4300 rpm. Taxable hp: 39.2. Net torque: 235 at 3200 rpm. Five main bearings. Roller hydraulic valve lifters. Induction: Sequential multi-port fuel injection. VIN Code: 7. Built by Cadillac.

BROUGHAM BASE V-8

Overhead valve. Cast iron block. Displacement: 307 cid (5.0 liters). Bore and Stroke: 3.80 x 3.39 inches. Compression ratio: 8.0:1. Net brake hp: 140 at 3200 rpm. Taxable hp: 46.20. Net torque: 346 at 2000 rpm. Five main bearings. Hydraulic valve lifters. Carburetion: Four-barrel. VIN Code: Y. Built by Oldsmobile.

CADILLAC OPTIONAL V-8

Overhead valve. Cast iron block. Displacement: 307 cid (5.0 liters). Bore and Stroke: 3.80 x 3.39 inches. Taxable hp: 46.20. Five main bearings. Hydraulic valve lifters. Carburetion: Four-barrel. VIN Code: 9. Built by Oldsmobile.

CHASSIS

(Cimarron) Wheelbase: 101.2 inches. Overall Length: 177.8 inches. Height: 52.1 inches. Width: 65.0 inches. Front Tread: 55.4 inches. Rear Tread: 55.2 inches. Standard Tires: P195/70R14.

(DeVille) Wheelbase: 110.8 inches. Overall Length: 196.5 inches. Height: 55.0 inches. Width: 71.7 inches. Front Tread: 60.3 inches. Rear Tread: 59.8 inches. Standard Tires: P205/75R14.

(Fleetwood d'Elegance) Wheelbase: 110.8 inches. Overall Length: 196.5 inches. Height: 55.0 inches. Width: 71.7 inches. Front Tread: 60.3 inches. Rear Tread: 59.8 inches. Standard Tires: (Coupe DeVille and Fleetwood d'Elegance) Michelin P205/70R14. (Sedan DeVille) P205/75R14.

(Sixty Special) Wheelbase: 116.0 inches. Overall Length: 201.7 inches. Height: 55.0 inches. Width: 71.7 inches. Front Tread: 60.3 inches. Rear Tread: 59.8 inches. Standard Tires: P205/75R14.

(Seville) Wheelbase: 108.0 inches. Overall Length: 190.8 inches. Height: 53.7 inches. Width: 70.9 inches. Front Tread: 59.9 inches. Rear Tread: 59.9 inches. Standard Tires: P205/70R14. (Touring) Goodyear Eagle GT4 P205/75R15.

(Eldorado) Wheelbase: 108.0 inches. Overall Length: 191.2 inches. Height: 53.7 inches. Width: 71.3 inches. Front Tread: 59.9 inches. Rear Tread: 59.9 inches. Standard Tires: P205/70R14. (Touring) Goodyear Eagle GT4 P205/75R15.

(Allante) Wheelbase: 99.4 inches. Overall Length: 178.6 inches. Height: 52.2 inches. Width: 73.4 inches. Front Tread: 60.4 inches. Rear Tread: 60.4 inches. Standard Tires: Goodyear Eagle VL P225/55VR16.

(Brougham) Wheelbase: 121.5 inches. Overall Length: 221.0 inches. Height: 56.7 inches. Width: 75.3 inches. Front Tread: 61.7 inches. Rear Tread: 60.7 inches. Standard Tires: P225/60VR15.

TECHNICAL

Transmission: (Cimarron) Muncie-Getrag five-speed manual transmission, (DeVille, Fleetwood, Eldorado, Seville) THM 440-T4 four-speed automatic transmission (includes overdrive and viscous converter clutch), (Allante) THM F7 four-speed automatic transmission (includes overdrive, viscous converter clutch and electronic shift control), (Brougham) THM 200-4R TCC four-speed automatic transmission (includes overdrive and torque converter clutch). Steering: (All models except Brougham): power-assisted rack and pinion. Brougham: power-assisted recirculating ball. Ratios: DeVille, Fleetwood: 19.1:1, Seville, Eldorado: 16.5:1, Touring: 15.6:1, Allante: 15.6:1, Brougham: 15-13:1. Front Suspension: (All models except Brougham) Independent MacPherson strut with coil springs, strut-type shock absorbers (integral-in strut and electronic variable on Allante) and stabilizer bar, (Brougham) Independent with short/long arms, coil springs, direct acting shock absorbers and link-type stabilizer bar. Rear Suspension: (All models except Brougham) Fully independent with coil springs, automatic level control and strut-type superlift shock absorbers on all models except Cimarron, Allante and Brougham, (Allante) Integral-in strut electronic variable shock absorbers with no rear stabilizer, (Brougham) Four link, coil springs with automatic level control and direct acting shock absorbers. Brakes: (All models except Brougham and Allante) Power front disc and rear drum with Teves anti-lock system, (Allante) Front and rear power disc brakes with Bosch III anti-lock braking system. Body Construction: (All models except Brougham) Integral body-frame, (Brougham) Separate body on frame. Fuel Tank: (Cimarron) 13.6 gallons, (DeVille, Fleetwood) 18.0 gallons, (Eldorado, Seville) 18.8 gallons, (Allante) 22 gallons, (Brougham) 25 gallons.

OPTIONS

CIMARRON OPTIONS

Garage door opener. Vista Vent sun roof. Leather and Cashmere cloth seating area. Six-way power seat. Visor-vanity mirrors. Delco-GM Bose symphony sound system. Delco AM stereo/FM stereo electronically-tuned receiver with cassette player. Elelectronic instrument cluster. Aluminum alloy wheels. Door edge guards. Floor mats. Deck lid luggage rack, heavy-duty battery, 13 inches. Narrow strip whitewalls. Engine block heater.

DEVILLE OPTIONS

Cellular telephone. Automatic day/night mirror. Controlled-cycle wiper system. Rear window defogger. Dimming sentinel. Automatic door locks. Garage door opener. Illuminated entry system. Electrically-powered mirrors. Power driver seat recliner. Six-way power seat adjuster. Dual comfort 45/55 seats. Tilt-and-telescope steering wheel. Trumpet horn. Trunk lid release and power pull down. Twilight Sentinel. Visor-vanity mirrors. Delco-GM Bose symphony sound system. Delco AM stereo/FM stereo electronically- tuned receiver with cassette player. Universal citizens band transceiver. Cambria Cloth texture roof treatment. Two-tone paint. Formal Cabriolet roof. Digital instrument cluster. Wire wheel discs. Aluminum alloy wheels. Accent striping. Door edge guards. Fuel-filter door remote release. Leather seating areas. Fremist paint. Pearlmist paint. Reversible front and rear floor mats. Leather-trimmed steering wheel. Theft deterrent system. Trunk mat. Ride-and-handling package. Anti-lock braking system. Heavy-duty battery. Engine block heater. Puncture-sealing tires (not available with ride-and-handling package). Anti-lock braking. Engine block heater. Aluminum alloy wheels. DeVille Option Package B, includes door edge guards, front carpeted floor mats, six-way power passenger seat. DeVille Option Package C, includes items in Package B plus illuminated entry system, illuminated visor-vanity mirrors, trunk lid power pull down, Twilight Sentinel. DeVille Option Package D, includes items in Package C plus remote-release fuel-filler door, manual driver seat recliner and, trumpet horn ($894).

FLEETWOOD D'ELEGANCE, SIXTY SPECIAL OPTIONS

Cellular telephone. Memory seat. Automatic day/night mirror. Controlled-cycle windshield wiper system. Rear window defogger. Dimming sentinel. Automatic door locks. Garage door opener. Illuminated entry system. Electrically powered mirrors. Power driver seat recliner. Six-way power seat adjuster. Dual comfort 45/55 seats. Tilt-and-telescope steering wheel. Trumpet horn. Trunk lid release and power pull down. Twilight Sentinel. Visor-vanity mirrors. Delco-GM Bose symphony sound system. Delco AM stereo/FM stereo electronically-tuned receiver with cassette player. Universal citizens band transceiver. Cambria Cloth texture roof treatment. Two-tone paint. Formal Cabriolet roof. Digital instrument cluster. Wire wheel discs. Aluminum alloy wheels. Accent striping. Door edge guards. Fuel-filler door remote release. Leather seating areas. Firemist paint. Pearlmist paint. Reversible front and rear floor mats. Leather-trimmed steering wheel. Theft-deterrent system. Trunk mat. Ride-and-handling package. Anti-lock braking system (standard on Sixty Special). Heavy-duty battery. Engine block heater. Puncture-sealing tires (not available with ride-and-handling package). Anti-lock braking. Engine block heater.

ELDORADO OPTIONS

Cellular telephone. Automatic day/night mirror. Astroroof. Controlled-cycle windshield wiper system. Rear window defogger. Dimming sentinel. Automatic door locks. Garage door opener. Illuminated entry system. Electrically powered mirrors. Power driver seat recliner. Delco-GM Bose symphony sound system. Delco AM stereo/FM stereo electronically-tuned receiver with cassette player. Universal citizens band transceiver. Two-tone paint. Door edge guards. Fuel-Filler door remote release. Firemist paint. Pearlmist paint. Theft deterrent system. Trunk mat. Touring suspension. Heavy-duty battery. Engine block heater. Puncture-sealing tires (not available with Touring suspension). Cabriolet roof. Wire wheel discs. Wide brushed and bright body side accent molding. Anti-lock braking. Engine block heater.

1988 Cadillac, Sedan DeVille

1988 Cadillac, Seville Elegante, sedan

SEVILLE OPTIONS

Cellular telephone. Automatic day/night mirror. Astroroof. Controlled-cycle windshield wiper system. Rear window defogger. Dimming sentinel. Automatic door locks. Garage door opener. Illuminated entry system. Electrically powered mirrors. Power driver seat recliner. Delco-GM Bose symphony sound system. Delco AM stereo/FM stereo electronically-tuned receiver with cassette player. Universal citizens band transceiver. Two-tone paint. Door edge guards. Fuel-Filler door remote release. Firemist paint. Pearlmist paint. Mid-tone paint treatment. Theft deterrent system. Trunk mat. Touring suspension. Heavy-duty battery. Engine block heater. Puncture-sealing tires (not available with Touring suspension). Cabriolet roof. Wire wheel discs. Wide brushed and bright body side accent molding. Anti-lock braking. Engine block heater. Puncture-sealing tires (not available with Touring suspension). Cabriolet roof. Wire wheel discs. Wide brushed and bright body side accent molding.

BROUGHAM OPTIONS

Memory seat, automatic day/night mirror. Twilight Sentinel. Astroroof. Automatic door locks. Guidematic headlight control. Six-way power front seat. Adjustable rear seat reading lights. Rear window defogger. Garage door opener. Electrically-powered exterior mirrors. Power front seat recliner. Tilt-and-telescope steering wheel.

Visor-vanity lighted mirrors. Delco electronically-tuned receiver with cassette tape. Remote locking fuel filler door. Theft deterrent system. Security option package. Wire wheels. Wire wheel discs. Accent striping. Door edge guards. Floor mats. Leather seating areas. Firemist paint. Leather-trimmed steering wheel. Electronic level control. Trailering package. Heavy-duty battery. Engine block heater. Puncture-sealing tires. Engine block heater. Heavy-duty ride package. Trailer towing package. Wire wheels. Brougham Option Package B, includes door edge guards, carpeted front and rear floor mats, six- way power passenger seat adjuster, trunk mat: $385. Brougham Option Package C, includes items from package B plus illuminated vanity mirrors, rear sail panel reading lights, power trunk lid pull down. Twilight Sentinel.

HISTORICAL

Production for the model-year totaled 270,844 compared with 282,562 the year previous. Cadillac's share of the U.S. car market was 2.52 percent. On the auto-show circuit, Cadillac displayed its Voyage concept car. The aerodynamic four-door Sedan was designed for fuel efficiency and stability at speeds up to 200 mph. The Voyage also featured a rear-vision video camera that alerted the driver to oncoming vehicles by projecting images on a color monitor located on the instrument panel.

Phil Hall

1988 Cadillac, Cimarron, sedan

1989

OVERVIEW

Cadillac for 1989 offered six car lines powered by V-8 engines. The Cimarron was not produced for 1989. New model highlights included longer and restyled DeVille and Fleetwood models, a more powerful Allante and refinements in the Seville, Eldorado and Brougham. The Seville was now available in limited-edition Seville Touring Sedan (STS) form. This new model was equipped with a re-tuned European-feel suspension package for more precise steering control and a firmer feel of the road. The limited-production Fleetwood Sixty Special Sedan had new front leather seats created by Italian designer Giorgelto Giugiaro. The Allante received a substantial power boost to 200 hp, which made it capable of 0-60 mph acceleration in less than 8.5 seconds. New comfort and convenience features included an express-down driver's window, an electrochromic inside rearview mirror, an ElectriClear windshield and an oil life indicator. Cadillac's 4.5-liter, digitally fuel-injected V-8 was the power plant for the DeVille, Fleetwood, Seville and Eldorado models. Cadillac claimed its cars, capable of 0-60 mph in less than 10 seconds, were the fastest domestically-produced luxury cars available.

Above: **1989 Cadillac, Fleetwood sedan**

Norm Larson

I.D. DATA

The 17-symbol serial number was located on top of the instrument panel, where it was visible through the windshield. The first symbol 1=U.S.-built vehicle. The second symbol G=General Motors. The third symbol 6=Cadillac. The fourth symbol indicated carline/the fifth symbol indicated series as follows: C/B=Fleetwood d'Elegance, C/D= DeVille, C/S= Fleetwood Sixty Special, D/W=Brougham, E/L=Eldorado, J/G=Cimarron, K/S=Seville and V/R=Allante. The sixth symbol incated body stytle: 1=two-door Coupe/Sedan GM/Fisher Style Nos. 11, 27, 37, 47, 57 or 97, 3=two-door Convertible GM/Fisher Style No. 67, 5=four-door Sedan GM/Fisher style nos. 19, 23, 33 or 69. The seventh symbol indicates the type of restaint system: 1=manual belts, 3=Manual belts with driver's air bag, 4=automatic belts. The eighth symbol identified the engine: Y=5.0L V-8, 5=4.5L V-8, 8=4.5L V-8 and 9=5.0L V-8. The ninth symbol was a check digit. The 10th symbol was a number indicating model year: K=1989. The 11th symbol indicates the GM assembly plant: U=Hamtramck, Mich. (Allante), 4=Orion, Mich. (DeVille), 9=Detroit (Cadillac). The next group of numbers was the sequential production code starting with 100001. The Fisher Body tag on the cowl, under the hood includes additional information.

DEVILLE - SERIES 6C/D - V-8

The Cadillac Coupe DeVille and Sedan DeVille shared a distinctive new interior and exterior appearance as well as a more spacious passenger compartment and increased trunk capacity for 1989. The overall length of the coupe increased 5.8 inches to 202.5 inches, while that of the sedan moved up 8.8 inches to 205.2 inches. The sedan's wheelbase was also expanded 3.0 inches to 113.8 inches. The front overhang of both models increased 2.4 inches to 44.1 inches. Their rear overhang was increased 3.4 inches to 47.2 inches. New front sheet metal, a new grille, new quarter panels and a new hood were used. A new fascia was used to improve air flow. Bright headlight bezels and cornering lights were also featured along with a rear-mounted power antenna. At the rear a new deck lid, taillight and fascia were adopted. Highlighting the 1989 model's profile were new rear wheel "eyebrow" openings and lower body side color accent moldings. The Sedan, in addition to having new rear doors, had an integrated center-high-mounted stop light. If the Sedan was ordered with the optional full-padded vinyl roof, an electroluminescent wreath-and-crest sail ornament was installed. The sedan's longer wheelbase provided additional interior space. Trunk capacity was increased from 16.1 cubic feet to 18.4 cubic feet on the Sedan and 18.1 cubic feet on the Coupe. The jack was relocated to a position under the trunk floor, which now had a flat surface area. "Tiffany" carpeting was used for the trunk. The DeVille models now had new front and rear reversible and washable floor mats with a new retention device. A driver-side express-down window was standard, as were electrically-operated car-colored outside rearview mirrors, and an AM/FM stereo signal-seeking radio with scanner, digital display, cassette player, five-band graphic equalizer and extended-range front speakers. A new Delco/Bose II Symphony sound system was optional, as was a digital compact disc player that was integrated with the Bose II radio. Other new options included an electrochromic automatic day/night rearview mirror with a three-position sensitivity switch and a heated windshield. Aluminum touring wheels were now available as an option.

DEVILLE – SERIES C/D - V-8

Model Number	Body/Style No.	Body Type & Seating	Factory Price	Shipping Weight	Production Total
C/D	1	2D Coupe	25,285	3,397	4,108
C/D	5	4D Sedan	25,760	3,470	122,693

FLEETWOOD - SERIES 6C/B - V-8

The Cadillac Fleetwood was available as a Coupe and a Sedan for 1989. Both versions shared the DeVille's new sheet metal and added interior and exterior dimensions. Both Fleetwoods had new rear fender skirts. A fully-padded vinyl roof was standard on the Sedan. The Coupe featured a standard formal Cabriolet roof. The electroluminescent wreath-and-crest sail panel ornament was standard for the Sedan. The Fleetwood's seats were of a tufted design and had Elite cloth inserts with Primavera cloth bolsters. The new center arm rest offered as an option for the DeVille was standard for the Fleetwood interior, which also had the revisions provided for the DeVille. Except on cars fitted with the optional Astroroof, all Fleetwood Sedans had new illuminated overhead vanity mirrors. The Fleetwood's revised and enlarged trunk was identical to the DeVille's. The Fleetwood also had the floor mats, driver's side express-down power window, new mirrors and heated windshield as optrional equipment as the DeVille did. The Fleetwood interior featured a real wood nameplate on the glovebox with "Fleetwood" in gold script. The interior trim was in high-gloss American walnut. Joining the standard features found on 1989 DeVilles were the Fleetwood's remote-release fuel-filler door, a trumpet horn and wire wheel covers.

FLEETWOOD – SERIES C/B - V-8

Model Number	Body/Style No.	Body Type & Seating	Factory Price	Shipping Weight	Production Total
C/B	1	2D Coupe	30,365	3,459	23,294
C/B	5	4D Sedan	30,840	3,545	26,641

FLEETWOOD SIXTY SPECIAL-SERIES 6C/S-V-8

Cadillac described the 1989 Fleetwood Sixty Special as a "luxuriously-equipped up-level sedan with all-new styling...[and] a unique and sumptuous seating package trimmed in ultrasoft leather." In line with DeVille and

1989 Cadillac, Sedan DeVille

1989 Cadillac, Allante' convertible

1989 Cadillac, Fleetwood sedan

Fleetwood models, the Sixty Special (available in five new colors and 11 colors in all) had new sheet metal and styling components. It also had a larger-capacity trunk and new comfort and convenience options. A fully-padded vinyl roof was standard, but could be a delete option. The electroluminescent wreath-and-crest sail panel ornamentation was standard. The Sixty Special interior featured a new exclusive ITAL/Giugiaro seat trim style with "Ultrasoft" leather available in three colors. The front seat now had a unique "Split-Frame" arrangement that allowed independent vertical adjustment of the lower cushion relative to the seat back. Wider headrests were also used. The new center arm rest used on the Fleetwood was also found on the Sixty Special, as were the revised rear seats. The Sixty Special's front arm rest opened to the rear for rear seat access. The rear seat center arm rest had a storage compartment. Map pockets were installed in the front seat backs. Added to the Fleetwood trim was an identification plaque on the quarter panel and glovebox.

FLEETWOOD SIXTY SPECIAL – SERIES C/S – V-8

Model Number	Body/Style No.	Body Type & Seating	Factory Price	Shipping Weight	Production Total
C/S	5	4D Sedan	34,840	3,598	2,007

BROUGHAM - SERIES 6D/W - V-8

The traditional rear-wheel-drive 1989 Brougham was identified by its restyled grille and front-end panel molding. The header molding no longer had an embedded script. The Cadillac script was now located on the grille. The premier formal-padded roof option was offered in five new colors for a total of 12 choices. The Brougham interior included Cadillac's new carpeted and reversible floor mats with a retention device. A 100-amp generator was standard. New standard features consisted of a controlled-cycle windshield-wiper system, cruise control, electronic level control, electrically- powered chrome outside mirrors, a trumpet horn and a power trunk lid release.

BROUGHAM—SERIES D/W—V-8

Model Number	Body/Style No.	Body Type & Seating	Factory Price	Shipping Weight	Production Total
D/W	5	4D Sedan	25,699	4,190	28,926

NOTE 1: An additional 12,212 Broughams were produced with the d'Elegance option.

ELDORADO - SERIES 6E/L - V-8

The Eldorado continued to be available as the Eldorado Coupe and as the Eldorado Biarritz, which was ordered as Option Code YP3. A new White Diamond color was introduced, making a total choice of 18 colors for the Eldorado buyer. The Black Metallic roof of 1988 was replaced with a Sable Black version. The Biarritz roof was revised via the elimination of the bright bead adjacent to the roof molding. New options consisted of an electrochromic mirror, a Delco/Bose Symphony sound system and a digital disc player. New standard features consisted of

an accent molding, remote fuel-door release, front license plate mounting, an AM/FM stereo radio used on the Sixty Special and aluminum alloy wheels with a snowflake finish. Interior changes for 1989 were headlined by a high-gloss bird's-eye maple wood trim for the instrument panel, front console and door panels that were installed on the Eldorado Biarritz and standard on Eldorados with the B20 Appliqués option. A passive vehicle anti-theft system (VATS) that disengaged the starter, fuel pump and ECM was standard. The heater/defroster and bi-level air modes were revised to provide a more gradual and comfortable transition from warm to cool airflow.

ELDORADO—SERIES E/L–V-8

Model Number	Body/Style No.	Body Type & Seating	Factory Price	Shipping Weight	Production Total
6E	L57	2D Coupe	26,915	3,422	20,633

NOTE 2: An additional 7,174 Eldorados were produced with the Biarritz option.

SEVILLE - SERIES 6K/S - V-8

The Seville offered several interior improvements and new standard features. Cadillac depicted the Touring Sedan option (Code YP6) as featuring "European styling, exclusive appointments, performance and road manners that make a driver's car in the European tradition." The Seville's color choice was revised to include White Diamond finish for the standard Seville and the replacement of Black Metallic with Sable Black. A total of 18 colors were offered. The bird's-eye maple trim also used for the Eldorado was standard for the Seville. The 1998 Elegante seat was now standard. The Seville also had the VATS installed on the 1989 Eldorado. New standard equipment included Cadillac's electrochromic day/night mirror, an engine-oil-life indicator, driver side express-down window and Delco/Bose II Symphony sound system. Except for the Eldorado's accent molding and snowflake wheels, the Seville shared that model's new standard equipment. Power front passenger and driver recliners and 15-inch cast-aluminum lace wheels were also standard for the Seville. It featured hand-stitched beechwood ultrasoft leather seating areas, anti-lock braking, a touring suspension, a 3.3:1 drive ratio, and 15-inch cast-aluminum alloy wheels. The STS interior was fitted with a 12-way power front seat, manual articulating front seat headrests, rear bucket seats with integral headrests, a center rear console and rear storage compartment, leather-wrapped front and rear door trim panels, door-pull straps, overhead pull straps, high-gloss elm burl wood appliqués (on the door trim panels, switch plates, horn pad, horn bar, instrument panel and front and rear consoles), and a deck lid liner in Tara material with an "STS" logo. Other standard STS features consisted of an illuminated entry system, a theft-deterrent system and a trunk mat.

Model Number	Body/Style No.	Body Type & Seating	Factory Price	Shipping Weight	Production Total
K/S	5	4D Sedan	29,935	3,422	20,422

NOTE 3: An additional 1,893 Sevilles were produced with the Touring Sedan option.

ALLANTE - SERIES 6V/R - V-8

The Allante was refined for 1989 by virtue of a larger 4.5-liter port-fuel-injected V-8 engine that provided increased power and improved performance. With 10 percent greater displacement, new low-restriction exhaust manifolds and an improved-flow air cleaner, the Allante's engine had a 17 percent increase in horsepower and a 13 percent increase in torque. Its 0-60 mph time was improved from 9.5 to 8.3 seconds. The time needed to get from 40 to 80 mph dropped from 12.3 to 10.3 seconds. The Allante's top speed increased from 125 to 135 mph. Central door unlocking was now available. Several improvements took place in the Allante's soft top. A new seat design was used with a softer foam on the cushions and back wings, as well as softer wrinkled leather trim and French seams for the wings and head restraints. Significant technical developments were also part of the 1989 Allante package. A new speed-dependent suspension provided for a variety of ride-and-handling characteristics. For higher speeds the focus was on stability without a significant loss of ride quality. This system also monitored braking and acceleration to reduce the rate of fore/aft movement. A new variable-assist steering system reduced pump output flow as engine speed increased. It also reduced parking and low-speed effort while increasing steering effort and precision at higher speeds.

ALLANTE–SERIES V/R–V-8

Model Number	Body/Style No.	Body Type & Seating	Factory Price	Shipping Weight	Production Total
V/R	5	2D Convertible	57,183	3,492	3,296

ENGINE

DEVILLE, FLEETWOOD, SEVILLE, ELDORADO BASE V-8

Overhead valve. Aluminum block with cast iron liners. Displacement: 273 cid (4.5 liters). Bore and Stroke: 3.62 x 3.31 inches. Compression ratio: 9.0:1. Net brake hp: 155 at 4000 rpm. Taxable hp: 42.00. Net torque: 240 at 2800 rpm. Five main bearings. Roller hydraulic valve lifters. Induction: Digital fuel injection. VIN Code: 5. Built by Cadillac.

1989 Cadillac, Coupe de Ville

ALLANTE BASE V-8

Overhead valve. Aluminum block with cast iron liners. Displacement: 273 cid (4.5 liters). Bore and Stroke: 3.62 x 3.31 inches. Compression ratio: 9.0:1. Net brake hp: 200 at 4300 rpm. Taxable hp: 42.00. Net torque: 270 at 3200 rpm. Five main bearings. Roller hydraulic valve lifters. Induction: Sequential multiport fuel injection. VIN Code: 8. Built by Cadillac.

BROUGHAM BASE V-8

Overhead valve. Cast iron block. Displacement: 307 cid (5.0 liters). Bore and Stroke: 3.80 x 3.39 inches. Compression ratio: 8.0:1. Net brake hp: 140 at 3200 rpm. Taxable hp: 46.20. Net torque: 346 at 2000 rpm. Five main bearings. Hydraulic valve lifters. Carburetion: Four-barrel. VIN Code: Y. Built by Oldsmobile.

CADILLAC OPTIONAL V-8

Overhead valve. Cast iron block. Displacement: 307 cid (5.0 liters). Bore and Stroke: 3.80 x 3.39 inches. Taxable hp: 46.20. Five main bearings. Hydraulic valve lifters. Carburetion: Four-barrel. VIN Code: 9. Built by Oldsmobile.

CHASSIS

(DeVille) Wheelbase: 110.8 inches. Overall Length: 196.5 inches. Height: 55.0 inches. Width: 71.7 inches. Front Tread: 60.3 inches. Rear Tread: 59.8 inches. Standard Tires: P225/75R15.

(Fleetwood d'Elegance) Wheelbase: 110.8 inches. Overall Length: 196.5 inches. Height: 55.0 inches. Width: 71.7 inches. Front Tread: 60.3 inches. Rear Tread: 59.8 inches. Standard Tires: (Coupe DeVille and Fleetwood d'Elegance) Michelin P205/70R14. (Sedan DeVille) P225/75R15.

(Sixty Special) Wheelbase: 116.0 inches. Overall Length: 201.7 inches. Height: 55.0 inches. Width: 71.7 inches. Front Tread: 60.3 inches. Rear Tread: 59.8 inches. Standard Tires: P225/75R15.

(Seville) Wheelbase: 108.0 inches. Overall Length: 190.8 inches. Height: 53.7 inches. Width: 70.9 inches. Front Tread: 59.9 inches. Rear Tread: 59.9 inches. Standard Tires: P205/70R15.

(Eldorado) Wheelbase: 108.0 inches. Overall Length: 191.2 inches. Height: 53.7 inches. Width: 71.3 inches.

Front Tread: 59.9 inches. Rear Tread: 59.9 inches. Standard Tires: P205/70R15.

(Allante) Wheelbase: 99.4 inches. Overall Length: 178.6 inches. Height: 52.2 inches. Width: 73.4 inches. Front Tread: 60.4 inches. Rear Tread: 60.4 inches. Standard Tires: Goodyear Eagle VL P225/55VR16.

(Brougham) Wheelbase: 121.5 inches. Overall Length: 221.0 inches. Height: 56.7 inches. Width: 75.3 inches. Front Tread: 61.7 inches. Rear Tread: 60.7 inches. Standard Tires: P225/75R15.

TECHNICAL

Transmission: (DeVille, Fleetwood, Eldorado, Seville) THM 440-T4 automatic four-speed (includes overdrive and viscous converter clutch), (Allante) THM F7 automatic four-speed (includes overdrive, viscous converter clutch and electronic shift control), (Brougham) THM 200-4R automatic four-speed (includes overdrive and torque converter clutch). Steering: (All models except Brougham): Power-assisted rack and pinion. Brougham: Power-assisted recirculating ball. Ratios: DeVille, Fleetwood: 19.1:1, Seville, Eldorado: 16.5:1, Touring: 15.6:1, Allante: 15.6:1, Brougham: 15-13:1. Front Suspension: (All models except Brougham) Independent MacPherson strut with coil springs, strut-type shock absorbers (integral-in strut and electronic variable on Allante) and stabilizer bar. (Brougham) Independent with short/long arms, coil springs, direct acting shock absorbers and link-type stabilizer bar. Rear Suspension: (All models except Brougham): fully independent with coil springs. Automatic level control and strut-type superlift shock absorbers on all models except Allante and Brougham. Allante: Integral-in strut electronic variable shock absorbers with no rear stabilizer. Brougham: Four link, coil springs with automatic level control and direct acting shock absorbers. Brakes: (All models except Brougham and Allante): Power-assisted front disc/rear drum with Teves anti-lock braking system. Allante: Power-assisted front disc/rear disc, Bosch III anti-lock braking system. Brougham: Power-assisted front disc/rear drum. Body Construction: (All models except Brougham): Integral body-frame, Brougham: Separate body on frame. Fuel Tank: (DeVille, Fleetwood) 18.0 gallons, (Eldorado, Seville) 18.8 gallons, (Allante) 22 gallons, (Brougham) 25 gallons.

OPTIONS

DEVILLE OPTIONS

Accent striping ($75) Anti-lock braking system ($925). Storage front arm rest ($70). Astroroof ($1355). California emissions and testing ($100). California emissions label ($100). Rear window defogger ($195). Heated windshield defogger ($250). Automatic door locks ($185). Carpeted rear floor mats ($25). Gold ornamentation package (395). Trailer towing package ($120). Digital instrument cluster

($250). Leather seating area ($560). Automatic day/night mirror ($80). Firemist paint ($240). Monotone lower accent color (no charge). Delco-Bose sound system with cassette ($576). Delco-Bose sound system with compact disc system ($872). Manual passenger seat recliner ($45). Power passenger seat recliner ($95-$410). Formal Cabriolet roof on Coupe DeVille ($825). Full-padded vinyl roof on Sedan DeVille ($825). Leather-trimmed steering wheel ($115). Theft-deterrent system ($225). Trunk mat ($36). Wire locking wheel discs ($365). Aluminum alloy wheels on Coupe DeVille ($480). DeVille Option Package B, includes door edge guards, front carpeted floor mats, six-way power passenger seat ($324). DeVille Option Package C, includes items in Package B, plus illuminated-entry system, illuminated visor-vanity mirrors, trunk lid power pull down, Twilight Sentinel: ($739). DeVille Option Package D, includes items in Package C plus remote release fuel filler door, manual driver seat recliner, trumpet horn: ($894). Brougham Option Package B, includes door edge guards, carpeted front and rear floor mats, six-way power passenger seat adjuster, trunk mat: $385.

FLEETWOOD OPTIONS

Accent molding ($150). Astroroof ($1,355). California emissions and testing ($100). Heated windshield defogger ($250). Automatic door locks ($185). Gold ornamentation package ($395). Leather seating area ($560). Two-position driver's side memory seat ($235). Automatic day/night mirror ($80). Firemist paint ($240). Monotone lower accent color (no charge). Delco-Bose sound system with cassette ($576). Delco-Bose with compact disc system ($872). Power driver seat recliner ($95). Power passenger seat recliner ($95-$410). Leather-trimmed steering wheel ($115). Vinyl roof delete ($374 credit). Theft-deterrent system ($225). Stylized aluminum wheels ($115).

SIXTY SPECIAL OPTIONS

California emissions and testing ($100). Rear window defogger ($195). Heated windshield defogger ($250). Automatic door locks ($185). Gold ornamentation package ($395). Two-position driver's side memory seat ($235). Automatic day/night mirror ($80). Firemist paint ($240). Monotone lower accent color (no charge). Delco-Bose sound system with cassette ($576). Delco-Bose with compact disc system ($872). Power passenger seat recliner ($95-$410). Vinyl roof delete ($374 credit). Theft-deterrent system ($225). Stylized aluminum wheels ($115).

BROUGHAM OPTIONS

Accent striping ($75). Astroroof ($1,355). California emissions and testing ($100). California emissions label ($100). Coachbuilder delete package ($389 credit). Rear window defogger ($195). Brougham d'Elegance cloth ($2,286). Brougham d'Elegance leather ($2,846).

Automatic door locks ($185). Remote release fuel filler door ($65). Gold ornamentation package ($395). Heavy-duty coachbuilder/livery package, includes heavy-duty ride package ($299). Leather seating area, not available with d'Elegance option ($560). Automatic day/night mirror ($80). Firemist paint ($240). Base radio with cassette tape player ($309). Power passenger seat recliner ($95-$410). Premier formal vinyl roof ($1,195). Leather-trimmed steering wheel ($115). Theft deterrent system ($225). Wire locking wheel discs ($445). Wire wheels ($1,000). Heavy-duty ride package ($120). Trailer Towing package ($299). Brougham Option Package B, includes door edge guards, carpeted front and rear floor mats, six-way power passenger seat adjuster, trunk mat ($385). Brougham Option Package C, includes items from Package B plus illuminated vanity mirrors, rear sail panel reading lights, power trunk lid pull down, Twilight Sentinel ($743).

ELDORADO OPTIONS

Accent striping ($75). Anti-lock braking system ($925). Bird's-eye maple appliqués ($2435, but included in Eldorado Biarritz package). Astroroof ($1355). Biarritz-Eldorado leather ($3,325). Biarritz-Eldorado cloth ($2875). California emissions and testing ($100). Cellular mobile telephone ($1975). Cellular mobile telephone provision ($395, but included with optional analog instrument cluster). Rear window defogger ($195). Automatic door locks ($185). Gold ornamentation package ($395). Leather seating area ($450). Automatic day/night mirror ($80). Firemist paint ($240, but not available with two-tone paint). Primary firemist paint for Eldorados with two-tone paint ($190). Secondary Firemist paint for Eldorado with two-tone paint ($50). White diamond paint ($240). Monotone lower accent color (no charge). Delco-Bose sound system with compact disc player ($872). Power passenger seat recliner ($95-$410). Full padded vinyl roof package ($1,095). Full cabriolet roof ($1,095). Theft-deterrent system ($225). White sidewall P215/65R15 tires ($76). FE2 touring suspension including stiffer front springs, larger-diameter front stabilizer bar, a rear stabilizer bar and faster steering and 3.33:1 final drive ratio ($155). Engine block heater, $45. Wire locking wheel discs ($235).

SEVILLE OPTIONS

Accent molding ($150). Anti-lock braking system ($925). Astroroof ($1,355). California emissions and testing ($100). Cellular mobile telephone ($1,975). Cellular mobile telephone provision ($395, but included in analog instrument cluster). Rear window defogger ($195 but standard with STS). Automatic door locks ($185, but included in STS package). Gold ornamentation package ($395). Leather seating area ($450, but included in STS). Automatic day/night mirror ($80). Firemist paint ($240,

but not available with two-tone paint). Primary Firemist paint for Seville with two-tone paint ($190). Secondary Firemist paint for Seville with two-tone paint ($50). White Diamond paint ($240). Two-tone paint ($225, but not available with STS). Delco-Bose sound system with compact disc player ($872). Power passenger seat recliner ($95-$410). Full padded viny roof ($1,095, but not available with STS). Full Cabriolet roof ($1,095, but not available with STS or full padded vinyl roof). Phaeton roof ($1,195, but not available with STS or full-padded vinyl roof). Seville touring sedan ($5,754). Theft-deterrent system ($225, but included with STS ($225). P215/65R15 white sidewall tires ($76 on cars with FE2 suspension and not available with STS). Touring suspension ($115, but included with STS). Wire locking wheel discs($235, but not available with STS). Aluminum alloy wheels (no charge with FE2 suspension, but not available with STS). Seville touring sedan option YP6 including FE2 touring suspension ($5,754). FE2 touring suspension including stiffer front springs, larger-diameter front stabilizer bar, a rear stabilizer bar and faster steering and 3.33:1 final drive ratio ($155). Engine block heater, $45,

ALLANTE OPTIONS

Accent striping ($75). California emissions label ($100). Cellular mobile telephone ($1,975). Cellular mobile telephone provision ($395). Analog instrument cluster (no charge). Power passenger seat recliner ($95-$410).

HISTORICAL

Cadillac had 1,605 dealers at the start of the 1989 calendar-year. Compared to the 1988 model-year, Cadillac increased its market share from 2.52 percent to 2.70 percent. Model-year output totaled 276,138 compared to 270,844 the year previous. Following up the 1988 Voyage concept car, Cadillac engineers created the Solitaire rear-wheel drive coupe for display on the show circuit. It was powered by a dual overhead cam V-12 with port fuel injection, jointly produced by Cadillac and Lotus. The Solitaire featured a memory system that automatically tilted front seats forward for easy exit of back seat occupants. Its aerodynamic front fender skirts opened when the front wheels were turned. It used two miniature video cameras in place of exterior and interior rearview mirrors. The cameras transmitted color images to video screens on the instrument panel.

1989 Cadillac, Seville, STS sedan

1990

OVERVIEW

Highlights of the 1990 Cadillacs included a new soft top and the world's first front-wheel-drive Traction Control system for the Allante. A passive restraint system was installed in every Cadillac. Also for 1990, anti-lock brake systems were available as either standard equipment or as an option on all Cadillac models. Cadillac's 4.5-liter V-8 continued to be a Cadillac exclusive, available only in its full-size, front-wheel drive models. For 1990, the engine benefited from sequential port fuel injection and a higher compression ratio. Horsepower was now 180 with no consequent reduction in fuel economy.

I.D. DATA

The 17-symbol serial number was located on top of the instrument panel, where it was visible through the windshield. The first symbol 1=U.S.-built vehicle. The second symbol G=General Motors. The third symbol 6=Cadillac. The fourth symbol indicated car line/the fifth symbol indicated series as follows: C/B=Fleetwood, C/D=DeVille, C/S= Fleetwood Sixty Special, D/W=Brougham, E/L=Eldorado, K/S=Seville, K/Y=Seville Touring Sedan (STS), V/R=Allante Convertible Hardtop and V/S=Allante Convertible. The sixth symbol incated

Above: **1990 Cadillac, Allante' convertible**

body style: 1=two-door Coupe/Sedan GM/Fisher Style Nos. 11, 27, 37, 47, 57 or 97, 3=two-door Convertible GM/Fisher Style No. 67, 5=four-door Sedan GM/Fisher style nos. 19, 23, 33 or 69. The seventh symbol indicates the type of restaint system: 1=manual belts, 3=Manual belts with driver's air bag, 4=automatic belts. The eighth symbol identified the engine: Y=5.0L V-8, 3=4.5L V-8, 7=5.7L V-8 and 9=5.0L V-8. The ninth symbol was a check digit. The 10th symbol was a number indicating model year: L=1990. The 11th symbol indicates the GM assembly plant: U=Hamtramck, Mich. (Allante), 4=Orion, Mich. (DeVille), 9=Detroit (Cadillac). The next group of numbers was the sequential production code starting with 100001. The Fisher Body tag on the cowl, under the hood includes additional information.

DEVILLE-SERIES 6C/D-V-8

The best-selling luxury automobile in America, the 1990 version of the DeVille was powered by a more powerful 4.5-liter V-8 engine. Its horsepower was increased from 155 to 190, while torque moved up from 240 to 245 pound-feet. A new windshield wiper system with enhanced overall operation was adopted. Features that were previously optional, that were now standard on the DeVille, consisted of a center front seat armrest with a

flip-open storage area, door edge guards, manual driver and passenger seat recliners, a leather-trimmed steering wheel rim and a driver's side supplemental inflatable restraint (S.I.R.) system. Five new exterior colors were offered: Slate Gray, Light Auburn, Dark Auburn, Medium Slate Gray and Dark Slate Gray. A long list of advances and improvements highlighted the 1990 DeVille interior. Two new Primavera cloth colors, Slate Gray and Dark Auburn, were introduced. A total of five colors were offered. These two colors were also available in the Sierra grain leather trim, joining six carryover colors from 1989. New standard driver and vanity mirrors with mirror covers were also installed. A new front seat back buckle anchor (on track) was used to provide convenience in locating the buckle from any position. The use of the S.I.R. resulted in the elimination of the steering wheel telescoping function. The Express-Open Webasto Astroroof was improved to allow the roof window to open with a single one-second touch on the switch. It could be stopped at any position by tapping the switch a second time. Changes in Cadillac's engine for 1990 included the use of a dual level intake manifold, lightweight pistons, larger valve cylinder heads, new magnesium valve covers and new BCM software. The optional cast-aluminum lace wheels offered for the DeVille featured window areas of either silver or gray depending on the car's lower accent molding color. A chrome wreath-and-crest were used.

DEVILLE—SERIES 6C/D — V-8

Model Number	Body/Style No.	Body Type & Seating	Factory Price	Shipping Weight	Production Total
C/D	1	2D Coupe	26,960	3,486	2,438
C/D	5	4D Sedan	27,540	3,466	131,717

FLEETWOOD-SERIES 6C/B-V-8

All of the new or improved features introduced for the 1990 DeVilles were also found on the Fleetwood Cadillacs. The Elite cloth used for the 1989 Fleetwood seats was replaced by new Ardmore cloth. The Fleetwood's standard aluminum lace wheels differed slightly from the DeVille's by having a silver background for the center cap and a chrome wreath in association with a crest in traditional Cadillac colors. Wire wheel discs were optional.

FLEETWOOD — SERIES 6C/B — V-8

Model Number	Body/Style No.	Body Type & Seating	Factory Price	Shipping Weight	Production Total
C/B	1	2D Coupe	32,400	3,538	17,569
C/B	5	4D Sedan	32,980	3,618	22,889

FLEETWOOD SIXTY SPECIAL - SERIES 6C/S - V-8

Cadillac's depiction of the 1990 Fleetwood Sixty Special was of a car "for those buyers who seek luxury with power." Added to the Fleetwood's list of 1990 features were a number of items appropriate to the Sixty Special's status.

Three new exterior colors, Slate Gray, Medium Slate Gray and Dark Slate Gray, were available for the Sixty Special. Eleven colors were offered. A new ultrasoft leather slate gray color, for a total of three, was also available.

FLEETWOOD SIXTY SPECIAL— SERIES 6C/S–V-8

Model Number	Body/Style No.	Body Type & Seating	Factory Price	Shipping Weight	Production Total
C/S	5	4D Sedan	36,980	3,657	1,824

BROUGHAM-SERIES 6D/W-V-8

The 1990 Brougham featured what Cadillac proclaimed as "contemporary yet classic exterior and interior restyling." This view was justified by a major revamping of the long-lived Brougham package. Three new colors, Brownstone, Maple Red and Light Antelope, were introduced. A total of 12 colors was offered. A new wide lower body side colored accent molding was standard. The moldings were Silver Frost or Light Antelope depending on exterior paint color. Three exterior colors could be ordered with matching color accent moldings. Silver Frost and Light Antelope were available only as monotone. The Brougham's front end appearance was revised by the use of halogen composite headlights, new end caps, rub strip and bumper filler, plus a new windshield pillar pad and drip molding. In profile, a number of restyling efforts were evident. A new combination turn signal/parking/side marker light was used. The opera light was moved forward and a new bright chrome center pillar was used. New front and rear body-color door edge guards were standard as were new colored wide lower accent moldings. At the rear a new deck lid molding for the license plate opening was found. A new formal padded full vinyl roof was standard.

1990 Cadillac, Fleetwood sedan

1990 Cadillac, Brougham sedan

Significant changes took place in the Brougham's interior. Two new colors for the Primavera cloth upholstery, antelope and dark maple red, were introduced. A total of four colors were offered. Revisions to the Brougham's seating areas consisted of the replacement of Royal Prima with Primavera cloth, outboard front seat cushions contoured on the standard Brougham for increased lateral support, a new standard front seat center armrest with storage compartment and a change in the d'Elegance seat to a 55/45 configuration. A black walnut burl trim was used for the instrument panel, doors and steering wheel horn pad. Both a power driver seat recliner and an electronic digital instrument panel were now standard. An improved electronic climate control system with three automatic and two manual settings was adopted. The standard AM/FM radio with a preset graphic equalizer, cassette tape player and signal seeking and scanner feature with digital display was also upgraded. Both a new compact disc player and an electrochromic inside rearview mirror were optional. Previous options that were made standard for 1990 included: heated outside mirrors, door edge guards, carpeted floor mats, front license mounting provisions and trunk mat. The power plant and chassis of the Brougham benefited from the use of a new standard anti-lock braking system. A 5.7-liter V-8 with throttle body fuel injection was included with the coachbuilder package (which was also revised for 1990) and trailer towing packages. The 5.7-liter V-8 came with an 8.5-inch ring gear and 3.08:1 final drive ratio as well as a one-time Level 3 Gas Guzzler tax! In addition, the option code V4S model had a specific interior trim design including tufted multi-button seats, three overhead assist handles, six-way power passenger seat adjuster, illuminated driver and passenger visor-vanity mirrors, rear sail panel reading lights, Twilight Sentinel, power trunk lid pulldown and exterior/interior identification.

BROUGHAM—SERIES 6D/W—V-8

Model Number	Body/Style No.	Body Type & Seating	Factory Price	Shipping Weight	Production Total
D/W	5	4D Sedan	27,400	4,283	21,529

Note 1: An additional 12,212 Broughams were equipped with the d'Elegance option.

ELDORADO - SERIES 6E/L - V-8

Cadillac's personal luxury coupe gained added distinction for 1990 via its exterior and interior restyling. It also enjoyed the added power of the 4.5-liter Cadillac V-8. Five new colors, for a total of 17, were available for the Eldorado. The new colors were Light Auburn, Dark Auburn, Crimson (not available for Biarritz), Medium Slate Gray and Dark Slate Gray. The 1990 Eldorado's front end was revised by the use of new bumper molding, a body-color front valance panel and bumper guards changed to Gray, from body color. The Eldorado's body side appearance was altered by its new standard body molding and revised accent stripes. At the rear was found a new bumper molding, revised back-up light lenses, a new license plate pocket, a relocated reflex (moved to the rear-end panel) and a new deck lid pull-down molding. A central door-unlocking system was added to the optional automatic door lock option. Turning the key in either door unlocked the door. Holding the key in turned position for 1.5 seconds unlocked the other door. Three new Mayfair cloth colors, Slate Gray, Antelope and Garnet (for a total of four), were offered. Nine Sierra grain leather colors were available for the standard Eldorado. Among these were two new choices: Slate Gray and Dark Auburn. These colors, plus Black, were available for the Sierra grain leather of the Biarritz, for a total of nine colors. Leather seating areas were now standard for the Biarritz. Both versions of the Eldorado had modified seating styles for 1990. The standard model had a seat cushion providing improved lateral and lumbar support. The seat back pockets were removed on the standard model. Both versions had new molded side panels. The optional leather seating area now included the power passenger seat recliner. A revised vinyl center front armrest and new carpeted rubber-backed floor mats with retention needles were also used. Suspension changes for 1990 involved a new direct-acting front stabilizer shaft for improved ride control and a standard ride-and-handling structural package. Optional new 15-inch cast-aluminum wheels were offered, except for cars with the touring suspension. Eight items that were optional in 1989, and now standard for the 1990 Eldorado, were side and deck lid accent striping, a rear window defogger, heated outside rearview mirrors, door edge guards, front and rear carpeted floor mats, an illuminated entry system, leather seating areas (for the Eldorado Biarritz), illuminated driver and passenger visor-vanity mirrors and a trunk mat. The Eldorado Biarritz, Option Code YP3, was distinguished by its two-tone paint treatment (monotone was also available), a formal Cabriolet roof, opera lights, "Biarritz" sail panel identification, wire wheel discs (cast-aluminum snowflake wheels were available), a specific interior design, specific front bucket seats, bird's-eye maple appliqués, power driver and passenger seat recliners, power lumbar support adjusters for driver and passenger seats and deluxe front and rear floor carpet mats. Broadening the Eldorado's market appeal was the

1990 Cadillac, Fleetwood coupe

introduction of the Touring Coupe model. Its Beechwood leather and bird's-eye maple wood interior provided an ambiance that Cadillac said was "intentionally designed with fewer chrome appointments." Other Touring Coupe features included an extra-wide rocker panel molding, a touring suspension, an anti-lock braking system and forged aluminum wheels.

ELDORADO – SERIES 6E/L – V-8

Model Number	Body/Style No.	Body Type & Seating	Factory Price	Shipping Weight	Production Total
E/L	1	2D Coupe	28,855	3,426	13,610

Note 2: An additional 1,507 Eldorados with the touring coupe option were built.
Note 3: An additional 7,174 Eldorados with the Biarritz option were built.

SEVILLE-SERIES 6K/S-V-8

The 1990 Seville largely shared the changes made in the Eldorado for 1990. There were a few exceptions however, as detailed below. The Seville was offered in 16 colors. Four new hues were Light Auburn, Dark Auburn, Medium Slate Gray and Dark Slate Gray. New body side reflexes were used. The corner turn signal lights were relocated to the bumper. A new white crystalline taillight lens was used. Interior developments consisted of two new Sierra grain leather color choices, Slate Gray and Dark Auburn, for a total of nine. The Seville's seat was revamped to provide for envelope-type seat back pockets and molded side panels.

SEVILLE – SERIES 6K/S – V-8

Model Number	Body/Style No.	Body Type & Seating	Factory Price	Shipping Weight	Production Total
K/S	5	4D Sedan	31,830	3,481	31,235

SEVILLE TOURING SEDAN-SERIES 6K/Y-V-8

The Seville Touring Sedan was now built entirely at Detroit/Hamtramck. According to GM coding, it was part of the "K" car line like other Sevilles, but it was in its own new "Y" series. It had new, body color, front and rear lower fascias with a black bead, plus a body-color rocker molding that also had a black bead. The rear of the car was updated by use of a larger "STS" cloisonné deck lid emblem and a dual-outlet exhaust system. Larger 16-inch diamond-cut-finish forged-aluminum wheels, with larger Goodyear Eagle GT4 P215/60R16 tires, were also introduced for 1990.

SEVILLE TOURING SEDAN – SERIES 6K/Y – V-8

Model Number	Body/Style No.	Body Type & Seating	Factory Price	Shipping Weight	Production Total
K/Y	5	4D Sedan	36,320	3,557	1,893

ALLANTE CONVERTIBLE HARDTOP-SERIES 6V/R-V-8

The Allante was available in two body styles for 1990. The Convertible Hardtop included both a convertible top and a removable, all-aluminum hardtop. The standard and optional content of the two models was nearly identical, but there were some minor variations between the two models. The Convertible Hardtop's standard digital instrument cluster was an extra-cost feature for the Convertible. Pearl White finish was available at no charge on the Convertible Hardtop, but cost extra on the Convertible. The only exterior change for 1990 was the addition of a new Beige Metallic color providing a total of eight color choices for the Allante. Natural Beige-colored durosoft leather was also available. Other revised or new items for 1990 included a standard S.I.R. driver-side airbag system, a smaller steering wheel with a thicker rim cross-section, a standard Delco-Bose compact digital disc player and an improved cellular telephone option. A Traction Control system providing increased steering ability and improved stability when accelerating, as well as increased traction on slippery surfaces, was standard. New chassis calibration involved revised strut valving and the use of gas-charged struts. A new direct-acting front stabilizer shaft was also used. Shift points for the Allante's transmission were changed to 40 and 60 mph from 1989's 25 and 60 mph.

ALLANTE CONVERTIBLE HARDTOP – SERIES 6Y/R – V-8

Model Number	Body/Style No.	Body Type & Seating	Factory Price	Shipping Weight	Production Total
Y/R	3	2D Convertible Hardtop	57,183	3,522	Note 4

ALLANTE CONVERTIBLE-SERIES 6V/S-V-8

The new Allante Convertible was offered as a convertible only and did not include a hardtop. An analog instrument cluster was standard in the Convertible. A digital instrument cluster was an extra-cost item. Pearl White finish cost extra on the Convertible.

ALLANTE CONVERTIBLE – SERIES 6Y/S – V-8

Model Number	Body/Style No.	Body Type & Seating	Factory Price	Shipping Weight	Production Total
Y/S	3	2D Convertible	51,550	3,470	Note 4

Note 4: Allante production totaled 3,101.

ENGINE

DEVILLE, FLEETWOOD, SEVILLE, ELDORADO BASE V-8

Overhead valve. Aluminum block with cast-iron liners. Displacement: 273 cid (4.5 liters). Bore and Stroke: 3.62 x 3.31 inches. Compression ratio: 9.5:1. Net brake hp: 180 at 4300 rpm. Taxable hp: 42.00. Net torque: 240 lbs.-ft. at 3000 rpm. Five main bearings. Roller hydraulic valve lifters. Induction: Sequential port fuel injection. VIN Code: 6. Built by Cadillac.

ALLANTE BASE V-8

Overhead valve. Aluminum block with cast-iron liners. Displacement: 273 cid (4.5 liters). Bore and Stroke: 3.62 x 3.31 inches. Compression ratio: 9.0:1. Net brake hp: 200

1990 Cadillac, Sedan De Ville

at 4400 rpm. Taxable hp: 42.00. Net torque: 270 lbs.-ft. at 3200 rpm. Five main bearings. Roller hydraulic valve lifters. Induction: Sequential multiport fuel injection. VIN Code: 8. Built by Cadillac.

BROUGHAM BASE V-8
Overhead valve. Cast-iron block. Displacement: 307 cid (5.0 liters). Bore and Stroke: 3.80 x 3.39 inches. Compression ratio: 8.0:1. Net brake hp: 140 at 3200 rpm. Taxable hp: 46.20. Net torque: 346 lbs.-ft. at 2000 rpm. Five main bearings. Hydraulic valve lifters. Carburetion: Four-barrel. VIN Code: Y. Built by Oldsmobile.

CADILLAC OPTIONAL V-8
Overhead valve. Cast-iron block. Displacement: 307 cid (5.0 liters). Bore and Stroke: 3.80 x 3.39 inches. Taxable hp: 46.20. Five main bearings. Hydraulic valve lifters. Carburetion: Four-barrel. VIN Code: 9. Built by Oldsmobile.

COACHBUILDER AVAILABLE V-8
Overhead valve. Cast-iron block . Displacement: 350 cid (5.7 liters). Bore and stroke: 4.00 x 3.48. Compression ratio: 9.3:1. Net brake hp: 175 at 4200 rpm. Taxable hp: 51.20. Net torque: 400 lbs.-ft. at 2000 rpm. Five main bearings. Hydraulic valve lifters. Induction: Fuel injection. VIN Code: 7. Built by Chevrolet.

CHASSIS

(Coupe DeVille) Wheelbase: 110.8 inches. Overall Length: 202.7 inches. Height: 54.9 inches. Width: 73.3 inches. Front Tread: 60.3 inches. Rear Tread: 59.8 inches. Standard Tires: P205/70R15.

(Sedan DeVille) Wheelbase: 113.8 inches. Overall Length: 205.6 inches. Height: 55.2 inches. Width: 73.3 inches. Front Tread: 60.3 inches. Rear Tread: 59.8 inches. Standard Tires: P225/75R15.

(Fleetwood Coupe) Wheelbase: 110.8 inches. Overall Length: 202.7 inches. Height: 54.9 inches. Width: 73.3 inches. Front Tread: 60.3 inches. Rear Tread: 59.8 inches. Standard Tires: P205/70R15.

(Fleetwood Sedan) Wheelbase: 113.8 inches. Overall Length: 205.6 inches. Height: 55.2 inches. Width: 73.3 inches. Front Tread: 60.3 inches. Rear Tread: 59.8 inches. Standard Tires: P205/70R15.

(Sixty Special) Wheelbase: 113.8 inches. Overall Length: 205.6 inches. Height: 55.2 inches. Width: 73.3 inches. Front Tread: 60.3 inches. Rear Tread: 59.8 inches. Standard Tires: P205/70R15.

(Brougham) Wheelbase: 121.5 inches. Overall Length: 221 inches. Height: 56.7 inches. Width: 76.5 inches. Front Tread: 61.7 inches. Rear Tread: 60.7 inches. Standard Tires: P225/75R15.

(Seville) Wheelbase: 108 inches. Overall Length: 190.8 inches. Height: 53.7 inches. Width: 72 inches. Front Tread: 59.9 inches. Rear Tread: 59.9 inches. Standard Tires: P215/65R15.

(Eldorado) Wheelbase: 108 inches. Overall Length: 191.4 inches. Height: 53.7 inches. Width: 72.4 inches. Front Tread: 59.9 inches. Rear Tread: 59.9 inches. Standard Tires: P215/65R15.

(Allante) Wheelbase: 99.4 inches. Overall Length: 178.7 inches. Height: 52.2 inches. Width: 73.5 inches. Front Tread: 60.4 inches. Rear Tread: 60.4 inches. Standard Tires: Goodyear Eagle VL P225/55VR16.

TECHNICAL

Transmission: (DeVille, Fleetwood, Eldorado, Seville) THM 440T4 automatic four-speed (includes overdrive and viscous converter clutch), (Allante) THM F7 automatic four-speed transaxle (includes overdrive, viscous converter clutch and electronic shift control), (Brougham) THM 200-4R automatic four-speed (includes overdrive and torque converter clutch), (Brougham with Coachbuilder Package or Trailer Towing Package) THM-700-automatic 4R four-speed (includes overdrive and a torque converter clutch). This transmission is also fitted with a modified prop shaft and 8.5 inches. Steering: (All models except Brougham): Power-assisted rack and pinion. Brougham: Power-assisted recirculating ball. Ratios: DeVille, Fleetwood: 18.6:1, Seville, Eldorado: 16.5:1, Touring: 15.6:1, Allante: 15.6:1, Brougham: 15-13:1. Front Suspension: (All models except Brougham) Independent MacPherson strut with coil springs, strut-type shock absorbers (integral-in strut and electronic variable on Allante) and stabilizer bar, (Brougham) Independent with short/long arms, coil springs, direct acting shock absorbers and link-type stabilizer bar. Rear Suspension: (All models except Brougham): fully independent with coil springs. Automatic level control and strut-type superlift shock

absorbers on all models except Allante and Brougham. Allante: Integral-in strut electronic variable shock absorbers with no rear stabilizer. Brougham: Four link, coil springs with automatic level control and direct acting shock absorbers. Brakes: (All models except Brougham and Allante): Power assisted front disc/rear drum with Teves anti-lock braking system, Allante: Power assisted front disc/rear drum, Bosch III anti-lock braking system, Brougham: Power assisted front disc/rear drum, Bosch ABS. Body Construction: (All models except Brougham): Integral body-frame, Brougham: Separate body on frame. Fuel Tank: (DeVille, Fleetwood) 18.0 gallons, (Eldorado, Seville) 18.8 gallons, (Allante) 22 gallons, (Brougham) 25 gallons.

OPTIONS

DEVILLE OPTIONS

Accent striping ($75). Anti-lock braking system ($925). Storage front armrest ($70). Astroroof ($1,355). California emissions and testing ($100). California emissions label ($100). Rear window defogger ($195). Heated windshield defogger ($250). Automatic door locks ($185). Carpeted rear floor mats ($25). Gold ornamentation package ($395). Trailer towing package ($120). Digital instrument cluster ($250). Leather seating area ($560). Automatic day/night mirror ($80). Firemist paint ($240). Monotone lower accent color (no charge). Delco-Bose sound system with cassette ($576). Delco-Bose sound system with compact disc system ($872). Manual passenger seat recliner ($45). Power passenger seat recliner ($95-$410). Formal Cabriolet roof on Coupe DeVille ($825). Full-padded vinyl roof on Sedan DeVille ($825). Leather-trimmed steering wheel ($115). Theft-deterrent system ($225). Trunk mat ($36). Wire locking wheel discs ($365). Aluminum alloy wheels on Coupe DeVille ($480). DeVille Option Package B, includes door edge guards, front carpeted floor mats, six-way power passenger seat ($324). DeVille Option Package C, includes items in Package B, plus illuminated-entry system, illuminated visor-vanity mirrors, trunk lid power pull down, Twilight Sentinel: ($739). DeVille Option Package D, includes items in Package C plus remote release fuel filler door, manual driver seat recliner, trumpet horn: ($894). Brougham Option Package B, includes door edge guards, carpeted front and rear floor mats, six-way power passenger seat adjuster, trunk mat: ($385).

FLEETWOOD OPTIONS

Accent molding ($150). Astroroof ($1355). California emissions and testing ($100). Heated windshield defogger ($250). Automatic door locks ($185). Gold ornamentation package ($395). Leather seating area ($560). Two-position driver's side memory seat ($235). Automatic day/night mirror ($80). Firemist paint ($240). Monotone lower accent color (no charge). Delco-Bose sound system with

1990 Cadillac, Seville sedan

1990 Cadillac, Eldorado Touring Coupe

cassette ($576). Delco-Bose with compact disc system ($872). Power driver seat recliner ($95). Power passenger seat recliner ($95-$410). Leather-trimmed steering wheel ($115). Vinyl roof delete ($374 credit). Theft-deterrent system ($225). Stylized aluminum wheels ($115).

SIXTY SPECIAL OPTIONS

California emissions and testing ($100). Rear window defogger ($195). Heated windshield defogger ($250). Automatic door locks ($185). Gold ornamentation package ($395). Two-position driver's side memory seat ($235). Automatic day/night mirror ($80). Firemist paint ($240). Monotone lower accent color (no charge). Delco-Bose sound system with cassette ($576). Delco-Bose with compact disc system ($872). Power passenger seat recliner ($95-$410). Vinyl roof delete ($374 credit). Theft-deterrent system ($225). Stylized aluminum wheels ($115).

BROUGHAM OPTIONS

Accent striping ($75). Astroroof ($1,355). California emissions and testing ($100). California emissions label ($100). Coachbuilder delete package ($389 credit). Rear window defogger ($195). Brougham d'Elegance cloth ($2,286). Brougham d'Elegance leather ($2,846). Automatic door locks ($185). Remote release fuel filler door ($65). Gold ornamentation package ($395). Heavy-duty coachbuilder/livery package, includes heavy-duty ride package ($299). Leather seating area, not available with d'Elegance option ($560). Automatic day/night mirror ($80). Firemist paint ($240). Base radio with cassette tape player ($309). Power passenger seat recliner ($95-$410).

Premier formal vinyl roof ($1,195). Leather-trimmed steering wheel ($115). Theft deterrent system ($225). Wire locking wheel discs ($445). Wire wheels ($1,000). Heavy-duty ride package ($120). Trailer Towing package ($299). Brougham Option Package B, includes door edge guards, carpeted front and rear floor mats, six-way power passenger seat adjuster, trunk mat ($385). Brougham Option Package C, includes items from Package B plus illuminated vanity mirrors, rear sail panel reading lights, power trunk lid pull down, Twilight Sentinel ($743).

ELDORADO OPTIONS
Accent striping ($75). Anti-lock braking system ($925). Bird's-eye maple appliqués ($2,435, but included in Eldorado Biarritz package). Astroroof ($1,355). Biarritz-Eldorado leather ($3,325). Biarritz-Eldorado cloth ($2,875). California emissions and testing ($100). Cellular mobile telephone ($1,975). Cellular mobile telephone provision ($395, but included with optional analog instrument cluster). Rear window defogger ($195). Automatic door locks ($185). Gold ornamentation package ($395). Leather seating area ($450). Automatic day/night mirror ($80). Firemist paint ($240, but not available with two-tone paint). Primary firemist paint for Eldorados with two-tone paint ($190). Secondary Firemist paint for Eldorado with two-tone paint ($50). White diamond paint ($240). Monotone lower accent color (no charge). Delco-Bose sound system with compact disc player ($872). Power passenger seat recliner ($95-$410). Full padded vinyl roof package ($1,095). Full cabriolet roof ($1,095). Theft-deterrent system ($225). White sidewall P215/65R15 tires ($76). FE2 touring suspension including stiffer front springs, larger-diameter front stabilizer bar, a rear stabilizer bar and faster steering and 3.33:1 final drive ratio ($155). Engine block heater, $45. Wire locking wheel discs ($235).

SEVILLE OPTIONS
Accent molding ($150). Anti-lock braking system ($925). Astroroof ($1,355). California emissions and testing ($100). Cellular mobile telephone ($1,975). Cellular mobile telephone provision ($395, but included in analog instrument cluster). Rear window defogger ($195 but standard with STS). Automatic door locks ($185, but included in STS package). Gold ornamentation package ($395). Leather seating area ($450, but included in STS). Automatic day/night mirror ($80). Firemist paint ($240, but not available with two-tone paint). Primary Firemist paint for Seville with two-tone paint ($190). Secondary Firemist paint for Seville with two-tone paint ($50). White Diamond paint ($240). Two-tone paint ($225, but not available with STS). Delco-Bose sound system with compact disc player ($872). Power passenger seat recliner ($95-$410). Full padded viny roof ($1,095, but not available with STS). Full Cabriolet roof ($1,095, but not available with STS or full padded vinyl roof). Phaeton roof ($1,195, but not available with STS or full-padded vinyl roof). Seville touring sedan ($5,754). Theft-deterrent system ($225, but included with STS ($225). P215/65R15 white sidewall tires ($76 on cars with FE2 suspension and not available with STS). Touring suspension ($115, but included with STS). Wire locking wheel discs($235, but not available with STS). Aluminum alloy wheels (no charge with FE2 suspension, but not available with STS). Seville touring sedan option YP6 including FE2 touring suspension ($5,754). FE2 touring suspension including stiffer front springs, larger-diameter front stabilizer bar, a rear stabilizer bar and faster steering and 3.33:1 final drive ratio ($155). Engine block heater, ($45).

ALLANTE OPTIONS
Accent striping ($75). California emissions label ($100). Cellular mobile telephone ($1,975). Cellular mobile telephone provision ($395). Analog instrument cluster (no charge). Power passenger seat recliner ($95-$410).

HISTORICAL
Cadillac's model-year production totaled 268,698 compared with 276,138 the year previous. Its share of the automotive market moved up to 2.8 percent. John Grettenberger, who had served as Cadillac general manager since January 1984, was credited by many industry observers as having played a major role in improving Cadillac's quality. Cadillac's newest concept car was the Aurora, a name that would later in the decade be adopted by Oldsmobile. Cadillac's version of the Aurora sedan used many features already part of regular-production cars, such as Traction Control, the 4.5-liter V-8 and electronically adjustable struts. Innovative equipment on the car included all-wheel drive, four-passenger inflatable restraints and a sun roof that the driver could adjust automatically to darken, all of which had the potential for inclusion on future Cadillacs. Another new item was the ETAK in-car navigation system that used a CD- ROM to store maps for all the United States. Aurora's ETAK maps were displayed on a working full-color flat screen liquid crystal display.

1990 Cadillac, Seville STS, sedan

1991

OVERVIEW

Anti-lock brakes became standard equipment in all Cadillacs in 1991. The 4.5-liter V-8 formerly used to power most Cadillacs was replaced by a more powerful 4.9-liter V-8 with port fuel injection. This new engine saw service in DeVille/Fleetwood, Eldorado and Seville models. Also new and coupled to the 4.9-liter V-8, was the 4T60-E electronically controlled four-speed automatic transmission with overdrive. The rear-wheel drive Brougham sedan's standard 5.0-liter V-8 received fuel injection and delivered 21 percent more horsepower (up to 170) over the previously carbureted unit. Computer Command Ride was new to Fleetwood, Seville and Eldorado and automatically adjusted struts to provide increased damping and road control as those vehicles' speed increased. The Fleetwood 60 Special was redesigned and a Commercial Chassis was re-introduced.

I.D. DATA

The 17-symbol serial number was located on top of the instrument panel, where it was visible through the windshield. The first symbol 1=U.S.-built vehicle. The second symbol G=General Motors. The third symbol 6=Cadillac.

Above: **1991 Cadillac, Allante' convertible**

The fourth symbol indicated car line. The fifth symbol indicated series as follows: C/B=Fleetwood, C/D=DeVille, C/G=-Fleetwood Sixty Special, C/Z=Commercial Chassis, D/W=Brougham, E/L=Eldorado, K/S=Seville, K/Y=Seville Touring Sedan (STS), V/R=Allante Convertible Hardtop and V/S=Allante Convertible. The sixth symbol incated body style: 1=two-door Coupe/Sedan GM/Fisher Style Nos. 11, 27, 37, 47, 57 or 97, 3=two-door Convertible GM/Fisher Style No. 67, 5=four-door Sedan GM/Fisher style nos. 19, 23, 33 or 69. The seventh symbol indicates the type of restaint system: 1=manual belts, 3=Manual belts with driver's air bag, 4=automatic belts. The eighth symbol identified the engine: B=L26 4.9L V-8, E=L03 5.0L V-8, 7=LLO 5.7L V-8 and 8=LQ6 4.5L V-8. The ninth symbol was a check digit. The 10th symbol was a number indicating model year: M=1991. The 11th symbol indicates the GM assembly plant: U=Hamtramck, Mich. (Allante), 4=Orion, Mich. (DeVille), 9=Detroit (Cadillac). The next group of numbers was the sequential production code starting with 100001. The Fisher Body tag on the cowl, under the hood includes additional information.

DEVILLE-SERIES 6C/D-V-8

The Coupe DeVille and Sedan DeVille were powered by the new 4.9-liter V-8 mated to the 4T60-E electronically

controlled four-speed automatic transmission with overdrive. This engine replaced the previously standard 4.5-liter V-8. An improved version of the Teves anti-lock braking system was also now standard equipment. Other new standard features of the DeVille series included structural enhancements for improved crashworthiness, 15-inch cast aluminum wheels and a larger, higher-capacity front braking system. Computer Command Ride was optional and offered three damping modes to enhance ride-and-handling characteristics. Formerly optional, but made standard equipment in 1991 were side and deck lid accent striping, a rear window defogger with heated outside mirrors, Twilight Sentinel and automatic door locks with a new central door unlocking system. Appearance-wise, the DeVille featured a new power dome hood, a wider grille with a grid design and integral "Cadillac" script, revised front bumper guards, a revised rear bumper rub strip and a "4.9 Port Fuel Injection V-8" deck lid emblem. Inside, EZ-Kool solar-control glass for all windows was made standard, Esteem seat cloth replaced the previously used Primavera and an engine-oil-life indicator became standard. A Phaeton roof was optional for the Sedan DeVille, while both a Cold Weather Package and a Security Package were also new options. The former included a heated windshield system and engine block heater, while the latter featured remote keyless entry, illuminated entry and a theft-deterrent system.

DEVILLE – SERIES 6C/D – V-8

Model Number	Body/Style No.	Body Type & Seating	Factory Price	Shipping Weight	Production Total
C/D	1	2D Coupe	30,205	3,545	Note 2
C/D	5	4D Sedan	30,455	3623	Note 3

Note 1: Cadillac tallied DeVille and Fleetwood production together with no series breakout available.
Note 2: DeVille/Fleetwood Coupe production totaled 12,134 with no further breakout available.
Note 3: DeVille/Fleetwood Sedan production totaled 135,776 with no further breakout available.

DEVILLE TOURING SEDAN-SERIES 6C/T-V-8

Joining the Coupe DeVille and Sedan DeVille in 1991 was a Touring version of the Sedan DeVille. It was also powered by the new 4.9-liter V-8 mated to the 4T60-E electronically controlled four-speed automatic transmission with overdrive.

DEVILLE TOURING SEDAN
–SERIES 6C/T – V-8

Model Number	Body/Style No.	Body Type & Seating	Factory Price	Shipping Weight	Production Total
C/T	5	4D Touring Sedan	33,455	Note 4	Note 4

Note 4: See Note 3 above

FLEETWOOD-SERIES 6C/B-V-8

As in previous years, much of what was updated on DeVille models also found its way into the Fleetwood Coupe and Sedan. This included the 4.9-liter V-8, rated at 200 hp and the 4T60-E four-speed automatic transmission with overdrive, viscous converter clutch and electronic shift control. Deviating from the updates in the DeVille listing, Fleetwood models received Computer Command Ride as standard equipment, the previously optional electrochromic automatic day/night mirror as standard equipment and cast-aluminum lace wheels as an option. Inside, again deviating from DeVille updates, was a new White Sierra Grain Leather color was added to the seven colors available in Sedans and six in Coupes. Also new was darker stained American Walnut wood appliqués and the optional Custom Seating Package including driver memory seat and driver/passenger seats power recliners. Outside, again, different from the DeVille refinements, was the body side inserts with integral "Fleetwood" lettering replacing the previously-seen script on the rear quarter panels.

FLEETWOOD–SERIES 6C/B–V-8

Model Number	Body/Style No.	Body Type & Seating	Factory Price	Shipping Weight	Production Total
C/B	1	2D Coupe	34,675	3,594	Note 5
C/B	5	4D Sedan	34,925	3,676	Note 6

Note 5: See Note 2 above.
Note 6: See Note 3 above.

FLEETWOOD SIXTY SPECIAL-SERIES 6C/G-V-8

Cadillac's limited-production, executive-class Sedan mimicked the updates of the Fleetwood Coupe and Sedan. Unique to the Sixty Special was its new body style designator: 6CG69, a "Sixty Special" plaque on the rear quarter panels, a "Sixty Special" nameplate replacing previously used engine plaque at the rear and the optional Express-Open Astroroof. Updates included a new standard front seat armrest that included a cupholder, a coinholder and storage for CDs. The power front floor storage drawer formerly offered was eliminated to accommodate rear climate-control outlets. With the new 4.9-liter V-8 and 4T60-E transmission, the Sixty Special's final drive ratio was 2.73:1. Also, the 4.9-liter V-8 featured the improved CS144 Generation II alternator that provided a higher power output. The 140-amp alternator provided increased air flow and could withstand higher-temperature operation. The leather interior of the Sixty Special was styled by famed Italian designer Giugiaro of Milan. The

1991 Cadillac, Eldorado Touring Coupe

hand-crafted leather was offered in three color choices. A six-position memory feature was added as standard to the front seats, which had 22 power adjustments. Also, the Sixty Special's wiper system was refined to provide a wider clearing pattern with less blade chatter and greater resistance to snow and ice fatigue. Eleven exterior color selections were available in 1991.

FLEETWOOD SIXTY SPECIAL – SERIES 6C/G–V-8

Model Number	Body/Style No.	Body Type & Seating	Factory Price	Shipping Weight	Production Total
C/G	5	4D Sedan	38,325	3,707	Note 7

Note 7: See Note 3 above.

COMMERCIAL CHASSIS-SERIES 6C/Z-V-8

Not offered since 1990, a factory-produced commercial chassis returned to the Cadillac lineup this year. It was designed for sale to the builders of "professional vehicles" such as hearses and stretch limousines. Information about the commercial chassis was not given in most references aimed at the general public.

COMMERCIAL CHASSIS– SERIES 6C/Z – V-8

Model Number	Body/Style No.	Body Type & Seating	Factory Price	Shipping Weight	Production Total
C/Z	5	Chassis	NA	NA	NA

BROUGHAM-SERIES 6D/W-V-8

Cadillac's Brougham series again consisted of the Brougham Sedan and the special-edition Brougham d'Elegance Sedan (option code V4S). Power was supplied by the revised 5.0-liter V-8 with throttle body injection (TBI). The "new" 5.0-liter V-8 was rated at 170 hp and featured roller-valve lifters for less friction and cast-iron exhaust manifolds contoured for minimal flow resistance. Available previously only with the Coachbuilder Package, the 185-hp 5.7-liter V-8 with TBI was now a stand-alone Brougham engine option. Both engines were paired with the 4L60 Hydra-Matic four-speed automatic transmission with overdrive. Final drive ratio was 3.08:1 (3.73:1 with Coachbuilder and Armor options). Formerly optional, but now standard features of the Brougham were rear sail panel reading lights, a passenger seat power recliner, a six-way power seat adjuster and a leather-trimmed steering wheel. New standard features included an electronic-variable-orifice steering system in which steering effort was reduced during low-speed driving and increased during high-speed maneuvers to improve stability. Outside, the Brougham received clearcoat paint as standard, with two new colors added (12 total): Victorian Red and Dark Antelope. Eleven vinyl top color choices were available. Brougham's stopping power was provided by the Bosch II anti-lock braking system. Standard tires were self-sealing P225/75R15 Uniroyals that had a distinctive gold letter treatment. An available trailer towing package gave the Brougham a towing capacity of 5,000 pounds.

The d'Elegance sedan featured a specific trim design with multi-button tufted seats. The d'Elegance again also featured Twilight Sentinel, a power trunk pull-down feature and specific exterior/interior ornamentation.

BROUGHAM–
SERIES 6D/W–V-8

Model Number	Body/Style No.	Body Type & Seating	Factory Price	Shipping Weight	Production Total
D/W	5	4D Sedan	30,225	4,282	27,231

ELDORADO-SERIES 6E/L-V-8

In addition to the previously-offered Eldorado coupe and special edition Eldorado Biarritz coupe (option code YP3), a special edition Eldorado Touring Coupe (option code YP5) joined the series for 1991. As with other Cadillacs, anti-lock braking became standard on Eldorados in 1991. Powering the coupes was the 4.9-liter V-8 mated to the 4T60-E electronically controlled four-speed automatic transmission with overdrive. The 4.9-liter V-8 with port fuel injection improved the Eldorado's 0-60 mph time to 8.2 seconds over the previously used 4.5-liter V-8. The transverse-mounted engine was comprised of an aluminum block with wet, cast-iron cylinder liners and cast-iron cylinder heads. It had a compression ratio of 9.5:1 and needed premium unleaded fuel with a minimum octane rating of 91. Eldorado coupes also received new focused engine mounts that aimed the mounts at the engine/transmission torque axis, which aided in isolating engine noise and reducing vibration. Computer Command Ride became standard equipment. Also new was the exterior color Polo Green, upping the total to 16 colors for Eldorados and 15 for Biarritz. New options included a heated windshield system that melted frost and ice five times faster than a conventional defroster and a Security Package that included remote keyless entry, automatic door locks with central door unlocking capability and theft-deterrent system. The 4.9-liter V-8's functions were controlled by Cadillac's GMP4 Powertrain Control Module (PCM) that sensed vital operating conditions, including engine rpm, intake manifold pressure and air temperature, outside air temperature, coolant temperature, exhaust gas oxygen content, throttle position, vehicle speed, accessory load level and brake operation. The PCM also functioned as a data storage system for service technicians

1991 Cadillac, Seville sedan

to diagnose malfunctions. Eldorado's Body Computer Module (BCM)—the heart of the car's sophisticated electronic information system—also provided driver and diagnostic information. The BCM also monitored and controlled functions such as air conditioning, Twilight Sentinel headlight operation, theft alarm and electric cooling fan. The Touring Coupe's final drive ratio was 3.33:1 and its suspension provided a more "international feel" of driving. This suspension package included a 23mm diameter front stabilizer bar, 16mm diameter rear stabilizer bar and 16-inch styled aluminum wheels. The steering system was modified to include a quicker ratio (2.97 turns lock-to-lock vs. 3.13) and a higher effort steering gear compared to the standard Eldorado. The Touring Coupe's coachwork featured body color front and rear fascias and rocker moldings, all with black bead edging. The Touring Coupe also featured a grille-mounted Cadillac wreath-and-crest emblem. A cloisonné emblem highlighted the rear deck lid, while the "Eldorado" script was dropped from the fenders and deck lid.

ELDORADO—SERIES 6E/L–V-8

Model Number	Body/Style No.	Body Type & Seating	Factory Price	Shipping Weight	Production Total
EL1	L57	2D Coupe	31,245	3,470	16,212

SEVILLE - SERIES 6K/S - V-8

Updates and revisions to the Seville Sedan mirrored those changes listed for the EldoradoThe final drive ratio for the Seville sedan was 2.97:1. A touring package with 15-inch cast aluminum wheels and Goodyear Eagle GT4 P215/65R15 tires was optional on the Seville sedan. High-gloss birdseye maple wood was used to accent the Seville's instrument panel and console. The 1991 Sevilles also received a new taillight treatment and neutral density back-up lights.

SEVILLE—SERIES 6K/S-V-8

Model Number	Body/Style No.	Body Type & Seating	Factory Price	Shipping Weight	Production Total
K/S	5	4D Sedan	33,935	3,513	Note 8

Note 8: Seville production totaled 26,431 with no further breakout available.

SEVILLE STS-SERIES 6K/Y-V-8

The STS received new, blue-tinted outside rearview mirrors as standard equipment and its seating area was revised. In addition to redesigned seats, new full Beechwood leather front bucket seats included six-way power seat adjusters, power recliners and power lumbar support for driver and passenger. There was also a full-width rear leather seat with integral headrests. The previously seen rear console was eliminated to accommodate a third, center rear seat passenger. Final drive ratio for the STS was 3.33:1. The STS was equipped with the firmer ride-and-handling of a touring suspension package. It included 23mm front and 16mm rear stabilizer bars, special 16-inch forged aluminum

wheels with Goodyear Eagle GT4 P215/60R16 tires. The STS exclusively featured elm burl high-gloss wood on all door panels, instrument panel and console. The 1991 STS also received the new taillight treatment and neutral density back-up lights.

SEVILLE STS—
SERIES 6K/Y-V-8

Model Number	Body/Style No.	Body Type & Seating	Factory Price	Shipping Weight	Production Total
K/Y	5	4D Tour Sedan	37,135	3,565	Note 9

Note 9: See Note 8 above.

ALLANTE CONVERTIBLE HARDTOP-SERIES 6V/R-V-8

The Allante Convertible Hardtop included both a convertible top and a removable all-aluminum hardtop. Allantes retained the 4.5-liter V-8 and F-7 four-speed automatic transaxle used previously. For 1991, this engine received a new air intake resonator for quieter performance. It took the edge off the induction "roar" (an example was hill driving), but left the exhaust note unchanged. For improved power output, the aluminum engine's cast iron cylinder heads featured straighter intake ports and were equipped with large, 45mm intake and 38mm exhaust valves. Exhaust was evacuated through thin-wall, cast iron manifolds that were shaped for minimum flow resistance. Also, to help reduce oil aeration, a new gearotor-type oil pump was added to the engine. Final drive ratio was 3.21:1. Allante continued to offer the Bosch III anti-lock braking system and traction control as standard equipment. The traction control system was refined for 1991 with the addition of rubber isolated plungers that reduced noise when the system was engaged. Allante's variable-assist rack-and-pinion power steering system was also improved with a revised pump and adapter that resulted in quieter operation and enhanced reliability.

ALLANTE CONVERTIBLE HARDTOP
SERIES 6 V/R—V-8

Model Number	Body Style No.	Body Type & Seating	Factory Price	Shipping Weight	Production Total
V/R	3	2Dconvertible hardtop	60,800	3,537	Note 10

Note 10: Allante production totaled 2,500 with no further breakout available.

ALLANTE CONVERTIBLE - SERIES 6V/S - V-8

The Allante Convertible had the same changes as the Allante Convertible Hardtop.

1991 Cadillac, Fleetwood sedan

Model Number	Body Style No.	Body Type & Seating	Factory Price	Shipping Weight	Production Total
V/S	3	2D convertible	55,250	3,480	Note 11

ENGINE

DEVILLE, FLEETWOOD, SEVILLE, ELDORADO BASE V-8

Overhead valve. Aluminum block with cast-iron liners. Displacement: 300 cid (4.9 liters). Bore and Stroke: 3.62 x 3.62 inches. Compression ratio: 9.5:1. Net brake hp: 200 at 4100 rpm. Taxable hp: 41.93. Net torque: 275 at 3000 rpm. Five main bearings. Roller hydraulic valve lifters. Induction: Multiport fuel injection. VIN Code: B; Option Code L26. Built by Cadillac.

ALLANTE BASE V-8

Overhead valve. Aluminum block with cast-iron liners. Displacement: 273 cid (4.5 liters). Bore and Stroke: 3.62 x 3.31 inches. Compression ratio: 9.0:1. Net brake hp: 200 at 4400 rpm. Taxable hp: 42.00. Net torque: 270 lbs.-ft. at 3200 rpm. Five main bearings. Roller hydraulic valve lifters. Induction: Multiport fuel injection. VIN Code: 8; Option Code L06. Built by Cadillac.

BROUGHAM BASE V-8

Overhead valve. Cast-iron block. Displacement: 305 cid (5.0 liters). Bore and Stroke: 3.74 x 3.48 inches. Compression ratio: 9.3:1. Net brake hp: 170 at 4200 rpm. Taxable hp: 44.8. Net torque: 255 lbs.-ft. at 2400 rpm. Five main bearings. Roller hydraulic valve lifters. Induction: Throttle Body Injection. VIN Code: E; Option Code L03.

BROUGHAM, COACHBUILDER, TOWING PACKAGE BASE V-8, CADILLAC OPTIONAL V-8

Overhead valve. Cast-iron block. Displacement: 350 cid (5.7 liters). Bore and stroke: 4.00 x 3.48. Compression ratio: 9.8:1. Net brake hp: 185 at 4200 rpm. Taxable hp: 51.20. Net torque: 300 lbs.-ft. at 2400 rpm. Five main bearings. Roller hydraulic valve lifters. Induction: Throttle Body Injection. VIN Code: 7; Option Code LL0. Built by Chevrolet.

CHASSIS

(Coupe DeVille) Wheelbase: 110.8 inches. Overall Length: 202.6 inches. Height: 54.9 inches. Width: 73.4 inches. Front Tread: 60.3 inches. Rear Tread: 59.8 inches. Standard Tires: P205/70R15.

(Sedan DeVille) Wheelbase: 113.8 inches. Overall Length: 205.6 inches. Height: 55.2 inches. Width: 73.4 inches. Front Tread: 60.3 inches. Rear Tread: 59.8 inches. Standard Tires: P205/70R15.

(DeVille Touring Sedan) Wheelbase: 113.8 inches. Overall Length: 205.6 inches. Height: 55.2 inches. Width: 73.4 inches. Front Tread: 60.3 inches. Rear Tread: 59.8 inches. Standard Tires: P215/65R15 Goodyear Eagle GT4.

(Fleetwood Coupe) Wheelbase: 110.8 inches. Overall Length: 202.6 inches. Height: 54.9 inches. Width: 73.4 inches. Front Tread: 60.3 inches. Rear Tread: 59.8 inches. Standard Tires: P205/70R15.

(Fleetwood Sedan) Wheelbase: 113.8 inches. Overall Length: 205.6 inches. Height: 55.2 inches. Width: 73.4 inches. Front Tread: 60.3 inches. Rear Tread: 59.8 inches. Standard Tires: P205/70R15.

(Sixty Special) Wheelbase: 113.8 inches. Overall Length: 205.6 inches. Height: 55.2 inches. Width: 73.4 inches. Front Tread: 60.3 inches. Rear Tread: 59.8 inches. Standard Tires: P205/70R15.

(Brougham) Wheelbase: 121.5 inches. Overall Length: 221 inches. Height: 57.4 inches. Width: 76.5 inches. Front Tread: 61.7 inches. Rear Tread: 60.7 inches. Standard Tires: P225/75R15.

(Seville) Wheelbase: 108 inches. Overall Length: 190.8 inches. Height: 53.7 inches. Width: 72 inches. Front Tread: 59.9 inches. Rear Tread: 59.9 inches. Standard Tires: P205/70R15.

(Seville STS) Wheelbase: 108 inches. Overall Length: 190.8 inches. Height: 53.7 inches. Width: 72 inches. Front Tread: 59.9 inches. Rear Tread: 59.9 inches. Standard Tires: 215/60R16 with 16-inch wheels.

(Eldorado) Wheelbase: 108 inches. Overall Length: 191.4 inches. Height: 53.7 inches. Width: 72.4 inches. Front Tread: 59.9 inches. Rear Tread: 59.9 inches. Standard Tires: P205/70R15.

(Allante) Wheelbase: 99.4 inches. Overall Length: 178.7 inches. Height: 51.0-51.2 inches. Width: 73.5 inches. Front Tread: 60.4 inches. Rear Tread: 60.4 inches. Standard Tires: Goodyear Eagle VL P225/55VR16.

TECHNICAL

Transmission: (DeVille, Fleetwood, Eldorado, Seville) 4T60-E electronically controlled four-speed automatic with overdrive (includes viscous converter clutch), (Allante) THM-F7 four-speed automatic (includes viscous converter clutch), (Brougham) THM 4L60 four-speed automatic with overdrive (includes torque converter clutch). Steering: (All except Brougham) Power-assisted rack-and-pinion, (Brougham) Power-

assisted recirculating ball. Front Suspension: (All except Brougham) Independent MacPherson strut with coil springs, strut-type shock absorbers (integral-in strut and electronic variable on Allante and Computer Command Ride on Fleetwood, Seville, Eldorado) and stabilizer bar, (Brougham) Independent with short/long arms, coil springs, direct acting shock absorbers and link-type stabilizer bar. Rear Suspension: (DeVille, Fleetwood) fully independent with coil springs, automatic level control and (DeVille) strut-type superlift shock absorbers (Fleetwood) Computer Command Ride, (Eldorado, Seville) Fully independent transverse monoleaf with automatic level control and Computer Command Ride, no rear stabilizer, (Allante) Fully independent transverse monoleaf with integral-in strut electronic variable shock absorbers, no rear stabilizer, (Brougham) Four link, coil springs with automatic level control and direct acting shock absorbers and stabilizer bar. Brakes: (All except Allante) Power assisted front disc/rear drum with Teves anti-lock braking system (Eldorado, Seville, Brougham used Bosch II ABS), (Allante) Power assisted front and rear disc with Bosch III anti-lock braking system. Body Construction: (All except Brougham) Integral body-frame, (Brougham) Separate body on frame. Fuel Tank: (DeVille, Fleetwood) 18.0 gallons, (Eldorado, Seville) 18.8 gallons, (Allante) 22.0 gallons, (Brougham) 25.0 gallons.

OPTIONS

DEVILLE OPTIONS

Coupe DeVille Spring Edition package, includes cast-aluminum wheels, front and rear carpeted floor mats, illuminated entry, leather seating, illuminated vanity mirrors, six-way power passenger seat, full Cabriolet roof and gold ornamentation ($1,481). Option package B ($320). Option package C ($586). Option package D ($1,045). Security package ($385). Cold weather package ($369). Digital instrument cluster ($250). Illuminated entry system ($90). Auto day/night mirror ($110). Astroroof ($1,550). Coachbuilders package for Sedan DeVille ($1,000). Gold Ornamentation package ($395). Heavy-duty Livery Package for Sedan DeVille ($1,000). Leather seating ($570). Firemist paint ($240). Lower accent Firemist paint ($50). Two-tone paint for Sedan DeVille ($225). Delco-Bose sound system ($575), Delco-Bose sound system with CD ($872). Formal Cabriolet roof for Coupe DeVille ($925). Full Cabriolet roof for Coupe DeVille ($1,095). Phaeton roof for Sedan DeVille ($1,095). Locking wire wheel discs ($235). Lace cast-aluminum wheels ($235). FX3 Computer Command Ride ($380).

FLEETWOOD, FLEETWOOD SIXTY SPECIAL OPTIONS

Security package ($295). Cold weather package ($369). Custom seating package ($425). Astroroof ($1,550). Gold Ornamentation package ($395). Leather seating ($570). Delco-Bose sound system ($575). Delco-Bose sound system with CD ($872).

ELDORADO OPTIONS

Eldorado Spring Special package including cast-aluminum wheels, full Cabriolet roof, leather seating, Delco Bose sound System and gold ornamentation ($115). YP3 Biarritz option ($3,275). YP5 Touring Coupe option ($2,050). Birdseye maple wood appliqué ($245). Security package ($480). Heated windshield system ($309). Astroroof ($1,550). Gold Ornamentation package ($395). Leather seating ($555). Auto day/night mirror ($110). Firemist paint ($240). Lower accent Firemist paint ($50). White Diamond paint ($240). Delco-Bose sound system

1991 Cadillac, Seville, STS sedan

($575). Delco-Bose sound system with CD ($872). Full vinyl roof ($1,095). Full Cabriolet roof ($1,095). P215/65R15 white sidewall tires with FE2 Touring suspension ($76). Locking wire wheel discs ($235). Cast-aluminum wheels ($115). FE2 Touring Suspension package ($155 or standard with Touring Coupe package).

SEVILLE OPTIONS
Heated windshield system ($309). Astroroof ($1,550). Gold Ornamentation package ($395). Leather seating ($460). Auto day/night mirror ($110). Firemist paint ($240). Lower accent Firemist paint ($50). White Diamond paint ($240). Delco-Bose sound system ($575). Delco-Bose sound system with CD ($872). Phaeton roof ($1,195). P215/65R15 white sidewall tires, with FE2 Touring suspension only ($76). Locking wire wheel discs ($235). FE2 Touring suspension package ($155, but standard on Seville Touring Sedan).

BROUGHAM OPTIONS
Option package B ($325). Option package C ($685). Option package C for Brougham with d'Elegance package ($360). Astroroof ($1,550). Coachbuilder package ($139 credit). Brougham d'Elegance cloth Interior ($1,875). Brougham d'Elegance leather interior ($2,445). Gold Ornamentation package ($395). Leather seating ($570).

Livery package ($299). Auto day/night mirror ($110). Firemist paint ($240). Lower accent Firemist paint ($50). CD music system ($396). Full vinyl roof ($925). Locking wire wheel discs ($445). Wire wheels ($1,000). 5.7-liter V-8 ($250). V92 trailer towing package ($550).

ALLANTE OPTIONS
Digital instrument cluster for convertible only ($495). Pearl White paint for convertible only ($700).

HISTORICAL
Cadillac's model-year production totaled 220,284 compared with 268,698 the year previous. Based on sales of 213,288 automobiles in 1991 (compared to 258,168 the year before), Cadillac's share of the U.S. market was 2.61 percent compared with 2.78 percent in 1990.

1991 Cadillac, Sedan DeVille

1991 Cadillac, Brougham sedan

1992

OVERVIEW

The 1992 Seville and Eldorado models were Cadillac's first totally new offerings since the luxury automaker was reorganized in 1987 as an autonomous General Motors division. Fleetwood models received traction control as standard equipment, while the DeVille models offered this function as an option. The Brougham sedan retained its distinction as America's longest production vehicle, but it was not subject to "gas guzzler" taxes in 1992. The Federal Luxury Tax did apply to the Brougham, as well as to the Allante. The commercial chassis car line was dropped again.

I.D. DATA

The 17-symbol serial number was located on top of the instrument panel, where it was visible through the windshield. The first symbol 1=U.S.-built vehicle. The second symbol G=General Motors. The third symbol 6=Cadillac. The fourth symbol indicated car line/the fifth symbol indicated series as follows: C/B=Fleetwood, C/D=DeVille, C/G=Fleetwood Sixty Special, C/T=DeVille Touring Sedan, D/W=Brougham, E/L=Eldorado, K/S=Seville, K/Y=Seville Touring Sedan (STS), V/R=Allante

Above: **1992 Cadillac, Eldorado Touring coupe**

Convertible Hardtop and V/S=Allante Convertible. The sixth symbol incated body style: 1=two-door Coupe/Sedan GM/Fisher Style Nos. 11, 27, 37, 47, 57 or 97, 3=two-door Convertible GM/Fisher Style No. 67, 5=four-door Sedan GM/Fisher style nos. 19, 23, 33 or 69. The seventh symbol indicates the type of restaint system: 1=manual belts, 2=Manual belts with dual airbags, 3=Manual belts with driver's air bag, 4=automatic belts, 5=Automatic belts with airbags. The eighth symbol identified the engine: B=L26 4.9L V-8, E=L03 5.0L V-8, 7=LLO 5.7L V-8 and 8=LQ6 4.5L V-8. The ninth symbol was a check digit. The 10th symbol was a number indicating model year: N=1992. The 11th symbol indicates the GM assembly plant: U=Hamtramck, Mich. (Allante), 4=Orion, Mich. (DeVille), R=Arlington, Texas. The next group of numbers was the sequential production code starting with 100001. The Fisher Body tag on the cowl, under the hood includes additional information.

DEVILLE-SERIES 6C/D-V-8

The basic DeVille lineup again consisted of a Coupe DeVille and a Sedan DeVille. Both were again powered by the 4.9-liter V-8 mated to the 4T60-E electronically-controlled four-speed automatic transmission with overdrive. The DeVille's V-8 received platinum-tipped spark plugs with a 100,000-mile replacement interval as

standard equipment. Other new standard items (formerly offered as optional equipment) were an electrochromic automatic day/night inside rearview mirror, a six-way power adjuster for the front passenger seat and front and rear carpeted floor mats. New options included brake-only traction control (available only with Computer Command Ride), which regulated tire spin during acceleration, driver's side electrochromic outside rearview mirror and Delco-Bose Gold Series CD sound system. New DeVille features included six exterior colors: Slate Green, Light Beige (monotone only), Taupe, Autumn Brown, Academy Gray and Dark Plum, three new lower accent molding colors: Light Beige, Academy Gray and Dark Plum, and three new interior colors: Light Gray, Neutral and Taupe. The DeVille's throttle position sensor and throttle body design were upgraded to provide improved throttle feel.

DEVILLE–SERIES 6C/D–V-8

Model Number	Body/Style No.	Body Type & Seating	Factory Price	Shipping Weight	Production Total
C/D	1	2D Coupe	31,740	3,519	Note 2
C/D	5	4D Sedan	31,740	3,591	Note 3

Note 1: Cadillac tallied DeVille and Fleetwood production together with no series breakout available.
Note 2: DeVille/Fleetwood coupe production totaled 8,423 with no further breakout available.
Note 3: DeVille/Fleetwood sedan production totaled 133,808 with no further breakout available.

DEVILLE TOURING SEDAN-SERIES 6C/D-V-8

The DeVille Touring Sedan was also powered by the 4.9-liter V-8 mated to the 4T60-E electronically controlled four-speed automatic transmission with overdrive. Other changes included revised seating consisting of new split-frame Dual Comfort front seats trimmed in Beechwood leather with six-way power adjusters, power recliners and manual headrests. The rear seat was also redesigned and now featured two individual headrests. The Touring Sedan also featured a wide, chrome-plated body side molding with "Touring Sedan" identification located on the forward edge of the front doors, body-color front and rear fascias and body-color "sport" door handles. Only monotone color choices were available on the Touring Sedan, including five new colors: Slate Green, Light Beige, Royal Maroon, Academy Gray and Dark Plum. A vinyl top could not be ordered. A quicker 17:1 steering gear was exclusive to the Touring Sedan.

DEVILLE TOURING SEDAN – SERIES 6C/T – V-8

Model Number	Body/Style No.	Body Type & Seating	Factory Price	Shipping Weight	Production Total
C/T	5	4D Tour Sedan	35,190	3,627	Note 4

Note 4: See Note 3 above.

FLEETWOOD-SERIES 6C/B-V-8

The new exterior and interior colors available listed for DeVilles were also part of the changes for the 1992 Fleetwoods. Returning to power the Fleetwood Coupe and Sedan was the 4.9-liter V-8 paired with the 4T60-E

1992 Cadillac, Eldorado coupe

electronically controlled four-speed automatic transmission with overdrive. New standard features included the brake-only traction control system, 100,000-mile replacement interval, platinum-tipped spark plugs and a driver's side electrochromic outside rearview mirror. A new option was the Delco-Bose Gold Series CD sound system. Fleetwood models also received upgrades to the exhaust system and throttle body design. The Fleetwood's power-assisted rack-and-pinion steering system was refined, with its power steering pump, gear assembly and tie-rod ends being upgraded. Suspension modifications were also carried out to the Fleetwood's struts, rear stabilizer bar, rear springs and toe links to improve durability.

FLEETWOOD – SERIES 6C/B – V-8

Model Number	Body/Style No.	Body Type & Seating	Factory Price	Shipping Weight	Production Total
C/B	1	2D Coupe	36,360	3,566	Note 5
C/B	5	4D Sedan	36,360	3,642	Note 6

Note 5: See Note 2 above.
Note 6: See Note 3 above.

FLEETWOOD SIXTY SPECIAL-SERIES 6C/G-V-8

The Sixty Special's new features mirrored those of the Fleetwood Coupe and Sedan with the exception of two new interior leather colors: Light Gray and Black. The new, standard brake-only traction control system used the same integral front bearing wheel-speed sensors as the Teves anti-lock braking system. The traction control system applied pulses of brake pressure to a drive wheel if it began to spin. This system was fully functional up to 24 mph, with the traction control operation gradually phased out between 24 and 30 mph.

FLEETWOOD SIXTY SPECIAL
–SERIES 6C/G–V-8

Model Number	Body/Style No.	Body Type & Seating	Factory Price	Shipping Weight	Production Total
C/G	5	4D Sedan	39,860	3,653	Note 7

Note 7: See Note 3 above.

BROUGHAM-SERIES 6D/W-V-8

Cadillac's only rear-wheel-drive sedan—again also available in d'Elegance trim (option code V4S)—was basically a carryover from the previous year, except that Brougham's appearance was improved by a new, more durable base coat/clear coat paint process. The 5.0-liter V-8 coupled to

the Hydra-Matic 4L60 four-speed automatic transmission with overdrive remained as the standard powertrain. The 5.7-liter V-8 was again optional equipment, but required when trailer towing. Also, Coachbuilder or Armoring options were ordered. The Brougham again also was available with the Funeral Coach Package (option code B9Q) for aftermarket conversion to funeral service. In this configuration, only the 5.0-liter V-8 was offered.

BROUGHAM—SERIES 6D/W—V-8

Model Number	Body/Style No.	Body Type & Seating	Factory Price	Shipping Weight	Production Total
D/W5	5	4D Sedan	31,740	4,276	13,761

ELDORADO-SERIES 6E/L-V-8
Inside and out, it was an all-new Eldorado Coupe and Touring Coupe (option code YP5) for 1992. The Eldorado returned to a traditional hardtop configuration with the "door glass into roof" design rather than a full door frame. The luxury Coupe was over 10 inches longer than the previous year's model. Structurally, the Eldorado's unibody construction was improved with the addition of crush zones for enhanced safety and an integrated, solid feel. The returning 4.9-liter V-8 received 100,000-mile replacement interval, platinum-tipped spark plugs and was again coupled to the 4T60-E electronically controlled four-speed automatic transmission with overdrive. The Eldorado's redesigned appearance included a larger flush-glass windshield, flush-glass door and rear-quarter windows, revamped front fenders, revamped rear quarter panels, a hood with a stand-up ornament, body-color fascias with rub strips, a chrome-plated grille, revised parking, and signal and cornering lights, flush door handles, revamped body side moldings with bright upper strip and integral "Eldorado" or "Touring Coupe" lettering with gray border, low-gloss black rocker moldings, a new center-high-mounted stoplight integrated into package shelf, new taillight assemblies, a new rear fascia, a new deck lid with a revised locking emblem and new "Eldorado" lettering integrated into the rear license plate pocket. New Bistro Cloth trim was used and seats were redesigned for enhanced comfort. The standard climate control system was improved with an upgraded electronic solar sensor and adjustable outlets with five-speed fan control. Optional equipment included more supple leather seating areas, a Sport Interior package that included a full floor console with a shift lever and analog instrument cluster, heated front seats (available only with leather) and a Delco-Bose Gold Series CD sound system. The Touring Coupe featured a monochromatic paint scheme, a specific body-color front fascia and integral foglights. Final drive ratio for the Touring Coupe was 3.33:1. Computer Command Ride was standard equipment and featured four electronically-controlled struts that were re-valved for stiffer suspension qualities. The Touring Coupe rode on specific 16-inch aluminum wheels and on Goodyear Eagle GA P225/60HR16 tires.

ELDORADO—SERIES 6E/L—V-8

Model Number	Body/Style No.	Body Type & Seating	Factory Price	Shipping Weight	Production Total
E/L	1	2D Coupe	32,470	3,604	31,151

SEVILLE-SERIES 6K/S-V-8
While the refinements/upgrades of the all-new Seville basically mirrored those of the Eldorado, the overall appearance of each of the two models was kept distinct. According to Cadillac's exterior design studio, the Seville was nicknamed the "greyhound" because of its rounded, muscular look (the Eldorado was nicknamed the "needle" because of its sharp, razor edge styling and angular body lines). The all-new Seville's overall length of 203.9 inches was 13.1 inches longer than the previous year's measure. As with the Eldorado, the Seville's electronic systems were streamlined. A new simplified main computer called the Instrument Panel Cluster eliminated the Body Control Module offered previously. It integrated Powertrain Control Module functions. The Seville's source of power was again the 4.9-liter V-8 mated to the 4T60-E electronically controlled four-speed automatic transmission with overdrive. The Seville featured composite headlights and wraparound parking, signal and cornering lights. In the rear, the center high-mounted stop light ran the entire length of the deck lid. Inside, interior volume was increased 6.5 cubic feet to 119.5 cubic feet.

SEVILLE—SERIES 6K/S—V-8

Model Number	Body/Style No.	Body Type & Seating	Factory Price	Shipping Weight	Production Total
K/S	5	4D Sedan	34,975	3,648	Note 8

Note 8: Seville production totaled 43,953 with no further breakout available.

SEVILLE TOURING SEDAN - SERIES 6K/Y - V-8
The SeVille lineup again included a Seville Touring Sedan or STS model. The Seville Touring Sedan had a body-color grille that featured a pewter color wreath-and-crest emblem.

SEVILLE TOURING SEDAN — SERIES 6K/Y—V-8

Model Number	Body/Style No.	Body Type & Seating	Factory Price	Shipping Weight	Production Total
K/Y	5	4D Tour Sedan	37,975	3,721	Note 9

Note 9: See Note 8 above.

ALLANTE HARDTOP CONVERTIBLE - SERIES 6V/R - V-8
The all-new 1993 convertible was launched early in spring 1992, so the 1992 Allante was basically a carry-over from the year previous. It was again offered in convertible hardtop configurations and was powered by the 4.5-liter V-8 paired with the F-7 four-speed automatic transaxle.

Model Number	Body/Style No.	Body Type & Seating	Factory Price	Shipping Weight	Production Total
V/R3	3	2D Convertible Hardtop	62,790	3,555	Note 10

Note 10: Allante production totaled 1,931 with no further breakout available.

ALLANTE HARDTOP CONVERTIBLE-SERIES 6V/S-V-8

The all-new 1993 Allante convertible was powered by the 4.5-liter V-8 paired with the F-7 four-speed automatic transaxle.

ALLANTE CONVERTIBLE – SERIES 6V/S – V-8

Model Number	Body/Style No.	Body Type & Seating	Factory Price	Shipping Weight	Production Total
Y/S	3	2D Convertible	57,170	3,491	Note 11

Note 11: See Note 10 above.

ENGINE

DEVILLE, FLEETWOOD, SEVILLE, ELDORADO BASE V-8

Overhead valve. Aluminum block with cast-iron liners. Displacement: 300 cid (4.9 liters). Bore and Stroke: 3.62 x 3.62 inches. Compression ratio: 9.5:1. Net brake hp: 200 at 4100 rpm. Taxable hp: 41.93. Net torque: 275 at 3000 rpm. Five main bearings. Roller hydraulic valve lifters. Induction: Multiport fuel injection. VIN Code: B; Option Code L26. Built by Cadillac.

ALLANTE BASE V-8

Overhead valve. Aluminum block with cast-iron liners. Displacement: 273 cid (4.5 liters). Bore and Stroke: 3.62 x 3.31 inches. Compression ratio: 9.0:1. Net brake hp: 200 at 4400 rpm. Taxable hp: 42.00. Net torque: 270 lbs.-ft. at 3200 rpm. Five main bearings. Roller hydraulic valve lifters. Induction: Multiport fuel injection. VIN Code: 8; Option Code L06. Built by Cadillac.

BROUGHAM BASE V-8

Overhead valve. Cast-iron block . Displacement: 305 cid (5.0 liters). Bore and Stroke: 3.74 x 3.48 inches. Compression ratio: 9.3:1. Net brake hp: 170 at 4200 rpm. Taxable hp: 44.8. Net torque: 255 lbs.-ft. at 2400 rpm. Five main bearings. Roller hydraulic valve lifters.

1992 Cadillac, Coupe De Ville

Induction: Throttle Body Injection. VIN Code: E; Option Code L03.

BROUGHAM COACHBUILDER, TOWING PACKAGE BASE V-8, CADILLAC OPTIONAL V-8

Overhead valve. Cast-iron block . Displacement: 350 cid (5.7 liters). Bore and stroke: 4.00 x 3.48. Compression ratio: 9.8:1. Net brake hp: 185 at 4200 rpm. Taxable hp: 51.20. Net torque: 300 lbs.-ft. at 2400 rpm. Five main bearings. Roller hydraulic valve lifters. Induction: Throttle Body Injection. VIN Code: 7; Option Code L05. Built by Chevrolet.

CHASSIS

(Coupe DeVille) Wheelbase: 110.8 inches. Overall Length: 205.1 inches. Height: 54.4 inches. Width: 73.4 inches. Front Tread: 60.2 inches. Rear Tread: 59.9 inches. Standard Tires: P205/70R15.

(Sedan DeVille) Wheelbase: 113.8 inches. Overall Length: 208 inches. Height: 55 inches. Width: 73.4 inches. Front Tread: 60.2 inches. Rear Tread: 59.9 inches. Standard Tires: P205/70R15.

(DeVille Touring Sedan) Wheelbase: 113.8 inches. Overall Length: 208 inches. Height: 55 inches. Width: 73.4 inches. Front Tread: 60.2 inches. Rear Tread: 59.9 inches. Standard Tires: P215/65R15 Goodyear Eagle GT4.

(Fleetwood Coupe) Wheelbase: 110.8 inches. Overall Length: 205.1 inches. Height: 54.4 inches. Width: 73.4 inches. Front Tread: 60.2 inches. Rear Tread: 59.9 inches. Standard Tires: P205/70R15.

(Fleetwood Sedan) Wheelbase: 113.8 inches. Overall Length: 208 inches. Height: 55.0 nches. Width: 73.4 inches. Front Tread: 60.2 inches. Rear Tread: 59.9 inches. Standard Tires: P205/70R15.

(Sixty Special) Wheelbase: 113.8 inches. Overall Length: 208 inches. Height: 55 inches. Width: 73.4 inches. Front Tread: 60.2 inches. Rear Tread: 59.9 inches. Standard Tires: P205/70R15.

(Brougham) Wheelbase: 121.5 inches. Overall Length: 221 inches. Height: 57.4 inches. Width: 76.5 inches. Front Tread: 61.7 inches. Rear Tread: 60.7 inches. Standard Tires: P225/75R15.

(Seville) Wheelbase: 111 inches. Overall Length: 203.9 inches. Height: 54 inches. Width: 74.4 inches. Front Tread: 60.9 inches. Rear Tread: 60.9 inches. Standard Tires: P225/60R15.

(Seville STS) Wheelbase: 111 inches. Overall Length: 203.9 inches. Height: 54 inches. Width: 74.4 inches. Front Tread: 60.9 inches. Rear Tread: 60.9 inches. Standard Tires: P225/60R15 with 16-inch wheels.

(Eldorado) Wheelbase: 108 inches. Overall Length: 202.2 inches. Height: 54 inches. Width: 74.8 inches. Front Tread: 60.9 inches. Rear Tread: 59.9 inches. Standard Tires: P225/60R15.

(Eldorado Touring Coupe) Wheelbase: 108 inches. Overall Length: 202.2 inches. Height: 54 inches. Width: 74.8 inches. Front Tread: 60.9 inches. Rear Tread: 59.9 inches. Standard Tires: P225/60R15.

(Allante Soft Top) Wheelbase: 99.4 inches. Overall Length: 178.7 inches. Height: 51 inches. Width: 73.5 inches. Front Tread: 60.4 inches. Rear Tread: 60.4 inches. Standard Tires: Goodyear Eagle GA P225/60HR16.

(Allante Both Tops) Wheelbase: 99.4 inches. Overall Length: 178.7 inches. Height: 51.2 inches. Width: 73.5 inches. Front Tread: 60.4 inches. Rear Tread: 60.4 inches. Standard Tires: Goodyear Eagle GA P225/60HR16.

TECHNICAL

Transmission: (DeVille, Fleetwood, Eldorado, Seville) 4T60-E electronically controlled four-speed automatic with overdrive (includes viscous converter clutch), (Allante) THM-F7 four-speed automatic (includes viscous converter clutch), (Brougham) THM 4L60 four-speed automatic with overdrive (includes torque converter clutch). Steering: (All except Brougham) Power-assisted rack-and-pinion, (Brougham) Power-assisted recirculating ball. Front Suspension: (All except Brougham) Independent MacPherson strut with coil springs, strut-type shock absorbers (integral-in strut and electronic variable on Allante and Computer Command Ride on Fleetwood, Seville, Eldorado) and stabilizer bar, (Brougham) Independent with short/long arms, coil springs, direct acting shock absorbers and link-type stabilizer bar. Rear Suspension: (DeVille, Fleetwood) fully independent with coil springs, automatic level control and (DeVille) strut-type superlift shock absorbers (Fleetwood) Computer Command Ride, (Eldorado, Seville) Fully independent transverse monoleaf with automatic level control and Computer Command Ride, no rear stabilizer, (Allante) Fully independent transverse monoleaf with integral-in strut electronic variable shock absorbers, no rear stabilizer, (Brougham) Four link, coil springs with automatic level control and direct acting shock absorbers and stabilizer bar. Brakes: (All except Eldorado, Seville, Allante) Power assisted front disc/rear drum with Teves anti-lock braking system (Brougham used Bosch II ABS), (Eldorado, Seville) Power assisted front and rear disc with Bosch II anti-lock braking system, (Allante) Power assisted front and rear disc with Bosch III anti-lock braking system. Body Construction: (All except Brougham) Integral body-frame, (Brougham) Separate body on frame. Fuel Tank: (DeVille, Fleetwood) 18.0 gallons, (Eldorado, Seville) 18.8 gallons, (Allante) 22.0 gallons, (Brougham) 25.0 gallons.

OPTIONS

DEVILLE OPTIONS

Option package B ($356). Option package C ($803). Security package ($295). Cold weather package ($369). Digital instrument cluster ($495). Astroroof ($1,550). Coachbuilders package for Sedan Deville ($1,000). Gold Ornamentation package ($395). Heavy-duty livery package for Sedan Deville ($1,000). Leather seating ($570). Firemist paint ($190). Delco-Bose sound system ($575). Delco-Bose sound system with CD ($872). Formal Cabriolet roof for Coupe Deville ($925). Full Cabriolet

1992 Cadillac, Sedan DeVille

roof for Coupe Deville ($1,095). Phaeton roof for Sedan Deville ($1,095). Locking wire wheel discs ($235). Lace cast-aluminum wheels ($235). NW9 traction control ($175). FX3 speed-sensitive suspension ($380).

FLEETWOOD AND SIXTY SPECIAL OPTIONS

Security package ($295). Cold weather package ($369). Custom seating package ($425). Astroroof ($1,550). Gold Ornamentation package ($395). Leather seating ($570). Firemist paint ($190). Delco-Bose sound system ($575). Delco-Bose sound system with CD ($872). Full vinyl roof, except Coupe ($925).

ELDORADO OPTIONS

YP5 Touring Coupe Option ($4,000). Option package B ($181). Security package ($480). Seating package ($340). Accent striping ($75). Heated front seats ($120). Astroroof ($1,550). Gold Ornamentation package ($395). Heated windshield ($309). Leather seating ($650). Auto day/night mirror ($110). Firemist paint ($240). Gold/White Diamond paint ($240). Delco-Bose sound system with CD and cassette ($972). Sport interior ($146). P225/60R16 white sidewall tires ($76).

SEVILLE OPTIONS

Option package B ($181). Security package ($480). Seating package ($340). Sport interior ($146). Accent striping ($75). Heated front seats ($120). Heated windshield system ($309). Astroroof ($1,550). Leather seating ($650). Auto day/night mirror ($110). Firemist paint ($240). Gold/White Diamond paint ($240). Delco-Bose sound system with CD and cassette ($972).

BROUGHAM OPTIONS

Option package B ($325). Option package C ($685). Option package C for d'Elegance ($360). Astroroof ($1,550). Coachbuilder Package ($295). Funeral Coach package ($1,680 credit). Brougham d'Elegance cloth interior ($1,875). Brougham d'Elegance leather interior ($2,445). Gold Ornamentation package ($395). Leather seating for Brougham d'Elegance ($570). Auto Day/Night Mirror ($110). Firemist Paint ($240). Radio with CD and cassette ($396). Full vinyl roof ($925). Locking wire wheel discs ($445). Wire wheels ($1,000). 5.7-liter V-8 ($250). V4P trailer towing package ($550).

ALLANTE OPTIONS

Digital Instrument Cluster for convertible only ($495). Pearl White paint for convertible only ($700).

HISTORICAL

Cadillac's model-year production totaled 233,027 compared with 220,284 the year previous. Based on sales of 214,176 automobiles in 1992 (compared to 213,288 in 1991) Cadillac's share of the U.S. market remained at 2.61 percent. A 1993 Allante convertible was selected as the pace car for the 1992 Indianapolis 500.

1992 Cadillac, Seville show car

1993

OVERVIEW

It was Cadillac's 90th Anniversary and also a year of "musical chairs" for the names of the automaker's products. The previously offered Brougham sedan was now called the Fleetwood, with the Brougham moniker reserved for an upscale option package available on the Fleetwood sedan. The former Fleetwood series, comprised of a coupe and sedan, was discontinued. The previously available Fleetwood Sixty Special was now simply called the Sixty Special. The Allante convertible was greatly revamped (launched early in spring 1992), but it was the final year for the luxury two-seater. Eldorado added a Sport Coupe package and Sport Appearance Package to "dress-up" the personal luxury coupe. The Northstar powertrain, with "limp-home" capability (after loss of all engine coolant) also debuted in 1993.

I.D. DATA

The 17-symbol serial number was located on top of the instrument panel, where it was visible through the windshield. The first symbol 1=U.S.-built vehicle. The second symbol G=General Motors. The third symbol 6=Cadillac. The fourth symbol indicated car line/the fifth symbol indicated series as follows: C/B=Sixty Special, C/D=DeVille, C/T=DeVille Touring, D/W=Brougham, E/L=Eldorado, K/S=Seville, K/Y=Seville Touring Sedan (STS) and V/S=Allante Convertible. The sixth symbol incated body style: 1=two-door Coupe/Sedan GM/Fisher Style Nos. 11, 27, 37, 47, 57 or 97, 3=two-door Convertible GM/Fisher Style No. 67, 5=four-door Sedan GM/Fisher style nos. 19, 23, 33 or 69. The seventh symbol indicates the type of restaint system: 1=manual belts, 2=Manual belts with dual airbags, 3=Manual belts with driver's air bag, 4=automatic belts, 5=Automatic belts with airbags. The eighth symbol identified the engine: B=L26 4.9L V-8, Y=LD8 4.6L V-8, 7=L05 5.7L V-8 and 9=L37 4.6L V-8. The ninth symbol was a check digit. The 10th symbol was a number indicating model year: P=1993. The 11th symbol indicates the GM assembly plant: U=Hamtramck, Mich. (Allante), 4=Orion, Mich. (DeVille), R=Arlington, Texas. The next group of numbers was the sequential production code starting with 100001. The Fisher Body tag on the cowl, under the hood includes additional information.

DEVILLE-SERIES 6C/D-V-8

The DeVille series lineup returned intact from the year previous, but "America's best-selling luxury car" received several upgrades, including speed-sensitive steering and speed-sensitive suspension as standard equipment. Speed-

Above: **1993 Cadillac, Allante', convertible**

sensitive steering varied the amount of steering effort required of the driver in proportion to the vehicle's speed. The DeVille's power-assisted rack-and-pinion steering's ratio was 17.6:1 with 2.97 turns required lock-to-lock. Speed- sensitive suspension automatically selected from three settings—comfort, normal and firm—to provide optimal ride-and-handling characteristics at all operating speeds. The 4.9-liter V-8 and 4T60-E electronically-controlled four-speed automatic transmission with overdrive again was the DeVille's power source. A new feature for 1993 was the Generation II CS144 alternator that delivered 140 amps of power. The CS144 incorporated a self-cooling design for optimal reliability. Final drive ratio for the Coupe DeVille and Sedan DeVille was 2.73:1. Exterior improvements included a revised grille for a "bolder" appearance and formal cabriolet roof on the Coupe DeVille. The DeVille continued to offer a driver's side airbag, solar control glass all-around, Pass-Key II anti-theft system and Twilight Sentinel headlight system as standard fare. Remote keyless entry, traction control and Astroroof remained on the optional equipment list.

DEVILLE – SERIES 6C/D – V-8

Model Number	Body/Style No.	Body Type & Seating	Factory Price	Shipping Weight	Production Total
C/D	1	2D Coupe	33915	3519	4,711
C/D	5	4D Sedan	32990	3605	Note 2

Note 1: Cadillac tallied DeVille and Sixty Special production together with no series breakout available.
Note 2: DeVille/Sixty Special sedan production totaled 125,963 with no further breakout available.

DEVILLE TOURING-SERIES 6C/T-V-8

The DeVille Touring Sedan had a new blacked-out quarter window molding treatment. The Touring Sedan also featured speed-sensitive steering and suspension systems, as well as traction control, as standard-equipment items. The outside of the Touring Sedan was distinguished by a grille-mounted wreath-and-crest emblem, front and rear body-color fascia, body-color door handles and chrome-plated body side door moldings with "Touring Sedan" identification. Inside, Beechwood color leather was used and the leather-trimmed steering wheel included a tilt feature and driver's side airbag. The instrument panel and doors were trimmed with American Walnut wood inserts.

DEVILLE TOURING—SERIES 6C/T—V-8

Model Number	Body/Style No.	Body Type & Seating	Factory Price	Shipping Weight	Production Total
C/T	5	4D Tour Sedan	36,310	3,651	Note 3

Note 3: See Note 2 above.

SIXTY SPECIAL-SERIES 6C/B-V-8

No longer using the Fleetwood name, the Sixty Special's refinements were in line with those of the DeVilles. Already employing speed-sensitive suspension and traction control as standard fare, the Sixty Special added speed-sensitive steering to the list. Front end styling was revised with a "bolder" appearing grille. Inside, front seating was a 45/55 design for the driver and two front passengers. The new styled seats featured French stitching and included front Dual Comfort, six-way power seat adjusters, manual recliners, adjustable headrests and seat back pockets. An Ultra Seating Package was optional and included a split frame design that allowed for adjustment of the lower seat cushion independently of the seat back. A trunk convenience net was a new standard item on the Sixty Special. The net, mounted transversely across the trunk compartment, secured items from rolling or sliding. Pass-Key II anti-theft system was also a standard feature.

SIXTY SPECIAL—SERIES 6C/B—V-8

Model Number	Body/Style No.	Body Type & Seating	Factory Price	Shipping Weight	Production Total
C/B	5	4D Sedan	37,230	3,649	Note 4

Note 4: See Note 2 above.

FLEETWOOD BROUGHAM-SERIES 6D/W

The overall length of America's longest regular production car increased 4.1 inches to 225.1 inches and with that change Cadillac also renamed the former Brougham sedan, calling it the Fleetwood Brougham. The wheelbase remained at 121.5 inches. The formerly standard 5.0-liter V-8 was discontinued and the previously optional 5.7-liter V-8 was now the power plant for the Fleetwood series. This V-8 featured a new starter motor that turned the engine more quickly and enhanced reliability. The 5.7-liter V-8 was rated at 185 hp and 300 pound-feet of torque. It was paired with the 4L60 Hydra-Matic four-speed automatic transmission. The standard axle ratio for the Fleetwood was 2.56:1 while the Brougham's was 3.08:1. Bosch ASRIIU traction control was standard equipment. The 1993 Fleetwood Sedan met mandated 1997 federal standards for dynamic side impact testing and featured dual airbags as standard equipment. The exterior of the Fleetwood featured larger, flush-glass design windshield and back window. The front view was updated with a new grille integrated into the hood. New aerodynamic outside rearview mirrors and flush door handles matched the body color. Fleetwood offered 20.8 cubic feet of trunk space (up 1.2 cubic feet over 1992). Interior volume was 125.2 cubic feet. Inside, Fleetwood offered split frame

1993 Cadillac, Sedan DeVille

seat construction with power seat recliners as standard items. New indicators to aid the driver included: door ajar, oil level, oil change and low engine coolant. Other new features included Power Drain Protection (exclusive to Fleetwood), which protected the battery if lights were left on by automatically shutting off lights after 10 minutes of inactivity. The Fleetwood Brougham package included a full vinyl top (which could be deleted), sail panel badging, specific seat design with six-way driver's seat memory and heated and three-position lumbar front seats, instrument panel badging and rear seat storage armrest. Other packages available for the Fleetwood included Coachbuilder Limousine with a 7,200 pound capacity, Heavy-Duty Livery and Funeral Coach.

FLEETWOOD BROUGHAM—
SERIES 6D/W–V-8

Model Number	Body/Style No.	Body Type & Seating	Factory Price	Shipping Weight	Production Total
D/W	5	4D Sedan	33990	4418	31,774

ELDORADO-SERIES 6E/L-V-8

All-new in design the year before, the Eldorado gained not only more members in its series, but also the Cadillac-exclusive Northstar engine under the hood of two of those members. An Eldorado Sport Coupe joined the ranks already consisting of the base coupe and Eldorado Touring Coupe. The Sport Coupe could be ordered either with a Sport Appearance Package (SAP) or Sport Performance Package (SPP—of which the SAP was included). It was both the Touring Coupe and Sport Coupe with SPP that featured the Northstar 4.6-liter, 32-valve, dual overhead cam V-8 engine. Both the block and cylinder head assembly of the Northstar engine were constructed of cast aluminum. The Northstar's compression ratio was 10.3:1. Mated to the Northstar was the all-new 4T80-E electronically controlled four-speed automatic transmission with torque converter clutch. Designed specifically for the Northstar engine, the 4T80-E featured equal-length drive axles to help eliminate torque steer. The Eldorado and Eldorado Sport Coupe with SAP were powered by the 4.9-liter V-8 paired with the 4T60-E electronically controlled four-speed automatic transmission with overdrive. The Powertrain Control System integrated engine and transmission functions to deliver controlled power to the drive wheels. New standard features for the Eldorado included speed-sensitive steering, a multi-link short/long arm (SLA) rear suspension and dual airbags. The SLA suspension system included a short upper control arm, a longer lower control arm, shock absorbers and an additional lateral link. This system, introduced on the early-launch 1993 Allante, provided increased ride stability as well as improved steering responsiveness. Another new feature for 1993 was the high-density polyethylene fuel tank, which replaced the previous welded steel tank and provided better crashworthiness, corrosion

resistance and improved thermal management. Bistro knit cloth was standard with Nuance leather seating areas optional (with heated front seats part of the package). A new option for Eldorados was the express-open sun roof. In addition to the Northstar V-8, the Sport Coupe with SPP also featured traction control, road sensing suspension and low-rolling resistance Michelin XW4 P225/60R16 tires. Road sensing suspension included four specially equipped struts with two damping rates: soft and firm. Under most conditions, the system operated in the soft mode. It shifted to firm mode when more control was needed. Steering ratio for the Sport Coupe was 15.6:1 with 2.65 turns required lock-to-lock. Outside, the Sport Coupe was distinguished by a chrome grille with wreath-and-crest ornament in the center. In the rear, a specific fascia was used to accommodate the dual exhaust. Also, on SPP-equipped models, a "Northstar" engine identification plaque was located on the deck lid. Sport Coupes featured three cloth seat color selections and eight leather choices. Optional was an electrochromic inside rearview mirror. The Touring Coupe also featured SLA rear suspension, road sensing suspension and speed-sensitive steering. Standard tires were Goodyear Eagle GA P225/60ZR16 radials mounted on cast-aluminum wheels. A new option was chrome wheels. Other standard fare for the Touring Coupe included GM's Pass-Key II anti-theft system, a 7000-rpm tachometer, a 150-mph speedometer, an electrochromic inside rearview mirror and leather seating in five color choices, including a new Saddle color.

ELDORADO—SERIES 6E/L—V-8

Model Number	Body/Style No.	Body Type & Seating	Factory Price	Shipping Weight	Production Total
E/L	1	2D Coupe	33,990	3,604	21,473

SEVILLE-SERIES 6K/S-V-8

The Seville Sedan had refinements and upgrades similar to the base Eldorado. The Seville again used the 4.9-liter V-8 and 4T60-E automatic transmission. Final drive ratio for the Seville was 2.97:1.

SEVILLE—SERIES 6K/S—V-8

Model Number	Body/Style No.	Body Type & Seating	Factory Price	Shipping Weight	Production Total
K/S	5	4D Sedan	36,990	3,648	Note 5

Note 5: Seville production totaled 37,239 with no further breakout available.

SEVILLE TOURING-SERIES 6K/Y-V-8

The Seville Touring Sedan (STS) had refinements and upgrades matching those made to the Eldorado Touring Coupe. The STS received the new Northstar 4.6-liter V-8 and 4T80-E automatic transmission. Final drive ratio for the STS was 3.71:1. In addition to the Northstar engine, STS featured the new Bosch ASRIIU traction control system. Designed to eliminate wheel spin on slippery road surfaces, the system reduced engine torque

by shutting down up to five cylinders simultaneously while applying the brakes. The STS was distinguished by its monochromatic paint scheme, "STS" badging and "Northstar" engine plaque. The STS also featured a body-color grille with wreath-and-crest emblem, specific rocker molding and bright dual exhaust outlets. New standard features for the STS included solar control glass and two new exterior colors: Academy Gray and Dark Cherry Red Metallic.

SEVILLE STS–SERIES 6K/Y–V-8

Model Number	Body/Style No.	Body Type & Seating	Factory Price	Shipping Weight	Production Total
K/Y	5	4D Sedan	41,990	3,721	Note 6

Note 6: See note 5 above.

ALLANTE CONVERTIBLE-SERIES 6V/S-V-8

The redesigned 1993 Allante convertible was launched in 1992. Its early debut introduced the world to the Northstar V-8 engine, which now powered the Allante. As with all other Northstar applications, the 4.6-liter V-8 was paired with the 4T80-E electronically-controlled four-speed automatic transmission. The Northstar debut featured highly efficient compound-geometry valve/port designs and "quiet coil" Direct Ignition System designed to operate at high rpm levels without loss of spark synchronization. The engine's dual stream injector Fluid Induction System was another innovation. This system was isolated from underhood heat sources and cooled the fuel during operation, which enhanced performance. The 4T80-E transmission featured a controlled-flow, dual lubricating system that provided proper lubrication under all operating conditions. Free-wheeling clutches ensured consistent shifting quality. In its final year of production, the Allante was vastly upgraded with the addition of road sensing suspension, speed-sensitive steering and the new-generation Bosch ASRIIU traction control system. The convertible also benefited from receiving the short/long arm (SLA) rear suspension that improved steering responsiveness. Other new standard features of the Allante included revised 16-inch cast-aluminum wheels fitted with Goodyear Eagle GA P225/60ZR16 tires and a 23-gallon polyethylene fuel tank. Chrome wheels were a new option. Outside, a new Maroon soft top was offered and the removal aluminum hardtop remained available as an option. A new, three-inch front fascia spoiler enhanced high-speed aerodynamics while new, one-piece side window glass improved weather sealing and acoustics. Three new clearcoat paint colors were offered: Pearl Red, Pearl Flax and Polo Green, upping the total to eight colors available. The Allante also featured a headlight washer system, new outside electric heated rearview mirrors with a foldaway design and blue tinted glass. New Nuance leather-trimmed bucket seats were orthopedically designed to provide optimal support and comfort. The

seats had power eight-way metaphoric adjustments and a new four-way power lumbar control. The console included a transmission shift selector that was slightly offset 20 degrees toward the driver for ease of shifting. The Allante also featured the new Pass-Key II anti-theft system as a standard item.

ALLANTE–SERIES 6V/S–V-8

Model Number	Body/Style No.	Body Type & Seating	Factory Price	Shipping Weight	Production Total
V/S	S67	2D Convertible	59,975	3,752	4,670

ENGINE

ELDORADO WITH SPP BASE V-8
Northstar Overhead valve. Dual overhead cam. Aluminum block with cast-iron liners. Aluminum cylinder heads. Displacement: 279 cid (4.6 liters). Taxable hp: 42.90. Bore and Stroke: 3.66 x 3.31 inches. Compression ratio: 10.3:1. Net brake hp: 270 at 5600 rpm. Net torque: 300 lbs.-ft. at 4000 rpm. Direct acting hydraulic tappets. Induction: Tuned port injection. VIN Code: 9; Option Code L37. Built by Cadillac.

ELDORADO TOURING COUPE, SEVILLE TOURING SEDAN, ALLANTE BASE V-8
Northstar Overhead valve. Dual overhead cam. Aluminum block with cast-iron liners. Aluminum cylinder heads. Displacement: 279 cid (4.6 liters). Taxable hp: 42.90. Bore and Stroke: 3.66 x 3.31 inches. Compression ratio: 10.3:1. Net brake hp: 295 at 6000 rpm. Net torque: 290 lbs.-ft. at 4400 rpm. Direct acting hydraulic tappets. Induction: Tuned port injection. VIN Code: Y; Option Code LD8. Built by Cadillac.

DEVILLE, SIXTY SPECIAL, SEVILLE, ELDORADO BASE V-8
Overhead valve. Aluminum block with cast-iron liners. Displacement: 300 cid (4.9 liters). Bore and Stroke: 3.62 x 3.62 inches. Compression ratio: 9.5:1. Net brake hp: 200 at 4100 rpm. Taxable hp: 41.93. Net torque: 275 lbs.-ft. at 3000 rpm. Five main bearings. Roller hydraulic valve lifters. Induction: Multiport fuel injection. VIN Code: B; Option Code L26. Built by Cadillac.

1993 Cadillac, Seville, STS sedan

FLEETWOOD BASE V-8

Overhead valve. Cast-iron block . Displacement: 350 cid (5.7 liters). Bore and stroke: 4.00 x 3.48. Compression ratio: 9.8:1. Net brake hp: 185 at 4200 rpm. Taxable hp: 51.20. Net torque: 300 at 2400 rpm. Five main bearings. Roller hydraulic valve lifters. Induction: Throttle Body Injection. VIN Code: 7; Option Code L07. Built by Chevrolet.

CHASSIS

(Coupe DeVille) Wheelbase: 110.8 inches. Overall Length: 203.3 inches. Height: 54.8 inches. Width: 73.4 inches. Front Tread: 60.1 inches. Rear Tread: 60.1 inches. Standard Tires: Michelin P205/70R15.

(Sedan DeVille) Wheelbase: 113.7 inches. Overall Length: 206.3 inches. Height: 55.1 inches. Width: 73.4 inches. Front Tread: 60.1 inches. Rear Tread: 60 inches. Standard Tires: P205/70R15.

(DeVille Touring) Wheelbase: 113.7 inches. Overall Length: 206.3 inches. Height: 55.1 inches. Width: 73.4 inches. Front Tread: 60.1 inches. Rear Tread: 60 inches. Standard Tires: Goodyear Eagle P215/60R16.

(Sixty Special Sedan) Wheelbase: 113.7 inches. Overall Length: 206.3 inches. Height: 57.1 inches. Width: 78 inches. Front Tread: 60.1 inches. Rear Tread: 60 inches. Standard Tires: P205/70R15.

(Fleetwood Brougham) Wheelbase: 121.5 inches. Overall Length: 225.1 inches. Height: 57.4 inches. Width: 76.5 inches. Front Tread: 61.7 inches. Rear Tread: 60.7 inches. Standard Tires: Michelin P235/70R15.

(Seville) Wheelbase: 111 inches. Overall Length: 204.4 inches. Height: 54 inches. Width: 74.4 inches. Front Tread: 60.9 inches. Rear Tread: 60.9 inches. Standard Tires: Michelin P225/60R16.

(Seville STS) Wheelbase: 111 inches. Overall Length: 204.4 inches. Height: 54 inches. Width: 74.4 inches. Front Tread: 60.9 inches. Rear Tread: 60.9 inches. Standard Tires: Goodyear Eagle GA P225/60ZR16.

(Eldorado) Wheelbase: 108 inches. Overall Length: 202.2 inches. Height: 54 inches. Width: 75.5 inches. Front Tread: 60.9 inches. Rear Tread: 60.9 inches. Standard Tires: Michelin P225/60R16.

(Eldorado Touring Coupe) Wheelbase: 108 inches. Overall Length: 202.2 inches. Height: 54 inches. Width: 75.5 inches. Front Tread: 60.9 inches. Rear Tread: 59.9 inches. Standard Tires: Goodyear Eagle GA P225/60ZR16.

(Allante Convertible) Wheelbase: 99.4 inches. Overall Length: 178.7 inches. Height: 51.5 inches. Width: 73.7 inches. Front Tread: 60.4 inches. Rear Tread: 60.4 inches. Standard Tires: Goodyear Eagle GA P225/60ZR16.

TECHNICAL

Transmission: (DeVille, Sixty Special, Eldorado, Seville) 4T60-E electronically controlled four-speed automatic with overdrive (includes viscous converter clutch), (Eldorado Touring Coupe, Eldorado Sport Coupe with Sport Performance Package, Seville Touring Sedan, Allante) 4T80-E electronically controlled four-speed automatic including torque converter clutch, (Fleetwood) THM 4L60 four-speed automatic with overdrive (includes torque converter clutch). Steering: (All except Fleetwood) Power-assisted rack-and-pinion, speed-sensitive, (Fleetwood) Power-assisted recirculating ball, speed-sensitive, variable assist. Front Suspension: (All except Fleetwood) Independent MacPherson strut with coil springs, strut-type shock absorbers (Eldorado Sport Coupe used electronic variable damping shock absorbers with road sensing suspension) and stabilizer bar, (Fleetwood) Independent with short/long arms, coil springs, direct acting shock absorbers and stabilizer bar. Rear Suspension: (DeVille, Sixty Special) Fully independent with coil springs, automatic level control and speed-sensitive suspension, (Eldorado, Seville) Fully independent, coil springs, short/long arm with automatic level control and speed-sensitive suspension (Eldorado Sport Coupe used electronic variable damping shock absorbers with road sensing suspension), (Eldorado Touring Coupe, Seville Touring Sedan). Fully independent, short/long arm with automatic level control, electronic variable damping shock absorbers with road sensing suspension, (Allante). Independent, short/long arm with coil springs, electronic variable damping shock absorbers with road sensing suspension and stabilizer bar, (Fleetwood) Four link, coil springs with automatic level control and direct acting shock absorbers and stabilizer bar. Brakes: (All except Eldorado, Seville, Allante). Power assisted front disc/rear drum with Teves anti-lock braking system (Fleetwood used Bosch II ABS), (Eldorado, Seville, Allante). Power assisted front and rear disc with Bosch II anti-lock braking system. Body Construction: (All except Fleetwood) Integral body-frame, (Fleetwood) Separate body on frame. Fuel Tank: (DeVille, Sixty Special) 18.0 gallons, (Eldorado, Seville Touring Sedan) 20.0 gallons, (Seville) 18.0 gallons, (Allante) 22.0 gallons, (Fleetwood) 23.0 gallons.

OPTIONS

DEVILLE OPTIONS

Option package B for Deville ($356). Option package B for DeVille Touring ($266). Option package C for Deville

($833). Option package C for DeVille Touring ($406). Security package ($295). Cold weather package ($369). Digital instrument cluster ($495). Astroroof ($1,550). Coachbuilders package for Sedan Deville ($1,000). Gold ornamentation package ($395). Heavy-duty livery package for Sedan Deville ($1,000). Leather seating ($570). Firemist paint ($190). Delco-Bose sound system ($575). Delco-Bose sound system with CD ($872). Full vinyl roof for Sedan Deville ($925). Full Cabriolet roof for Coupe Deville ($170). Phaeton roof for Sedan Deville ($1,095). Locking wire wheel discs ($235). Lace cast-aluminum wheels ($235). Chrome wheels ($1,195). NW9 traction control ($175).

SIXTY SPECIAL OPTIONS

Security package ($295). Cold weather package ($369). Custom seating package ($425). Ultra seating package ($3,500). Astroroof ($1,550). Gold ornamentation package ($395). Leather seating ($570). Firemist paint ($190). Delco-Bose sound system ($575). Delco-Bose sound system with CD ($872). Chrome wheels ($1,195).

ELDORADO OPTIONS

YP5 Touring Coupe option ($5,000). YP7 Sport Appearance package ($875). V4Z Sport Performance package ($3,000). Security package ($480). Accent striping ($75). Heated front seats ($120). Astroroof ($1,550). Heated windshield ($309). Leather seating ($650). Power lumbar support ($292). Auto day/night mirror ($110). Firemist paint ($240). Gold/White Diamond paint ($240). Delco-Bose sound system with CD and cassette ($972). P225/60R16 white sidewall tires ($76). Chrome wheels ($1,195).

SEVILLE OPTIONS

Security package ($480). Sport interior ($146). Full console ($146). Accent striping ($75). Heated front seats ($120). Heated windshield system ($309). Astroroof ($1,550). Leather seating ($650). Power lumber support ($292). Auto day/night mirror ($110). Firemist paint ($240). Gold/White Diamond paint ($240). Delco-Bose sound system with CD and cassette ($972). Chrome wheels ($1,195).

FLEETWOOD OPTIONS

Security package ($545). Astroroof ($1,550). Coachbuilder package (NC)). Funeral Coach package (($1,405 credit). Brougham cloth interior ($1,680). Brougham leather interior ($2,250). Heavy-duty livery package ($150). Leather seating in Fleetwood ($570). Auto day/night mirror ($110). Firemist paint ($190). AM/FM stereo radio with CD and cassette ($396). Full vinyl roof ($925). Full-size spare tire ($51). V4P trailer towing package ($70).

ALLANTE OPTIONS

Digital instrument cluster ($495). Pearlcoat Flax/White paint ($700).

HISTORICAL

Cadillac's model-year production totaled 225,830 compared with 233,027 the year previous. Based on sales of 204,159 automobiles in 1993 (compared 214,176 the year before), Cadillac's share of the U.S. market was 2.40 percent compared with 2.61 the year previous.

1993 Cadillac, Seville, STS sedan

1994

OVERVIEW

Cadillac thinned its ranks considerably in 1994, dropping both the Allante Convertible and Sixty Special Sedan as well as eliminating the Coupe DeVille. All series except the Fleetwood were "realigned." The DeVille (now identified on the car with a capital "D") series was now comprised of the Sedan DeVille and the Concours. The Eldorado Sport Coupe formerly offered was discontinued and the Eldorado series consisted of the "base" coupe and Eldorado Touring Coupe (ETC). The two trim levels of Seville offered were now distinguished as the Seville Luxury Sedan (SLS) and Seville Touring Sedan (STS). Other than the Sedan DeVille and Fleetwood, powered by 4.9-liter V-8 and 5.7-liter V-8 engines, respectively, the Northstar 4.6-liter V-8 was used in all other Cadillacs. Every Cadillac met 1997 federal mandates for dynamic side impact standards and all models featured steel safety cage construction, side door beams and front and rear crush zones.

I.D. DATA

The 17-symbol serial number was located on top of the instrument panel, where it was visible through the windshield. The first symbol 1=U.S.-built vehicle. The second symbol G=General Motors. The third symbol 6=Cadillac. The fourth symbol indicated car line/the fifth symbol indicated series as follows: D/H=Commercial Chassis, D/W=Fleetwood, E/L=Eldorado, E/T=Eldorado Touring, K/D=DeVille, K/F=Concours, K/S=Seville (SLS), K/Y=Seville (STS). The sixth symbol incated body style: 1=two-door Coupe/Sedan GM/Fisher Style Nos. 27, 37, 47, 57 or 97, 5=four-door Sedan GM/Fisher style nos. 19, 69. The seventh symbol indicates the type of restaint system: 1=manual belts, 2=Manual belts with dual airbags, 3=Manual belts with driver's air bag, 4=Automatic belts, 5=Automatic belts with airbags, 6=Manual belts with dual front airbags. The eighth symbol identified the engine: B=L26 4.9L V-8, P=LT1 5.7L V-8, Y=LD8 4.6L V-8

1994 Cadillac, Sedan De Ville

Above: **1994 Cadillac, Eldorado Touring Coupe**

1994 Cadillac, Eldorado Coupe

and 9=L37 4.6L V-8. The ninth symbol was a check digit. The 10th symbol was a number indicating model year: R=1994. The 11th symbol indicates the GM assembly plant: U=Hamtramck, Mich. (Allante), 4=Orion, Mich. (DeVille) and R=Arlington, Texas. The next group of numbers was the sequential production code starting with 100001. The Fisher Body tag on the cowl, under the hood includes additional information.

DEVILLE-SERIES 6K/D-V-8

The 1994 DeVille was a completely redesigned automobile and was offered only in sedan form. The Coupe DeVille was dropped. Body trim identified the sedan as a "DeVILLE" rather than a "DeVille." The Sedan DeVille was the lone Cadillac to use the 4.9-liter V-8. This sequential-port fuel-injected engine was refined for 1994, receiving a redesigned intake manifold for quieter operation and a single longitudinal exhaust that lowered exhaust restriction and improved engine performance. The accompanying 4T60-E electronically controlled four-speed automatic transmission was also used exclusively in the Sedan DeVille. It, too, was upgraded, receiving a new third clutch package, premium gear set and rocker pin chain, all of which enhanced wear resistance and reliability. Engine power was applied to the transmission via a viscous converter clutch. The transfer of this power was controlled via a single Powertrain Control Module, which managed engine and transmission functions as a single unit. DeVilles featured speed-sensitive steering, speed-sensitive suspension, short/long arm rear suspension and a Bosch ABSII antilock braking system as standard equipment. Full-speed traction control was optional. With the speed-sensitive steering, the Sedan DeVille's steering ratio was 15.5:1 with 2.97 turns required lock-to-lock. The DeVille's interior was also revamped. Dual airbags were standard fare, as was a new HD6 air conditioning compressor (for use with R-134a refrigerant). The interior noise level was reduced via a fiberglass dash mat and noise-absorbing material located in the engine compartment shock towers. A full-perimeter door sealing system that included dual door weatherstrips dampened road noise. The DeVille grew 4.4 inches wider, 3.9 inches longer and 1.3 inches taller, but its sleeker body lines

reduced coefficient of drag from 0.38 to 0.35. The front and rear bumpers featured a chrome-colored molding that flowed into the body side molding, which encircled the car. DeVille block lettering was etched into the body side molding on the front doors. Also new were body-color dual outside rearview mirrors. The rear of the DeVille featured tall, thin taillights. Thirteen exterior color choices were available including the new White Diamond, Light and Medium Montana Blue, Calypso Green and Mocha. Standard safety equipment included anti-lock-out automatic door locking with central door unlocking and remote keyless entry. All Cadillacs were equipped with Pass-Key II theft deterrent system.

DEVILLE—SERIES 6K/D—V-8

Model Number	Body/Style No.	Body Type & Seating	Factory Price	Shipping Weight	Production Total
K/D	5	4D Sedan	32,990	3,758	Note 1

Note 1: DeVille production totaled 120,352 with no further breakout available.

DEVILLE CONCOURS-SERIES 6K/F-V-8

The DeVille Concours was powered by the Northstar 4.6-liter V-8 coupled to the 4T80-E electronically-controlled four-speed automatic transmission with viscous converter clutch. In addition to the standard features found on the Sedan DeVille, the Concours added road-sensing suspension and Bosch ASRIIU traction control. Inside the Concours had Nuance leather seating, specific instrument panel badging, Zebrano wood trim and a new 11-speaker Delco Electronics active audio system. Outside, the Concours' unique features included a grille-mounted wreath-and- crest emblem, ribbed side molding, specific cast aluminum wheels with Goodyear Eagle GA P225/60HR16 tires, dual exhaust outlets and a "32V Northstar" badge. Chrome wheels were optional. The front and rear bumper assemblies featured an Argent color fascia molding that flowed into the body side molding. "Cadillac Concours" lettering was etched into the molding on the front doors.

CONCOURS—SERIES 6K/F—V-8

Model Number	Body/Style No.	Body Type & Seating	Factory Price	Shipping Weight	Production Total
K/F	5	4D Sedan	36590	3985	Note 2

Note 2: See Note 1 above.

FLEETWOOD-SERIES 6D/W-V-8

The Fleetwood sedan and upscale optional Brougham package for the "base" sedan again comprised the Fleetwood series. Also, the optional Coachbuilder Limousine, Funeral Coach and Trailer Towing packages were again available. In 1994, all Fleetwoods were powered by the Gen II 5.7-liter V-8 with sequential port fuel injection and the new Opti-Spark ignition system. Opti-Spark was an angle-based spark delivery system that ensured precisely timed, high-energy spark needed for optimum fuel efficiency

and low emissions. The Gen II V-8 was mated to the new 4L60-E electronically controlled four-speed automatic transmission, which replaced the previously used 4L60 unit. The 4L60-E transmission featured altitude compensation and over-rev protection. The transmission shared the same key information with the Powertrain Control Module as the engine to maintain consistent shifting, even in higher altitude, as well as automatically upshifting out of D1 (first gear) to second to protect the engine. New standard features of the Fleetwood included a four-spoke steering wheel, HD6 air conditioning compressor (for use of R-134a refrigerant), a turn-signal-activated "flash-to-pass" feature that allowed the driver to signal the driver in front of intent to pass via bright headlights (the system worked whether the headlights were on or not) and a DEFOG feature added to the Climate Control system. The DEFOG function directed 65 percent of the air to the windshield for clearing and 35 percent to the floor heat ducts. The Fleetwood's interior carpet was 18-ounce Twilight plush, which gave the appearance of wool with a nylon yarn. Chrome wheels were a new option for Fleetwood in 1994. The Brougham package again offered a full vinyl top (again a delete option), specific sail panel and instrument panel badging, specific seating (cloth or leather), specific cast-aluminum wheels and a 2.93 axle ratio.

FLEETWOOD—SERIES 6D/W—V-8

Model Number	Body/Style No.	Body Type & Seating	Factory Price	Shipping Weight	Production Total
D/W	5	4D Sedan	33,990	4,478	27,473

ELDORADO-SERIES 6E/L-V-8

The Northstar 4.6-liter V-8 and 4T80-E electronically controlled four-speed automatic transmission with viscous converter clutch were now part of the base Eldorado's power train. The short/long arm rear suspension introduced the year before was upgraded with an aluminum alloy lower control arm replacing the previous cast iron unit. This resulted in reduced unsprung mass, which enhanced ride quality. Also new were urethane engine cradle mounts that reduced powertrain vibration. A road-sensing suspension was now standard on the base Eldorado. Nuance leather seating was optional in the Eldorado and four new colors

1994 Cadillac, Seville, Luxury Sedan

were available: Dark Blue, Mocha, Dark Cherry and Beechwood. Interior noise levels were reduced in 1994 due to the use of thicker front fender closeout panels and cotton sound-absorbing added to door panels and rear package shelf. Windshield thickness was also increased .9mm for enhanced isolation of wind noise. Outside, a "32V Northstar" badge was located on the deck lid and dual exhaust outlets were also new.

ELDORADO—SERIES 6E/L—V-8

Model Number	Body/Style No.	Body Type & Seating	Factory Price	Shipping Weight	Production Total
E/L	1	2D Coupe	37,290	3,774	Note 3

Note 3: Eldorado production totaled 24,947 with no further breakout available.

ELDORADO TOURING-SERIES 6E/T-V-8

The Northstar 4.6-liter V-8 and 4T80-E electronically controlled four-speed automatic transmission with viscous converter clutch was also the power source for the Eldorado Touring Coupe (ETC). It also had the upgraded SLA suspension with an aluminum alloy lower control arm and the urethane engine cradle mounts. Other new features shared with the Eldorado included a leather-wrapped four-spoke steering wheel, timer and reset buttons that allowed the driver to clock driving time using "stopwatch" functions, the DEFOG feature of the Climate Control system, trunk convenience net and the HD6 air conditioning compressor (for use of R-134a refrigerant). New standard safety equipment included anti-lockout, automatic door locking with central door unlocking and remote keyless entry. ETC models were offered in 11 exterior color choices, including the new Medium Montana Blue, Mocha, Calypso Green, Platinum and Frost Beige.

ELDORADO TOURING— SERIES 6E/T – V-8

Series No.	Body/Style No.	Body Type & Seating	Factory Price	Shipping Weight	Production Total
E/T	1	2D Coupe	40,590	3,819	Note 4

Note 4: See Note 3 above.

SEVILLE SLS-SERIES 6K/S-V-8

Cadillac's K car line now featured a Seville Luxury Sedan (or SLS) that utilized the Northstar 4.6-liter V-8 and 4T80-E electronically controlled four-speed automatic transmission with viscous converter clutch. Standard equipment included speed-sensitive steering, road-sensing suspension, short/long arm rear suspension, anti-lock brakes and Bosch ASRIIU traction control. Other new features mirrored those listed for the Eldorado. The SLS was distinguished by a chrome-plated grille with stand-up wreath-and-crest hood ornament and "SLS" badging.

Series No.	Body/Style No.	Body Type & Seating	Factory Price	Shipping Weight	Prod.
K/S	5	4D Sedan	40,990	3,831	Note 5

Note 5: Seville production totaled 46,713 with no further breakout available.

SEVILLE SLS-SERIES 6K/S-V-8

The Seville series also inclued the Seville Touring Sedan (or STS). It also utilized the Northstar 4.6-liter V-8 and 4T80-E electronically controlled four-speed automatic transmission with viscous converter clutch. Standard equipment included speed-sensitive steering, road-sensing suspension, short/long arm rear suspension, anti-lock brakes and Bosch ASRIIU traction control. New STS features mirrored those listed for the Eldorado Touring Coupe. The STS featured a body-color grille with integrated wreath-and-crest emblem, body side cladding and "STS" badged wheels.

SEVILLE STS—SERIES 6K/S—V-8

Series No.	Body/Style No.	Body Type & Seating	Factory Price	Shipping Weight	Production Total
K/Y	5	4D Sedan	44,890	3,893	Note 6

Note 6: See Note 5 above.

COMMERCIAL CHASSIS (REAR-WHEEL DRIVE)-SERIES 6D/H-V-8

Cadillac once again offered this configuration to builders of "professional cars" like airport limousines and funeral vehicles. The Commercial Chassis designation was used. The big chassis-only product was based on the Fleetwood Brougham "D" series platform.

ENGINE

CONCOURS, ELDORADO, SEVILLE LUXURY SEDAN (SLS) BASE V-8

Northstar Overhead valve. Dual overhead cam. Aluminum block with cast-iron liners. Aluminum cylinder heads. Displacement: 279 cid (4.6 liters). Bore and Stroke: 3.66 x 3.31 inches. Compression ratio: 10.3:1. Net brake hp: 270 at 5600 rpm. Taxable hp: 42.90. Net torque: 300 at 4000 rpm. Direct acting hydraulic tappets. Induction: Tuned port injection. VIN Code: 9; Option Code L37. Built by Cadillac.

ELDORADO TOURING COUPE (ETC), SEVILLE TOURING SEDAN (STS) BASE V-8

Northstar Overhead valve. Dual overhead cam. Aluminum block with cast-iron liners. Aluminum cylinder heads. Displacement: 279 cid (4.6 liters). Bore and Stroke: 3.66 x 3.31 inches. Compression ratio: 10.3:1. Net brake hp: 295 at 6000 rpm. Taxable hp: 42.90. Net torque: 290 at 4400 rpm. Direct acting hydraulic tappets. Induction: Tuned port injection. VIN Code: Y; Option Code LD8. Built by Cadillac.

SEDAN DEVILLE BASE V-8

Overhead valve. Aluminum block with cast-iron liners. Displacement: 300 cid (4.9 liters). Bore and Stroke: 3.62 x 3.62 inches. Compression ratio: 9.5:1. Net brake hp: 200 at 4100 rpm. Taxable hp: 41.93. Net torque: 275 at 3000 rpm. Five main bearings. Roller hydraulic valve lifters. Induction: Multiport port injection. VIN Code: B; Option Code L26. Built by Cadillac.

1994 Cadillac, Fleetwood sedan

FLEETWOOD BASE V-8

Overhead valve. Cast-iron block . Displacement: 350 cid (5.7 liters). Bore and stroke: 4.00 x 3.48. Compression ratio: 9.7:1. Net brake hp: 260 at 5000 rpm. Taxable hp: 51.20. Net torque: 335 at 2400 rpm. Roller hydraulic valve lifters. Induction: Multiport port Injection. VIN Code: P; Option Code LT1. Built by Chevrolet.

CHASSIS

(Sedan DeVille) Wheelbase: 113.7 inches. Overall Length: 209.7 inches. Height: 56.3 inches. Width: 75.5 inches. Front Tread: 60.9 inches. Rear Tread: 60.9 inches. Standard Tires: Michelin P215/70R15.

(Concours) Wheelbase: 113.7 inches. Overall Length: 209.7 inches. Height: 56 inches. Width: 75.5 inches. Front Tread: 60.9 inches. Rear Tread: 60.9 inches. Standard Tires: Goodyear Eagle GA P225/60HR16.

(Fleetwood Brougham) Wheelbase: 121.5 inches. Overall Length: 225.1 inches. Height: 57.1 inches. Width: 78 inches. Front Tread: 60.7 inches. Rear Tread: 60.7 inches. Standard Tires: Michelin P235/70R15.

(Seville SLS) Wheelbase: 111 inches. Overall Length: 204.1 inches. Height: 54.5 inches. Width: 74.2 inches. Front Tread: 60.9 inches. Rear Tread: 60.9 inches. Standard Tires: Michelin P225/60R16.

(Seville STS) Wheelbase: 111 inches. Overall Length: 204.1 inches. Height: 54.5 inches. Width: 74.2 inches. Front Tread: 60.9 inches. Rear Tread: 60.9 inches. Standard Tires: Goodyear Eagle GA P225/60ZR16.

(Eldorado) Wheelbase: 108 inches. Overall Length: 202.2 inches. Height: 53.9 inches. Width: 75.5 inches. Front Tread: 60.9 inches. Rear Tread: 60.9 inches. Standard Tires: Michelin P225/60R16.

(Eldorado Touring Coupe) Wheelbase: 108 inches. Overall Length: 202.2 inches. Height: 53.9 inches. Width: 75.5 inches. Front Tread: 60.9 inches. Rear Tread: 60.9 inches. Standard Tires: Goodyear Eagle GA P225/60ZR16.

TECHNICAL

Transmission: (Sedan DeVille) 4T60-E electronically controlled four-speed automatic with overdrive (includes viscous converter clutch), (DeVille Concours, Eldorado, Seville) 4T80-E electronically controlled four-speed automatic (includes viscous converter clutch), (Fleetwood) 4L60-E electronically controlled four-speed automatic (includes torque converter clutch). Steering: (All except Fleetwood) Power-assisted rack-and-pinion, speed-sensitive, (Fleetwood) Power-assisted recirculating ball, speed-sensitive, variable assist. Front Suspension: (All except Fleetwood) Independent MacPherson strut with coil springs, strut-type shock absorbers (DeVille Concours used electronic variable rate dampers) and stabilizer bar, (Fleetwood) Independent with short/long arms, coil springs, direct acting shock absorbers and stabilizer bar. Rear Suspension: (Sedan DeVille) Fully independent, short/long arm with automatic level control and speed-sensitive suspension, (DeVille Concours, Seville, Eldorado) Fully independent, coil springs, short/long arm with automatic level control and electronic variable dampers with road sensing suspension, (Fleetwood) Four link, coil springs with automatic level control, direct acting shock absorbers and stabilizer bar. Brakes: (all except Fleetwood) Power assisted front and rear disc with Bosch II anti-lock braking system, (Fleetwood) Power assisted front disc/rear drum with Bosch anti-lock braking system. Body Construction: (All except Fleetwood) Integral body-frame, (Fleetwood) Separate body on frame. Fuel Tank: (all except Fleetwood) 20.0 gallons, (Fleetwood) 23.0 gallons.

OPTIONS

DEVILLE OPTIONS

Option package 1SB for Sedan DeVille ($428). Astroroof ($1,550). Alarm system for Sedan DeVille ($295). White Diamond paint ($500). ETR AM/FM stereo radio with cassette ($274,but standard in Concours). ETR AM/FM stereo radio with cassette and CD for Sedan DeVille ($670). ETR AM/FM stereo radio with cassette and CD for Concours ($396). Heated windshield for Sedan DeVille ($309). Heated front seats for Sedan DeVille ($310). Heated front seats for Concours ($120). Leather Seats ($785, but standard in Concours). Body side stripe ($75). Chrome wheels ($1,195). NW9 Traction Control on Sedan Deville ($175).

ELDORADO OPTIONS

V4C Sport Interior package ($146). Alarm System ($295, but standard in ETC). Bodyside Striping for base Eldorado ($75). Heated front seats ($120). Astroroof ($1,550). Heated windshield ($309). Leather seating ($650, but standard in ETC). Power lumbar support ($292,but standard in ETC). Auto day/night mirror ($87, but standard in ETC). White Diamond Paint ($500). Delco-Bose sound system with CD and cassette ($972). P225/60R16 white sidewall tires for base Eldorado ($76). Chrome wheels ($1,195).

SEVILLE OPTIONS

V4C Sport Interior package ($146). Alarm System ($295, but standard in STS). Bodyside Striping for Seville SLS ($75). Heated front seats ($120). Heated windshield ($309). Astroroof ($1,550). Leather seating ($650,

but standard in STS). Power lumbar support ($292, but standard in STS). Auto day/night mirror ($87, but standard in STS). White Diamond paint ($500). Delco-Bose sound system with CD and cassette ($972). Chrome wheels ($1,195).

FLEETWOOD OPTIONS

Security package ($545). Astroroof ($1,550). Coachbuilder package ($755). Funeral Coach package ($910 credit). Brougham cloth interior ($1,680). Brougham leather interior ($2,250). Heavy-duty Livery package ($150). Leather seating in base Fleetwood ($570). Auto day/night mirror ($110). Sungate windshield ($50). ETR AM/FM stereo radio with CD and cassette ($396). Full vinyl roof on base Fleetwood ($925). Full-size spare tire ($95). Chrome wheels ($1,195). V92 trailer towing package ($70).

HISTORICAL

Cadillac's model-year production totaled 219,485 compared with 225,830 the year previous. Based on sales of 210,686 automobiles in 1994 (compared to 204,159 the year before) Cadillac's share of the U.S. market was 2.3 percent compared to 2.4 percent the year previous. The Cadillac LSE (Luxury Sedan Euro-Style) show car was exhibited at the major 1994 auto shows. The LSE, a five-passenger sedan finished in Ruby Red, was, according to Cadillac, the "vision for an entry-level luxury sedan for the mid-1990s." It was powered by a 3.0-liter dual-overhead-cam V-6 rated at 200 hp and its wheelbase measured 107.5 inches. The aim of the LSE was to broaden Cadillac's appeal to young, affluent buyers.

1994 Cadillac, DeVille Concours, sedan

1995

OVERVIEW

It was the 80th Anniversary of the Cadillac V-8 engine. The 1995 Cadillac lineup mirrored the previous year's offerings. New on all Cadillacs was the PG260 Planetary Gear Starter that featured improved corrosion protection with added lubricants and improved sealing around the drive shaft. The front-wheel-drive Cadillacs received structural refinements to improve body stiffness and limit vibration. These revisions included new steering column struts that tied in to the cross-car beam behind the instrument panel, longitudinal braces in the trunk compartment and a more rigid urethane seal where all stationary glass surfaces mount to the body. All front-wheel-drivers also benefited from a newly designed, quieter exhaust system that included a larger muffler and longer tailpipe.

I.D. DATA

The 17-symbol serial number was located on top of the instrument panel, where it was visible through the windshield. The first symbol 1=U.S.-built vehicle. The second symbol G=General Motors. The third symbol 6=Cadillac. The fourth symbol indicated carline. The fifth symbol indicated series as follows: D/W=Fleetwood, E/

L=Eldorado, E/T=Eldorado Touring, K/D=DeVille, K/F=Concours, K/S=Seville (SLS), K/Y=Seville (STS). The sixth symbol indicated body style: 1=two-door Coupe/Sedan GM/Fisher Style Nos. 27, 37, 47, 57 or 97, 5=four-door Sedan GM/Fisher style nos. 19, 69. The seventh symbol indicated the type of restraint system: 1=manual belts, 2=Manual belts with dual airbags, 3=Manual belts with driver's air bag, 4=Automatic belts, 5=Automatic belts with airbags, 6=Manual belts with dual front airbags. The eighth symbol identified the engine: B=L26 4.9L V-8, P=LT1 5.7L V-8, Y=LD8 4.6L V-8 and 9=L37 4.6L V-8. The ninth symbol was a check digit. The 10th symbol indicated model year: S=1995. The 11th symbol indicated the GM assembly plant: U=Hamtramck, Mich. (Allante), 4=Orion, Mich. (DeVille) and R=Arlington, Texas. The next group of numbers was the sequential production code starting with 001. The Fisher Body tag on the cowl, under the hood includes additional information.

DEVILLE - SERIES 6K/D - V-8

Sedan DeVille retained the powertrain used the year previous. Formerly optional features that were made standard on the Sedan DeVille included Bosch ASR5 (Anti-Slip Regulation) traction control, 20-second illuminated entry, an airbag electronic sensing and diagnostic module, an electronic gear selector display

Above: **1995 Cadillac, DeVille Concours, sedan**

and windshield wiper-activated headlights. Other new standard features included a trunk lid power pull-down and door edge guards deleted (both 1994 running changes), a trunk cargo net, an underhood light, deck lid lock ornamentation in red and black, new accent striping and three additional exterior waterborne paint colors: Shale, Pearl Red and Amethyst. Inside, Saratoga interior cloth was standard with one new color offered: Neutral Shale. In the optional Nuance leather, Neutral Shale and Cappuccino Cream were new color choices. New optional equipment included an electronic compass inside the rearview mirror, a programmable garage door opener and a sun roof with illuminated driver and front passenger vanity mirrors and rear reading lights.

DEVILLE — SERIES 6K/D–V-8

Model Number	Body/Style No.	Body Type & Seating	Factory Price	Shipping Weight	Production Total
K/D	5	4D Sedan	34,900	3758	Note 1

DeVille production totaled 109,066 with no further breakout available.

DEVILLE CONCOURS - SERIES 6K/F - V-8

The DeVille Concours sedan's Northstar engine was upgraded by five horsepower (from 270 to 275) due to receiving a new fluid-induction system that increased air flow efficiency through smoother intake tuning tubes. In addition to the upgrades listed above for the Sedan DeVille, the DeVille Concours received the Integrated Chassis Control System (ICCS) that improved stopping distance, increased braking stability and reduced unnecessary reaction of the traction-control system in low-speed, tight-turning-radius maneuvers. The Concours sedan also featured a traction-control disable switch located in the glovebox. Other unique-to-Concours features included the programmable garage door opener as standard fare, a rear seat storage arm rest, 16-inch cast-aluminum wheels with diamond-cut finish wreath-and-crest center caps, pre-loaded damper-valving suspension components, a stiffening brace package for the Northstar V-8 to reduce vibration and two additional color choices for standard Nuance leather seating: Neutral Shale and Cappuccino Cream.

CONCOURS — SERIES 6K/F — V-8

Model Number	Body/Style No.	Body Type & Seating	Factory Price	Shipping Weight	Production Total
K/F	5	4D Sedan	39,400	3,985	Note 2

Note 2: See Note 1 above.

FLEETWOOD - SERIES 6D/W - V-8

The Gen II 5.7-liter V-8 that powered the Fleetwood sedan and Fleetwoods with the Brougham package was upgraded for 1995. In addition to the aforementioned PG260 starter that all Cadillacs received, the rear-wheel-drive Fleetwood's V-8 now also featured Quiet Cam. This revised camshaft design, in conjunction with new sound and vibration reducing composite rocker arm covers, decreased engine mechanical noise and eliminated valve noise on the outside of the car. Again, the 4L60-E electronically-controlled four-speed automatic transmission saw service with the Gen II V-8. For 1995, the 4L60-E featured a 298mm torque converter clutch assembly that had a higher torque capacity, which enhanced the unit's durability. Former options, now standard, included remote keyless entry, central door unlocking and automatic door locks and electrochromic inside rearview mirror. The Brougham sedan added a programmable garage door opener and an upgraded electronic lumbar system for seat adjustments. Also, the optional V4R security package was restructured to include the theft deterrent system and auto lock/unlock fuel filler door. For 1995, Fleetwoods also received increased capacity of the Electronic Control Unit that provided more convenient traction-control on/off capability. A toggle switch in the glovebox allowed the traction-control to be switched off and on without restarting the engine. The Fleetwood could be ordered as the V4U Coachbuilder Limousine Package, B9Q Funeral Coach Package or R1P Heavy-Duty Sedan Package.

FLEETWOOD—SERIES 6D/W–V-8

Model Number	Body/Style No.	Body Type & Seating	Factory Price	Shipping Weight	Production Total
D/W	5	4D Sedan	35,595	4,477	27,350

ELDORADO - SERIES 6E/L- V-8

The Eldorado coupe was powered by the Northstar 4.6-liter V-8 mated to the 4T80-E electronically controlled four-speed automatic transmission with viscous converter clutch. Due to the aforementioned new fluid-induction system the Northstar received in 1995, the Eldorado's horsepower rating increased by five over the previous year. The appearance of the "base" Eldorado was greatly refined with newly-designed front and rear fascias, a chrome grille with a body-color perimeter and a new integrated wreath-and-crest emblem. Inside, the Eldorado received windshield wiper-activated headlights, 20-second illuminated entry, electronic gear selector display, airbag electronic sensing and diagnostic module and new Charisma cloth replaced the previous Bistro cloth and was available in Neutral Shade (cloth and leather). Powertrain

1995 Cadillac, Seville, STS sedan

and chassis refinements included the aforementioned PG260 starter motor and fluid-induction system, as well as the Integrated Chassis Control System that featured steering wheel angle sensor, four-channel anti-lock brake system and ASR5 traction control. The Northstar V-8 received a stiffening brace package to reduce vibration. The Eldorado was stiffened via steering column struts tied in to the cross-car beam, behind the instrument panel, as well as corner gussets that replaced front shock tower to radiator tie-bar braces. New options included a electronic compass in the inside rearview mirror, a programmable garage door opener, chrome wheels (common to the Seville Luxury Sedan), a rear seat storage arm rest and two Nuance leather seating color choices: Neutral Shale and Cappuccino Cream.

ELDORADO—SERIES 6E/L–V-8

Model Number	Body/Style No.	Body Type & Seating	Factory Price	Shipping Weight	Production Total
E/L	1	2D Coupe	38,220	3,774	Note 3

Note 3: Eldorado production totaled 25,230 with no further breakout available.

ELDORADO TOURING-SERIES 6E/T-V-8

The Eldorado Touring (Coupe) also had five more horsepower than last year. Additionally, the ETC also gained torque and delivered 295 pound-feet (up from 290). Other standard features unique to the Touring Coupe included an "ETC" deck lid badge (there was no Touring Coupe identification on the doors), body-color license plate frames with "ELDORADO" lettering, five new exterior waterborne color choices: Shale, Pearl Red, Amethyst, Cotillion White and Light Montana Blue, and four new Nuance leather seating color choices: Neutral Shale, Cappuccino Cream, Dark Blue and Dark Cherry. Also revised on the ETC was its body color grille.

ELDORADO TOURING—SERIES 6E/T–V-8

Model Number	Body/Style No.	Body Type & Seating	Factory Price	Shipping Weight	Production Total
E/T	1	2D Coupe	41,535	3,818	Note 4

Note 4: See Note 3 above.

SEVILLE-SERIES 6K/S-V-8

The Seville series again used the Northstar 4.6-liter V-8 and 4T80-E electronically controlled four-speed automatic transmission with viscous converter clutch. Engine, chassis and interior upgrades/refinements for the SLS basically mirrored the Eldorado coupe.

SEVILLE SLS – SERIES 6K/S – V-8

Model Number	Body/Style No.	Body Type & Seating	Factory Price	Shipping Weight	Produc
K/S	5	4D Sedan	41,935	3,950	Note 5

Note 5: Seville production totaled 38,931 with no further breakout available.

1995 Cadillac, Sedan De Ville

1995 Cadillac, Eldorado coupe

SEVILLE TOURING SEDAN-SERIES 6K/Y-V-8

Engine, chassis and interior upgrades/refinements for the STS's mimicked those for the Eldorado ETC.

SEVILLE STS—SERIES 6K/Y—V-8

Model Number	Body/Style No.	Body Type & Seating	Factory Price	Shipping Weight	Production Total
K/Y	5	4D Sedan	45935	3950	Note 6

Note 6: See Note 5 above.

ENGINE

DE VILLE CONCOURS, ELDORADO, SEVILLE LUXURY SEDAN BASE V-8

Northstar overhead valve. Dual overhead cam. Aluminum block with cast iron liners. Aluminum cylinder heads. Displacement: 279 cid (4.6 liters). Bore and Stroke: 3.66 x 3.31 inches. Compression ratio: 10.3:1. Net brake hp: 275 at 5600 rpm. Taxable hp: 42.90. Net torque: 300 at 4000 rpm. Direct acting hydraulic tappets. Induction: Tuned port injection. VIN Code: 9; Option Code L37. Built by Cadillac.

ELDORADO TOURING COUPE, SEVILLE TOURING SEDAN BASE V-8

Northstar overhead valve. Dual overhead cam. Aluminum block with cast iron liners. Aluminum cylinder heads. Displacement: 279 cid (4.6 liters). Bore and Stroke: 3.66 x 3.31 inches. Compression ratio: 10.3:1. Net brake hp: 300 at 6000 rpm. Taxable hp: 42.90. Net torque: 295 at 4400 rpm. Direct acting hydraulic tappets. Induction: Tuned port injection. VIN Code: Y; Option Code LD8. Built by Cadillac.

SEDAN DE VILLE BASE V-8

Overhead valve. Aluminum block with cast iron liners. Displacement: 300 cid (4.9 liters). Bore and Stroke: 3.62 x 3.62 inches. Compression ratio: 9.5:1. Net brake hp: 200 at 4 rpm. Taxable hp: 41.93. Net torque: 275 at 3000 rpm. Five main bearings. Roller hydraulic valve lifters. Induction: Multiport port injection. VIN Code: B; Option Code L26. Built by Cadillac.

FLEETWOOD BASE V-8

Overhead valve. Cast iron block. Displacement: 350 cid (5.7 liters). Bore and stroke: 4.00 x 3.48. Compression ratio: 10.5:1. Net brake hp: 260 at 5000 rpm. Taxable hp: 51.20. Net torque: 335 at 2400 rpm. Roller hydraulic valve lifters. Induction: Multiport port Injection. VIN Code: P; Option Code LT1. Built by Chevrolet.

CHASSIS

(Sedan DeVille) Wheelbase: 113.7 inches. Overall Length: 209.7 inches. Height: 56.3 inches. Width: 75.5 inches. Front Tread: 60.9 inches. Rear Tread: 60.9 inches. Standard Tires: Michelin P215/70R15.

(Concours) Wheelbase: 113.7 inches. Overall Length: 209.7 inches. Height: 56 inches. Width: 75.5 inches. Front Tread: 60.9 inches. Rear Tread: 60.9 inches. Standard Tires: Goodyear Eagle GA P225/60HR16.

(Fleetwood Brougham) Wheelbase: 121.5 nches. Overall Length: 225.1 inches. Height: 57.1 inches. Width: 78 inches. Front Tread: 60.7 inches. Rear Tread: 60.7 inches. Standard Tires: Michelin P235/70R15.

(Seville SLS) Wheelbase: 111 inches. Overall Length: 204.1 inches. Height: 54.5 inches. Width: 74.2 inches. Front Tread: 60.9 inches. Rear Tread: 60.9 inches. Standard Tires: Michelin P225/60R16.

(Seville STS) Wheelbase: 111 inches. Overall Length: 204.1 inches. Height: 54.5 inches. Width: 74.2 inches. Front Tread: 60.9 inches. Rear Tread: 60.9 inches. Standard Tires: Goodyear Eagle GA P225/60ZR16.

(Eldorado) Wheelbase: 108 inches. Overall Length: 202.2 inches. Height: 53.9 inches. Width: 75.5 inches. Front Tread: 60.9 inches. Rear Tread: 60.9 inches. Standard Tires: Michelin P225/60R16.

(Eldorado Touring Coupe) Wheelbase: 108 inches. Overall Length: 202.2 inches. Height: 53.9 inches. Width: 75.5 inches. Front Tread: 60.9 inches. Rear Tread: 60.9 inches. Standard Tires: Goodyear Eagle GA P225/60ZR16.

TECHNICAL

Transmission: (Sedan DeVille) 4T60-E electronically-controlled four-speed automatic with overdrive (includes viscous converter clutch), (DeVille Concours, Eldorado, Seville) 4T80-E electronically controlled four-speed automatic (includes viscous converter clutch), (Fleetwood) 4L60-E electronically controlled four-speed automatic (includes torque converter clutch). Steering: (All except Fleetwood) Power-assisted rack-and-pinion, speed-sensitive, (Fleetwood) Power-assisted recirculating ball, speed-sensitive, variable assist. Front Suspension: (All except Fleetwood) Independent MacPherson strut with

1995 Cadillac, Eldorado Touring Coupe

coil springs, strut-type shock absorbers (DeVille Concours used electronic variable rate dampers) and stabilizer bar, (Fleetwood) Independent with short/long arms, coil springs, direct acting shock absorbers and stabilizer bar. Rear Suspension: (Sedan DeVille) Fully independent, short/long arm with automatic level control and speed-sensitive suspension, (DeVille Concours, Seville, Eldorado) Fully independent, coil springs, short/long arm with automatic level control and electronic variable dampers with road sensing suspension, (Fleetwood) Four link, coil springs with automatic level control, direct acting shock absorbers and stabilizer bar. Brakes: (all except Fleetwood) Power assisted front and rear disc with Bosch anti-lock braking system, (Fleetwood) Power assisted front disc/rear drum with Bosch anti-lock braking system, Body Construction: (All except Fleetwood) Integral body-frame, (Fleetwood) Separate body on frame. Fuel Tank: (all except Fleetwood) 20.0 gallons, (Fleetwood) 23.0 gallons.

OPTIONS

DEVILLE OPTIONS

Option Package 1SB for Sedan DeVille ($428). Astroroof ($1,550-$1,700). Garage door opener ($107). Theft deterrent system for Sedan DeVille ($295). White Diamond paint ($500). Pearl Red paint ($500). Electrochromic automatic day/night driver's side mirror for Sedan DeVille ($87). ETR AM/FM stereo radio with cassette ($274, but standard in Concours). ETR AM/FM stereo radio with cassette and CD in Sedan DeVille ($670). ETR AM/FM stereo radio with cassette and CD in DeVille Concours ($396). Heated windshield in Sedan DeVille ($309). Heated front seats ($120). Leather seats ($785, but standard in Concours). Chrome wheels ($1,195). V92 3,000-lb. trailer towing package for Concours ($110).

ELDORADO OPTIONS

UY9 Sport interior package ($146). Theft deterrent system ($295, but standard in ETC). Garage door opener ($107). Accent striping for base Eldorado ($75). Heated front seats ($120). Astroroof ($1,550). Heated windshield ($309). Leather seating ($650, but standard in ETC). Power lumbar support ($292, but standard in ETC). Electrochromic automatic day/night driver's side rearview mirror ($87, but standard in ETC). White Diamond paint ($500). Pearl Red paint ($500). Delco-Bose sound system with CD and cassette ($972). P225/60R16 white sidewall tires for base Eldorado ($76). Chrome wheels ($1,195).

SEVILLE OPTIONS

UY9 Sport interior package ($146). Theft deterrent system ($295, but standard in STS). Electronic compass ($). Garage door opener ($107). Accent striping for SLS ($75). Heated front seats ($120). Heated windshield ($309). Astroroof ($1,550). Leather seating for SLS ($650). Power lumbar support for SLS ($292). Electrochromic automatic day/night driver's side mirror for SLS ($87). White Diamond paint ($500). Pearl Red paint ($500). Delco-Bose sound system with CD and cassette ($972). Chrome wheels ($1,195).

FLEETWOOD OPTIONS

Security package ($360). Theft-deterrent system ($295). Astroroof ($1,550). Garage door opener ($107). Coachbuilder package ($755). Funeral Coach package ($910 credit). Brougham cloth interior ($1,680). Brougham leather interior ($2,250). Heavy-Duty Livery package ($150). Leather seating in base Fleetwood ($570). Heated front seats ($120). Sungate windshield ($50). ETR AM/FM stereo radio with CD and cassette ($396). Full vinyl roof on base Fleetwood ($925). Full-size spare tire ($95). Chrome wheels ($1,195). 7,000-lb. Trailer Towing package for base Fleetwood ($215).

HISTORICAL

Cadillac's model-year production totaled 200,577, compared with 219,485 the year previous. Based on sales of 180,504 automobiles in 1995 (versus 210,686 the year before), Cadillac's share of the U.S. market was 2.1 percent compared with 2.3 the year previous.

1995 Cadillac, Fleetwood sedan

1995 Cadillac, Seville, Luxury Sedan

1996

OVERVIEW

The Northstar V-8, in either its 275- or 300-hp format, now powered all front-wheel-drive Cadillacs. The Arlington, Texas-produced Fleetwood (with or without the optional Fleetwood Brougham package) was the lone front-engine, rear-wheel-drive Cadillac. However, this was its final year of production. Introduced in early-1996, as a 1997 model, was the all-new rear-wheel-drive Catera. This midsize luxury sedan was a joint venture between Cadillac and Opel. It was assembled in Germany and used a 3.0-liter dual-overhead-cam V-6. All 1996 Cadillacs received daytime running lights and a new dark gray remote keyless entry fob, with light gray buttons and white icons. The fob functions were: lock, unlock, trunk open and fuel door open. The fobs were identified on back with a "one" or "two" indication, allowing two separate drivers to personalize seat positions. All front-wheel-drive Cadillacs featured an ignition key anti-lockout feature that protected the driver from accidental lockout.

I.D. DATA

The 17-symbol serial number was located on top of the instrument panel, where it was visible through the

Above: **The 1996 Cadillacs combined traditional luxury with exciting technology.**

windshield. The first symbol 1=U.S.-built vehicle. The second symbol G=General Motors. The third symbol 6=Cadillac. The fourth symbol indicated carline/the fifth symbol indicated series as follows: D/W=Fleetwood, E/L=Eldorado, E/T=Eldorado Touring, K/D=DeVille, K/F=Concours, K/S=Seville (SLS), K/Y=Seville (STS). The sixth symbol indicated body style: 1=two-door Coupe/Sedan GM/Fisher Style Nos. 27, 37, 47, 57 or 97, 5=four-door Sedan GM/Fisher style nos. 19, 69. The seventh symbol indicated the type of restraint system: 1=manual belts or 5=Automatic belts with airbags. The eighth symbol identified the engine: P=LT1 5.7L V-8, Y=LD8 4.6L V-8 and 9=L37 4.6L V-8. The ninth symbol was a check digit. The 10th symbol indicated model year: T=1996. The 11th symbol indicated the GM assembly plant: U=Hamtramck, Mich. (Allante) and R=Arlington, Texas. The next group of numbers was the sequential production code starting with 001. The Fisher Body tag on the cowl, under the hood includes additional information.

DEVILLE-SERIES 6K/D-V-8

The Sedan DeVille used the 275-hp 4.6-liter Northstar V-8 mated to the 4T80-E electronically-controlled four-speed automatic transmission with viscous converter clutch. This combination replaced the formerly standard 4.9-liter V-8 and 4T60-E four-speed transmission. Sedan DeVille's new

1996 Cadillac, Fleetwood sedan

final-drive ratio was 3.11:1. A more powerful Powertrain Control Module (PCM) with microprocessors monitored and directed DeVille engine/transmission operations. Clock speed of the PCM microprocessor was increased from 2.1 megahertz to 3.4 megahertz, which improved processing time 63 percent. Memory size was increased from 64 kilobytes to 96 kilobytes per microprocessor, allowing the PCM to provide more software functionality. For improved throttle response and reduced exhaust emissions, a mass airflow sensor was added. This sensor continually measured the volume of air entering the engine and supplied that information to the PCM. In addition, the PCM was moved from the passenger compartment to the air cleaner housing. This enhanced engine harness reliability by reducing wiring lengths and minimized the number of wires passed through the front of the dash. Improved design precision fuel injectors delivered precise fuel metering, which contributed to more efficient fuel control. The Sedan DeVille received the Integrated Chassis Control System (ICCS) for 1996. The ICCS featured a steering wheel angle position sensor that read the steering angle of the vehicle and transmitted that position to the brake, traction control and Road Sensing Suspension controller units, which calibrated these systems for improved control and quicker stops. Optional on the 1996 DeVille was a 3,000-lb. trailer towing package that included a wiring harness with oil cooler lines from the oil cooler adapter to the radiator and a radiator end tank to provide extra engine cooling when towing large loads. An "Electro-motor" electronic cruise control replaced the previous vacuum-operated system. A revised wheel design (in fine grain cast aluminum or chrome finish) incorporated a wreath-and-crest center cap.

DEVILLE – SERIES 6K/D – V-8

Model Number	Body/Style No.	Body Type & Seating	Factory Price	Shipping Weight	Production Total
K/D	5	4D Sedan	35,995	3,959	Note 1

Note 1: DeVille production totaled ,251 with no further breakout available.

CONCOURS - SERIES 6K/F - V-8

The Concours sedan again featured the 300-hp Northstar engine coupled to the 4T80-E transmission. Its final drive ratio was revised from 3.11:1 to 3.71:1 for

improved acceleration and passing performance. New standard features unique to the Concours sedan included Magnasteer electro-magnetic variable-assist power steering (which replaced the previous speed-sensitive steering), the Rainsense Wiper System that automatically activated in inclement weather and a Continuously Variable Road Sensing Suspension. This was a refinement of the previous Road Sensing Suspension and offered improved damping for a smoother ride. Additionally, the Concours sedan's Delco Electronics Active Audio System could be upgraded to include a factory-installed, trunk-mounted 12-compact disc changer. Also, a Cadillac-exclusive convenience feature offered in the Concours sedan was the Dual-Mode (analog and digital) voice-activated cell phone, which was available in a portable or non-portable package.

CONCOURS – SERIES 6K/F – V-8

Model Number	Body/Style No.	Body Type & Seating	Factory Price	Shipping Weight	Production Total
K/F	5	4D Sedan	40,495	3,981	Note 2

Note 2: See Note 1 above.

FLEETWOOD-SERIES 6D/W-V-8

In its final year of production, the revisions to the Fleetwood sedan and optional Brougham package model were mainly of a "creature comfort" nature. Fleetwoods were again powered by the Gen II 5.7-liter V-8 paired with the 4L60-E electronically controlled four-speed automatic transmission. Final drive ratio for Fleetwood was 2.56:1, while the Brougham's was 3.42:1. Inside, the Fleetwood received "Electro-motor" electronic cruise control and a new center arm rest with dual cupholder, coinholder and CD/cassette storage. Fleetwood models were also pre-wired to accommodate the optional Dual-Mode cell phone. Also new was a six-speaker entertainment system that could be upgraded with the factory-installed, trunk-mounted CD changer. Again, the Fleetwood could also be ordered as the V4U Coachbuilder Limousine package, B9Q Funeral Coach package or R1P Heavy-Duty Sedan package with heavy-duty components required for continuous commercial service.

FLEETWOOD—SERIES 6D/W—V-8

Model Number	Body/Style No.	Body Type & Seating	Factory Price	Shipping Weight	Production Total
D/W	5	4D Sedan	36,995	4,461	15,101

ELDORADO-SERIES 6E/L-V-8

The Eldorado coupe was again powered by the 275-hp Northstar 4.6-liter V-8. A 4T80-E electronically-controlled four-speed automatic transmission was linked to the engine via a viscous converter clutch. The final drive ratio was 3.11:1. Inside the "base" coupe, the seats were redesigned to improve comfort. Eight-way memory seats were available as an option. These featured adjustability

for two different drivers. The seats were designed to reveal a hand-crafted look through French seam stitching. Other new features included new dark gray trim on the power seat and power window switches, trim plates, cluster area and radio face plate. The old speed-density air/fuel control system was replaced with a mass airflow sensor. A more powerful Powertrain Control Module (PCM) was used to help reduce exhaust emissions. The PCM was moved from the passenger compartment to the air cleaner housing to enhance its reliability. "Electro-motor" electronic cruise control replaced the previous vacuum-operated system. A new Sea Mist Green exterior color choice was offered. New options included a Dual-Mode voice-activated cell phone and one new leather seating color choice: Sea Mist Green. When leather seating was ordered, a new lamination process was used to bond the leather to the trim pad to reduce wrinkles. Also new for 1996 was a computer algorithm in the PCM that anticipated air conditioner compressor load cycling to eliminate the drive line disturbances associated with A/C operation while driving. The Road Sensing Suspension module used wheel displacement to calculate body velocities, which eliminated the need for body accelerometers.

ELDORADO—SERIES 6E/L–V-8

Model Number	Body/Style No.	Body Type & Seating	Factory Price	Shipping Weight	Production Total
E/L	1	2D Coupe	39,595	3,765	Note 3

Note 3: Eldorado production totaled 20,816 with no further breakout available.

ELDORADO TOURING COUPE (ETC)-SERIES 6E/T-V-8

The Eldorado Touring Coupe (ETC) again used the 300-hp Northstar engine mated to the 4T80-E electronically controlled four-speed automatic transmission linked with a viscous converter clutch. Final drive ratio was 3.71:1. The ETC featured a completely redesigned interior. The entertainment system, climate control system and DIC controls were all integrated into a full center console. Relocating these controls from their previous location on the instrument panel allowed for the widening of the analog gauge cluster, making it appear "international" with large speedometer and tachometer dials. New features of the ETC included the Dual-Mode cell phone, the Rainsense Wiper System, a traction-control-off switch and a valet lockout button that deactivated the trunk, fuel door and garage door opener functions located in the glovebox. The ETC also received Magnasteer variable-assist power steering, as well as a Continuously Variable Road Sensing Suspension for improved ride comfort. In the event of an airbag deployment in the ETC, the interior lights were illuminated after one second and remained on for 25 minutes, unless manually switched off. Also, automatic door locks unlocked 15 seconds after deployment.

ELDORADO TOURING – SERIES 6E/T – V-8

Model Number	Body/Style No.	Body Type & Seating	Factory Price	Shipping Weight	Production Total
E/T	1	2D Coupe	42,995	3,801	Note 4

See Note 3 above.

1996 Cadillac, Seville, STS sedan

1996 Cadillac, Seville, STS sedan

1996 Cadillac, Fleetwood sedan

1996 Cadillac, Seville sedan

SEVILLE-SERIES 6K/S-V-8

As in the previous year, the refinements to the "base" Eldorado coupe were carried through to the Seville Luxury Sedan (SLS). The SLS was powered by the 275-hp Northstar 4.6-liter V-8 were paired with the 4T80-E electronically controlled four-speed automatic transmission with viscous converter clutch.

SEVILLE SLS – SERIES 6K/S – V-8

Model Number	Body/Style No.	Body Type & Seating	Factory Price	Shipping Weight	Production Total
K/S	5	4D Sedan	42,995	3,832	Note 5

Note 5: Seville production totaled 38,238 with no further breakout available.

SEVILLE-SERIES 6K/S-V-8

As in the previous year, the refinements in the Eldorado Touring Coupe were carried through to the Seville Touring Sedan (STS). The STS used the 300-hp Northstar V-8 paired with the 4T80-E electronically controlled four-speed automatic transmission with viscous converter clutch.

SEVILLE STS – SERIES 6K/Y – V-8

Model Number	Body/Style No.	Body Type & Seating	Factory Price	Shipping Weight	Produc
K/Y	5	4D Sedan	47,495	3,869	Note 6

Note 6: See Note 5 above.

ENGINE

SEDAN DE VILLE, ELDORADO, SEVILLE LUXURY SEDAN BASE V-8

Northstar Overhead valve. Dual overhead cam. Aluminum block with cast iron liners. Aluminum cylinder heads. Displacement: 279 cid (4.6 liters). Bore and Stroke: 3.66 x 3.31 inches. Compression ratio: 10.3:1. Net brake hp: 275 at 5600 rpm. Taxable hp: 42.90. Net torque: 300 at 4000 rpm. Direct acting hydraulic tappets. Induction: Tuned port injection. VIN Code: 9; Option Code L37. Built by Cadillac.

DE VILLE CONCOURS, ELDORADO TOURING COUPE, SEVILLE TOURING SEDAN BASE V-8

Northstar Overhead valve. Dual overhead cam. Aluminum block with cast iron liners. Aluminum cylinder heads. Displacement: 279 cid (4.6 liters). Bore and Stroke: 3.66 x 3.31 inches. Compression ratio: 10.3:1. Net brake hp: 300 at 6000 rpm. Taxable hp: 42.90. Net torque: 295 at 4400 rpm. Direct acting hydraulic tappets. Induction: Tuned port injection. VIN Code: Y; Option Code LD8. Built by Cadillac.

FLEETWOOD BASE V-8

Overhead valve. Cast iron block. Displacement: 350 cid (5.7 liters). Bore and stroke: 4.00 x 3.48. Compression ratio: 10.0:1. Net brake hp: 260 at 5000 rpm. Taxable hp: 51.20. Net torque: 330 at 2400 rpm. Roller hydraulic valve lifters. Induction: Multiport port Injection. VIN Code: P; Option Code LT1. Built by Chevrolet.

CHASSIS

(Sedan DeVille) Wheelbase: 113.7 inches. Overall Length: 209.7 inches. Height: 56.3 inches. Width: 75.5 inches. Front Tread: 60.9 inches. Rear Tread: 60.9 inches. Standard Tires: Michelin P215/70R15.

(Concours) Wheelbase: 113.7 inches. Overall Length: 209.7 inches. Height: 56 inches. Width: 75.5 inches. Front Tread: 60.9 inches. Rear Tread: 60.9 inches. Standard Tires: Goodyear Eagle GA P225/60HR16.

(Fleetwood Brougham) Wheelbase: 121.5 inches. Overall Length: 225.1 inches. Height: 57.1 inches. Width: 78 inches. Front Tread: 60.7 inches. Rear Tread: 60.7 inches. Standard Tires: Michelin P235/70R15.

(Seville SLS) Wheelbase: 111 inches. Overall Length: 204.1 inches. Height: 54.5 inches. Width: 74.2 inches. Front Tread: 60.9 inches. Rear Tread: 60.9 inches. Standard Tires: Michelin P225/60R16.

(Seville STS) Wheelbase: 111 inches. Overall Length: 204.1 inches. Height: 54.5 inches. Width: 74.2 inches. Front Tread: 60.9 inches. Rear Tread: 60.9 inches. Standard Tires: Goodyear Eagle GA P225/60ZR16.

(Eldorado) Wheelbase: 108 inches. Overall Length: 202.2 inches. Height: 53.9 inches. Width: 75.5 inches. Front Tread: 60.9 inches. Rear Tread: 60.9 inches. Standard Tires: Michelin P225/60R16.

(Eldorado Touring Coupe) Wheelbase: 108 inches. Overall Length: 202.2 inches. Height: 53.9 inches. Width: 75.5 inches. Front Tread: 60.9 inches. Rear Tread: 60.9 inches. Standard Tires: Goodyear Eagle GA P225/60ZR16.

TECHNICAL

Transmission: (DeVille, Eldorado, Seville) 4T80-E electronically controlled four-speed automatic (includes viscous converter clutch), (Fleetwood) 4L60-E electronically controlled four-speed automatic (includes torque converter clutch). Steering: (All except Fleetwood) Power-assisted rack-and-pinion, speed-sensitive (Magnasteer on DeVille Concours, Eldorado Touring Coupe and Seville Touring Sedan), (Fleetwood) Power-assisted recirculating ball, speed-sensitive, variable assist. Front Suspension: (Sedan DeVille, Eldorado, Seville Luxury Sedan) Independent MacPherson strut with coil springs, strut-type shock absorbers and stabilizer bar and electronic variable road sensing suspension, (DeVille Concours, Eldorado Touring Coupe, Seville Touring Sedan) Independent MacPherson strut with coil springs, strut-type shock absorbers and stabilizer bar and electronic continuously variable road sensing suspension, (Fleetwood) Independent with short/long arms, coil springs, direct acting shock absorbers and stabilizer bar. Rear Suspension: (Sedan DeVille, Eldorado, Seville Luxury Sedan) Fully independent, short/long arm with automatic level control and electronic variable road sensing suspension, (DeVille Concours, Eldorado Touring Coupe, Seville Touring Sedan) Fully independent, coil springs, short/long arm with automatic level control and electronic continuously variable road sensing suspension, (Fleetwood) Four link, coil springs with automatic level control, direct acting shock absorbers and stabilizer bar. Brakes: (all except Fleetwood) Power assisted front and rear disc with Bosch anti-lock braking system, (Fleetwood) Power assisted front disc/rear drum with Bosch anti-lock braking system, Body Construction: (All except Fleetwood) Integral body-frame, (Fleetwood) Separate body on frame. Fuel Tank: (all except Fleetwood) 20.0 gallons, (Fleetwood) 23.0 gallons

OPTIONS

DEVILLE OPTIONS

WA4 Special Edition package for Sedan DeVille including gold ornamentation, chrome wheels and simulated convertible top ($1,590). Option Package 1SB for Sedan DeVille ($530). Astroroof ($1,550-$1,700). Garage door opener ($107). Theft deterrent system for Sedan DeVille ($295). White Diamond paint ($500). Pearl Red paint ($500). ETR AM/FM stereo radio with cassette for Sedan DeVille ($274). ETR AM/FM stereo radio with cassette and CD for Sedan DeVille ($869). ETR AM/FM stereo

1996 Cadillac, Eldorado, ETC coupe

radio with cassette and CD for DeVille Concours ($595). Digital signal processing sound system for Sedan DeVille ($1,064). Digital signal processing sound system for DeVille Concours ($790). Heated windshield on Sedan DeVille ($377). Memory driver's seat for Sedan DeVille ($235). Heated leather seats ($225). Leather seats in Sedan DeVille ($785). Chrome Wheels ($1,195). V92 3,000-lb. trailer towing package ($110).

ELDORADO OPTIONS

UY9 Sport interior package ($146). Theft deterrent system for base Eldorado ($295). Garage door opener ($107). Accent striping for base Eldorado ($75). Heated leather front seats ($225). Astroroof ($1,550). Heated windshield ($377). Leather seating in base Eldorado ($785). Dual power lumbar support in base Eldorado ($292). Memory driver's seat in base Eldorado ($235). Electrochromic automatic day/night driver's side mirror in base Eldorado ($87). White Diamond paint ($500). Pearl Red paint ($500). Bose sound system with cassette ($723). Bose sound sysatem with cassette and CD changer ($1,318). Bose sound system with digital signal processing ($1,513). P225/60R16 white sidewall tires for base Eldorado ($76). P225/60ZR16 black sidewall tires for Eldorado Touring Coupe ($250). Chrome Wheels ($1,195).

SEVILLE OPTIONS

UY9 Sport interior package ($146). Theft deterrent system for SLS ($295). Garage door opener ($107). Accent striping for SLS ($75). Heated leather front seats ($225). Astroroof ($1,550). Heated windshield ($377). Leather seating in SLS ($785). Power lumbar support in SLS ($292). Memory driver's seat in base SLS ($225).

Electrochromic automatic day/night driver's side mirror in SLS ($87). White Diamond paint ($500). Pearl Red paint ($500). Bose sound system with cassette ($723). Bose sound sysatem with cassette and CD changer ($1,318). Bose sound system with digital signal processing ($1,513). P225/60ZR16 black sidewall tires for STS ($250). Chrome Wheels ($1,195).

FLEETWOOD OPTIONS

Security Package ($360). Theft deterrent system ($295). Astroroof ($1,550). Garage door opener ($107). Coachbuilder package ($755). Funeral Coach package ($910 credit). Brougham cloth interior ($1,680). Brougham leather interior ($2,465). Heavy-duty Livery package ($150). Leather seating in base Fleetwood ($785). Sungate windshield ($50). ETR AM/FM stereo radio with CD and cassette ($200). Full vinyl roof for base Fleetwood ($925). Full-size spare tire ($95). Chrome wheels ($1,195). V4P 7,000-lb. trailer towing package for Fleetwood ($215).

HISTORICAL

Cadillac's model-year production totaled 174,406 compared with 200,577 the year previous. Based on sales of 170,379 automobiles in 1996 (vs. 180,504 the year before), Cadillac's share of the U.S. market was 2100 percent, compared with 2.1 the year previous. The 1996 sales figure listed included 1,676 early-launch 1997 Catera sedans sold in the 1996 model-year. In September 1996, faulty computer chips force the recall of 587,000 Cadillacs.

1996 Cadillac, Deville sedan

1997

OVERVIEW

This marked the first time since 1988 (when the underachieving V-6-powered Cimarron was discontinued) that Cadillac offered something other than a V-8 engine. The all-new Catera used a 200-hp dual-overhead-cam V-6. The DeVille ranks were bolstered with the addition of the d'Elegance sedan joining the existing DeVille and DeVille Concours sedans. All DeVille and Catera models now featured side airbags as standard equipment and the exclusive-to-Cadillac OnStar communication system also debuted as an option on all front-wheel-drive models in 1997. All Cadillacs also received improved anti-lockout protection.

I.D. DATA

The 17-symbol serial number was located on top of the instrument panel, where it was visible through the windshield. The first symbol 1=U.S.-built vehicle or W=German-built vehicle. The second symbol G=General Motors or O=Opel of Germany. The third symbol 6=Cadillac. The fourth symbol indicated carline/the fifth symbol indicated series as follows: E/L=Eldorado, E/T=Eldorado Touring, K/D=DeVille, K/E=DeVille D'Elegance, K/F=Concours,

Above: **1997 Cadillac, Eldorado coupe**

K/S=Seville (SLS), K/Y=Seville Touring (STS), V/R=Catera. The sixth symbol indicated body style: 1=two-door Coupe/Sedan GM/Fisher Style Nos. 27, 37, 47 or 57, 5=four-door Sedan GM/Fisher style nos. 19, 69. The seventh symbol indicated the type of restraint system: 2=Manual belts with dual airbags, 4=Automatic belts. The eighth symbol identified the engine: R=L81 3.0-liter V-6, Y=LD8 4.6L V-8 and 9=L37 4.6L V-8. The ninth symbol was a check digit. The 10th symbol indicates model year: V=1997. The 11th symbol indicates the GM assembly plant: U=Hamtramck, Mich. (Allante) and R=Russelsheim, Germany. The next group of numbers was the sequential production code starting with 001. The Fisher Body tag on the cowl, under the hood includes additional information.

CATERA - SERIES 6V/R - V-6

Launched during the 1996 model-year, the midsize 1997 Catera sports sedan was a joint venture automobile developed by Cadillac and Adam Opel AG and built by Opel in Ruesselsheim, Germany. It was based on the European Opel Omega sedan platform. The five-passenger, rear-wheel-drive sedan was imported into the United States and sold and serviced by more than 765 Cadillac dealers nationwide. Optional items included leather seating with front/rear seat heaters, a Bose audio

system, an automatic power sun roof, a garage door opener and five-spoke alloy wheels in either natural or chrome finish. The Catera power train consisted of a 200-hp 3.0-liter dual-overhead-cam V-6 with Dual-Ram induction paired with a 4L30-E electronically controlled four-speed automatic transmission with overdrive. This transmission featured easy-to-select Sport, Normal and Winter driving modes. The turning circle of the Catera was 34.1 feet. Interior volume measured 111.2 cubic feet with an additional 14.5 cubic feet of trunk space. The rear bench seat featured a three-piece fold-down seat back for carrying long objects. The Catera's instrument panel had analog gauges, including a tachometer. The Catera exterior featured a contoured black chrome grille with integrated wreath-and-crest emblem and single-piece front fascia.

CATERA – SERIES 6V/R – V-8

Model Number	Body/Style No.	Body Type & Seating	Factory Price	Shipping Weight	Production Total
V/R	5	4D Sedan	2,9995	3,770	25,411

Note 1: Production total based on number of cars imported into U.S.

DEVILLE - SERIES 6K/D-V-8

The DeVille offered Cadillac buyers luxury. It was powered by the 275-hp Northstar V-8 paired with the 4T80-E electronically-controlled four-speed automatic transmission with viscous converter clutch. Key new standard features of the DeVille series included side airbags, Magnasteer electromagnetic variable-assist power steering (already standard on Concours) and a revised seat appearance. The DeVille sedan received a revamped hood (with more emphasis on the power dome), a new front fascia, new fenders, new rear upper and lower fascias, new body side moldings and refinements to both the anti-lock brake system and and the traction-control systems. One of the most notable changes to the 1997 DeVille was in profile, with the rear wheel opening being enlarged and the wheels being pulled out 10mm per side. Other new DeVille series features included the instrument panel pad, HVAC outlets with chrome finish and trunk storage dividers. New hydraulic shocks offered damping rates higher than the "firm" setting available with the previous road sensing suspension. A new lower control arm design put the unit's main bushing in line with the wheel center, which allowed the bushing to directly absorb cornering loads. The front brake discs were enlarged by one inch (to 11.9 inches in diameter) for additional stopping power. The optional OnStar communication system used onboard electronics in conjunction with global positioning system satellite technology to offer around-the-clock driver security in emergency situations.

DEVILLE—SERIES 6K/D—V-8

Model Number	Body/Style No.	Body Type & Seating	Factory Price	Shipping Weight	Production Total
K/D	5	4D Sedan	36,995	4,015	Note 2

Note 2: DeVille production totaled 99,601 with no further breakout available.

DE VILLE D'ELEGANCE-SERIES 6K/E-V-8

The DeVille d'Elegance offered an even higher degree of motoring luxury. It was also powered by the 275-hp version of the Northstar V-8 paired with the 4T80-E electronically controlled four-speed automatic transmission with viscous converter clutch. It had the new standard features

1997 Cadillac, De Ville Concours, sedan

of the DeVille series including side airbags, Magnasteer electromagnetic variable-assist power steering, a revised seat appearance, a revamped hood (with more emphasis on the power dome), a new front fascia, new fenders, new rear upper and lower fascias, new body side moldings, and refinements to both the anti-lock-brake system and traction-control system. Like the DeVille, the d'Elegance sedan sported a new chrome grille and its features included a new personalization programmable package and a memory package. Unique to the d'Elegance was a gold tone exterior ornamentation package and Rainsense windshield wiper system. It shared the other new DeVille series features listed above for the base DeVille.

DE VILLE D'ELEGANCE—SERIES 6K/E – V-8

Model Number	Body/Style No.	Body Type & Seating	Factory Price	Shipping Weight	Production Total
K/E	5	4D Sedan	39,995	4,050	Note 3

Note 3: See Note 2 above.

DEVILLE CONCOURS-SERIES 6K/F-V-8

The DeVille Concours was "repositioned" as a sportier sedan for performance-minded buyers. The Concours again used the 300-hp Northstar V-8 paired with the 4T80-E electronically-controlled four-speed automatic transmission with viscous converter clutch. Magnasteer electromagnetic variable-assist power steering was standard. The Concours sedan also had the personalization programmable package, the memory package and the Rainsense windshield wiper system. Concours exclusives included road texture detection, which increased the effectiveness of the anti-lock braking system. StabiliTrak, an electronic chassis system that helped the driver control the car on slippery surfaces, was also standard. Due to a full center console, the Concours sedan's revised interior now accommodated five passengers. Other new features included the instrument panel pad, HVAC outlets with chrome finish, re-rated hydraulic shocks, a new lower control arm design and larger front brake discs.

DE VILLE CONCOURS – SERIES 6K/F – V-8

Model Number	Body/Style No.	Body Type & Seating	Factory Price	Shipping Weight	Production Total
K/F	5	4D Sedan	41,995	4,055	Note 4

Note 4: See Note 2 above.

ELDORADO-SERIES 6E/L-V-8

The Eldorado was had the Northstar V-8 and 4T80-E automatic transmission. New standard features included Magnasteer, hydraulic shocks with a higher damping rate, a new lower control arm design to better absorb cornering load, one-inch larger front brake discs, trunk storage dividers, an improved headliner, acoustic refinements and more "user friendly" climate control readouts. All 1997 Eldorados were manufactured with an analog gauge cluster, a full center console and dual zone climate

control as standard fare. The Eldorado coupe received a new personalization programmable package that included auto door locks, exterior lighting, activation verification and battery storage. Eldorados offered the OnStar communication system as optional equipment.

ELDORADO—SERIES 6E/L—V-8

Model Number	Body/Style No.	Body Type & Seating	Factory Price	Shipping Weight	Produc
E/L	1	2D Coupe	37,995	3,843	Note 5

Note 5: Eldorado production totaled 18,102 with no further breakout available.

ELDORADO TOURING COUPE (ETC)-SERIES 6E/L-V-8

The ETC added road texture detection to aid anti-lock braking effectiveness, the StabiliTrak system to help the driver maintain control on slippery surfaces and 11 additional driver information center (DIC) messages, including: headlights suggested, ice possible (outside temperature of 36 degrees or lower) and check fuel gauge. The ETC also received a new personalization programmable package that included choice of memory

1997 Cadillac, Catera, sedan

1997 Cadillac, De Ville sedan

1997 Cadillac, De Ville sedan

recall with remote keyless entry, key in ignition or memory switches, HVAC settings, radio preset settings, battery storage mode, perimeter lighting, activation verification and auto door lock. Also new to the ETC was a memory package that featured eight-way seat adjustments and exit, outside rearview mirror adjustments and lumbar support positions. Eldorados offered the OnStar communication system as optional equipment.

ELDORADO TOURING – SERIES 6E/T – V-8

Model Number	Body/Style No.	Body Type & Seating	Factory Price	Shipping Weight	Production Total
E/T	1	2D Coupe	41,395	3,876	Note 6

Note 6: See Note 5 above.

SEVILLE-SERIES 6K/S-V-8

The Seville Luxury Sedan (SLS) again reflected the changes that occurred to the Eldorado coupe.

SEVILLE SLS– SERIES 6K/S–V-8

Model Number	Body/Style No.	Body Type & Seating	Factory Price	Shipping Weight	Production Total
K/S	5	4D Sedan	39,995	3,901	Note 7

Note 7: Seville production totaled 42,117 with no further breakout available.

SEVILLE TOURING SEDAN - SERIES 6K/Y - V-8

The Seville Touring Sedan (STS) again reflected the changes that occurred on the Eldorado Touring Coupe (ETC).

SEVILLE STS– SERIES 6K/Y–V-8

Model Number.	Body/Style No.	Body Type & Seating	Factory Price	Shipping Weight	Production Total
K/Y	5	4D Sedan	44,995	3,960	Note 5

Note 8: See Note 7 above.

ENGINE

CATERA BASE V-6

54-degree dual overhead cam V-6. Cast iron block. Aluminum cylinder heads. Displacement: 181-cid (3.0 liters). Bore and stroke: 3.40 x 3.40 inches. Compression ratio: 10.0:1. Brake hp: 200 @ 6000 rpm. Torque: 192 lb.-ft. at 3600 rpm. Variable Dual-Ram induction system.

DE VILLE D'ELEGANCE, ELDORADO, SEVILLE LUXURY SEDAN BASE V-8

Northstar Overhead valve. Dual overhead cam. Aluminum block with cast iron liners. Aluminum cylinder heads. Displacement: 279 cid (4.6 liters). Bore and Stroke: 3.66 x 3.31 inches. Compression ratio: 10.3:1. Net brake hp: 275 at 5600 rpm. Taxable hp: 42.90. Net torque: 300 at 4000 rpm. Direct acting hydraulic tappets. Induction: Tuned port injection. VIN Code: 9; Option Code L37. Built by Cadillac.

DE VILLE CONCOURS, ELDORADO TOURING COUPE, SEVILLE TOURING SEDAN BASE V-8

Northstar Overhead valve. Dual overhead cam. Aluminum block with cast iron liners. Aluminum cylinder heads. Displacement: 279 cid (4.6 liters). Bore and Stroke: 3.66 x 3.31 inches. Compression ratio: 10.3:1. Net brake hp: 300 at 6000 rpm. Taxable hp: 42.90. Net torque: 295 at 4400 rpm. Direct acting hydraulic tappets. Induction: Tuned port injection. VIN Code: Y; Option Code LD8. Built by Cadillac.

CHASSIS

(Catera) Wheelbase: 107.4 inches. Overall Length: 194 inches. Height: 56.3 inches. Width: 70.3 inches. Front Tread: 59.3 inches. Rear Tread: 59.8 inches. Standard Tires: Goodyear Eagle GS-A P225/55HR16.

(DeVille) Wheelbase: 113.7 inches. Overall Length: 209.7 inches. Height: 56.4 inches. Width: 76.5 inches. Front Tread: 60.9 inches. Rear Tread: 60.9 inches. Standard Tires: Michelin P225/60SR16.

(DeVille D'Elegance) 113.7 inches. Overall Length: 209.7 inches. Height: 56.4 inches. Width: 76.5 inches. Front

1997 Cadillac, Seville, STS sedan

Tread: 60.9 inches. Rear Tread: 60.9 inches. Standard Tires: Michelin P225/60SR16.

(Concours) Wheelbase: 113.7 inches. Overall Length: 209.7 inches. Height: 56 inches. Width: 75.5 inches. Front Tread: 60.9 inches. Rear Tread: 60.9 inches. Standard Tires: Goodyear Eagle RS-A P225/60HR16.

(Seville SLS) Wheelbase: 111 inches. Overall Length: 204.1 inches. Height: 54.5 inches. Width: 74.2 inches. Front Tread: 60.9 inches. Rear Tread: 60.9 inches. Standard Tires: Michelin P225/60SR16.

(Seville STS) Wheelbase: 111 inches. Overall Length: 204.1 inches. Height: 54.5 inches. Width: 74.2 inches. Front Tread: 60.9 inches. Rear Tread: 60.9 inches. Standard Tires: Goodyear Eagle GA P225/60ZR16.

(Eldorado) Wheelbase: 108 inches. Overall Length: 202.2 inches. Height: 53.6 inches. Width: 75.5 inches. Front Tread: 60.9 inches. Rear Tread: 60.9 inches. Standard Tires: Michelin P225/60SR16.

(Eldorado Touring Coupe) Wheelbase: 108 inches. Overall Length: 202.2 inches. Height: 53.6 inches. Width: 75.5 inches. Front Tread: 60.9 inches. Rear Tread: 60.9 inches. Standard Tires: Goodyear Eagle GA P225/60ZR16.

TECHNICAL

Transmission: (Catera) 4L30-E electronically controlled four-speed automatic transmission with overdrive, (DeVille, Eldorado, Seville) 4T80-E electronically controlled four-speed automatic (includes viscous converter clutch), Steering: (Catera) Recirculating ball, speed-sensitive, (DeVille, Eldorado, Seville) Power-assisted rack-and-pinion, Magnasteer. Front Suspension: (Catera) MacPherson strut, lower control arms with hydro bushing, coil spring and stabilizer bar, gas preloaded dampers, continuously variable road sensing suspension, (DeVille/d'Elegance, Eldorado, Seville Luxury Sedan) Independent MacPherson strut with coil springs, strut-type shock absorbers and stabilizer bar and MacPherson strut dampers, (DeVille Concours, Eldorado Touring Coupe, Seville Touring Sedan) Independent MacPherson strut with coil springs, strut-type shock absorbers and stabilizer bar and electronic continuously variable road sensing suspension. Rear Suspension: (Catera) Multi-link, coil spring and stabilizer bar, gas preloaded dampers, continuously variable road sensing suspension, (DeVille/d'Elegance, Eldorado, Seville Luxury Sedan) Fully independent, short/long arm and stabilizer bar with automatic level control and electronic continuously variable road sensing suspension, (DeVille Concours, Eldorado Touring Coupe, Seville Touring Sedan). Fully independent, coil springs, short/long arm and stabilizer bar with automatic level control and electronic continuously variable road sensing suspension. Brakes: (Catera) dual circuit front and rear disc with anti-lock, (DeVille, Eldorado, Seville) Power assisted front and rear disc with Bosch anti-lock braking system. Body Construction: (all) Integral body-frame. Fuel Tank: (Catera) 18.0 gallons (DeVille, Eldorado, Seville) 20.0 gallons.

OPTIONS
CATERA OPTIONS

Garage door opener ($107). Heated seats ($400). Bose sound system ($723). Electric sun roof ($995). Five-spoke

1997 Cadillac, Seville, STS sedan

aluminum wheels: ($355). Five-spoke chrome wheels ($1,195).

DEVILLE OPTIONS

WA7 Comfort/Convenience package for base DeVille ($642). WA8 Safety/Security package ($502). Astroroof ($1,550). White Diamond paint ($500). Pearl Red paint ($500). Heavy-duty livery package DeVille only ($160). Heated front seats ($225). Leather seats DeVille only ($785). Active audio sound system with cassette for DeVille ($274). Active audio sound system with cassette and CD changer in DeVille ($869). Active audio sound system with cassette and CD changer in DeVille d'Elegance and DeVille Concours ($595). Active audio sound system with cassette and CD changer in DeVille d'Elegance and DeVille Concours with Digital Signal Processing in DeVille ($1,064). Active audio sound system with cassette and CD changer in DeVille d'Elegance and DeVille Concours ($790). Chrome wheels ($1,195). V92 3,000-lb. trailer towing package ($110).

ELDORADO OPTIONS

WA7 Memory/Personalization package ($437). WA8 Safety/Security package ($502). WA9 Sport Interior package ($1,223). Garage door opener ($107). Accent Striping (Eldorado) ($75). Heated Front Seats ($225). Astroroof ($1,550). White Diamond paint ($500). Pearl Red paint ($500). Bose Sound System with Cassette ($723, with Cassette & CD Changer ($1,318, with Digital Signal Processing ($1,513). P225/60SR16 white sidewall tires (Eldorado) ($76). P225/60ZR16 BSW Tires (Touring Coupe) ($250). Chrome Wheels ($1,195).

SEVILLE OPTIONS

WA7 Memory/Personalization package ($437). WA8 Safety/Security package ($502). WA9 Sport Interior package ($1,223). Garage door opener ($107). Accent striping for LS ($75). Heated front seats ($225). Astroroof ($1,550). White Diamond paint ($500). Pearl Red paint ($500). Bose sound system with cassette ($723). Bose sound system with cassette and CD Changer ($1,318). Bose sound system with digital signal processing ($1,513). P225/60ZR16 black sidewall tires for STS ($250). Chrome wheels ($1,195).

HISTORICAL

Cadillac's model-year production totaled 159,820 compared with 174,406 the year previous (this figure does not include the 25,411 imported Cateras). Based on sales of 182,624 automobiles in 1997 (versus 170,379 the year before), Cadillac's share of the U.S. market was 2.2 percent compared with 2.0 the year previous. In May 1997, Cadillac announced the Catera would be produced domestically at its next redesign.

1997 Cadillac, De Ville sedan

1998

OVERVIEW

All Cadillac models offered the year previous were carried over to 1998. The all-new 1998 Seville, not available until December 1997, was designed to lead Cadillac into the "global" market, with exports to 40 countries. Both left- and right-hand drive versions were built at Cadillac's Detroit-Hamtramck assembly facility. StabiliTrak was now offered on all front-wheel-drive Cadillacs. The Catera joined the rest of the lineup in offering the OnStar communications system as optional equipment.

I.D. DATA

The 17-symbol serial number was located on top of the instrument panel, where it was visible through the windshield. The first symbol 1=U.S.-built vehicle or W=German-built vehicle. The second symbol G=General Motors or O=Opel of Germany. The third symbol 6=Cadillac. The fourth symbol indicated carline/the fifth symbol indicated series as follows: E/L=Eldorado, E/T=Eldorado Touring, K/D=DeVille, K/E=DeVille D'Elegance, K/F=Concours, K/S=Seville (SLS), K/Y=Seville Touring (STS), V/R=Catera. The sixth symbol indicated body style: 1=two-door Coupe/Sedan GM/Fisher Style Nos. 27, 37, 47 or

Above: **1998 Cadillac, Eldorado Touring Coupe**

57, 5=four-door Sedan GM/Fisher style nos. 19, 69. The seventh symbol indicated the type of restraint system: 2=Manual belts with dual airbags, 4=Automatic belts. The eighth symbol identified the engine: R=L81 3.0-liter V-6, Y=LD8 4.6L V-8 and 9=L37 4.6L V-8. The ninth symbol was a check digit. The 10th symbol indicated model year: W=1998. The 11th symbol indicated the GM assembly plant: U=Hamtramck, Mich. (Allante) and R=Russelsheim, Germany. The next group of numbers was the sequential production code starting with 001. The Fisher Body tag on the cowl, under the hood included additional information.

CATERA - SERIES 6V/R - V-6

In its sophomore year, the Catera received several upgrades. The entry-luxury sedan continued to be powered by the 3.0-liter dual-overhead-cam V-6 mated to the 4L30-E electronically-controlled four-speed automatic transmission with overdrive. New standard features included an upgrade to the Bosch ABS/ASR 5.3 anti-lock brake and traction-control system. The previous system controlled engine output to keep the engine from overpowering the tires on slippery roads. The enhanced system added brake control to the two rear wheels. If one wheel slipped, the system applied the brake to that wheel, transferring drive torque to the wheel that had more

traction. Other new features included three additional exterior colors: Sky, Cocoa and Platinum, as well as the radio that now featured Theftlock as a security measure. Power outlets were modified to better accommodate cell phones and other accessories and the outlets retained power with the key off. Also new, in the event of an accident that activated front airbags the interior lights came on and the doors unlocked automatically 15 seconds after deployment. In addition, a new airbag warning label was applied to the passenger visor. The Catera now offered GM's OnStar in-vehicle communications system as optional equipment. Also new on the option list was a Bose entertainment system that included an in-dash, single-slot CD player, a radio data system (RDS), a weather band and GM's Theftlock theft deterrent system. The RDS function received digital data in the form of traffic reports or emergency broadcasts that could be monitored any time, even breaking into a CD or cassette in play.

CATERA—SERIES 6V/R—V-8

Model Number	Body/Style No.	Body Type & Seating	Factory Price	Shipping Weight	Production Total
V/R	5	4D Sedan	29,995	3,770	25,755

Note 1: Production total is that reported by Opel for 1998 passenger vehicle production in Germany. Since no 1997 production is reported, this appears to be the total for both years

DEVILLE - SERIES 6K/D - V-8

This year the StabiliTrak stability control system was offered on the DeVille as part of a safety/security option package that also included an electronic passenger mirror, audible theft deterrent system and programmable garage door opener. The DeVille series offered four new exterior colors for 1998: Baltic Blue, Gold Firemist, Moonstone and Crimson Pearl. Inside, two new interior color choices were available: Camel (available only in leather) and Pewter (available in cloth or leather in the DeVille). Additionally, the series' personalization feature added two new locking modes to the three that already existed: all doors lock when shifting out of park and only the driver's door unlocks when the key is turned off and all doors lock when shifting out of park and unlock when the key is turned off. Also, the remote keyless entry fob added a feature: when the lock button was pressed, the horn sounded to verify that the doors were locked. All DeVilles now came with an airbag warning label affixed to the passenger visor and each received a revised electrochromic day/night inside rearview mirror. The radio installed in DeVille series sedans also received a mute button and Theftlock, while radio data system (RDS) and weather band were offered as part of the optional Active Audio sound system. RDS allowed broadcasters to deliver a 1,200-bits-per-second data stream along with audio content. The Concours' standard radio received an in-dash, single-slot CD player.

The OnStar in-vehicle communications system was again offered to DeVille buyers.

DEVILLE—SERIES 6K/D—V-8

Model Number	Body/Style No.	Body Type & Seating	Factory Price	Shipping Weight	Produc
K/D	5	4D Sedan	37,695	4,063	Note 2

Note 2: DeVille production totaled 111,030 with no further breakout available.

DEVILLE D'ELEGANCE-SERIES 6K/E-V-8

Like the DeVille, the DeVille d'Elegance again used the 275-hp version of the Northstar 4.6-liter V-8 coupled to the 4T80-E electronically-controlled four-speed automatic transmission with viscous converter clutch. The StabiliTrak was offered in the safety/security option package. The D'Elegance also got the other DeVille upgrades for 1998. The new Pewter interior was available in leather only in the D'Elegance.

DEVILLE D'ELEGANCE — SERIES 6K/E—V-8

Model Number	Body/Style No.	Body Type & Seating	Factory Price	Shipping Weight	Production Total
K/E	5	4D Sedan	41,295	4,052	Note 3

Note 3: See Note 2 above.

DEVILLE CONCOURS - SERIES 6K/F - V-8

The Concours featured the 300-hp Northstar V-8 coupled to the 4T80-E electronically-controlled four-speed automatic transmission with viscous converter clutch. StabiliTrak stability control was standard equipment The Concours also got the new Baltic Blue, Gold Firemist, Moonstone and Crimson Pearl exterior colors. Inside, two new interior color choices were available in leather only, Camel and Pewter. The Concours' standard radio also received an in-dash, single-slot CD player. Unique new standard Concours features included restyled 16-inch cast-aluminum wheels and the next generation of Magnasteer that reacted to lateral acceleration, as well as speed. When the cornering rate was sensed by an on-board lateral accelerometer, steering effort was automatically increased to enhance the driver's feel of the road. Both the d'Elegance and Concours added heated front seats to their list of standard fare. The OnStar in-vehicle communications system was a dealer-installed option.

DEVILLE D'ELEGANCE — SERIES 6K/F — V-8

Model Number	Body/Style No.	Body Type & Seating	Factory Price	Shipping Weight	Production Total
K/F	5	4D Sedan	42,295	4,012	Note 4

Note 4: See Note 2 above.

ELDORADO - SERIES 6E/L - V-8

No change occurred in either the Eldorado series. Eldorado series coupes offered four new exterior color choices: Baltic Blue, Gold Firemist, Moonstone and Crimson Pearl. Two new interior color selections called Camel (available only in leather) and Pewter (available in cloth or leather in the

Eldorado) were seen. All Eldorados received an airbag warning label affixed to the passenger visor, a redesigned electrochromic day/night inside rearview mirror and new radio with a Bose speaker system that included a mute button and Theftlock theft-deterrent system. An optional radio selection included radio data system (RDS) and weather band. The optional personalization feature was also upgraded with two new door locking modes as well as the remote keyless entry fob gaining an additional doors-locked verification feature. The OnStar communications system was again a dealer-installed option. StabiliTrak was now optional on the "base" coupe.

ELDORADO — SERIES 6E/L – V-8

Model Number	Body/Style No.	Body Type & Seating	Factory Price	Shipping Weight	Production Total
E/L	1	2D Coupe	38,495	3,843	Note 5

Note 5: Eldorado production totaled 18,415 with no further breakout available.

ELDORADO ETC-SERIES 6E/T-V-8

The ETC got the same upgrades as the base Eldorado. The StabiliTrak stability control system was optional on the "base" coupe. Unique new standard features found on the ETC included heated front seats and the next-generation of Magnasteer.

ELDORADO TOURING COUPE (ETC)—SERIES 6E/T—V-8

Model Number	Body/Style No.	Body Type & Seating	Factory Price	Shipping Weight	Production Total
E/T	1	2D Coupe	42,695	3,876	Note 6

Note 6: See Note 5 above.

SEVILLE SLS - SERIES 6K/S - V-8

The 1998 edition of the Seville was exclusively redesigned. It was now Cadillac's leading-edge "global market" product. To back up this world-product positioning, the 1998 Seville was introduced at both the Frankfurt in Germany and Tokyo auto show in Japan in the fall of 1997. The SLS was again powered by the 275-hp Northstar V-8 paired with the 4T80-E electronically-controlled four-speed automatic transmission with viscous converter clutch. The new Seville was computer-designed to meet all world standards for front, side and rear impact, as well as those for roof crush resistance and offset crashes. A one-piece floor panel extended from the front of the dash to the rear of the trunk, minimizing joints and seams. The interior body side rings were stamped from a single laser-welded blank, saving weight and improving build quality. A pair of hydroformed tubes swept up from the base of the windshield into the roof and back down to the rear wheelwells. These tubes helped form a safety cage around the passenger compartment, while improving torsional and beaming stiffness of the body structure. Compared to the previous year's sedan, the 1998 Seville's was shorter, but on a longer wheelbase. It had a wider stance that contributed to its 120.4 cubic feet of interior space. Up front, the Seville featured projection-beam headlights that included a rectangular high beam. The SLS sedan's grille was bright-finished in silver with a chrome edging and contained an integral full color wreath-and-crest emblem. Instead of having fog lights n the lower grille like the STS,

1998 Cadillac, De Ville d'Elegance, sedan

1998 Cadillac, Catera, sedan

the SLS used extended horizontal bars to cover that area. The Seville's hood featured a powerdome to enhance the image of the Northstar V-8. A high deck lid was retained at the rear, which improved both aerodynamics and trunk space. A subtle rocker panel deflector ahead of the rear wheels added functional character as well as eliminating aero drag. The wheels on the SLS had a larger, more aggressive look. The new Seville featured Bosch 5.0 four-channel anti-lock braking and all-speed traction control as standard fare. The Seville also featured a "smart" electrical system based on 16 electronic control modules linked together into a network capable of transferring data at 10,400 bytes per second. Inside, the SLS featured printed leather inserts for seat and door trim. To reduce interior noise, the Seville used 5mm-thick door glass and doors sealed with triple rubber seals. New standard equipment on the Seville included Magnasteer III speed-sensitive power rack-and-pinion steering and Pass-Key III theft deterrent system. The OnStar in-vehicle communications system and a high-performance Bose 4.0 425-watt eight-speaker stereo system was optional on the SLS.

SEVILLE SLS–SERIES 6K/S–V-8

Model Number	Body/Style No.	Body Type & Seating	Factory Price	Shipping Weight	Produc
K/S	5	4D Sedan	42,495	3,972	Note 7

Note 7: Seville production totaled 33,270 with no further breakout available.

SEVILLE STS-SERIES 6K/Y-V-8

The STS used the more powerful 300-hp Northstar V-8 and the transmission was programmed for performance shifting via sensors in the vehicle, including a lateral

acceleration sensor from StabiliTrak, which was standard. The STS sedan's grille was body color with an argent monochrome integral wreath-and-crest emblem. Foglights were positioned in the lower grille. The wheels on the STS featured a more open spoke design to reveal large-capacity brakes. The STS continued to use fine-perforated leather trim panels for both seats and doors. The STS steering wheel (optional on SLS) had a power tilt-and-telescope feature. The 1998 STS was the first car to offer adaptive seating technology as optional equipment. Adaptive seating, via a network of 10 air cells located in the front bucket seats, automatically recognized occupant position and adjusted the seats' support to custom-fit every individual.

SEVILLE STS– SERIES 6K/Y–V–8

Model Number	Body/Style No.	Body Type & Seating	Factory Price	Shipping Weight	Production Total
K/Y	5	4D Sedan	46,995	4,001	Note 8

Note 8: See Note 7 above.

ENGINE

CATERA BASE V-6

54-degree dual overhead cam V-6. Cast iron block. Aluminum cylinder heads. Displacement: 181-cid (3.0 liters). Bore and stroke: 3.40 x 3.40 inches. Compression ratio: 10.0:1. Brake hp: 200 @ 6000 rpm. Torque: 192 lb.-ft. at 3600 rpm. Variable Dual-Ram induction system.

DE VILLE D'ELEGANCE, ELDORADO, SEVILLE LUXURY SEDAN BASE V-8

Northstar Overhead valve. Dual overhead cam. Aluminum block with cast iron liners. Aluminum cylinder heads.

Displacement: 279 cid (4.6 liters). Bore and Stroke: 3.66 x 3.31 inches. Compression ratio: 10.3:1. Net brake hp: 275 at 5600 rpm. Taxable hp: 42.90. Net torque: 300 at 4000 rpm. Direct acting hydraulic tappets. Induction: Tuned port injection. VIN Code: 9; Option Code L37. Built by Cadillac.

DE VILLE CONCOURS, ELDORADO TOURING COUPE, SEVILLE TOURING SEDAN BASE V-8

Northstar Overhead valve. Dual overhead cam. Aluminum block with cast iron liners. Aluminum cylinder heads. Displacement: 279 cid (4.6 liters). Bore and Stroke: 3.66 x 3.31 inches. Compression ratio: 10.3:1. Net brake hp: 300 at 6000 rpm. Taxable hp: 42.90. Net torque: 295 at 4400 rpm. Direct acting hydraulic tappets. Induction: Tuned port injection. VIN Code: Y; Option Code LD8. Built by Cadillac.

CHASSIS

(Catera) Wheelbase: 107.4 inches. Overall Length: 194 inches. Height: 56.3 inches. Width: 70.3 inches. Front Tread: 59.3 inches. Rear Tread: 59.8 inches. Standard Tires: Goodyear Eagle RS-A P225/55HR16.

(DeVille) Wheelbase: 113.8 inches. Overall Length: 209.8 inches. Height: 56 inches. Width: 76.5 inches. Front Tread: 60.9 inches. Rear Tread: 60.9 inches. Standard Tires: Michelin P225/60SR16.

(DeVille D'Elegance) 113.8 inches. Overall Length: 209.8 inches. Height: 56 inches. Width: 76.5 inches. Front Tread: 60.9 inches. Rear Tread: 60.9 inches. Standard Tires: Michelin P225/60SR16.

(Concours) Wheelbase: 113.8 inches. Overall Length: 209.8 inches. Height: 56 inches. Width: 76.5 inches. Front Tread: 60.9 inches. Rear Tread: 60.9 inches. Standard Tires: Goodyear Eagle RS-A P225/60HR16,.

(Seville SLS) Wheelbase: 112.2 inches. Overall Length: 201 inches. Height: 55.4 inches. Width: 75 inches. Front Tread: 62.7 inches. Rear Tread: 62.3 inches. Standard Tires: Goodyear Eagle LS P235/60HR16.

(Seville STS) Wheelbase: 112.2 inches. Overall Length: 201 inches. Height: 55.4 inches. Width: 75 inches. Front Tread: 62.7 inches. Rear Tread: 62.3 inches. Standard Tires: Goodyear Eagle LS P235/60HR16.

(Eldorado) Wheelbase: 108 inches. Overall Length: 200.6 inches. Height: 53.6 inches. Width: 75.5 inches. Front Tread: 60.9 inches. Rear Tread: 60.9 inches. Standard Tires: Michelin P225/60SR16.

(Eldorado Touring Coupe) Wheelbase: 108 inches. Overall Length: 200.6 inches. Height: 53.6 inches. Width: 75.5 inches. Front Tread: 60.9 inches. Rear Tread: 60.9 inches. Standard Tires: Goodyear Eagle RS-A P225/60HR16.

TECHNICAL

Transmission: (Catera) 4L30-E electronically controlled four-speed automatic transmission with overdrive, (DeVille, Eldorado, Seville) 4T80-E electronically controlled four-speed automatic (includes viscous converter clutch), Steering: (Catera) Recirculating ball, speed-sensitive, (DeVille, Eldorado, Seville) Power-assisted rack-and- pinion, Magnasteer. Front Suspension: (Catera) MacPherson trut, lower control arms with hydro bushing, coil spring and stabilizer bar, gas preloaded dampers, (DeVille/d'Elegance, Eldorado) Independent MacPherson strut with coil springs, strut-type shock absorbers and stabilizer bar and MacPherson strut dampers, (DeVille Concours, Eldorado Touring Coupe, Seville Luxury Sedan, Seville Touring Sedan) Inependent MacPherson strut with coil springs, stabilizer bar and electronic continuously variable road sensing suspension. Rear Suspension: (Catera) Multi-link, coil spring and stabilizer bar, gas preloaded dampers, (DeVille/d'Elegance, Eldorado) Fully independent, short/long arm, rear shock with airlift and stabilizer bar with automatic level control, (DeVille Concours, Eldorado Touring Coupe). Fully independent, coil springs, short/long arm and stabilizer bar with automatic leve control and electronic continuously variable road sensing suspension, (Seville Luxury Sedan, Seville Touring Sedan) Independent, multi-link, aluminum control arms, lateral toe links, coil springs, stabilizer bar with automatic level control and electronic continuously variable road sensing suspension. Brakes: (Catera) dual circuit front and rear disc with Bosch anti-lock braking system, (DeVille, Eldorado) Power assisted front and rear disc with Bosch anti-lock braking system (Concours had road texture detection), (Seville) power front and rear disc with four-channel anti-lock braking system and StabiliTrak. Body Construction: (all) Integral body-frame. Fuel Tank: (Catera) 18.0 gallons (DeVille, Eldorado) 20.0 gallons, (Seville) 18.5 gallons.

OPTIONS

CATERA OPTIONS

Heated seats ($400). Bose sound system ($973). Electric sun roof ($995). Power rear sunshade ($295). Five-spoke chrome wheels ($795).

DEVILLE OPTIONS

R8J Special Edition package for DeVille only ($2,497). WA7 Comfort/Convenience package for DeVille only ($867). WA8 Safety/Security package for DeVille and DeVille d'Elegance ($995). WA8 Safety/Security

package for Concours ($502). Express-open sun roof ($1,550). White Diamond paint ($500). Crimson Pearl paint ($500). Heavy-duty livery package for DeVille only ($160). Leather seats for DeVille only ($785). Active audio sound system with cassette and CD for DeVille ($670). Active audio sound system with cassette and CD and digital signal processing for DeVille ($770). Active audio sound system with cassette and CD and digital signal processing for Deville d'Elegance or DeVille Concours. Trunk-mounted 12-disc CD changer ($595). Trunk storage system ($265). Chrome wheels ($795, but standard on DeVille d'Elegance). V92 3,000-lb. trailer towing package ($110).

ELDORADO OPTIONS

R8H Autumn Classic edition ($2,418). WA7 Comfort/ Convenience package ($867). WA8 Safety/Security package for Eldorado ($502). WA8 Safety/Security package for Touring Coupe ($207). Accent Striping for Eldorado ($75). Astroroof ($1,550). White Diamond paint ($500). Crimson Pearl paint ($500). Leather seats for Eldorado ($785). Bose sound system with cassette and CD for Eldorado ($1,119). Bose sound system with cassette and CD and digital signal processing for Eldorado ($1,219). Trunk-mounted 12-disc CD changer ($595). P225/60SR16 white sidewall tires for Eldorado ($76). P225/60ZR16 black sidewall tires for Touring Coupe ($250). Trunk storage system ($265). Chrome wheels ($795). StabiliTrak chassis control system ($495).

SEVILLE OPTIONS

1SB Convenience package ($596). 1SC Personalization package ($1,698). Wood trim package ($495). Accent striping for Seville SLS ($75). Heated seats package for Seville STS ($632). Adaptive Seat package for Seville STS ($1,202). Express-open sun roof ($1,550). Engine block heater ($18). White Diamond paint ($500). Crimson Pearl paint ($500). Console-mounted 6-disc CD changer ($500). Bose high-performance entertainment system for Seville SLS ($1,250). Bose high-performance entertainment system for Seville STS ($300). Trunk storage system ($265). P235/60ZR16 black sidewall tires for Seville ($250). Chrome wheels ($795).

HISTORICAL

Cadillac's model-year production totaled 162,715 compared with 159,820 the year previous (this figure does not include the Cateras imported from Germany).

1998 Cadillac, Eldorado, coupe

1999

OVERVIEW

The Catera gained an optional Sport Package model and an all-new 1999-1/2 Eldorado Touring Coupe debuted in the middle of the model year. The big news for Cadillac in 1999 does not fall within the scope of this catalog, that being the debut of the luxury sport utility vehicle named Escalade. Optional equipment in 1999 included the innovative massaging lumbar seat to provide maximum driver comfort.

I.D. DATA

The 17-symbol serial number was located on top of the instrument panel, where it was visible through the windshield. The first symbol 1=U.S.-built vehicle or W=German-built vehicle. The second symbol G=General Motors or O=Opel of Germany. The third symbol 6=Cadillac. The fourth symbol indicated carline/the fifth symbol indicated series as follows: E/L=Eldorado, E/T=Eldorado Touring, K/D=DeVille, K/E=DeVille D'Elegance, K/F=Concours, K/S=Seville (SLS), K/Y=Seville Touring (STS), V/R=Catera. The sixth symbol indicated body style: 1=two-door Coupe/Sedan GM/Fisher Style Nos. 27, 37, 47 or 57, 5=four-door Sedan GM/Fisher style nos. 19, 69. The

Above: **1999 Cadillac, Catera, sedan**

seventh symbol indicated the type of restraint system: 2=Manual belts with front airbags, 4=Automatic belts with front and side airbags. The eighth symbol identified the engine: R=L81 3.0-liter V-6, Y=LD8 4.6L V-8 and 9=L37 4.6L V-8. The ninth symbol was a check digit. The 10th symbol indicates model year: X=1999. The 11th symbol indicated the GM assembly plant: U=Hamtramck, Mich. (Allante) and R=Russelsheim, Germany. The next group of numbers was the sequential production code starting with 001. The Fisher Body tag on the cowl, under the hood includes additional information.

CATERA-SERIES 6V/R-V-6

In addition to the sedan that "zigs," the 1999 Catera lineup offered a Sport model option package that allowed the driver, as Cadillac claimed, "to zig with no fear." The 1999 Catera was the first Cadillac to meet low emissions vehicle (LEV) standards, significantly reducing smog-causing exhaust emissions. To meet the standards, the Catera featured new power train control computers, an electronic throttle control and wide-range heated exhaust oxygen sensors. The Catera also received a new fuel tank and evaporative emission system to more efficiently recover vapors during refueling. Standard equipment in the Catera with cloth interior included dual front and front side air bags, an integrated rear window antenna, an anti-

lockout system, 4-wheel power ABS disc brakes, a digital clock, an electronic Dual-Zone climate control system, rear ventilation outlets in the center console, continuous outside temperature and ice sensing displays, cruise control, an electric rear window defogger, power door locks, a programmable auto lock system, a stainless steel dual exhaust system, Solar-Ray tinted glass, illuminated entry, an analog instrument cluster, an on-board diagnostics system, a full-featured sound system with Theftlock, a manually-reclining front passenger seat, an 8-way power driver's seat, remote keyless entry, cloth front bucket seats with lumbar support, a cloth bench rear seat with split-folding armrest, a leather-trimmed steering wheel with fingertip entertainment controls, speed-sensitive power steering, a theft-deterrent system, Goodyear Eagle tires, automatic transmission, dual padded sun visors, 16-inch cast-aluminum wheels, express-type power windows and a controlled-cycle windshield wiper/washer system. The Catera with leather interior added an audible theft-deterrent system, leather seat trim, an 8-way power passenger seat and a memory mirrors system. The Catera Sport sedan featured ZJ1 suspension that was set up for more aggressive handling and response. The ZJ1 package included stiffer front and rear springs, struts and shocks with increased compression and rebound performance, enhanced valving for the rear shocks, automatic leveling system, specific seven-spoke machined aluminum 16-inch wheels and Goodyear Eagle H-rated tires. The Catera Sport sedan's exterior color choices were Ebony, Ivory and Platinum while the interior was Ebony leather. Other Sport model features included next-generation dual front and side airbags, a rear spoiler and specific rocker panel moldings.

CATERA — SERIES 6V/R — V-8

Model Number	Body/Style No.	Body Type & Seating	Factory Price	Shipping Weight	Production Total
V/R	5	4D Sedan	31,775	3,770	16,493

Note 1: Production total is that reported by Opel for 1999 production in Germany.

DEVILLE - SERIES 6K/D - V-8

The all-sedan DeVille series again used the 275-hp Northstar 4.6-liter V-8 and 4T80-E automatic transmission. An anti-theft alarm and inside compass mirror were standard. An enhanced air bag sensing and diagnostic module (SDM) recorded vehicle speed, engine rpm, throttle position and brake use in the last five seconds prior to air bag deployment, in addition to seat belt use and air bag system readiness. The DeVille's standard equipment included Next Generation dual front and side air bags, 4-wheel power ABS disc brakes, a digital clock, an electronic Dual-Zone climate control system with recirculation and mode control, rear ventilation outlets in the center console, continuous outside temperature and ice sensing displays, a central door-unlocking system, child safety security locks, a driver's information center, a

stainless steel exhaust system, a digital fuel gauge, Solar-Ray tinted glass, illuminated entry, an analog instrument cluster, dual heated power outside rearview mirrors (driver's electrochromatic), an on-board diagnostics system, a full-featured sound system with casette and Theftlock, power reclining front seats with 8-way power driver's seat, remote keyless entry, a leather-trimmed tilting 4-spoke steering wheel with fingertip entertainment controls, Magnasteer variable-assist speed-sensitive power rack-and-pinion steering, Michelin XW4 S-rated all-season tires, 4-speed automatic transmission, Twilight Sentinel, 16-inch cast-aluminum wheels, express-type power windows and a controlled-cycle windshield wiper/washer system.

DEVILLE — SERIES 6K/D — V-8

Model Number	Body/Style No.	Body Type & Seating	Factory Price	Shipping Weight	Production Total
K/D	5	4D Sedan	38,630	3,978	Note 2

Note 2: DeVille production totaled 112,253 with no further breakout available.

DEVILLE D'ELEGANCE - SERIES 6K/E - V-8

In addition to or instead of the DeVille's standard equipment, the DeVille d'Elegance included dual exhausts, a 4-way power lumbar support for driver and front passenger seats, the Memory package, rear compartment overhead illuminated vanity mirrors (not on cars with the optional sun roof), an Active Audio sound system with single-slot CD, 12-way power heated driver and front passenger seating and an audible theft-deterrent system.

DEVILLE D'ELEGANCE — SERIES 6K/E — V-8

Model Number	Body/Style No.	Body Type & Seating	Factory Price	Shipping Weight	Production Total
K/E	5	4D Sedan	42,730	4,049	Note 3

Note 3: See Note 2 above.

DEVILLE CONCOURS - SERIES 6K/F - V-8

The DeVille Concours added or substituted a number of features to the standard equipment list of the DeVille d'Elegance. These included the 300-hp Northstar V-8, an analog fuel gauge, an analog instrument panel with digital displays for many functions including gear selection, telltales and other driver information, Nuance perforated leather seating areas, 4-way lumbar support individual driver and passenger bucket front seats, electrically-heated right- and left-hand outside rearview mirrors (driver's electrochromatic) and H-rated Goodyear Eagle tires.

DEVILLE CONCOURS — SERIES 6K/F — V-8

Model Number	Body/Style No.	Body Type & Seating	Factory Price	Shipping Weight	Produc
K/F	5	4D Sedan	43,230	4,047	Note 4

Note 4: See Note 2 above.

ELDORADO - SERIES 6E/L - V-8

The base Eldorado Coupe's standard equipment included Next Generation dual front air bags, a rear-mounted

power antenna, an ignition anti-lockout system, a braking-and-shifting interlock system, 4-wheel power ABS disc brakes, a multi-featured electronic climate control system with recirculation and mode control, a digital display clock, cruise control, an electric rear window defogger with front side window outlets, electric power door locks, a programmable door auto lock system, a central door-unlocking system, a driver's information center, the 275-hp Northstar V-8, a dual elliptical stainless steel exhaust system, remote keyless entry, an analog fuel gauge, Solar-Ray tinted glass, illuminated entry, an analog instrument cluster with fule gauges and monitors, an auto day/night inside electrochromatic rearview mirror with electric compass, dual illuminated front visor-vanity mirrors, dual heated power outside rearview mirrors (driver's electrochromatic), an on-board Diagnostic II system, a full-featured sound system with casette and Theftlock, power reclining front bucket seats with 8-way power driver's seat, a leather-trimmed tilting 4-spoke steering wheel with redundant controls, Magnasteer variable-assist speed-sensitive power rack-and-pinion steering, a Pass-Key II theft-deterrent system, Michelin XW4 S-rated all-season tires, a four-speed automatic transmission, Twilight Sentinel, dual padded sun visors with extensions, 16-inch cast-aluminum wheels, express-type power windows and a controlled-cycle windshield wiper/washer system with Demand Wash.

ELDORADO — SERIES 6E/L — V-8

Model Number	Body/Style No.	Body Type & Seating	Factory Price	Shipping Weight	Production Total
E/L	1	2D Coupe	39,235	3,825	Note 5

Note 5: Eldorado production totaled 16,172 with no further breakout available.

ELDORADO TOURING (ETC) - SERIES 6E - V-8

The Eldorado Touring Coupe (ETC) received a mid-model-year update (it went into production in January 1999 and was available to customers as a 1999-1/2 model by March). The revised ETC included new body color inserts on side and fascia moldings, which replaced the previous chrome inserts, new seven-spoke wheels with wreath-and-crest center cap, new P235/60HR16 tires and new "ETC" deck lid logo with a simplified design. As compared to the base Eldorado Coupe's standard equipment, the ETC added or substituted the 300-hp Northstar V-8, perforated Nuance leather seating surfaces, 4-way power lumbar support in the driver and front passenger seats, curb-view type heated outside rearview mirrors, a Bose Digital Signal Processing premium sound system with cassette player and single-slot CD player, 12-way power driver and front passenger seats, Goodyear Eagle tires and a Rainsense windshield wiper system.

ELDORADO TOURING COUPE (ETC) — SERIES 6E/T — V-8

Model Number	Body/Style No.	Body Type & Seating	Factory Price	Shipping Weight	Production Total
E/T	1	2D Coupe	43,495	3,856	Note 6

Note 6: See Note 5 above.

SLS - SERIES 6K/S - V-8

The Seville SLS, coming off a major redesign the previous year, returned in much the same format. Standard equipment included Next Generation dual front and front side air bags, an ignition anti-lockout system, a braking-and-shifting interlock system, 4-wheel power ABS disc brakes, a multi-featured electronic Dual-Zone climate control system with recirculation and mode control, a digital display clock, cruise control, an electric rear window defogger with front side window outlets, electric power door locks, a programmable door auto lock system, a central door-unlocking system, child safety security locks, a driver's information center, the 275-hp Northstar V-8, a twin oval stainless steel exhaust system, remote

1999 Cadillac, De Ville Concours sedan

keyless entry, Solar-Ray tinted glass, illuminated entry, an analog instrument cluster with fule gauges and monitors and a redundant digital speedometer, an electrochromatic inside rearview mirror, dual illuminated front visor-vanity mirrors, dual heated power outside rearview mirrors (driver's electrochromatic), an on-board Diagnostic II system, a high-performance 250-watt 8-speaker sound system with cassette and single-slot CD player with Theftlock, leather trimmed front bucket seats, a leather-trimmed rear bench seat with fold-down center arm rest, a 10-way power driver's seat including recliner, a leather-trimmed tilting 4-spoke steering wheel with redundant controls, Magnasteer, a Passkey III audible theft-deterrent system, Goodyear Integrity tires, a four-speed automatic transmission, Twilight Sentinel, dual padded sun visors with extensions, 16-inch cast-aluminum wheels, express-type power windows and a controlled-cycle windshield wiper/washer system.

SEVILLE SLS – SERIES 6K/S – V-8

Model Number	Body/Style No.	Body Type & Seating	Factory Price	Shipping Weight	Production Total
K/S	5	4D Sedan	43,355	3,976	Note 7

Note 7: Seville production totaled 42,452 with no further breakout available.

STS - SERIES 6K/Y - V-8

The Seville STS was the sporty version of Cadillac's higher-priced sedan. As compared to the base Eldorado Coupe's standard equipment, the ETC added or substituted a diversity antenna, a Bose 4.0 Digital Signal Processing high-performance sound system with cassette player, single-slot CD player and auto volume control, the 300-hp Northstar V-8, a stainless steel exhaust system with twin rectangular tips, a Memory package, 4-way power lumbar support in the driver and front passenger seats, curb-view type heated outside rearview mirrors, 14-way power driver and front passenger seats, a 4-spoke tilting and telescoping steering wheel and a Rainsense windshield wiper system.

SEVILLE STS – SERIES 6K/Y – V-8

Model Number	Body/Style No.	Body Type & Seating	Factory Price	Shipping Weight	Production Total
K/Y	5	4D Sedan	47,850	4,001	Note 8

Note 8: See Note 7 above.

ENGINE

CATERA BASE V-6

54-degree dual overhead cam V-6. Cast iron block. Aluminum cylinder heads. Displacement: 181-cid (3.0 liters). Bore and stroke: 3.40 x 3.40 inches. Compression ratio: 10.0:1. Brake hp: 200 @ 6000 rpm. Torque: 192 lb.-ft. at 3600 rpm. Variable Dual-Ram induction system.

DE VILLE D'ELEGANCE, ELDORADO, SEVILLE LUXURY SEDAN BASE V-8

Northstar Overhead valve. Dual overhead cam. Aluminum block with cast iron liners. Aluminum cylinder heads.

1999 Cadillac, Catera, sport sedan

Displacement: 279 cid (4.6 liters). Bore and Stroke: 3.66 x 3.31 inches. Compression ratio: 10.3:1. Net brake hp: 275 at 5600 rpm. Taxable hp: 42.90. Net torque: 300 at 4000 rpm. Direct acting hydraulic tappets. Induction: Tuned port injection. VIN Code: 9; Option Code L37. Built by Cadillac.

DE VILLE CONCOURS, ELDORADO TOURING COUPE, SEVILLE TOURING SEDAN BASE V-8

Northstar Overhead valve. Dual overhead cam. Aluminum block with cast iron liners. Aluminum cylinder heads. Displacement: 279 cid (4.6 liters). Bore and Stroke: 3.66 x 3.31 inches. Compression ratio: 10.3:1. Net brake hp: 300 at 6000 rpm. Taxable hp: 42.90. Net torque: 295 at 4400 rpm. Direct acting hydraulic tappets. Induction: Tuned port injection. VIN Code: Y; Option Code LD8. Built by Cadillac.

CHASSIS

(Catera) Wheelbase: 107.4 inches. Overall Length: 194 inches. Height: 56.3 inches. Width: 70.3 inches. Front Tread: 59.3 inches. Rear Tread: 59.8 inches. Standard Tires: Goodyear Eagle RS-A P225/55HR16.

(DeVille) Wheelbase: 113.8 inches. Overall Length: 209.8 inches. Height: 56 inches. Width: 76.5 inches. Front Tread: 60.9 inches. Rear Tread: 60.9 inches. Standard Tires: Michelin P225/60SR16.

(DeVille d'Elegance) 113.8 inches. Overall Length: 209.8 inches. Height: 56 inches. Width: 76.5 inches. Front Tread: 60.9 inches. Rear Tread: 60.9 inches. Standard Tires: Michelin P225/60SR16.

(Concours) Wheelbase: 113.8 inches. Overall Length: 209.8 inches. Height: 56 inches. Width: 76.5 inches. Front Tread: 60.9 inches. Rear Tread: 60.9 inches. Standard Tires: Goodyear Eagle RS-A P225/60HR16,.

(Seville SLS) Wheelbase: 112.2 inches. Overall Length: 201 inches. Height: 55.4 inches. Width: 75 inches. Front Tread: 62.7 inches. Rear Tread: 62.3 inches. Standard Tires: Goodyear Eagle LS P235/60SR16.

(Seville STS) Wheelbase: 112.2 inches. Overall Length: 201 inches. Height: 55.4 inches. Width: 75 inches. Front Tread: 62.7 inches. Rear Tread: 62.3 inches. Standard Tires: Goodyear Eagle LS P235/60SR16.

(Eldorado) Wheelbase: 108 inches. Overall Length: 200.6 inches. Height: 53.6 inches. Width: 75.5 inches. Front Tread: 60.9 inches. Rear Tread: 60.9 inches. Standard Tires: Michelin P225/60SR16.

(Eldorado Touring Coupe) Wheelbase: 108 inches. Overall Length: 200.6 inches. Height: 53.6 inches. Width: 75.5 inches. Front Tread: 60.9 inches. Rear Tread: 60.9 inches. Standard Tires: Goodyear Eagle RS-A P225/60HR16.

TECHNICAL

Transmission: (Catera) 4L30-E electronically controlled four-speed automatic transmission with overdrive, (DeVille, Eldorado, Seville) 4T80-E electronically controlled four-speed automatic (includes viscous converter clutch), Steering: (Catera) Recirculating ball, speed-sensitive, (DeVille, Eldorado, Seville) Power-assisted rack-and-pinion, Magnasteer. Front Suspension: (Catera) MacPherson strut, lower control arms with hydro bushing, coil spring and stabilizer bar, gas preloaded dampers, (DeVille/d'Elegance, Eldorado) Independent MacPherson strut with coil springs, strut-type shock absorbers and stabilizer bar and MacPherson strut dampers, (DeVille Concours, Eldorado Touring Coupe, Seville Luxury Sedan, Seville Touring Sedan) Independent MacPherson strut with coil springs, stabilizer bar and electronic continuously variable road sensing suspension. Rear Suspension: (Catera) Multi-link, coil spring and stabilizer bar, gas preloaded dampers, (DeVille/d'Elegance, Eldorado) Fully independent, short/long arm, rear shock with airlift and stabilizer bar with automatic level control, (DeVille Concours, Eldorado Touring Coupe) Fully independent, coil springs, short/long arm and stabilizer bar with automatic level control and electronic continuously variable road sensing suspension, (Seville Luxury Sedan, Seville Touring Sedan) Independent, multi-link, aluminum control arms, lateral toe links, coil springs, stabilizer bar with automatic level control and electronic continuously variable road sensing suspension. Brakes: (Catera) dual circuit front and rear disc with Bosch anti-lock braking system, (DeVille, Eldorado) Power assisted front and rear disc with Bosch anti-lock braking system (Concours had road texture detection), (Seville) power front and rear disc with four-channel anti-lock braking system and StabiliTrak. Body Construction: (all) Integral body-frame. Fuel Tank: (Catera) 16.0 gallons, (DeVille, Eldorado) 20.0 gallons, (Seville) 18.5 gallons

OPTIONS
CATERA OPTIONS
Sport package ($795). Heated seats ($425). Bose sound system ($973). Electric sun roof ($995). Power rear sunshade ($295). Five-spoke chrome wheels ($795).

DEVILLE OPTIONS
WA7 Comfort/Convenience package for base DeVille only ($867). Express Open sun roof ($1,550). White Diamond paint ($500). Crimson Pearl paint ($500). Leather seats in DeVille only ($785). Massaging lumbar

seats in DeVille d'Elegance or DeVille Concours ($200). Active Audio sound system with cassette and CD for DeVille ($670). Active Audio sound system with cassette and CD and Digital Signal Processing in base DeVille ($770). Active Audio sound system with cassette and CD and Digital Signal Processing in DeVille d'Elegance or DeVille Concours ($). Trunk-mounted 12-disc CD changer ($595). Trunk storage system ($265). Chrome wheels ($795, but standard on DeVille d'Elegance. V92 3,000-lb. Trailer Towing package ($110).

ELDORADO OPTIONS

WA7 Comfort/Convenience package ($867). Accent striping on base Eldorado ($75). Sun roof ($1,550). White Diamond paint ($500). Crimson Pearl paint ($500). Leather seats in base Eldorado ($785). Massaging lumbar seats in Eldorado Touring Coupe ($200). Bose sound system with cassette and CD and Digital Signal Processing for base Eldorado ($1,219). Trunk-mounted 12-disc CD changer ($595). P225/60ZR16 black sidewall tires for Eldorado Touring Coupe ($250). Trunk storage system ($265). Chrome wheels ($795). StabiliTrak chassis control system for DeVille or DeVille d'Elegance ($495). StabiliTrak chassis control system for Eldorado ($495).

SEVILLE OPTIONS

1SB SLS Convenience package ($598). 1SC SLS Personalization package ($1,698). 1SE SLS Adaptive Seat package ($2,401). 1SD STS Convenience package ($632). 1SE STS Adaptive Seat package ($1,627). Wood trim package ($495). Accent striping for SLS ($75). Massaging lumbar seats for STS ($200). Express Open sun roof ($1,550). Engine block heater ($18). White Diamond paint ($500). Crimson Pearl paint ($500). Console-mounted 6-disc CD changer ($500). Bose high-performance entertainment system for SLS ($1,250). Bose high-performance entertainment system for STS ($300). Trunk storage system ($265). P235/60ZR16 black sidewall tires for STS ($250). Chrome wheels ($795).

HISTORICAL

Cadillac, within its future design theme of "The Fusion of Art & Science," debuted its Evoq concept car on the 1999 auto show circuit to rave reviews. It was powered by a 405-hp 4.2-liter Northstar V-8 topped by an integrated supercharger/intercooler system. Other Evoq features included an automatic transmission that featured Performance Algorithm Shifting, EyeCue head-up display and the Night Vision System borrowed from the 2000 DeVille. Cadillac also stunned the racing world when the luxury automaker announced it would compete in the 2000 24 Hours of Le Mans endurance race. The racing Cadillac, the prototype was named LMP (for Le Mans Prototype), was based on a Riley & Scott chassis fitted with a twin-turbocharged, intercooled 4.0-liter Northstar V-8 (not a regular production item). With a reported budget of $30 million spread over four years, the reason given for Cadillac to enter the competition arena was "image" and enhancing Cadillac's reputation as a global automobile.

1999 Cadillac, Eldorado, ETC coupe

2000

OVERVIEW

Cadillac's millennium-ending 2000 lineup featured completely restyled full-size DeVille sedans built on a much stiffened platform shared with some other GM marques. The end results was somewhat shorter and slightly narrower than the '99 model, but rode on a 1.5-inch longer wheelbase. The Catera received a facelift and the addition of a Sport version distinguished by 17-inch wheels and other exterior styling fillips. The Eldorado and Seville remained largely unchanged in appearance, but received tweaks to their Northstar V-8 engines. While Cadillac's impressive Evoq concept car hinted at future styling for the marque, the year's production models were characterized by technological razzle-dazzle such as a thermal-imaging Night Vision system, updates to the StabiliTrak system that included automatic shock-absorber dampening adjustment on individual wheels, LED taillights, Ultrasonic Rear Parking Assist and a system that prevented front-passenger air bags from deploying if the seat was unoccupied or contained a small child.

I.D. DATA

The 17-symbol serial number was located on top of the instrument panel, where it was visible through the wind-shield. The first symbol 1=U.S.-built vehicle or W=German-built vehicle. The second symbol G=General Motors or O=Opel of Germany. The third symbol 6=Cadillac. The fourth symbol indicated carline/the fifth symbol indicated series as follows: E/L=Eldorado, E/T=Eldorado Touring, K/D=DeVille, K/E=DeVille Luxury, K/F=DeVille Touring Sedan, K/S=Seville (SLS), K/Y=Seville Touring Sedan (STS), V/R=Catera. The sixth symbol indicated body style: 1=two-door Coupe/Sedan GM/Fisher Style Nos. 27, 37, 47 or 57, 5=four-door Sedan GM/Fisher Style nos. 19, 69. The seventh symbol indicates the type of restraint system: 2=Manual belts with front airbags, 4=Automatic belts with front and side airbags, 7=Manual belts with front and side airbags and rear side air bags. The eighth symbol identified the engine: R=L81 3.0-liter V-6, Y=LD8 4.6L V-8 and 9=L37 4.6L V-8. The ninth symbol was a check digit. The 10th symbol indicated model year: Y=2000. The 11th symbol indicated the GM assembly plant: B=Lansing, Michigan, U=Hamtramck, Michigan and R=Russelsheim, Germany. The next group of numbers was the sequential production code starting with 100001. The Fisher Body tag on the cowl, under the hood includes additional information.

Above: **2000 Cadillac, De Ville, DTS sedan**

CATERA-SERIES 6V/R-V-6

For its fourth year in the lineup, the nimble, Opel Omega-based Catera was Cadillac's "entry-level" luxury car. The 2000 model received a freshening up both inside and out. Retaining its overall European look, the Catera featured a new front fascia, new headlights and a redesigned hood that contoured around a smaller, matte-black, chrome grille. A new front cowl concealed the wet-arm windshield wipers and washer nozzles. The rear end was also reworked with a new fascia, separated left and right LED (light-emitting diode) taillights, a center brake light, revised Catera badging and a trademark Cadillac wreath-and-crest emblem. Standard equipment in the base Catera included a 3.0-liter DOHC V-6, a four-speed electronic overdrive transmission, a 310-amp battery with run down protection, an auto-leveling suspension, a front independent-strut suspension with anti-roll bar, front coil springs, a rear independent multi-link suspension with anti-roll bar, rear coil springs, speed-sensitive power steering, 4-wheel power ABS disc brakes, an 18-gallon fuel tank, body-color body-side moldings, monotone paint, aero-style halogen auto headlights, Daytime Running Lights, cornering lights, front fog lights, a high-mounted stoplight, 16-inch silver alloy wheels, a temporary spare tire, an electronic Dual-Zone climate control system with recirculation and mode control, rear ventilation outlets, a full-featured sound system with Theftlock, a diversity antenna, a power remote trunk release, cell phone pre-wiring, two accessory power outlets, a driver's foot rest, retained accessory power, a garage door opener, a full instrumentation display, dual air bags, a security system with ignition-system-disable function, tinted power windows, variable-intermittent windshield wipers with heated jets, front bucket seats with adjustable tilt headrests, 6-way power driver and front passenger seats with lumbar support, a 40-20-40 folding rear bench seat with tilting rear headrests and a center pass-through arm rest, adjustable-height front and rear seat belts with tensioners, leather seat trim, leatherette door panels, full carpeting with carpet mats, woodtone interior trim, a memory driver's seat, dual illuminated visor-vanity mirrors, an auto-dimming inside day/night rearview mirror, a full floor console, a lighted and locking glove box, a front cupholder, twin seat back storage pockets, a black rear window molding and body-color door handles. Updates to the Catera Sport included larger, 17-inch aluminum wheels shod with Goodyear Eagle H-rated all-season tires, high-intensity discharge (HID) Xenon headlights, and a rear spoiler. Catera interior changes included a re-shaped instrument panel and center console—the latter equipped with an additional auxiliary power outlet—and a new center stack for the entertainment system and climate controls. Other interior changes included new door trim panels with integrated door handles, and latch-type storage bins front and rear.

Side-impact air bags were standard on all 2000 Cateras. The new, three-button OnStar system came standard, replacing the first-generation OnStar unit.

CATERA – SERIES 6V/R–V-8

Model Number	Body/Style No.	Body Type & Seating	Factory Price	Shipping Weight	Production Total
V/R	5	4D Sedan	31,010	3,770	17,730

Note 1: Production total is that reported by Opel for 2000 production in Germany.

DEVILLE - SERIES 6K/D - V-8

The 2000 Cadillac DeVille was new on the outside and new on the inside. It was the 50th anniversary of the DeVille nameplate. The new version was shorter and narrower than its predecessor. Cadillac's flagship sedan was promoted as a "sophisticated American luxury car." Firsts that became available on these models included Night Vision thermal-imaging technology that permitted drivers to "see" well beyond the range of their headlights at night or under reduced visibilty conditions and Ultrasonic Rear Parking Assist, which used rear-mounted sensors to warn drivers of obstacles during back-up maneuvers. Standard equipment included a 4.6-liter DOHC V-8, a four-speed electronic overdrive transmission, a battery with run down protection, a 140-amp alternator, front-wheel drive, traction control, a 3.11:1 rear axle, a rear independent multi-link suspension with anti-roll bar, rear coil springs, power rack-and-pinion steering whith vehicle-speed-sensing assist, 4-wheel power ABS disc brakes, an 18.5-gallon fuel tank, side impact bars, front and rear body-color bumpers, clearcoat monotone paint, a body side accent stripe, aero-composite halogen auto headlights, Daytime Running Lights with delay-off feature, cornering lights, an underhood light, left- and right-hand power remote body-colored heated outside rearview mirrors, 16x7-inch silver alloy wheels, a compact spare tire, an electronic Dual-Zone climate control system with recirculation, mode control and an air filter, a rear ventilation outlets, a full-featured sound system with Theftlock, a diversity antenna, a leather-trimmed steering wheel with fingertip entertainment system controls, cruise control, power door locks with two-stage unlock, a power fuel filler door release, cell phone pre-wiring, three accessory power outlets, retained accessory power, a full instrumentation display, dual driver/passenger/front side

2000 Cadillac, Catera, sedan

air bags, a security system with ignition-system-disable function, tinted power windows, a 40-20-40 split-bench front seat with adjustable tilt headrests, a front center arm rest with storage provisions, 6-way power driver and front passenger seats, a rear bench seat with fixed headrests and a pass-through storage-type center arm rest, cloth door trim insets, a full cloth headliner, adjustable-height front and rear seat belts with tensioners, color-keyed full carpeting with carpet mats, simulated wood instrument panel trim, fading interior dome and reading lights, four door curb lights, illuminated entry, a leather-wrapped tilt steering wheel, auto-dimming inside day/night rearview mirror, a mini overhead console with storage, a lighted and locking glove box, trunk carpeting, a trunk light, a chrome grille, chrome side window moldings, a black windshield molding, a black rear window molding and body-color door handles.

DEVILLE–SERIES 6K/D–V-8

Model Number	Body/Style No.	Body Type & Seating	Factory Price	Shipping Weight	Production Total
K/D	5	4D Sedan	38,630	3,978	Note 2

Note 2: DeVille production totaled 98,456 with no further breakout available

DEVILLE LUXURY (DHS)-SERIES 6K/E-V-8

The opulent d'Elegance became the DeVille High Luxury Sedan (DHS). Its standard equipment was based on the list printed above for the base DeVille, with the foilowing substitutions or additions: 16 x 7-inch chrome alloy wheels, a premium full-featured sound system, a diversity antenna, an enhanced instrument panel display showing additional functions, sun blinds, rain-detecting windshield wipers, a rear power blind, a 40-20-40 split-bench front seat with heated cushion, a heated rear bench seat with tilt headrests, leather seat trim, leatherette door trim inserts, genuine wood instrument panel trim, a wood gear shift knob, a memory driver's seat with two settings, a tilt-telescope steering wheel and an illuminated rear vanity mirror.

DEVILLE LUXURY (DHS) – SERIES 6K/E – V-8

Model Number	Body/Style No.	Body Type & Seating	Factory Price	Shipping Weight	Production Total
K/E	5	4D Sedan	45,595	4,049	Note 3

Note 3: See Note 2 above.

DEVILLE TOURING SEDAN (DTS) - SERIES 6K/E - V-8

The sportiest version of the DeVille, previously called the Concours, became the DeVille Touring Sedan (DTS). The standard equipment list for this car started where the DHS left off and the following features were added or substituted: a 3.71:1 rear axle ratio, the Auto Ride Control suspension system, an adaptive auto-leveling suspension, an electronic stability system, an underhood light, 17 x 7.5 silver alloy wheels, P235/55HR17 performance A/S

black sidewall tires, 40-40 front bucket seats with heated cushions, a heated rear bench seat with fixed headrests, a leather-wrapped tilt steering wheel and a full-length center console.

DEVILLE TOURING SEDAN (DTS) – SERIES 6K/F – V-8

Model Number	Body/Style No.	Body Type & Seating	Factory Price	Shipping Weight	Production Total
K/F	5	4D Sedan	45,595	4,047	Note 4

Note 4: See Note 2 above.

ELDORADO SPORT COUPE (ESC)-SERIES 6E/L-V-8

With the demise of the Lincoln Mark VIII and the Buick Riviera, the 2000 Cadillac Eldorado was the only luxury coupe still being produced in North America. The base Eldorado was rebadged ESC (for Eldorado Sport Coupe). Styling was carried over from 1999. Big news was an extensive redesign of the Northstar 4.6-liter V-8 engines, which allowed it to run smoothly, quietly and efficiently on regular gasoline. The base Eldorado continued to use the 275-hp Northstar V-8. The 4T80-E electronically controlled four-speed automatic transmission with viscous converter clutch was again used. Standard equipment also included a 770-amp battery with run down protection, a 140-amp alternator, front-wheel drive, traction control, a 3.11:1 rear axle, a dual stainless steel exhaust system with chrome tip, an auto-leveling comfort ride suspension, a front independent-strut suspension with anti-roll bar, front coil springs, a rear independent multi-link suspension with anti-roll bar, rear coil springs, power rack-and-pinion steering with vehicle-speed-sensing assist, 4-wheel power ABS disc brakes, a 19-gallon fuel tank, aero-composite halogen fully-auto headlights, Daytime Running Lights with delay-off feature, additional exterior lights including cornering lights, front fog-and-driving lights, an underhood light, left- and right-hand power remote body-colored heated outside rearview mirrors, 16x7-inch silver alloy wheels, a compact spare tire, an electronic Dual-Zone climate control system with recirculation, mode control and an air filter, a rear ventilation outlets, a full-featured sound system with Theftlock, a power antenna, power door locks with two-stage unlock, a power fuel filler door

2000 Cadillac, Catera, Sport sedan

release, remote keyless entry, two accessory power outlets, front and rear cigar lighters, retained accessory power, a smoker's package, a full instrumentation display, dual driver/passenger/front side air bags, a security system with ignition-system-disable function, 40-40 front bucket seats with adjustable tilt headrests, a front center arm rest with storage provisions, 6-way power driver and front passenger seats, a rear bench seat with fixed headrests and a center arm rest, rear seat belts with tensioners, leather upholstery with leatherette door trim inserts, a full cloth headliner, full carpet foor covering with carpeted floor mats, genuine wood instrument panel trim, fading interior dome and reading lights, four door curb lights, illuminated entry, a leather-wrapped tilt steering wheel, dual illuminated visor-vanity mirrors, an auto-dimming inside day/night rearview mirror, a carpeted trunk lid, a cargo net, a trunk light, concealed cargo storage, a chrome grille, chrome side window moldings, a black windshield molding, a black rear window molding and body-color door handles.

ELDORADO ESC – SERIES 6E/L – V-8

Model Number	Body/Style No.	Body Type & Seating	Factory Price	Shipping Weight	Production Total
E/L	1	2D Coupe	39,665	3,825	Note 5

Note 5: Eldorado production totaled 13,993 with no further breakout available.

ELDORADO TOURING COUPE (ETC)-SERIES 6E/T-V-8

The more powerful and better-handling Eldorado Touring Coupe (ETC) gave buyers a choice between rides that were either cushier or more sporting. The ETC's Northstar V-8 churned out 300 hp. It was also linked to the 4T80-E electronically controlled four-speed automatic transmission. In addition to or in place of ESC equipment, the ETC included a 3.71:1 rear axle, the electronic stability system, a touring ride suspension, Auto Ride Control, P225/60HR16 all-season black sidewall tires, a premium sound system, a storage type rear seat center armrest, a leather-wrapped gearshifter, a 2-settings memory driver's seat and a body-color grille.

ELDORADO ETC – SERIES 6E/T – V-8

Model Number	Body/Style No.	Body Type & Seating	Factory Price	Shipping Weight	Production Total
E/T	1	2D Coupe	43,240	3,856	Note 6

Note 6: See Note 5 above.

2000 Cadillac, Catera, Sport sedan

SEVILLE LUXURY SEDAN (SLS) - SERIES 6K-V-8

Largely unchanged in outward appearance, Seville returned for 2000 with a significantly refined Northstar V-8. Targeted by Cadillac to impact the global luxury-sedan market, Sevilles were veritable gadget-laden showcases of American automotive technology. Standard were improved versions of both StabiliTrak and Cadillac's Continuously Variable Road-Sensing Suspension (CVRSS) which, in combination with Magnasteer variable-assist, speed-sensitive power rack-and-pinion steering and the road-texture detection system, greatly enhanced vehicle performance and passenger safety. New for 2000 was a system to prevent deployment of the front-passenger air bag if the seat was empty or occupied by a small child. Also new was an ultrasonic rear parking assist and GM's advanced three-button OnStar communications service. Performance Algorithm Shifting (PAS) allowed the four-speed automatic transmission to perform more like a manual transmission under spirited driving conditions. Inside, Sevilles were even more luxurious than before with leather, optional Zebrano wood, improved interior storage, an advanced sound system and seats using inflatable air cells to adjust for comfort and support. Standard equipment also included a 770-amp battery with run down protection, a 138-amp alternator, front-wheel drive, traction control, a 3.71:1 rear axle, a stainless steel exhaust system with chrome tip, an adaptive auto-leveling comfort ride suspension, a front independent-strut suspension with anti-roll bar, front coil springs, a rear independent multi-link suspension with anti-roll bar, rear coil springs, power rack-and-pinion steering with vehicle-speed-sensing assist, 4-wheel power ABS disc brakes, an 18.5-gallon fuel tank, a front license plate bracket, a rear lip spoiler, side impact bars, front and rear body-color bumpers, a body-color body side molding, clearcoat monotone paint, projector-beam halogen fully-auto headlights,16x7-inch silver alloy wheels, P235/60SR16 all-season black sidewall tires, a compact spare tire, an electronic Dual-Zone climate control system with recirculation, mode control and an air filter, a rear ventilation outlets, a full-featured sound system with Theftlock, a power antenna, a steering wheel with radio controls, two accessory power outlets, front and rear cigar lighters, retained accessory power, a smoker's package, a full instrumentation display, dual driver/passenger/front side air bags, a security system with ignition-system-disable function, tinted 1-touch power windows, variable-intermiitent windshield wipers, a sun visor strip, a rear window defroster, front height-adjustable seat belts with tensioners, leather upholstery with leatherette door trim inserts, a full cloth headliner, genuine wood instrument panel trim, a leather-wrapped gearshifter, full-feature interior lighting, four door curb lights, illuminated entry, a leather-wrapped tilt steering wheel, dual illuminated visor-vanity mirrors, dual auxiliary visors, a lighted and locking glove box, front and rear cupholders, two seat back storage pockets, driver and passenger door bins, a chrome grille, chrome side

window moldings, a black windshield molding, a black rear window molding and body-color door handles.

SEVILLE SLS–SERIES 6K/S – V-8

Model Number	Body/Style No.	Body Type & Seating	Factory Price	Shipping Weight	Production Total
K/S	1	4D Sedan	44,475	3,970	Note 7

Note 7: Seville production totaled 34,592 with no further breakout available

SEVILLE TOURING SEDAN (STS) - SERIES 6K/Y-V-8

The more powerful Seville Touring Sedan (STS) gave buyers a choice between rides that were either cushier or more sporting. Even optional massaging lumbar seats were available in the STS. The STS's Northstar V-8 churned out 300 hp. It was also linked to the 4T80-E electronically controlled four-speed automatic transmission. In addition to or in place of ESC equipment, the ETC included additional exterior lighting, a premium sound system, a window grid diversity antenna, rain-detecting wipers, a storage type rear seat center armrest, a leather-wrapped gearshifter, a 2-settings memory driver's seat, and a power tilt-telescopic leather-wrapped steering wheel.

SEVILLE STS – SERIES 6K/Y – V-8

Model Number	Body/Style No.	Body Type & Seating	Factory Price	Shipping Weight	Production Total
K/Y	1	4D Sedan	49,075	4,001	Note 7

Note 8: See Note 7 above.

ENGINE

CATERA BASE V-6

54-degree dual overhead cam V-6. Cast iron block. Aluminum cylinder heads. Displacement: 181-cid (3.0 liters). Bore and stroke: 3.40 x 3.40 inches. Compression ratio: 10.0:1. Brake hp: 200 @ 6000 rpm. Torque: 192 lb.-ft. at 3600 rpm. Variable Dual-Ram induction system.

DE VILLE, DEVILLE LUXURY, ELDORADO ESC, SEVILLE SLS BASE V-8

Northstar Overhead valve. Dual overhead cam. Aluminum block with cast iron liners. Aluminum cylinder heads. Displacement: 279 cid (4.6 liters). Bore and Stroke: 3.66 x 3.31 inches. Compression ratio: 10.0:1. Net brake hp: 275 at 5600 rpm. Taxable hp: 42.90. Net torque: 300 at 4000 rpm. Direct acting hydraulic tappets. Induction: Tuned port injection. VIN Code: 9. Option Code L37. Built by Cadillac.

DE VILLE STS, ELDORADO ETC, SEVILLE STS SEDAN BASE V-8

Northstar Overhead valve. Dual overhead cam. Aluminum block with cast iron liners. Aluminum cylinder heads. Displacement: 279 cid (4.6 liters). Bore and Stroke: 3.66 x 3.31 inches. Compression ratio: 10.3:1. Net brake hp: 300 at 6000 rpm. Taxable hp: 42.90. Net torque: 295 at 4400 rpm. Direct acting hydraulic tappets. Induction: Tuned port injection. VIN Code: Y. Option Code LD8. Built by Cadillac.

CHASSIS

(Catera) Wheelbase: 107.4 inches. Overall Length: 192.2 inches. Height: 56.3 inches. Width: 70.3 inches. Front Tread: 59.3 inches. Rear Tread: 59.8 inches. Standard Tires: Goodyear Eagle RS-A P225/55HR16.

(DeVille) Wheelbase: 115.3 inches. Overall Length: 207.2 inches. Height: 56.7 inches. Width: 74.5 inches. Front Tread: 62.7 inches. Rear Tread: 62.2 inches. Standard Tires: Michelin P225/60SR16.

(DeVille DHS) 115.3 inches. Overall Length: 207.2 inches. Height: 56.7 inches. Width: 74.5 inches. Front Tread: 62.7 inches. Rear Tread: 62.2 inches. Standard Tires: Michelin P225/60SR16.

(DeVille DTS) 115.3 inches. Overall Length: 207.2 inches. Height: 56.7 inches. Width: 74.5 inches. Front Tread: 62.7 inches. Rear Tread: 62.2 inches. Standard Tires: Goodyear P235/55HR17.

(Seville SLS) Wheelbase: 112.2 inches. Overall Length: 201 inches. Height: 55.7 inches. Width: 75 inches. Front Tread: 62.7 inches. Rear Tread: 62.3 inches. Standard Tires: Goodyear Integrity P235/60R16.

(Seville STS) Wheelbase: 112.2 inches. Overall Length: 201 inches. Height: 55.4 inches. Width: 75 inches. Front Tread: 62.7 inches. Rear Tread: 62.3 inches. Standard Tires: Goodyear Eagle LS P235/60R16.

(Eldorado ESC) Wheelbase: 108 inches. Overall Length: 200.6 inches. Height: 53.6 inches. Width: 75.5 inches. Front Tread: 60.9 inches. Rear Tread: 60.9 inches. Standard Tires: Michelin XW4 P225/60R16.

(Eldorado ETC) Wheelbase: 108 inches. Overall Length: 200.6 inches. Height: 53.6 inches. Width: 75.5 inches. Front Tread: 60.9 inches. Rear Tread: 60.9 inches. Standard Tires: Goodyear Eagle RS-A P235/60R16.

2000 Cadillac, DeVille, sedan

TECHNICAL

Transmission: (Catera) 4L30-E electronically controlled four-speed automatic transmission with overdrive, (DeVille, Eldorado, Seville) 4T80-E electronically controlled four-speed automatic overdrive (includes viscous torque converter clutch) Steering: (Catera) Recirculating ball, speed-sensitive, (DeVille, Eldorado, Seville) Power-assisted rack-and-pinion, Magnasteer. Front Suspension: (Catera) MacPherson strut, lower control arms with hydro bushing, coil spring and stabilizer bar, gas preloaded dampers, (DeVille/DHS, Eldorado ESC), Independent MacPherson strut-type with coil springs and stabilizer bar, (DeVille Concours, Eldorado ETC, Seville SLS, Seville STS), Independent MacPherson strut-type with coil springs, stabilizer bar and electronic continuously variable road sensing suspension. Rear Suspension: (Catera) Multi-link, coil spring and stabilizer bar, gas preloaded dampers, (DeVille/DHS, Eldorado ESC), Fully independent, short/long arm, rear shock with airlift and stabilizer bar with automatic level control, (DeVille DTS, Eldorado ETC), Fully independent, coil springs, short/long arm and stabilizer bar with automatic level control and electronic continuously variable road sensing suspension, (Seville SLS, Seville STS), Independent, multi-link, aluminum control arms, lateral toe links, coil springs, stabilizer bar with automatic level control, StabiliTrak and electronic continuously variable road sensing suspension. Brakes: (Catera) dual circuit front and rear disc with Bosch anti-lock braking system, (DeVille, Eldorado), Power assisted front and rear disc with Delco-Bosch anti-lock braking system, (Seville) power front and rear disc with four-channel anti-lock braking system and road texture detection. Body Construction: (all) Integral body-frame. Fuel Tank: (Catera) 16.0 gals, (DeVille) 18.5 gallons, (Eldorado) 19.0 gallons, (Seville) 18.5 gallons.

OPTIONS

CATERA OPTIONS

CF5 sun roof with express open ($995). DE1 rear power sun shade ($295). KA1 heated front and rear seats ($400). P05 chrome wheels ($795). UL6 Bose sound system with CD, cassette player, eight speakers, signal-seeking AM/FM stereo with seek and scan, digital display, single-slot CD player, weather band, radio data system (RDS) and theftlock ($973).

DE VILLE OPTIONS

Trunk storage system ($265). 86U Crimson Pearl paint ($650). 93U White Diamond paint ($650). AC9 adaptive front seats for either model, requires comfort-and-convenience package ($995). AW9 rear seat side air bags ($295, but not available with livery package ($295). CF5 sun roof with express open ($1,550). N30 wood trim package for DTS, including woodgrained steering wheel and shift knob ($595). N94 chrome wheels for DTS ($795). QC6 chrome wheels for base DeVille ($795). U1R AM/FM stereo with cassette, single-slot CD, theftlock and eight speakers in base DeVille ($300). U1Z glovebox-mounted 6-disc CD changer ($595). UM9 AM/FM stereo with cassette, mini disc, weather band, theftlock, digital signal processing, radio data system and eight-speaker Bose acoustic system ($300). UV2 night vision system, requires safety-and-security option ($1,995). UY4 onboard CD-Rom-based navigation system, requires premium audio system and 6-disc CD changer ($1,995). V92 3000-lb. Trailer towing provisions for DTS ($110). W20 livery package for base DeVille, includes rocker-type on/off switch, accent striping deleted, engine oil cooler, full-size spare tire, rear reading lights, dimming rear visor-vanity mirrors and white sidewall ($160, but not available on cars with the AW9 or V92 options). WA7 comfort and convenience package for base DeVille, includes 4-way power lumbar support, memory package, trunk mat and heated seats ($1,095). WA7 comfort and convenience package for DTS, includes memory package, trunk mat, tilt-and-telescope steering wheel ($695). WA8 safety and security package for base DeVille and DHS, includes Stabilitrak, ultrasonic rear parking assist and 3-channel garage door opener ($895). WA8 safety and security package for DTS, includes ultrasonic rear parking assist and 3-channel garage door opener ($400). WJ7 leather seats for base DeVille ($785).

ELDORADO OPTIONS

Accent stripe for ESC, requires D98 accent stripe color (no charge). 86U Crimson Pearl paint ($650). 93U White Diamond paint ($650). BNN trunk storage system ($265) CF5 sun roof with express open, deletes sun glass storage compartment ($1,550). JL4 Stabilitrak for ESC ($495). N26 chrome wheels for ETC ($795). N30 wood steering wheel ($395). QC8 chrome wheels for ESC ($795). QDC P235/60ZR16 Goodyear Eagle LS tires for ETC ($250). U1S 12-disc trunk-mounted disc changer ($595). UG1 programmable garage door opener ($107). UM5 Bose

**2000 Cadillac, Seville, STS sedan,
Cunningham Edition pace car**

sound system with cassette player, AM/FM stereo, digital signal processing, single-slot CD player, weather band, radio data system (RDS), theftlock and Bose amplified speaker system for ESC ($1,219). WA7 comfort and convenience package for ESC, includes 4-way lumbar support, memory package and heated front seats ($867).

SEVILLE OPTIONS

1SB Seville SLS Convenience package including 4-way power lumbar support, RainSense windshield wiper system and 3-channel programmable garage door opener ($598). 1SC Seville SLS Personalization package, including 4-way power lumbar support, memory package, RainSense windshield wiper system, heated front and rear seats and 3-channel programmable garage door opener $1,627. 1SD Seville STS heated seats package, includes heated front and rear seats a 3-channel programmable garage door opener ($632). 1SE Seville SLS Adaptive Seat package, includes driver and front passenger adaptive seats, memory package, RainSense windshield wiper system, heated front and rear seats, power tilt and telescope steering column and 3-channel programmable garage door opener ($2,401). 1SE Seville STS Adaptive Seat package, includes driver and front passenger adaptive seats, heated front and rear seats and 3-channel programmable garage door opener ($1,627). Wood Trim Package ($595). Accent Striping (SLS) $75. Express Open Sun roof ($1,550). Engine. Block Heater $18. 86U Crimson Pearl paint ($650). 93U White Diamond paint ($650). CF5 sun roof with express open ($1,550). D98 accent stripe color for SLS ($75). FE9 emissions requirements (no cost, but not available with YF5). K05 engine block heater ($18). N30 wood trim package, includes wood steering wheel and gearshifter ($795). P05 chrome wheels for Seville STS ($795). PX2 chrome wheels for Seville SLS ($795). QDC P235/60ZR16 Goodyear Eagle LS tires for STS ($250). U1Z 6-disc console-mounted disc changer ($595). UD7 ultrasonic rear parking assist ($295). UM5 Bose sound system with cassette player, AM/FM stereo, digital signal processing, single-slot CD player, weather band, radio data system (RDS), auto volume control, theftlock, Bose 425-watts 4.0 music system and eight Bose speakers ($950 and not available with UM9). UM9 Bose High-Performance Entertainment System for Seville SLS ($1,250). UM9 Bose High-Performance Entertainment System for Seville STS ($300). UY4 On Board Navigation for Seville SLS ($2,945). UY4 On Board Navigation for Seville STS ($1,995). YE5 California emissions (no charge).

HISTORICAL

As announced during 1999, Cadillac fielded cars to compete in the 24 Hours of Le Mans endurance race. The four racing Cadillacs, named LMP (for Le Mans Prototype), were based on a Riley & Scott chassis fitted with a twin-turbocharged, intercooled 4.0-liter Northstar V-8s (not a regular production item). While the cars were not ultimately victorious, valuable lessons were learned by the Cadillac contingent and optimism prevailed for a better showing in 2001. One bright spot in Cadillac's Le Mans experience was the performance of the Night Vision systems on its race cars. Derived from thermal-imaging technology developed for the military, Night Vision was one element of the technological wizardry that typified 2000 Cadillacs. Standard and optional features such as Night Vision, StabiliTrak, CVRSS, PAS, Ultrasonic Rear Parking Assist, OnStar, and hands-free cellular phone operation—to name a few—brought world attention to Cadillac's state-of-the-art engineering and commitment to excellence.

2000 Cadillac, DeVille, sedan

2001

OVERVIEW

The Catera, built in Russelsheim, Germany, got redesigned headlights for 2001. New solar glass reduced temperatures inside the cars by up to 18 degrees. New ventilated rear disc brakes were also introduced. Cadillac's OnStar service was upgraded with new features, including Internet access. Eight-way power seats became standard equipment in mid-2001. Catera prices increased about $500. A voice-controlled "infotainment" system was a new DeVille option. It combined a Bose music system with a map-based navigation system, communications, a voice memo recorder, a personal data assistant interface and e-mail capability. The DeVille DHS and DTS also got a standard automatic windshield wiper system and a trunk-entrapment release. The upgraded OnStar was standard and a system that automatically monitored tire pressures was optional for all models. DeVilles were made in Hamtramck, Michigan. Production of Cadillac Eldorados, formerly carried out in the Hamtramck factory, was relocated to the Lansing Craft Center, in Lansing, Michigan, for 2001. Not much else changed, but the Eldorado's OnStar system got the upgrades. Sevilles continued to be built in Hamtramck. The Seville

engine now complied to new NLEV emissions standards. An optional new STS Sport package included 17-inch performance tires, a revised suspension, tire pressure monitoring and infotainment system.

I.D. DATA

The 17-symbol serial number was located on top of the instrument panel, where it was visible through the windshield. The first symbol 1=U.S.-built vehicle or W=German-built vehicle. The second symbol G=General Motors or O=Opel of Germany. The third symbol 6=Cadillac. The fourth symbol indicated carline/the fifth symbol indicated series as follows: E/L=Eldorado, E/T=Eldorado Touring, K/D=DeVille, K/E=DeVille Luxury, K/F=DeVille Touring Sedan, K/S=Seville (SLS), K/Y=Seville Touring Sedan (STS), V/R=Catera. The sixth symbol indicated body style: 1=two-door Coupe/Sedan GM/Fisher Style Nos. 27, 37, 47 or 57, 5=four-door Sedan GM/Fisher style nos. 19, 69. The seventh symbol indicated the type of restraint system: 2=Manual belts with front airbags, 4=Automatic belts with front and side airbags, 7=Manual belts with front and side airbags and rear side air bags. The eighth symbol identified the engine: R=L81 3.0-liter V-6, Y=LD8 4.6L V-8 and 9=L37 4.6L V-8. The ninth symbol was a check digit. The 10th symbol indicated model year:

Above: **2001 Cadillac, Eldorado, Sport Coupe**

1=2001. The 11th symbol indicates the GM assembly plant: B=Lansing, Michigan, U=Hamtramck, Michigan and R=Russelsheim, Germany. The next group of numbers was the sequential production code starting with 100001. The Fisher Body tag on the cowl, under the hood includes additional information.

CATERA-SERIES 6V/R-V-6

Changes in the Catera for 2001 included the new 2.6 version of OnStar, the vented rear disac brakes, the Solar Protect windshield and projector-beam headlights. The Catera Sport got new seats. Standard equipment in the base Catera included a 3.0-liter DOHC 24-valve V-6, a four-speed electronic overdrive transmission, a 310-amp battery with run down protection, an engine oil cooler, a 120-amp alternator, a driver-selectable programmable transmission, traction control, a 3.90:1 rear axle, a front independent-strut suspension with anti-roll bar, front coil springs, a rear independent multi-link suspension with anti-roll bar, rear coil springs, speed-sensitive power steering, 4-wheel power ABS disc brakes, an 18-gallon fuel tank, front fog lights, a high-mounted stoplight, 16-inch silver alloy wheels, a temporary spare tire, an electronic Dual-Zone climate control system with recirculation and mode control, rear ventilation outlets, a full-featured sound system with Theftlock, a diversity antenna, a leather-trimmed steering wheel with fingertip entertainment system controls, a power remote trunk release, cell phone pre-wiring, two accessory power outlets, a driver's foot rest, retained accessory power, a garage door opener, a full instrumentation display, dual air bags, a security system with ignition-system-disable function, tinted power windows, variable-intermiitent windshield wipers with heated jets, 8-way power driver and front passenger seats with lumbar support, a 40-20-40 folding rear bench seat with tilting rear headrests and a center pass-through arm rest, leather seat trim, leatherette door panels, full carpeting with carpet mats, woodtone interior trim, a memory driver's seat, an auto-dimming inside day/night rearview mirror, a full floor console, a lighted and locking glove box, a front cupholder, a trunk light, and body-color door handles.

CATERA—SERIES 6V/R—V-8

Model Number	Body/Style No.	Body Type & Seating	Factory Price	Shipping Weight	Production Total
V/R	5	4D Sedan	31,305	3,770	297

Note 1: Production total is that reported by Opel for 2001 production in Germany.

DEVILLE-SERIES 6K/D-V-8

DeVilles had few big changes this year. A tire-pressure-monitoring system was available. Instead of Parisian Blue or Polo Green paint, DeVille buyers were offered a new shade of Graphite along with the other previous options. A new Dark Gray interior color was added.

All DeVilles were now certified low-emissions vehicles. Standard equipment included a 4.6-liter DOHC 32-valve V-8, a four-speed electronic overdrive transmission, a battery with run down protection, a 140-amp alternator, front-wheel drive, traction control, a 3.11:1 rear axle, a stainless steel exhaust system, an auto-leveling comfort ride suspension, a front independent-strut suspension with anti-roll bar, front coil springs, a rear independent multi-link suspension with anti-roll bar, rear coil springs, power rack-and-pinion steering whith vehicle-speed-sensing assist, 4-wheel power ABS disc brakes, an 18.5-gallon fuel tank, front and rear body-color bumpers, 16 x 7-inch cast-aluminum wheels, an electronic Dual-Zone climate control system with recirculation, mode control and an air filter, a rear ventilation outlets, a full-featured sound system with Theftlock, a leather-trimmed steering wheel with fingertip entertainment system controls, three accessory power outlets, unction, tinted power windows, variable-intermiitent windshield wipers, a sun visor strip, a rear window defroster, a 40-20-40 split-bench front seat with adjustable tilt headrests, a front center arm rest with storage provisions, 6-way power driver and front passenger seats, cloth door trim insets, a full cloth headliner, adjustable-height front and rear seat belts with tensioners, a leather-wrapped tilt steering wheel, dual illuminated visor-vanity mirrors, driver and passenger door bins, trunk carpeting, a cargo net, a trunk light, a chrome grille, chrome side window moldings, a black windshield molding, a black rear window molding and body-color door handles.

DEVILLE—SERIES 6K/D —V-8

Model Number	Body/Style No.	Body Type & Seating	Factory Price	Shipping Weight	Production Total
K/D	5	4D Sedan	40,495	3,978	Note 2

Note 2: DeVille production totaled 90,140 with no further breakout available

DEVILLE LUXURY (DHS)-SERIES 6K/E-V-8

Standard equipment for the DeVille High-luxury Sedan (DHS) was based on DeVille features, plus the foillowing substitutions or additions: 16 x 7-inch chrome cast-aluminum wheels, a premium full-featured sound system, a diversity antenna, an enhanced instrument panel display showing additional functions, rear power blinds, rain-

2001 Cadillac, De Ville, DHS sedan

detecting windshield wipers, a rear power blind, a 40-20-40 split-bench front seat with heated cushion, a heated rear bench seat with tilt headrests, leather seat trim, leatherette door trim inserts, genuine wood instrument panel trim, a wood gear shift knob, a memory driver's seat with two settings, a tilt-telescope steering wheel, an illuminated rear vanity mirror and carpeted cargo mats.

DEVILLE LUXURY (DHS) – SERIES 6K/E – V-8

Model Number	Body/Style No.	Body Type & Seating	Factory Price	Shipping Weight	Production Total
K/E	5	4D Sedan	46,267	4049	Note 3

Note 3: See Note 2 above.

DEVILLE TOURING SEDAN (DTS)-SERIES 6K/E-V-8

The standard equipment list for the DeVille Touring Sedan (DTS) started at the DHS level and the following features were added or substituted: a 300-hp Northstar V-8, a 3.71:1 rear axle ratio, the Auto Ride Control suspension system, an adaptive auto-leveling suspension, an electronic stability system, an underhood light, 17 x 7.5 silver alloy wheels, P235/55HR17 performance A/S black sidewall tires, 40-40 front bucket seats with heated cushions, a heated rear bench seat with fixed headrests, a leather-wrapped tilt steering wheel, a full-length center console and a mini overhead console with storage.

DEVILLE TOURING SEDAN (DTS) – SERIES 6K/F – V-8

Model Number	Body/Style No.	Body Type & Seating	Factory Price	Shipping Weight	Production Total
K/F	5	4D Sedan	46,267	4,047	Note 4

Note 4: See Note 2 above.

ELDORADO SPORT COUPE (ESC)-SERIES 6E/L-V-8

Eldorados offered a new Sequoia exterior color and a new Dark Gray interior color. No longer available was the Bose sound system with mini disc player. The base Eldorado continued to use the 275-hp Northstar V-8. The 4T80-E electronically controlled four-speed automatic transmission with viscous converter clutch was again used. Standard equipment also included a 770-amp battery

2001 Cadillac, Seville, SLS sedan

with run down protection, a 140-amp alternator, front-wheel drive, traction control, a 3.11:1 rear axle, a dual stainless steel exhaust system with chrome tip, an auto-leveling comfort ride suspension, a front independent-strut suspension with anti-roll bar, front coil springs, a rear independent multi-link suspension with anti-roll bar, rear coil springs, power rack-and-pinion steering with vehicle-speed-sensing assist, 4-wheel power ABS disc brakes, side impact bars, front and rear body-color bumpers with a chrome bumper insert, 16x7-inch cast-aluminum wheels, a compact spare tire, an electronic Dual-Zone climate control system with recirculation, mode control and an air filter, a rear ventilation outlets, a full-featured sound system with Theftlock, a power antenna, a steering wheel with radio controls, two accessory power outlets, front and rear cigar lighters, retained accessory power, a smoker's package, a full instrumentation display, dual driver/passenger/front side air bags, a security system with ignition-system-disable function, tinted 1-touch power windows, variable-intermiitent windshield wipers, a rear window defroster, a 40-40 front bucket seats, 6-way power driver and front passenger seats, leather upholstery with leatherette door trim inserts, a full cloth headliner, full carpet foor covering with carpeted floor mats, genuine wood instrument panel trim, fading interior dome and reading lights, four door curb lights, illuminated entry, a leather-wrapped tilt steering wheel, a full-length center console, a carpeted trunk lid, a cargo net, a trunk light, concealed cargo storage, a chrome grille, chrome side window moldings, a black windshield molding, a black rear window molding and body-color door handles.

ELDORADO ESC – SERIES 6E/L – V-8

Model Number	Body/Style No.	Body Type & Seating	Factory Price	Shipping Weight	Production Total
E/L	1	2D Coupe	40,036	3,825	Note 5

Note 5: Eldorado production totaled 14,834 with no further breakout available.

ELDORADO TOURING COUPE (ETC)-SERIES 6E/T-V-8

The more powerful and better-handling Eldorado Touring Coupe (ETC) gave buyers a choice between rides that were either cushier or more sporting. The ETC's Northstar V-8 churned out 300 hp. It was also linked to the 4T80-E electronically controlled four-speed automatic transmission. In addition to or in place of ESC equipment, the ETC included a 3.71:1 rear axle, the electronic stability system, a touring ride suspension, Auto Ride Control, P225/60HR16 all-season black sidewall tires, a premium sound system, a storage type rear seat center armrest, a leather-wrapped gearshifter, a two-settings memory driver's seat and a body-color grille.

Model Number	Body/Style No.	Body Type & Seating	Factory Price	Shipping Weight	Production Total
E/T	1	2D Coupe	43,611	3,856	Note 6

Note 6: See Note 5 above.

SEVILLE LUXURY SEDAN (SLS)-SERIES 6K-V-8

The optional new STS Sport package was one of three new packages for this car line. A revised suspension, high-intensity discharge headlights, tire pressure monitoring, a hands-free cell phone and the infotainment system were all new options. The upgraded OnStar system was standard in the STS and optional in the SLS. Standard equipment also included a 770-amp battery with run down protection, a 138-amp alternator, front-wheel drive, traction control, a 3.71:1 rear axle, a stainless steel exhaust system with chrome tip, an adaptive auto-leveling comfort ride suspension, 4-wheel power ABS disc brakes, an 18.5-gallon fuel tank, a front license plate bracket, a rear lip spoiler, side impact bars, front and rear body-color bumpers, projector-beam halogen fully-auto headlights, Daytime Running Lights with delay-off feature, additional exterior lights including cornering lights, front fog-and-driving lights, an underhood light, left- and right-hand power remote body-colored heated outside rearview mirrors, 16x7-inch silver alloy wheels, an electronic Dual-Zone climate control system with recirculation, mode control and an air filter, a rear ventilation outlets, a full-featured sound system with Theftlock, a power antenna, a steering wheel with radio controls, cruise control, power door locks with two-stage unlock, a power fuel filler door release, remote keyless entry, a full instrumentation display, dual driver/passenger/front side air bags, a security system with ignition-system-disable function, tinted 1-touch power windows, variable-intermiitent windshield wipers, a sun visor strip, a rear window defroster, front bucket seats with power-adjustable tilt headrests, a front center arm rest with storage provisions, 6-way power driver and front passenger seats, leather upholstery with leatherette door trim inserts, genuine wood instrument panel trim, a leather-wrapped gearshifter, full-feature interior lighting, four door curb lights, illuminated entry, a leather-wrapped tilt steering wheel, dual illuminated visor-vanity mirrors, dual auxiliary visors, an auto-dimming inside day/night rearview mirror, a full-length center console, a mini overhead console with storage pockets, a lighted and locking glove box, front and rear cupholders, two seat back storage pockets, driver and passenger door bins, trunk carpeting, a carpeted trunk lid, a cargo net, cargo tie downs, a trunk light, concealed cargo storage, a chrome grille, chrome side window moldings, a black windshield molding, a black rear window molding and body-color door handles.

Series No.	Body/Style No.	Body Type & Seating	Factory Price	Shipping Weight	Production Total
K/S	1	4D Sedan	41,935	3,970	Note 7

Note 7: Seville production totaled 25,169 with no further breakout available.

SEVILLE TOURING SEDAN (STS)-SERIES 6K/Y-V-8

The more powerful Seville Touring Sedan (STS) gave buyers a choice between rides that were either cushier or more sporting. Even optional massaging lumbar seats were available in the STS. The STS's Northstar V-8 churned out 300 hp. It was also linked to the 4T80-E electronically controlled four-speed automatic transmission. In addition to or in place of ESC equipment, the ETC included additional exterior lighting, a premium sound system, a window grid diversity antenna, rain-detecting wipers, a storage type rear seat center armrest, a leather-wrapped gearshifter, a 2-settings memory driver's seat, a rear seat with tilting headrests and a power tilt-telescopic leather-wrapped steering wheel.

Model Number	Body/Style No.	Body Type & Seating	Factory Price	Shipping Weight	Production Total
K/Y	1	4D Sedan	48,045	4,001	Note 7

Note 8: See Note 7 above.

ENGINE

CATERA BASE V-6

54-degree dual overhead cam V-6. Cast iron block. Aluminum cylinder heads. Displacement: 181-cid (3.0 liters). Bore and stroke: 3.40 x 3.40 inches. Compression ratio: 10.0:1. Brake hp: 200 @ 6000 rpm. Torque: 192 lb.-ft. at 3600 rpm. Variable Dual-Ram induction system.

DE VILLE, DEVILLE LUXURY, ELDORADO ESC, SEVILLE SLS BASE V-8

Northstar Overhead valve. Dual overhead cam. Aluminum block with cast iron liners. Aluminum cylinder heads. Displacement: 279 cid (4.6 liters). Bore and Stroke: 3.66 x 3.31 inches. Compression ratio: 10.0:1. Net brake hp: 275

2001 Cadillac, Catera, Sport sedan

at 5600 rpm. Taxable hp: 42.90. Net torque: 300 at 4000 rpm. Direct acting hydraulic tappets. Induction: Tuned port injection. VIN Code: 9. Option Code L37. Built by Cadillac.

DE VILLE STS, ELDORADO ETC, SEVILLE STS SEDAN BASE V-8

Northstar Overhead valve. Dual overhead cam. Aluminum block with cast iron liners. Aluminum cylinder heads. Displacement: 279 cid (4.6 liters). Bore and Stroke: 3.66 x 3.31 inches. Compression ratio: 10.3:1. Net brake hp: 300 at 6000 rpm. Taxable hp: 42.90. Net torque: 295 at 4400 rpm. Direct acting hydraulic tappets. Induction: Tuned port injection. VIN Code: Y. Option Code LD8. Built by Cadillac.

CHASSIS

(Catera) Wheelbase: 107.4 inches. Overall Length: 192.2 inches. Height: 56.4 inches. Width: 70.3 inches. Front Tread: 59.3 inches. Rear Tread: 59.8 inches. Standard Tires: Goodyear Eagle RS-A P225/55HR16.

(DeVille) Wheelbase: 115.3 inches. Overall Length: 207.2 inches. Height: 56.7 inches. Width: 74.5 inches. Front Tread: 62.7 inches. Rear Tread: 62.2 inches. Standard Tires: Michelin P225/60SR16.

(DeVille DHS) 115.3 inches. Overall Length: 207.2 inches. Height: 56.7 inches. Width: 74.5 inches. Front Tread: 62.7 inches. Rear Tread: 62.2 inches. Standard Tires: Michelin P225/60SR16.

(DeVille DTS) 115.3 inches. Overall Length: 207.2 inches. Height: 56.7 inches. Width: 74.5 inches. Front Tread: 62.7 inches. Rear Tread: 62.2 inches. Standard Tires: Goodyear P235/55HR17.

(Seville SLS) Wheelbase: 112.2 inches. Overall Length: 201 inches. Height: 55.7 inches. Width: 75 inches. Front Tread: 62.7 inches. Rear Tread: 62.3 inches. Standard Tires: Goodyear Integrity P235/60R16.

(Seville STS) Wheelbase: 112.2 inches. Overall Length: 201 inches. Height: 55.4 inches. Width: 75 inches. Front Tread: 62.7 inches. Rear Tread: 62.3 inches. Standard Tires: Goodyear Eagle LS P235/60R16.

(Eldorado ESC) Wheelbase: 108 inches. Overall Length: 200.6 inches. Height: 53.6 inches. Width: 75.5 inches. Front Tread: 60.9 inches. Rear Tread: 60.9 inches. Standard Tires: Michelin XW4 P225/60R16.

(Eldorado ETC) Wheelbase: 108 inches. Overall Length: 200.6 inches. Height: 53.6 inches. Width: 75.5 inches. Front Tread: 60.9 inches. Rear Tread: 60.9 inches. Standard Tires: Goodyear Eagle RS-A P235/60R16.

TECHNICAL

Transmission: (Catera) 4L30-E electronically controlled four-speed automatic transmission with overdrive, (DeVille, Eldorado, Seville) 4T80-E electronically controlled four-speed automatic overdrive (includes viscous torque converter clutch). Steering: (Catera) Recirculating ball, speed-sensitive, (DeVille, Eldorado, Seville) Power-assisted rack-and-pinion, Magnasteer. Front Suspension: (Catera) MacPherson strut, lower control arms with hydro bushing, coil spring and stabilizer bar, gas preloaded dampers, (DeVille/DHS, Eldorado ESC), Independent MacPherson strut-type with coil springs and stabilizer bar, (DeVille Concours, Eldorado ETC, Seville SLS, Seville STS), Independent MacPherson strut-type with coil springs, stabilizer bar and electronic continuously variable road sensing suspension. Rear Suspension:

2001 Cadillac, Catera, sedan

(Catera), Multi-link, coil spring and stabilizer bar, gas preloaded dampers, (DeVille/DHS, Eldorado ESC), Fully independent, short/long arm, rear shock with airlift and stabilizer bar with automatic level control, (DeVille DTS, Eldorado ETC), Fully independent, coil springs, short/long arm and stabilizer bar with automatic level control and electronic continuously variable road sensing suspension, (Seville SLS, Seville STS), Independent, multi-link, aluminum control arms, lateral toe links, coil springs, stabilizer bar with automatic level control, StabiliTrak and electronic continuously variable road sensing suspension. Brakes: (Catera) dual circuit front and rear disc with Bosch anti-lock braking system, (DeVille, Eldorado) Power assisted front and rear disc with Delco-Bosch anti-lock braking system, (Seville) power front and rear disc with four-channel anti-lock braking system and road texture detection. Body Construction: (all) Integral body-frame. Fuel Tank: (Catera) 16.0 gals, (DeVille) 18.5 gallons, (Eldorado) 19.0 gallons, (Seville) 18.5 gallons.

OPTIONS

CATERA OPTIONS

CF5 sun roof with express open ($995). DE1 rear power sun shade ($295). KA1 heated front and rear seats ($400). P05 chrome wheels ($795). UL5 Bose sound system with CD, cassette player, eight speakers, signal-seeking AM/FM stereo with seek and scan, digital display, single-slot CD player, weather band, radio data system (RDS) and theftlock ($973). T24 Sport package includes 8-way power passenger seat, memory package, audible theft-deterrent system, 3-channel garage door opener, rear spoiler, heated front seats, 17-inch alloy wheels, P235/45R17 all-season black sidewall tires, Xenon high-intensity-discharge headlights and sport suspension ($2,510, but not available with P05 or TW1). TW1 eqipment group, includes 8-way power passenger seat, memory package, audible theft-deterrent system, 3-channel garage door opener ($995).

DE VILLE OPTIONS

Nuance leather seat trim in base DeVille ($785). 86U Crimson Pearl paint ($650). 93U White Diamond paint ($650). AC9 adaptive front seats for either model, requires comfort-and-convenience package ($995). AW9 rear seat side air bags ($295). CF5 sun roof with express open ($1,550). N30 wood trim package for DTS, including woodgrained steering wheel and shift knob ($595). N94 17-inch chrome wheels for DTS ($795). QC6 chrome wheels for base DeVille ($795). U1Z glovebox-mounted 6-disc CD changer ($595). UV2 night vision system, requires safety-and-security option ($1,995). UY4 onboard CD-ROM-based navigation system, requires premium audio system and 6-disc CD changer ($1,995). WA7 comfort and convenience package for base DeVille, includes 4-way power lumbar support, memory package,

trunk mat and heated seats ($1,095). WA8 safety and security package for base DeVille and DHS, includes Stabilitrak, ultrasonic rear parking assist and 3-channel garage door opener ($1,045). WA8 safety and security package for DTS, includes ultrasonic rear parking assist and 3-channel garage door opener ($550). WA9 comfort and convenience package for DTS, includes memory package, trunk mat and power tilt-and-telescope stering wheels ($695).

ELDORADO OPTIONS

86U Crimson Pearl paint ($650). 93U White Diamond paint ($650). CF5 sun roof with express open, deletes sun glass storage compartment ($1,550). JL4 Stabilitrak for ESC ($495). N26 chrome wheels for ETC ($795). N30 wood steering wheel ($395). QC8 chrome wheels for ESC ($795). QDC P235/60ZR16 Goodyear Eagle LS tires for ETC ($250). U1S 12-disc trunk-mounted disc changer ($595). UG1 programmable garage door opener ($107). UM5 Bose sound system with cassette player, AM/FM stereo, digital signal processing, single-slot CD player, weather band, radio data system (RDS), theftlock and Bose amplified speaker system for ESC ($1,219). WA7 comfort and convenience package for ESC, includes 4-way lumbar support, memory package and heated front seats ($950).

2001 Cadillac, Catera, sedan

In 2001, the Cadillac LMP car raced at Le Mans in France.

SEVILLE OPTIONS

1SB Seville SLS Convenience package including heated front and rear seats and power tilt and telesope steering wheel ($1,100, but not with 1SC). 1SC Seville SLS Premium Luxury package, including memory package, heated front and rear seats, power tilt and telesope steering wheel, Bose 4.0 stereo with CD and cassette, 16-inch chrome wheels and ultrasonic parking assist ($3,140). 1SD Seville STS Luxury package includes Bose 4.0 stereo with CD and cassette, 16-inch chrome wheels, wood trim package, wood steering wheel and wood-trimmed gearshift knob ($1,985, but not available with 1SE or 1SF). 1SE Seville STS Premium Luxury package, including Bose 4.0 stereo with CD and cassette, 17-inch chrome wheels, ultrasonic parking assist, wood trim package, P235/55R17 Goodyear Eagle LS tires, high-intensity-discharge headlights and tire pressure monitoring, not available with 1SD or 1SF ($2,930). 1SF Seville STS Premium Luxury package, including Bose 4.0 stereo with CD and cassette, 17-inch chrome wheels, ultrasonic parking assist, wood trim package, wood steering wheel, wood gearshifter, P235/55R17 Goodyear Eagle LS tires, high-intensity-discharge headlights and tire pressure monitoring and portable hands-free cell phone, not available with 1SE or 1SD ($6,400). 86U Crimson Pearl paint ($650). 93U White Diamond paint ($650). CF5 sun roof with express open ($1,550). K05 engine block heater ($35). N30 wood trim package, includes wood steering wheel and gearshifter ($595 and requires 1SB or 1SC). PX2 16-inch chrome wheels for Seville SLS ($795). QWM P235/55WR17 Goodyear Eagle LS tires for STS ($250 and 1SE or 1SF required). U1Z 6-disc console-mounted disc changer ($595). U45 Bose 4.0 sound system with infotainment radio, includes AM/FM stereo cassette, weather band, digital signal processing, radio data system, personal digital assistant (e-mail), text messaging, remote vehicle control, Theftlock and eight speakers ($1,995 and requires UV8 or 1SF). UD7 ultrasonic rear parking assist ($295). UM5 Bose sound system with cassette player, AM/FM stereo, digital signal processing, single-slot CD player, weather band, radio data system (RDS), auto volume control, theftlock, Bose 425-watts 4.0 music system and eight Bose speakers ($950 and not available with UM9). UV8 portable integrated hands-free cell phone ($675). UY4 On Board Navigation for Seville SLS ($2,945). UY4 On Board Navigation for Seville STS ($1,995).

HISTORICAL

Cadillac, based at 100 Renaissance Center in downtown Detroit, was now headed by general manager Mark R. LaNeve. Model-year production of 130,143 cars was counted. Calendar-year production included 1,424 new 2002 CTS models, 8,171 Eldorados, 98,420 DeVilles and 25,421 Sevilles for a total of 133,436 units. Calendar-year sales came to 140,267 units, which was a 1.7 percent share of the total U.S. market. The total included 9,764 Cateras, 95,354 DeVilles, 9,859 Eldorados and 25,290 Sevilles.

2001 Cadillac, Eldorado, Touring Coupe

2002

OVERVIEW

The Catera was gone. New for 2002 was a long list of minor refinements for DeVille full-size luxury sedans ranging from suspension improvements to new electronics systems and upgraded sound systems. For the Lansing-built Eldorado the only real revisions were changed engine oil specifications and extended oil change intervals. Eldorado output ended in March 2002. The Seville received new badging, some new space-age electronics and the extended oil change arrangement. Later in the year came two new body colors and communication system upgrades to accommodate cellular integration and XM Satellite Radio. The biggest 2002 news was a 2003 model bowing in the spring. The CTS replaced the over-age Catera sedan. Being technically a 2003 car, it is covered in the next section. However, Cadillac did build 661 as early as November 2001, 763 in December 2001 and 47,072 in calendar-year 2002.

I.D. DATA

The 17-symbol serial number was located on top of the instrument panel, where it was visible through the windshield. The first symbol 1=U.S.-built vehicle. The second symbol G=General Motors. The third symbol 6=Cadillac. (Together the first three symbols were now called the World Make Identifier and were the same for all Cadillacs). The fourth symbol indicated car line/the fifth symbol indicated series as follows: E/L=Eldorado, E/T=Eldorado Touring, K/D=DeVille, K/E=DeVille Luxury, K/F=DeVille Touring Sedan, K/S=Seville (SLS), K/Y=Seville Touring Sedan (STS). The sixth symbol indicated body style: 1=two-door Coupe/Sedan GM/Fisher Style No. 57, 5=four-door Sedan GM/Fisher style no. 69. The seventh symbol indicated the type of restraint system: 2=Manual belts with front airbags, 4=Automatic belts with front and side airbags, 7=Manual belts with front and side airbags and rear side air bags. The eighth symbol identified the engine: Y=LD8 4.6L V-8 and 9=L37 4.6L V-8. The ninth symbol was a check digit. The 10th symbol indicated model year: 2=2002. The 11th symbol indicates the GM assembly plant: B=Lansing, Michigan, U=Hamtramck, Michigan. The next group of numbers was the sequential production code starting with 100001. The Fisher Body tag on the cowl, under the hood included additional information.

DEVILLE-SERIES 6K/D-V-8

A new DVD-based navigation system incorporating voice recognition technology was optional on all DeVilles. The

Above: **2002 Cadillac, DeVille sedan**

screen on the system could even be used to view movies. Also optional was XM Satellite Radio with up to 100 subscription channels available across the country. A new phone integration kit permitted hands-free operation of cell phones. Oil change specifications were upgraded and oil-change intervals were extended to 12,500 miles. Also new were express-up front windows, dual-stage air bag inflators and revised badging. Standard equipment included a 275-hp 4.6-liter DOHC 32-valve V-8, a four-speed electronic overdrive transmission, front-wheel drive, 16 x 7-inch alloy wheels, P225/60SR16 mud-and-snow tires, a spacesaver spare tire on a steel spare wheel, 4-wheel independent suspension, a front stabilizer bar, a rear stabilizer bar, a self-leveling suspension, ventilated front disc/solid rear disc ABS brakes, a traction-control system, side-mounted air bags, rear door child safety locks, child seat anchors, a trunk interior emergency release, safety belts, front headrests, rear headrests, a remote anti-theft system, an engine immobilizer, daytime running lights, dusk-sensing headlights, variable-intermittent windshield wipers, a rear window defogger, a cloth split-bench front seat with pass-through style center storage armrest, remote power door locks, four 1-touch power windows, heated power-operated outside rearview mirrors (with electrochromatic auto-dimming driver's mirror), a full-featured AM/FM 8-speaker sound system with cassette and CD players, a grid-type diversity antenna, cruise control, speed-proportional power tilt steering with redundant controls on steering wheel, a remote trunk lid release, front door pockets, front seat back storage, a cargo net, retained accessory power, three-zone climate control, an auto-dimming inside rearview mirror, dual illuminating vanity mirrors, a leather-wrapped steering wheel, front and rear floor mats, a clock, a low-fuel monitor, a compass and the OnStar telecommunications service.

DEVILLE—SERIES 6K/D—V-8

Model Number	Body/Style No.	Body Type & Seating	Factory Price	Shipping Weight	Production Total
K/D	5	4D Sedan	42,590	3,978	Note 1

Note 1: DeVille production totaled 91,006 with no further breakout available.

DEVILLE LUXURY (DHS)-SERIES 6K/E-V-8

Standard equipment for the DeVille High-luxury Sedan (DHS) was based on DeVille features, plus the following substitutions or additions: 16 x 7-inch chrome cast-aluminum wheels, variable-intermittent rain-sensing windshield wipers, 8-way power heated front seats with adjustable lumbar support, a heated rear seat, leather upholstery, Bose premium sound system, a tilt-and-telescope steering wheel, easy-entry rear seat access, a leather-and-wood steering wheel and memory settings (seats, wheel and mirrors) for two.

DEVILLE LUXURY (DHS) — SERIES 6K/E—V-8

Model Number	Body/Style No.	Body Type & Seating	Factory Price	Shipping Weight	Production Total
K/E	5	4D Sedan	47,250	4,049	Note 2

Note 2: See Note 1 above.

DEVILLE TOURING SEDAN (DTS)-SERIES 6K/E-V-8

The standard equipment list for the DeVille Touring Sedan (DTS) started at the DHS level and the following features were added or substituted: a 300-hp Northstar V-8, the Auto Ride Control active suspension system, an adaptive auto-leveling suspension, an electronic stability system, an underhood light, 17 x 7.5 silver alloy wheels, P235/55HR17 performance A/S black sidewall tires, 40-40 front bucket seats with heated cushions, a heated rear bench seat with fixed headrests, a leather-wrapped tilt steering wheel and a full-length center console.

DEVILLE TOURING SEDAN (DTS)—SERIES 6K/F — V-8

Model Number	Body/Style No.	Body Type & Seating	Factory Price	Shipping Weight	Production Total
K/F	5	4D Sedan	47,250	4,047	Note 3

Note 3: See Note 1 above.

ELDORADO SPORT COUPE (ESC)-SERIES 6E/L-V-8

In its last half year of existence, the Eldorado had no real changes other than extended oil life intervals. Standard equipment included a 275-hp 4.6-liter DOHC 32-valve V-8, a four-speed electronic overdrive transmission, front-wheel drive, 16 x 7-inch alloy wheels, P225/60SR16 all-season tires, a spacesaver spare tire on a steel spare wheel, 4-wheel independent suspension, a front stabilizer bar, a rear stabilizer bar, a self-leveling suspension, ventilated front disc/solid rear disc ABS brakes, a traction-control system, child seat anchors, a trunk interior emergency release, safety belts, front headrests, a remote anti-theft system, an engine immobilizer, daytime running lights, dusk-sensing headlights, variable-intermittent windshield wipers, a rear window defogger, 8-way power heated leather front bucket seats with adjustable lumbar support, a leather rear bench seat with folding storage-type center armrest, rear seat heating ducts, remote power door locks, 1-touch power windows, heated power-operated outside rearview mirrors (with electrochromatic auto-dimming

2002 Cadillac, DeVille sedan

driver's mirror), a full-featured AM/FM 6-speaker sound system with cassette and CD players, a power antenna, cruise control, speed-proportional power tilt steering with redundant controls on steering wheel, a remote trunk lid release, front door pockets, front seat back storage, a cargo net, a front center console with leather trim and storage provisions, retained accessory power, dual-zone climate control, an auto-dimming inside rearview mirror, front and rear reading lights, dual illuminating vanity mirrors, a leather-wrapped steering wheel, wood instrument panel trim, wood-and-leather door trim, front and rear floor mats, a clock, an external-termperature display, a low-fuel monitor, a compass and the OnStar telecommunications service.

ELDORADO ESC—SERIES 6E/L—V-8

Model Number	Body/Style No.	Body Type & Seating	Factory Price	Shipping Weight	Production Total
E/L	1	2D Coupe	42,130	3,825	Note 4

Note 4: Eldorado production totaled 7,052 with no further breakout available.

ELDORADO TOURING COUPE (ETC)-SERIES 6E/T-V-8

The more powerful and better-handling Eldorado Touring Coupe (ETC) added or substituted a 300-hp Northstar V-8, an active suspension system, an electronic stability system, rain-sensing windshield wipers, P235/60HR16 tires, a Bose premium brand sound system, wood-and-leather trim on the center console and memorized seat-wheel-mirror settings for two.

ELDORADO ETC—SERIES 6E/T—V-8

Model Number	Body/Style No.	Body Type & Seating	Factory Price	Shipping Weight	Production Total
E/T	1	2D Coupe	45,265	3,856	Note 5

Note 5: See Note 4 above.

SEVILLE LUXURY SEDAN (SLS) - SERIES 6K-V-8

The 2002 Seville had redesigned Cadillac wreath-and-crest badges, the advanced voice-recognition navigation system and stretched oil change intervals. Late-2002 versions were made available in two new exterior colors and came with provisions for cell phones and XM Satellite Radio. Standard equipment included a 275-hp 4.6-liter DOHC 32-valve V-8, a four-speed electronic overdrive transmission, front-wheel drive, 16 x 7-inch

2002 Cadillac, Deville sedan

alloy wheels, P235/60SR16 tires, a spacesaver spare tire on a steel spare wheel, 4-wheel independent suspension, a front stabilizer bar, a rear stabilizer bar, a self-leveling suspension, ventilated front disc/solid rear disc ABS brakes, stability control, front side-mounted air bags, a traction-control system, rear door child safety locks, child seat anchors, a trunk interior emergency release, safety belts, front and rear headrests, a remote anti-theft system, an engine immobilizer, daytime running lights, dusk-sensing headlights, cornering lights, variable-intermittent rain-sensing windshield wipers, a rear window defogger, 10-way power heated leather front bucket seats with adjustable lumbar support, a heated leather rear bench seat with folding storage-type pass-through center armrest, remote power door locks, four 1-touch power windows, heated power-operated outside rearview mirrors (with electrochromatic auto-dimming driver's mirror), a full-featured AM/FM 8-speaker sound system with cassette and CD players, a diversity antenna, cruise control, speed-proportional power tilt steering with redundant controls on steering wheel, a remote trunk lid release, front door pockets, front seat back storage, a cargo net, a front center console with storage provisions, a universal remote transmitter, retained accessory power, triple-zone climate control, an auto-dimming inside rearview mirror, front and rear reading lights, dual illuminating vanity mirrors, a leather-wrapped steering wheel, front and rear floor mats, a clock, an external-temperature display, a low-fuel monitor, a compass and the OnStar telecommunications service.

SEVILLE SLS—SERIES 6K/S—V-8

Model Number	Body/Style No.	Body Type & Seating	Factory Price	Shipping Weight	Production Total
K/S	1	4D Sedan	44,039	3,970	Note 6

Note 6: Seville production totaled 25,160 with no further breakout available.

SEVILLE TOURING SEDAN (STS)- SERIES 6K/Y-V-8

The more powerful Seville Touring Sedan (STS) gave buyers a choice between rides that were either cushier or more sporting. Even optional massaging lumbar seats were available in the STS. The STS's Northstar V-8 churned out 300 hp. It was also linked to the 4T80-E electronically controlled four-speed automatic transmission. In addition to or in place of ESC equipment, the ETC included additional exterior lighting, a premium sound system, a leather-wrapped gearshifter, a two-settings memory driver's seat, an easy access rear seat and a power tilt-telescopic leather-wrapped steering wheel.

SEVILLE STS – SERIES 6K/Y – V-8

Model Number	Body/Style No.	Body Type & Seating	Factory Price	Shipping Weight	Production Total
K/Y	1	4D Sedan	49,345	4,001	Note 7

Note 7: See Note 6 above.

ENGINE

DE VILLE, DEVILLE LUXURY, ELDORADO ESC, SEVILLE SLS BASE V-8

Northstar Overhead valve. Dual overhead cam. Aluminum block with cast iron liners. Aluminum cylinder heads. Displacement: 279 cid (4.6 liters). Bore and Stroke: 3.66 x 3.31 inches. Compression ratio: 10.0:1. Net brake hp: 275 at 5600 rpm. Taxable hp: 42.90. Net torque: 300 at 4000 rpm. Direct acting hydraulic tappets. Induction: Tuned port injection. VIN Code: 9. Option Code L37. Built by Cadillac.

DE VILLE STS, ELDORADO ETC, SEVILLE STS SEDAN BASE V-8

Northstar Overhead valve. Dual overhead cam. Aluminum block with cast iron liners. Aluminum cylinder heads. Displacement: 279 cid (4.6 liters). Bore and Stroke: 3.66 x 3.31 inches. Compression ratio: 10.3:1. Net brake hp: 300 at 6000 rpm. Taxable hp: 42.90. Net torque: 295 at 4400 rpm. Direct acting hydraulic tappets. Induction: Tuned port injection. VIN Code: Y. Option Code LD8. Built by Cadillac.

CHASSIS

(DeVille) Wheelbase: 115.3 inches. Overall Length: 207.2 inches. Height: 56.7 inches. Width: 74.5 inches. Front Tread: 62.7 inches. Rear Tread: 62.2 inches. Standard Tires: P225/60SR16.

(DeVille DHS) 115.3 inches. Overall Length: 207.2 inches. Height: 56.7 inches. Width: 74.5 inches. Front Tread: 62.7 inches. Rear Tread: 62.2 inches. Standard Tires: P225/60SR16.

(DeVille DTS) 115.3 inches. Overall Length: 207.2 inches. Height: 56.7 inches. Width: 74.5 inches. Front Tread: 62.7 inches. Rear Tread: 62.2 inches. Standard Tires: P235/55HR17.

(Seville SLS) Wheelbase: 112.2 inches. Overall Length: 201 inches. Height: 55.7 inches. Width: 75 inches. Front Tread: 62.7 inches. Rear Tread: 62.3 inches. Standard Tires: P235/60SR16.

(Seville STS) Wheelbase: 112.2 inches. Overall Length: 201 inches. Height: 55.4 inches. Width: 75 inches. Front Tread: 62.7 inches. Rear Tread: 62.3 inches. Standard Tires: P235/60SR16.

(Eldorado ESC) Wheelbase: 108 inches. Overall Length: 200.6 inches. Height: 53.6 inches. Width: 75.5 inches. Front Tread: 60.9 inches. Rear Tread: 60.9 inches. Standard Tires: P225/60SR16.

(Eldorado ETC) Wheelbase: 108 inches. Overall Length: 200.6 inches. Height: 53.6 inches. Width: 75.5 inches. Front Tread: 60.9 inches. Rear Tread: 60.9 inches. Standard Tires: P235/60HR16.

TECHNICAL

Transmission: (DeVille, Eldorado, Seville) 4T80-E electronically controlled four-speed automatic overdrive (includes viscous torque converter clutch), Steering: (DeVille, Eldorado, Seville) Power-assisted rack-and-pinion, Magnasteer. Front Suspension: (DeVille/DHS, Eldorado ESC) Independent MacPherson strut-type with coil springs and stabilizer bar, (DeVille Concours, Eldorado ETC, Seville SLS, Seville STS) Independent MacPherson strut-type with coil springs, stabilizer bar and electronic continuously variable road sensing suspension. Rear Suspension: (DeVille/DHS, Eldorado ESC) Fully independent, short/long arm, rear shock with airlift and stabilizer bar with automatic level control, (DeVille DTS, Eldorado ETC) Fully independent, coil springs, short/long arm and stabilizer bar with automatic level control and electronic continuously variable road sensing suspension, (Seville SLS, Seville STS) Independent, multi-link, aluminum control arms, lateral toe links, coil springs, stabilizer bar with automatic level control, StabiliTrak and electronic continuously variable road sensing suspension. Brakes: (DeVille, Eldorado) Power assisted front and rear disc with Delco-Bosch anti-lock braking system, (Seville) power front and rear disc with four-channel anti-lock braking system and road texture detection. Body Construction: (all) Integral body-frame. Fuel Tank: (DeVille) 18.5 gallons, (Eldorado) 19.0 gallons, (Seville) 18.5 gallons.

OPTIONS

DE VILLE OPTIONS

86U Crimson Pearl paint ($650). 93U White Diamond paint ($650). AC9 adaptive front seats for either model, requires comfort-and-convenience package ($995). AW9 rear seat side air bags ($295). CF5 sun roof with express open ($1,550). N30 wood trim package for DTS, including woodgrained steering wheel and shift knob ($595). N94 17-inch chrome wheels for DTS ($795). QC6 chrome wheels for base DeVille ($795). R6M New Jersey surcharge (no cost). U1Z glovebox-mounted 6-disc CD changer ($595). U2K XM Satellite Radio ($295). U3R Advanced Vehicle Navigation system ($1,995). UV2 night vision system, requires safety-and-security option ($2,250). UV8 cellular integration package ($325). WA7 comfort and convenience package for base DeVille, includes four-way power lumbar support, memory package, trunk mat and heated seats ($1,095). WA8 safety and security package for Base DeVille, includes ultrasonic rear parking assist and 3-channel garage door opener ($550). WA8 safety and

security package for DeVille DHS, includes StabiliTrak, ultrasonic rear parking assist and 3-channel garage door opener ($895). WA9 Premium Luxury package for DTS, includes rear side air bags, memory package, trunk mat, deck lid tie-down, wood-trimmed steering wheel, wood-trimmed gear selector, power tilt-and-telescope steering wheel, ultrasonic rear parking assist and 3-channel programmable garage door opener ($1,985).

ELDORADO OPTIONS

1SA base equipment group, includes vehicle with standard equipment (no cost). 1SB Luxury package for ESC, includes StabiliTrack, wood steering wheel, 16-inch seven-spoke chrome wheels, and full-featured Bose sound system ($2,900). 1SC Luxury package for ETC, includes 16-inch seven-spoke chrome wheels and 12-disc CD changer ($1,390). 86U Crimson Pearl paint ($650). 93U White Diamond paint ($650). CF5 sun roof with express open, deletes sun glass storage compartment ($1,550). FE9 federal emissions override not available with NC7, YF5 or NG1 (no cost). NB8 California and Northeast States emissions override, requires FE9 (no cost). NC7 federal emissions override requires YF5 or NG1 (no cost). NG1 Northest States emissions override, not available with FE9, YF5 or NB8 (no cost). R6M New Jersey costsurcharge, required in New Jersey (no cost). UG1 programmable garage door opener ($107). YF5 California emissions requirements, not available with FE9, NG1 or NB8 (no cost).

SEVILLE OPTIONS

1SA base vehicle package, includes vehicle with standard equipment (no cost). 1SB Seville SLS Luxury package including vehicle with standard equipment, memory settings for two and power tilt-and-telesope steering wheel ($675, but not available with 1SA or 1SC). 1SC Seville SLS Premium Luxury package, including memory package, heated front and rear seats, power tilt and telesope steering wheel, Bose 4.0 stereo with CD and cassette, 16-inch chrome wheels and ultrasonic parking assist ($3,015). 1SD Seville STS Premium Luxury package includes Bose 4.0 stereo with CD and cassette, 16-inch chrome wheels, wood trim package, wood steering wheel and wood-trimmed gearshift knob ($1,985, but not available with 1SE or 1SF). 1SE Seville STS Premium Luxury package, including Bose 4.0 stereo with CD and cassette, 17-inch chrome wheels, ultrasonic parking assist, wood trim package, P235/55R17 Goodyear Eagle LS tires, high-intensity-discharge headlights and tire pressure monitoring, not available with 1SD or 1SF ($2,635). 1SF Seville STS Premium Performance package, including 1SE, integrated hands-free cellular kit, express-open sun roof and advanced voice-recognition vehicle navigation system ($5,305 but not available with 1SA, 1SD or 1SE).

86U Crimson Pearl paint ($650). 93U White Diamond paint ($650). CF5 sun roof with express open ($1,550). K05 engine block heater ($45). P05 16-inch chrome wheels ($795). QWM P235/55WR17 Goodyear Eagle LS tires for STS ($250 and 1SE required). R6M New Jersey surcharge (no cost). U1Z 6-disc console-mounted disc changer ($595). U2K XM Satellite Radio ($295). U3R Advanced Vehicle Navigation system ($1,995). UM5 Bose sound system with cassette player, AM/FM stereo, digital signal processing, single-slot CD player, weather band, radio data system (RDS), auto volume control, theftlock, Bose 425-watts 4.0 music system and eight Bose speakers ($950, but requires 1SB, included in 1SC and not available with UR3). UV8 portable integrated hands-free cell phone kit ($325).

HISTORICAL

Cadillac, based at 100 Renaissance Center in downtown Detroit, was now headed by general manager Mark R. LaNeve. Model-year production of 123,218 DeVilles, Eldorados and Sevilles was counted. Calendar-year production included 47,072 new 2003 CTS models, 2,721 Eldorados, 86,849 DeVilles and 23,428 Sevilles for a total of 160,070 units. Calendar-year sales came to 150,104 units. The total included 244 Cateras and 149,860 domestically-produced Cadillacs. The Escalade SUV, with calendar-year sales of 49,644 units, played a significant role in giving Cadillac a 1.2 percent share of the total U.S. light-vehicle market. This vehicle is, however, beyond the scope of this catalog.

2002 Cadillac, Seville, sedan

2002 Cadillac, DeVille, DHS sedan

2003

OVERVIEW

The all-new CTS sport sedan made its first appearance early in calendar-year 2002 as a 2003 model. It was built in Lansing, Michigan and was the replacement for the German-made Catera. It was the first car to be assembled in GM's all-new Grand River plant. Prices started in the $30,000 range. The 2003 DeVille got a tire-pressure-monitoring system and turn signal repeaters in the outside rearview mirrors as standard features. The base model had redesigned taillights and a new, movable front safety belt attachment. XM Satellite Radio and a DVD navigation system were optional for all DeVilles. The Seville got some new options like XM Satellite Radio and magnetic ride control. Chrome wheels were optional for the Seville STS.

I.D. DATA

The 17-symbol serial number was located on top of the instrument panel, where it was visible through the windshield. The first symbol 1=U.S.-built vehicle. The second symbol G=General Motors. The third symbol 6=Cadillac. (Together the first three symbols were now called the World Make Identifier and were the same for

Above: **2003 Cadillac, DeVille sedan**

all Cadillacs). The fourth symbol indicated carline/the fifth symbol indicated series as follows: D/G=CTS, D/M=CTS, D/R=CTS RH Drive, D/U=CTS RH Drive, K/D=DeVille, K/E=DeVille Luxury, K/F=DeVille Touring Sedan, K/S=Seville (SLS), K/Y=Seville Touring Sedan (STS), Y/V=XLR roadster. The sixth symbol indicated body style: 1=two-door Coupe/Sedan GM/Fisher Style No. 57, 3=convertible/roadster, 5=four-door Sedan GM/Fisher style no. 69. The seventh symbol indicated the type of restraint system: 2=Manual belts with front airbags, 4=Automatic belts with front and side airbags, 7=Manual belts with front and side airbags and rear side air bags. The eighth symbol identified the engine: N=LA3 3.2-liter V-6, Y=LD8 4.6L V-8 and 9=L37 4.6L V-8. The ninth symbol was a check digit. The 10th symbol indicated model year: 3=2003. The 11th symbol indicated the GM assembly plant: B=Lansing, Michigan, U=Hamtramck, Michigan. The next group of numbers was the sequential production code starting with 100001. The Fisher Body tag on the cowl, under the hood included additional information.

CTS-SERIES 6D/G-D/M-D/R-D/U-V-6

The rear-wheel-drive CTS is considered an entry-level sports sedan. It has a radically-style wedge-shaped body that some consider awkward. A bit larger in proportions

than its European competition, the CTS has a roomy interior. The only engine is a 3.2-liter 220-hp 24-valve DOHC V-6 that can be linked to a five-speed manual gearbox or a five-speed automatic transmission. The CTS features a taught ride and precise steering. The CTS comes equipped just one way, but offers two option packages, the first stressing luxury and the second highlighting the handling aspects. Standard equipment included 16 x 7-inch wheels, P225/55HR16 all-season tires, a spacesaver spare tire, 4-wheel independent suspension, a front stabilizer bar, a rear stabilizer bar, ventilated front and rear disc ABS brakes, a traction-control system, front side-mounted air bags, front and rear head air bags, front seat belt pre-tensioners, rear door child safety locks, safety belts, front headrests, rear headrests, an anti-theft system, an engine immobilizer, daytime running lights, dusk-sensing headlights, auto-delay-off headlights, front fog lights, cornering lights, variable-intermittent windshield wipers, a rear window defogger, 8-way power driver's bucket seat, front passenger bucket seat, rear bench seat with folding center armrest, power door locks, two 1-touch power windows, heated power-operated outside rearview mirrors, an AM/FM cassette stereo system with seven speakers, a power diversity antenna, cruise control, power steering, a tilt adjustable steering wheel with audio and cruise controls, front and rear cupholders, a remote trunk lid release, front and rear door pockets, front seat back storage, a cargo net, a front 12-volt power outlet, a front center console with storage, retained accessory power, dual-zone climate control, an auto-dimming inside rearview mirror, front and rear reading lights, dual illuminating vanity mirrors, a leather-wrapped steering wheel, wood-and-leather shift knob trim, front and rear floor mats, a trunk light, a tachometer, a clock, a low-fuel monitor and the OnStar telecommunications service. Upgrading to the Luxury package added a power passenger seat, an audible anti-theft system, a memory package for two, a programmable garage door opener, an electronic voice recorder and wood trim on the steering wheel, shifter and door handles. The Luxury/Sport package added all Luxury options plus, a sport-tuned suspension, 17-inch wheels and tires, speed-sensitive power steering, high-performance brake linings and StabiliTrak.

2003 Cadillac, XLR roadster

CTS—SERIES 6D/G —V-6

Model Number	Body/Style No.	Body Type & Seating	Factory Price	Shipping Weight	Produc
D/G	5	4D Sedan	29,990	3,568	Note 1

Note 1: CTS 2003 model-year production totaled 75,011.

DEVILLE-SERIES 6K/D-V-8

The 2003 DeVille got a new tire-pressure-monitoring system. All models, the right- and left-hand side-view mirrors were now equipped with turn-signal indicators. All DeVilles also had redesigned taillights and a new, movable front safety belt attachment. The onboard navigation system was now an option for the base DeVille. Another new extra was XM Satellite Radio. Additional standard equipment for the base model included a 275-hp 4.6-liter DOHC 32-valve V-8, a four-speed electronic overdrive transmission, front-wheel drive, 16 x 7-inch alloy wheels, 4-wheel independent suspension, a front stabilizer bar, a rear stabilizer bar, a self-leveling suspension, ventilated front disc/solid rear disc ABS brakes, a traction-control system, side-mounted air bags, rear door child safety locks, child seat anchors, a remote anti-theft system, an engine immobilizer, daytime running lights, dusk-sensing headlights, variable-intermittent windshield wipers, a rear window defogger, a cloth split-bench front seat with pass-through style center storage armrest, remote power door locks, four 1-touch power windows, heated power-operated outside rearview mirrors (with electrochromatic auto-dimming driver's mirror), a full-featured AM/FM 8-speaker sound system with cassette and CD players, a grid-type diversity antenna, cruise control, speed-proportional power tilt steering with redundant controls on steering wheel, three-zone climate control, an auto-dimming inside rearview mirror, dual illuminating vanity mirrors, a leather-wrapped steering wheel, a clock, a low-fuel monitor, a compass and the OnStar telecommunications service.

DEVILLE—SERIES 6K/D—V-8

Model Number	Body/Style No.	Body Type & Seating	Factory Price	Shipping Weight	Produc
K/D	5	4D Sedan	44,345	3,984	Note 2

Note 2: DeVille production totaled 82,085 with no further breakout available.

DEVILLE LUXURY (DHS)-SERIES 6K/E-V-8

Standard equipment for the DeVille High-luxury Sedan (DHS) was based on DeVille features, plus the following substitutions or additions: 16 x 7-inch chrome cast-aluminum wheels, variable-intermittent rain-sensing windshield wipers, 8-way power heated front seats with adjustable lumbar support, a heated rear seat, leather upholstery, a Bose premium sound system, a tilt-and-telescope steering wheel, easy-entry rear seat access, a leather-and-wood steering wheel and memory settings (seats, wheel and mirrors) for two drivers.

DEVILLE LUXURY (DHS)–
SERIES 6K/E–V-8

Series No.	Body/Style No.	Body Type & Seating	Factory Price	Shipping Weight	Production Total
K/E	5	4D Sedan	49,995	4,048	Note 3

Note 3: See Note 2 above.

DEVILLE TOURING SEDAN (DTS)-SERIES 6K/E-V-8

The standard equipment list for the DeVille Touring Sedan (DTS) started at the DHS level and the following features were added or substituted: a 300-hp Northstar V-8, the Auto Ride Control active suspension system, an adaptive auto-leveling suspension, an electronic stability system, an underhood light, 17 x 7.5 silver alloy wheels, P235/55HR17 performance A/S black sidewall tires, 40-40 front bucket seats with heated cushions, a heated rear bench seat with fixed headrests, a leather-wrapped tilt steering wheel and a full-length center console.

DEVILLE TOURING SEDAN (DTS) – SERIES 6K/F – V-8

Model Number	Body/Style No.	Body Type & Seating	Factory Price	Shipping Weight	Production Total
K/F	5	4D Sedan	48,995	4,044	Note 4

Note 4: See Note 2 above.

SEVILLE LUXURY SEDAN (SLS)-SERIES 6K-V-8

For 2003 the SLS got a new body-color grille and fog lamps as part of a monochromatic appearance treatment. New options included, you guessed it, XM Satellite Radio and DVD navigation. Standard equipment included a 275-hp 4.6-liter DOHC 32-valve V-8, a four-speed electronic overdrive transmission, front-wheel drive, 16 x 7-inch alloy wheels, 4-wheel independent suspension, a front stabilizer bar, a rear stabilizer bar, a self-leveling suspension, ventilated front disc/solid rear disc ABS brakes, stability control, front side-mounted air bags, a traction-control system, a remote anti-theft system, an engine immobilizer, daytime running lights, dusk-sensing headlights, cornering lights, variable-intermittent rain-sensing windshield wipers, a rear window defogger, 10-way power heated leather front bucket seats with adjustable lumbar support, a heated leather rear bench seat with folding storage-type pass-through center armrest, remote power door locks, four 1-touch power windows, heated power-operated outside rearview mirrors (with electrochromatic auto-dimming driver's mirror), a full-featured AM/FM 8-speaker sound system with cassette and CD players, a diversity antenna, cruise control, speed-proportional power tilt steering with redundant controls on steering wheel, a remote trunk lid release, front door pockets, front seat back storage, a cargo net, a front center console with storage provisions, a universal remote transmitter, retained accessory power, triple-zone climate control, an auto-dimming inside rearview mirror, front and rear reading lights, dual illuminating vanity mirrors, a leather-wrapped steering wheel, front and rear floor

mats, a clock, an external-temperature display, a low-fuel monitor, a compass and the OnStar telecommunications service.

SEVILLE SLS – SERIES 6K/S–V-8

Model Number	Body/Style No.	Body Type & Seating	Factory Price	Shipping Weight	Production Total
K/S	1	4D Sedan	45,395	3,992	Note 5

Note 5: Seville production totaled 19,836 with no further breakout available.

SEVILLE TOURING SEDAN (STS)-SERIES 6K/Y-V-8

The 300-hp Seville Touring Sedan (STS) gave buyers a choice between the soft ride of the SLS and a more sporting ride in the STS. The 300-hp Northstar V-8 was linked to the 4T80-E electronically controlled four-speed automatic transmission. In addition to or in place of SLS equipment, the STS included additional exterior lighting, a premium sound system, a leather-wrapped gearshifter, a two-settings memory driver's seat, an easy access rear seat and a power tilt-telescopic leather-wrapped steering wheel.

SEVILLE STS–SERIES 6K/Y–V-8

Model Number	Body/Style No.	Body Type & Seating	Factory Price	Shipping Weight	Production Total
K/Y	1	4D Sedan	51,695	4,027	Note 6

Note 6: See Note 5 above.

ENGINE

CTS BASE V-6

Dual overhead cam V-6. Displacement: 3175 cc (3.2 liters). Bore and Stroke: 3.44 (87.5 mm) x 3.46 (88.0) mm. Compression ratio: 10.0:1. Net brake hp: 220 at 6000 rpm. Net torque: 300 at 3400 rpm. Sequential fuel injection. VIN Code: N. Option Code LA3. Built by Cadillac.

DE VILLE, DEVILLE LUXURY, SEVILLE SLS BASE V-8

Northstar Overhead valve. Dual overhead cam. Aluminum block with cast iron liners. Aluminum cylinder heads. Displacement: 279 cid (4.6 liters). Bore and Stroke: 3.66 x 3.31 inches. Compression ratio: 10.0:1. Net brake hp: 275 at 5600 rpm. Taxable hp: 42.90. Net torque: 300 at 4000 rpm. Direct acting hydraulic tappets. Induction: Tuned port injection. VIN Code: 9. Option Code L37. Built by Cadillac.

DE VILLE STS, SEVILLE STS SEDAN BASE V-8

Northstar Overhead valve. Dual overhead cam. Aluminum block with cast iron liners. Aluminum cylinder heads. Displacement: 279 cid (4.6 liters). Bore and Stroke: 3.66 x 3.31 inches. Compression ratio: 10.3:1. Net brake hp: 300 at 6000 rpm. Taxable hp: 42.90. Net torque: 295 at 4400 rpm. Direct acting hydraulic tappets. Induction: Tuned

port injection. VIN Code: Y. Option Code LD8. Built by Cadillac.

CHASSIS

(CTS) Wheelbase: 113.4 inches. Overall Length: 190.1 inches. Height: 56.7 inches. Width: 70.6 inches. Standard Tires: P225/55HR16 all-season.

(DeVille) Wheelbase: 115.3 inches. Overall Length: 207.2 inches. Height: 56.7 inches. Width: 74.5 inches. Front Tread: 62.7 inches. Rear Tread: 62.2 inches. Standard Tires: P225/60SR16.

(DeVille DHS) 115.3 inches. Overall Length: 207.2 inches. Height: 56.7 inches. Width: 74.5 inches. Front Tread: 62.7 inches. Rear Tread: 62.2 inches. Standard Tires: P225/60SR16.

(DeVille DTS) 115.3 inches. Overall Length: 207.2 inches. Height: 56.7 inches. Width: 74.5 inches. Front Tread: 62.7 inches. Rear Tread: 62.2 inches. Standard Tires: P235/55HR17.

(Seville SLS) Wheelbase: 112.2 inches. Overall Length: 201 inches. Height: 55.7 inches. Width: 75 inches. Front Tread: 62.7 inches. Rear Tread: 62.3 inches. Standard Tires: P235/60SR16.

(Seville STS) Wheelbase: 112.2 inches. Overall Length: 201 inches. Height: 55.4 inches. Width: 75 inches. Front Tread: 62.7 inches. Rear Tread: 62.3 inches. Standard Tires: P235/60SR16.

TECHNICAL

Transmission: (CTS) Five-speed manual transmission standard, five-speed automatic transmission optional. (DeVille, Seville) 4T80-E electronically controlled four-speed automatic overdrive (includes viscous torque converter clutch). Steering: (CTS) Power-assisted rack-and-pinion, (DeVille, Seville) Power-assisted rack-and-pinion, Magnasteer. Front Suspension: (DeVille/DHS) Independent MacPherson strut-type with coil springs and stabilizer bar, (DeVille Concours, Seville SLS, Seville STS) Independent MacPherson strut-type with coil springs, stabilizer bar and electronic continuously variable road sensing suspension. Rear Suspension: (DeVille/DHS) Fully independent, short/long arm, rear shock with airlift and stabilizer bar with automatic level control, (DeVille DTS) Fully independent, coil springs, short/long arm and stabilizer bar with automatic level control and electronic continuously variable road sensing suspension, (Seville SLS, Seville STS) Independent, multi-link, aluminum control arms, lateral toe links, coil springs, stabilizer bar with automatic level control, StabiliTrak and electronic

continuously variable road sensing suspension. Brakes: (DeVille) Power assisted front and rear disc with Delco-Bosch anti-lock braking system, (Seville) power front and rear disc with four-channel anti-lock braking system and road texture detection. Body Construction: (all) Integral body-frame. Fuel Tank: (DeVille) 18.5 gallons, (Seville) 18.5 gallons.

OPTIONS

CTS OPTIONS

4U premium paint ($650). 1SA CTS standard package (no cost). 1SB CTS Luxury package ($2,000). 1SC CTS Luxury Sport package ($3,500). AM9 split-folding rear seat ($300). CF5 express-open sun roof ($1,100). K05 engine block heater ($60). KA1 heated front seats ($400). M82 5-speed automatic transmission ($1,200). PX0 16-inch bright-finish alloy wheels ($795). TT6 high-intensity discharge headlights ($500). U2S Bose sound system with 6-CD changer ($1,275). UV2 Bose sound system with 6-CD changer and CD navigation ($2,700).

DE VILLE OPTIONS

86U Crimson Pearl paint ($650). 93U White Diamond paint ($650). AC9 adaptive front seats for either model, requires comfort-and-convenience package ($995). AW9 rear seat side air bags ($295). CF5 sun roof with express open ($1,550). N30 wood trim package for DTS, including woodgrained steering wheel and shift knob ($595). N94 17-inch chrome wheels for DTS ($795). QC6 chrome wheels for base DeVille ($795). R6M New Jersey surcharge (no cost). U1Z glovebox-mounted 6-disc CD changer ($595). U2K XM Satellite Radio ($295). U3R Advanced Vehicle Navigation system ($1,995). UV2 night vision system, requires safety-and-security option ($2,250). UV8 cellular integration package ($325). WA7 comfort and convenience package for base DeVille, includes four-way power lumbar support, memory package, trunk mat and heated seats ($1,095). WA8 safety and security package for Base DeVille, includes ultrasonic rear parking assist and 3-channel garage door opener ($550). WA8 safety and security package for DeVille DHS, includes StabiliTrak, ultrasonic rear parking assist and 3-channel garage door opener ($895). WA9 Premium Luxury package for DTS, includes rear side air bags, memory package, trunk mat, deck lid tie-down, wood-trimmed steering wheel, wood-trimmed gear selector, power tilt-and-telescope steering wheel, ultrasonic rear parking assist and 3-channel programmable garage door opener ($1,985).

SEVILLE OPTIONS

1SA base vehicle package, includes vehicle with standard equipment (no cost). 1SB Seville SLS Luxury package including vehicle with standard equipment, memory settings for two and power tilt-and-telescope steering

wheel ($675, but not available with 1SA or 1SC). 1SC Seville SLS Premium Luxury package, including memory package, heated front and rear seats, power tilt and telesope steering wheel, Bose 4.0 stereo with CD and cassette, 16-inch chrome wheels and ultrasonic parking assist ($3,015). 1SD Seville STS Premium Luxury package includes Bose 4.0 stereo with CD and cassette, 16-inch chrome wheels, wood trim package, wood steering wheel and wood-trimmed gearshift knob ($1,985, but not available with 1SE or 1SF). 1SE Seville STS Premium Luxury package, including Bose 4.0 stereo with CD and cassette, 17-inch chrome wheels, ultrasonic parking assist, wood trim package, P235/55R17 Goodyear Eagle LS tires, high-intensity-discharge headlights and tire pressure monitoring, not available with 1SD or 1SF ($2,635). 1SF Seville STS Premium Performance package, including 1SE, integrated hands-free cellular kit, express-open sun roof and advanced voice-regiognition vehicle navigation system ($5,305 but not available with 1SA, 1SD or 1SE). 86U Crimson Pearl paint ($650). 93U White Diamond paint ($650). CF5 sun roof with express open ($1,550). K05 engine block heater ($45). P05 16-inch chrome wheels ($795). QWM P235/55WR17 Goodyear Eagle LS tires for STS ($250 and 1SE required). R6M New Jersey surcharge (no cost). U1Z 6-disc console-mounted disc changer ($595). U2K XM Satellite Radio ($295). U3R Advanced Vehicle Navigation system ($1,995). UM5 Bose sound system with cassette player, AM/FM stereo, digital signal processing, single-slot CD player, weather band, radio data system (RDS), auto volume control, theftlock, Bose 425-watts 4.0 music system and eight Bose speakers ($950, but requires 1SB, included in 1SC and not available with UR3). UV8 portable integrated hands-free cell phone kit ($325).

HISTORICAL

Cadillac celebrated its 100th anniversary in 2003. In honor of this occassion, Krause Publications joined with Cadillac to produce the book *Cadillac: 100 Years of Innovation* authored by Angelo Van Bogart. Model-year production of 176,932 CTS, DeVille and Seville models was counted. Calendar-year production included 59,250 CTS sedans, 82,965 DeVille sedans, 15,619 Seville sedans and 1,731 XLR roadsters for a total of 159,565 units. Calendar-year sales came to 151,298 units. The total included 15 imported cars and 151,283 domestically-produced Cadillacs. The Escalade SUV, with calendar-year sales of 64,792 units, again played a significant role in Cadillac's total sales figure and helped the company earn a 1.3 percent share of the total U.S. light-vehicle market.

A new generation of 21st century-styled Cadillacs debuted in 2003.

2004

OVERVIEW

For the 2004 model year, the breakthrough era of Cadillac vehicles reached full flight with two all-new entries in new segments-the XLR luxury roadster and SRX luxury utility (which is not covered in this catalog since it qualifies as a light truck). In addition, 2004 ushered in new varieties of some of Cadillac's most significant products, with the CTS-V performance version, the new Platinum version of the Escalade ESV (another SUV) and a special armored version of the DeVille, available in both standard sedan and stretch models. "This is a truly historic time for Cadillac," said Mark LaNeve, Cadillac general manager. "The complete Cadillac lineup for the 2004 model year is more compelling than at any time in the past 50 years. The product renaissance we began several years ago is now in full force."

I.D. DATA

The 17-symbol serial number was located on top of the instrument panel, where it was visible through the windshield. The first symbol 1=U.S.-built vehicle. The second symbol G=General Motors. The third symbol 6=Cadillac. (Together the first three symbols were now called the World Make Identifier and were the same for all Cadillacs). The fourth symbol indicated carline/the fifth symbol indicated series as follows: D/M=CTS, D/N=CTS-V, D/R CTS RH Drive, K/D=DeVille, K/E=DeVille Luxury, K/F=DeVille Touring Sedan, K/S=Seville (SLS), K/Y=Seville Touring Sedan (STS), Y/V=XLR roadster. The sixth symbol indicated body style: 1=two-door Coupe/Sedan GM/Fisher Style No. 57, 3=convertible/roadster, 5=four-door Sedan GM/Fisher style no. 69. The seventh symbol indicated the type of restraint system: 2=Manual belts with front airbags, 4=Automatic belts with front and side airbags, 7=Manual belts with front and side airbags and rear side air bags. The eighth symbol identified the engine: A=LH2 4.6-liter SFI V-8, M=LY9 2.6-liter MFI V-6, N=LA3 3.2-liter MFI V-6, S=LS6 5.7-liter SFI V-8, Y=LD8 4.6-liter SFI V-8, 7=LY7 3.6-liter SFI V-6, 9=L37 4.6-liter SFI V-8. The ninth symbol was a check digit. The 10th symbol indicated model year: 4=2004. The 11th symbol indicated the GM assembly plant: B=Lansing, Michigan, U=Hamtramck, Michigan, 5=Bowling Green, Kentucky. The next group of numbers was the sequential production code starting with 100001. The Fisher Body tag on the cowl, under the hood included additional information.

Above: **2004 Cadillac, Seville, SLS sedan**

XLR - SERIES 6Y/V-V-8

The 2004 Cadillac XLR roadster could trace its roots to the 1999 Evoq concept car. Cadillac stunned the automotive world with the audacious Evoq, which was unveiled at the North American International Auto Show in Detroit. The first production-type XLR was built in the spring of 2003 on a dedicated assembly line at General Motors' Bowling Green Assembly Plant in Bowling Green, Kentucky. Shipments to Cadillac dealers were set for midyear 2003. Replete with a dynamic design, advanced technology and a unique blend of luxury and performance, the Cadillac XLR brought a striking new presence to the elite international luxury-roadster class. The vehicle underscored its vibrant visual statement with a performance-oriented chassis and structure and an all-new 4.6L Northstar V-8 VVT (variable valve timing) rear-wheel-drive engine. This combination made it the lightest, most powerful vehicle in its class. "The XLR is a luxury roadster with performance car roots," said Jay Spenchian, XLR marketing director. "Beneath its stunning exterior style, XLR has a patented performance car architecture that is ideal for a roadster and serves as a strong foundation for a car designed for great agility and bona fide luxury." Under its skin, the XLR offered a harmonious blend of technologies and materials meant to add pleasure, not complexity, to the driving experience. Innovative features included a heads-up display, adaptive cruise control, Magnetic Ride Control, StabiliTrak, heated and cooled seats, keyless access with push-button start and DVD navigation and entertainment. The XLR was a contemporary expression of Cadillac's heritage of landmark design and advanced technology. Inspired by the design of the stealth fighter airplane in much the same way that Bill Mitchell's tail fin came from the P38 airplane, the sporty XLR took Cadillac performance to an entirely new level. Bold and "edgy," yet elegant and refined, the XLR's crisp linear design created a dramatic presence and modern icon for luxury and performance, while paying tribute to the marque's rich history. The XLR's strong grille represented a modern expression of past Cadillac grille-styling motifs. The vertical headlights, on the other hand, expressed the company's current design philosophy.

2004 Cadillac, XLR roadster

The XLR offered the ultimate convenience of a retractable hard top. Compared to soft-top convertibles, the retractable hardtop was quieter with the top up, more secure and more visually pleasing. Car Top Systems (CTS) GmbH of Germany developed the XLR top. By pushing and holding a single button, the XLR could be converted from a coupe into an open roadster in less than 30 seconds. The top assembly for the XLR was installed as a complete module and contributed to the car's overall structural rigidity. The top structure was crafted of aluminum and magnesium, with composite exterior panels. It featured a heated glass backlight and glass rear-quarter windows. The XLR's interior design epitomized contemporary luxury. Unique eucalyptus wood and striking aluminum accents were combined to provide a luxurious and inviting environment. The gauges were designed in conjunction with the Italian luxury brand Bulgari. The XLR's Northstar V-8 VVT engine was a 90-degree, DOHC, four-valves-per-cylinder engine featuring an aluminum block and cylinder heads and a valve train configuration with roller finger followers. The engine was extensively re-engineered for the luxury roadster and was the Northstar's first adaptation to rear-wheel-drive (RWD) and all-wheel-drive (AWD) configurations. Other Northstar firsts on the XLR included four-cam continuously-variable valve timing (VVT), electronically-controlled, hydraulically-actuated intake and exhaust cam phasers on all four camshafts (for extra control), electronic throttle control (ETC), low-restriction intake and exhaust manifolds, low-restriction cylinder head ports, close-coupled catalytic converters mounted directly adjacent to the exhaust manifolds and a new air-induction system that was redesigned for enhanced capacity and noise attenuation. It also used a more powerful engine control module (ECM) and included a high-speed local area network (LAN) communication system dedicated to engine and transmission control. A new engine-mounting system was employed and a more rigid block structure help provide outstanding operating smoothness and quietness. The V-8 provided smooth, refined performance throughout its entire operating range. Though quiet, it was tuned to give the driver feedback from the environment. It operated even more cleanly and efficiently than its predecessors, with excellent reliability and durability. The XLR featured the first longitudinal application of the 4.6L Northstar V-8, which was mated to a Hydra-Matic 5L50-E five-speed automatic transmission. Developed to manage the high torque and horsepower of the XLR engine, it represented one of the most technologically-advanced transmissions on any highway or autobahn in the industry. The 5L50-E transmission was a modified version of the Hydra-Matic 5L40-E transmission used in the Cadillac CTS. Another advantage of Cadillac's roadster was the rear mounting of the transmission. This helped give the XLR a virtual 50/50

front-to-rear weight distribution for superior balance and also provided a roomy footwell. The XLR's backbone, upon which the car's dynamic capabilities rested, was based on GM's new performance-car architecture. This unique and patented structure was comprised of steel hydroformed perimeter frame rails, an enclosed structural "tunnel," an aluminum cockpit structure and balsa-cored composite floors. Providing rigidity without bulk and exceptional resistance to torsional and bending forces, this architecture was the basis for the XLR's outstanding ride-and-handling characteristics. The suspension system used double wishbones at each corner, combined with transverse-mounted, composite leaf springs front and rear. The system was designed to maintain firm control over wheel motion, while delivering a composed and compliant ride quality. During normal driving, the chassis exhibits comfortable and confident handling characteristics, but when pushed harder, the car remains stable and secure with outstanding road holding. The XLR could provide a maximum lateral G-force of more than 0.9. The XLR had Michelin ZP tires with advanced "run flat" technology that eliminated the need for a spare tire, while providing outstanding overall tire performance. The XLR came with Magnetic Ride Control or electronically-controlled, magnetic-fluid-based, real-time damping. The system employed four wheel-to-body displacement sensors to measure wheel motion over the road surface, then adjusted the shock damping at speeds approaching one millisecond, five times faster than previous "real time" damping systems. The system maintains tire contact with the road surface and keeps the body on an even plane, with smooth, well-controlled body motions even during aggressive maneuvers or on uneven road surfaces. The XLR had adaptive cruise control (ACC). ACC uses a radar sensor, mounted at the front of the car, to detect objects in its path. If the lane ahead is clear, the system will maintain the set speed, just like conventional cruise control. When a vehicle is detected in the same lane in front of the car, the system will adjust vehicle speed to help maintain a constant following distance, set by the driver. If a vehicle or object in the path of the car is stationary or moving at significantly slower speed, the system provides visible and audible alerts to the driver. ACC is set by a conventional stalk-mounted control, but is monitored through a graphic representation in the head-up display. One of the XLR's foremost convenience features was Keyless Access. This allowed a driver to keep the key fob in a pocket or purse. The XLR's seats were both heated and cooled in the back and the cushion. A 7-inch color touch screen mounted in the upper center console gave driver and passenger access to DVD navigation, a nine-speaker world-class Bose audio system with a six-CD in-dash changer and digital signal processing modes, XM Satellite Radio (continental U.S. only) and DVD entertainment (available in Park position

only). The XLR also came equipped with OnStar and a head-up display that projected key driver information onto the windshield.

XLR—SERIES 6Y/V—V-8

Model Number	Body/Style No.	Body Type & Seating	Factory Price	Shipping Weight	Production Total
Y/V	3	2D Roadster	76,200	3,647	N/A

CTS 3.2-SERIES 6D/M-D/R-V-6

Fashioned by Cadillac's bold designers and featuring an "edgy" appearance, the first-year CTS racked up strong sales of 37,976 units, well ahead of the 30,000 units projected for 2002-2003. The 2004 CTS featured suspension and interior changes. The re-tuned base suspension featured new shocks and new shock mounts. The interior refinements, included a body-colored center armrest and a color-keyed center console. The instrument cluster got a temperature gauge, bright white lighting and chrome accents on the ashtray. Power adjustable lumbar support was now optional with power seats. The Sport package was now available across the entire model lineup. This package featured newly-designed 17 x 7.5-inch cast-aluminum wheels with a choice of painted or polished finish, Goodyear Eagle RS-A P225/50VR17 all-season tires, StabiliTrak, performance brake linings, variable assist steering and rear load-leveling. Other CTS standard equipment included a 3.2-liter DOHC V-6, a Getrag five-speed manual gearbox, 16 x 7-inch wheels, 4-wheel independent suspension, a front stabilizer bar, a rear stabilizer bar, ventilated front and rear disc ABS brakes, a traction-control system, front side-mounted air bags, front and rear head air bags, an anti-theft system, an engine immobilizer, daytime running lights, dusk-sensing headlights, auto-delay-off headlights, front fog lights, cornering lights, variable-intermittent windshield wipers, a rear window defogger, 8-way power driver's bucket seat, front passenger bucket seat, rear bench seat with folding center armrest, power door locks, two 1-touch power windows, heated power-operated outside rearview mirrors, an AM/FM cassette stereo system with

2004 Cadillac, CTS V-Series, sedan

seven speakers, a power diversity antenna, cruise control, power steering, a tilt adjustable steering wheel with audio and cruise controls, front and rear cupholders, a remote trunk lid release, front and rear door pockets, front seat back storage, a cargo net, a front 12-volt power outlet, a front center console with storage, retained accessory power, dual-zone climate control, a leather-wrapped steering wheel, wood-and-leather shift knob trim, a tachometer, a clock, a low-fuel monitor and the OnStar telecommunications service. Upgrading to the Luxury package added a power passenger seat, an audible anti-theft system, a memory package for two, a programmable garage dor opener, an electronic voice recorder and wood trim on the steering wheel, shifter and door handles. The Luxury/Sport package added all Luxury options plus, a sport-tuned suspension, 17-inch wheels and tires, speed-sensitive power steering, high-performance brake linings and StabiliTrak.

CTS 3.2–SERIES 6D/M–V-6

Model Number	Body/Style No.	Body Type & Seating	Factory Price	Shipping Weight	Production Total
D/M	5	4D Sedan	31,060	3,568	N/A

CTS 3.6 VVT-SERIES 6D/M-D/R-V-6

The already successful CTS sedan got an all-new, more powerful engine that incorporated features and technology packaged to deliver high performance and refinement. This 3.6-liter VVT (variable valve timing) V-6 was available for cars with automatic transmission only. It was the first V-6 to demonstrate a new GM strategy aimed at developing world-class engines with fully contemporary features at a competitive cost structure that permitted use of the engine in a global mix of vehicles. The 3.6-liter global V-6 developed 255 hp (190 kw) at 6200 rpm and 255 lb.-ft. of torque (346 Nm) at 3200 rpm. It came only with the 5L40-E automatic transmission. The adoption of fully-variable valve timing for both intake and exhaust valves provided outstanding flexibility, fuel economy and emissions reduction. Compared to an existing GM 3.2-liter DOHC V-6, the 3.6L V-6 VVT develops 20 percent more peak power, a 13 percent increase in peak torque and a 24 percent increase in torque-integral (the amount of torque available at most points throughout the rpm range). Although minimizing or eliminating all sources of undesirable engine noise was a priority, the interior sound level was carefully optimized to be rich and rewarding. The focus on reducing noise, vibration and harshness (NVH) did not compromise horsepower output. The V-6 VVT featured specially-isolated cam covers to decouple them from vibration created by the combustion process. A structural aluminum oil pan, attached by a full-circle mounting, enhanced bending stiffness and mitigated "drumming" from the oil pan. Polymer-coated piston skirts helped them track more smoothly and quietly

in their bores. Pressure-actuated piston-oil squirters helped cool the pistons, contributing to performance and durability, and helping to minimize typical noises. The well-known "hiss" from the PCV valve was eliminated by using two dissimilar-sized flow-metering holes, while equal-length intake manifold runners minimized half-order noise content. A forged-steel crankshaft ensured the durability required of high-specific-output engines and provided an extra degree of robustness. Flexible oil pan configurations facilitated the engine's adaptability for all drive train layouts. On the CTS models equipped with the new engine, a dual-outlet performance exhaust system was fitted.

CTS 3.6 VVT – SERIES 6D/M – V-6

Model Number	Body/Style No.	Body Type & Seating	Factory Price	Shipping Weight	Production Total
D/M	5	4D Sedan	31,060	3,694	N/A

CTS-V-SERIES 6D/N-V-8

The 2004 CTS-V was Cadillac's ambitious entry into the low-volume, high-performance luxury car niche and was the first GM vehicle to wear the division's V-Series badge. All work for the CTS-V was engineered by the newly-formed GM Performance Division, a unit created as an in-house expertise center formed to develop enthusiast-oriented versions of production models. No engineering, design or assembly functions were outsourced. This made the CTS-V a true all-GM offering. It represented a highly-refined performance sedan designed and engineered for enthusiasts. Based on GM's rear-wheel-drive Sigma architecture–also the foundation for the CTS sedan, SRX luxury utility and coming STS luxury sedan–the CTS-V incorporated a series of high-performance refinements that were tested on the world's most renowned tracks, including Germany's famed Nürburgring. The result was the most powerful production Cadillac ever. It was positioned to compete with the BMW M-series, the Audi S-series and the AMG Mercedes. The CTS-V was engineered with near 50/50 weight distribution and could hit 60 mph in about 4.6 seconds, but it also provided more than raw power. The exterior was revised with purposeful

2004 Cadillac, CTS sedan

enhancements, including seven-spoke 18-inch flangeless wheels, dual investment-cast-stainless-steel exhaust tips, and badging that incorporated the distinctive Cadillac V-Series emblem. Interior revisions included suede seat inserts to hold the driver in place during high-speed maneuvering, accent stitching, driver and passenger adjustable lumbar support, satin chrome accents, and aluminum accents. In order to manage high-output horsepower and torque from the LS6 engine – and to ensure desired noise and vibration characteristics–a host of performance modifications were made. The extremely-robust front and rear suspensions included larger shocks, larger springs, heftier stabilizer bars, performance tuned bushings and strategically placed reinforcements on the larger, hydroformed, front and rear cradles. The extra-robust differential housing optimized performance as well as cooling. Focused engine mountings ensured that the high-output powerplant was optimally supported to minimize idle vibration, ensure optimized tuning of engine mounts and achieve appropriate ride-and-handling characteristics. Performance tuning of the steering system took into account the increased weight of the vehicle, which was approximately 264 lbs. heavier than the base CTS. A steel tower-to-tower brace beefed up the cross-vehicle structure and aided steering response and linearity. A heavy-duty, increased-diameter prop shaft and heavier CV joints helped handle higher torque requirements. A significantly-larger, extremely-robust Nürburgring-tuned Brembo brake system provided world-class braking unmatched in a high-performance luxury car. A dual-exhaust system with larger-diameter pipes ensured minimal back-pressure for engine performance. A tunable, remote-mounted shifter provided better transmission packaging, more precise shift feel and improved noise/vibration characteristics. A dual-mass flywheel reduced the potential for gear and drive-away rattles. A four-channel/four-selection-mode StabiliTrak chassis-control system enabled the driver to switch between four stability settings, including a "less-governed" competition mode for the performance enthusiast. An undercarriage, front-positioned belly pan enhanced aerodynamics and engine cooling and reduced vehicle lift at high speeds. GM's 5.7-liter, overhead valve (OHV) LS6 V-8 went under the hood. The two-valves-per-cylinder power plant delivered some 400-hp at 6000 rpm and 395 lb. ft. of torque at 4800 rpm. The engine – a variant of that found in the Corvette ZO6–was mated with a six-speed manual Tremec T56 (M12) transmission. The LS6 provided the CTS-V with successful, track-proven performance, outstanding reliability and durability and smooth, quiet operation. The LS6 block reduced internal "windage" by managing airflow more efficiently. The over-travel windows allowed air to move more freely between cylinder bays, reducing back pressure and freeing the pistons' downward

movement. The steel billet LS6 camshaft contributed to horsepower gains over previous LS engines. The cam opened the valves faster and higher, allowing more air to flow more quickly in and out of the combustion chambers. To accommodate valve operation with the high-lift cam, the LS6 valve springs were stiffer and sturdier. They were constructed from tightly-wound steel wire for a higher spring rate. A new induction system enabled the CTS-V engine to "breathe" as much as possible. Three inlets in the front of the car (two facing forward and one that channeled air in from the side) routed air directly to the induction box, resulting in increased horsepower. A special composite (glass-reinforced nylon resin) intake manifold on the LS6 was designed for high airflow into the intake ports. Plenum volume was optimized and the intake runners were molded to eliminate dead spots and increase the volume of air flowing to the cylinder heads. The fuel injectors used on the LS6 engine delivered fuel at a rate of 3.55 grams per second. A high-volume mass airflow sensor with integral inlet air temperature sensor increased air-intake volume and enabled the power train control module (PCM) to adjust for optimal performance at any given air temperature. The exhaust manifolds on the CTS-V engine were pointed more downward to permit close-mounting of dual catalytic converters. The manifolds were also configured to permit as much flow as possible into the vehicle's dual-exhaust system to reduce back pressure. The CTS-V dual-exhaust system was constructed of 2.5-inch diameter stainless steel pipe and the catalytic converters were located directly behind the exhaust manifolds. The CTS-V oil pan's deeper sump enabled passage of the steering gear from a location specific to the vehicle. A newly-designed water pump was lighter and more compact. A unique nylon cover with closed-cell foam under the nylon, was fitted over the top of the engine to provide better acoustics. The specifically-designed cover tied into the exterior of the vehicle and featured the Cadillac wreath-and-crest emblem in its center and V-Series identification over each cylinder bank.

CTS-V—SERIES 6D/N—V-8

Model Number	Body/Style No.	Body Type & Seating	Factory Price	Shipping Weight	Production Total
D/N	5	4D Sedan	49,995	3,847	N/A

DEVILLE-SERIES 6K/D-V-8

The 2004 DeVille gained heated and cooled seats and a heated steering wheel for 2004, along with new exterior colors. The DeVille also debuted a state-of-the-art armored edition for 2004. Designed to provide an added level of security, this extraordinary DeVille was intended for executives, officials and others who required a high level of protection as they traveled. The armored DeVille was available in both standard sedan and 8-inch stretch models, with a range of options to suit individual customer

requirements. Details of this model are not included below for security reasons. Additional standard equipment for the base model included a 275-hp 4.6-liter DOHC 32-valve V-8, a four-speed electronic overdrive transmission, front-wheel drive, 16 x 7-inch alloy wheels, 4-wheel independent suspension, a front stabilizer bar, a rear stabilizer bar, a self-leveling suspension, ventilated front disc/solid rear disc ABS brakes, a traction-control system, side-mounted air bags, a remote anti-theft system, an engine immobilizer, daytime running lights, dusk-sensing headlights, variable-intermittent windshield wipers, a rear window defogger, a cloth split-bench front seat with pass-through style center storage armrest, remote power door locks, four 1-touch power windows, heated power-operated outside rearview mirrors (with electrochromatic auto-dimming driver's mirror), a full-featured AM/FM 8-speaker sound system with cassette and CD players, a grid-type diversity antenna, cruise control, speed-proportional power tilt steering with redundant controls on steering wheel, a remote trunk lid release, retained accessory power, three-zone climate control, an auto-dimming inside rearview mirror, dual illuminating vanity mirrors, a leather-wrapped steering wheel, a clock, a low-fuel monitor, a compass and the OnStar telecommunications service.

DEVILLE—SERIES 6K/D—V-8

Model Number	Body/Style No.	Body Type & Seating	Factory Price	Shipping Weight	Production Total
K/D	5	4D Sedan	45,745	3,984	N/A

DEVILLE LUXURY (DHS)-SERIES 6K/E-V-8

Standard equipment for the DeVille High-luxury Sedan (DHS) was based on DeVille features, plus the following substitutions or additions: 16 x 7-inch chrome cast-aluminum wheels, variable-intermittent rain-sensing windshield wipers, 8-way power heated front seats with adjustable lumbar support, a heated rear seat, leather upholstery, a Bose premium sound system, a tilt-and-telescope steering wheel, easy-entry rear seat access, a leather-and-wood steering wheel and memory settings (seats, wheel and mirrors) for two drivers.

2004 Cadillac, XLR roadster

DEVILLE LUXURY (DHS) — SERIES 6K/E — V-8

Model Number	Body/Style No.	Body Type & Seating	Factory Price	Shipping Weight	Production Total
K/E	5	4D Sedan	50,895	4,048	N/A

DEVILLE TOURING SEDAN (DTS) - SERIES 6K/E - V-8

The standard equipment list for the DeVille Touring Sedan (DTS) started at the DHS level and the following features were added or substituted: a 300-hp Northstar V-8, the Auto Ride Control active suspension system, an adaptive auto-leveling suspension, an electronic stability system, an underhood light, 17 x 7.5 silver alloy wheels, P235/55HR17 performance A/S black sidewall tires, 40-40 front bucket seats with heated cushions, a heated rear bench seat with fixed headrests, a leather-wrapped tilt steering wheel and a full-length center console.

DEVILLE TOURING SEDAN (DTS) — SERIES 6K/F — V-8

Series No.	Body/Style No.	Body Type & Seating	Factory Price	Shipping Weight	Production Total
K/F	5	4D Sedan	50,895	4,044	N/A

SEVILLE LUXURY SEDAN (SLS)-SERIES 6K-V-8

The 2004 model year is one of transition for Seville. In May 2003, Cadillac discontinued the STS model to make way for the all-new Sigma-architecture based 2005 STS performance sedan, which was set to start production in the summer of 2004. As a result, the only Seville for the 2004 model year was be the SLS, which was unchanged from the 2003 version. The SLS was scheduled to come to the end of its production run in December 2003. In addition, Cadillac planned to retire the Seville nameplate after the SLS ended production. Standard equipment included a 275-hp 4.6-liter DOHC 32-valve V-8, a four-speed electronic overdrive transmission, front-wheel drive, 16 x 7-inch alloy wheels, 4-wheel independent suspension, a front stabilizer bar, a rear stabilizer bar, a self-leveling suspension, ventilated front disc/solid rear disc ABS brakes, stability control, front side-mounted air bags, a traction-control system, a remote anti-theft system, an engine immobilizer, daytime running lights, dusk-sensing headlights, cornering lights, variable-intermittent rain-sensing windshield wipers, a rear window defogger, 10-way power heated leather front bucket seats with adjustable lumbar support, a heated leather rear bench seat with folding storage-type pass-through center armrest, remote power door locks, four 1-touch power windows, heated power-operated outside rearview mirrors, a full-featured AM/FM 8-speaker sound system with cassette and CD players, a diversity antenna, cruise control, speed-proportional power tilt steering with redundant controls on steering wheel, a universal remote transmitter, retained accessory power, triple-zone climate control, an auto-dimming inside rearview mirror, a leather-wrapped steering wheel, front and rear floor mats, a clock, an

external-termperature display, a low-fuel monitor, a compass and the OnStar telecommunications service.

SEVILLE SLS–SERIES 6K/S–V-8

Model Number	Body/Style No.	Body Type & Seating	Factory Price	Shipping Weight	Production Total
K/S	1	4D Sedan	46,620	3,992	N/A

ENGINE

CTS BASE V-6 (MANUAL TRANSMISSION)

Dual overhead cam V-6. Four valves per cylinder. Cast iron block. Cast aluminum head. Displacement: 194 cid (3.2 liters). Bore and Stroke: 3.44 (87.5 mm) x 3.46 (88.0) mm. Compression ratio: 10.0:1. Net brake hp: 220 at 6000 rpm. Net torque: 220 at 3400 rpm. Returnless sequential fuel injection. VIN Code: N. Option Code LA3. Built by Cadillac.

CTS V-6 (AUTOMATIC TRANSMISSION)

Roller-follower dual overhead cam V-6. Four valves per cylinder. Cast aluminum block. Cast aluminum head. Displacement: 217 cid (3.2 liters). Bore and Stroke: 3.70 (94 mm) x 3.37 (85.0) mm. Compression ratio: 10.2:1. Net brake hp: 255 at 6200 rpm. Net torque: 220 at 3200 rpm. Bosch Motoronic sequential fuel injection. VIN Code: N. Option Code LA3. Built by Cadillac.

XLR ROADSTER BASE NORTHSTAR V-8

Overhead valve. Dual overhead cam. Four valves per cylinder. Four-cam continuously-variable valve timing. Cast-aluminum block. Cast-aluminum cylinder heads. Displacement: 279 cid (4.6 liters). Bore and Stroke: 3.66 x 3.31 inches. Compression ratio: 10.5:1. Net brake hp: 320 at 6400 rpm. Net torque: 310 at 4400 rpm. Direct acting hydraulic tappets. Sequential electronic fuel injection. VIN Code: A. Option Code LH2. Built by Cadillac.

DE VILLE, DEVILLE LUXURY, SEVILLE SLS BASE V-8

Northstar Overhead valve. Dual overhead cam. Aluminum block with cast iron liners. Aluminum cylinder heads. Displacement: 279 cid (4.6 liters). Bore and Stroke: 3.66 x 3.31 inches. Compression ratio: 10.0:1. Net brake hp: 275 at 5600 rpm. Taxable hp: 42.90. Net torque: 300 at 4000 rpm. Direct acting hydraulic tappets. Induction: Tuned port injection. VIN Code: 9. Option Code L37. Built by Cadillac.

DE VILLE STS, SEVILLE STS SEDAN BASE V-8

Northstar Overhead valve. Dual overhead cam. Aluminum block with cast iron liners. Aluminum cylinder heads. Displacement: 279 cid (4.6 liters). Bore and Stroke: 3.66 x 3.31 inches. Compression ratio: 10.3:1. Net brake hp: 300 at 6000 rpm. Taxable hp: 42.90. Net torque: 295 at 4400 rpm. Direct acting hydraulic tappets. Induction: Tuned port injection. VIN Code: Y. Option Code LD8. Built by Cadillac.

CTS/V BASE V-8

Overhead valve. Hydraulic roller cam. Aluminum block with cast iron liners. Aluminum cylinder heads. Displacement: 346 cid (5.7 liters). Bore and Stroke: 3.90 x 3.62 inches. Compression ratio: 10.5:1. Net brake hp: 400 at 6000 rpm. Taxable hp: 49.00. Net torque: 395 at 4800 rpm. Direct acting hydraulic tappets. Sequential multi-port fuel injection. VIN Code: S. Option Code LS6. Built by Chevrolet.

CHASSIS

(XLR) Wheelbase: 105.7 inches. Overall Length: 177.7 inches. Height: 50.4 inches. Width: 72.3 inches. Front tread: 62.2 inches. Rear tread: 62.2 inches. Standard Front Tires: Michelin ZP extended-mobility P235/50R18. Standard Rear Tires: Michelin ZP extended-mobility P235/50R18.

(CTS) Wheelbase: 113.4 inches. Overall Length: 190.1 inches. Height: 56.7 inches. Width: 70.6 inches. Front tread: 60 inches. Rear tread: 60 inches. Standard Tires: Goodyear Eagle RS-A P225/55HR16 all-season.

(CTS Sport) Wheelbase: 113.4 inches. Overall Length: 190.1 inches. Height: 56.7 inches. Width: 71 inches. Front tread: 60 inches. Rear tread: 60 inches. Standard Tires: Goodyear Eagle RS-A P225/50VR17 all-season.

(CTS/V Sport) Wheelbase: 113.4 inches. Overall Length: 194.5 inches. Height: 58.1 inches. Width: 70.6 inches. Front tread: 62 inches. Rear tread: 62 inches. Standard Tires: P245/45R18 x 8.5 inch.

(DeVille) Wheelbase: 115.3 inches. Overall Length: 207 inches. Height: 56.7 inches. Width: 74.4 inches. Front Tread: 62.6 inches. Rear Tread: 62.1 inches. Standard Tires: Michelin P225/60SR16 all-season black sidewall.

(DeVille DHS) Wheelbase: 115.3 inches. Overall Length: 207 inches. Height: 56.7 inches. Width: 74.4

2004 Cadillac, DeVille, DTS sedan

inches. Front Tread: 62.6 inches. Rear Tread: 62.1 inches. Standard Tires: Michelin P225/60SR16 all-season black sidewall.

(DeVille DTS) Wheelbase: 115.3 inches. Overall Length: 207 inches. Height: 56.7 inches. Width: 74.4 inches. Front Tread: 62.6 inches. Rear Tread: 62.1 inches. Standard Tires: Michelin P235/55HR17 all-season black sidewall performance radials.

(Seville SLS) Wheelbase: 112.2 inches. Overall Length: 201 inches. Height: 55.7 inches. Width: 75 inches. Front Tread: 62.7 inches. Rear Tread: 62.4 inches. Standard Tires: Michelin Symmetry S-rated P225/60R16.

NOTE: Model-year production, option lists and option-installation rates were not available at time of publication.

HISTORICAL

Cadillac continued to celebrate its 100th anniversary in 2004. Cadillac continued its racing program in 2004. CST/V racing cars had a successful season and ran for the manufacturer's cup. An important new phase in Cadillac history was the launch of the Cadillac brand in China in early June of the year.

In 2003, Cadillac's Sixteen show car was introduced.

2005

For the 2005 model year, Cadillac refined its entire lineup and introduced an all-new STS.

XLR

Since it debuted in 2003, the XLR drew positive response from the press, public and dealers alike. Buyers of 2005 XLRs could choose either a Dark or Light Eucalyptus interior and Blue Steel exterior paint (replacing Thunder Gray). Cadillac described the 2005 XLR as "a contemporary expression of Cadillac's heritage of landmark design and advanced technology."

CTS

The CTS was the first passenger car to showcase the design motifs that all 2005 models reflected. Its bold styling and sharp creases stood as a modern interpretation of the strikingly beautiful cars that made Cadillac famous. The CTS continued to be built on GM's acclaimed Sigma rear-wheel-drive architecture. For 2005, CTS buyers had more product choices, including a new entry-level model with a 210-hp 2.8-liter engine and single exhaust system. The higher-end CTS with the 3.6L V-6 VVT engine received a new six-speed manual transmission. Also new were 16-inch painted wheels, 16-inch machined wheels, a restyled instrument cluster and new Stealth Gray, Sand Storm and Moonstone exterior colors.

CTS/V

An essential part of Cadillac's product plan was to re-establish its heritage for performance with new high-powered automobiles. The new V-Series played a critical role in this effort. The CTS-V blended the best of what Cadillac had to offer in terms of sophistication and luxury performance into the most powerful production model Cadillac ever offered. The 400-hp sports sedan was based on Cadillac's performance-oriented rear-drive Sigma architecture. The CTS-V was designed for performance enthusiasts and served as the foundation for the CTS-V race car.

DE VILLE

Cadillac controlled nearly 50 percent of the North American large-luxury-sedan market segment and the 2005 DeVille was designed to keep things that way. It offered three new exterior colors called Green Silk, Light Cashmere and Glacier Gold. Sixth-generation OnStar hardware with upgraded hands-free capability was introduced.

STS

The 2005 STS replaced the Seville. It combined the best of the brand into a luxury-performance sedan designed to deliver precision craftsmanship, exceptional performance and sophisticated luxury. Based on GM's rear-wheel-drive Sigma architecture, the STS was available with a 255-hp 3.6L V-6 in a rear-wheel-drive configuration or with the 320-hp Northstar 4.6L V-8 in rear- and all-wheel-drive variations. Both engines incorporated variable valve timing (VVT) and both were mated to the widely acclaimed Hydra-Matic five-speed automatic transmission with Driver Shift Control.

2005 Cadillac CTS-V sedan

Price Guide

SECTION TWO

The prices listed here represent a sample of Cadillacs taken from the *2005 Old Cars Price Guide*. If you do not see your car here, check the 2005 edition of *Standard Guide to Cars and Prices* published by Krause Publications or contact your local chapter of the Cadillac-La Salle Club, Inc. for more information.

Vehicle Condition Scale

1. **Excellent.** Restored to current maximum professional standards of quality in every area or perfect original with components operating and appearing as new. A 95-plus point show car that is not driven.

2. **Fine.** Well-restored or a combination of superior restoration and excellent original parts. An extremely well-maintained original vehicle showing minimal wear.

3. **Very good.** Completely operable original or older restoration. A good amateur restoration, or a combination of well-done restoration and good operable components or partially restored car with parts necessary to complete and/or valuable NOS parts.

4. **Good.** A driveable vehicle needed no work or only minor work to be functional. A deteriorated restoration or poor amateur restoration. All components may need restoration to be "excellent" but the car is useable "as is."

5. **Restorable.** Needs complete restoration of body, chassis, and interior. May or may not be running. Isn't weathered or stripped to the point of being useful only for parts.

6. **Parts car.** May or may not be running but it weathered, wrecked and/or stripped to the point of being useful primarily for parts.

	6	5	4	3	2	1
1903 Model A, 1-cyl.						
Rbt	1,600	4,800	8,000	16,000	28,000	40,000
Tonn Rbt	1,640	4,920	8,200	16,400	28,700	41,000
1910 Model 30, 4-cyl.						
Rds	1,600	4,800	8,000	16,000	28,000	40,000
demi T&C	1,640	4,920	8,200	16,400	28,700	41,000
Tr	1,560	4,680	7,800	15,600	27,300	39,000
Limo	1,480	4,440	7,400	14,800	25,900	37,000
1912 Model 30, 4-cyl.						
Rds	1,800	5,400	9,000	18,000	31,500	45,000
4P Phae	1,840	5,520	9,200	18,400	32,200	46,000
5P Tr	1,880	5,640	9,400	18,800	32,900	47,000
Cpe	1,560	4,680	7,800	15,600	27,300	39,000
Limo	1,640	4,920	8,200	16,400	28,700	41,000
1914 Model 30, 4-cyl.						
Rds	1,840	5,520	9,200	18,400	32,200	46,000
Phae	1,880	5,640	9,400	18,800	32,900	47,000
5P Tr	1,920	5,760	9,600	19,200	33,600	48,000
7P Tr	1,960	5,880	9,800	19,600	34,300	49,000
Lan Cpe	1,560	4,680	7,800	15,600	27,300	39,000
Encl dr Limo	1,640	4,920	8,200	16,400	28,700	41,000
Limo	1,680	5,040	8,400	16,800	29,400	42,000
1917 Model 55, V-8						
Rds	1,880	5,640	9,400	18,800	32,900	47,000
Clb Rds	1,920	5,760	9,600	19,200	33,600	48,000

	6	5	4	3	2	1
Conv	1,840	5,520	9,200	18,400	32,200	46,000
Cpe	1,480	4,440	7,400	14,800	25,900	37,000
Vic	1,520	4,560	7,600	15,200	26,600	38,000
Brgm	1,480	4,440	7,400	14,800	25,900	37,000
Limo	1,600	4,800	8,000	16,000	28,000	40,000
Imp Limo	1,680	5,040	8,400	16,800	29,400	42,000
7P Lan'let	1,760	5,280	8,800	17,600	30,800	44,000
1920-21 Type 59, V-8						
Rds	1,720	5,160	8,600	17,200	30,100	43,000
Phae	1,760	5,280	8,800	17,600	30,800	44,000
Tr	1,680	5,040	8,400	16,800	29,400	42,000
Vic	1,360	4,080	6,800	13,600	23,800	34,000
Sed	1,320	3,960	6,600	13,200	23,100	33,000
Cpe	1,360	4,080	6,800	13,600	23,800	34,000
Sub	1,320	3,960	6,600	13,200	23,100	33,000
Limo	1,480	4,440	7,400	14,800	25,900	37,000
Twn Brgm	1,520	4,560	7,600	15,200	26,600	38,000
Imp Limo	1,560	4,680	7,800	15,600	27,300	39,000
NOTE: Coupe and Town Brougham dropped for 1921.						
1926-27 Series 314, V-8						
Cpe	1,520	4,560	7,600	15,200	26,600	38,000
Vic	1,560	4,680	7,800	15,600	27,300	39,000
5P Brgm	1,520	4,560	7,600	15,200	26,600	38,000
5P Sed	1,200	3,600	6,000	12,000	21,000	30,000
7P Sed	1,240	3,720	6,200	12,400	21,700	31,000
Imp Sed	1,200	3,600	6,000	12,000	21,000	30,000

1926-27 Custom Line, V-8

	6	5	4	3	2	1
Rds	3,360	10,080	16,800	33,600	58,800	84,000
Tr	3,360	10,080	16,800	33,600	58,800	84,000
Phae	3,440	10,320	17,200	34,400	60,200	86,000
Cpe	1,920	5,760	9,600	19,200	33,600	48,000
Sed	1,640	4,920	8,200	16,400	28,700	41,000
Sub	1,680	5,040	8,400	16,800	29,400	42,000
Imp Sed	1,840	5,520	9,200	18,400	32,200	46,000

1930 Series 353, V-8, 140" wb Fisher Custom Line

	6	5	4	3	2	1
Conv	4,320	12,960	21,600	43,200	75,600	108,000
2P Cpe	2,800	8,400	14,000	28,000	49,000	70,000
Twn Sed	1,800	5,400	9,000	18,000	31,500	45,000
Sed	1,760	5,280	8,800	17,600	30,800	44,000
7P Sed	1,840	5,520	9,200	18,400	32,200	46,000
7P Imp Sed	2,080	6,240	10,400	20,800	36,400	52,000
5P Cpe	2,160	6,480	10,800	21,600	37,800	54,000

1930 Fleetwood Line, V-8

	6	5	4	3	2	1
Rds	4,960	14,880	24,800	49,600	86,800	124,000
5P Sed	1,880	5,640	9,400	18,800	32,900	47,000
Sed Cabr	4,320	12,960	21,600	43,200	75,600	108,000
5P Imp	2,080	6,240	10,400	20,800	36,400	52,000
7P Sed	1,880	5,640	9,400	18,800	32,900	47,000
7P Imp	2,080	6,240	10,400	20,800	36,400	52,000
Trans Cabr	5,040	15,120	25,200	50,400	88,200	126,000
Trans Limo Brgm	4,800	14,400	24,000	48,000	84,000	120,000
Clb Cabr	4,960	14,880	24,800	49,600	86,800	124,000
A/W Phae	5,360	16,080	26,800	53,600	93,800	134,000
A/W State Imp	5,520	16,560	27,600	55,200	96,600	138,000

1930 Fleetwood Custom Line, V-16, 148" wb

	6	5	4	3	2	1
Rds	12,960	38,880	64,800	129,600	226,800	324,000
Phae	13,760	41,280	68,800	137,600	240,800	344,000

1930 "Flat Windshield" Models

	6	5	4	3	2	1
A/W Phae	13,960	41,880	69,800	139,600	244,300	349,000
Conv	12,960	38,880	64,800	129,600	226,800	324,000
Cpe	4,800	14,400	24,000	48,000	84,000	120,000
Clb Sed	4,560	13,680	22,800	45,600	79,800	114,000
5P OS Sed	4,560	13,680	22,800	45,600	79,800	114,000
5P Sed Cabr	10,960	32,880	54,800	109,600	191,800	274,000
Imp Cabr	10,960	32,880	54,800	109,600	191,800	274,000
7P Sed	4,800	14,400	24,000	48,000	84,000	120,000
7P Imp Sed	4,960	14,880	24,800	49,600	86,800	124,000
Twn Cabr 4212	11,160	33,480	55,800	111,600	195,300	279,000
Twn Cabr 4220	11,160	33,480	55,800	111,600	195,300	279,000
Twn Cabr 4225	11,160	33,480	55,800	111,600	195,300	279,000
Limo Brgm	7,960	23,880	39,800	79,600	139,300	199,000
Twn Brgm 05	7,960	23,880	39,800	79,600	139,300	199,000

1930 Madame X Models, V-16

	6	5	4	3	2	1
5P OS Imp	6,760	20,280	33,800	67,600	118,300	169,000
5P Imp	6,560	19,680	32,800	65,600	114,800	164,000
Twn Cabr 4312	12,560	37,680	62,800	125,600	219,800	314,000
Twn Cabr 4320	12,560	37,680	62,800	125,600	219,800	314,000
Twn Cabr 4325	12,560	37,680	62,800	125,600	219,800	314,000
Limo Brgm	9,360	28,080	46,800	93,600	163,800	234,000

1936 Series 60, V-8, 121" wb

	6	5	4	3	2	1
2d Conv	2,480	7,440	12,400	24,800	43,400	62,000
2d 2P Cpe	1,280	3,840	6,400	12,800	22,400	32,000
4d Tr Sed	1,040	3,120	5,200	10,400	18,200	26,000

1936 Series 70, V-8, 131" wb, Fleetwood bodies

	6	5	4	3	2	1
2d Conv	2,720	8,160	13,600	27,200	47,600	68,000
2d 2P Cpe	1,320	3,960	6,600	13,200	23,100	33,000
4d Conv Sed	2,800	8,400	14,000	28,000	49,000	70,000
4d Tr Sed	1,200	3,600	6,000	12,000	21,000	30,000

1936 Series 75, V-8, 138" wb, Fleetwood bodies

	6	5	4	3	2	1
4d Sed	1,600	4,800	8,000	16,000	28,000	40,000
4d Tr Sed	1,640	4,920	8,200	16,400	28,700	41,000
4d Conv Sed	2,960	8,880	14,800	29,600	51,800	74,000
4d Fml Sed	1,600	4,800	8,000	16,000	28,000	40,000
4d Twn Sed	1,640	4,920	8,200	16,400	28,700	41,000
4d 7P Sed	1,680	5,040	8,400	16,800	29,400	42,000
4d 7P Tr Sed	1,800	5,400	9,000	18,000	31,500	45,000
4d Imp Sed	1,840	5,520	9,200	18,400	32,200	46,000
4d Imp Tr Sed	1,880	5,640	9,400	18,800	32,900	47,000
4d Twn Car	2,080	6,240	10,400	20,800	36,400	52,000

1936 Series 80, V-12, 131" wb, Fleetwood bodies

	6	5	4	3	2	1
2d Conv	3,120	9,360	15,600	31,200	54,600	78,000
4d Conv Sed	3,200	9,600	16,000	32,000	56,000	80,000
2d Cpe	1,880	5,640	9,400	18,800	32,900	47,000
4d Tr Sed	1,760	5,280	8,800	17,600	30,800	44,000

1936 Series 85, V-12, 138" wb, Fleetwood bodies

	6	5	4	3	2	1
4d Sed	1,800	5,400	9,000	18,000	31,500	45,000
4d Tr Sed	1,840	5,520	9,200	18,400	32,200	46,000
4d Conv Sed	2,960	8,880	14,800	29,600	51,800	74,000
4d Fml Sed	1,960	5,880	9,800	19,600	34,300	49,000
4d Twn Sed	2,000	6,000	10,000	20,000	35,000	50,000
4d 7P Sed	1,960	5,880	9,800	19,600	34,300	49,000
4d 7P Tr Sed	2,000	6,000	10,000	20,000	35,000	50,000
4d Imp Sed	2,080	6,240	10,400	20,800	36,400	52,000
4d Imp Tr Sed	2,160	6,480	10,800	21,600	37,800	54,000
4d Twn Car	2,480	7,440	12,400	24,800	43,400	62,000

1936 Series 90, V-16, 154" wb, Fleetwood bodies

	6	5	4	3	2	1
2d 2P Conv	4,960	14,880	24,800	49,600	86,800	124,000
4d Conv Sed	5,200	15,600	26,000	52,000	91,000	130,000
2d 2P Cpe	3,760	11,280	18,800	37,600	65,800	94,000
2d Aero Cpe	4,320	12,960	21,600	43,200	75,600	108,000
4d Sed	3,600	10,800	18,000	36,000	63,000	90,000
4d Twn Sed	3,600	10,800	18,000	36,000	63,000	90,000
4d 7P Sed	3,680	11,040	18,400	36,800	64,400	92,000
4d 5P Imp Cabr	5,360	16,080	26,800	53,600	93,800	134,000
4d 7P Imp Cabr	5,360	16,080	26,800	53,600	93,800	134,000
4d Imp Sed	5,560	16,680	27,800	55,600	97,300	139,000
4d Twn Cabr	5,760	17,280	28,800	57,600	100,800	144,000
4d Twn Lan	5,200	15,600	26,000	52,000	91,000	130,000
4d 5P Conv	5,360	16,080	26,800	53,600	93,800	134,000

1937 Series 60, V-8, 124" wb

	6	5	4	3	2	1
2d Conv	2,280	6,840	11,400	22,800	39,900	57,000
4d Conv Sed	2,360	7,080	11,800	23,600	41,300	59,000
2d 2P Cpe	1,280	3,840	6,400	12,800	22,400	32,000
4d Tr Sed	1,080	3,240	5,400	10,800	18,900	27,000

1937 Series 65, V-8, 131" wb

	6	5	4	3	2	1
4d Tr Sed	1,160	3,480	5,800	11,600	20,300	29,000

1939 Series 61, V-8, 126" wb

	6	5	4	3	2	1
2d Conv	2,560	7,680	12,800	25,600	44,800	64,000
4d Conv Sed	2,640	7,920	13,200	26,400	46,200	66,000
2d Cpe	1,280	3,840	6,400	12,800	22,400	32,000
4d Tr Sed	1,160	3,480	5,800	11,600	20,300	29,000

1939 Series 60 Special, V-8, 127" wb, Fleetwood

	6	5	4	3	2	1
4d Sed	1,680	5,040	8,400	16,800	29,400	42,000
4d S/R Sed	1,760	5,280	8,800	17,600	30,800	44,000
4d S/R Imp Sed	1,880	5,640	9,400	18,800	32,900	47,000

1939 Series 75, V-8, 141" wb, Fleetwood bodies

	6	5	4	3	2	1
2d Conv	3,040	9,120	15,200	30,400	53,200	76,000
4d Conv Sed Trk	3,120	9,360	15,600	31,200	54,600	78,000
2d 4P Cpe	1,480	4,440	7,400	14,800	25,900	37,000
2d 5P Cpe	1,520	4,560	7,600	15,200	26,600	38,000
4d Tr Sed	1,400	4,200	7,000	14,000	24,500	35,000
4d Div Tr Sed	1,440	4,320	7,200	14,400	25,200	36,000
4d Twn Sed Trk	1,480	4,440	7,400	14,800	25,900	37,000
4d Fml Sed Trk	1,520	4,560	7,600	15,200	26,600	38,000
4d 7P Fml Sed Trk	1,600	4,800	8,000	16,000	28,000	40,000
4d 7P Tr Sed	1,560	4,680	7,800	15,600	27,300	39,000
4d 7P Tr Imp Sed	1,600	4,800	8,000	16,000	28,000	40,000
4d Bus Tr Sed	1,480	4,440	7,400	14,800	25,900	37,000
4d 8P Tr Imp Sed	1,680	5,040	8,400	16,800	29,400	42,000
4d Twn Car Trk	1,720	5,160	8,600	17,200	30,100	43,000

1939 Series 90, V-16, 141" wb, Fleetwood bodies

	6	5	4	3	2	1
2d Conv	3,760	11,280	18,800	37,600	65,800	94,000
4d Conv Sed	4,160	12,480	20,800	41,600	72,800	104,000
2d 4P Cpe	3,360	10,080	16,800	33,600	58,800	84,000
2d 5P Cpe	3,280	9,840	16,400	32,800	57,400	82,000
4d 5P Tr Sed	2,720	8,160	13,600	27,200	47,600	68,000
4d Twn Sed Trk	2,800	8,400	14,000	28,000	49,000	70,000
4d Div Tr Sed	2,800	8,400	14,000	28,000	49,000	70,000
4d 7P Tr Sed	2,800	8,400	14,000	28,000	49,000	70,000
4d 7P Imp Tr Sed	2,880	8,640	14,400	28,800	50,400	72,000
4d Fml Sed Trk	2,880	8,640	14,400	28,800	50,400	72,000
4d 7P Fml Sed Trk	2,960	8,880	14,800	29,600	51,800	74,000
4d Twn Car Trk	3,360	10,080	16,800	33,600	58,800	84,000

1941 Series 61, V-8, 126" wb

	6	5	4	3	2	1
2d FBk	1,050	3,100	5,200	10,400	18,200	26,000
2d DeL FBk	1,100	3,250	5,400	10,800	18,900	27,000
4d Sed FBk	950	2,900	4,800	9,600	16,800	24,000
4d DeL Sed FBk	1,100	3,350	5,600	11,200	19,600	28,000

1941 Series 62, V-8, 126" wb

	6	5	4	3	2	1
2d Conv	2,500	7,550	12,600	25,200	44,100	63,000
4d Conv Sed	2,450	7,300	12,200	24,400	42,700	61,000
2d Cpe	1,300	3,850	6,400	12,800	22,400	32,000
2d DeL Cpe	1,300	3,950	6,600	13,200	23,100	33,000
4d Sed	900	2,650	4,400	8,800	15,400	22,000
4d DeL Sed	900	2,750	4,600	9,200	16,100	23,000

1941 Series 63, V-8, 126" wb

	6	5	4	3	2	1
4d Sed FBk	1,100	3,350	5,600	11,200	19,600	28,000

1941 Series 60 Special, V-8, 126" wb, Fleetwood

	6	5	4	3	2	1
4d Sed	1,700	5,050	8,400	16,800	29,400	42,000
4d S/R Sed	1,800	5,400	9,000	18,000	31,500	45,000

NOTE: Add $1,500 for division window.

1941 Series 67, V-8, 138" wb

	6	5	4	3	2	1
4d 5P Sed	1,050	3,100	5,200	10,400	18,200	26,000
4d Imp Sed	1,100	3,250	5,400	10,800	18,900	27,000
4d 7P Sed	1,050	3,100	5,200	10,400	18,200	26,000
4d 7P Imp Sed	1,100	3,350	5,600	11,200	19,600	28,000

1941 Series 75, V-8, 136-1/2" wb

	6	5	4	3	2	1
4d 5P Sed	1,100	3,250	5,400	10,800	18,900	27,000
4d 5P Imp Sed	1,150	3,400	5,700	11,400	20,000	28,500
4d 7P Sed	1,150	3,400	5,700	11,400	20,000	28,500
4d 9P Bus Sed	1,100	3,350	5,600	11,200	19,600	28,000
4d 7P Imp Sed	1,150	3,500	5,800	11,600	20,300	29,000
4d Bus Imp Sed	1,100	3,250	5,400	10,800	18,900	27,000
4d 5P Fml Sed	1,150	3,500	5,800	11,600	20,300	29,000
4d 7P Fml Sed	1,150	3,500	5,800	11,600	20,300	29,000

1948 Series 61, V-8, 126" wb

	6	5	4	3	2	1
2d FBk	1,200	3,600	6,000	12,000	21,000	30,000
4d 5P Sed	1,080	3,240	5,400	10,800	18,900	27,000

1948 Series 62, V-8, 126" wb

	6	5	4	3	2	1
2d Conv	2,440	7,320	12,200	24,400	42,700	61,000
2d Clb Cpe	1,240	3,720	6,200	12,400	21,700	31,000
4d 5P Sed	1,160	3,480	5,800	11,600	20,300	29,000

1948 Series 60 Special, V-8, 133" wb, Fleetwood

	6	5	4	3	2	1
4d Sed	1,240	3,720	6,200	12,400	21,700	31,000

1948 Series 75, V-8, 136" wb, Fleetwood

	6	5	4	3	2	1
4d 5P Sed	1,240	3,720	6,200	12,400	21,700	31,000
4d 7P Sed	1,280	3,840	6,400	12,800	22,400	32,000
4d 7P Imp Sed	1,440	4,320	7,200	14,400	25,200	36,000
4d 9P Bus Sed	1,280	3,840	6,400	12,800	22,400	32,000
4d 9P Bus Imp	1,360	4,080	6,800	13,600	23,800	34,000

1949 Series 61, V-8, 126" wb

	6	5	4	3	2	1
2d FBk	1,240	3,720	6,200	12,400	21,700	31,000
4d Sed	1,120	3,360	5,600	11,200	19,600	28,000

1949 Series 62, V-8, 126" wb

	6	5	4	3	2	1
2d FBk	1,280	3,840	6,400	12,800	22,400	32,000
4d 5P Sed	1,200	3,600	6,000	12,000	21,000	30,000
2d HT Cpe DeV	1,800	5,400	9,000	18,000	31,500	45,000
2d Conv	2,520	7,560	12,600	25,200	44,100	63,000

1949 Series 60 Special, V-8, 133" wb, Fleetwood

	6	5	4	3	2	1
4d 5P Sed	1,280	3,840	6,400	12,800	22,400	32,000

1949 Series 75, V-8, 136" wb, Fleetwood

	6	5	4	3	2	1
4d 5P Sed	1,280	3,840	6,400	12,800	22,400	32,000
4d 7P Sed	1,320	3,960	6,600	13,200	23,100	33,000
4d 7P Imp Sed	1,480	4,440	7,400	14,800	25,900	37,000
4d 9P Bus Sed	1,320	3,960	6,600	13,200	23,100	33,000
4d 9P Bus Imp	1,400	4,200	7,000	14,000	24,500	35,000

Left Column

	6	5	4	3	2	1
1953 Series 62, V-8						
4d Sed	960	2,880	4,800	9,600	16,800	24,000
2d HT	1,400	4,200	7,000	14,000	24,500	35,000
2d HT Cpe DeV	1,760	5,280	8,800	17,600	30,800	44,000
2d Conv	2,160	6,480	10,800	21,600	37,800	54,000
2d Eldo Conv	4,440	13,320	22,200	44,400	77,700	111,000
1953 Series 60S, V-8						
4d Sed	1,440	4,320	7,200	14,400	25,200	36,000
1953 Series 75, V-8, Fleetwood						
4d 7P Sed	1,480	4,440	7,400	14,800	25,900	37,000
4d Imp Sed	1,560	4,680	7,800	15,600	27,300	39,000
1959 Series 62, V-8						
4d 4W HT	1,000	3,000	5,000	10,000	17,500	25,000
4d 6W HT	960	2,880	4,800	9,600	16,800	24,000
2d HT	1,200	3,600	6,000	12,000	21,000	30,000
2d Conv	2,120	6,360	10,600	21,200	37,100	53,000
1959 Series 63 DeVille, V-8						
2d HT Cpe DeV	1,480	4,440	7,400	14,800	25,900	37,000
4d 4W HT	1,080	3,240	5,400	10,800	18,900	27,000
4d 6W HT	1,040	3,120	5,200	10,400	18,200	26,000
1959 Series Eldorado, V-8						
4d HT Brgm	1,480	4,440	7,400	14,800	25,900	37,000
2d HT Sev	1,640	4,920	8,200	16,400	28,700	41,000
2d Brtz Conv	2,800	8,400	14,000	28,000	49,000	70,000
1959 Fleetwood 60 Special, V-8						
4d 6P Sed	1,240	3,720	6,200	12,400	21,700	31,000
1959 Fleetwood Series 75, V-8						
4d 9P Sed	1,320	3,960	6,600	13,200	23,100	33,000
4d Limo	1,400	4,200	7,000	14,000	24,500	35,000
1963 Series 62, V-8						
4d 4W HT	680	2,040	3,400	6,800	11,900	17,000
4d 6W HT	664	1,992	3,320	6,640	11,620	16,600
2d HT	800	2,400	4,000	8,000	14,000	20,000
2d Conv	1,200	3,600	6,000	12,000	21,000	30,000
1963 Series 63 DeVille, V-8						
4d 4W HT	720	2,160	3,600	7,200	12,600	18,000
4d 6W HT	704	2,112	3,520	7,040	12,320	17,600
4d HT Pk Ave	700	2,100	3,500	7,000	12,250	17,500
2d HT Cpe DeV	1,000	3,000	5,000	10,000	17,500	25,000
1963 Eldorado Series, V-8						
2d Brtz Conv	1,400	4,200	7,000	14,000	24,500	35,000
1963 Fleetwood 60 Special, V-8						
4d 6P HT	760	2,280	3,800	7,600	13,300	19,000
1963 Fleetwood 75 Series, V-8						
4d 9P Sed	840	2,520	4,200	8,400	14,700	21,000
4d 9P Limo	1,000	3,000	5,000	10,000	17,500	25,000
1964 Series 62, V-8						
4d 4W HT	720	2,160	3,600	7,200	12,600	18,000
4d 6W HT	712	2,136	3,560	7,120	12,460	17,800
2d HT	880	2,640	4,400	8,800	15,400	22,000
1964 Series 63 DeVille, V-8						
4d 4W HT	728	2,184	3,640	7,280	12,740	18,200
4d 6W HT	720	2,160	3,600	7,200	12,600	18,000
2d HT Cpe DeV	1,040	3,120	5,200	10,400	18,200	26,000
2d Conv	1,240	3,720	6,200	12,400	21,700	31,000
1964 Eldorado Series, V-8						
2d Conv	1,440	4,320	7,200	14,400	25,200	36,000
1964 Fleetwood 60 Special, V-8						

Right Column

	6	5	4	3	2	1
4d 6P HT	880	2,640	4,400	8,800	15,400	22,000
1964 Fleetwood 75 Series, V-8						
4d 9P Sed	880	2,640	4,400	8,800	15,400	22,000
4d 9P Limo	1,000	3,000	5,000	10,000	17,500	25,000
1967 Calais, V-8, 129.5" wb						
4d HT	640	1,920	3,200	6,400	11,200	16,000
2d HT	700	2,100	3,500	7,000	12,250	17,500
1967 DeVille, V-8, 129.5" wb						
4d HT	664	1,992	3,320	6,640	11,620	16,600
2d HT	760	2,280	3,800	7,600	13,300	19,000
2d Conv	1,000	3,000	5,000	10,000	17,500	25,000
1967 Fleetwood Eldorado, V-8, 120" wb						
2d HT	760	2,280	3,800	7,600	13,300	19,000
1967 Sixty-Special, V-8, 133" wb						
4d Sed	680	2,040	3,400	6,800	11,900	17,000
1967 Fleetwood Brougham, V-8, 133" wb						
4d Sed	680	2,040	3,400	6,800	11,900	17,000
1967 Seventy-Five Series, V-8, 149.8" wb						
4d Sed	720	2,160	3,600	7,200	12,600	18,000
4d Limo	760	2,280	3,800	7,600	13,300	19,000
1974 Calais, V-8						
2d HT	496	1,488	2,480	4,960	8,680	12,400
4d HT	488	1,464	2,440	4,880	8,540	12,200
1974 DeVille, V-8						
2d HT	516	1,548	2,580	5,160	9,030	12,900
4d HT	508	1,524	2,540	5,080	8,890	12,700
1974 Fleetwood Brougham, V-8						
4d Sed	640	1,920	3,200	6,400	11,200	16,000
1974 Fleetwood Eldorado, V-8						
2d HT	640	1,920	3,200	6,400	11,200	16,000
2d Conv	880	2,640	4,400	8,800	15,400	22,000
1974 Fleetwood 75, V-8						
4d Sed	620	1,860	3,100	6,200	10,850	15,500
4d Limo	640	1,920	3,200	6,400	11,200	16,000

NOTE: Add 20 percent for Talisman Brougham. Add 10 percent for padded top on Series 75. Add 10 percent for sunroof on DeVille/60/Eldorado.

1979 DeVille, V-8						
2d Cpe	360	1,080	1,800	3,600	6,300	9,000
4d Sed	248	744	1,240	2,480	4,340	6,200

NOTE: Add 5 percent for Phaeton Special Edition.

1979 Eldorado, V-8						
2d Cpe	560	1,680	2,800	5,600	9,800	14,000

NOTE: Add 15 percent for Biarritz.

1979 Fleetwood Brougham, V-8						
4d Sed	260	780	1,300	2,600	4,550	6,500
1979 Fleetwood Limo						
4d Sed	388	1,164	1,940	3,880	6,790	9,700
4d Fml Sed	396	1,188	1,980	3,960	6,930	9,900

NOTE: Deduct 12 percent for diesel.

4d Sed	224	672	1,120	2,240	3,920	5,600
1984 Seville, V-8						
4d Sed	272	816	1,360	2,720	4,760	6,800
1984 DeVille, V-8						
2d Sed	264	792	1,320	2,640	4,620	6,600
4d Sed	240	720	1,200	2,400	4,200	6,000
1984 Eldorado, V-8						
2d Cpe	520	1,560	2,600	5,200	9,100	13,000
2d Conv	960	2,880	4,800	9,600	16,800	24,000

NOTE: Add 15 percent for Biarritz.

1984 Fleetwood Brougham, V-8						
2d Sed	360	1,080	1,800	3,600	6,300	9,000
4d Sed	260	780	1,300	2,600	4,550	6,500
1984 Fleetwood, V-8						
4d Sed	380	1,140	1,900	3,800	6,650	9,500
4d Fml Limo	388	1,164	1,940	3,880	6,790	9,700

	6	5	4	3	2	1
1987 Cimarron						
4d Sed, 4-cyl.	236	708	1,180	2,360	4,130	5,900
4d Sed, V-6	240	720	1,200	2,400	4,200	6,000
1987 Seville, V-8						
4d Sed	364	1,092	1,820	3,640	6,370	9,100
1987 DeVille, V-8						
4d Sed	252	756	1,260	2,520	4,410	6,300
2d Cpe	248	744	1,240	2,480	4,340	6,200
1987 Fleetwood, V-8						
4d Sed d'Elegance	396	1,188	1,980	3,960	6,930	9,900
4d Sed, 60 Spl	400	1,200	2,000	4,000	7,000	10,000
1987 Eldorado, V-8						
2d Cpe	524	1,572	2,620	5,240	9,170	13,100
1987 Brougham, V-8						
4d Sed	416	1,248	2,080	4,160	7,280	10,400
1987 Fleetwood 75 Series, V-8						
4d Limo	580	1,740	2,900	5,800	10,150	14,500
4d Fml	560	1,680	2,800	5,600	9,800	14,000
1987 Allante, V-8						
2d Conv	920	2,760	4,600	9,200	16,100	23,000
1990 Seville, V-8						
4d Sed	560	1,680	2,800	5,600	9,800	14,000
4d Sed STS	640	1,920	3,200	6,400	11,200	16,000
1990 DeVille, V-8						
2d Cpe	580	1,740	2,900	5,800	10,150	14,500
4d Sed	568	1,704	2,840	5,680	9,940	14,200
1990 Fleetwood, V-8						
2d Cpe	620	1,860	3,100	6,200	10,850	15,500
4d Sed	628	1,884	3,140	6,280	10,990	15,700
4d Sed 605	680	2,040	3,400	6,800	11,900	17,000
1990 Eldorado, V-8						
2d Cpe	640	1,920	3,200	6,400	11,200	16,000
1990 Brougham, V-8						
4d Sed	640	1,920	3,200	6,400	11,200	16,000
1990 Allante						
2d Conv	960	2,880	4,800	9,600	16,800	24,000
NOTE: Add $3,000 for hardtop.						
1996 Seville, V-8						
4d SLS Sed	650	2,000	3,300	6,600	11,600	16,500
4d STS Sed	700	2,100	3,500	7,000	12,300	17,500
1996 Deville, V-8						
4d Sed	550	1,700	2,800	5,600	9,800	14,000
4d Concours Sed	600	1,850	3,100	6,200	10,900	15,500
1996 Fleetwood, V-8						
4d Sed	650	1,900	3,200	6,400	11,200	16,000
1996 Eldorado, V-8						
2d Cpe	650	1,900	3,200	6,400	11,200	16,000
2d Trg Cpe	650	2,000	3,300	6,600	11,600	16,500
1997 Catera, V-6						
4d Sed	400	1,200	2,000	4,000	7,000	10,000
1997 Seville, V-8						
4d SLS Sed	660	1,980	3,300	6,600	11,550	16,500
4d STS Sed	700	2,100	3,500	7,000	12,250	17,500
1997 Deville, V-8						
4d Sed	560	1,680	2,800	5,600	9,800	14,000
4d d'Elegance Sed	600	1,800	3,000	6,000	10,500	15,000
4d Concours Sed	620	1,860	3,100	6,200	10,850	15,500
1997 Eldorado, V-8						
2d Cpe	640	1,920	3,200	6,400	11,200	16,000
2d Trg Cpe	660	1,980	3,300	6,600	11,550	16,500

Jack Tallman

LEADERSHIP RESTS ON ACHIEVEMENT

Cadillac WAS FIRST
TO USE THE SELF-STARTER

RENÉ ROBERT CAVELIER,
SIEUR de la SALLE
EXPLORER OF THE MISSISSIPPI

If there is one basic advancement which has had more to do with the success of the automobile than any other—that advancement is undoubtedly the self-starter. And, as has been the case with so many other fundamental improvements in the motor car, the self-starter was a Cadillac achievement. Not only did Cadillac introduce the self-starter, but it perfected it as well—and gave it to motordom as a never-ending source of convenience and satisfaction. . . . This is but a typical example of the pioneering which has carried Cadillac to world dominance as a motor car builder—and which is so admirably exemplified in today's great Cadillacs and La Salles. In their Fisher No Draft Ventilation, individually-controlled; their sensitive full-range ride regulators; their eight, twelve and sixteen cylinder engines; and their marvelous comfort and performance—the new Cadillacs and La Salles are in the finest tradition of Cadillac leadership . . . . These distinguished cars are now on display throughout America, and you are cordially invited to appraise them at any time. La Salle list prices start at $2245, Cadillac at $2695, f. o. b. Detroit.

The self-starter was first placed on an experimental Cadillac car in the spring of 1911, and soon thereafter was incorporated in all Cadillac cars as standard equipment—the first time it was so employed.

THE CADILLAC V-8 TOWN SEDAN